HUMAN RESOURCE DEVELOP

THEORY AND PRACTICE

JEFF GOLD, RICH HOLDEN   OWELL

First published 2010 by
PALGRAVE MACMILLAN

Palgrave Macmillan in the UK is an imprint of Macmillan Publishers Limited, registered in England, company number 785998, of Houndmills, Basingstoke, Hampshire RG21 6XS.

Palgrave Macmillan in the US is a division of St Martin's Press LLC, 175 Fifth Avenue, New York, NY 10010.

Palgrave Macmillan is the global academic imprint of the above companies and has companies and representatives throughout the world.

Palgrave® and Macmillan® are registered trademarks in the United States, the United Kingdom, Europe and other countries.

ISBN-13: 978–0–230–21687–7

This book is printed on paper suitable for recycling and made from fully managed and sustained forest sources. Logging, pulping and manufacturing processes are expected to conform to the environmental regulations of the country of origin.

A catalogue record for this book is available from the British Library.

A catalog record for this book is available from the Library of Congress.

10 9 8 7 6 5 4 3 2 1
19 18 17 16 15 14 13 12 11 10

Printed in China

Contents

List of Figures

List of Tables

About the Editors

Julie Beardwell is Academic Support Manager, Corporate Development at Leicester Business School, De Montfort University. During the development and writing of this text, she was an Associate Dean at Leeds Business School, responsible for postgraduate and professional programmes. She has over 15 years' experience of designing, leading and delivering programmes in HRM. Julie is also Chief Moderator, Standards for the CIPD and is a Chartered Fellow of the Institute.

Jeff Gold is Principal Lecturer in Organisation Learning at Leeds Business School, Leeds Metropolitan University and Leadership Fellow at Leeds University where he coordinates the Northern Leadership Academy. He has led a range of seminars and workshops on leadership with a particular emphasis on participation and distribution. He is the co-author of *Management Development, Strategies for Action* (with Alan Mumford), published by the CIPD in 2004, and the fourth edition of his *Human Resource Management* (with John Bratton) was published in 2007 by Palgrave Macmillan.

Rick Holden is Principal Lecturer (Research) at Leeds Business School, Leeds Metropolitan University. His research interests include enterprise education and training, and the graduate labour market and teaching skills, and he has published extensively in these areas. He chaired the 2005 International Conference on HRD Research and Practice across Europe. Prior to joining Leeds Met, Rick was Training Manager for the Confectionery Division of Cadbury Schweppes. He is Editor of the journal *Education & Training* and Vice Chair of the University Forum for HRD Research Committee.

Paul Iles is Running Stream Professor of HRD at Leeds Business School, Leeds Metropolitan University. He is a chartered psychologist and a Chartered Fellow of the CIPD. He has published and made presentations on a variety of HRD issues, including leadership and management development, team building and organizational learning, career development, coaching, mentoring, organizational change and development, international and comparative HRD and recently talent management.

Jim Stewart is Running Stream Professor of HRD at Leeds Business School, Leeds Metropolitan University. He has held previous professorial and academic appointments at Nottingham and Wolverhampton Business Schools. As an active researcher, Jim has undertaken projects funded by the UK government, the EU, ESRC and LSC among others. He is the author and co-author/editor of 12 books and numerous articles, most of which draw on these research projects. Jim is Chair of the University Forum for HRD and holds three national roles with the CIPD, including Chief Examiner for Learning and Development.

Notes on the Contributors

Catherine Burrell is Principal Lecturer in Organizational Behaviour at Leeds Business School.

Dave Chesley is Senior Lecturer at Leeds Business School and Course Leader of the Post-graduate Certificate in Management.

David Devins is Principal Research Fellow in the Policy Research Institute at Leeds Metropolitan University. His primary research interests lie in a variety of aspects of enterprise development.

Catherine Glaister is Associate Senior Lecturer at Leeds Business School.

Vivienne Griggs is Senior Lecturer at Leeds Business School where she teaches Learning and Development and Business Skills modules on undergraduate programmes, postgraduate/professional HR courses and the Executive MBA. Prior to joining Leeds Metropolitan in 2003, she had 12 years' experience as an HR manager at BT.

Vicky Harte is Research Officer in the Institute for Enterprise at Leeds Metropolitan University where she undertakes research and evaluation of the many aspects of enterprise education, entrepreneurs and entrepreneurial activity in relation to curriculum design and assessment, learning and teaching encompassed within the 'student learning experience'.

Niki Kyriakidou is Lecturer in Human Resource Management and Organizational Behaviour at Leeds Metropolitan University. She received her PhD and Masters in HRM from the University of Leeds; and her Bachelor degree in Political Science and Public Administration from Athens University. She is a scholar of the Greek State Scholarship Foundation.

Patrick McCauley is an HR specialist and Fellow of the CIPD. Patrick has combined management consultancy and training with a successful academic career, most recently as a Senior Lecturer in Human Resource Management at Leeds Metropolitan University.

Hazel Kershaw-Solomon is Senior Lecturer in Human Resource Management at Leeds Business School.

Chitra Meetoo is completing a PhD at Leeds Business School on distributed leadership in self-directed teams. She is a graduate member of the CIPD and a fellow of the Northern Leadership Academy. She works as a part-time lecturer at Leeds Metropolitan University.

Helen Rodgers is Senior Lecturer in Human Resource Management at Leeds Business School. She gained her PhD at Kent University and researches in aspects of gender at work and strategic learning.

Joanna Smith is Subject Group Leader for Human Resource Management and Organizational Behaviour at Leeds Business School.

Hilary Sommerlad is Professor of Law and Society and Director of the Centre for Research into Diversity in the Professions at Leeds Metropolitan University. The centre brings together staff from a wide range of disciplines to engage in research and act as a resource for practitioners and policy makers.

Crystal Ling Zhang is Lecturer in Human Resource Management and Organizational Behaviour at Leeds Metropolitan University. Her PhD focused on cognitive style and processes of acculturation for cross-cultural travellers. Her recent work has focused on the extent to which cognitive style can be meaningfully applied to facilitate learning over the process of acculturation at the level of the organization as well as the individual.

Preface

This book has a number of origins. The first is a recognized lack by a number of members of the University Forum for Human Resource Development (HRD) of a suitable HRD text for teaching the subject at undergraduate level. This was especially recognized by staff at Leeds Business School and this is related to the second origin. In early 2007, Leeds Business School appointed two Running Stream Professors in HRD, which led to a suggestion by Jeff Gold, one of the editors, that the school now had the necessary resources to produce such a book. The final origin was agreement in the Human Resource Management/Organizational Behaviour subject group of the school that a project to produce the book was both possible and desirable and so a formal proposal was produced and submitted to the publishers.

The main purpose of the book is to provide a learning and teaching resource to academics and students. We have in mind second and final year undergraduates as the primary readership but would ourselves be happy to use the book with postgraduate and professional students, especially those studying for CIPD qualifications. As a learning and teaching resource, the book has a number of standard features in every chapter. These include clear learning outcomes, activities, reflective and discussion questions, examples of HRD practice, summaries and suggestions for further reading. All these features are intended to make the book a resource and so amenable to various approaches to its use. For example, it is not necessary and we don't expect every reader to start on page one and keep reading to the last page. The chapters can be read and studied in any order. That said, we have organized the content into what to us is a useful logic and have signalled that by the structure of parts and the names of those parts. We recognize that our logic is only one of a number of possible ways of interpreting the subject and so expect others to apply their own and different logic. The contents of the book will cope with that without problems. However, for newcomers to the study of HRD, we suggest you start with Chapter 1, Encountering Human Resource Development.

As editors, we want to thank a number of people, starting with our contributors and in many cases co-authors. They have responded in the main with good cheer to our changing and urgent demands on their time and expertise. We also want to thank the reviewers of our original proposal and some draft chapters. While it is true to say that we were not in agreement with all their comments and suggestions, we were and are grateful for the food for thought they gave us and those comments and suggestions we have applied, which have undoubtedly improved the book. We also want to thank Ursula Gavin and her colleagues at Palgrave Macmillan for supporting the project, especially for their understanding in relation to missed and changing deadlines. Finally, on behalf of all the authors as well as the editors, we want to thank our partners, spouses, families and other colleagues for their patience while we brought the project to fruition. We are confident that it has been worthwhile in producing a usable and valuable resource and we hope readers reach a similar conclusion.

Acknowledgements

The author(s)/editor(s) and publishers wish to thank the following for permission to reproduce copyright material:

The BBC for permission to republish excerpts from 'Equal Opportunities and Diversity at the BBC', accessed at http:www.bbc.co.uk/info/policies/diversity.shtml#commitments on 28 July 2009; T. Garavan and C. Gubbins for Fig. 3.2, taken from their conference paper, *The changing context and role of the HRD professional*, presented at the 8th International Conference on HRD Research and Practice across Europe, Oxford, June 2007; UK Civil Service for Fig. 3.3, 'The business partner model in the UK civil service', 2005; Learning and Skills Research Centre for Fig. 5.1 'Myers-Briggs Type Indicator', Table 5.1 'Thorne and Gough's summary of the MBTI types', Fig. 5.6 'Coffield et al.'s families of learning styles', in Coffield, F., Moseley, D., Hall, E. and Ecclestone, K. (2004) *Learning Styles and Pedagogy in Post-16 Learning: A Systematic and Critical Review*, Learning and Skills Research Centre; Steve J. Armstrong for Fig. 5.2 'Cognitive Style Index Scale'; Peter Honey Publications for Fig. 5.4 'Dimensions of Honey and Mumford's learning cycle', Figs 10.6 and 10.8 'Honey and Mumford's learning cycle and styles', in Peter Honey and Alan Mumford, *The Learning Styles Questionnaire, 80-Item Version*, Peter Honey Publications, 2006; Roger Beale for the 'Bonding' cartoon in Chapter 7; Cengage for Fig. 8.1 'Classic experimental design', in de Vaus, *Surveys for Social Research*, 1993; HM Treasury for Fig. 8.2 'The ROAMEF cycle', HM Treasury, 2003, *The Green Book, Appraisal and Evaluation in Central Government*; Mike Rix for HRD in Practice 9.2, 'Learning in projects at Intraining NTP Consulting'; Berrett-Koehler Publishers for Fig. 8.4 'Levels of evaluation for training', adapted from Kirkpatrick, *Evaluating Training Programs*, 1998; Taylor & Francis publishers for Fig. 9.1, 'Contested possibilities in HRD' in Gold, J. and Smith, V. (2003) Advances towards a learning movement: translations at work, *Human Resource Development International*, 6(2): 139–52, and Fig. 18.2, 'Knowledge migration in IEs and international JVs', adapted from International HRD alliances in viable knowledge migration and development: the Czech Academic Link Project, *Human Resource Development International*, (2003) 6(3), Taylor & Francis Ltd, http://www.informaworld.com, reprinted by permission of the publisher; CIPD for Fig. 10.2 'MD and economic success', Fig. 10.4 'A virtuous learning cycle for MD', Fig. 10.5 'Triangle of effectiveness', and Fig. 10.7 'Types of MD', in Mumford and Gold, *Management Development: Strategies for Action*, 2004; Mike Hender for HRD in Practice 10.2, 'Action learning with the All Sector Management & Leadership Programme Strategic Forum', from www.sfbn-mandl.org.uk/alfl_success_stories.htm, accessed 4 February 2009; Table 12.1 'Belbin's team roles', reproduced by kind permission of Belbin Associates (www.belbin.com) from www.belbin.com/rte.asp?id=10; Emeraldinsight for Table 15.1 'Provision of training by small businesses', Matlay, Vocational education and training in Britain: a small business perspective, *Education and Training*, 1999; CEML for 'The Business Improvement Tool for Entrepreneurs', 2002, in Chapter 15; Nicholas Theodorakopoulos for Fig. 15.2 'A model of small business learning' from Theodorakopoulos and Wyer, *Small business growth and the use of networks*, paper presented at the 24th ISBA Conference, 2001; The Law Society for Table 16.1; Universities UK for

Table 17.1 'Trends in student numbers at UK HE institutions: 1994/95–2005/06' from www.universitiesuk.ac.uk/statistics; Warwick Institute for Employment Research for Table 17.2 'Classification of graduate jobs', (www2.warwick.ac.uk/fac/soc/ier/research/completed/7yrs2) and Figs 17.1 and 17.2, in Elias and Purcell, *Measuring Change in the Graduate Labour Market*, 2003; The Open University Centre for Higher Education Research and Information for Fig. 17.3, 'Perceptions of the degree programme five years on', from Brennan, J. (2008) *The Flexible Professional in the Knowledge Society (REFLEX): Overview Report*.

Every effort has been made to trace rights holders, but if any have been inadvertently overlooked the publishers would be pleased to make the necessary arrangements at the first opportunity.

List of Abbreviations

AAC	Australian Apprenticeship Centre		**LMX**	leader–member exchange (theory)
AQTF	Australian Quality Training Framework		**LO**	learning organization
AR	action research		**LSC**	Learning and Skills Council
BA	British Airways		**LSI**	Learning Style Inventory
BAA	British Airports Authority		**LSQ**	Learning Styles Questionnaire
CCT	cross-cultural training		**MBTI**	Myers-Briggs Type Indicator
CD-ROM	compact disc read only memory		**MD**	Management Development
CEHR	Commission for Equality and Human Rights		**ML**	Management Learning
CEML	Council for Excellence in Management and Leadership		**MLD**	Management and Leadership Development
CHRD	Critical HRD		**NCVO**	National Council for Voluntary Organizations
CIPD	Chartered Institute of Personnel and Development		**NHRD**	National HRD
CIT	continuous improvement team		**NOS**	National Occupational Standards
CoPs	communities of practice		**NQF**	National Qualification Framework
CPD	continuing professional development		**NVQ**	National Vocational Qualification
CSI	Cognitive Style Index		**OD**	Organization Development
CSR	corporate social responsibility		**OECD**	Organization for Economic Co-operation and Development
CU	corporate university		**OL**	Organizational Learning
EHR	equality and human rights		**PCN**	parent country national
EI	emotional intelligence		**PDP**	personal development plan
ELD	employee-led development		**QCA**	Qualifications and Curriculum Authority
EO	equal opportunities		**RDA**	Regional Development Agency
FDI	foreign direct investment		**RTO**	registered training organization (Australia)
FE	further education		**SDT**	self-directed team
FSC	future search conference		**SHRD**	Strategic HRD
GTO	group training organization (Australia)		**SME**	small and medium-sized enterprise
HCN	host country national		**SMWT**	self-managed work team
HE	higher education		**SNVQ**	Scottish National Vocational Qualification
HEPI	Higher Education Policy Institute		**SSC**	Sector Skills Council
HESA	Higher Education Statistics Agency		**SSDA**	Sector Skills Development Agency
HR	Human Resources		**STS**	sociotechnical systems
HRD	Human Resource Development		**SVQ**	Scottish Vocational Qualification
HRM	Human Resource Management		**T5**	Terminal 5 (Heathrow Airport)
ICT	information and communication technologies		**TCN**	transcountry/third country national
IiP	Investors in People		**T group**	training group
IPM	Institute of Personnel Development		**TM**	talent management
ISC	Industry Skills Council (Australia)		**TNA**	training needs analysis
IT	information technology		**TP**	training package (Australia)
JV	joint venture		**TQM**	Total Quality Management
LD	Leadership Development		**ULR**	union learning representative
LL	lifelong learning		**VET**	vocational education and training
			ZPD	zone of proximal development

HAVE A LOOK

Chapter 1
Encountering HRD

Encountering HRD

1

Jim Stewart, Julie Beardwell, Jeff Gold, Paul Iles and Rick Holden

Chapter learning outcomes

After studying this chapter, you should be able to:

- Consider the implementation of Human Resource Development (HRD) during change

- Establish why HRD is necessary

- Understand the purpose and direction of this book

Chapter outline

Introduction

This book is about Human Resource Development (HRD). You may ask what this is about and whether it warrants your attention and time. At one level, HRD might be considered as another subject to study, consisting of a body of knowledge to master and perhaps some skills to practise, just like any other subject. You might even think it is connected to other subjects like Human Resource Management (HRM), so if you like the idea of adding something on people learning to your repertoire, HRD could be a good option. However, we think it is more than just another subject, because the concern of HRD is not just about particular knowledge and skills but how so much of our lives now and in the future is tied to how we cope with a wide range of factors to which we all have to respond, for example dealing with the latest mobile phone technologies, getting your CV ready for employment, settling into a job, leading others or making sure lots of people get their act together on a significant project of change. HRD is concerned with all these aspects of life and many more. However, to make the point more clearly and more vividly, we would like you to examine a recent event where things seemed to go wrong and since we are talking about a £4.3bn project that was meant to present a number of organizations in the best possible light, we think it nicely exemplifies why a failure to understand HRD was very much part of the problem. See what strikes you in this encounter with HRD.

Muppets!

Muppets is not the usual term applied by workers to their managers, is it? Perhaps it is, or, more likely, it is a term brought out for special occasions. In this case, it was used by a rather mischievous airline pilot on 27 March 2008 on the occasion of the opening of Terminal 5 (T5) at Heathrow Airport in London. The full quotation was:

> It's the same muppets that made our lives a misery at Terminals 1, 2, 3 and 4 running the show, we should NOT be that surprised.

The comment was one of a number that appeared that day on a rather popular pilots' forum on the internet, used to share an interesting form of knowledge – rumours and gossip. What is notable is how this forum allows pilots to share their thoughts on a whole range of issues to do with flying and, as with so many web-based forums of this kind, we can learn quite a lot about the unofficial versions of what goes on in an organization. In this case, as indicated by the historic reference, it seems that the lessons of the past had not been learned and there seems to be an expectation of failure in the way managers at T5 manage projects of change.

What is also interesting about T5 is how the high expectations that it would solve what had become known as the 'Heathrow hassle' were quickly thrown into disarray within the first hours of its opening on 27 March. Soon after the first British Airways (BA) aircraft had left on time, things started to go wrong. There were problems with baggage handling, computer software, security screening of staff, car parking and transport and the lifts in the building failing. This all resulted in over 36,000 passengers being delayed, over 150 flights were cancelled and, at one point, over 23,000 bags had to be sorted manually. Some passengers had to camp out on the terminal floor and some aeroplanes left without luggage.

The chaotic images from T5 appeared on TV screens around the world, quickly turning a source of national pride into a 'national embarrassment'. BA had exclusive use of T5, and its spokesperson initially saw the problems as 'teething problems' and 'glitches' caused by 'staff familiarization'. However, as the problems worsened and the queues lengthened as check-ins were suspended, the company began to accept that this 'was not our finest hour', according to Chief Executive Willie Walsh. David Frost, director general of the British Chambers of Commerce, described events as a 'shambles', which sent a 'depressing message to businesses round the world'. It was, he said, 'a PR disaster'.[1]

Training and systems were quickly identified as the main reasons for the problems of T5. However, this was not how it was meant to be. T5 was planned and is operated by the British Airports Authority (BAA) and evidence would suggest that it had invested considerable amounts in training and systems to ensure successful completion of the project against the budget and the plan. It had been the largest construction project in Europe, employing around 4,000 workers at one time. Further, in an agreement between BAA and the London Learning and Skills Council (LSC), a Construction Training Centre sought to provide a supply of skilled workers who could be directly employed on the project and then elsewhere. In the early 2000s, there were recognized shortages of skilled workers in areas such as carpentry, bricklaying and steel erection. The centre seemed to provide a win–win opportunity for BAA, the LSC and the unions Unite and Amicus, providing job opportunities and training for local people. In 2005, 14 advanced apprentices started training as electricians and mechanical engineers. The apprentices, having completed level 2 qualifications at a college, were now able to do on-the-job training with theoretical support from the college, leading to a level 3 National Vocational Qualification (NVQ). The T5 project director declared his delight that the trainees were getting training and that there could not be 'a more exciting construction environment to learn in than T5'. A director of the LSC highlighted the value of such training in creating 'a world-class workforce'.

Nevertheless, despite this investment in skills in the construction of T5, when it came to the opening, training was identified as one of the main reasons for the difficulties. In a report from the House of Commons Transport Committee (2008), training was found to have been 'inadequate'. The committee had taken evidence from BA, BAA and the trade union Unite after questions in the House of Commons on 31 March 2008 relating to the 'disasters' at Heathrow. At the first session of evidence, BAA were seen as 'unhelpful and ill-prepared', with 'no satisfactory explanation as to how this national embarrassment had been allowed to unfold'.

The evidence on training suggested that all staff had attended courses but it had not been 'thorough'. The training had consisted of a film or slide followed by three days of 'familiarization' with the new building and site, 'an area the size of Hyde Park'. For two days out of the three, staff were shown around on a coach but there was no 'hands on training' and this was particularly important for the new baggage-handling system. Apparently, building delays prevented full testing, which would have allowed hands-on learning. However, for two years, BAA had held 'public trials' involving 15,000 members of the public and other 'stakeholders'. This allowed the exposure of problems and issues and improvements could be made. BAA told the committee that the tests might have been 'too uniform' and that 'the reality of the baggage that people put into the system was more diverse than our tests represented'.

In its evidence, Unite pointed to the failure of management to use the experience of the staff on what would work and how to work. Meetings with management had consisted of presentations. 'Deeper discussions' tended to ignore the warnings and the experience of staff 'who had worked there for years', focusing instead on the new technology and how management said it would be.

In its conclusion, the committee noted the revelation of 'serious failings' but also how the inquiry into events in March 2008 had enabled BAA, British Airways and Unite to work together on T5.

HRD encountered and this book

Having read this case, how far were you able to point to events and features that you might consider as HRD? Would it be the training of staff (or lack of it), or the attention to supplying skilled workers at the Construction Training Centre? These would normally be recognized as falling under the heading of HRD. But what about the failure to use the knowledge of staff 'who had worked there for years' or the use of internet forums to spread stories and gossip about the management at Heathrow (the 'muppets')? To include these sorts of consideration would suggest a rather broader understanding of HRD. Indeed, as a relatively young subject area, there are a variety of views about what HRD is and what it is not. You might spend some time gaining an initial understanding of the meaning of HRD and associated terms, its nature and scope (Chapter 2).

Clearly, there appears to have been a bit of history at Heathrow, with pilots pointing fingers at the managers and leaders, who don't seem to have learned from experience. This might raise questions about how managers (Chapter 10) and leaders (Chapter 11) can be developed. You might also wonder what the difference is between managers and leaders; suffice to say that there has been a considerable interest for many years in the development of managers and leaders. A key issue is whether managers and leaders were ready for the events as they unfolded. After all, there was a plan and presumably a strategy, which included investment in training. However, not all strategies are realized and unpredictable events can make the strategy appear inadequate. This is particularly evident in complex projects of change, which T5 undoubtedly was and is. How could the complexity of the change required be considered strategically and what role should HRD specialists have in such considerations (Chapter 3).

One of the most interesting features of the T5 project was its attention to investing in skills against a recognition of skilled worker shortages. There were agreements between key agencies, organizations and even trade unions to provide apprentice-level training leading to recognized qualifications. This was seen as part of a national need to create a 'world-class workforce'. As students of HRD, you might be interested in comparisons between different countries, their investment in skills and how the supply and quality of skills is matched to demand (Chapter 4). Policy can only go so far, however. It is how HRD is implemented and skills are applied that are valued and make the difference. This needs an understanding of how people learn (Chapter 5), how needs are identified (Chapter 6), how needs are translated through the design and delivery of learning events (Chapter 7) and how the application of skills is measured and valued (Chapter 8). In several ways, key ideas about effective implementation of HRD at T5 were not utilized. There were complaints about the lack of thoroughness of the training and, probably most importantly, the lack of opportunity to test things in practice and learn 'hands on'.

Did everyone assume that the 'familiarization' would be enough? One complaint was that management did not make use of experience in the form of lessons from the past and the understanding and knowledge of the existing workforce. They failed to understand the importance of learning at work and the knowledge embedded in the practice of the workforce (Chapter 9). The pilots were quick to highlight this through their electronic forum, as you probably do through your own membership of social networking sites such as Facebook and YouTube. Organizations are becoming increasingly aware of the power of e-learning (Chapter 14).

As you can hopefully see, an understanding of HRD can provide a wide consideration of key aspects of how organizations, projects and even countries work and deal with change. In each of the chapters referred to so far, you will find key ideas, theories and practice that could have been considered by the management and others at T5 – perhaps they were. In addition, we have also included other aspects we consider essential to this textbook. These include the importance of developing teams (Chapter 12), diversity in HRD (Chapter 13), small businesses (Chapter 15), continuing professional development and lifelong learning (Chapter 16), the particular needs of graduates (Chapter 17) and cross-cultural understanding (Chapter 18). In addition, because events tend to move so fast, we conclude with a chapter on the future of HRD and the tools to use in preparing for the future (Chapter 19).

We hope you find this book of value in your study of HRD. Our authors have all been briefed to present the key ideas and theories, with examples, where possible, of what works. In addition, in most chapters, there will be chance to do something, sometimes with others and sometimes using the internet. Let us know if you are learning. Contact us by email at:

Jeff Gold
j.gold@leedsmet.ac.uk

Rick Holden
r.holden@leedsmet.ac.uk

Paul Iles
p.iles@leedsmet.ac.uk

Jim Stewart
j.d.stewart@leedsmet.ac.uk

Julie Beardwell
j.beardwell@dmu.ac.uk

Note

1   All the quotes are taken from articles on the BBC News website, http://news.bbc.co.uk/, 28 March 2008.

Reference

House of Commons Transport Committee (2008) *The Opening of Heathrow Terminal 5*, 3 November, London, TSO.

SECTION 1 **LOOKING OUT**
MACRO CONSIDERATIONS OF HRD

The Nature and Scope of HRD

Jim Stewart, Jeff Gold, Paul Iles, Rick Holden and Julie Beardwell

2

Chapter learning outcomes

After studying this chapter, you should be able to:

- Describe the history and origins of HRD
- Debate the meanings associated with HRD theory and practice
- Evaluate the arguments provided in support of current debates
- Apply a range of concepts in critically assessing HRD practice

Chapter outline

Introduction

This book examines the idea of Human Resource Development (HRD). A general approach throughout the book is to focus on theoretical and conceptual understanding as well as the application of that understanding in practice. HRD is an area of professional practice as well as a subject of academic enquiry. The purpose of this first chapter is to look at the foundations of both. In other words, we will be concerned with discussing the results of academic theorizing and the results of research into professional practice. To achieve this purpose, we will provide a brief overview of the history and origins of the idea, identify the academic disciplines that have been drawn on to develop associated concepts and theories utilized within HRD, describe the various contexts in which HRD is argued to be practised and finally examine the current debates and emerging themes in HRD research.

Human Resource Development (HRD) takes capital letters for a reason. This reason is mostly associated with the interests of academics in universities (McGoldrick and Stewart, 1996). The capital letters denote a name and a proper noun that are used in academic titles of, for example, departments and personal titles such as Professor of Human Resource Development in universities. It is less common to see the term used in professional practice (Sambrook and Stewart, 2005). The words 'training' and 'development', used as both nouns and verbs, are more common in that context and sometimes are combined with the word 'learning', especially in personal and job titles. In fact, the Chartered Institute of Personnel and Development (CIPD), the professional body in the UK, use the words 'Learning and Development' rather than HRD in the title of its professional standards specifying the knowledge and skill requirements of professional practitioners (Harrison, 2005). It also titles its web pages as 'Learning, Training and Development'. So we can see here an immediate difference and distinction between HRD as a subject of academic enquiry and an area of professional practice. It is simply that HRD is more commonly used in academic contexts than it is in those of professional practice.

This simple difference also allows us to make a more important point. This is that HRD is a human construct. It does not have an objective or independent existence. In fact, 'it' is not even an 'it', at least not in the same sense that we say a chair is an 'it', as in 'it (the chair) has four legs and is used to sit on'. That being the case, we cannot describe and review the meaning and history of HRD as easily or in the same way as we might that of a chair. It is also the case that as a human construct, HRD does not have a settled and accepted meaning. Different people for different reasons argue different positions in relation to the meaning of HRD, and it is no easy or straightforward matter to determine whose argument might be right and whose might be wrong. In the end, there may be no definitive basis for making that judgement. Our own view is that this is the case, so in the end personal judgement has to be exercised in the face of ambiguity and uncertainty. The meaning of HRD is contested and subject to debate and argument. There is no definitive basis for deciding between the various arguments and positions. So, personal judgement, based on the best available evidence and a critical evaluation of and arguments built on that evidence, is the final determinant of a position on HRD. We will be using the term HRD as if it is indeed an 'it' in the rest of the chapter and most of the book. This is for the sake of brevity and ease of reading and should not be taken to negate our argument here.

The arguments made so far will be developed and expanded as this opening chapter proceeds. What is important at this point is that you are alerted to this overall uncertainty as you read what follows. We want you to exercise your personal judgement throughout this chapter and indeed throughout the book. It is best then to direct you on that path from the start. The Reflective questions below, as with others in the book, are designed to help you to achieve the objectives set for the chapter. These questions support the application and exercise of personal judgement. You will need to engage with others for this activity, which can be a group of colleagues or a seminar/tutorial group of students.

Reflective questions

1 What reasons can you think of for the greater use of HRD in academic contexts compared to professional practice contexts?

2 What implications other than ambiguity and uncertainty arise from HRD being a contested term?

3 What criteria might you use in judging the validity of evidence and the logic of arguments on the meaning of HRD?

History and origins of HRD

As with its meaning, there is also debate over the origins of the term HRD. Some argue that it can be traced to what is known as 'Organization Development' (OD), which began in the USA sometime in the 1940s (Blake, 1995) without, as it were, catching on. Others, including Blake, attribute the first specific formulation to the American writer Leonard Nadler (1970). The definition offered by Nadler of this then new term is instructive:

> HRD is organized learning experiences provided by employers, within a specified period of time, to bring about the possibility of performance improvement and/or personal growth (quoted in Nadler and Nadler, 1989, p. 4)

This definition is interesting for reasons that will become clear soon and so it will be useful to bear it in mind. It is also an important definition because it shaped debates and controversies that continue now. For example, there seem to be two purposes attached to HRD in the definition. One is the possibility of 'improving performance'. However, it also suggests a purpose of bringing about 'personal growth'. It might be worth asking whether there is no connection between these two possible outcomes but the definition certainly seems to imply this is the case. These two possible purposes are, however, the focus of disagreement between those who adopt what is known as a 'performative' focus for HRD and those who adopt what is known as a 'learning' focus (Rigg et al., 2007). We do not need to examine these debates here but for now just note that the term 'HRD' is American in origin and emerged in common usage there sometime in the 1970s.

Debate centred on a number of factors in the years that followed. One significant piece of work to attempt to settle that debate was commissioned by the American Society of Training and Development and conducted by Pat McLagan (1989). This produced a specification of the key activities of HRD professionals in their practice, which were argued to encompass all levels and foci of development in work organizations, for example career and organization as well as personal and professional development. Rather than settle matters, McLagan's work merely stimulated new avenues of research and debate. Notable among these have been the contributions of McLean (2004) and Swanson (2001), in their debates on the foundations and theories of HRD, and Lynham (2000) and others on theory building in HRD. Other writers have focused on the basic philosophy of HRD, for example Holton and Kuchinke (see McGoldrick et al., 2004, for a summary).

Adoption of the term HRD came later to Europe and the UK, where it did not really prove popular until the late 1980s and more particularly the 1990s. Two early UK references were in Mumford (1986) and Stewart (1989). A simpler debate than that seen in the USA occurred in the UK between Oxtoby and Coster (1992), later contributed to by Stewart (1992), and published in the professional journal *Training and Development*. This debate centred on the values inherent in referring to 'employees', and thus people, as 'resources' and so debated the validity and utility of the term 'HRD'. Themes similar to those raised by Oxtoby and Coster are still subject to scrutiny (see, for example, Kuchinke and Han, 2005). More sophisticated debates have since grown in the UK, including that of Lee (2004), who argues against any attempt to define HRD on the basis that, in uncertain and unpredictable times, this would give 'the appearance of being in control' and 'serve the political and social needs of the minute' (p. 38). An additional continuing theme in HRD debates is that of the relationship of the term to longer established concepts such as Human Resource Management (HRM). This is a theme addressed early by Stewart and McGoldrick (1996) and in their later work with Watson (McGoldrick et al., 2004). The term 'HRM' had become prominent in the UK from the late 1980s as a particular approach to managing people, again after earlier work in the USA. HRM is argued to be more strategic in its outlook than personnel management as a necessary response to globalization and the internationalization of technology through gaining the commitment of workers as a source of competitive advantage and increasing productivity (Bratton and Gold, 2007). HRD could be seen as a subset of the HRM movement, although we will argue it has become increasingly a movement in its own right.

Another continuing theme on both sides of the Atlantic is the relationship of HRD with education, training and development. Part of that theme is to define each of the concepts so that each can be distinguished from the others. Stewart (1999) is not alone in suggesting that it is a futile debate but it does continue to fascinate some. A final continuing theme is differentiating HRD from Strategic HRD (SHRD). This too might be argued to be futile, especially since some writers distinguish HRD from training on the basis that HRD is strategic while training is operational (Stewart and McGoldrick, 1996). Others insist on a difference between HRD and SHRD, for example Walton (1999).

Many of the debates referred to above concern and are informed by different views on the way HRD theory and practice draws on established academic disciplines, so we will examine those possibilities in the next section. Before moving on, the following Activity will be useful in furthering understanding of the debates that have led to the current views on HRD.

Activity

Access two articles from the journals below, which will help to answer the following questions:

1 What is meant by the notion of 'performative' perspectives of HRD?

2 What is meant by the notion of 'learning' perspectives of HRD?

3 What are the key differences between the two perspectives?

4 What in your view are the main arguments in favour of and against each perspective?

Human Resource Development International – www.tandf.co.uk/journals/routledge/13678868.html

Human Resource Development Quarterly – www.josseybass.com/WileyCDA/WileyTitle/productCd-HRDQ.html

Human Resource Development Review – http://hrd.sagepub.com/

Academic disciplines

It might seem a subject of little dispute to determine which academic disciplines underpin and inform HRD. That is part of the debate, however, at least as to which are the most significant and influential (see McGoldrick et al., 2004). What can be said with some confidence is that HRD is concerned with human behaviour, so disciplines concerned with understanding and explaining that behaviour are of some potential relevance to HRD (Stewart, 2007). These disciplines are referred to as the 'social sciences'. This generic heading is generally taken to include economics, politics, geography, sociology, social psychology, psychology and anthropology. Each of these can be and is argued to have informed and influenced the development of theory and understanding of HRD.

Psychology and its variants such as social psychology are probably not disputed as being central to the development of HRD. This is because the latter is focused on changing behaviour through learning, and psychology has been central in the development of learning theories. Chapter 5 recognizes this and it is rare to find a textbook on HRD that does not include some discussion of learning theory. Human behaviour, while in some senses always a phenomenon of individuals, occurs in social contexts. Individuals behave in the context of, in relation and response to and, mostly, in the company of other individuals. This raises the possibility that learning is as much a social process as an individual process, so even within the limited context of learning theories, those developed in psychology may not tell the whole story. This point aside, we know that as social beings humans congregate in groups of varying types and sizes, for example families, tribes, organizations and nations. Thus, social sciences such as social psychology, sociology and anthropology are also drawn on because of their contributions to understanding human behaviour in the context of human collectives. A specific example of recent and current topicality is the application of the concept of 'culture' in organization studies. This concept was originally developed in anthropology in the study of tribes, communities and societies (Stewart and McGoldrick, 1996). Its relevance and application within HRD is because of interest in applying the concept of 'culture' to the study of work organizations and the association of HRD with such organizations, as suggested by Nadler's definition, given above. There are those who argue that HRD is primarily if not exclusively concerned with human behaviour in the context of work organization. We will examine this in more detail in the next section. For now though, this argument in part supports the view that economics and to a lesser extent politics are also essential disciplines informing HRD theory and practice (McLean, 2004). An example of the application of economic theory is the notion of 'human capital', which seeks to explain investment in education and training as well as being used to justify such investment (see Becker, 1964). A related economic concept is that of 'return on investment', which is often argued to be the 'gold standard' of evaluating HRD activity (see Chapter 8). Politics is argued to be of relevance because of its central concern with the notion of power and how power is and can be exercised in human groups. Power is a key concept in OD and, as we saw earlier, OD is held to be a component of HRD. This is not the only reason though, as it is an axiom of organizations that power is essential to influence decision making, especially in relation to resource allocation, so HRD practitioners need to understand these processes if they are to secure resources to support their work (Harrison, 2005). Geography may seem the least likely social science to have relevance to HRD, and it certainly has not been as significant as the others discussed. However, with the theme of globalization now prominent, along with the economic and social problems facing groups, communities, regions, cities and nations, it would seem that geography is bound to become another source of understanding for those in HRD in future years (Marquardt et al., 2004).

This brief summary of academic disciplines suggests that HRD is not itself subject to independent theorizing or theory development. This view is not necessarily widely shared (Mankin, 2001) but it does have some support (Stewart, 2007). The summary also suggests that only the social sciences are of interest to HRD. This view is also open to challenge, since at least some of the natural sciences also have useful and relevant contributions to understanding human behaviour. This is perhaps most obviously the case with the natural sciences concerned with the development and application of evolutionary theory, for example zoology, ethology and biology. That there are connections between the natural and social sciences in theorizing and understanding human behaviour is best demonstrated by the development in recent years of 'hybrid' disciplines such as social biology and evolutionary psychology. Little use has been made to date of the natural sciences or the newer hybrid disciplines in developing HRD but they may become more significant in the future. Similarly, there are those who would wish to see a greater influence of the arts and humanities in HRD. This is part of a wider concern about the apparent failure of business schools to provide relevant ideas to actual business practice. There is a claim that the need to conform to rigorous models of scientific research loses the connection to the realities of practice (Ghoshal, 2005). Thus research into the practice of HRD can reveal the very human processes of talk, persuasion, use of rhetoric and storytelling in bringing about HRD activities and the valuing of such activities (Gold and Smith, 2003).

Contexts of practice

So far we have examined the origins and underlying academic disciplines of HRD and found that those questions are not easily settled. The same is true when we look at the contexts of HRD practice. The definition given earlier from Nadler illustrates this quite clearly. It specifically mentions and so focuses on 'employers'. An alternative definition provides a different view and different possibilities:

> HRD is constituted by planned interventions in organizational and individual learning processes. (Stewart, 2007, p. 66)

This definition allows for several additional contexts. First, the term 'organization' is not limited to those who engage in an employment relationship with individuals. Therefore, according to this definition, HRD can be and is practised by more than 'employers'. An example might be charitable organizations that rely on voluntary workers rather than employees. Another might be purely voluntary organizations such as interest or community groups. Second, the focus on 'planned interventions in individual learning processes' opens up a wide range of possibilities. These might include voluntary groups such as the Scout movement or local youth clubs. It might also be said to encompass what happens in schools during compulsory education. A more widely held view is that HRD does encompass further and higher education, since these two contexts have a firm focus on and purpose of planned interventions in individual learning processes (see, for example, Stewart and Knowles, 2003; Stewart and Harte, 2008).

The possible contexts of compulsory, further and higher education support a view that policies pursed by national governments are also a context of HRD practice. This context is associated with a number of different terms including national policies, vocational education and training (VET) and National HRD (NHRD). The latter term has recently become popular through the work of McLean (2004) in the USA, but VET is more common in Europe, including the UK. This focus on government interventions also raises the question of communities and whole societies being a context of HRD practice. There are other arguments to support this, for example much of the early work of OD practitioners in the USA and the UK centred on communities and community issues such as race relations. If we accept that HRD encompasses and includes OD, as suggested by McLagan (1989), those early programmes and others like them today are yet another context of HRD practice.

Activity

A number of government departments play a role in national HRD considerations. For example, go to www.berr.gov.uk/ for the Department for Business, Enterprise and Regulatory Reform and www.dius.gov.uk/ for the Department for Innovation, Universities and Skills. These departments cover policy in England but for Scotland, go to www.scotland.gov.uk/Topics/Education, for Wales, go to http://new.wales.gov.uk/topics/educationandskills/?lang=en and for Northern Ireland, go to www.delni.gov.uk/index/publications/pubs-sectoral/skills-strategy-ni.htm.

This brief discussion illustrates a number of important points. First, the definition of HRD that is adopted will influence and shape the contexts in which HRD is understood to be practised. The definition offered by Stewart might include families as a context of HRD practice, since parents engage in planned interventions in the learning processes of their children, but Nadler's definition would certainly exclude such a context. It might be reasonably argued that taking Stewart's definition to include families would be stretching the concept of HRD too far, and, in contrast, that Nadler's definition is too restrictive and excludes areas of legitimate interest to researchers and professional practitioners alike. Second, 'professional practice' may be both helpful and legitimate as the defining feature determining contexts. Thus, where professionals with expertise in developing human resources work and practise determines the contexts of HRD practice. Adopting this suggestion as a guiding principle would allow for those contexts suggested in this section but it would not stop debate. For example, many who work in higher education, although their job and title includes the word 'lecturer', would not see themselves as HRD practitioners and so would argue against such a label. But their job and everyday work is certainly included in Stewart's definition, irrespective of their particular subject, for example lecturers in mathematics, physics, history and sociology are all engaged in the common task of designing and delivering planned interventions in learning processes. Such lecturers might argue that they are primarily specialists in their subject. A counterargument might accept that premise but then point out that they need also to be specialists in supporting and facilitating learning since they work in education.

A final point to arise from the discussion of contexts of practice is that HRD has historically and traditionally been associated with training in work organizations and as a tool of management in that context, but as it has developed as an academic subject, the contexts of practice have been broadened to encompass arenas not previously seen as legitimate. We can now say with confidence that HRD occurs in informal as well as formal organizations, at national and perhaps supranational as well as organization levels and, with the rise of personal coaching, for example, also at individual levels outside organization contexts, especially since individuals are increasingly encouraged to become lifelong learners (see Chapter 16).

Reflective questions

1 How do the academic disciplines drawn on in researching and theorizing HRD influence the definition and meaning of the term?

2 Based on your understanding so far of the meaning of the term HRD, which academic disciplines have been and are most significant in shaping current definitions and meanings?

3 How does the definition of HRD influence contexts of practice? Which contexts of practice do you consider to be legitimate and why?

Key debates and emerging themes

We have seen that there are a number of areas of debate within HRD as both a field of academic enquiry and professional practice. These can be summarized as follows:

- Defining and attaching meaning to the term

- The possibility of theorizing HRD

- Assuming the possibility of theorizing, actual theories of HRD

- The significance, role and impact of various established academic disciplines in HRD theorizing

- The number and location of legitimate areas of HRD practice.

Some of these debates have been engaged in since the emergence of the term 'HRD', for example defining and attaching meaning to the term. Some are more recent and are still, to some extent, emerging themes, for example the possibility of theorizing HRD, which has, in chronological terms, actually emerged after early attempts to produce theories of HRD. This final section will identify a number of additional emerging themes in HRD debates.

The first theme is that of HRD in the development of small and medium-sized enterprises (SMEs). Debates here centre on at least three factors. The first is the extent to which HRD is practised in SMEs and the extent to which HRD theorizing has taken enough account of the different and variable contexts of small organizations (see Stewart and Beaver, 2004). The second factor is that of SME development in the sense of supporting and facilitating the establishment of new businesses and social enterprises. The key question here is what if any role is there for HRD and HRD practitioners in that process, especially in light of the growing consensus that learning and development in SMEs are best considered as informal processes (CBI, 2003)? The final focus is the role of higher education institutions in developing enterprising characteristics in university graduates. Related to this is the debate on the precise meaning of enterprise development in that context (Stewart and Harte, 2008).

A second emerging theme for debate is the value of adopting more precise foci for HRD research and practice. Such foci can be sector, function or method specific. Examples of the first of these include the public as opposed to the private sector, or even more specific sectors within that (see, for example, Sambrook and Stewart, 2007). An example of the second is Leadership Development (Chapter 11), which has in recent years attracted a good deal of research by HRD academics and specialization by HRD professionals. The third focus can be illustrated by a profusion of both research and practice interest in recent years in coaching as a method within HRD. All these varying foci and examples raise a similar question: is HRD different and therefore worthy of special attention in different sectors or functions, or when particular methods are adopted? This is not a question to be addressed in this chapter, but it is one that a full reading of the book may at least help to answer.

The third emerging theme and area of debate is the difference between HRD and its relationship with other foci of academic research and professional practice. We have already mentioned the relationship with HRM but there are others such as 'learning organization', 'Organizational Learning' and 'Knowledge Management'. All these share similarities with HRD, in that they have emerged as terms used in academic contexts as titles of departments and professorships, have their own academic and professional journals and also are applied in practice with people holding jobs in work organizations and government agencies with those or similar words used in their titles. The main issue is that the terms focus both academic enquiry and professional practice on the same social practices as does HRD (Stewart, 2005). The questions that arise therefore include: to what extent and how are they different from and the same as HRD?

The final emerging theme and area of debate is the most recent and is referred to as 'Critical HRD' (CHRD). This focus has emerged partly in response to the rise of critical management studies, although some of the themes addressed in CHRD such as ethics have a longer history than critical management as an area of debate (see, for example, Stewart, 1998; McGoldrick et al., 2004). CHRD questions the traditional and taken-for-granted assumptions of the purpose, nature, application and activities of HRD and raises issues to do with legitimacy, power, control and the economic and social context of HRD theory and practice. The term 'CHRD' became established in several academic conferences of the late 1990s and early 2000s and has led to a number of special editions of journals (Trehan et al., 2004, 2006) as well as edited collections in books (Elliott and Turnbull, 2005; Rigg et al., 2007).

CHRD does not represent a separate and particular strand in HRD research and practice, but provides alternative perspectives that can and do inform mainstream HRD theory and practice. Thus you will not find chapters on CHRD as such in this book, but you will find chapters that are informed to varying extents and in varying ways by work done by academics within CHRD. You will also find chapters that address some of the other emerging themes and areas of debate identified here. For example, there are chapters devoted to specific functions such as leadership and with specific contexts such as small businesses. The book therefore provides and examines current knowledge on emerging as well as established themes in HRD, and in doing so, also reviews and evaluates current debates on all those themes. To help to prepare you for getting the most out of the rest of the book, answer the Discussion questions below before moving on with your reading of the book.

Summary

- This chapter has introduced the term 'HRD' and briefly examined its origins and history as well as its core academic disciplines, contexts of practice and emerging themes and debates. We can conclude that HRD is not a simple or straightforward term and that it has no settled meaning.

- As a recent and abstract human construct, HRD is also subject to continuous and continuing debate. Such debate encompasses not just its definition and meaning but also the possibility of any theory of HRD as well as some additional emerging themes.

- There is a key debate among HRD professionals and academics between those who adopt a 'performative' focus for HRD and those who adopt a 'learning' focus.

- HRD is concerned with human behaviour and so disciplines in the social sciences concerned with understanding and explaining that behaviour are of some potential relevance to HRD.

- HRD is not restricted to work organizations and there has been growing interest in the practice of HRD in a range of contexts such as charities and voluntary contexts.

- At a national level, HRD is now a crucial emerging consideration, with a focus on government interventions in pursuit of national economic and social agendas.

- There are emerging themes of enquiry, practice and debate, which include sector-, function- and method-specific practice as well as the notion of Critical HRD.

Discussion questions

1 What does the term HRD mean to you?
2 How would you differentiate HRD from training and development in work organizations?
3 What is the value, if any, of using the term 'HRD' instead of training and development?
4 What is the value, if any, of the term 'CHRD'?
5 How does HRD relate to the term 'HRM'? How is it similar and different?
6 Which of the emerging themes within HRD research and writing are the most important and why?

Further reading

Lee, M.M., Stewart, J. and Woodall, J. (eds) (2004) *New Frontiers in Human Resource Development*, London, Routledge.

Lepak, D.P. and Snell, S.A. (1999) The human resource architecture: toward a theory of human capital allocation and development, *Academy of Management Review*, **24**(1): 31–48.

Stewart, J. and McGoldrick, J. (1996) *Human Resource Development: Perspectives, Strategies and Practice*, London, Pitman.

Swanson, R.A. (2001) Human resource development and its underlying theory, *Human Resource Development International*, **4**(3): 299–312.

References

Becker, G.S. (1964) *Human Capital*, New York, National Bureau of Economic Research.

Blake, R. (1995) Memories of HRD, *Training and Development*, **49**(3): 22–8.

Bratton, J. and Gold, J. (2007) *Human Resource Management: Theory and Practice,* Basingstoke, Palgrave Macmillan.

CBI (Confederation of British Industry) (2003) *Informality Works: A New Approach to Training for SMEs*, London, CBI.

Elliott, C. and Turnbull, S. (eds) (2005) *Critical Thinking in Human Resource Development*, London, Routledge.

Ghoshal, S. (2005) Bad management theories are destroying good management practices, *Academy of Management Learning and Education*, **4**(1): 75–81.

Gold, J. and Smith, V. (2003) Advances towards a learning movement: translations at work, *Human Resource Development International*, **6**(2): 139–52.

Harrison, R. (2005) *Learning and Development*, 4th edn, London, CIPD.

Kuchinke, K.P. and Han, H.-Y. (2005) Should caring be viewed as a competence? (Re-)Opening the dialogue over the limitations of competency frameworks in HRD, *Human Resource Development International*, **8**(3): 385–9.

Lee, M.M. (2004) A refusal to define HRD, in M.M. Lee, J. Stewart and J. Woodall (eds) *New Frontiers in Human Resource Development*, London, Routledge.

Lynham, S.A. (2000) Theory building in the human resource development profession, *Human Resource Development Quarterly*, **11**(2): 159–78.

McGoldrick, J. and Stewart, J. (1996) The HRM–HRD nexus, in J. Stewart and J. McGoldrick (eds) *HRD: Perspectives, Strategies and Practice*, London, Pitman.

McGoldrick, J., Stewart, J., Watson, S. (eds) (2004) *Understanding Human Resource Development: A Research Based Approach*, London, Routledge.

McLagan, P. (1989) *Models for HRD Practice*, Alexandra, VA, ASTD Press.

McLean, G.N. (2004) National human resource development: what in the world is it?, *Advances in Developing Human Resources*, **6**(3): 269–75.

Mankin, D. (2001) A model for human resource development, *Human Resource Development International*, **4**(1): 65–85.

Marquardt, M., Berger, N. and Loan, P. (2004) *HRD in the Age of Globalization: A Practical Guide to Workplace Learning in the Third Millennium*, New York, Basic Books.

Mumford, A. (ed.) (1986) *Handbook of Management Development*, 2nd cdn, Aldershot, Gower.

Nadler, L. (1970) *Developing Human Resources*, Austin, Learning Concepts.

Nadler, L. and Nadler, Z. (1989) *Developing Human Resources*, 3rd edn, San Francisco, Jossey-Bass.

Oxtoby, B. and Coster, P. (1992) HRD: a sticky label, *Training and Development*, **10**(9): 31–2.

Rigg, C., Stewart, J. and Trehan, K. (2007) *Critical Human Resource Development: Beyond Orthodoxy*, Harlow, FT/Prentice Hall.

Sambrook, S. and Stewart, J. (2005) A critical review of researching human resource development: the case of a pan-European project, in C. Elliott and S. Turnbull (eds) *Critical Thinking in Human Resource Development,* London, Routledge.

Sambrook, S. and Stewart, J. (2007) HRD in health and social care, in S. Sambrook and J. Stewart (eds) *Human Resource Development in the Public Sector*, London, Routledge.

Stewart, J. (1989) Bringing about organisation change: a framework, *Journal of European Industrial Training*, **13**(6): 31–5.

Stewart, J. (1992) Towards a model of HRD, *Training and Development*, **10**(10): 26–9.

Stewart, J. (1998) Intervention and assessment: the ethics of HRD, *Human Resource Development International*, **1**(1): 16–22.

Stewart, J. (1999) *Employee Development Practice*, London, FT/Pitman.

Stewart, J. (2005) The current state and status of HRD research, *Learning Organisation Journal*, **12**(1): 90–5.

Stewart, J. (2007) The ethics of HRD, in C. Rigg, J. Stewart and K. Trehan (eds) *Critical Human Resource Development: Beyond Orthodoxy*, Harlow, Prentice Hall.

Stewart, J. and Beaver, G. (eds) (2004) *HRD in Small Organisations: Research and Practice*, London, Routledge.

Stewart, J. and Harte, V. (2008) Enterprise education and its impact on career intentions, paper presented at the 9th International Conference on HRD Research and Practice across Europe, IESEG School of Management, Lille, 21–23 May.

Stewart, J. and Knowles, V. (2003) Mentoring in undergraduate business management programmes, *Journal of European Industrial Training*, **27**(3): 147–59.

Stewart, J. and McGoldrick, J. (1996) *Human Resource Development: Perspectives, Strategies and Practice*, London, Pitman.

Swanson, R.A. (2001) Human resource development and its underlying theory, *Human Resource Development International*, **4**(3): 299–312.

Trehan, K., Rigg, C. and Stewart, J. (2004) Special issue on Critical Human Resource Development, *Journal of European Industrial Training*, **28**(8/9): 611–24.

Trehan, K., Rigg, C. and Stewart, J. (2006) Special issue on Critical HRD, *International Journal of Training and Development*, **10**(1): 4–15.

Walton. J. (1999) *Strategic Human Resource Development,* London, FT/Prentice Hall.

Strategic HRD and the Learning and Development Function

3

Jim Stewart, Paul Iles, Jeff Gold, Rick Holden, Helen Rodgers and Hazel Kershaw-Solomon

Chapter learning outcomes

After studying this chapter, you should be able to:

- Explain the meaning of Strategic HRD (SHRD)
- Explain the key ideas informing an HRD strategy and policy
- Understand the link between change and HRD
- Assess the role of the learning and development professional

Chapter outline

Introduction

In a statement in the Foreword of the Leitch (2006) review of skills, it was suggested that:

> Without increased skills, we would condemn ourselves to a lingering decline in competitiveness, diminishing economic growth and a bleaker future for all.

This argument can be combined with significant changes in technology, global markets and customer requirements and such disturbances as the 'credit crunch' in 2008 and resource costs. As a consequence, HRD needs to be considered strategically by governments, organizations and individuals. Indeed, it is suggested that the move to make HRD more strategic provides a clear signal that learning and development are important. Bratton and Gold (2007) provide the following indicators of this move:

1 HRD emphasizes 'investment' in people rather than training as a 'cost', allowing a longer term perspective on outcomes and value-added.

2 HRD feeds other HRM polices such as recruitment for skills and retaining and rewarding talented employees as part of a qualitative difference between organizations and the development of a primary internal market with attention to continuous learning.

3 HRD is a key feature of a 'high road' HRM strategy (Cooke, 2000), which seeks to engender loyalty and commitment among employees. Through learning by employees, organization strategy itself can be transformed.

By adopting a more strategic view of HRD, organizations can consider learning at individual, group and organizational levels and as a source of competitive advantage. Learning occurs throughout the organization and is seen as a way of coping with change and generating innovation. Thus, Prahalad and Hamel (1990, p. 82) argue, 'collective learning' is an aspect of an organization's core competencies that other organizations cannot easily copy, and Ashton and Felstead (1995, p. 235) regard investment in skills as a 'litmus test' for a change in the way people are managed. One vital image that has emerged over the past decade is that of high performance working based on high-level skills and high discretion in work performance and decision making (ILO, 2000).

If HRD strategically becomes the concern of everyone, this has implications for those who specialize in its practice, and there has been growing interest in the profession of HRD. After many years of low interest and awareness, a growing number of HRD practitioners are seeking to advance their status through membership of the CIPD (Gold et al., 2003). In addition, there is more attention to the theoretical foundations of professional status, with journals and conferences devoted to HRD as a separate field of study rather than a small part of HRM. In this chapter, we will seek to explore the connection between Strategic HRD (SHRD) and the HRD function. First, we will consider strategy and the formation of HRD policies and plans, and then the link to change as a crucial source of understanding in SHRD. Finally, we will explore how the HRD function can benefit or otherwise from the enhanced status of HRD.

SHRD and HRD strategy

Attaching the word 'strategy' to organization functions is now so common that it is in danger of becoming meaningless. The word itself is associated with its own function of strategic management, which in these terms is seen to be a central part of general and senior management, for example a function of chief executives, managing directors, chief operating officers and other similar titles. It is also associated with the specialist and non-specialist contributions to organization management of top and senior functional managers, especially those with responsibility for finance, operations and perhaps marketing. The concern of top and senior managers with strategy follows from the history and development of the concept, which is mainly the application of economic theory to long-range planning and the long-term survival and prosperity in economic terms of business and commercial organizations. As with any and every other aspect and function of management, strategy has seen developments in theory and practice through academic research and academic and practitioner writing and publications.

In conventional terms, strategic management is concerned with ensuring the long-term survival of organizations. The key outcome of strategic management is a set of strategies that are themselves plans, programmes and activities and the resource allocations to support them. Strategies are based on an analysis of external and internal factors and a 'matching' process to ensure that the organization continues to be successful, especially in relation to formulating and achieving appropriate organizational-level performance goals and objectives in the face of competition from other organizations operating in the same markets. While it is of some value, it is a limited perspective on the meaning of strategy. What emerges from it for HRD is a view that top managers set out a vision and mission for an organization and develop organization or 'corporate' goals and strategy from which are derived business strategy and then functional strategy, including a strategy for HRD. This suggests a linear and static process, where fixed plans for HRD are formulated to contribute to the achievement of the business strategy, which in turn contributes to the achievement of the corporate strategy.

The logic of this understanding of strategic management and strategy is that HRD strategy is impossible in the absence of corporate and business strategy and that the purpose of HRD strategy is to support, or serve, business strategy. Stewart and McGoldrick (1996) adopt a different view of the strategic management process, which allows for a more proactive and processual contribution from HRD. In their nonlinear model of the strategy process, the focus is first on what they refer to as the 'strategic direction' of a given organization. This suggests the possibility of differences between what actually happens in practice in relation to long-term survival and what was and is determined and planned by top and senior managers. Stewart and McGoldrick go on to argue that strategic direction is the result of the interplay of a number of internal factors, the most significant of which are culture, leadership, the commitment of employees, and the approaches and responses to changed and changing internal and external conditions. They further argue that HRD in theory and practice has a major influence on each of these factors:

- shaping organizational culture

- developing current and future leaders

- building commitment among organization members

- anticipating and managing responses to changed conditions.

Thus, HRD is a strategic function as it has a significant impact on long-term survival. This view is supported by the work of Fredericks and Stewart (1996), who examine the connection between strategy and HRD from a processual rather than a functional perspective and argue that there are clear and mutually influencing relationships between organization structure (internally facing), organization strategy (externally facing), the actions and behaviours of organization members, management/leadership style and HRD policies and practices. So both pieces of work suggest that HRD is in and of itself strategic, since its practices have an impact on long-term survival.

SHRD

The previous point raises the question of whether there is any place for the concept of SHRD. If, as suggested above, HRD is by definition strategic, is there a need for and can there be any meaning attached to the concept of 'SHRD'? Many would argue such a need and therefore a distinction between HRD and SHRD, prominent among them Garavan (1991, 2007) and Walton (1999). Early work on SHRD by these authors adopted the conventional view of strategic management as being a long-term planning function in the hands (or perhaps brains) of top and senior managers. More recent work, summarized and applied by Garavan (2007), attempts to integrate both functional and processual perspectives on strategy to argue a meaning and space for SHRD. The main premise remains that HRD can be practised at an operational level without having connections with or relevance to corporate and business strategy or impact on long-term survival. This being the case, SHRD is distinguished from HRD, according to Garavan (2007, p. 11), because 'SHRD is a multi-level concept whose contribution to the organization is to enhance its performance in the long term'. It is perhaps a pity that in support of this claim, Garavan then quotes and cites the work of York, who actually writes about HRD rather than SHRD, rather suggesting that York is of the view that HRD is strategic in and of itself. This said, Garavan provides a detailed analysis of the literature on SHRD over the past 15 years as the basis for a persuasive argument on the nature and meaning of SHRD as a conceptual understanding of professional practice. His work does, however, leave the question of a clear distinction between HRD and SHRD open.

HRD strategies and plans

Despite the uncertainties over HRD and SHRD, it is nonetheless useful to apply the concept of 'strategy' in relation to HRD practice. In common with Stewart (1999), we adopt here a meaning in common usage, that an HRD strategy is a course of action intended to have long-term rather than short-term impact on significant rather than marginal areas of performance at organizational rather than individual level. The particular course of action will also have been arrived at through a series of decisions resulting from analysis of external as well as internal factors and be intended to directly contribute to matching organizational capability to changed and changing market conditions in order to achieve competitive advantage. If the particular organization in question does not operate in a market and so does not have competitors, the purpose will be related to whatever conditions affect long-term survival, for example satisfying funding and political stakeholders in the case of a public or quasi-public sector organization such as a university.

So HRD strategies are programmes and activities that make a contribution to long-term survival. Cultural change programmes around, for example, developing high levels of customer service through attitudes and values as well as knowledge and skills are a clear example of an HRD strategy. Others commonly include leadership and/or talent management programmes designed and intended to ensure a sufficient quantity and quality of future senior and top managers over, say, a 5-, 10- or 20-year period. Here 'quality' usually refers to a set of behavioural descriptors that reflect and express organizational values so as to ensure consistency and continuity in managerial and leadership style. Programmes to support the development of particular organizational forms, such as a 'learning organization' (see Chapter 9), can also be described as HRD strategy. The use of the word 'support' here is significant. HRD strategies are commonly components in a range of programmes and activities designed and intended to bring about the kinds of changes implicit in these examples. Other components will usually include related HR strategies in, for example, employer branding in support of recruitment and selection, job and work design, employee reward and performance management. These HRD and HR strategies will in turn be linked with business strategy, for example the development of new products and/or distribution channels that require new and different competencies. It should be clear from this that the meaning being attached to the notion of strategy here is consistent with the conventional view, which leads to HRD being seen as the 'servant' of corporate and business strategy. HRD in Practice 3.1 provides an example of how one organization gave more strategic importance to HRD.

Security firm focuses on learning

Learning and development will be top of the agenda for G4S Security Services (UK) this year, according to its new HR director. Valerie Dale, who took up the post in January, explained: 'Learning and development is something that needs to be properly embedded in the company's culture. We need to look at how we can be better, quicker and slicker on the development side.'

Dale intends to introduce cross-divisional placements within G4S Security Services, a division of FTSE 100 firm G4S, saying: 'We want to try to move away from the traditional chalk and talk method.' Dale explained that encouraging cross-functional placements – for example HR employees spending time in the finance department – was 'a healthy thing to do ... It can be used to build up a rapport and there's the opportunity to resolve one another's problems. It's a great career development opportunity.'

Dale added that she would like to oversee the development of better qualifications for the industry, providing skills for life. She said that there was 'a good business proposition there in terms of credibility'.

A UK leadership programme for senior members is also being set up and is expected to launch later this month. Dale said: 'That's an extremely important strategy for us. It's vital that leaders are leading and are not being dictatorial through being led by market forces.'

Dale is also considering using reward to encourage development. She explained: 'The old days of long service rewards are dead and buried. We should have some based on development, look-ing at recognized milestones and step-ping stones.'

Source: Adapted from Chubb, L. (2008) *People Management*, 6 March

Designing and implementing programmes that meet the characteristics described here are not the only contribution of HRD practice. Other programmes and activities will need to be designed, implemented and conducted. They may not have long-term impact or be focused on significant aspirations and ambitions but they will nevertheless consti-tute an important contribution. We might signal the difference by the term 'plan' rather than the word 'strategy'. HRD plans will then be concerned with shorter time horizons, usually a year, and will cover a number and range of programmes and activities. The focus of these programmes and activities will be 'operational' and intended to ensure that the day-to-day work of the organization can be accomplished. Examples might include:

- programmes to train new starters to replace staff losses as a result of labour turnover

- programmes to develop knowledge and skills associated with some new technology or system

- programmes to develop better teamwork

- programmes of supervisory or management development to prepare individuals for promotion in the immediate or short term.

Another useful way of distinguishing between HRD strategies and plans is to apply the notions of 'maintenance' and 'change'. These have been applied to HRD practice for many years and one example is the work of Fredericks and Stewart (1996) referred to above. The basic idea is that HRD 'maintenance' programmes and activities are intended to keep the organization as it is, and effective and efficient at what it currently does. This is achieved by HRD plans. In contrast to this, HRD 'change' programmes are designed and intended to make the organization different and develop it to be able to do new and different things effectively and efficiently. This is achieved by HRD strategies. We will examine the application of this notion later in the chapter when we look at the connec-tions between HRD and organizational change. Before that, there is one further related concept to be explained.

HRD policy

HRD policy is different from both strategy and plans. As we have seen, the latter two concepts are applied to programmes and activities – what HRD professionals do. Policy is a concept used to describe the framework within which decisions about programmes and activities are taken and which guides those decisions and their implementation. So policy is a set of principles that govern decisions and actions (Stewart, 1999). Such principles are not universal givens, however; they have to be determined and thus are a matter of human choice and decision. We will now describe a common process of determining policy as well as common features and content of HRD policy.

When looking at determining policy, it is as well to recognize that the process is not always and does not have to be a formal or deliberate process. Policy, like strategy, can emerge and be the cumulative result of ad hoc processes and decisions. Whether the result of formal and planned processes or an emergent and evolving process, there will be a number of factors influencing the formulation and content of HRD policy. These include:

External factors:

- Government policies and programmes

- Technological developments

- Social conditions, for example demographics and norms

- Competitor and stakeholder actions.

Internal factors:

- Organizational history and traditions

- Structure and culture

- Levels of management support

- Current performance and expected future performance

- Other organizational policies, especially related HR policies.

This list is taken from Stewart (1999) and he makes the important point that the factors do not operate separately and independently of each other. They all interact with and influence the impact of each other in complex processes that are hard to identify. One consequence of this is that even when policy making is planned and formalized, it will always be an iterative process. As well as being influenced by the factors identified above, policy making will also be influenced by the preferences, interests and needs of a variety of different groups involved in determining policy. These commonly include:

- Senior managers

- HRD professionals

- Trades unions representatives

- Other professional staff, especially HR and financial officers.

The specific content of any HRD policy will reflect the particular influence of the factors and groups identified here and how they interact. Resulting policies will commonly comprise a written statement of principles informing and shaping decisions in relation to a range of HRD applications. These will normally include the following:

- A statement of purpose and objectives

- A statement of priorities

- Roles and responsibilities of various groups and parties, for example senior managers, line managers, HRD professionals and individual employees

- Cost allocation policy and process

- Place of and access to records

- Application of policy to various different categories of employees

- Application of policy to various different approaches to and types of HRD practice, for example educational programmes and other forms of external development versus internal programmes.

It will be clear that there are connections between the concepts discussed so far. There is a need for some level of consistency and congruence between strategy, plans and policy. But this is not always the case in practice, since practice is not a matter of the simple application of theory or logic – organizations are much messier than that. What we have set out so far in this chapter represents what would be a textbook approach.

HRD and change

The formation of strategies in organizations of whatever kind have an inevitable link to change. Strategies are often a response to perceived change in the environment but they also set in motion desired changes within the organization. We know that the rate of change is never constant (Tushman et al., 1986) and that the effects of change can be studied over different timescales and at different levels – individual, group or team, department, whole organization, societal, national and international. In organizations, change is not always seen as an HRD issue, and whether change links to HRD depends on the various ways in which those who make strategy see learning as a key response. Gold and Smith (2003) found that some managers saw the need for change in terms of HRD as a principal component. In addition, it becomes possible for HRD specialists to have a role as facilitators or 'change agents' in ensuring that change can be managed and provide learning opportunities for others (McCracken and Wallace, 2000).

Types of change

It is not unusual to suggest that change and learning are the same thing. Certainly there seems to be some connection but we feel it is important to maintain some separation. We can think of some examples where change occurs, for example the installation of new equipment or a new procedure, but no one learns in terms of developing new skills or gaining knowledge. We can also find examples of people finding new possibilities for change that emerge from their learning at work. The latter possibility has been increasingly recognized as a source of new knowledge gained by individuals and shared with others, which can be captured for change in the organization as whole, but which can so easily be missed by managers (Bartlett and Ghoshal, 1997).

One thing that is clear – not all change is the same. Here we can make use of a distinction suggested by Hayes (2007) between 'incremental' and 'transformational' change. We present this as a dimension, as shown in Figure 3.1.

FIGURE 3.1 Incremental and transformational change

Incremental change occurs over a period of time but on a regular and continuous basis. However, such changes may hardly be noticed except that people are 'doing things better' through a process of 'tinkering, adaptation and modification' (Hayes 2007, p. 12). There is a link between change and continuous improvement and this is sometimes formalized in continuous improvement teams (CITs) and the Japanese Total Quality Management (TQM) principle of kaizan. This approach to change is connected to Toyota's lean manufacturing system, where changes for improvement are identified and implemented quickly by those closest to the work (Wall, 2005). As the small changes accumulate over time, it might be possible to identify some kind of transformation.

Activity

Kaizan is a development from TQM and you might like to explore some of the tools available to help people learn about improvement at work. Go to www.ifm.eng.cam.ac.uk/dstools/represent/tqm.html. Which of these tools could be used in your work?

One of the features of incremental change is that there is less difficulty or 'hassle' in making the changes identified (Buchanan and Boddy, 1992), whereas transformational change is considered to be a disturbance to the present and the creation of new dynamics that requires a break with the past. Rather than doing things better, the key question is: what can be done differently? For example, a manufacturing engineering company that shifts its purpose towards a design company because of the cost of manufacturing clearly makes a choice to change the path of its future development rather than remain in manufacturing.

How people in organizations understand the need for change also provides a close connection to the forms of learning suggested by Argyris and Schön (1978). First, single-loop learning is concerned with detecting errors and correcting them. There is no opportunity to challenge how things are done but incremental changes become possible. By contrast, there is double-loop learning, which challenges accepted practices based on particular assumptions that can be reconsidered. This can lead to new ideas and new practices. Bartunek and Moch (1987) use similar terms to describe frameworks of understanding for change. First-order change is concerned with incremental change that matches the shared understanding of those involved, while second-order change modifies how understanding occurs. They also add third-order change, which is concerned with developing the capacity to understand events as they occur, transcending single or particular ways of understanding to consider a variety of possibilities.

Hayes (2007) also considers how some organizations anticipate the need for change. They are 'proactive' in seeking opportunities for change, which they can initiate, as well as understanding threats, for which they can prepare. By contrast, and this is probably more common, organizations might only change when they have to – such organizations are 'reactive'.

Models of change management

Given the variation in types of change, it has become quite normal in the past 20 years to veer towards the transformational view, which provides a link to ideas about leaders who, through their vision, can inspire and motivate others for change (Stewart and McGoldrick, 1996). Transformational leaders connect strategy to culture and commitment. It is not surprising that one of the most well-known change models in organizations is concerned with 'leading change', based on the work of John Kotter. Kotter (1996, p. 35) put strong emphasis on the leading of change:

> Leadership defines what the future should look like, aligns people with that vision, and inspires them to make it happen.

The organizations he studied failed to achieve transformational change because of mistakes, which provided eight steps that leaders could follow to ensure success. These steps are:

- Establish a sense of urgency

- Form a powerful guiding coalition

- Create a vision

- Communicate the vision

- Empower others to act

- Create short-term wins

- Consolidate and build

- Institutionalize the new approaches.

While focusing on leaders, the model is very much in tune with other models of change based on the view that stages or steps can be used to guide change. Probably the most well-known and earliest model was by Kurt Lewin (1951), whose stages involved:

- *Unfreezing:* reducing those forces that maintain behaviour in its present form, and recognition of the need for change and improvement to occur

- *Movement:* development of new attitudes or behaviour and implementation of the change

- *Refreezing:* stabilizing change at the new level and reinforcement through supporting mechanisms, for example policies, structure or norms.

There is a range of other change models that provide stages or steps and this tends to reinforce the view that change can be planned or programmed and managed. Change could also be seen as a single disturbance to an organization, perhaps as part of a change in strategy, with a restoration of some kind of equilibrium in due course. HRD activities can also be part of the plan, provided at the appropriate stage in line with the strategy for change. For example, if a policy is implemented on discipline at work, training could be provided to enable new skills and behaviours to be learned and then reinforced through coaching and monitoring. Such steps can be easily predicted and built into the plan.

By contrast, and increasingly accepted as normal, change is seen as continuous and/or rather unpredictable. Weick (2000), for example, suggests that Lewin's stages should be freeze-rebalance-unfreeze, where the first step is to investigate and make visible what is happening, with rebalance concerned with reinterpreting and reordering activities. Unfreeze means to allow change to continue in an emergent way. Others such as Buchanan and Storey (1997, p. 127) see change as 'messy and untidy', with projects rarely following predictable stages. History, culture and contextual factors all have a role to play, so it becomes difficult to provide 'universal rules' for change management and leadership (Pettigrew and Whipp, 1993, p. 105). One organization we have worked with at least recognized this dilemma by advising change managers to build 'surprise, unpredictability and planning for the unplanned' into their models.

Most views of change recognize the importance of communication and one model seems to acknowledge this explicitly. Ford and Ford (2003) present a view of change as concerned with the shifting of current reality towards the creation of a new one. Since any organization of any size is composed of different groups and individuals, each with their own version of reality, it is the job of those leading change to 'author' new realities and this is achieved principally through conversations. This is a crucial feature where conversations between individuals and groups at work make and remake the realities they experience. People tell stories to each other about what is right and wrong and this includes why a particular project or process of change should or should not be considered worthy. Indeed, the whole organization can be considered as a network of conversation, which establishes the context, culture and history for change to occur or not. This puts great onus on change leaders to hold conversations with others and present good arguments for what they are seeking to achieve. Ford and Ford (2003) suggest a model composed of different conversations that need to be held. These are:

- *Initiative conversations:* asserting that there is an opportunity for change

- *Conversations for understanding:* explaining why change is needed and what would indicate satisfactory achievement, resulting in the involvement of others who know what they must do

- *Conversations for performance:* taking action and making things happen

- *Conversations for closure:* asserting what has been achieved and recognition of contributions.

This model should not be seen as another series of steps but rather as guidance to those leading and managing change of how it is only by talking with others that they can understand the variety of meanings present, which may help or hinder the change sought. They also need to present arguments and respond to counterarguments based on learning about the variety of meanings present in any situation.

Reflective question

For those seeking to lead change projects, what are the implications of groups and individuals holding different views of reality?

Change agents, skills and interventions

Different types of change and different models for implementing change require a variety of skills and knowledge of tools and techniques by those expected to lead and manage change. During the 1980s, this role was closely associated with transformational leaders who were expected to become 'change masters' (Kanter, 1985), relying on their charisma and vision to act as change champions and leaders of change. More recently, Kotter (2008) reasserts the importance of leaders to establish a sense of urgency as the first stage of his model. During the 1990s and 2000s, this role was expected to become part of the work of managers throughout the organization and functional specialists such as HRD practitioners as change agents. In addition, experts in change could also be employed from consultancies outside the organization. Whoever undertakes such a role, there are some key questions to consider:

- How do individuals behave in times of change?

- Does theory inform our understanding of human change processes?

- What interventions are needed in the change process?

- What are the keys to successful and sustainable change?

If you look at any organization behaviour textbook in relation to change, you will see that, from a personal perspective, change is often difficult, largely influenced by emotions and can require an involved process of individual readjustment and reframing of a person's work context and orientation. Individual reactions to change are many and varied depending on a complex interaction of history, context, situation and individual orientation to change and work. People frequently experience a complicated mix of both positive and negative responses to change. In addition, the flow of responses may fluctuate and intensify over time and may be connected to the way in which change is presented by managers and colleagues at work over time (Balogun et al., 2008). The responses to change at any given point in time include:

- resentment

- frustration

- anxiety

- dissatisfaction

- fear

- insecurity.

This list is not exhaustive but does show the range of responses to a situation of change and the potential for 'disaffection' (Kanter, 1985) or indeed resistance to a change process.

The potential and real difficulties in change at work have been recognized for many years. As a consequence, a wide range of intervention tools and techniques have been developed for change agents during the 1950s and 60s, as part of OD. This takes a whole organization approach to planned change and builds on the work of Lewin, whose change model we referred to above. In OD, change agents seek to diagnose problems and find interventions that are appropriate to assist the 'change effort' (Beckhard 1969, p. 101). Diagnosis will involve collecting data, possibly through surveys and interviews, before developing plans for intervention to improve the situation. The aim is to find a degree of consensus between different groups and individuals, finding and building common ground where conflict and disagreement exists. Schein (1969) sees the change agent as a process consultant who 'facilitates' interventions in an unbiased and positive way. We can see how such a view informs the way HRD and other initiatives that seek to promote learning at work are now implemented, which will be considered throughout this book, for example teamwork, Investors in People, management and leadership development and so on. Among those who work in the field of HRD, the roles of change agent and facilitator are seen as the most important (Nijhof and de Rijk, 1997).

As facilitators of change, there has been considerable attention given to the skills that need to be learned and practice. For example, Buchanan and Boddy (1992) provide a list of competencies for effective change agents, which include:

- clarity of specifying goals

- team-building activities

- communication skills

- negotiation skills

- influencing skills to gain commitment to goals.

Many organizations also specify facilitating change as a skill for managers. For example, a large UK financial services organization identifies 'driving change' as one of the competencies managers require.

Activity

You can learn more about OD by visiting the USA's OD Institute website – www.odinstitute.org/.

For useful materials on change, project management and competencies for change, go to the UK's Improvement and Development Agency website – www.idea.gov.uk/idk/core/page.do?pageId=5817020.

The HRD function

We noted above that while a degree of conceptual ambiguity exists as regards HRD and SHRD, it is nonetheless useful to think about the concept of strategy in relation to HRD practice. A degree of consensus exists among leading practitioners and academics that HRD can, and should, operate strategically within an organization. However, exactly what such practice should look like, how the function should be positioned and managed in terms of such a responsibility remains problematic. Certainly there is little empirical evidence to suggest that there may be a 'one size fits all'. This said, there are a number of critical questions that can legitimately be raised about the positioning, role and management of the function which are pertinent to all organizations, irrespective of size, sector and so on.

The HRD landscape is shifting. The CIPD talks about a shift from 'training' to 'learning' (Sloman, 2005), e-learning has transformed the provision in some organizations (for example BA), and there is a real claim that in recent years the HRD profession has acquired and consolidated a credible position distinct from HRM (see, for example, Gold et al., 2003). This said, it remains unclear as to the extent to which the changing landscape is being driven by a new 'breed' of HRD practitioners or whether HRD is responding to a set of forces both within and external to the organization (see, for example, Hendry et al., 1988; Gold and Smith, 2003). This ambiguity is reflected in the two ideas we explore below about how we might begin to think about the changing role of the HRD function. Each of these notions seeks to capture critical elements of the shifting landscape of HRD and offer a conceptual vehicle for onward travel.

Business partner

In abstract, the idea of a business partner is simple. In order to engage appropriately with the strategic development of the organization, HRD operates as a 'partner' alongside the various business units and as an agent to facilitate change in the organization. The word 'partner' is crucial, implying that HRD has an equal, credible and legitimate role to play in relation to the most important business decisions taken by the organization. The HRD function becomes responsible for aligning HRD with the business strategy and ensuring that HRD can add value at any level within the organization. In this model, HRD has a key leadership role, working in collaboration with other senior figures to help determine the vision and direction of the organization (Ulrich, 1997). Gubbins and Garavan (2007) add the word 'Strategic' and position the 'Strategic Business Partner' model on the right-hand side of a chart, which seeks to 'map' the changing nature of HRD professional roles from the traditional role – training intervention focused – to one of 'transformational strategic partner' – shown in Figure 3.2. This is not exactly a neat, linear continuum but it does usefully capture the point that the journey away from this traditional role may well involve a range of different pathways and configurations. (See Analoui (1994) for further discussion of the more 'traditional' and 'transactional' roles, and Gilley and Maycunich Gilley (2003) for the more 'transformational' roles.)

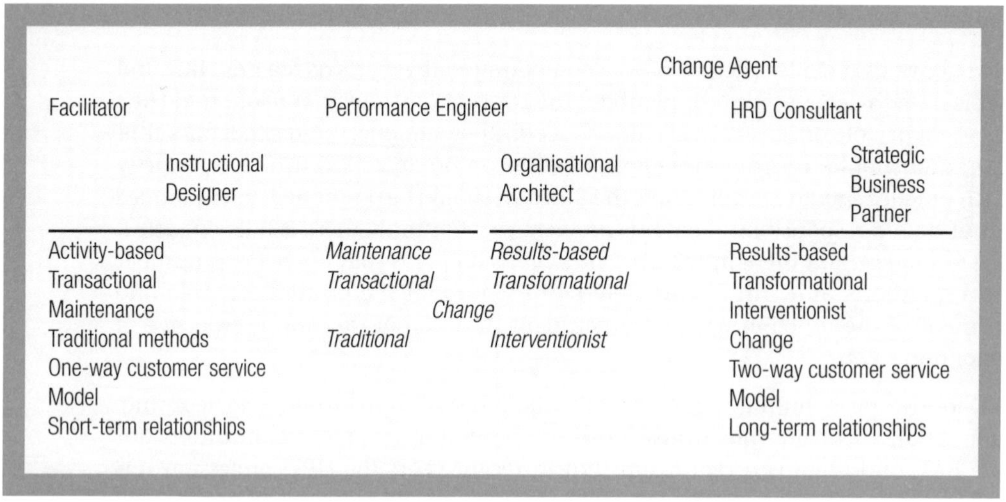

Change Agent
Facilitator
Performance Engineer
HRD Consultant
Instructional Designer
Organisational Architect
Strategic Business Partner
Activity-based
Transactional
Maintenance
Traditional methods
One-way customer service Model
Short-term relationships
Maintenance
Transactional
Change
Traditional
Results-based
Transformational
Interventionist
Results-based
Transformational
Interventionist
Change
Two-way customer service Model
Long-term relationships

FIGURE 3.2 Shifting roles of the HRD professional

SOURCE: Gubbins and Garavan (2007)

Focus: direction and sponsorship; team leadership; review HR value and impact
HR business partners
Centres of excellence
HR leadership team
Focus: strategic impact
Focus: high-quality HR expertise
Administrative service centres
Focus: cost-effective administrative HR services

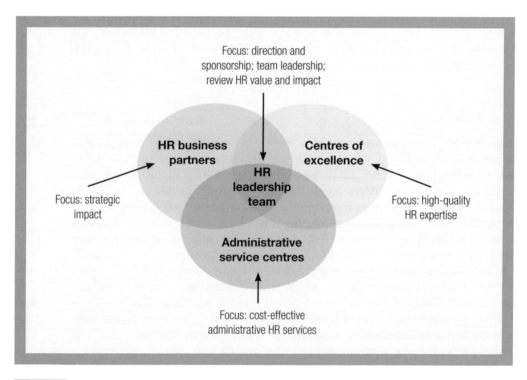

FIGURE 3.3 The business partner model in the UK civil service

SOURCE: Civil service (2005)

It is important to note that the business partner model may well seek to integrate a number of subfunctions. Three such subfunctions might be:

- *shared services:* routine 'transactional' services across organizations, for example standard training programmes

- *centres of excellence:* small teams of experts with specialist knowledge of cutting-edge HRD solutions, for example 'electronic' knowledge management, mentoring

- *strategic partners:* HR professionals working closely with business leaders influencing strategy and steering its implementation.

The essence of the business partner model is captured in Figure 3.3, which forms the basis for how the civil service, drawing on the work of Ulrich (1997), seeks to put the business partner model into practice within HR.

The corporate university

Some of the biggest companies in the world have established corporate universities (CUs) in recent years, for example BAE Systems, Motorola, McDonald's, Heineken, Lloyds TSB. Gibb (2008, p. 143) offers the following description of a corporate university:

> The CU shapes corporate culture by fostering leadership, creative thinking and problem solving. Strategic is the key word. The CU provides strategically relevant (learning) solutions for each job family within a corporation. It aspires to create a strategic learning organization that functions as the umbrella for a company's total education requirements.

Paton et al. (2007) seek to identify the key features that make corporate universities distinctive. Three are suggested:

1 *Corporate-level initiatives in large, highly complex and differentiated settings:* CUs will have a presence on the board. They may be distinct from the HRD function within large business units. They aim to deliver a specific corporate contribution, avoiding replication or duplication with what is managed or delivered at a local level.

2 *The pursuit of continuing corporate alignment:* The CU is seen as a vehicle by which control of HRD activities, broadly interpreted, can most effectively be aligned with strategic priorities, such as post-merger integration, customer loyalty, developing leadership.

3 *The raising of standards, expectations and impact:* For Paton et al. (2007), it is the CU that can really reflect the strategic priority afforded to learning. Issues might be ensuring the highest quality of provision including harnessing the best available technology to create a virtual learning platform across global sites.

A fourth feature of the model, of course, is the use of the term 'university'. Advocates of CUs claim this provides the critical symbolic factor. It raises the status of organizational learning (Chapter 9) to its very highest level. For example, Motorola defends its decision to create a corporate university, arguing:

> Motorola management has always tried to use words in ways that force people to rethink their assumptions. The term university will arouse curiosity and, we hope, raise the expectations of our workforce and our training and education staff. We could have

called it an educational resource facility but who would that have electrified? (Wiggen-horn, 1990)

One further feature of a CU is a possible influence beyond the boundary of the organization. In other words, the CU may seek to influence the training and development of the entire value chain, including customers and suppliers. An example is shown in HRD in Practice 3.2.

The Motorola University

The Motorola University is one of the most well-known CUs and is the inventor and creator of Six Sigma, in 1986, and holds the registered trademark for this quality improvement methodology. It offers green and black belt certification for Six Sigma and claims to 'practice what it preaches before it preaches it'. Based on the ability to apply the methodology internally, the Motorola University is able to update materials based on 'best practices'. Over $17bn in savings within Motorola have been documented, and in recent years, this has been extended to customers and suppliers.

John Emling, vice president of operations at the Kaydon Corporation, reports the benefits of working with Motorola University:

> We were practicing Lean in many of our plants, but we knew we could get more impact than Lean was delivering. Motorola University helped us integrate our lean techniques into an overall Six Sigma Business Improvement Methodology. Their coaching and customer support made it easy to ramp up to full adoption of Six Sigma without over investing in infrastructure. Their training and project coaching was solid. But most importantly, through their help in adopting the Six Sigma Management System, we are delivering sustainable bottom line impact to Kaydon shareholders.

Source: www.motorola.com/motorolauniversity.jsp

Critics of CUs (see, for example, Walton, 2005) have been concerned that most are simply rebadged training departments. This is an important point. It is easy to give the HRD function a new name but if its actual practice is little different, then the role has not changed.

HRD positioning and management

With this in mind, if we now try and translate this conceptual thinking into the implications for the positioning and day-to-day management of the HRD function, two important sets of questions arise: first in terms of a centralizing–decentralizing tension and second in relation to the capabilities of those aspiring to purportedly 'new' HRD roles. Hirsh and Tamkin's (2005) research sought to ascertain how, in practice, organizations align their HRD activity with business needs. Their findings uncover some underlying 'dilemmas'.

For example, they note that business needs can be both corporate and local, but which of these should influence what happens in terms of HRD practice at ground level? If line managers are taking greater responsibility for the training and development of their teams, this will act as a force towards devolvement including devolved budgets. A desire for 'just in time training' and tailored learning closer to the job reinforces such pressures. However, Hirsh and Tamkin's research shows that, for large organizations in particular, a perceived need to measure and control spend 'and to focus on corporate priorities' creates a powerful 'centralizing effect' (p. 33). Shared service initiatives, operating a call centre-type role, further reinforce centralizing tendencies and plans.

Hirsh and Tamkin (2005) report the case of Diageo, one of the world's leading drinks businesses. Diageo provides an interesting example of how a company has sought to deal with the corporate–local tension. A corporate policy is to devolve and embed training and learning throughout the business. However, Diageo differentiates between resources for strategic, company-wide priorities and those for more local and operational needs. A process called the 'organization and people review' aims to join and integrate the top-down view with the bottom-up view. HRD operates with local mangers to identify capability issues. This information is then 'amalgamated upwards' and a corporate perspective added at group level. This might be conceived of as an example of what Gibb (2008, p. 158) calls a 'hub and spoke' model.

Activity

'If only you'd asked us sooner' (Sloman, 2006, p. 13)

This is a reflection from the CIPD following its 2006 survey on learning and development. A key finding was that learning, training and development professionals do not have enough involvement in organizational change projects. Sloman notes: 'If the learning, training and development function isn't perceived as a key stakeholder, we won't be involved in the crucial decisions. As a result we'll only contribute late in the process … if at all.' Hence the title of the reflection.

Think about the title of the reflection and the key finding raised from the survey. How does this capture some of the issues we have been discussing in terms of a shifting landscape and a model of the HRD role to reflect and drive this?

Visit the CIPD's website and view the most recent survey findings – www.cipd. co.uk/subjects/lrnanddev/general/_reftrendtd.htm?IsSrchRes=1.

Also visit the Institute for Employment Studies website – www.employment-studies.co.uk/pubs – for a fuller discussion of Hirsh and Tamkin's research.

Numerous questions of capability flow from the different ways of thinking about how HRD might be positioned. Two of some significance are noted below; one external to the function and the other much closer to home.

One of the anticipated challenges noted by advocates of the business partner model concerns line management. If, as part of an intimate engagement with strategy, an implication is that line management take on board a much greater responsibility for the day-to-day, week-by-week development of their staff (the devolvement of responsibility discussed above), have they the capability to fulfil such a responsibility effectively? A recurrent concern flagged by the CIPD as a result of its annual learning and development survey work has been this very theme. Reflecting on the 2007 survey findings, Wain (2007, p. 25) notes, for example, that as only 6% of organizations reward managers for developing their people, 'no wonder it's not top priority for the other 94%'.

Second, to play any kind of leadership role at the strategic centre of the organization clearly has implications for the capabilities of senior HRD professionals. Two are considered critical; first, power and influence, and second, learning expertise. Stewart and McGoldrick (1996) argue that 'a strategy for augmenting influence is virtually imperative if the HRD department is to survive' and the reader will note that we have been discussing a role that is much more than mere 'survival'.

The following extract, drawn from research undertaken with HRD practitioners about the 'politics' of their role (Holden and Griggs, 2008), illustrates the lived experience of one HRD manager who works for a large UK car dealership as she seeks to develop a strategic presence within the organization:

> I do go to Board meetings but I'm not a director ... I mean I influence as much as I can but it's hard work, it really wears you down. I've tried to make HRD a lever of change and I have driven a lot through but it's a battle, it's a real struggle ... you've got to be permanently selling it and by nature HR people are not salespeople. It's the art of balancing what we need operationally, today, now, with what's best for the business in the longer term ... And one of the problems here is that if you're not an accountant you don't fit ... they're so insular they won't look outside the motor trade and so I can't say 'Look, it works here' ... they just won't see it ... and of course we're women ... I'm sorry but that's the case and all the other directors are men.

Reflecting on the factors that may enhance and detract from a high level of power and influence within an organization, the issue of gendered power relations in HRD raises some important questions (Hanscome and Cervero, 2003). The majority of HRD professionals in the UK are female.

In relation to learning, the necessary expertise goes beyond a technical proficiency in identifying and managing learning needs and provision. The strategic HRD role requires an understanding of knowledge management and organizational learning (Chapter 9) and, increasingly, an appreciation of how technology may be utilized as a strategic learning tool.

Pettinger (2002) combines the two factors of influence and expertise in a simple matrix, shown in Figure 3.4.

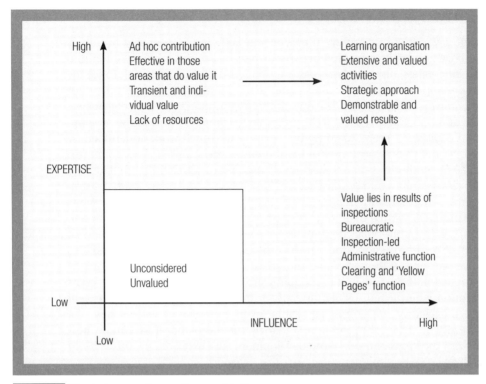

High ↑ Ad hoc contribution   Learning organisation
        Effective in those   Extensive and valued
        areas that do value it   activities
        Transient and indi-   ——→   Strategic approach
        vidual value   Demonstrable and
        Lack of resources   valued results

EXPERTISE   ↑

                                     Value lies in results of
                                     inspections
                                     Bureaucratic
                                     Inspection-led
        Unconsidered   Administrative function
        Unvalued   Clearing and 'Yellow
                                     Pages' function

Low ──→

                    INFLUENCE   High

        Low

FIGURE 3.4 The balance of expertise and influence

SOURCE: Pettinger (2002)

Before we conclude this chapter, two important additional considerations need to be addressed.

Outsourcing

Over recent years, a growing trend has been for various training tasks to be undertaken by external organizations. According to a survey by Capita Learning & Development (www.capita-ld.co.uk/) in 2005, two in five UK organizations now outsource training in one way or another. This might simply be to an external provider of training programmes. Here Richman and Trondsen (2004) suggest the term 'out-tasking' might be more appropriate. Alternatively, comprehensive outsourcing may see an external contractor take complete control of an organization's total HRD function. Simmonds and Gibson (2008) identify the impetus for outsourcing as cost, competence and capacity. They cite the example of Unilever, which has taken transactional activities and delivery outside, with transformational and strategic activities remaining in Unilever's remit. While the authors identify a set of problems with any outsourcing of HRD, they suggest that the administrative, operational and transactional-type activities can be overcome, but less so the strategic. A critical research need is to explore those organizations that have taken or are taking this step (Woodal et al., 2002).

Competing on costs not skills

We noted above a variety of ways that in practice an HRD function may move away from a model based on ad hoc training activity or planned maintenance (Fonda and Hayes, 1988). Nonetheless, an underlying assumption has been the aspiration to see the HRD function develop into a strategic player and where learning is seen as critical for organizational growth and prosperity. The flaw in this assumption is the lack of evidence that all organizations necessarily see it as appropriate to compete through the development of human capital. As Keep (2005) rightly reminds us, much work undertaken by organizations does not sit comfortably with the rhetoric of the knowledge economy (see also Grugulis, 2007). Rather, it is highly routinized, involves low discretion and relatively low skills. Keep (2005) argues that in some sectors, cost-based competition is still the strategic driving force, with a consequent pressure to deskill rather than upskill. This presents corporate HRD managers with a dilemma. They are caught at the pinch point between, on the one hand, wider public policy goals in terms of skills and education, together with rhetoric from their own profession, and, on the other hand, the hard business realities and competitive pressures of the sector and market in which they operate. Of course, it could still be argued that the function is engaging strategically with the business goals of the organization when it refuses demands for training and opportunities for skill enhancement, but clearly the enhanced status given to learning within, say, the corporate university model is inappropriate. It follows, therefore, that if we equate 'best practice' HRD with the kinds of models and developments discussed above, this is likely to remain, as Keep (2005) eloquently puts it, a 'minority sport'.

Summary

- Conventional views on strategy are based on top managers setting out a vision and mission for an organization and developing organization or 'corporate' goals and strategy from which are derived business strategy and then functional strategy, including a strategy for HRD.

- An alternative view is that HRD can have a key role to play in shaping organizational culture, developing current and future leaders, building commitment among organization members and anticipating and managing responses to changed conditions to ensure long-term survival.

- HRD strategy is a course of action that is intended to have a long-term rather than a short-term impact on significant rather than marginal areas of performance at organizational rather than individual level.

- HRD plans are concerned with shorter time horizons, usually a year, and will cover a number and range of programmes and activities. The focus of these programmes and activities will be 'operational' and intended to ensure that the day-to-day work of the organization can be accomplished.

- HRD policy describes the framework within which decisions about programmes and activities are taken and which guides those decisions and their implementation.

- Organization strategies imply change but are not always linked to HRD.

- Types of change can vary between incremental and transformational. Organizations can be proactive or reactive in anticipating the need for change.

- Various models of change inform the skills needed to manage and implement change at work.

- Change agents need to use ideas and tools for intervention in change projects and facilitate intervention in an unbiased and positive way.

- HRD practitioners can operate as a business partner to align HRD with business strategy.

- Many large organizations have developed corporate universities to raise the status of learning.

- The HRD role in organizations must manage key dilemmas relating to centralizing and decentralizing HRD activities and the balance between expertise and influence.

- Recent years have seen a trend toward outsourcing HRD activities such as training.

Discussion questions

1 Can HRD ever be considered strategic?
2 Investment or cost? How important is this 'litmus test' for HRD and why?
3 Is HRD necessary for long-term organization survival?
4 Does all change lead to learning?
5 What are the key skills of a change agent?
6 What value is the business partner model for HRD in practice?

Further reading

Chia, R. (2002) 'Rhizomic' model of organizational change and transformation: perspective from a metaphysics of change, *British Journal of Management*, **10**(3): 209–27.

Gold, J., Rodgers, H. and Smith, V. (2003) What is the future for the human resource development professional? A UK perspective, *Human Resource Development International*, **6**(4): 437–55.

Horwitz, F.M. (1999) The emergence of strategic training and development: the current state of play, *Journal of European Industrial Training,* **23**(4/5): 180–90.

Oliver, J. (2008) Action learning enabled strategy making, *Action Learning: Research and Practice*, **5**(2): 149–58.

Watson, S., Maxwell, G.A. and Farquharson, L. (2007) Line managers' views on adopting human resource roles: the case of Hilton (UK) hotels, *Employee Relations*, **29**(1): 30–49.

References

Analoui, F. (1994) Training and development: the role of trainers, *Journal of Management Development*, **13**(9): 61–72.

Argyris, C. and Schön, D. (1978) *Organizational Learning: A Theory of Action Perspective*, Reading, MA, Addison Wesley.

Ashton, D. and Felstead, A. (1995) Training and development, in D. Storey (ed.) *Human Resource Management: A Critical Text*, London, Routledge.

Balogun, J., Hope Hailey, V. and Johnson, G. (2008) *Exploring Strategic Change*, London, Pearson Education.

Bartlett, C. and Ghoshal, S. (1997) The myth of the generic manager: new personal competencies for new management roles, *California Management Review*, **40**(1): 92–116.

Bartunek, J.M. and Moch, M.K. (1987) First-order, second-order, and third-order change and organization development interventions: a cognitive approach, *Journal of Applied Behavioral Science*, **23**(4): 483–500.

Beckhard, R. (1969) *Organizational Development: Strategies and Models*, Reading, MA, Addison.

Bratton, J. and Gold, J. (2007) *Human Resource Management: Theory and Practice*, 4th edn, Basingstoke, Palgrave Macmillan.

Buchanan, D. and Boddy, D. (1992) *The Expertise of the Change Agent: Public Performance and Backstage Activity*, London, Prentice Hall.

Buchanan, D. and Storey, J. (1997) Role taking and role switching in organizational change: the four pluralities, in I. McLoughlin and M. Harris (eds) *Innovation, Organizational Change and Technology*, London, International Thomson.

Civil Service (2005) Modernising People Management, HR Business Partner Guide, http://hr.civilservice.gov.uk/downloads/bp_guide.pdf.

Cooke, F.L. (2000) Human resource strategy to improve organisational performance: a route for British firms?, Working Paper 9, ESRC Future of Work Programme, ESRC, Swindon.

Fonda, N. and Hayes, C. (1988) Education, training and business performance, *Oxford Review of Economic Policy*, **4**(3).

Ford, J. and Ford, L. (2003) Conversations and the authoring of change, in D. Holman and R. Thorpe (eds) *Management and Language*, London, Sage.

Fredericks, J. and Stewart, J. (1996) The strategy-HRD connection, in J. Stewart and J. McGoldrick (eds) *Human Resource Development: Perspectives, Strategies and Practice*, London, Pitman.

Garavan, T. (1991) Strategic human resource development, *Journal of European Industrial Training*, **15**(1): 17–31.

Garavan, T. (2007) A strategic perspective on human resource development, *Advances in Developing Human Resources*, **9**(1): 11–30.

Gibb, S. (2008) *Human Resource Development: Process, Practices and Perspectives*, 2nd edn, Basingstoke, Palgrave Macmillan.

Gilley, J.W. and Maycunich Gilley, A. (2003) *Strategically Integrated HRD: Six Transformational Roles in Creating Results-driven Programmes*, 2nd edn, Cambridge, Perseus.

Gold, J. and Smith, V. (2003) Advances towards a learning movement: translations at work, *Human Resource Development International*, **6**(2): 139–52.

Gold, J., Rodgers, H. and Smith, V. (2003) What is the future for the human resource development professional? A UK perspective, *Human Resource Development International*, **6**(4): 437–55.

Grugulis, I. (2007) *Skills, Training and Human Resource Development*, Basingstoke, Palgrave Macmillan.

Gubbins, C. and Garavan, T. (2007) The changing context and role of the HRD professional, 8th International Conference on HRD Research and Practice across Europe, Oxford, June.

Hanscome, L. and Cervero, R. (2003) The impact of gendered power relations in HRD, *Human Resource Development International*, **6**(4): 509–25.

Hayes, J. (2007) *The Theory and Practice of Change Management*, Basingstoke, Palgrave Macmillan.

Hendry, C., Pettigrew, A. and Sparrow, P.R. (1988) The forces that trigger training, *Personnel Management*, **20**(12): 28–32.

Hirsh, W. and Tamkin, P. (2005) *Planning Training for your Business*, report no. 422, Brighton, Institute of Employment Studies.

Holden, R. and Griggs, V. (2008) Teaching the politics of HRD: problems and possibilities, 9th International Conference on HRD Research and Practice across Europe, Lille, May.

ILO (International Labour Office) (2000) *High Performance Work Research: Project Case Studies*, Geneva, ILO.

Kanter, R.M. (1985) *The Change Masters: Corporate Entrepreneurs at Work*, London, Taylor and Francis.

Keep, E. (2005) The firm, society and social inclusion: addressing the societal value of HRD, keynote address, 6th International Conference on HRD Research and Practice across Europe, Leeds, May.

Kotter, J.P. (1996) *Leading Change*, Boston, MA, Harvard Business Press.

Kotter, J.P. (2008) *A Sense of Urgency*, Boston, MA, Harvard Business Press.

Leitch, S. (2006) *Prosperity for all in the Global Economy: World Class Skills*, London, HM Treasury.

Lewin, K. (1951) *Field Theory in Social Science*, New York, Harper and Row.

McCracken, M. and Wallace, M. (2000) Towards a redefinition of strategic HRD, *Journal of European Industrial Training*, **24**(5): 281–90.

Nijhof, W.J. and de Rijk, R.N. (1997) Roles, competences and outputs of HRD practitioners: a comparative study in four European countries, *Journal of European Industrial Training*, **21**(6/7): 247–55.

Paton, R., Peters, G., Storey, J. and Taylor, S. (2007) *Handbook of Corporate University Development*, London, Gower.

Pettigrew, A. and Whipp, R. (1993) *Managing Change for Competitive Success*, London, Wiley.

Pettinger, R. (2002) *Mastering Employee Development*, Basingstoke, Palgrave – now Palgrave Macmillan.

Prahalad, C.K. and Hamel, G. (1990) The core competence of the corporation, *Harvard Business Review*, **90**(3): 79–91.

Richman, H. and Trondsen, E. (2004) Outsourcing: what can it do to your job?, *Training and Development*, **58**(10): 68–73.

Schein, E. (1969) *Process Consultation: Its Role in Organization Development*, Reading, MA, Addison-Wesley.

Simmonds, D. and Gibson, R. (2008) A model for outsourcing HRD, *Journal of European Industrial Training*, **32**(1): 4–18.

Sloman, M. (2005) *Training to Learning: Change Agenda*, London, CIPD.

Sloman, M. (2006) If only you'd asked us sooner: involvement of learning and development professionals in organizational change, in *CIPD, Latest Trends in Learning Training and Development*, London, CIPD.

Stewart J. (1999) *Employee Development Practice*, London, FT/Pitman.

Stewart, J. and McGoldrick, J.A. (1996) *Human Resource Development: Perspectives, Strategies and Practice*, London, Pitman.

Tushman, M.L., Newman, W.H. and Romanelli, E. (1986) Convergence and upheaval: managing the unsteady pace of organizational evolution, *California Management Review*, **29**: 22–39.

Ulrich, D. (1997) *Human Resource Champions: The Next Agenda for Adding Value and Delivering Results*, Boston, Harvard Business School Press.

Wain, D. (2007) *Lies, Damned Lies and a Few Home Truths: Reflections on the 2007 Learning and Development Survey*, London, CIPD.

Wall, S.J. (2005) The protean organization: learning to love change, *Organizational Dynamics*, **34**(1): 37–46.

Walton, J. (2005) Would the real corporate university please stand up, *Journal of European Industrial Training*, **29**(1): 7–20.

Weick, K.E. (2000) Emergent change as universal in organizations, in M. Beer and N. Nohria (eds) *Breaking the Code of Change*, Boston, MA, Harvard Business School Press.

Wiggenhorn, W. (1990) Motorola U: when training becomes an education, *Harvard Business Review*, **68**(4): 71–83.

Woodall, J., Gourlay, S. and Short, D. (2002) Trends in outsourcing HRD in the UK: the implications for strategic HRD, *International Journal of Human Resource Development and Management*, **2**(1/2): 50–63.

National HRD Policies and Practice

Jeff Gold, Jim Stewart and Paul Iles

Chapter learning outcomes

After studying this chapter, you should be able to:

- Explain the meaning of National HRD (NHRD)
- Explain the key ideas informing NHRD
- Understand the key features of vocational and educational training systems
- Assess various models of NHRD
- Explain the policies and practices in different countries

Chapter outline

Introduction

The meaning of NHRD

The VET system

NHRD in the Czech Republic

NHRD in California

NHRD in Australia

Summary

Introduction

Rapid technological development, globalization and the internationalization of the labour market, greater customer expectations and competition on prices and quality are frequently presented as fundamental reasons why investment in skills should be of national concern. In the UK, the Leitch report (2006) highlighted skills as crucial to economic prosperity, productivity and the improvement of social justice. If the 19th century can be seen as a time when the UK could draw on a ready supply of natural resources, which could also include cheap labour, the 'hands' needed for the Industrial Revolution, the 20th century could be characterized as a continuation of a journey that ends with what became understood as a 'low skills equilibrium' (Finegold and Soskice, 1988), a self-reinforcing cycle of low-quality products and low skills. Leitch pointed to a 'different kind of revolution' in the 21st century, which requires a move to a 'service-led economy and high value-added industry', based on high skills. The UK government's response to Leitch (DIUS, 2007) made clear its agreement, highlighting that skills were a key reason why the country lagged behind other successful economies, although it should also be said that it is how skills are used, in combination with factors such as investment and innovative product strategies, that makes the impact on productivity (Keep et al., 2006). Nevertheless, to the extent that the government set out a plan to achieve a movement up 'the skills ladder' in England,[1] a national agenda for HRD has been established. In this chapter, we will be exploring the idea of a National HRD (NHRD). We will see that plans can certainly be one part of this idea but there has been recent interest in the connection of skills to the way communities develop, the health and wellbeing of people and the infrastructure to support rapid movements of people around the globe. There are different views of NHRD and these reflect the importance of history and culture and the trajectory set by such factors for skills and their formation. These pose interesting dilemmas for policy makers but also the response of key players in institutions. We will examine the various responses by focusing on NHRD in different contexts around the world, the USA, Australia and the Czech Republic, as well as the UK, which will be our main reference point.

The meaning of NHRD

The search for the meaning of a term usually requires a definition. However, it is widely agreed that HRD and NHRD are difficult to define (McLean, 2004). For the latter, there are bound to be differences in culture and history, which affect the meaning of NHRD from one country to another. HRD meanings can concern individuals, teams, organizations, regions, countries and even the globe. We see NHRD as an approach to how a country views the contribution of skills towards its economic and social life, which finds expression in the policies and practices of the state and its agents and organizations. For McLean, the concern for NHRD has arisen out of government interest in workforce development as a strategic issue. McLean provides a number of reasons for this interest, shown in Table 4.1.

TABLE 4.1 Growing interest in NHRD

- A lack of access to natural resources requires a focus on human resources as a primary resource, for example Japan and Korea

- Developing people can help to alleviate poverty and unemployment

- HRD can improve the quality of people's lives

- Coordination and cooperation can help a country or region to deal with the ambiguity of globalization

- Labour shortages, as a consequence of a proportionate decline in young people, require more attention to a skilled and upskilled workforce

- In many developing countries, AIDS/HIV is causing damage to the workforce now and in the future

- Technological advances require a response through upskilling the workforce

SOURCE: Adapted from McLean (2004, p. 272)

Reflective questions

1 How do the above factors affect the interest in HRD in your country or region?

2 What other factors influence a concern for workforce skills?

While NHRD is apparently a relatively new term, it is argued by Wang (2008) that interest in the importance of HRD and the contribution to a country's development has important roots in models and theories of development economics. During the 1950s and 60s, there was a strong interest in the idea and measurement of human capital and investment in skills. Policy makers employed the language of economics in seeking to develop manpower plans for the demand and supply of skills for the economy. Bennison (1980) shows that the key processes of planning are:

- determination of manpower requirements

- determination of supply of manpower

- development of policies to fill the gap between demand and supply.

In theory, using notions of supply and demand and the measurement of variables would enable movement towards equilibrium within the market. Of course, equilibrium may not produce the desired level of skills utilization; indeed, a consequence may well be a low demand for skills or skills of low quality. Left to itself, the market for skills may fail. This so-called 'market failure' can take two forms. First, there may not be enough incentive for employers to acquire those with skills to work for them, and second, employers may not be willing to bear the costs of training (Booth and Snower, 1996). In either situation or both, governments may wish to intervene to address the market failure. How much intervention will vary from country to country and be strongly connected to the cultural and historical factors that are manifest in the political stances taken.

We can make a general distinction between 'voluntarism', where a government sees its role as the encouragement of organizations to take responsibility for skills acquisition and HRD, and 'interventionism', where governments seek to influence decision making on HRD in the interests of the economy as a whole. More likely, there is a mix of the two approaches but probably with a preference towards one against the other, as shown in Figure 4.1.

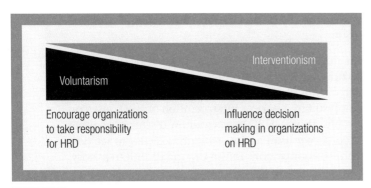

Voluntarism

Interventionism

Encourage organizations
to take responsibility
for HRD

Influence decision
making in organizations
on HRD

FIGURE 4.1 Voluntarism vs. interventionism in HRD

One way this contrast becomes manifest in policy terms is whether governments should impose a training levy on organizations to be returned as a fund to support training and development. In France for example, since the 1970s, a training levy is imposed on organizations annually as a proportion of payroll. If an organization provides HRD, it receives a grant. The question is whether this intervention has increased the amount and quality of HRD in French organizations. Research suggests that there has been an increase in training expenditure in French organizations (Greenhalgh, 2001). However, the downside has been an expensive system for administering the levies and grants, with the main benefits going to already trained mobile workers and training providers who have a ready-made market. These are just the sorts of criticism that led to the decline of the UK's levy system in the 1980s, as part of a move by the government towards a more voluntarist approach, which put more faith in decision makers in organizations to invest in HRD and skilled employees.

Activity

Work with a partner. Each person answers the question and then compare your findings.

What are the pros and cons of a training levy/grant system from the perspective of:

- governments
- employers
- citizens
- employees
- trade unions?

The choices to be made between voluntarism and intervention at a national level are a reflection of a country's social and cultural traditions. In many European countries, for example, there is a tradition of support for vocational education following compulsory school. The state provides support in the form of the infrastructure for vocational education and training (VET), its regulation and funding. Acceptance of the degree of intervention and support can become politically acknowledged by all parties, so that over time, consensus is achieved between the key players of government, employers and labour organizations.

There are, however, key debates on how much intervention is needed or how much should be left to employers. Human capital theory is concerned with ideas relating to the value in investing in people as a form of capital against which returns can be measured and assessed (Garrick, 1999). This can result in a narrow interpretation of HRD based on what is quickly tangible and measurable. That is, HRD needs to show a return like other expenditures and can be seen as a cost rather than an investment. It is easy to see how such an interpretation is made by many organizations in the UK and its link to history.

One link is the need to measure and compete in the 19th century. The work of Charles Babbage, mathematician and engineer, was instrumental in dividing work into its high-skill and low-skill elements. If work could be assigned to low skilled workers, costs could be reduced. This could occur even for high skilled work, if it could be divided into lower skilled elements. This process became known as the 'Babbage principle', which set in motion a path that focused on cost control and reduction, giving enormous influence to accountants, which has continued to this day. One further and connected influence is the way organizations come to be seen through the lens of a machine metaphor, which causes jobs to be seen as parts coordinated by a rational control system of measurement (Marsick and Williams, 1999). Learning has to fit against performance criteria, which set the standards for what is required but no more. There is little place for consideration of attitudes, feelings or the development of potential that cannot be measured against short-term targets. Thus HRD can easily become trapped by the constraints of measurement, especially in SMEs, where research has shown that there is little time for anything other than operational activities, controlled by narrow 'bottom-line' performance measures (Garengo et al., 2005).

These factors have all contributed to what has been seen as the 'low skills equilibrium' in the UK, which holds that the economy has been trapped in a cycle of low value-added, low skills and wages, coupled with high employment (Wilson and Hogarth, 2003). The key ideas here, first advanced by Finegold and Soskice (1988), are that products, under pressure to keep costs down, can be specified in low skills terms, thus, as argued by Wilson and Hogarth (2003, p. viii): 'Other things being equal, the lower the specification, the lower the skill intensity of the production process ... [and therefore] the lower demand for skill'. The apparent equilibrium is impervious to requests to increase skills levels, which provides a signal to the labour market of low skills requirements, and simultaneously constrains a move in the direction of higher skills because there is a lack of a well-educated and trained labour force (Keep, 1999).

How skills are understood and defined in an organization is a central concern in NHRD. Felstead et al. (2002), for example, point to the different uses of the word 'skill':

1   competence to carry out tasks successfully

2   the idea of hierarchical skill levels that are dependent on the complexities and discretions involved

3   the view that there are different types of skill, some generic and applicable in diverse work situations, and some specific and vocational and suitable for particular contexts.

The last point raises another key issue, regarding the extent to which skills can be regarded as generic and can therefore be provided as part of a VET system and preparation for work, or whether skills learned in the context of their use are more valued, in which case organizations need to take more responsibility. This remains a serious issue of contention in the UK (Payne, 2004). However, if organizations take responsibility for defining the meaning of skills, this can easily be set by the conditions of factors such as the structure of domestic markets, short-term financial pressure, models of competitive advantage based on economies of scale, central control, cost containment and standardization (Wilson and Hogarth, 2003), which all combine to design tasks to a low specification, requiring low skills and providing low value-added (Bloom et al., 2004). Therefore, even when there are reported skills deficiencies or gaps, it is quite possible that these remain low skills. Bloom et al. (2004, p. 12) talk about a 'latent skills gap', where organizations can accept and adjust to low-skill requirements, losing awareness of the restriction this imposes.

The challenge therefore is for organizations to break out of the low skills equilibrium, based on low specified products and services, and embrace high performance working in high-performing firms, which, according to the DTI (2005), have a focus on the long term and create a culture and employee relations characterized by pride, innovation and strong interpersonal relations. Skill development is focused on performance and learning is continuous and integrated into work (Sung and Ashton, 2005). High performance working and its connection with high skills provides a link to the idea of developmental humanism, where managers become more concerned with empowering employees through learning and skill development – a strong contrast to human capital theory. In many organizations, it is recognized that the key ingredient in products and especially services is the knowledge of the employees – the owners of intellectual capital acquired through their training and, more importantly, through their interaction with a network of customers, suppliers and each other. There are, however, some doubts that high performance working can be equated with high skills (Lloyd and Payne, 2004), representing an ideal of how work can be performed, which contrasts with the reality of low-skill work design. NHRD policy may be faced by extremes and polarization between high- and low-skill work practices.

Providing an escape from the low skills equilibrium requires some degree of coordination on the supply and demand for skills in order to move up the skills ladder. Based on their study of three of the 'tiger economies' – South Korea, Singapore and Taiwan – Green et al. (1999) point to the strategic role of the state in economic growth and the transformation of skills. It is never easy to systematically show a link between skills training and economic growth (Machin and Vignoles, 2001). It is argued, however, that given the longer term nature of returns to investment in skills, including the social as well as economic benefits, the state can play a 'matchmaking' role, which is more effective than allowing market forces to find their equilibrium. In the tiger economies, governments have been able to take a more informed, longer term view of skill requirements consistent with the targets for growth, and this in turn sets the direction for the supply of skills from schools, colleges/universities and trade institutions. The match-making occurs through a consistent and systematic gathering of information about skills requirements to set the direction for outputs by the education and training systems, combined with a process of persuading employers to demand skills, undertake workplace training and upgrade skills through targets, incentives and subsidy. Over time, as economic growth was achieved, the movement up the skills ladder was achieved. The crucial lesson from the study of these economies is less to do with choosing between voluntarism and intervention or manpower planning, and more to do with a consistent approach in developing institutions to supply skills based on forecasts of global economic developments, and simultaneously to influence demand towards high performance production. This pattern of NHRD appears in others countries, such as Australia (see below).

The crucial dilemma in NHRD between voluntarism and interventionism underpins some of the emerging models of NHRD identified by Cho and McLean (2004). One extreme form of interventionism would be a 'centralized model', imposed top down from central government, sometimes backed by a collectivist ideology as in China, or as a feature of centralized plans as in Mexico. The danger here is a squeezing out of private sector initiative and entrepreneurship, or the deadweight of administration and duplication as in France. The alternative decentralization or 'free-market model' leaves decisions on HRD to market forces, perhaps with stimulus and some persuasion from the government. Between the extremes are various efforts to gain the benefits of voluntarism and interventionism. As we will see, the UK, the USA and Australia all seek to provide an infrastructure for the supply of skills, but to varying degrees expect the market for skills to be 'demand led' from employers, where historical and cultural constraints may play a key role. European countries such as Austria, Germany and the Czech Republic take a more 'corporatist' approach, seeking to generate agreement between the key stakeholders of government, employers and trade unions. Between and perhaps above the demand-led and corporatists models lie the tiger economies with a 'matchmaking' model (Green et al., 1999), who seek to reconcile the dilemma of intervention and voluntarism by the intelligent use of forecasting data at government level to guide the supply infrastructure, and persuade and stimulate the demand for skills from organizations within the context of high growth and high skills aspirations. There is another angle on centralization and decentralization, where responsibility for policies is shared between a central or federal government and regions, states or devolved authorities, for example the USA, Australia and the UK. There are also efforts to move from one model towards another. For example, countries like the Czech Republic have sought transition from a centralized model towards a less interventionist corporatist model, and in France, there are efforts to move in the direction of a more market-oriented, demand-led model, although not without difficulties.

Reflective questions

1 Who do you think has most responsibility for ensuring a supply of skilled labour: government, employers or individuals?

2 What are the reasons for your answer?

The VET system

As we can see from the analysis of NHRD, apart from the extreme voluntarist models, in most cases, there is a role for government to ensure an adequate supply of skills to meet, to a greater or lesser extent, planned or forecasted requirements of the economy. Governments have a key role to play in establishing and supporting a VET infrastructure, composed of a variety of agencies, departments and processes working together as a system. Historically and culturally, it is crucial that the VET system is accepted as credible in terms of numbers and especially quality, indicated by the qualifications available and the standard of achievement. Qualifications often serve as a measurement by proxy of skills in an economy, and this process of equating skills with qualifications is referred to as 'credentialism'. There are some doubts as to the validity of this process (Fuller and Unwin, 1999). Nevertheless, qualifications provide a currency for a VET system, with debates about the value of one qualification process against another and considerations about who has the credentials to practise in an occupational area. For example, in many areas of professional work, restrictions on those who can practise are set by professional bodies such as the Law Society. In the UK, there are more than 400 professional bodies, although not all of them can control entry to professional practice. In other areas of work practice, there have been restrictions in the UK since the Statute of Artificers (1563), which made it a requirement to gain an apprenticeship to work in various crafts. Gaining an apprenticeship has traditionally been seen as a highly valid qualification to practise a skill.

Reflective questions

1 What are your credentials?

2 Do your qualifications, or those you are studying for, prove your ability to use certain skills?

The configuration of the VET system involving institutions, responsibilities and provision of resources will, of course, vary from country to country, although there are common features, as shown in Figure 4.2. There are also some attempts to bring consistency and compatibility between countries. For example, in the European Union (EU), under the 'Copenhagen Declaration' (EC, 2003), the member states have begun a process to develop:

- A single framework for transparency of competencies and qualifications

- A system of credit transfer for VET

- Common criteria and principles for quality in VET

- Common principles for the validation of non-formal and informal learning

- Information for lifelong guidance.

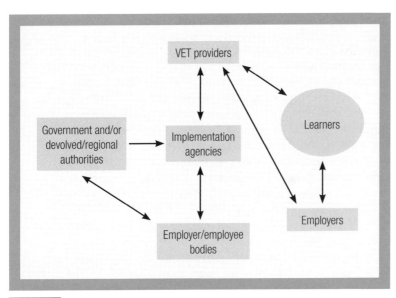

FIGURE 4.2 Configuration of VET systems

Activity

You might like to learn more about the EC's VET approaches by going to
http://ec.europa.eu/education/copenhagen/index_en.html.

We suggest that the main outcomes of a VET system are an educated and trained workforce. This may be measured by qualifications, although much training at work does not lead to qualifications. We have already examined the possible NRHD models that inform policy making at government and/or devolved authority and regional levels. Policies are implemented by agencies who may also provide funding for supporting and stimulating VET activities. Included among the agencies are those providing the framework and quality assurance for qualifications. Employer bodies attempt to allow employers voice to inform the working of the system and the standards required in qualifications. Employee bodies such as trade unions can also play a crucial role in ensuring that employees receive resources for HRD. While much HRD is provided by employers for learners, in crucial areas of youth development and adult learning, VET is supported and funded through providers. This includes institutions such as schools, universities and further education colleges, but also a large number of private providers. In the following sections, we will consider the working of the VET system in different countries and regions, starting with the UK.

The UK's VET system

We see the UK's VET system as one informed by the demand-led model of NHRD. The role of government and its agents has been to improve the training infrastructure, providing support and funding where market failure is identified. While we will focus mainly on what are now seen as the policies of England, there are links to the policies of Wales, Scotland and Northern Ireland.

Activity

For more details of skills strategy in Scotland, go to www.futureskillsscotland. org.uk. The Welsh Assembly's Education and Skills page is http://wales.gov. uk/topics/educationandskills/?lang=en, and for Northern Ireland, go to www. delni.gov.uk/index/successthroughskills.htm.

A crucial feature of the infrastructure has been the development of a National Qualification Framework (NQF) based on national vocational qualifications (NVQs, or SVQs in Scotland). Such qualifications cover most occupational areas and are work related by specifying the required outcomes expected in the performance of a task in a particular work role. Performance can be assessed against criteria or standards to achieve an NVQ. Skills and knowledge are reflected in the performance and achievement of an outcome. NVQs are organized into five levels of competence and Table 4.2 shows the general definitions at each level.

TABLE 4.2 Levels of competence in NVQs

Level	Description
Level 1	Competence that involves the application of knowledge in the performance of a range of varied work activities, most of which are routine and predictable
Level 2	Competence that involves the application of knowledge in a significant range of varied work activities, performed in a variety of contexts. Some of these activities are complex or non-routine and there is some individual responsibility or autonomy. Collaboration with others, perhaps through membership of a work group or team, is often a requirement
Level 3	Competence that involves the application of knowledge in a broad range of varied work activities performed in a wide variety of contexts, most of which are complex and non-routine. There is considerable responsibility and autonomy, and control or guidance of others is often required
Level 4	Competence that involves the application of knowledge in a broad range of complex, technical or professional work activities performed in a variety of contexts, with a substantial degree of personal responsibility and autonomy. Responsibility for the work of others and the allocation of resources is often present
Level 5	Competence that involves the application of a range of fundamental principles across a wide and often unpredictable variety of contexts. Substantial personal autonomy, often significant responsibility for the work of others and the allocation of substantial resources feature strongly, as do personal accountability for analysis, diagnosis, design, planning, execution and evaluation

SOURCE: www.qca.org.uk/14–19/qualifications/index_nvqs.htm

Each NVQ is based on the definition of National Occupational Standards (NOS) for occupational areas and purports to describe the performance of a competent person, including what is regarded as best practice. This requires some connection to what employers see as competent performance, which is achieved by the development and maintenance of NVQs by employer bodies. In particular, employers are represented by Sector Skills Councils (SSCs), although these are currently financed by the state. In the UK, 25 SSCs have been established since 2002, replacing a variety of national training organizations. They have a key role to play in relation to NOS and also, following the recommendations of Leitch (2006), the stimulation of demand for skills among employers in their sector. For example, Improve is the SSC for the food manufacturing sector, covering:

- bakery

- brewery

- dairy

- distillery

- drinks manufacturing

- food manufacturing and processing

- fresh produce

- meat and poultry

- sea fish

- confectionery.

Activity

Find out more about Improve at www.improveltd.co.uk. Also check www.ukces.org.uk/, the web page of the UK Commission for Employment and Skills, set up following the Leitch report to set a strategy for raising skills levels in the UK.

The number of NVQ certificates awarded provides an indicator of progress in the skill levels of the population. According to the Qualifications and Curriculum Authority (QCA),[2] there were 6,253,299 certificates awarded to 30 June 2007, an increase of 10.9% on the total awarded to 30 June 2006. In addition, it was reported that there was a growth in higher levels beyond level 2. The Leitch report (2006) has set targets for raising achievement in skill levels, aiming for 90% of adults to have at least a level 2 qualification, a shift in balance towards level 3 intermediate skills, with 500,000 people a year in apprenticeships and 40% of adults to have a level 4 or 5 qualification, equivalent to higher education.

Some organizations are making good use of NVQs in their own development programmes. An example is shown in HRD in Practice 4.1.

Vodaphone offers NVQ scheme to retail staff

Vodaphone UK is offering to put all its 2,200 retail staff through an NVQ-accredited development scheme to help them progress from trainee adviser to regional manager. The programme was launched in November 2007. It is expected to take three years to complete all six levels, which would be equivalent to 15 GCSEs and four A levels.

The scheme, created with NVQ specialist Elmfield, requires students to provide evidence of their experience and case studies showing they have attained certain standards. The case studies are reviewed by a regional or store manager and then assessed by Elmfield.

'There is a direct link between staff and customer satisfaction. We're confident that this scheme will give both a large boost', said Tom Devine, director of consumer sales at Vodaphone.

Source: *People Management* (26 June 2008)

While competence-based NVQs are now well established, from their inception in the 1980s, criticism has been levelled at the meaning of competence used that emphasizes outcomes against standards. It is claimed that this gives less attention to the importance of knowledge and understanding and providing support for developing skills (Grugulis, 2003). There have also been persistent doubts that the NVQ framework has the support of employers (Raggatt and Williams, 1999). For example, the standard set for level 2 may simply be too disconnected from the requirements and values of employers who pursue improvement and growth (Gold and Thorpe, 2008).

One frequent criticism is that they lack the rigour of academic qualifications such as GCSEs, A levels and degrees. This is a reflection of the cultural and historical tradition in the UK of separating thinking and doing, referred to earlier – it has created what is usually termed the 'academic/vocational divide'. Some attempt has been made to extend the NQF to show equivalence between academic and vocational qualifications. Thus an honours degree is equated with a level 4 NVQ and a Masters degree with a level 5 NVQ. In addition, following the Tomlinson report in 2004 and the *14–19 Education and Skills White Paper* in 2005 (DfES, 2005), the government set out to reform the school curriculum, including providing better vocational routes. This includes the development of 14–19 diplomas in vocational areas from 2008, which relate more closely to vocational skills and accommodate employment-based training through apprenticeships. The intention is to have 14 diploma routes by 2014, and crucial to their success will be recognition by employers and universities as well as young people, who need to regard diplomas as a viable alternative to traditional academic pathways.

The development of 14–19 diplomas is part of a broader concern with weaknesses in the UK supply of intermediate skills. Such skills have been traditionally related to craft skills acquired by serving an apprenticeship. In the 1980s, apprenticeships in the UK declined dramatically along with craft-based manufacturing. Rising unemployment among young people resulted in a youth training scheme but this was never seen as a replacement for apprenticeships and was regarded as a low standard qualification (Steedman et al., 1998). By contrast, countries such a Germany retained their apprenticeship systems, combining academic and technical skills with guidance from work experience, resulting in higher numbers of skilled workers (Grugulis, 2002).

The failure to provide sufficient numbers of apprentices in the UK is also a cause of the apparent skills gaps, filled in recent years by workers arriving from the EU. As a response, since the mid-1990s, and as part of the 14–19 reforms, there has been an attempt to recreate a 'golden pathway' to intermediate skills from basic skills through level 2 to 3, by the introduction of a framework of work-based training that leads to apprenticeship status. There are one-year programmes leading to a technical certificate at level 2 and two-year programmes leading to level 3. Apprenticeships are delivered by a combination of work-based and off-site training, undertaken by work-based learning providers and further education colleges. In 2005, the Apprenticeships Task Force (2005) reported that apprenticeships do improve business performance and cost-effective training, along with better retention of staff. However, not all employers see the value of apprenticeships, with many preferring to upgrade the skills of existing employees (Lewis et al., 2008). In addition, because what happens in the workplace is crucial in apprenticeships, there are bound to be variations in culture affecting the depth and breadth of opportunities for learning, including the chance to participate in skilled practices (Fuller and Unwin, 2003).

Activity

Check the 14–19 website at the renamed Department for Children, Schools and Families – www.dcsf.gov.uk/14–19/.

Read more about apprenticeships at www.apprenticeships.org.uk/.

The VET policy in England is implemented through a range of institutions throughout the country. It is characterized by a lack of consistency, in that changes are fairly frequent. There are also swings between the extent to which institutions operate at regional, subregional and local authority levels. There are also possible tensions at national level between agendas that emphasize skills, for example those from the renamed Department of Innovation, Universities and Skills, and those that emphasize business development, for example from the Department of Business, Enterprise and Regulatory Reform.

From 2000, the main approach has been informed by 'new regionalism' (Webb and Collis, 2000), with regions such as the northwest or Yorkshire forming the basis of thinking relating to development, competitiveness and growth. Throughout the country, Regional Development Agencies (RDAs) were established to create strategies for their region. RDAs were supplemented by a Learning and Skills Council (LSC), at first operating subregionally and then regionally to implement policies on skills including a key role of funding training places at work. The LSCs also provide contracts for supporting businesses through a network of Business Links. This now includes the main funding process for training, Train to Gain (TTG). As recommended by the Leitch review (2006), all government funding for training is channelled through TTG. This process provides advice to employers on training through a skills broker who completes a needs analysis of training before recommending a choice of providers. Employers are also encouraged to voluntarily take a 'skills pledge' to support staff to develop skills to at least level 2, although as we have indicated above, this is hardly an advanced level of skill. Reviews of TTG suggest that, in future, there will be more emphasis on level 3 (TTG, 2007). From 2010, the LSCs' responsibilities will be allocated to other agencies, including a Skills Funding Agency and a National Apprenticeship Service.

As we said above, there tend to be swings in policy with respect to the unit of implementation. Thus, there is more attention being paid to the responsibility being taken by local authorities as part of the government's *Review of Sub-national Economic Development and Regeneration* (HM Treasury, 2007). This can also include authorities working together as city regions (for more about city regions, go to www.idea.gov.uk/idk/core/page. do?pageId=4730940). There are also plans to break up the LSCs, allocating their responsibilities to local authorities and other agencies.

Changes in the supply infrastructure are one thing but for the VET system to work, there has to be a response from employers, and in the UK, this response remains voluntary. This means that employers have a choice about how much they invest in HRD activity, and it seems that many choose to minimize costs. Even in organizations that take strategic management seriously, HRD can still remain a subsidiary issue (Coleman and Keep, 2001), with costs kept low. This can leave a production process bound by a low product specification with an impact on the demand for skills (Green et al., 2003). Recent survey evidence (NESS, 2007) points to the fact that over one-third of employers provide no training, and that for 11% of those that do train, only health and safety or induction training is provided – with no skills development.

Trade unions could play a role within organizations to raise the profile of skills. Under the 2002 Employment Act, recognition can be granted to union learning representatives, who can promote the value of training and learning, including analysis of training needs, advice to members and arrangement of events for training and learning. They can also consult with employers on issues concerning members' training and learning, and are entitled to receive paid time off so they can be trained to carry out the role, attending courses with their union in order to acquire the skills to analyse needs and negotiate with employers (Lee and Cassell, 2004). According to the Union Learn website (www.unionlearn.org.uk/), Union Learn seeks to help unions to become learning organizations, to broker learning opportunities for its members and research union priorities on learning and skills.

Another source of possible stimulation, and one that certainly attempts to move skills and HRD into business plans, is the Investors in People (IiP) award, which has been operating since 1991. IiP provides a set of standards for training and development against which organizations can be assessed and reassessed on an agreed basis. It has survived with some copying in Australia, Germany and France (Bell et al., 2004). Recent evidence suggests that using the IiP standard can help to provide a framework for HRD and HRM policy generally, which increased investment in skills and can impact on performance (Tamkin et al., 2008). It was crucial, however, to integrate HR policies so that key links were recognized, for example skills development with promotion and remuneration.

The analysis of survey findings used regression analysis to make its claims but accepted that claims about causality could not be made. It can also be the case that IiP firms are already performing well against the standard and other measures so have the least to do to gain it (Down and Smith, 1998).

Activity

Form a group of three. Each person should visit the IiP home page – www.investorsinpeople.co.uk. Allocate tasks as follows and report back on findings:

1 One person should examine 'The Standard' and find a case study of its use.

2 One person should explore 'Profile Self Check' and find a case study of its use.

3 One person should examine 'IiP Interactive' and consider how it could be used at work.

Awards such as IiP can play a significant role in providing a language to talk about HRD and this can lead to action. This is part of what Gold and Smith (2003) refer to as the 'learning movement', where positive talk about HRD and skills can become self-fulfilling. It also features the positive orientation of decision makers about HRD and those who judge the results. However, central to the process were those who continued the positive talk as persuaders of others – this is not easy and requires stubbornness and good skills of negotiation and argument. Without these, and the support from senior managers, HRD talk can easily be relegated behind other sorts of talk. Needless to say, there also needs to be a close examination of what kinds of products and services are being designed that require higher skills or lower skills. In the remaining sections, we will consider how other countries tackle some of the issues raised in this section. We begin with the Czech Republic.

Reflective questions

1 What do you think are the advantages and disadvantages of an NVQ for an individual seeking work compared with a professional or academic qualification?

2 Why do you think this?

NHRD in the Czech Republic

There is a very high level of youth participation in post-compulsory education in the Czech Republic – official estimates of the rate vary, but all put it at above 90% (and as high as 96%), well above the EU average.

Participation was at high levels during the Communist era, and has remained at high levels since then, due to the long history of support for the value of education in Czech society. Case study research conducted in the Czech Republic revealed that the high participation of young people resulted from cultural factors, rather than specific policy initiatives (see LSC, 2008).

The wider education system in the Czech Republic is undergoing change, which is mainly centrally designed and driven but relies on local implementation. The need for reform is driven by the requirement to better align the vocational training system with labour market needs – particularly foreign-owned businesses located in the Czech Republic – and increase the supply of skilled workers. The Czech economy relies heavily on immigrant labour, associated in part with high levels of foreign direct investment (FDI), which requires higher level and different skills than those available in the local labour market:

Several reforms have been introduced to address this issue, modelled on lessons learned and policies adopted in other EU member states, particularly the UK. These reforms bear some resemblance to features of the English post-16 education and training landscape:

- Vocational curriculum reform – focusing more on delivering skills and outcomes relevant to the labour market, including transferable skills

- Introduction of an NQF to specify standards of qualification and assessment. This will involve partial as well as full qualifications

- Introduction of a 'national career framework', which will indicate employers' skills needs across different job roles

- 'Sector councils' established, involving employers and other organizations in the design of new curricula

- Introduction of approved assessors to separate training provision and assessment/ verification of qualifications

- Establishment of HRD 'advisory councils' in each region.

These reforms have been designed and implemented mainly through EU funding. There is little political will to commit state funds to education, with the Czech Republic allocating a relatively low proportion of its GDP to the education budget. EU funding is finite, so one of the critical factors is the extent to which the country will be prepared to sustain funding for the reforms when the EU investment comes to an end.

The Czech Republic has not yet made consistent use of financial incentives to encourage participation of either individuals or employers in training, although there is some evidence of incentives being offered to employers in regions with high levels of unemployment and support for large foreign companies. Other measures designed to stimulate demand have had a limited impact to date, even when subsidized training is offered. For example, the central government funded retraining courses for people who are unemployed and looking for work, or in employment and seeking to change jobs. Take-up of these courses is low, with only around 10% of the target groups participating. This seems to be due to barriers relating to wider social and employment policies. There are changes being introduced in social policy to address this problem. The Czech example illustrates the importance of ensuring that measures to stimulate demand for learning are effectively aligned with employment and social policies.

NHRD in California

California, the most populous state in the USA, has prospered in recent years as new industries (for example high-tech Silicon Valley) have replaced old ones (for example cold war defence industries and manufacturing), and its universities, especially the University of California, are seen as world-class research institutions. In many respects, the Californian VET system is demand led to a large extent, as many adult individuals pursue VET, often at their own expense, and many companies and organizations fund and undertake in-house education and training of their existing employees. Much adult self-funded provision is undertaken in the California 'community college system', dispro-portionately large in California, often chosen by students for two years and usually seen as an asset, providing low-cost, local higher education and industry-recognized certifi-cates and credentials. However, it has been mainly focused on 'transfer' and articulation agreements with four-year universities, such as California State University (that is, it offers undergraduate and graduate programmes, although recently it has moved into providing more workforce development and contract training).

In this sense, California would be placed at the voluntarist end of the spectrum given in Figure 4.1. However, there are a number of interesting ways in which a more interven-tionist stance has been adopted in recent years, moving it more towards a matchmaking model. California has made recent changes to its public policy initiatives in response both to federal government drivers and its specific situation:

1   There is a Master Plan for Education, dating from 1960, which is reviewed, renewed and coordinated by the California Post-secondary Education Commis-sion, established in 1974.

2   The current governor (2009), with an Austrian VET background, is leading changes, especially in CTE (career and technical education). The 1984 Federal Perkins Vocational Education & Applied Technology Act (now 2006) delivers funding to help develop integrated CTE courses in 15 industry sectors in the school system.

3   The 1998 Federal Workforce Investment Act established a state Workforce Investment Board and 50 local boards in California to coordinate and develop a strategy for 'workforce development'. The boards have to have at least 50% business representation, alongside elected officials, and their role is to identify HRD providers, monitor the effectiveness of HRD and analyse the local labour market.

4   A bipartisan California Economic Strategy Panel was established in 1993 to develop an overall vision and strategy and complete the 'regional economies project'.

5   An Employment Training Panel, established in 1983, provides publicly funded workplace-based customized training to new and existing employees, especially those facing out-of-state, especially global, competition. This training is provided by a range of public, private and non-profit education and training providers. It is funded by the 'employment training tax' paid by employers, and is intended to target threatened firms (although in practice it may not always be used in this way).

These initiatives show how the state is moving to involve businesses with government in a more matchmaking model direction, rather than adopting a purely voluntarist position.

The USA has a federal structure, in which states and localities, such as local school districts, retain significant power. There is no single agency responsible for policy in youth/adult education and training. National government departments (for example the US Department of Education) are responsible for some aspects of policy, with substantial variations in education practice and funding levels. This means that it is difficult to discern a coherent approach or fully national policy. Individuals and employers, but not necessarily employee or employer associations, are seen as playing a key role in financing adult education. Within California, VET is fragmented across both levels of governance (federal, state, local) and state departments (California Department of Education, Community Colleges Chancellors Office, Employment Development Department, Department of Social Services, Department of Industrial Relations).

The main drivers for change in VET, pushing California away from a purely voluntarist model, have been the new economy and the 'new California'. In the former, globalization, technological change and the need to compete in the knowledge economy have placed a premium on high-skill jobs and lifelong learning. Local jobs in many services, nursing and construction have experienced skill shortages. The culture is generally seen as innovative, entrepreneurial and pro-education, but prioritizing academic education and the four-year college degree. VET is sometimes seen as stigmatizing minorities (denying college and so on) and a lower status than academic education.

The new California embraces increasing diversity and immigration, including an ageing population and especially Latino/Hispanic immigration (a projected 70% increase between 2000 and 2020 means Latinos are likely to become a majority by 2040). However, levels of education and English fluency tend to be lower than other groups. Drop-out rates are a particular problem for some minorities (especially African-Americans and Latinos) and immigrants and their children. These two factors have led to changes in VET policy for both youths and adults.

NHRD in Australia

We see Australia's NHRD model as moving towards that of matchmaking, with recognition since the 1990s – when there was high youth unemployment and a decline in traditional apprenticeships – of the need to move towards a high skilled, high productivity economy within a global economy based on ITC and knowledge-intensive work. For adults, mainly the existing workforce, there has been the need to reskill and upskill, with recent attempts to encourage older workers to undertake apprenticeship training and stimulate 'recognition of prior learning', allowing alternative pathways to qualifications. A national training system has been developing since the early 1990s and is seen to be effective by most stakeholders. The key features of the system are training packages (TPs), which are composed of competency standards, assured by the Australian Quality Training Framework (AQTF) and delivered by over 4000 registered training organizations (RTOs) in compliance with the standard set by the AQTF to ensure high quality. In addition, there is a single system of qualifications that form the Australian Qualifications Framework, providing coverage from senior secondary certificates of education to PhDs.

There has been a quadrupling of the numbers of apprentices and trainees since the 1990s, although there is concern about the high numbers of cancellations and withdrawals from apprenticeships and trainees. Delivery of apprenticeships and traineeship occurs through the Australian Apprenticeship Centres (AACs), which engage with employers to market and promote apprenticeships. Targets are set with the Common-wealth Department for Education, Science and Training.

RTOs deliver training and qualifications against the requirements of TPs, and group training organizations (GTOs) provide a leasing process with employers. These provide a crucial feature for engagement with employers. AACs, GTOs and RTOs all have field staff – 'shoe leathers' – who cover regions, making use of the training system and incentives. Training contracts are set with employers and trainees.

As a consequence, training is now seen as a key requirement with relatively high levels of participation and there is acceptance by all stakeholders of the importance of skills. The training system and infrastructure provides consistency and quality but is being used flexibly with increased uptake of VET in schools and some evidence of dual accred-itation. Student satisfaction with VET at schools contributes to the reason for increased staying on rates to year 12. There is acceptance of VET study within the senior secondary certificate and use in university entrance.

Evidence suggests that there has been a strong take-up of TPs by employers, including over half of large and medium-sized enterprises who use TPs to provide accreditation for employees. It has also been found that TPs are benefiting staff who would not have received training or qualifications in organizations, and they are shaping other HRM activities such as recruitment and performance management. It is argued that the enthusiasm for TPs is the result of including key stakeholders in their creation, although some doubts remain about the competence approach.

TPs allow a flexible and responsive approach to skills to be taken, as shown in HRD in Practice 4.2.

HRD in Practice 4.2

Fitness trainers for children: pilot Australian apprenticeship programme

This project will pilot an Australian apprenticeship programme that facilit-ates the skill acquisition for fitness train-ers to specialize in the delivery of exercise to children and young adolescents.

It is estimated that there are 1,335 gyms or fitness centres in Australia cater-ing to the needs of 1.6 million people. This gives an average attendance rate of about 1.75 times a week per individual. It is further estimated that the industry has been growing at the rate of 15% per year over the past three to five years and is expected to continue at the same rate over the next few years.

The fitness industry offers enormous potential for qualified people to become self-employed and run their own small businesses. Opportunities for self-employment are not limited to those in metropolitan areas but present a real possibility for those in rural, regional and isolated areas.

Learner demand and training delivery is currently focusing on the high-profile, glamorous occupations of gym instructor and personal trainer. It is imperative to promote and facilitate the training for fit-ness professionals to deal with the future needs of the Australian population.

It is well documented that Australia is facing a crisis of childhood obesity. It is estimated that 25% of Australian children are overweight or obese and this number is increasing by 1% every year. So there is an urgent need for qualified fitness professionals to deliver exercise to children.

The pilot project will aim to address fitness professionals' skill shortages. The pilot apprenticeship programme will:

- deliver the 'Certificate IV in Fitness', with participants undertaking the children's trainer specialization

- be implemented via an Australian apprenticeship delivery strategy, a combination of formal on and off-the-job competency-based training
- promote delivery strategies and outcomes to RTOs, Australian apprenticeship centres, the fitness and health industries, government and other relevant stakeholders as an effective model for implementation nationally
- encourage the uptake of training in the children's trainer specialization.

Ten Industry Skills Councils (ISCs) are tasked with the stewardship of TPs including their development, maintenance and review. ISCs are run by boards that include representatives from industry associations, Chambers of Commerce and employers. ISCs attempt to consult with all parties, including unions, in their work, feeding the skill requirement of sectors to ongoing strategic considerations at Commonwealth and states/territories levels. Targets are set within the *2005–08 Commonwealth-State Agreement for Skilling Australia's Workforce* (DEST, 2006), and incorporated by the states/territories into bilateral agreements, which are reviewed annually.

One of the most interesting features of the progress in Australia has been an interest and willingness to explore and experiment with new ideas. While there have been a number of policies and developments, these have mostly been concerned with boosting the numbers and quality of skilled participants in the workforce. There is also the issue of how skills are utilized; it is quite possible that even where employers see the value of skills in their workforce, they persist in the methods of work practice that underutilize skills. As a consequence, there have been a number of projects to analyse the range of interconnected factors that shape skills formation within an ecosystem (Buchanan et al., 2001).

Activity

Details and resources about the skills ecosystem projects can be found at www.skillecosystem.net/. For more details of the VET system in Australia, go to www.dest.gov.au/sectors/training_skills/default2.htm.

Summary

- It is clear from this chapter that NHRD is not yet a settled or fully accepted term. It is also clear, however, that national governments seek to influence, shape and, in some cases, determine and direct VET.

- Societal-level HRD is a feature of HRD practice and a context for that practice. Governments tend to have policies on VET, which they implement through a variety of structural and financial mechanisms and related agencies.

- The approaches adopted vary but with sufficient similarity and purpose that they can be classified on a continuum between voluntarism and interventionism. Examples can be found from different countries that illustrate different points on this continuum.

- In the UK, various policies have been implemented to shape and influence the behaviour of employers and individual citizens in order to stimulate a high skills economy. There are, however, sound reasons to doubt the potential and actual success of these policies in achieving their aims.

- The main outcomes of a VET system are an educated and trained workforce. This may be measured by qualifications, although much training at work does not lead to qualifications.

- The UK's VET system is informed by the demand-led model of NHRD. The role of the governments/authorities of England, Wales, Scotland and Northern Ireland and their agents has been to improve the training infrastructure, providing support and funding where market failure is identified. The system is characterized by frequent changes with respect to the unit of implementation.

- The Czech Republic has high levels of youth participation in post-compulsory education. The need for reform is driven by the requirement to better align the vocational training system with labour market needs – particularly foreign-owned businesses located in the Czech Republic – and to increase the supply of skilled workers. One critical factor is the extent to which the Czech Republic will be prepared to sustain funding for the reforms when the EU investment comes to an end.

- The Californian VET system is to a large extent demand led, as many adult individuals pursue VET, often at their own expense, and many companies and organizations fund and undertake in-house education and training of their existing employees. Much adult self-funded provision is undertaken in the California community college system, disproportionately large in California, and usually seen as an asset, providing low-cost, local higher education and industry-recognized certificates and credentials. California has made recent changes to its public policy initiatives, moving to involve businesses with government in a more matchmaking model direction, rather than adopting a purely voluntarist position.

- Australia's NHRD model has been moving towards that of matchmaking, with recognition since the 1990s of the need to move towards a high skilled, high productivity economy within a global economy based on ITC and knowledge-intensive work. Training is now seen as a key requirement with relatively high levels of participation and there is acceptance by all stakeholders of the importance of skills. The training system and infrastructure provides consistency and quality but is being used flexibly, with increased uptake of VET in schools and some evidence of dual accreditation.

Discussion questions

1 Can there be a National HRD?

2 How far should NHRD polices relate to economic and social wellbeing?

3 Who should be responsible for investment in HRD?

4 Is a high skilled, high productivity workforce possible?

5 What are the key features for a successful VET system?

6 What are the main similarities and differences between NHRD in the Czech Republic, Australia and California?

7 How does each NHRD compare with that in the UK?

8 What lessons do you think could be learned by and applied in the UK from the NHRD systems described here?

Further reading

Murray, A. and Skarlind, A. (2005) Does vocational training matter for young adults in the labour market?, *European Journal of Vocational Training*, **34**: 16–27.

Smith, A. (2006) Engagement or irrelevance? HRD and the world of policy and practice, *Human Resource Development Review*, **5**(4): 395–9.

Stevens, M. (1999) Human capital theory and UK vocational training policy, *Oxford Review of Economic Policy*, **15**: 16–32.

Wang, G. and Swanson, R. (2008) The idea of national HRD: an analysis based on economics and theory development methodology, *Human Resource Development Review*, **7**(1): 79–106.

Notes

1 It is worth saying at the outset that most UK government statements on these issues apply only to England. The governments and assemblies of Wales, Scotland and Northern Ireland have their own plans.

2 In Scotland, check the Scottish Qualifications Authority – www.sqa.org.uk. The QCA's website on NVQs is www.qca.org.uk/qca_7133.aspx.

References

Apprenticeships Task Force (2005) *Final Report*, London, Apprenticeships Task Force.

Bell, E., Taylor, R. and Hoque, K. (2004) *Workplace Training and the High Skills Vision: Where Does Investors in People Fit in?*, Warwick, Centre for Skills, Knowledge and Organizational Performance (SKOPE).

Bennison, M. (1980) *The IMS Approach to Manpower Planning*, Brighton, Institute of Manpower Studies.

Bloom, N., Conway, N., Mole, K. et al. (2004) *Solving the Skills Gap*, AIM Research Paper, London, Advanced Institute of Management.

Booth, A.L. and Snower, D.J. (1996) Does the free market produce enough skills?, in A.L. Booth and D.J. Snower (eds) *Acquiring Skills: Market Failures, Their Symptoms and Policy Responses*, Cambridge, Cambridge University Press.

Buchanan, J., Schofield, K., Briggs, C. et al. (2001) *Beyond Flexibility: Skills and Work in the Future*, Sydney, NSW Board of Vocational Education and Training.

Cho, E. and McLean, G.N. (2004) What we discovered about NHRD and what it means for HRD, *Advances in Developing Human Resources*, **6**(3): 382–93.

Coleman, E. and Keep, E. (2001) Background literature review for PIU project on workforce development, research paper for the Performance and Innovation Unit, Cabinet Office, London.

DEST (Department of Education, Science and Training, Australia) (2006) *2005–08 Commonwealth-State Agreement for Skilling Australia's Workforce*, Canberra, DEST.

DfES (Department for Education and Skills) (2005) *14–19 Education and Skills*, White Paper, London, DfES.

DIUS (Department of Innovation, Universities and Skills) (2007) *World Class Skills: Implementing the Leitch Review of Skills in England*, London, DIUS.

Down, S. and Smith, S. (1998) It pays to be nice to people, *Personnel Review*, **27**(2): 143–55.

DTI (Department of Trade and Industry) (2005) *People, Strategy and Performance: Results from the Second Work and Enterprise Business Survey*, London, DTI.

EC (European Commission) (2003) *Enhanced Co-operation in Vocational Education and Training*, Brussels, EC.

Felstead, A., Gallie, D. and Green, F. (2002) *Work Skills in Britain 1986–2001*, London, DfES.

Finegold, D. and Soskice, D. (1988) The failure of training in Britain: analysis and prescription, *Oxford Review of Economic Policy*, **4**: 21–53.

Fuller, A. and Unwin, L. (1999) Credentialism, national targets, and the learning society: perspectives on educational attainment in the UK steel industry, *Journal of Education Policy*, **14**(6): 605–17.

Fuller, A. and Unwin, L. (2003) Learning as apprentices in the contemporary UK workplace: creating and managing expansive and restrictive participation, *Journal of Education and Work*, **16**(4): 407–26.

Garengo, P., Biazzo, S. and Bititci, U. (2005) Performance measurement systems in SMEs: a review for a research agenda, *International Journal of Management Reviews*, **7**(1): 25–47.

Garrick, J. (1999) The dominant discourse of learning at work, in D. Boud and J. Garrick (eds) *Understanding Learning at Work*, London, Routledge.

Gold, J. and Smith, V. (2003) Advances towards a learning movement: translations at work, *Human Resource Development International*, **6**(2): 139–52.

Gold, J. and Thorpe, R. (2008) Training, it's a load of crap: the story of the hairdresser and his suit, *Human Resource Development International*, **11**(4): 385– 99.

Green, F., Ashton, D., James, D. and Sung, J. (1999) The role of the state in skill formation: evidence from the Republic of Korea, Taiwan and Singapore, *Oxford Review of Economic Policy*, **15**(1): 82–96.

Green, F., Mayhew, K. and Molloy, E. (2003) *Employer Perspectives Survey*, Warwick, Centre for Skills, Knowledge and Organizational Performance.

Greenhalgh, C. (2001) Does an employer training levy work? The incidence of and returns to adult vocational training in France and Britain, Research Paper 14, Oxford, SKOPE.

Grugulis, I. (2002) Skills and qualifications: the contribution of NVQs to raising skills levels, Research Paper 36, Warwick, SKOPE.

Grugulis, I. (2003) The contribution of national vocational qualifications to the growth of skills in the UK, *British Journal of Industrial Relations*, **41**(3): 457–75.

HM Treasury (2007) *Review of Sub-national Economic Development and Regeneration,* London, HM Treasury.

Keep, E. (1999) Employer attitudes towards adult learning, Skills Task Force Research Paper 15, London, DfEE.

Keep, E., Mayhew, K. and Payne, J. (2006) From skills revolution to productivity miracle: not as easy as it sounds?, *Oxford Review of Economic Policy,* **22**(4): 539–59.

Lee, B. and Cassell, C. (2004) Electronic routes to change? A survey of website support for trade union learning representatives, *International*

Journal of Knowledge, Culture and Change Management, **4**: 701–11.

Leitch, S. (2006) Prosperity for all in the global economy – world class skills, London, HM Treasury.

Lewis, P., Ryan, P. and Gospel, H. (2008) A hard sell? The prospects for apprenticeship in British retailing, *Human Resource Management Journal*, **18**(1): 3–19.

Lloyd, C. and Payne, J. (2004) Just another bandwagon? A critical look at the role of the high performance workplace as vehicle for the UK high skills project, SKOPE Research Paper 49, Oxford University.

LSC (2008) *World-class Comparisons: Research Report*, Coventry, Learning and Skills Council.

Machin, A. and Vignoles, S. (2001) *The Economic Benefits of Training to the Individual, the Firm and the Economy: The Key Issues*, London, Cabinet Office.

McLean, G.N. (2004) National human resource development: what in the world is it?, *Advances in Developing Human Resources*, **6**(3): 269–75.

Marsick, V. and Watkins, K. (1999) Envisioning new organizations for learning, in D. Boud and J. Garrick (eds) *Understanding Learning at Work*, London, Routledge.

NESS (National Employers Skills Survey) (2007) *Employers Skills Survey: Main Report*, Coventry, Learning and Skills Council.

Payne, J. (2004) *The Changing Meaning of Skill*, Issues Paper 1, University of Warwick, SKOPE.

Raggatt, P. and Williams, S. (1999) *Government, Markets and Vocational Qualifications: An Anatomy of Policy*, London, Falmer.

Steedman, H., Gospel, H. and Ryan, P. (1998) *Apprenticeship: A Strategy for Growth*, Centre for Economic Performance, London, LSE.

Sung, J. and Ashton, D. (2005) *High Performance Work Practices: Linking Strategy and Skills to Performance Outcomes*, London, DTI.

Tamkin, P., Cowling, M. and Hunt, W. (2008) *People and the Bottom Line*, Brighton, Institute of Employment Studies.

TTG (Train to Gain) (2007) *A Plan for Growth, November 2007–July 2011*, Coventry, Learning and Skills Council.

Wang, G. (2008) National HRD: new paradigm or reinvention of the wheel?, *Journal of European Industrial Training*, **32**(4): 303–16.

Webb, D. and Collis, C. (2000) Regional development agencies and the new regionalism in England, *Regional Studies*, **34**: 857–64.

Wilson, R. and Hogarth, T. with Bosworth, D. et al. (2003) *Tackling the Low Skills Equilibrium: A Review of Issues and Some New Evidence,* London, DTI.

SECTION 1 CASE STUDY

Pre-employment training for cabin crew

Ryanair is Europe's largest low-cost airline, with over 163 aircraft operating from 28 European bases. Crewlink is one of a number of contract cabin crew agencies who supply cabin crew to Ryanair on a subcontract basis.

Potential applicants are invited to an open day, which takes place throughout Europe each month. A presentation is given, followed by interviews to assess candidates against the following key selection criteria:

- Experienced in a customer services environment and comfortable in a selling role
- Physically fit with a good attendance record
- Hard working, flexible and willing to operate on a shift roster
- Over 18 years of age
- Between 5'2" (1.57m) and 6'2" (1.85m), with weight in proportion to height
- Of normal vision (contact lenses acceptable)
- Able to swim well

- In possession of a valid EU passport
- Fluent in English (both written and spoken)
- Ideally possessing knowledge of a second European language
- Prepared to live within one hour's travelling time of any Ryanair base
- Prepared to work unsociable hours, any day of the year, at any time including weekends
- Ready to meet the challenge of dealing with people and demanding situations
- Friendly and outgoing with a lively personality
- Flexible to work at any base within the Ryanair network.

Candidates who are successful at the open day are offered a place on a Ryanair training course. This is an intensive six-week programme, which runs from 9.00 to 5.30, Monday to Friday and includes some weekends. A considerable amount of study is involved and candidates are required to sit examinations as part of the assessment process. The course has a 95% pass rate.

Candidates are required to pay for this training themselves: the course costs €1,750 if paid in full, or €2,000 with a €500 deposit and the remainder paid by monthly salary deduction. Candidates are not paid during the six weeks of the course, but those who successfully complete all aspects of the training programme are offered a three-year employment contract with Crewlink to work as cabin crew for Ryanair. Over the first six months, they will receive a new joiners allowance totalling €1,200. New contract crew also earn on average €1,200 per month plus travel benefits. There is a 12-month probationary period but candidates who meet Ryanair's performance criteria are likely to be offered a permanent contract with Ryanair.

SOURCE: www.crewlink.ie

Questions

1 What are the advantages and disadvantages of this approach for Crewlink and Ryanair?

2 What are the advantages and disadvantages of this approach for prospective cabin crew?

3 How might the effectiveness of the training course be assessed?

4 How transferable is this approach to other organizations?

SECTION 2 **LOOKING IN**
PRINCIPLES OF HRD

Learning Theories and Principles

5

Crystal Ling Zhang, Niki Kyriakidou and David Chesley

Chapter learning outcomes

After studying this chapter, you should be able to:

- Understand the nature of learning and its importance in the context of an organization
- Define 'learning' and explain the learning theories
- Understand various models of learning styles and their complexity
- Understand how to apply learning theories in the organization

Chapter outline

Introduction

Learning is a human phenomenon, essential to growth and development, and occurring throughout life. It is itself as much an experience as is the subject of the learning. We not only learn to be better (at whatever), but have the opportunity to 'learn how to learn' better or faster. The effectiveness of learning can itself be manipulated. HRD is concerned with the provision of learning and the development of opportunities that support the achievement of business strategies and the improvement of organizational, team and individual performance (Armstrong and Baron, 2002). An understanding of learning is therefore crucial for anyone involved in HRD – trainers, consultants and facilitators, assessors of qualifications and, especially, managers and leaders. As Sadler-Smith (2006, p. 2) points out, 'learning is at the heart of *organization*'. However, there is also a connection between views about how work should occur and ideas about learning. Such ideas will inform a manager's understanding of behaviour at work, and the motivation and skills required.

We will begin this chapter with a broad examination of the social changes that have made learning such a central concept in contemporary society and discuss the definition of 'learning' and its implications for HRD.

What is learning?

Before defining learning, we must distinguish between 'education', 'training' and 'learning'. According to Mayo and Lank (1994):

- *Education* is the exposure to new knowledge, concepts and ideas in a relatively programmed way. It is normally aimed at increasing knowledge, or modifying attitudes and beliefs.

- *Training* includes those solutions to a learning need that involve being taught or shown a way of doing things. It is essentially skill oriented.

- *Learning* is employee need centred and starts with the individual as a beneficiary.

In this context, it can be argued that learning is a knowledge-creating process through transforming experience (Kolb, 1984), but it is also a knowledge-skills-insight process because people can do something different and/or become more aware of what they know and can do when they learn. According to Honey and Mumford (1996):

> Learning has happened when people can demonstrate that they know something that did not know before (insights and realizations, as well as facts) and/or when they can do something they could not do before (skills).

Important aspects of learning are:

- *knowledge* – what someone knows

- *skills* – what someone can do

- *employee attitudes* – the beliefs that shape how they do things

- *experience* – what someone has actually done.

For the first three elements, learning can be demonstrated as an end result or outcome (Mumford and Gold, 2004). For the last element, there needs to be a process through which people achieve outcomes or otherwise. In the process, people do things actively and passively, which may result in outcomes, and this is also a part of learning. So, learning is both a process and the outcomes achieved.

Another distinction can be made between learning and development. 'Learning' refers to the acquisition of knowledge, skills and experience for fulfilling current needs, whereas 'development' refers to an increase to an existing skill or qualification for future needs and career prospects. According to Mumford and Gold (2004), development embraces all the activities through which people learn.

Activity

Form a group of four. Each person should identify the factors influencing their learning and development process. Share your findings with each other and produce a list of factors. Use this list throughout the chapter to identify if there are theories and models to support your ideas.

The changing world of work and organization

Rifkin (1995) describes the 'end of work' as the result of the technological revolution that took place at the end of the 20th century. According to many authors, information and communication technologies (ICT) had a great impact on the competitive advantage of firms, their survival and the future of workplace jobs. Globalization has played a significant role in the changing nature of organizations and their impact on the relationships that individuals have with employing organizations (frequent job/career moves, short-term employment contracts, different working patterns). The features of modern organizations are flexibility, quality consciousness, customer orientation and improvement of their performance to remain competitive (Beardwell and Clayton, 2007).

Activity

Go to the ESRC Future of Work programme website – www.leeds.ac.uk/esrcfutureofwork/, and explore the changing world of work and organizations. Also visit www.qca.org.uk/qca_6091.aspx, to consider how changes in society are affecting the curriculum of schools. How significant is 'learning' in the findings?

In this changing context, the skill needs of firms are increasing and are expected to increase in the future because of globalization and technological change. The most significant change over the past decade has been the increase in the number of people employed in managerial, professional and service occupations. For example, the proportion of people in the UK employed in managerial and professional occupations increased by almost 1.6 million people between 1991 and 2001 (DfEE, 2001). Business and public service associate professionals have also seen a significant increase. There were 211,000 more science and technology professionals (for example engineers and scientists) in 2001 than there were in 1991. Numbers employed in technical and specialized sales occupations have increased substantially with the creation of an additional 153,000 new jobs.

While this review of the changing sectoral and occupational pattern of employment provides some useful insight into the changing demand for skills, it is only a partial picture. In particular, the relationship between specific sectors and occupations and the types of skill and qualification required in order to perform a job effectively is changing constantly for a range of reasons, including the introduction of new technologies, changes in work organization, regulatory requirements or changes in customer demand. This suggests an increase in high skilled graduate jobs but an alternative interpretation is also possible.

According to Green (1999), perceptions of real skill change might occur as a result of changes in job requirements. This is normally the case where employers demand higher levels of qualifications for what is essentially the same job ('credentialism'). Some commentators argue that the increased demand for qualifications by employers does not necessarily correspond with an increase in the skill content of jobs. As Gallie (1994) notes, skill levels might have increased either because a person had moved into a higher level job or because the existing job had been restructured in a way that increased its skill content. For example, the analysis so far has not considered the changing nature of occupations themselves. While the actual occupational titles and classification systems remain stable, the actual content of particular jobs may have changed – it may have become more or less skilled (Green et al., 2001). On a more general basis, it is worth noting that the value of qualifications and acquisition of skills change over time as the supply of and demand for them changes.

If this is currently the case, it is crucial to understand the significance and implications of ongoing skill rises within the workplace and the relevant premiums to the learning and development of employees within organizations. However, this case for understanding learning is not just restricted to the workplace; we now live in an age of lifelong learning, which commentators such as Green (2002, p. 611) suggest is a 'dominant and organizing discourse in education and training policy', and the terms 'learning society', 'learning cities', 'learning regions' and so on are widely used to indicate the need to respond to the speed of change in our world today (see Chapter 16). The following sections examine some of the key theories, ideas and models of learning used to inform practice and debates about learning in the various contexts.

Activity

With a partner, discuss whether you see qualifications as a necessary route to show evidence of skill acquisition. How will you ensure that you will be ready for changes in skill requirements over time?

Learning theories

Learning theories are crucial, but one important point needs to be made at the outset – human beings learn throughout their lives but much of this learning is hardly recognized because it happens informally without conscious awareness. Michael Eraut (2000) refers to this as 'non-formal learning'. By contrast, HRD is mainly concerned with more formal approaches, where learning is more explicitly recognized. Theories are used to explain how learning occurs and this is made more explicit in more formal events, although there is growing attention to the value of informal and implicit learning (see Chapter 9).

There are a large number of ideas considered as learning theories. We intend to provide a broad overview and consider their use in HRD. Learning theories can be loosely divided into four categories:

- *Behavioural theories* – the learner sits and listens, or does as they are told

- *Cognitive theories* – require mental involvement for the active thinking learner

- *Social and sociocultural learning theories* – stress the importance of learning new behaviours by observing and adopting the behaviours, attitudes and emotional reactions of others and actions in the context of practice.

The following sections will provide a historical overview of some of the most well-known learning theories commonly used in HRD. In general, learning theories have had an evident shift from the behavioural experiments with animals and explanations of children learning in the 20th century, to the 1960s' adult learning focus. The distinction between dependent learning in the former cases and self-directed learning in the latter group was well recognized by researchers in the 1960s (Knowles, 1973). The adult learner's past accumulated experience is also acknowledged as one of the resources for learning. Furthermore, their increasing readiness, the internalized motivation (Knowles, 1984) and the problem-centred orientation to learning were all characteristics for the premise of 'andragogy' (Greek word meaning 'man-leading', that is, for adult learners), compared with 'pedagogy' (child-leading, that is, for child learners) (Knowles, 1973). Due to the complexity and richness of the field, this chapter can only introduce the debate and more reading will be required to understand the details. It should be noted that the explanations found in these theories are contested and no one theory provides a 'perfect' answer of learning processes in work settings.

Activity

Go to www.infed.org/thinkers/et-knowl.htm and read about the ideas and life of Malcolm Knowles. In pairs, discuss the differences between adult learners and children learners.

Behavioural approach to learning

Learning theories were started from 19th century, when the earliest experimental psychologists observed the learning process through animals. Deeply rooted in the positivistic tradition, this school of psychologists intended to seek the laws of learning. The best-known representatives of this school are Russian scientist Ivan Pavlov (1849–1936) and American psychologist Burrhus Skinner (1904–90). They argued that learning is a result of reinforcement from an individual's experience. Researchers from this school of thought – behaviourism – were interested in behaviours that could be observed, measured and controlled. Any internal cognitive and mental activities in people's minds were excluded due to their inaccessibility.

Pavlov's (1927) research is considered important to learning in organizations and demonstrated how internal mental activities could be measured and observed. He argued that all learning could be explained by the phenomenon of classical or 'Pavlovian' conditioning. Pavlov started the experiment by training dogs to salivate in response to food:

- In Stage 1, no learning is involved since dogs have an automatic and instinctive salivation response to the sight of food.

- In Stage 2, Pavlov combined the food with a new stimulus – the sound of the bell – where the dogs in the experiment would salivate to the new stimulus if it were repeatedly associated with food.

- In Stage 3, after successful conditioning, Pavlov found dogs could be conditioned to salivate to the sound of a variety of stimuli (bells, tones, buzzers) even when no food appeared.

These experiments demonstrated how physiological reflexes could be conditioned to respond to a new situation and a new stimulus. Stage 2 demonstrates a state of learning, whereas in Stage 3, learning has already taken place when the stimulus–response has been bonded.

Skinner (1953) advanced the ideas of Pavlov and developed a theory called 'operant conditioning' from his research on the impact of reward and punishment on animal learning. He observed how rats learned to obtain food by pulling a lever, that is, subjects learn to operate on the environment to achieve a certain goal. This kind of learning refers to a response that has some effect on the situation or environment. With a different emphasis on positive reward (positive reinforcer), Skinner stressed that a response would also be learned when the subject associated the behavioural response to a punishment (negative reinforcer). Positive reinforcement in work settings could be a form of reward, such as money, promotion, recognition or praise from a manager, whereas negative reinforcement refers to unpleasant stimuli, such as a threat or criticism. Behaviour could be 'shaped' by reinforcement, while established behaviours could be maintained by intermittent reinforcement (Nye, 2000).

Behaviourism does seem to underpin how a lot of work is designed, where tasks are broken down into specific actions that must be performed against a specified standard. Practice will make perfect, through reinforcement and feedback but then the behaviour can be repeated over time, so long as the conditions of the task do not change. For those involved in helping staff to learn the required behaviours, objectives can be set, which state what a person can do against a set criteria after the learning has occurred. Sometimes these are specified as 'outcomes' (as at the start of each chapter in this book). It could be argued that such specification will help people to learn and enable the setting of goals and the seeking of feedback on performance, although not everyone seeks feedback (VandeWalle and Cummings, 1997).

Cognitive learning theory

With its positivist origin, the behaviourist approach has been criticized for its ignorance of the individual's internal mental activity. The question of how and why people learn was investigated by another group of researchers, who focused more on the learner. In the 1920s and 30s, psychologists Wolfgang Köhler (1887–1967) and Jean Piaget (1896–1980) demonstrated the limitation of behaviourist research and that learning is actually more complicated than stimulus–response development. Köhler observed the learning processes of chimpanzees using a stick as a tool to reach fruit and bring the fruit into the cage, and argued that the animal's problem-solving skills developed through insight rather than a simple stimulus–response association. By observing the way children adjust to their environment, Piaget also concluded that the simple behaviourist school could not explain children's learning. He believed learning occurs as a sequence, in which information is processed in different distinct stages: the stimulus perception stage, the sense-making stage and finally the restructuring and storage phrase.

These critiques of behaviourism resulted in a field of psychology known as 'cognitivism', which gives greater attention to what behaviourists tend to ignore – how people process information by thinking, using the resources of memory. The analogy of a computer seems relevant. People register inputs from the environment through their senses and these are processed into memory or rejected. Learning is concerned with acquiring new information that connects to what is already stored but makes an adjustment in the sense of it. The idea of 'schema' is used to explain how information is organized into knowledge patterns that can be called upon when needed. Schemas can also affect what is chosen for attention in how we perceive (Derry, 1996). Cognitive learning in HRD helps people to build meaningful patterns that can lead to new insights, discover new ways of understanding through seeing relationships, or even challenge existing patterns to produce new ways of seeing and understanding.

Cognitive styles

As people choose what to attend to, according to existing patterns of cognition, this can also affect what is ignored. People establish particular ways of thinking and understanding, which will affect what they are prepared to try to do. Patterns of thinking can settle into styles and this has been a key interest among cognitive theorists for many years. For example, Swiss psychoanalyst Carl Jung (1875–1961) formulated a model of cognitive styles or personality types – the introverted and the extroverted – and further subdivided them into four function types: thinking, feeling, sensation and intuition (Jung, 1923). Thinking and feeling were associated with a rational way of information processing, while sensation and intuition were associated with an irrational manner. Jung's work and theory have had a great impact on later researchers, for example Isabel Myers (1897–1980) and David Kolb (1939–).

Based on Jung's early work, and to make the work more accessible, Myers (1962) developed a measure of cognitive style called the Myers-Briggs Type Indicator (MBTI). The MBTI extended and redefined the Jungian concepts of 'rational' and 'irrational' and referred to them as 'judgement' and 'perception' respectively. The instrument has a series of questions associated with four bipolar discontinuous scales: extraversion and introversion, sensing and intuition, thinking and feeling, and judging and perceiving, as shown as Figure 5.1.

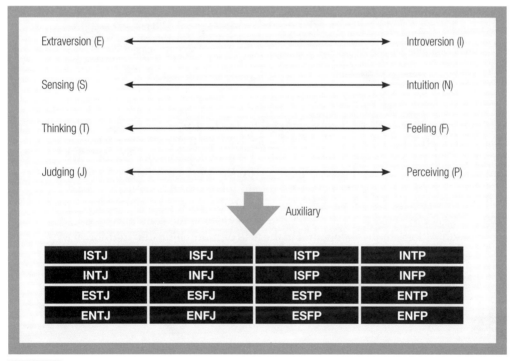

FIGURE 5.1 Myers-Briggs Type Indicator (MBTI)

SOURCE: Coffield et al. (2004, p. 48)

Myers also proposed the possible mixing of the different function types from Jung (1923), so that the possible matching of various types results in Myers' 16 distinct personality types (Figure 5.1). There are three versions of the MBTI, which vary according to the length of the questionnaire: the abbreviated form of 50 items, the standard 93-item Form M and the long 126-item Form G (Myers and McCaulley, 1985), each assigned to produce one of the 16 combinations of preferences, in terms of cognitive, behavioural, affective and perceptual perspectives. Thorne and Gough (1999) summarize the 10 most common MBTI types, based on their positive and negative traits, as shown in Table 5.1.

TABLE 5.1. Thorne and Gough's (1999) summary of the MBTI types

Type	Positive traits	Negative traits
INFP	Artistic, reflective, sensitive	Careless, lazy
INFJ	Sincere, sympathetic, unassuming	Submissive, weak
INTP	Candid, ingenious, shrewd	Complicated, rebellious
INTJ	Discreet, industrious, logical	Deliberate, methodical
ISTJ	Calm, stable, steady	Cautious, conventional
ENFP	Enthusiastic, outgoing, spontaneous	Changeable, impulsive
ENFJ	Active, pleasant, sociable	Demanding, impatient
ENTP	Enterprising, friendly, resourceful	Headstrong, self-centred
ENTJ	Ambitious, forceful, optimistic	Aggressive, egotistical
ESTJ	Contented, energetic, practical	Prejudiced, self-satisfied

SOURCE: Coffield et al. (2004, p. 48)

Following Jung's proposal, Myers' theory shares the idea that style is one part of the observable expression of a relatively stable personality type. Even though some researchers (for example Bayne, 1994) stress the versatility of individuals to move beyond their dominant function to exploit or develop 'auxiliary preferences', both Jung and Myers believed that the personality type would become dominant by adulthood and this versatility would be restricted by the individual's strong and habituated preferences (Coffield et al., 2004). Myers promoted her theory from a purely academic context to a wider audience in organizations, high schools, and in the field of counselling and marital relations. As such, the MBTI has been widely accepted as a research instrument and is one of most popular personality measures, having been translated into a number of languages (Furnham and Stringfield, 1993).

Activity

Visit the Myers & Briggs Foundation – www.myersbriggs.org. Find out about the use of this instrument in everyday life.

There has been and continues to be much interest in cognition with the development of a range of tests to enable people to understand how they process information, which identify a person's cognitive style. In the 1960s, Wallach (1962), Gardner (1962) and Hudson (1968) developed definitions of cognitive style and linked the concepts of individual style, thinking and behaviour. Since the 1970s, the emphasis of the research was further developed and applied in pedagogical settings (Sternberg and Grigorenko, 2001). Cognitive style has been widely recognized by researchers as the individual's consistent differences in information processing (Kogan, 1971; Messick, 1976; Allinson and Hayes, 1994; Riding and Rayner, 1998). Witkin and Goodenough (1981) pointed out that cognitive style has more consideration for the manner rather than the content of an activity, that is, there are individual differences in how people perceive, think, solve problems, learn and relate to others. It relates to how information is processed rather than the content of the information that is processed.

The Cognitive Style Index (CSI), developed by Chris Allinson and John Hayes (1994), is one of the most well-known and reliable tests used in organizational settings. Working with a split brain metaphor, Allinson and Hayes (1996, p. 122) suggested that:

> Intuition, characteristic of right-brain orientation, refers to immediate judgment based on feeling and the adoption of a global perspective. Analysis, characteristic of left-brain orientation, refers to judgment based on mental reasoning and a focus on detail.

The resulting theory of the intuitive–analytical dimensions of cognitive style is captured by the CSI. It has a self-report format, with 38 statements requiring a choice among true-uncertain-false answers. The score for the CSI ranges from 0 to 76, with a theoretical mean of 39; the closer the score is to 76, the more analytical the respondent is deemed to be, while the nearer the score is to 0, the more intuitive the respondent is, as shown in Figure 5.2.

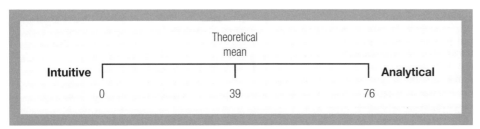

FIGURE 5.2 Cognitive Style Index scale

SOURCE: Armstrong (1999, p. 74)

The CSI has been widely used as a tool on a national and international basis. It has been translated into several languages (Lofstrom, 2002) and used for cross-cultural studies. Coffield et al. (2004, p. 138) argue that 'the CSI has the best psychometric credentials' out of 71 learning styles models that they reviewed and assessed.

Although the CSI has a reputation of being the most reliable instrument for organizational settings, there have been challenges from other scholars on its degree of simplification of the individual's information processing (Sadler-Smith, 2006; Hodgkinson and Clarke, 2007). They argue that there is interaction and interdependence between the different styles, that is, intuition and analysis are not contrasting opposites, but are two dimensions, ranging from high to low on each, which can be combined to generate four quadrants, such as high intuition and high analytic or high intuition and low analytic.

Experiential learning

Both behavioural and cognitive learning theories are considered to be part of the 'standard paradigm of learning' (Beckett and Hager, 2002, p. 98). Behaviourism is mainly concerned with stimulation from the outside that elicits a response, and cognitivism is concerned with how information is processed under the influence of existing knowledge, stored in the brain as schema. Over the past 30 years, while research in both theories has continued, there has been strong interest in the interaction between a person and their environment. Both the person and the environment, whether it is other people or physical things like books, working or just living, can provide experience that can become a source of learning.

The use of experience in learning has it roots in the work of John Dewey and Kurt Lewin, but the most well-known experiential learning theory was developed by Kolb (1976). His experiential learning model is based on a 'learning cycle' and his main contribution has been to re-evaluate the conventional definition of cognitive style. He refers to 'learning style' as a 'differential preference for learning, which changes slightly from situation to situation. At the same time, there is some long-term stability in learning style' (Kolb, 2000, p. 8). The stages in Kolb's learning cycle are concrete experience (CE), reflective observation (RO), abstract conceptualization (AC) and active experimentation (AE), shown in Figure 5.3. Ideally:

- learners can involve themselves in new experiences openly and without bias (CE)

- reflect on the new experience and observe it objectively from many angles (RO)

- formulate and generalize the observation into a logical concept (AC)

- test the concept in a new situation (AE).

The tension in the abstract–concrete dimension is between relying on conceptual interpretation or on immediate experience in order to grasp hold of experience, while the tension in the active–reflective dimension is between relying on internal reflection or external manipulation in order to transform experience (Coffield et al., 2004). To help individuals to assess their approach to learning, Kolb (1976) developed the Learning Style Inventory (LSI), which provides information on the individual's relative emphasis on the four abilities in the learning cycle.

Activity

Go to www.learningandteaching.info/learning/experience.htm for more information on experiential learning. If you want to learn more about Dewey, go to http://dewey.pragmatism.org/. For more on Lewin, try www.infed.org/thinkers/et-lewin.htm.

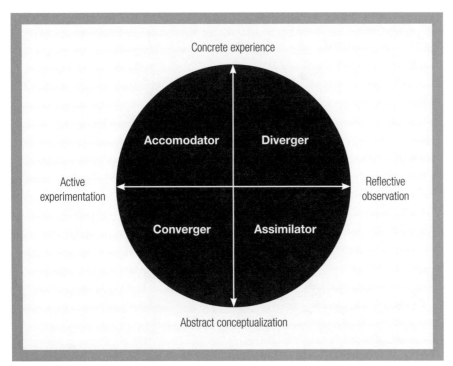

Concrete experience

Accomodator   Diverger

Active
experimentation   Reflective
observation

Converger   Assimilator

Abstract conceptualization

FIGURE 5.3 Kolb's experiential learning cycle and basic learning styles

SOURCE: Kolb et al. (2001, p. 229)

While there are disagreements regarding Kolb's theory and his LSI, his work has attracted considerable interest since the 1970s and has influenced the development of other models of learning style. Peter Honey and Alan Mumford (2006) believe that each learning style in the learning cycle, shown in Figure 5.4, has its own characteristics, each with its own unique strengths and weaknesses.

Honey and Mumford (2006, p. 43) emphasize that 'no single style has an overwhelming advantage over any other. Each has strengths and weaknesses but the strengths may be especially important in one situation, but not in another instance.' Learning styles are identified by completing the Honey and Mumford Learning Styles Questionnaire (LSQ), designed specifically for managers and professionals. It asks questions about general behavioural tendencies rather than just learning, as is the case with Kolb's LSI. The LSQ consists of questions with simple agree or disagree answers, which probe the preferences for the four learning styles. As a detailed practical manual with simple language for management people, Honey and Mumford try to make people aware of their strengths in the four types of learning styles.

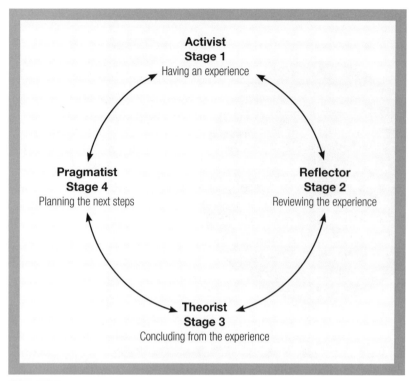

Activist
Stage 1
Having an experience

Reflector
Stage 2
Reviewing the experience

Theorist
Stage 3
Concluding from the experience

Pragmatist
Stage 4
Planning the next steps

FIGURE 5.4 Dimensions of Honey and Mumford's learning cycle

SOURCE: Honey and Mumford (2006)

Experiential learning cycles have enabled some interesting developments in helping students to become more self-directed, as shown in HRD in Practice 5.1.

HRD in Practice 5.1

Problem-based learning

Tutors at Leeds Metropolitan University have sought to help students to become more self-directed in the study of change in international contexts. The module emphasizes that individual experience is an important learning resource that individuals draw on when facing difficult and ambiguous situations. This reservoir of experience is consciously used as a rich resource for learning. This is based on the principle that as adult learners, students attach a great deal of meaning to learning gained through experience. Further, and following Kolb's learning cycle, through review, reflection on and analysis of experience, greater depth can be provided to learning.

The module lasts one semester and covers three phases:

• *Phase 1: familiarization*. Learners are introduced to the processes and methodology that highlight the distinctive inter- and multidisciplinary nature of the module. Each student is able to identify existing styles of learning and

problem management. Students learn about the idea of learning as a cycle as theorized by Kolb and their own preferred and less preferred learning styles.
- *Phase 2: research*. Learners are provided with a case study simulation of an actual international business problem. The case study incorporates material that encourages an inter- and multidisciplinary approach to research and developing understanding.
- *Phase 3: dramatization*. Learners are formed into negotiating teams and are required to prepare for participation in a role-playing exercise.

A key outcome of the module was the use of knowledge in practice in addition to becoming more self-directed as learners. As one student recorded:

'I became more confident during the role play when I was able to put theory into practice. I learned how to persuade others and express my own opinions. We were able to test the use of knowledge in the role play. We were no longer passive students.'

The use of the LSI and LSQ has not been without criticism. Sugarman (1985) argued that the LSI's psychometric evaluation was limited and low in quality, based on the small sample size. Allinson and Hayes (1990) also point out the ambiguity between Kolb's LSI and the LSQ and suggest that more research needs to be conducted to test validity. Duffy and Duffy (2002, cited in Coffield et al., 2004) were unable to validate the four learning styles and two bipolar dimensions using both exploratory and confirmatory factor analysis and were also unable to employ such psychometric tests as a predictor of students' academic performance. Such studies cast doubts on the utility of the LSQ.

Research on learning styles has continued. One of the most interesting models has been developed by Lynn Curry (1983, 1987) and is referred to as Curry's 'onion' model of learning styles. She reviewed the psychometric qualities of different learning style instruments and categorized them according to the three-layered 'onion' model, shown in Figure 5.5.

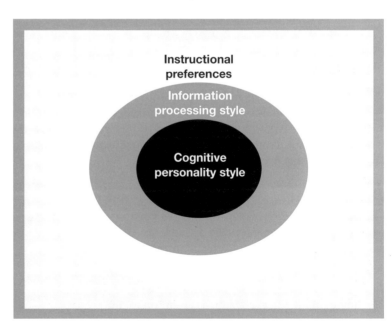

FIGURE 5.5 Curry's 'onion' model of learning styles
SOURCE: Curry (1983, 1987)

The categories are instructional preferences, information-processing style and cognitive personality style. In Curry's model, the inner layer (cognitive personality style) is more stable and significant in complex learning, while the outer layer of instructional preferences is easier to modify and influence, but less important in learning.

Reflective question

How would you develop training based on the different learning styles?
Go to www.support4learning.org.uk/education/learning_styles.cfm for more information.

Learning style or cognitive style?

There has been some confusion over the concepts of 'learning style' and 'cognitive style' for many years. Four different arguments have been attempted to contribute to the nature of individual style:

1   Some researchers (Entwistle, 1981; Campbell, 1991; Riding and Cheema, 1991; Coffield et al., 2004) argue that these terms are used loosely and interchangeably. Riding and Cheema (1991) argue that:

    The terms cognitive style and learning style have been much used by theorists, but what they mean still remains very much up to its author.

2   It is argued that cognitive style is different from learning style and can only be considered as a subcomponent of learning style (Dunn and Dunn, 1993). With the argument that learning style is a biological and developmental set of personality characteristics, Dunn and Dunn (1993, p. 2) remarked that:

    learning style is more than merely whether a child remembers new and difficult information most easily by hearing, seeing, reading, writing, illustrating, verbalizing, or actively experiencing; perceptual or modality strength is only one part of learning style. It also is more than whether a person processes information sequentially, analytically, or in a 'left-brain' mode rather than in a holistic, simultaneous, global, 'right-brain' fashion; that, too, is only one important component of learning style. It is more than how someone responds to the environment in which learning must occur or whether information is absorbed concretely or abstractly; those variables contribute to style but, again, are only part of the total construct.

3   Another school acknowledges that learning style has a more rigid meaning and it mainly focuses on the information-processing style in a learning environment and learning activities (Claxton and Ralston, 1978; Riding and Rayner, 2002). Claxton and Ralston (1978) define learning style as a student's consistent way of responding to and using stimuli in the context of learning. As the precursor of learning style, cognitive style has a wider concern about how information can be processed in a wider variety of settings, rather than just the learning context.

    Riding and Rayner (2002, p. 51) went on to argue that:

learning style is an individual set of differences that include not only a stated personal preference for instruction or an association with a particular form of learning activity but also individual differences found in intellectual or personal psychology.

While the two terms – 'learning style' and 'learning strategy' – are used interchangeably by some (Cronbach and Snow, 1977), Sternberg and Grigorenko (2001) and Riding and Rayner (2002) distinguish between learning style and learning strategy – the former referring to an individual's fixed trait, while the latter is generally used for more task- and context-dependent situations.

4   Some researchers attempt to make sense of the confusing field and review the origin and development of cognitive style and learning style (Curry, 1983; Riding and Rayner, 2002; Coffield et al., 2004). Coffield et al. (2004) summarized a continuum of learning styles, claiming that it is based on the extent to which the developers of learning style models and instruments appear to believe that learning styles are fixed, as shown in Figure 5.6.

At the left end of the continuum, researchers strongly believe in the influence of genetics on fixed, inherited traits, and the interaction of personality and cognition. At the right end of the continuum, theorists place more emphasis on personal factors such as motivation, environmental factors, and the effects of the environment on the individual's cognitive style.

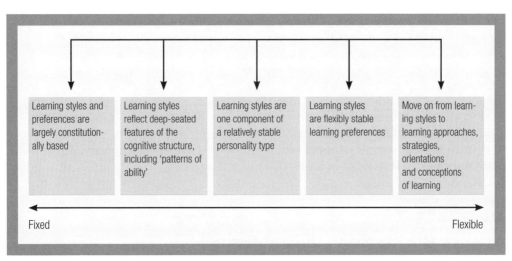

FIGURE 5.6 Coffield et al.'s families of learning styles

SOURCE: Coffield et al. (2004, p. 9)

Social and sociocultural learning theories

As approaches to measuring preferences for learning or problem solving, both cognitive styles and learning styles have been criticized for their focus on individuals and their distortion of the contextual factors that affect how a person learns and works (Reynolds, 1997). Being identified with a particular kind of style can also lead to stereotyping. For example, if you are classified as an 'activist' under the LSQ framework, this can create expectations of how you will or will not learn. Holman et al. (1997) also critique learning styles for the individual emphasis and suggest giving more importance to social conditions and interactions with others.

For example, social learning theorist Albert Bandura (1977) argues that learning is a dynamic interplay between the person, the environment and behaviour. He emphasizes how the environment explicitly affects learners (Gold et al., 2009). Learning occurs through indirect observation and modelling, for example a child observes their mother, remembers the observed behaviour and practises those learned behaviours. The social learning approach involves four interrelated processes: attention, memory, motor and motivation (Bandura, 1977).

Another theory that considers the effect of social factors is based on the work of Russian social psychologist, Lev Vygotsky, who in the 1920s and early 1930s developed a socio-cultural activity approach to learning. This approach to learning gives more attention to the importance of social interaction in the learning process. Learning is more than just what happens internally, it is also the fruit of interactions from the social to the individual. Two crucial contributions from Vygotsky are the 'mediating tools' between subject and goal in the learning action, and the idea of a 'zone of proximal development' (ZPD). By 'mediating tools', Vygotsky (1982) meant the obvious physical tools needed to complete an action such as a table, a chair and so on, and the psychological tools such as writing, language and so on. All these tools mediate how individuals think, feel and behave.

For consideration of ZPD, Vygotsky's theory gives importance to identifying the learner's lower and upper limits of ability, that is, the learner's optimal performance level or the ZPD. According to Vygotsky, learning occurs by the introduction of new mediating tools, physical or psychological or both. These tools could potentially enable individuals to perform better but also cause disturbance to existing ways of understanding and behaving. Such a learning process is achievable only with support or 'scaffolding'. In this approach, learning is the consideration of existing capacity and the skill to find solutions to problems that an individual is facing and moving towards more advanced learning that is relative to the existing capacity. An example is shown in HRD in Practice 5.2.

HRD in Practice 5.2

Mark Riley Hairdressers in Huddersfield

Mark Riley is a well-known hairdresser in Huddersfield, whose views about learning and development were typical of many in his kind of business. More concerned about survival than growth, he had a poor record in responding to, and was even antagonistic towards, formal training initiatives, being highly sceptical of the benefits of such initiatives. Mark was 'stuck' and 'struggling' with the running of his business, and this had been the pattern for many years, even though he knew he had a 'a gold mine', which could be exploited.

It took a meeting with Brian to unlock Mark's potential. Working with Brian, a business mentor, Mark soon identified 'major inefficiencies' in current operations that were causing cash flow problems; indeed, the business was a 'mess'. One change needed was a supervisory infra-structure, which would allow Mark more time to focus on operational and financial performance. He could also take time away from 'cutting hair' to meet Brian to talk business and think strategically. Part of this talk was to articulate Mark's vision of the 'Mark Riley Experience', based on a 'journey of wellbeing for customers' and growth of the business to 10 salons across Yorkshire by 2010.

Brian could work out with Mark what he needed to do; he could also work out how far and how fast he could take him. Mentoring could be provided to work in tune with Mark's capabilities, interests and desires, but also to stretch Mark into uncharted waters. Once again, this future could only be talked about with someone who understood Mark, but this very process also created the space for conversations to become more strategic.

Within six months, Mark had a strategy for growth and development and two new salons, with plans for two more in the next year.

Activity

Go to http://tip.psychology.org/bandura.html for more information about Bandura's work. Vygotsky's work is particularly important in the training of teachers. Go to www.gtce.org.uk/research/romtopics/rom_teachingandlearning/vygotsky_dec03/ for more information.

A further development of social approaches to learning is found in the work of Lave and Wenger (1991), who used the term 'situated learning' to emphasize the development of knowledge and expertise through activity and practice in work situations. This is a form of 'natural learning', which highlights the context and culture in which learning occurs. In contrast to the classical psychologically driven theories of learning developed mainly in the laboratory or classroom settings, situated learning theories occur in workplace settings. It is argued that learning is about participation in a 'community of practice'. For example, a community of practice occurs in the system of apprenticeships in carpentry, and the legal and medical professions. This system is developed through instances of formal and informal learning in various work activities. The term 'legitimate peripheral participation' was developed by Lave and Wenger (1991) to refer to the learning process from apprentice to expert.

Learning principles

All activities in HRD imply a view of how learning occurs, whether this is made explicit or not. As we have suggested, for much of the last century, the very process of organizing tended to imply a particular approach to learning based on behaviourism and mechanistic assumptions about humans. The contrasting theories of cognitive learning and experiential learning gained more favour towards the last quarter of the 20th century, along with recognition of the difference between pedagogical and andragogical notions of learning (Knowles, 1973) and the move towards knowledge-based organizations. There is also far more interest in everyday learning now, which is socially and culturally enabled and constrained, but which can be harnessed as a source of competitive advantage (see Chapter 9). All these theories have some value and it is the task of those involved to derive key principles for good practice. We will attempt to do this in the following sections.

Application of behavioural theories

Behaviourism deals with cause and effect, and learning practices based on behavioural theories predominantly use external stimuli to arouse a behavioural response. These theories explain how training effectiveness is improved by understanding the following:

- People respond to reinforcement (such as rewards) within training

- Reinforcement is a motivator to participate in training

- Responses to stimuli are dependent on the individual, so the instruction needs to be oriented to the individual

- Effectiveness of rewards must be individually determined, that is, different strokes for different folks

- HRD programmes should progress from the simple to the complex

- HRD programmes should include sensitization, practice and feedback to managers and employees – potentially through the growing use of coaches and mentors at work.

However, behaviourism has gained a notorious reputation, with its association with the ruthless efficiency of industrial organizations and rigid systems of bureaucracies (Gold et al., 2009), and ignores the emotions, preferences or motivations of learners who could process information differently.

Application of cognitive theories

Cognitive theories focus on mental processes such as memory, aptitude, intelligence and lateral thinking. Adult learners ought to be given the opportunity to build on prior experience rather than starting anew. The learning practice should take into account the social, cultural and environmental contexts and must recognize the dynamic nature of change and the role of previous experience. It must also acknowledge the different ways people give meaning to, and make sense of, their experiences. Implementing cognitive and learning style theories requires the following:

- Learner understanding should be a central feature of any design

- Learners are active and will learn more if they have some control over the learning process

- Information should be organized to facilitate learning rather than control learning

- Learners progress from the simple to the complex (not complicated, but holistic and complex)

- Learners need to learn how to learn, by understanding and testing out learning or cognitive styles or trying new ones.

The last point about learning to learn has become a particularly strong feature of debates about learning in recent years. There has been an emphasis on people taking more responsibility for learning and this has government backing as part of a policy of lifelong learning. Similarly, professionals are frequently required to undergo continuing professional development (see Chapter 16). A number of commentators, such as Brookfield (1986), call for more self-direction in learning and part of this encouragement requires individuals to develop learning skills and understand their learning preferences.

Application of social and sociocultural learning theories

Social and sociocultural learning theories stress the importance of learning new behaviours through observing and adopting the behaviours, attitudes and emotional reactions of others. Organizations can take advantage of our understanding of these theories by facilitating the appropriate informal and formal communication processes. A key aspect involves setting up apprenticeship or mentoring schemes – partnering a trainee with a tradesperson or mentor. Guidelines for a learning practice should include the following:

- Learning occurs through exposure to others, both formally and informally

- Interaction with others in the course of everyday practice is a source of learning

- Learning can also be inhibited by exposure to others as well as individual feelings about their abilities

- Learners acquire new skills and knowledge when they see these as relevant to what they do in practice

- Culture and history play a role in what people learn, which may be positive or otherwise

- Learners may need help to be able to cope with new tasks or solve problems.

A positive work climate will aid the application of learning about work, and that climate should include positive and genuine feedback about their efforts. A supportive environment enhances positive outcomes when individuals attempt to utilize their new learning in the workplace. Learners can be stretched to try new actions with appropriate support and this can occur every day by watching others, doing work and talking about it, especially through sharing stories about problems (Brown and Duiguid, 1991).

Summary

- Learning is a lifelong process and HRD is concerned with providing learning opportunities for the work context. There has been a growing interest in implementing good learning practices in organizations.

- Learning is concerned with the acquisition of knowledge, skills and attitudes through experiences. Learning is both the process of acquisition and the outcomes achieved.

- Learning theories have been evolved through several stages in history – from the observation of animal behaviour to the development of learning in children and adults.

- Globalization and technological change have implications for what skills and knowledge are needed and how learning occurs.

- Learning occurs both informally and formally at work, and differs between children and adults.

- Behaviourist theories start with Pavlovian conditioning and the importance of reinforcement in the learning process. Behaviourist ideas on learning have a close connection with mechanistic assumptions on work design and organization.

- Cognitive approaches to learning emphasize that individuals perceive stimulus, evaluate feedback, store and use information. Research on cognitive and learning styles enables the measurement and diagnosis of preferences, although there are concerns about the validity of such measures.

- Social and sociocultural learning theories suggest that individuals learn and develop through observation and modelling. They stress the importance of the community of practice and the hands-on experience of learning in the workplace rather than in a classroom or laboratory environment.

Discussion questions

1 Why is learning important in the workplace?
2 What are the main differences between the behavioural and cognitive approaches to learning? Identify the key players in each respective school of thinking and explain their work.
3 What do you understand by the concepts of 'punishment' and the 'learning cycle'? Illustrate with examples from work or college.
4 What are learning style and cognitive style?

5 What is the difference between learning style and cognitive style?

6 Why is the concept of 'learning style' important for managers and employees?

7 How does culture affect learning?

8 What cultures influence how your class learns?

Further reading

Billett, S. (2001) *Learning in the Workplace: Strategies for Effective Practice*, Crows Nest, NSW, Allen & Unwin.

Coffield, F., Moseley, D., Hall, E. and Ecclestone, K. (2004) *Learning Styles and Pedagogy in Post-16 Learning: A Systematic and Critical Review*, London, Learning and Skills Research Centre.

Mumford, A. and Gold, J. (2004) *Management Development: Strategies for Action*, London, CIPD.

Nailon, D., DelaHaye, B. and Brownlee, J. (2007) Learning and leading: how beliefs about learning can be used to promote effective leadership, *Development and Learning in Organizations*, **20**(4): 6–9.

Wenger, E. (1999) *Communities of Practice: Learning, Meaning and Identity*, Cambridge, Cambridge University Press.

References

Allinson, C.W. and Hayes, J. (1990) Validity of the Learning Styles Questionnaire, *Psychological Reports*, **67**: 859–66.

Allinson, C.W. and Hayes, J. (1994) Cognitive style and its relevance for management practice, *British Journal of Management*, **5**(1): 53–72.

Allinson, C.W. and Hayes, J. (1996) The cognitive style index: a measure of intuition-analysis for organizational research, *Journal of Management Studies*, **33**(1): 119–35.

Armstrong, M. and Baron, A. (2002) *Strategic HRM: The Key to Improved Business Performance*, London, CIPD.

Armstrong, S. (1999) Cognitive style and dyadic interaction: a study of supervisors and subordinates engaged in working relationships, unpublished PhD thesis, University of Leeds.

Bandura, A. (1977) *Social Learning Theory,* Englewood Cliffs, NJ, Prentice Hall.

Bayne, R. (1994) The 'big five' versus the Myers-Briggs, *Psychologist*, **7**(1).

Beardwell, J. and Clayton, T. (2007) *Human Resource Management: A Contemporary Approach*, 5th edn, Harlow, Pearson Education.

Beckett, D. and Hager, P. (2002) *Life, Work and Learning: Practice in Postmodernity*, London, Routledge.

Brookfield, S. (1986) *Understanding and Facilitating Adult Learning*, Milton Keynes, Open University Press.

Brown, J.S. and Duguid, P. (1991) Organizational learning and communities of practice: toward a unified view of working, learning, and innovation, *Organization Science*, **2**(1): 40–57.

Campbell, B.J. (1991) Planning for a student learning style, *Journal of Education for Business*, **66**(6): 356–8.

Claxton, C.S. and Ralston, Y. (1978) Learning styles, in C.S. Claxton and Y. Ralston (eds) *Learning Styles: Their Impact on Teaching and Administration,* Washington, DC, American Association for Higher Education.

Coffield, F., Moseley, D., Hall, E. and Ecclestone, K. (2004) *Learning Styles and Pedagogy in Post-16 Learning: A Systematic and Critical Review,* London, Learning and Skills Research Centre.

Cronbach, L.J. and Snow, R.E. (1977) *Aptitudes and Instructional Methods*, New York, Wiley.

Curry, L. (1983) *Learning Styles in Continuing Medical Education*, Ottawa, Canadian Medical Association.

Curry, L. (1987) *Integrating Concepts of Cognitive Learning Styles: A Review with Attention to Psychometric Standards*, Ottawa, Canadian College of Health Services Executives.

Derry, S. (1996) Cognitive schema theory in the constructivist debate, *Educational Psychologist*, **31**(3/4): 163–74.

DfEE (Department for Education and Employment) (2001) The changing graduate labour market, *Skills and Enterprise Briefing*, (2), May.

Duffy, A. and Duffy, T. (2002) Psychometic properties of Honey and Mumford's Learning Styles Questionnaire (LSQ), *Personality and Individual Differences*, **33**: 147–63.

Dunn, R. and Dunn, K. (1993) *Teaching Secondary Students through their Individual Learning Styles: Practical Approaches for Grades 7–12,* Boston, Allyn & Bacon.

Entwistle, N. (1981) *Styles of Learning and Teaching*, Chichester, Wiley.

Eraut, M. (2000) Non-formal learning, implicit learning and tacit knowledge in professional work, in F. Coffield (ed.) *The Necessity of Informal Learning*, Bristol, Policy Press.

Furnham, A. and Stringfield, P. (1993) Personality and occupational behaviour: Myers-Briggs Type Indicator correlates of managerial practices in two cultures, *Human Relations*, **46**(7): 827–40.

Gallie, D. (1994) Patterns of skill change: upskilling, deskilling, or polarization?, in R. Penn, M. Rose and J. Rubery (eds) *Skill and Occupational Change*, Oxford, Oxford University Press.

Gardner, R.W. (1962) Cognitive controls in adaptation: research and measurement, in S. Messick and J. Ross (ed.) *Measurement in Personality and Cognition*, New York, Wiley.

Gold, J., Thorpe, R. and Mumford, A. (2009) How leaders and managers learn, in J. Gold, R. Thorpe and A. Mumford (eds) *Handbook of Management and Leadership Development,* Aldershot, Gower Press (in press).

Green, A. (2002) The many faces of lifelong learning: recent education policy trends in Europe, *Journal of Education Policy*, **17**(6): 611–26.

Green, F. (1999) *The Market Value of Generic Skills*, Skills Task Force Research Paper No. 8, Sudbury, DfEE.

Green, F., Ashton, D. and Felstead, A. (2001) Estimating the determinants and supply of computing, problem-solving, communication, social and teamworking skills, *Oxford Review of Economic Policy*, **53**(3): 406–33.

Hodgkinson, G.P. and Clarke, I. (2007) Exploring the cognitive significance of oranizational strategizing: a dual-process framework and research agenda, *Human Relations*, **60**: 243–55.

Holman, D., Pavlica, K. and Thorpe, R. (1997) Rethinking Kolb's theory of experiential learning in management education, *Management Learning*, **28**(2): 135–48.

Honey, P. and Mumford, A. (1982) *The Manual of Learning Styles*, Maidenhead, P. Honey.

Honey, P. and Mumford, A. (1996) *Managing the Learning Environment*, Maidenhead, P. Honey.

Honey, P. and Mumford, A. (2006) *The Learning Styles Questionnaire: 80 Item Version*, Maidenhead, P. Honey.

Hudson, L. (1968) *Frames of Mind: Ability, Perception and Self-perception in the Arts and Science*, London, Methuen.

Jung, C. (1923) *Psychological Types*, London, Pantheon Books.

Knowles, M. (1973) *Adult Learner: A Neglected Species*, Houston, Gulf Publishing.

Knowles, M.S. (1984) *Andragogy in Action: Applying Modern Principles of Adult Education*, San Francisco, Jossey-Bass.

Kogan, N. (1971) Educational implications of cognitive styles, in G.S. Lesser (ed.) *Psychology and Educational Practice,* Glenview, IL, Scott Foresman.

Kolb, D.A. (1976) Management and the learning process, *California Management Review*, **18**(3): 21–31.

Kolb, D.A. (1984) *Experiential Learning: Experience as the Source of Learning and Development*, Englewood Cliffs, NJ, Prentice Hall.

Kolb, D.A. (2000) *Facilitator's Guide to Learning*, Boston, Hay/McBer.

Kolb, D.A., Boyatzis, R.E. and Mainemelis, C. (2001) Experiential learning theory: previous research and new directions, in R.J. Sternberg and L.F. Zhang (eds) *Perspectives on Thinking, Learning, and Cognitive Styles*, Mahwah, NJ, Lawrence Erlbaum.

Lave, J. and Wenger, E. (1991) *Situated Learning: Legitimate Peripheral Participation*, Cambridge, Cambridge University Press.

Lofstrom, E. (2002) Person-situation interactions in SMEs: a study of cognitive style and sources of job satisfaction, in M. Valcke and D. Gombeir (eds) *Learning Styles: Reliability and Validity,* proceedings of the 7th Annual European Learning Styles Information Network Conference, 26–28 June, University of Ghent.

Mayo, A. and Lank, E. (1994) *The Power of Learning,* London, Institute of Personnel Management.

Messick, S. (1976) Personality consistencies in cognition and creativity, in S. Messick (ed.) *Individuality in Learning*, San Francisco, CA, Jossey-Bass.

Mumford, A. and Gold, J. (2004) *Management Development: Strategies for Action*, London, CIPD.

Myers, I.B. (1962) *Manual: The Myers Briggs Type Indicator,* Palo Alto, CA, Consulting Psychologists Press.

Myers, I.B. and McCaulley, M.H. (1985) *Manual: A Guide to the Development and Use of the Myers-Briggs Type Indicator*, Palo Alto, CA, Consulting Psychologists Press.

Nye, R.D. (2000) B.F. Skinner and radical behaviourism, in R.D. Nye, *Three Psychologies: Perspectives from Freud, Skinner, and Rogers*, 6th edn, Belmont, CA, Wadsworth.

Pavlov, I.P. (1927) *Conditioned Reflexes: An Investigation of the Physiological Activity of the Cerebral Cortex*, transl. and ed. G. Anrep, London, Oxford University Press.

Reynolds, M. (1997) Learning styles: a critique, *Management Learning,* 28(2): 115–33.

Riding, R. and Cheema, I. (1991) Cognitive styles: an overview and integration, *Educational Psychology*, 11(3/4): 193–215.

Riding, R. and Douglas, G. (1993) The effect of cognitive style and mode of presentation on learning performance, *British Journal of Educational Psychology*, 63: 297–307.

Riding, R. and Rayner, S. (1998) *Cognitive Styles and Learning Strategies: Understanding Style Differences in Learning and Behaviour*, London, David Fulton.

Riding, R. and Rayner, S. (2002) *Cognitive Styles and Learning Strategies: Understanding Style Differences in Learning and Behaviour*, 5th edn, London, David Fulton.

Rifkin, J. (1995) *The End of Work: The Decline of the Global Labor Force and the Dawn of the Post-market Era*, New York, Tarcher/Putnam.

Sadler-Smith, E. (2006) *Learning and Development for Managers*, Oxford, Blackwell.

Skinner, B.F. (1953) *Science and Human Behavior*, New York, Macmillan.

Sternberg, R.J. and Grigorenkow, E.L. (2001) A capsule history of theory and research on styles, in R.J. Sternberg and L.F. Zhang (eds) *Perspectives on Thinking, Learning and Cognitive Styles*, Mahwah, NJ, Lawrence Erlbaum.

Sugarman, L. (1985) Kolb's model of experiential learning: touchstone for trainers, students, counselors and clients, *Journal of Counseling and Development*, 64(40): 264–8.

Thorne, A. and Gough, H. (1999) *Portraits of Type: An MBTI Research Compendium*, 2nd edn, Gainesville, FL, Center for Applications of Psychological Type.

VandeWalle, D. and Cummings, L.L. (1997) An empirical test of goal orientation as a predictor of feedback-seeking behaviour, *Journal of Applied Psychology*, 82: 390–400.

Vygotsky, L.S. (1982) *Collected Works,* Moscow, Pedagogica.

Wallach, M.A. (1962) Commentary: active-analytical vs. passive-global cognitive functioning, in S. Messick and J. Ross (eds) *Measurement in Personality and Cognition*, New York, Wiley.

Witkin, H.A. (1976) Cognitive styles in academic performance and in teacher-student relations, in S. Messick (ed.) *Individuality in Learning*, San Francisco, CA, Jossey-Bass.

Witkin, H.A. (1978) *Cognitive Styles in Personal and Cultural Adaptation,* Worcester, MA, Clark University Press.

Witkin, H.A. and Goodenough, D.R. (1981) *Cognitive Style: Essence and Origins,* New York, International Universities Press.

The Identification of Training Needs

6

Vivienne Griggs, Patrick McCauley, Catherine Glaister, Rick Holden and Jeff Gold

Chapter learning outcomes

After studying this chapter, you should be able to:

- Explain the meaning of 'training need'
- Understand three types of training need in relation to knowledge, skills and attitudes
- Understand inward and outward approaches to, and closed and open perspectives of, training problems
- Identify a range of key indicators of training need
- Distinguish between three different levels of training need: organizational, job and individual
- Understand a systematic process for the identification of training needs

Chapter outline

Introduction

The meaning of training need

Types of training need

Indicators of training needs

The identification and assessment of training needs

Problems with the identification of training needs

Summary

Introduction

Perceived as crucial to our success as a nation, the government constantly urges employers to carry out more training, pointing out (predictably enough) that the UK's record for investing in training compares unfavourably with our economic competitors. For example, recent estimates in the UK suggested that 'one third of employers do not train their staff and eight million employees receive no kind of training at all every year' (John Denham, secretary of state for innovation, universities and skills, 18 June 2008). But what is training and does it differ from learning or indeed development? The terms 'training', 'development' and 'learning' are often used interchangeably. While understandable, this can mask important distinctions. The CIPD defines training as 'an instructor led, content based intervention, leading to desired changes in behavior' and learning as 'a self directed, work-based process, leading to increased adaptive potential' (Sloman, 2005). These are clearly different types of practice. We would argue that the lines between these categories cannot be firmly drawn, and there must be and should be interchange between the two terms. For the purposes of clarity, however, in this chapter we will use the term 'training' to refer to the analysis of needs, as needs analysis has long been referred to as 'training needs analysis'. We would argue, however, that once a gap has been identified in terms of knowledge, skills or attitude, a range of options are open in terms of how to address this gap – some of these would be what the CIPD would define as 'training', others as 'learning'. This will be recognized and both terms are used in Chapter 7, which considers the provision of appropriate training and learning solutions.

The meaning of training need

Originating with the Industrial Training Boards (see Reid et al., 2004, for a useful positioning of the ITBs within the evolution of HRD), the use of a structured approach to the identification, planning, delivery and evaluation of training has long been advocated. This four-stage process, shown in Figure 6.1, has been widely adopted. It is systematic and emphasizes 'logical and sequential planning and action' (Buckley and Caple, 2007, p. 24).

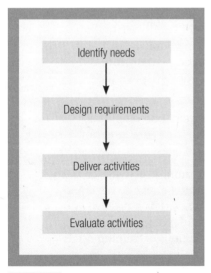

FIGURE 6.1 A four-stage training model

The model matches conventional wisdom of the need for rationality and efficiency with an emphasis on cost-effectiveness. However, the process is not so neat, ordered and predictable in real life and within real organizations. Although often criticized for its inflexibility, simplicity and lack of consideration of contextual issues, we would argue that the systematic model still provides a practical tool to analyse and manage these processes within organizations today. It is only a model, but its simplicity can be seen as its strength, and it can be applied widely and usefully across a range of organizations, with consideration of organizational context being built in at each stage. The model is reflected in how Chapters 6, 7 and 8 unfold. Here, our focus is on the first stage in the model, while Chapter 7 addresses stages two and three, and Chapter 8 deals with evaluation. We move now to a consideration of training needs.

It is axiomatic that any expression of a training need must be justified in terms of improving how people are working and, by implication, how the organization is performing. This requires an identification of what is not working so well, where it is not working and how significant this is. Without this, expenditure on training or any HRD activity is difficult to justify, according to conventional views (Moore and Dutton, 1978). According to Bratton and Gold (2007, p. 329), 'assessing and analysis of training needs is concerned with identifying gaps between work performance and standards of work or performance criteria that have a training solution'. This gap is categorized in terms of the knowledge, skills and attitudes that are required for the job and how these can be learned through HRD. It could be added that this apparent training need only really exists when clearly identified training helps to address organizational problems or exploit organizational opportunities. There must be a purposeful problem-solving approach if training is to make a worthwhile contribution to the health and prosperity of the organization. Many organizations' training activities come unstuck at this first hurdle. One of the most persistent findings is that training needs are often not identified (Boydell and Leary, 1996). This is discussed by Kearns and Miller (1993), who question why so few organizations have any clear idea of the value-added they achieve from their training investment. They offer some incisive suggestions:

- It is generally assumed that training per se is a 'good thing'

- Senior management may support whatever training activities are being arranged, presumably because they sanctioned them in the first place

- Vague assumptions are made about vague improvements in vague measures of performance, for example management skills, communication, organizational culture, and these improvements are (predictably and appropriately) vaguely attributable to allegedly related training events

- Trainers are notoriously defensive about the value of their role, and often hide behind notions of how esoteric and ephemeral their contributions are, and how philistine it is to try to impose crude measures of cost-effectiveness.

Other points could be added – especially the tendency to initiate training activities in the face of an organizational crisis or period of great change, so as to be seen to be 'doing something'. We will be discussing the identification of training needs as a positive and proactive attempt to engage with the real strategic and operational problems and opportunities of the organization. Clearly, there can be different perceptions of training needs from different points of view.

Consider the following scenario:

A university designs and delivers an MSc programme in employee relations. It is intended as a training and developmental programme for practising and aspiring HR managers wishing to specialize in this field. One of the postgraduate students is an area officer of a national trade union, seconded to the programme on full pay for a year by his employer.

How might the actual training needs of the trade unionist compare to and contrast with the training needs of the HR managers on the programme? How could this possible set of conflicts be resolved?

Types of training need

We look now to different types of training need that can exist within an organization. To shape the discussion in this section, a broad distinction is made between:

- knowledge

- skills

- attitude.

This distinction is one that is part of training and education's conventional wisdom and is derived from the work of an American educational expert Dr Benjamin Bloom (1956) and others who sought to develop a taxonomy of learning behaviours that could be used in the design and assessment of learning. The so-called 'Bloom's taxonomy' consists of three domains of learning, cognitive, psychomotor and affective, which broadly cover the distinction we have made. Thus knowledge connects to the cognitive domain in Bloom's taxonomy, skill connects to the psychomotor domain and attitude connects to the affective domain. Each domain has been elaborated to provide a useful way of considering learning and development needs, objectives of processes and assessment. (For more on Bloom's taxonomy of learning objectives, go to www.learningandteaching. info/learning/bloomtax.htm, and also see Chapter 7.)

Reflective question

Do you think objectives are necessary for learning?

Knowledge

It is evident that knowledge, its creation, management and use are key ingredients of products and services and that many organizations are now knowledge based (OECD,

1996), and that as 'knowledge workers', employees provide the source of an organization's intellectual capital (Edvinsson and Malone, 1997).

All staff will need to know what to do in order fulfil their particular roles and how to do it, a distinction made by Ryle ([1949]1984) between 'knowing-that', 'knowing-what' and 'knowing-how' (see also Chapter 9). Thus, many staff need a sound knowledge of their professional or technical specialisms. This is probably the easiest to identify, if one takes a steady-state perception of the specialism. However, it has become increasingly important to update knowledge through continuing professional development and lifelong learning (see also Chapter 16). In addition, there is a need to know about the particular environment within which their specialism operates and the organization's policies and procedures. For example, HR managers will need a broad knowledge of the technology of the industry within which they work, lawyers specializing in unfair dismissal need a knowledge of personnel practice, accountants dealing in corporate fraud need to know about the workings of city institutions and so on.

Knowledge is strongly connected to Bloom's (1956) cognitive domain and has been further elaborated to included comprehension, application, analysis, synthesis and evaluation. You may recognize such words from the objectives or outcomes specified in modules at your college. More recently, Anderson and Krathwohl (2001) modified the cognitive domain to indicate the importance of creating knowledge as a higher order form of knowing; it is one that clearly chimes with the growing interest in knowledge production and management (see also Chapter 9).

Skill

Knowledge in itself is rarely sufficient to ensure satisfactory performance; it almost invariably needs to be combined with the development of the necessary skills. Imagine the damage that could be caused by a plumber, a car mechanic or even a brain surgeon with impressive theoretical knowledge but no task-related skills. There are debates, however, on the meaning of the term 'skill'. For example, and as we saw in Chapter 3, Felstead et al. (2002), suggested that skill can mean:

- competence to carry out tasks successfully

- the idea of hierarchical skill levels that are dependent on the complexities and discretions involved

- the view that there are different types of skills, some generic and applicable in diverse work situations and some specific and vocational and suitable for particular contexts.

The current trend is to emphasize 'competence' and/or 'competency'. The subtle difference in spelling is not insignificant. 'Competence' refers to abilities to perform within an occupational area to a standard required in employment. A person is competent if the output of their work meets written standards as specified by performance criteria and evidence required. In the UK, such standards form the basis of NVQs (SVQs in Scotland), which are set within the NQF and are a crucial feature of the VET system (see also Chapter 4).

'Competency', on the other hand, is concerned with behaviour and perhaps the best-known view of competency is from Boyatzis (1982), who was concerned with a manager's characteristics or abilities (see also Chapter 12) that allow them to achieve effective or superior performance. The CIPD's (2008, p. 1) definition is:

> the behaviours that employees must have, or must acquire, to input into a situation in order to achieve high levels of performance.

Armstrong (2002) suggests three key aspects of competence:

- *Input:* knowledge, skills and personal attributes
- *Process:* the behaviour required to convert the input into outputs
- *Output:* the outcomes achieved.

Thus, competence or competency are concerned not only with the inputs and processes of behaviour but also with the outcomes of people's behaviours.

Whichever stance is taken, competences or competencies allow a specification of what skills someone needs to have and use at work and therefore allow training needs to be assessed. For example, here is how a large financial services organization in the UK sets out its competencies:

- self-control
- self-development
- personal organization
- positive approach
- delivering results
- providing solutions
- systemic thinking
- attention to detail
- creating customer service
- delivering customer service
- continuous improvement
- developing people
- working with others
- influencing
- leading
- delivering the vision
- change and creativity.

For each competency, there is a definition and description, with indicators that enable assessment and measurement. For example, the competency of 'creating customer service' is indicated by:

- anticipating emerging customer needs and planning accordingly

- identifying the customers who will be of value to the company

- recommending changes to current ways of working that will improve customer service

- arranging the collection of customer satisfaction data and acting on them.

Competency frameworks such as these provide a statement of the skills as behaviours needed at work and provide the benchmark against which employees can be assessed for training needs.

Activity

A Woman's Touch is a building and domestic repairs business set up four years ago. It employs exclusively female craftspeople. This exploits an obvious niche market of women who need repairs and home improvements but feel more comfortable admitting another woman into their homes. It was soon found that there was a secondary market of practically incompetent and technophobic men who were less uneasy admitting their limitations to a woman.

The business has grown hugely – and even has a branch in Spain serving British ex-pats. The chief executive now wishes to create a specialist training college for her staff, with the main task being induction of new recruits. The 'hard' competencies to be taught will be common to anyone pursuing the relevant crafts. The 'soft' competencies, however, will need a great deal of consideration.

What are your suggestions for a soft competencies' framework for the employees of A Woman's Touch?

An interesting example of an online competency framework for Primary Care Trusts
in the NHS can be found at www.natpact.nhs.uk/competency_framework/.

Attitudes

An attitude is usually understood as a particular mental state of a person, which can be positive or negative, affecting judgements, decision making and motivation. Attitudes concern people, including oneself, situations past, present and future as well as social phenomena such as work organizations and jobs (Gibb, 2002). Attitudes are one aspect of what Krathwohl et al. (1964) referred to as the 'affective' domain of learning. This includes not just attitudes but also emotions, values, feelings, motivation, beliefs and interests. As you might imagine, such terms are highly connected to each other and we will use attitudes as a general term to cover them all.

Attitudes will affect how work is carried out; therefore an organization might seek to employ people who show the right 'attitudinal commitment' (Guest, 1989, p. 49), and this attention to attitudes is one of the distinguishing features of HRM (Bratton and Gold, 2007). There are some attitudes universally appropriate for all jobs – such as enthusiasm and conscientiousness. However, there may be specific attitudes necessary for particular jobs. This may involve particular attitudes on flexibility, customer care, cost control, quality and so on. Organizations are becoming increasingly aware of the importance of identifying attitudes in their recruitment as a requirement for skill development – a recent policy statement at ASDA, for example, stated: 'Recruit for attitude, train for skill.'

There are different views about attitudes and this stems mainly from the problem that we are talking about someone's mental state, which we cannot directly perceive. What we perceive are their behaviours; we then construct assumptions about the nature of the attitudes that have motivated or driven the behaviours. This is a well-known feature of social psychology called 'attribution theory'. One view, argued by those who work with behavioural theories of learning, is that attitudes, because they cannot be seen directly, cannot be learned; only the behaviour can be changed through the right stimulus and reinforcement. However, an alternative view would highlight attitudes as crucial to performance and training. For example, Noe (1986, p. 737) presented a formula of what he terms 'trainability', a function of ability, motivation, and perceptions of the work environment: trainability = f (ability, motivation, work environment perceptions).

In this formula, motivation indicates that learners need to have a degree of enthusiasm or a positive attitude towards training as well as abilities relating to knowing or skill acquisition. The third part of the formula, work environment perceptions, is one that will have an impact on attitudes, especially feelings about whether new ideas or new skills learned through training can be used and applied at work and whether others, such as managers, will support use and application. This is a feature of what is often referred to as an organization's 'learning climate' (see also Chapter 9).

HRD in Practice 6.1

Health and safety training: too much fuss?

A training manager was tasked with delivering health and safety training to a cohort of managers and team leaders. As part of the training needs analysis, he consulted each of the members of the cohort to ask them about their safety problems and their suggestions for items to include in the programme. The first person interviewed was an experienced manager who 10 years previously had been the victim of a dreadful industrial accident – his arm was trapped in a conveyor belt and he had to have it amputated. When asked for his initial thought on safety training, he responded spontaneously: 'There's too much fuss made about all this **** safety!' The training manager was speechless, and left wondering, if losing an arm in an industrial accident didn't commit this man to an attitude of safety consciousness, what hope could there be for his three-day training programme?

Can such attitudes be changed? Are attitude-change programmes possible at work? Consider also health and safety, discrimination and prejudice and ethical awareness.

It has been necessary to look at knowledge, skills and attitudes separately for the purpose of explaining them. However, most training needs will involve a combination of all three. The case study at the end of Chapter 8 addresses training for lunchtime supervisors in schools in Hull. One issue is the extent to which the training needs identified in this case provide a challenging mix of knowledge, skills and attitudes.

Indicators of training needs

A systematic approach to training, as indicated by Figure 6.1, suggests something more than guesswork or intuition in identifying training needs (McGehee and Thayer, 1961). There needs to be an objective and rigorous process of data collection followed by analysis to allow informed decision making about whether a training solution is required or not. There are key questions relating to what sort of information within an organization may suggest the need for training intervention and how best this information might be analysed and made sense of in terms of the most effective actions to take.

Before we search for these indicators, we need to focus on the purpose of the training. One view is that we need to be clear about the business objectives the training is intended to achieve. This is what Chiu et al. (1999) refer to a 'business-oriented' approach, with an emphasis on business outcomes, possibly at the expense of individual needs. Most training is oriented towards 'intermediate objectives' such as 'improving supervisory skills' and it is merely assumed that this will have an ultimately beneficial impact on the effectiveness of the organization. Instead, the focus should be on designing the training to meet the ultimate business objective. For instance, instead of the bland aim of improving supervisory skills, data could be collected on the real problems facing the business, for example scrap rates, production costs, absenteeism and so on. We could then examine how these indicators can be influenced (for good or ill) by supervisors' ability to perform their role. Thus the direct link to organizational and job effectiveness is identified immediately and measures of success can be built into the exercise upfront. With this approach in mind, these are some of the possible indicators of training needs:

- *Output:* Where output is below established standards, there may well be a training problem. The possible reasons for poor output are varied – poor technical skills, poor information flow, limited supervision and so on.

- *Varying standards:* Where standards of performance vary significantly between broadly similar groups of employees, there is likely to be training need. The reasons for the differences must be ascertained and good practice identified and disseminated.

- *Time:* If standard times are not being met, there may be a training need. Also there is a need to identify unproductive time use and train staff to use time more effectively.

- *Turnover and absenteeism:* 'People join organizations but they leave managers.' High turnover may well indicate unsatisfactory treatment or conditions. It may also indicate poor induction and/or occupational training.

- *Delays:* Bottlenecks in operational processes may be due to limited knowledge or skills. Improved managerial or technical performance (brought about by better training) may address the problem.

- *Complaints:* Complaints from customers (especially influential ones) are often the impetus required to ensure that relevant training needs are met.

In reality, of course, there may well be a complex mix of factors that highlight a need for training. Consider HRD in Practice 6.2, which looks at the recent difficulties the BBC has experienced.

BBC trains to meet technology challenges

In 2008, the BBC was fined a record £400,000 by Ofcom for faking winners and misleading audiences in a series of competitions on TV and radio. The watchdog criticized the BBC for serious breaches of its editorial standards. When the breaches were revealed, the BBC responded by putting more than 19,000 staff through a series of 'Safeguarding Trust' training workshops led by senior programme makers and based around real-life editorial scenarios.

At the same time, however, the BBC sought to deflect any suggestion that the problems had arisen because of reductions in training spend. Caroline Prendergast, the corporation's training and development director, said the BBC had not cut its training budget and that training remained a high priority, pointing to the fact that the BBC's learning board was chaired by the deputy director general.

Prendergast identified changes to technology and audience tastes as the biggest learning and development challenges facing the industry. 'Technology is changing all the time and for us that means having to train people to produce programmes that will work across different platforms, such as MP3 players and mobile phones.' Prendergast also pointed to an increasingly mobile workforce, which was forcing the corporation to review and revise its delivery of training: 'We have to look at tailoring things to different situations.' Thus, online learning is playing an increasingly important role, alongside more traditional methods.

Source: Phillips (2008)

HRD in Practice 6.2 illustrates that while the specific stimulus for the 'Safeguarding Trust' training was the critical Ofcom report, the organization's training effort is not purely reactive. The biggest training challenges it faces are driven by change – technological changes, workforce changes and changes in audience tastes. Importantly, it also highlights that in practice there may well be an uneasy relationship between training and aspects of change within an organization.

One of the most crucial indicators for considering training, learning and development needs more widely is change at work. Of course, any change can vary in scope, depth and duration; however, it is recognized there is often a connection between change and identifying needs for training and learning, or at least there ought to be. Research by Reed and Vakola (2006) suggests that, traditionally, training needs are not sufficiently connected to change or cultural issues.

In contrast to the business-oriented approach, Chiu et al. (1999) also refer to the 'trainee-centred' approach, which gives more emphasis to individuals working out their own needs through self-assessment and using feedback from others, and which we consider below. Sloman (2005) suggests that the shift towards learning based on self-direction and learning from work is a key development of current times.

Activity

Form a group of three or four. Using either the university where you are studying or an organization where you have some work experience, think about some of the main challenges you consider to be affecting the organization. Identify three and describe the main indicators of these challenges. Consider the extent to which there may be training needs present.

The identification and assessment of training needs

Having considered certain indicators of training need, we will now examine the various processes available for the systematic identification of training needs. A systematic needs assessment can guide the subsequent stages of design, delivery and evaluation; indeed, it can be used to specify a number of key features for the implementation and evaluation of the training (see also Chapters 7 and 8). It is primarily conducted to determine where training is needed, what needs to be taught and who needs to be trained (Goldstein, 1993).

Levels of training need

It is useful to think of training needs existing at three levels. This was first suggested by McGehee and Thayer (1961) and has subsequently been advocated by others such as Boydell and Leary (1996) in the UK. These levels are organization, job and individual.

At the organizational level, the concern is with the whole organization – starting with strategy and objectives, key measurements and indicators, change projects, and more ephemeral features such as organizational climate and culture. At the level of the job, the concern is with a neutral view of work, which may cover a particular job or group of jobs in a section or department. Systematic processes are used to collect data and analyse how work should be done against some standard. Skills, knowledge and attitudes can be specified. Finally, and apparently at the end of the chain, is the person. The task here is to assess performance against the measurement standards for the job. It is assumed that each person has a responsibility to perform against the standard and receive training if they cannot meet the standard.

At each of these levels, there are a range of methods available. We shall be discussing each of these levels separately. However, a perceived training problem will often need to be dealt with at all three levels simultaneously. Reid et al. (2004) note an interesting example. In 2003, the Scottish Executive initiated a training needs analysis (TNA) for the NHS, focusing on the area of public involvement and facilitating the greater recognition of patient diversity. Training needs were identified at all levels:

- *At the organizational level*, training was needed to ensure a supply of staff with the necessary skills and flexibility for promotion and transfers; also training was needed to support a culture where staff would think strategically and try to see the global picture.

- *At the job level*, training was needed to facilitate a wide range of reforms, for example to develop nursing staff as managers as well as carers.

- *At the individual level*, training was needed to remedy the many significant skill gaps identified through individual appraisal interviews.

It has long been recognized that there needs to be some consideration for integrating the three levels (Moore and Dutton, 1978), taking a more holistic view of the connections between the vertical, horizontal and lateral aspects. This has been a view advocated by OD practitioners who take a more systemic or activity-based view of organizations (see also Chapter 3).

Organization-level needs

The first level of analysis may be at the level of the whole organization, assessing what skills the organization has now and what it requires now and in the future. It focuses on the congruence between training objectives with such factors as the organizational strategy, the available resources, constraints and support for the transfer of learning to the workplace (Salas and Cannon-Bowers, 2001). Depending on the size of the organization, it may also be necessary to conduct this analysis at the level of the division, the department and the team. We must not underestimate the importance of training in facilitating the pursuit of corporate goals. Lack of training may even make the goals unattainable. For example, in March 2008, Terminal 5 opened at Heathrow Airport and very soon descended into chaos – with many delayed and cancelled flights and thousands of bags misdirected or even lost. In a report to the House of Commons Transport Committee (House of Commons, 2008), British Airways admitted that a failure to adequately address training needs to operate the new systems contributed to the Terminal 5 fiasco (see also Chapter 1).

A clear understanding of the organization's strategy is a prerequisite to consideration of needs. For organizations that choose to compete on the basis of quality, highly skilled workers are essential; for those that compete on cost, they are an unjustifiable extravagance – and large sections of the British economy still compete on cost (Redman and Wilkinson, 2006). Identifying organization-level needs is concerned with considering which of the organization's goals can be achieved through training and whether any particular areas of the organization require investment in training, but this has to fit with the competitive strategy of the organization. A logistics company in the north of England delivering a low-cost, high-volume service focuses the identification of needs on those that are essential to delivery of each order, while a successful building society in the same locality adopts a longer term strategy, considering skill requirements to enable growth and competitive advantage in the future. This level of review may be appropriate for corporate and HR planning processes. In addition, Hackett (2003) identifies new products, new technology, work processes or systems and new legislation as specific drivers of learning needs.

The type of need you might identify in this kind of analysis could be needs that apply to the whole of the organization, such as a new computer system, or a new strategic focus following a merger or organizational change. Reid et al. (2004) identify four types of organization-level review: global; competence and performance management; critical incident; learner centred.

We now consider some of the strategies and procedures available when identifying training needs at the organizational level:

- *Analysis of the culture of the organization:* Obviously this is vital when trying to 'engineer' a change in culture, if this is ever possible (Alvesson, 2002). However, in any situation, understanding an organization's values and desired outcomes allows consideration of acceptability and receptiveness to change implied by any HRD interventions. For example, research on the success of many Asian firms shows that it has been built on their collectivist cultural orientation to developing and sharing learning in teams (Lucas et al., 2006). In this way, cultural indicators will have a distinct influence on the identification process.

- *Skills audit:* This is a process to identify the relevant skills or competences required by the organization and then assess whether these are present. It is necessary to consult widely with management, service departments, line managers, team leaders, prospective trainees, who may all be fertile sources of information.

- *Standards of performance and competency framework:* Once established, an assessment is made of the shortfall between these required standards and the actual ones being achieved. Gibb (2002) stresses that the observation and assessment of learning and development needs should take place within a context of performance management in the organization so that the needs will relate to business development.

- *HR plan:* This describes – quantitatively and qualitatively – the capabilities of the current workforce and the anticipated future requirements in terms of skills and performance levels. It can help to develop an understanding of training needs, in the sense that identified shortfalls, or gaps, can be met, in part, with training. Thus an HR plan is likely to include training proposals designed to address changing skill needs and performance deficiencies.

- *Analysis and synthesis of appraisal records:* Training needs will have been identified for specific individuals through the appraisal discussions. These may well build up over the whole organization to indicate a wider, more general pattern of training needs.

- *Critical incidents:* This involves the collection of data from a wide range of activities where the work makes what is regarded as a significant contribution. It can be argued that this covers all activities, or should do. However, it is increasingly recognized that interactions with clients and customers are important sources of understanding in knowledge-based work and professional work (Gold and Thorpe, 2007). Incidents can be positive or negative but, crucially, provide a story about what happened, what people did and why it was significant. This is a long-established technique first presented by Flanagan (1954) and can be used for different purposes, but collating such data from significant incidents can reveal key patterns that indicate training needs.

- *Useful sources of written information available within the organization:* This may include corporate plans, personnel records, and reports from training, joint consultative or safety committees. All are increasingly available on management information systems.

- *External research:* Government reports, national and local employment statistics and so on can all prove useful.

The analysis at this level could be conducted by the management team, the HR department or an outside consultant. In addition to these methods, there are other approaches that allow a whole organization diagnosis of needs. For example, in the 1980s and 90s, Total Quality Management (TQM) provided tools for engendering a culture of continuous improvement. The European Foundation for Quality Management (www.efqm.org) provides an excellence model, which allows an organization to be assessed against nine criteria such as leadership, customer results and people results. The assessment is based on data from across the organization and reveals possibilities for improvement including training, learning and development needs.

The government's Investors in People (IiP) standard also promotes and enables training needs analysis. Organizations committed to gaining IiP recognition are provided with tools to show them exactly how good they are and what areas they can focus on to enable further improvements and productivity gains (see also Chapter 4).

Job-level training needs

Following the more generic training needs of the organization, the next stage is to consider the requirements of each particular job. This considers what someone must learn to be able to do in order to do the job effectively. A range of methods is outlined below:

- *Job analysis or job training analysis:* This is the process of examining a job in order to identify its component parts. With relation to the responsibilities of the job holder, what knowledge, skills and attitudes are required to perform the role effectively? A job analysis will usually consist of three components:

  - *The job description:* an outline of the purpose and responsibilities of the job – the obvious starting point for the analysis

  - *The personnel specification:* a description of the qualities required of an employee in order to be able to discharge those responsibilities adequately – this details the organization's criteria for selection, but prior training may be an element, as may be future trainability; perhaps most important of all, the personnel specification may prevent the problem of recruiting unsuitable staff and then trying to 'train away' the problem

  - *The job specification* – perhaps better called the 'training specification': a description of the knowledge, skills and attitudes required of the job holder.

- *Problem-centred analysis:* Similar to a job analysis but the focus will be on areas of performance where problems generally occur.

- *Key task analysis:* Again similar to job analysis but prioritizing the elements within the job that have the greatest impact on performance. Each key task is analysed to see what knowledge, skills and attitude are required. Bee and Bee (2003) assert this will be the six to eight most important tasks or functions performed in the job.

- *Competency analysis:* Uses a competency framework to consider which competencies are required in a job or work area.

Reflective question

Think about these two scenarios:

1 A job, for example a contact centre adviser, that is closely defined and prescriptive and where new starters are frequent.

2 A job, for example a health and safety executive, where legislation determines necessary changes to some requirements of the role but others remain unchanged.

What type of job-level analysis do you consider might be appropriate in each scenario?

Job-level analysis can also include more generic role or occupational analysis. Reid et al. (2004) use the example of NVQs. Sector Skills Councils (SSCs) have drawn up competence statements for a range of roles. National Occupational Standards (NOS) describe what a person needs to do, know and understand in their job to carry out their role in a consistent and competent way. These are the building blocks for UK qualifications and business improvement tools and are developed by groups of employers for their employees through an SSC or a standards setting body. NOS can be used to inform the content of training as they specify in detail what constitutes good practice.

Activity

Form a group of three and go to www.ukstandards.co.uk/About_occupational_standards/For_Employers_and_businesses.aspx to find out more about National Occupational Standards.

Then go to www.ukstandards.co.uk/Find_Occupational_Standards.aspx and each person choose one 'area of learning' such as Accounting and Finance or Performing Arts. Then pick one document, such as Achieving Personal Effectiveness in Accounting and Finance, download it and report back on how this framework could be used for identifying training needs. Share your findings.

Identifying job-level training needs is often an important part of the 'planned maintenance' of an organization and a necessary response to changing conditions and new problems.

Individual-level training needs

Consider this, probably apocryphal, reflection on behalf of a senior manager, following a major organizational restructure and relocation:

> We've designed the organization structure very rationally; we've set up all the necessary control mechanisms; we've designed all the jobs intelligently. The problem is that the jobs all have to be done by idiosyncratic, temperamental and sometimes downright hostile people.

Obviously, considering the training needs of a particular job does not signify that everyone starting the job will require training in all those areas. A new starter may already have training or experience that matches the requirements of the job. Consequently, this stage concentrates on which individuals require training and what their particular needs are. It is essentially matching the skills of the person to the skills of the job and ascertaining where gaps exist. We can point to a variety of approaches and, mostly, this level of analysis is completed as part of a performance management process. A CIPD (2005) survey found that 62% of respondents used performance management activities to set objectives and personal development plans, and 36% provided coaching and/or mentoring, career management and/or succession planning. CIPD also indicated that performance management had a development purpose and a control purpose, which can create tensions and difficulties. This is partly to do with judgements about a person's performance and the decisions that can be made as a consequence. Such decisions are seen by employees as feedback, with a variety of responses, as shown in Figure 6.2.

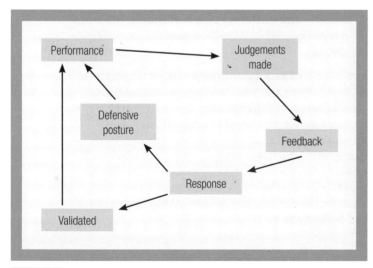

FIGURE 6.2 Responses to feedback

The crucial variable is 'validated'. If feedback is positive or negative, and the response is accepted, this can lead to improved performance, perhaps by undertaking training if gaps are identified. However, if the response is a defensive posture, the identification of needs might not be accepted and this could lead to a negative impact on performance. DeNisi and Kluger (2000) suggest that feedback can help someone to focus on what to do or learn and this will improve performance, but it can also affect a person's view of 'self' and the response can be emotional and detrimental to performance. VandeWalle and Cummings (1997) suggest a key factor is learning goal orientation, where people have a willingness to develop new skills and master new situations. Such people are proactive in seeking feedback and making good use of it. With these considerations on feedback, we now consider some of the methods:

- *Performance standards:* Where there are clear performance standards in place, these can be used as an indication of gaps in performance and potential learning needs, for example a sales executive who regularly misses their sales target of completing 20 sales per day.

- *Comparative methods:* Where there is a clear framework of performance standards and a comprehensive system of training records in place, it is then possible to try to discover the sort of competencies that correlate with good performance. For example, it may be that the most effective team leaders have excellent planning skills, while the poorer ones are noticeably weak in this area.

- *Direct observation:* There is a long history of observation at work for assessing training needs. Traditionally this been connected to time and motion studies[1] producing quantitative data. In more recent years, the value of qualitative data has been recognized, which is more suitable for discussion with employees.

- *Individual appraisal:* Many organizations use performance appraisal to review individual performance and this is often linked to a development review and the production of a personal development plan. This may or may not be competency based (see above). Together with other forms of appraisal, this can be valuable in identifying barriers to effective performance including lack of training (Hackett, 2003), but appraisal has long been recognized as a political process with potentially negative outcomes (Poon, 2004).

- *Multisource feedback:* A wider range of feedback sources may also be appropriate in the identification of training needs. For example, 360 degree appraisal is a system of collecting feedback from peers and subordinates, and can potentially include other viewpoints such as customers and suppliers. It may also be valuable to seek feedback from mentors and coaches. However, this approach to feedback can soon become counterproductive if mainly used for control and judgement purposes (Fletcher, 2001). Smither et al. (2005) looked at multisource feedback in 24 studies but found that much depended on factors such as reactions to feedback, orientation, beliefs about change and taking action if the process was to lead to improved performance.

- *Assessment and development centres:* These are most likely to be used for managers or graduates and would include a range of exercises designed to assess performance and encourage reflection on personal development. The focus is often skills rather than knowledge based. A key issue is whether the purpose is assessment, as for selection, or development that results in an accepted personal development plan for participants. The two purposes can become confused and as Woodruffe (2000, p. 32) warns: 'Assessment centres masquerading as development centres are wolves in sheep's clothing.'

Go to www.shl.com/SHL/uk/Products/, one of the main providers of development centre methods. Examine the different methods on offer and consider which you feel you would be happy/unhappy to take.

- *Self-assessment:* In recent years, much greater attention has been placed on self-assessment; encouraging individuals to take greater responsibility for the identification of their own needs. Reflection and self-assessment are key elements of many professional courses and in such a context an individual should be able to identify areas where they require development. This is also useful in addressing needs that are not apparent to observers, who may focus on results rather than behaviours and attitudes. For example, a manager may deliver a presentation that is well received by the audience but may lack confidence in their own performance and therefore have spent longer than necessary in preparation. Training to address this need may be beneficial to future performance but would not have been identified by an outside observer. The use of technology may also play a role in self-assessment. One tool, for example, might be an online test and, increasingly, organizations request employees to complete initial appraisal assessments online. However, there is a danger that self-reported needs could be a wish list of courses, which may not tie in with the organization's objectives. Campbell and Lee (1988, p. 307) argued that self-appraisal is an 'important developmental and motivation tool for individuals', but there are likely to be differences between a person's self-appraisal and the appraisal of their superior.

Reflective question

Think about any paid employment you are doing or have recently undertaken. To what extent can you identify individual training needs in relation to yourself?

Problems with the identification of training needs

The identification of training needs forms a fundamental and critical component in the training process and, more broadly, in HRD. However, it is important to acknowledge some potential issues. In practice, identification of needs is often ad hoc rather than systematic, and organizations undertaking a systematic approach do not always complete all three levels of analysis. Political and pragmatic considerations may influence an organization to be highly targeted in its TNA, for example individuals in the 'public eye', new starters or high potential individuals. Complex scenarios may initially be interpreted incorrectly and result in misleading training need assessments. (see HRD in Practice 6.3).

Sales training

In a large call centre organization, customer services and telesales were structured as separate departments. As part of the launch of a new product, the telesales centre was asked to promote and capture sales. Telesales agents were recruited through an agency and given training in the product, sales and customer service techniques. The initial results showed that sales were high, agents were motivated in their work and targets were being met. However, the customer service department received a high volume of complaints. The substance of the complaints was that telesales staff were sometimes rude to customers, hung up the phone in an abrupt manner if it became clear that the customer was not going to purchase, and even put through sales that were not sanctioned by the customer.

Customer service managers questioned the quality of training undertaken by the telesales agents. However, it came to light that the agents were paid commission for the level of sales they achieved. Customer service targets were measured but not rewarded and no sanctions were applied for orders that were subsequently cancelled.

There are a number of important issues and questions that emanate from an uncritical adoption of a systematic approach to training needs identification and assessment. These include, first, the issue of whether reliance on formal needs assessment results in a narrow focus on training rather than encouraging a more creative process and a culture of learning. Consider, for example, the case of companies offering a training allowance for individuals to spend as they choose, as part of an employee-led development scheme (Hamblett and Holden, 2000). The aim of such schemes is to generate greater enthusiasm for learning and stimulate new opportunities. Pettinger (2002) presents an interesting illustration of a greeting cards company that insists its staff do 30 days' training per year – as long as one event is directly work related, they can do whatever they want.

Second, a focus on the current requirements may ignore changes in the working environment, thus developing skills for today rather than tomorrow (or even worse for yesterday). For example, a study of the changing role of practice nurses revealed new requirements in the areas of counselling skills and health promotion, which are not included in traditional nurses' training programmes (Ross et al., 1994). It has been suggested for some time now that instead of regarding TNA as a one-off process, it should become continuous (Moore and Dutton, 1978). We have seen that organizations can produce a vast amount of data relating to their performance and operations at different levels. Such data can help to identify needs and allow employees to recognize opportunities from work. However, this does require a positive learning climate with support from line managers and others, with the roles of coaching and mentoring seen as particularly important. Increasingly, the skill of 'developing others' has appeared in competency frameworks for managers (IRS, 2001). A key difficulty comes from failing to secure senior management commitment. Many HRD programmes fail to reach their goals because of organizational constraints and conflicts (Salas and Cannon-Bowers, 2001). These should be identified upfront and senior managers engaged to ensure they can be overcome.

Third, identifying the wrong need, or where the need is only partially related to training, will hamper the success of the training if it is not targeting the real performance problem. One problem involves distinguishing training needs and training wants. This may be a particular problem in the context of the self-assessment of training needs. Further, identifying a gap between actual and desired performance does not necessarily indicate a training need. A wider review of performance issues and HR practices is required to ensure that the need can or should be met through training. HR departments themselves may be a constraint because they may have a vested interest in delivering particular sorts of training and development. This relates to a wider debate about the role of HR. In a traditional training environment, there may be a preference for formal training delivery at the expense of other more work-based methods. Further, HR may develop approaches it considers 'good' for its employees, which reflect the wants and desires of HR departments and their senior managers, rather than a proper analysis of the requirements of work activity. This is a reflection of the inherent tension between the business-oriented approach and the trainee-centred approach referred to by Chiu et al. (1999). The top-down approach of the former is certainly more prevalent in larger organizations but would be less suited to smaller organizations and other contexts (see also Chapter 15).

Fourth, TNA involves the collection of data but how can we ensure the data are reliable and valid. For example, where performance appraisal is used as a means of identifying needs, factors such as the frequency of appraisal and whether it is linked to performance-related pay may influence the validity of the data received. Is an employee likely to be honest about identifying their weak points if the discussion links to the reward for their performance?

Finally, the stakeholders at each level of analysis may have conflicting priorities. HRD initiatives can easily become a wish list for managers who make assumptions for others about what they are required to learn (Hicks and Hennessy, 1997). This is often connected to management views of how change occurs in organizations. Apart from the failure to see training needs as an essential aspect of change (Reed and Vakola, 2006), there are also failures to understand the cultural and historical influences that affect responsiveness to communication for change and readiness to change (Bernerth, 2004). Once again, we can highlight the importance of the roles of managers to support learning and become aware of the continuous developmental requirements of their interactions with employees.

Summary

- A training need is defined as the gap between the knowledge, skills and attitude possessed by the target individual or group and those needed to perform required occupational roles.

- Training needs will often involve a combination of knowledge, skills and attitudes, which provides a challenge for effective intervention.

- A range of potential indicators of training needs exists in all organizations. These include data on organizational performance, signs and indications of organizational problems (for example complaints, turnover) and needs related to organizational change.

- If effective training is to be implemented, training needs must be carefully analysed and assessed. A useful framework involves analysis and assessment at three levels: the organization, the job or occupation and the individual.

- At each level, techniques are available to the trainer to generate a specification of what is required to meet identified needs.

- The identification and assessment of training needs is not necessarily straightforward. Pursued mechanistically, a focus on current requirements may ignore changes on the horizon.

- Gathering the appropriate data may be difficult particularly in politically sensitive areas within the organization. Stakeholders at different levels in the organization may have different, if not conflicting priorities, thus making it difficult to achieve 'consensus' surrounding training need specifications.

Discussion questions

1 What are the three main levels at which training needs are assessed and who could assist in the identification of needs at each of these levels?

2 Consider any job you have held. What were the main responsibilities you had to discharge? What were the main qualities the organization demanded from applicants for the job (for example qualification, experience, communication ability, motivation)? What are the knowledge, skills and attitudes needed to perform the job adequately?

3 What are three potential problems with the use of appraisals to identify training needs?

4 Should all training be business oriented? Discuss this with reference to identifying training needs.

5 Consider how this chapter links with the earlier chapters in the book. Can you identify any synergies or possible tensions?

Further reading

Anderson, G. (1994) A proactive model of training needs analysis, *Journal of European Industrial Training*, **18**(3): 23–8.

Ballantyne, I. and Povah, N. (2004) *Assessment and Development Centres*, London, Gower.

Bowman, J. and Wilson, J. (2008) Different roles, different perspectives: perceptions about the purpose of training needs analysis, *Industrial and Commercial Training*, **40**(1): 38–41.

Gould, D., Kelly, D., White, I. and Chidgey, J. (2004) Training needs analysis: a literature review and reappraisal, *International Journal of Nursing Studies*, **41**(5): 471–86.

Palmer, R. (2005) *The Identification of Learning Needs*, London, Kogan Page.

Ruona, W. and Gibson, S. (2004) The making of twenty-first-century HR: an analysis of the convergence of HRM, HRD, and OD, *Human Resource Management*, **43**(1): 49–66.

Note

1   Time and motion study, also known as work study or industrial engineering, has its roots in Taylorism. Taylorism saw benefits in the extensive streamlining of the processes involved in work tasks. The link to training and development is that the 'time and motion' study would break down tasks into the various physical movements required and then determine an appropriate time to fulfill each movement effectively. See, for example, Benyon (1973) for a lively account of some of the difficulties caused by such practice within the Ford Motor Company.

References

Alvesson, M. (2002) *Understanding Organizational Culture*, London, Sage.

Anderson, L.W. and Krathwohl, D.R. (eds) (2001) *A Taxonomy for Learning, Teaching, and Assessing: A Revision of Bloom's Taxonomy of Educational Objectives*, New York, Longman.

Armstrong, M. (2002) *Employee Reward*, 3rd edn, London, CIPD.

Bee, R. and Bee, F. (2003) *Learning Needs Analysis and Evaluation*, London, CIPD.

Benyon, H. (1973) *Working for Ford*, Harmondsworth, Penguin.

Bernerth, J. (2004) Expanding our understanding of the change message, *Human Resource Development Review*, **3**(1): 36–52.

Bloom, B.S. (ed.) (1956) *Taxonomy of Educational Objectives: The Classification of Educational Goals*, Handbook I, Cognitive Domain, New York, McKay.

Boyatzis, R.E. (1982) *The Competent Manager: A Model for Effective Performance*, London, Wiley.

Boydell, T. and Leary, M. (1996) *The Identification of Training Needs*, London, CIPD.

Bratton, J. and Gold, J. (2007) *Human Resource Management: Theory and Practice*, Basingstoke, Palgrave Macmillan.

Buckley, R. and Caple, J. (2007) *The Theory and Practice of Training*, 5th edn, London, Kogan Page.

Campbell, D.J. and Lee, C. (1988) Self-appraisal in performance evaluation: development versus evaluation, *Academy of Management Review*, **13**(2): 302–14.

Chiu, W., Thompson, D., Mak, W. and Lo, K. (1999) Re-thinking training needs analysis: a proposed framework for literature review, *Personnel Review*, **28**(1/2): 77–90.

CIPD (Chartered Institute of Personnel and Development) (2005) *Performance Management*, London, CIPD.

CIPD (Chartered Institute of Personnel and Development) (2008) Competency and competency frameworks factsheet, www.cipd.co.uk/subjects/perfmangmt/competnces/comptfrmwk.htm.

DeNisi, A.S. and Kluger, A.N. (2000) Feedback effectiveness: can 360-degree feedback be improved?, *Academy of Management Executive*, **14**(1): 129–39.

Edvinsson, L. and Malone, M.S. (1997) *Intellectual Capital*, New York, Harper.

Felstead, A., Gallie, D. and Green, F. (2002) *Work Skills in Britain 1986–2001*, London, DfES.

Flanagan, J.C. (1954) The critical incident technique, *Psychological Bulletin*, **51**(4): 327–58.

Fletcher C. (2001) Performance appraisal and management: the developing research agenda, *Journal of Occupational and Organizational Psychology*, **74**(4): 473–87.

Gibb, S. (2002) *Learning and Development*, Basingstoke, Palgrave – now Palgrave Macmillan.

Gold, J. and Thorpe, R. (2007) Collective CPD in a law firm, paper presented to the Academy of HRD Conference, Indianapolis, February.

Goldstein, L. (1993) *Training in Organizations*, Pacific Grove, CA, Brooks/Cole.

Guest, D. (1989) HRM: implications for industrial relations, in J. Storey (ed.) *New Perspectives on Human Resource Management*, London, Routledge.

Hackett, P. (2003) *Training Practice*, London, CIPD.

Hamblett, J. and Holden, R. (2000) Employee-led development: another piece of left luggage?, *Personnel Review*, **29**(4): 509–20.

Hicks, C. and Hennessy, D. (1997) Identifying training objectives: the role of negotiation, *Journal of Nursing Management*, **5**(5): 263–5.

House of Commons (2008) The opening of Heathrow Terminal 5, House of Commons Transport Committee, HC 543, London, TSO.

IRS (Industrial Relations Services) (2001) *Competency Frameworks in UK Organizations*, London, IRS.

Kearns, P. and Miller, T. (1993) The financial return from training and development: hard facts or act of faith?, *Transition*, October.

Kenney, J. and Reid, M. (1986) *Training Interventions,* London, IPM.

Krathwohl, D.R., Bloom, B.S. and Masia, B.B. (1964) *Taxonomy of Educational Objectives: The Classification of Educational Goals*, Handbook II, *Affective Domain*, New York, David McKay.

Lucas, R., Lupton, B. and Mathieson, H. (2006) *Human Resource Management in an International Context*, London, CIPD.

McClelland, S. (1994) Training needs assessment data-gathering methods: part 4, on-site observations, *Journal of European Industrial Training*, **18**(5): 4–7.

McGehee, W. and Thayer, P.W. (1961) *Training in Business and Industry*, New York, John Wiley.

Moore, M. and Dutton, P. (1978) Training needs analysis: a review and critique, *Academy of Management Review*, **3**(3): 532–45.

Noe, R.A. (1986) Trainees' attributes and attitudes: neglected influences on training effectiveness, *Academy of Management Review*, **11**(4): 736–49.

OECD (Organization for Economic Co-operation and Development) (1996) *The Knowledge-Based Economy*, Paris, OECD.

Pettinger, R. (2002) *Mastering Employee Development*, Basingstoke, Palgrave – now Palgrave Macmillan.

Phillips, L. (2008) BBC trains to meet technology change, *People Management*, **14**(19): 8.

Poon, J.M. (2004) Effects of performance appraisal politics on job satisfaction and turnover intention, *Personnel Review*, **33**(3): 322–34.

Redman, T. and Wilkinson, A. (2006) *Contemporary Human Resource Management: Text and Cases*, London, Pearson.

Reed, J. and Vakola, M. (2006) What role can a training needs analysis play in organizational change?, *Journal of Organizational Change Management*, **19**(3): 393–407.

Reid, M.A., Barrington, H. and Brown, M. (2004) *Human Resource Development: Beyond Training Interventions*, London, CIPD.

Ross, F., Bower, P. and Sibbald, B. (1994) Practice nurses: characteristics, workload and training needs, *British Journal of General Practice,* **44**: 15–18.

Ryle, G. ([1949]1984) *The Concept of Mind*, Chicago, University of Chicago Press.

Salas, E. and Cannon-Bowers, J.A. (2001) The science of training: a decade of progress, *Annual Review of Psychology*, **52**: 471–99.

Smither, J., London, M. and Reilly, R.R. (2005) Does performance improve following multisource feedback? A theoretical model, meta-analysis and review of empirical findings, *Personnel Psychology*, **58**(1): 33–66.

Sloman, M. (2005) *Training to Learning: Change Agenda*, London, CIPD.

VandeWalle, D. and Cummings, L.L. (1997) A test of the influence of goal orientation on the feedback-seeking process, *Journal of Applied Psychology*, **82**(3): 390–400.

Woodruffe, C. (2000) *Development and Assessment Centres: Identifying and Developing Competence,* London, CIPD.

The Design and Delivery of Training

Catherine Glaister, Rick Holden, Vivienne Griggs and Patrick McCauley

7

Chapter learning outcomes

After studying this chapter, you should be able to:

- Understand the relationship between the identification of training needs and the subsequent design and delivery of training and learning

- Identify and explain the range of factors that will influence decisions about training and learning strategies and methods

- Juxtapose ideas about, and principles of, effective learning with practical considerations such as trainee characteristics, costs, trainer capabilities

- Identify a wide range of training and learning methods available to meet identified needs and explain the relative strengths and weaknesses of these approaches

- Understand the decisions necessary to determine fit for purpose training and learning solutions

Chapter outline

Introduction

Designing training

Training and learning methods

Trends and issues

Summary

Introduction

IF A WORD OF THIS GOES BEYOND THE STAFF TRAINING ROOM, SULLIVAN, YOU'RE DEAD

BONDING

©Roger Beale

Lucy Kellaway (2005), writing in the *Financial Times*, argues that the real issue in training is not that employers do not spend enough on training, 'but that they do not pitch it right'. This captures the essence of this chapter. It is about the design and delivery of effective training and learning. The observant reader will have noticed we have complemented the term 'training' with that of 'learning'. It will be recalled that at the start of Chapter 6, we noted the issue of a potentially confusing terminology. We noted our position that a 'training' method was not necessarily the same as a 'learning' method. Our position in this chapter is that if we only consider possible 'training' solutions, we are potentially ignoring a range of interventions that are more appropriately labelled 'learning'. Thus, in this chapter, the terms are deliberately used interchangeably, to convey that a broad range of solutions may need to be part of decision making. For a fuller discussion on this issue, see the CIPD publication *Training to Learning* (Sloman, 2005).

In Chapter 6, we examined the importance of carefully identifying training needs before committing resources to meet those needs. An analysis of the job or task provides the cornerstone for progressing towards interventions, which will, in time, meet and remove any training gap. Building on this framework, this chapter explores a range of factors to address in the design of training and learning – such as the characteristics of the trainees, and how best to utilize our understanding of what we know about how individuals and groups learn most effectively. Inevitably, issues of cost and available resources are also part of these design considerations. The second half of the chapter looks at how these various design considerations can be translated into practice. What alternative methods of delivery might be possible? Can a skill need be effectively delivered using e-learning, and what implications does a preferred method of delivery have in terms of trainer capabilities?

While the chapter unfolds in this way, there is clearly an inextricable relationship between design and delivery. The choice of a particular method, or combination of methods, needs to be fit for purpose. A particular strategy might appear highly appropriate in terms of its ability to meet the main objectives, but is unrealistic in terms of costs or because it requires considerable time away from work, which is likely to be opposed and resisted by those involved. Many a training intervention has floundered because those responsible for its design and delivery had not thought carefully enough about the cultural context in which the programme was being implemented.

The case of Harvey Nicholls (HRD in Practice 7.1) provides an interesting example of the how one large UK retailer seeks to put training into practice. The reader might usefully reflect back to this case throughout our more detailed discussion of design and delivery practice issues as they unfold in the remainder of the chapter.

HRD in Practice 7.1

Learning and development at Harvey Nichols

According to its website (www.harvey-nicholscareers.com): 'Harvey Nichols is an international luxury lifestyle store, renowned both in the UK and internationally for the breadth and depth of its exclusive fashion merchandise', with stores in the UK and abroad.

The embedding of clear brand values – providing a feel-good experience, being exclusive but accessible, and providing fashion leadership – into everyday performance and behaviours within the company was seen as key to business success. Originating from a project begun in 2003, project teams involving representatives from all levels of the business undertook extensive consultation and developed a set of people values and behaviours.

A creative approach to learning and development has since played a key role in making the people values and behaviours a reality within the business. Together with the incorporation of desirable behaviours within the performance management system itself, a top-down cascade approach was introduced, beginning with launch events held by directors. These included role plays of desirable and undesirable behaviours. Subsequently, for departmental managers, there were a series of one-day 'train the trainer' courses to equip them with the skills to help them train their staff on a day-to-day, week-by-week basis, using discussions and workplace-based training exercises.

People values	Behaviours
Eager to engage with customers in order to deliver a great experience	Being welcoming – using eye contact and positive body language
Willing to go the extra mile	Actively helping customers and colleagues
Enthusiastic and positive	Listening to customers and colleagues
People who like people	Looking for how to say 'yes'
Strong clear communicators	Encouraging colleagues to work as a team

In this way, Harvey Nichols was signalling its desire to move away from generic training courses for all sales assistants. Traditional training was rejected and replaced with methods that allowed for immediate feedback, ongoing support, and flexibility, recognizing the difficulty of precisely defining the skills involved in 'reading the customer'. Transfer of training problems and barriers were thus minimized.

To complement the training and development initiatives, Harvey Nichols launched the 'Brand Champion Scheme'. Staff were asked to identify examples of the values and behaviours in action by nominating peers for rewards based on exceptional performance. With this in place to reward excellence, attention was also placed on how to ensure development of poorer performance. Again, a belief in the importance of workplace learning underpinned the approach, with a further development of the line manager's skill in workplace coaching.

Source: Adapted from Sloman (2005)

Designing training

Training provision is big business in the UK. According to the *National Employers Skills Survey 2007*, the UK spent over £36bn on training activity in 2007 (LSC, 2008). There is no shortage of training providers anxious to get organizations to sign up to their particular set of training solutions. Yet for all this activity and hype, there are nagging doubts as to whether the money spent on training is always well spent. Of course, one of the difficulties here is that we lack sound ways and means to ascertain value for money. This is a theme addressed in the next chapter. Other reasons for legitimate concerns are a failure to identify needs effectively and a failure to design appropriate training to meet the identified training needs. It is the latter issue that we will address in this chapter. Reference to the model of training activity noted in Chapter 6 suggests that it is but a simple step from the identification of training to the implementation and delivery of some form of training event or programme. In practice, it is a little more complex than this.

Activity

Consider the following scenario:

Thornlea is a family-controlled, medium-sized, 'high-spec' engineering company specializing in components for the defence industry. Although profitable, recent market pressures have resulted in a new business plan, which has seen a layer of the organizational hierarchy removed. The eight supervisors are now known as 'team leaders' but have received no guidance as to whether they should be doing anything differently. When the suppliers of new computer-controlled machinery were delivering on-the-job training, there were few problems, but since they have left, supervisors, or rather the team leaders, complain that they aren't equipped to handle the problems.

Is it obvious how such training needs may best be met?

While the broad thrust of the required training at Thornlea is reasonably clear, how best to meet this need raises all kinds of questions. Should the training be completed away from work? This is not a big company – is there someone within the organization (perhaps a senior manager) capable of leading such a training effort or will external help be needed? Is the nature of the training more focused on skills or knowledge? Among the eight supervisors, are there not likely to be differences (age, experience, personality) that might need to be taken on board in any training provision? Thus there is a mix of issues and questions facing whoever assumes the responsibility for some sort of training effort to meet this need.

In Figure 7.1, a range of 'design' issues is summarized. Careful analysis of these is important, both in terms of choosing an appropriate training strategy and then planning and designing it. We would argue this is the case for formal training events as well as less traditional options including workplace learning. An initial distinction is useful. The spheres labelled 1, 2 and 3 are what we would describe as 'design principles'. Spheres 4, 5 and 6 are a number of (potentially) 'complicating factors'. At the heart of design principles are issues about purpose (for example what we hope to achieve) and harnessing our understanding of the learning process. The pressure on many organizations today means that they may well start with the complicating factors. A trainer might ask: 'How much can I spend on this?' and then work backwards. However, acknowledging a consensus among professional bodies such as the CIPD and the Institute of Training and Occupational Learning, good practice suggests that organizations should begin with the former and then address the complicating factors. This is the path we will follow. Having considered the identification of training needs in Chapter 6, we begin with purpose and objectives.

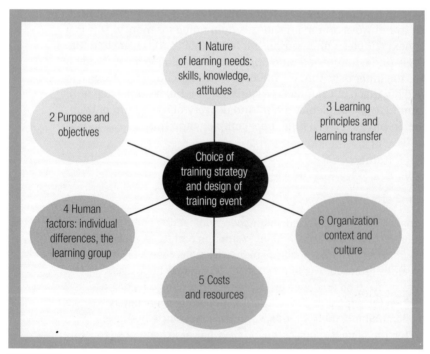

FIGURE 7.1 A training design framework

Purpose and objectives

A well-prepared statement of intent ('The purpose of this training is to … '), together with a set of unambiguous objectives, is important for three reasons:

1 It provides the link between the training needs analysis and the design and delivery of training, enabling the trainer/manager to consider which path to follow in order to achieve the end goal.

2 It reduces uncertainty and doubt on behalf of prospective trainees.

3 It offers a basis upon which evaluation can subsequently be undertaken (see also Chapter 8).

The acronym SMART offers a highly practical tool to help to determine the appropriate objectives. It stands for:

- Specific – objectives should specify what they want to achieve

- Measurable – the extent to which objectives have been met

- Achievable – are the objectives achievable and attainable?

- Realistic – are the objectives realistically achievable with the available resources?

- Time – within what time frame are objectives to be achieved?

SMART objectives are not the preserve of the training world. The example below shows how the SMART criteria have been used to formulate a training objective in the area of financial accounting, helping the trainer/manager to address design and delivery issues.

> By the end of a two-hour workshop, trainees will be able to create a profit and loss spreadsheet using Excel 2007 and utilize summation and subtraction formulae with complete accuracy.

Drawing on the work of Bloom (1956) and his development of taxonomies of learning in the areas of knowledge, skills and attitudes (see also Chapter 6), it is important to acknowledge that while it may be relatively straightforward to construct a SMART objective for a basic skill or knowledge need, this becomes more difficult for attitudes and more complex combinations of knowledge and skill. A good example is the construction of objectives for leadership training and development.

Activity

Working with a partner, visit the website of the training provider, Fenman, and look particularly at the section devoted to training objectives – www.fenman. co.uk/cat/product_info/training_objectives.pdf.

Consider the following questions:

1 What sort of words are best suited to objectives and what words are best avoided?

2 What may make the setting of SMART objectives difficult? Think, for

example, about a scenario requiring leadership training for senior managers.

3 Write a SMART objective for a student about to go on a three-month placement as part of their degree.

Learning principles and transfer of learning

The subject of learning is vast and complex, and has a huge literature. Consider for a moment the amount of learning achieved by a three-year old child, without any engagement in the processes so favoured by the institutions established as the guardians and gatekeepers of learning – schools, universities, training centres and so on.

Chapter 5 provides fuller treatment of learning theories. In this chapter, our approach to the bewildering array of avenues one could take in pursuit of 'understanding learning' is characterized by two key criteria:

- learning is central to effective training

- pragmatism.

Thus, with acknowledgement, but little more, to the body of knowledge about learning, we move to identify a set of learning principles – a set of rules or guidelines that can usefully guide the design of learning events at a practical and workable level. Two illustrations help us make this point. Skinner (1950) is known for his work with rats and pigeons. Through the judicious provision of food to 'reward' appropriate behaviour, Skinner, in effect, 'trained' pigeons to dance and play ping pong. For our purposes here, it is the principle that learning is likely to be more effective when it is reinforced through appropriate reward. Our second illustration draws on research into individual differences. One such difference might be that we learn in different ways, with different styles (Kolb, 1984; Honey and Mumford, 1992). The learning principle here is that learning is likely to be more effective when it is geared to the individual.

Thus, the psychology and sociology of learning have yielded a number of general principles that apply to most learning situations. These principles are that learning is likely to be more effective when:

- clear goals and targets are established

- it is carefully and thoughtfully sequenced and structured

- learners receive relevant feedback

- it is appropriately rewarded and reinforced

- the learner is actively involved

- it engages understanding

- it is meaningful to the individual/group in terms of their job responsibilities.

One observation on these principles might be that they are little more than common sense, or, more critically, 'they are too obvious'. However, our experience of teaching trainers over the past 20 years suggests that whatever the level of common sense and however obvious they may appear to be at first sight, they have had a rather disappointing impact on the average trainer or manager in industry. There is a further point. Taken singly, a point such as the provision of feedback may be obvious. But when taken in combination, some considerable complexity results – which is far from obvious and requires much thought and consideration. Beard and Wilson (2006) generate a helpful way to think about how trainers (and managers with responsibility for training) might engage with important learning principles in their design and delivery of training. They use the analogy of a combination lock to create a diagnostic tool. Unpicking a combination lock is complex, and much the same is the case for training and learning. Their 'Learning Combination Lock' consists of six 'dials':

1   *The learning environment* – for example training rooms, space, organizational culture

2   *Learning activities* – for example individual/collaborative, passive/active

3   *Communicating through the senses* – for example visuals, sounds

4   *Emotions in learning* – for example nervousness, antipathy, aggression

5   *Stimulating intelligence* – for example logical, spatial, interpersonal

6   *Understanding ways of learning* – for example activist, pragmatist, intuitive.

Thus, adjustment of each of the dials, depending on the situation, provides a systematic approach for considering the learning design – in effect, it enables the trainer or manager to 'unlock the door' of individual learning. (Go to www.engsc.ac.uk/resources/learning/experiential.asp for more details.)

If training has taken place away from work, how learning will be transferred back to a work situation is a further important consideration impacting on design, and should not be left to chance. Transfer of learning is a key problem in HRD (Cromwell and Kolb, 2004). It could be argued that effective transfer of learning is most likely when the learning principles are satisfied but this may not suffice. One of the most significant models of training transfer in HRD has been provided by Baldwin and Ford (1988), shown in Figure 7.2. The model identifies six linkages that are required for the achievement of the learning and retention of new knowledge and skills and their application into various activities at work (generalization) and further application over time (maintenance).

The particular nature of the work environment, the opportunities to use the learning and the level of support within the workplace to assist application from managers and others are all factors worth some consideration. Trainees might be encouraged to consider what they think might arise by way of transfer and to develop action plans accordingly. Recently, Holton et al. (2007) have developed a Learning Transfer System Inventory (LTSI) to help organizations identify the key barriers to transfer (see also Chapter 9 for details).

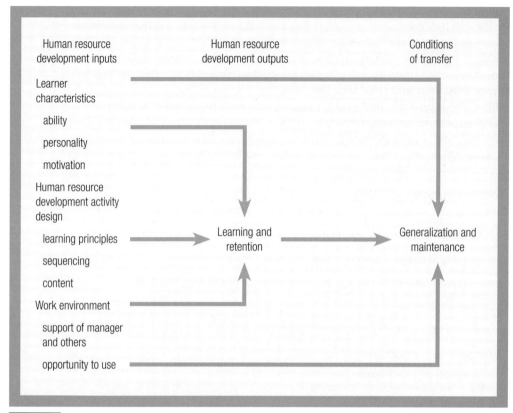

FIGURE 7.2 A model of the transfer of training

SOURCE: Adapted from Baldwin and Ford (1988)

We move now to the first of our 'complicating factors', a range of 'human' or people issues.

Human factors

It is perhaps a little unfair to regard people as a complicating factor but consider the following short case, which demonstrates why we have taken this stance.

The reluctant learner

Reflecting on the first of a two-day in-house 'effective communication' course, the two trainers consider that it has been a successful day. They felt the objectives had largely been met – apart, that is, from Joanna. From the outset, Joanna had been 'troublesome'. She arrived a little late. She interrupted proceedings several times only to make comments about the poor communication skills of certain managers in the organization. For the first group exercise after lunch, she seemed to be on another planet and was clearly all packed up and ready to leave half an hour before the scheduled finish time. The trainers resolve to have a quiet word with Joanna first thing the next morning. After some hesitancy, Joanna opens up. She feels she has been sent on the course unnecessarily. She acknowledges a clash with her boss but feels that it is him, not her, that needs training. No consultation about the course was undertaken – she simply received an email on Monday saying 'Attend on Wednesday.' To cap it all, Wednesday was Joanna's birthday.

1 What do you consider to be the main problems here?

2 Why should this have an impact on the learning process?

3 What principles of learning are involved?

The case of the reluctant learner illustrates how individual differences due to their circumstances and characteristics can cause difficulties. Knowles' work on adult learning (see, for example, Knowles and Swanson, 2005) indicates that individual differences, in terms of motivation to learn and the extent to which individuals are self-directed and 'ready to learn', are likely to be particularly relevant in relation to achieving success in any training intervention. Thinking back to Chapter 6, the way in which training needs are identified may also be an important influence in terms of motivation and readiness to learn. For example, an ambitious high performer, who has been identified as having potential for promotion and has been sent on a programme to help them achieve their aims, would arguably have a different mindset to an individual with problematic performance issues (Joanna perhaps?), who has been sent on a programme in order to address these.

There is a range of other factors, including learning styles, which we have already noted as an important principle of learning. The phrase 'I'm too old to learn' is still commonly heard and reflects two further potentially important differences. First, research evidence suggests that cognitive capabilities such as short-term memory and information processing do decline with age (Stammers and Patrick, 1975). Second, and possibly more importantly, is the individual's 'perception' that they are too old to learn, which links back to our point about an individual's learning 'disposition'. Previous experiences of learning, positive or negative, in terms of education more generally and learning at work in particular add further complexity. Buckley and Caple (2007) also suggest the importance of background and emotional disposition (including culture and social class) as factors influencing learning.

Acknowledgment and recognition of individual differences are clearly important in any consideration of how best to meet an identified training need. If training is one to one (discussed later in this chapter), there may be some real prospect of this being taken on board. But, much training takes place in a group context.

Reflective questions

1 What particular challenges might a lecturer face when teaching groups of students?

2 Are these similar for a trainer working within, for example, a chain of hotels or for a large car dealership?

Clearly a group is simply a collection of individuals and hence the differences and issues discussed above may be compounded. While there is much truth in the phrase 'know your audience', there are likely to be practical issues in terms of the amount of information available to the trainer/manager in terms of design and, critically, the extent to which individual differences can be catered for in a group situation. This said, some training needs can only really be tackled through groupwork (see also Chapter 12). Furthermore, many trainers would argue that groups can be fun to work with. If the dynamics of a group situation can be effectively harnessed by the trainer, a richer learning experience may well result.

Thus far we have considered the trainee, whether as an individual or in a group context. What about the trainer? Just as a group of trainees may reflect a complicated mix of individual differences, so might any group of trainers. These will include levels and nature of competence, nature of skills (stand up delivery versus facilitation, skills to assess and so on), motivation and orientation. Honey (2007), in an extension to his work on learning styles, notes that trainers also have 'styles' and suggests that there may be a tendency to use them as an excuse: 'I'm an activist so I work best with learners who are also activist. That's just the way I am.' Trainers who are best equipped to help diverse learners are those who:

• know their own strengths and how this translates into their approach and style

• are alert to differences among their participants

• adjust their approach style to cater for a range of different learning style preferences.

Costs and resources

From time to time we hear of stories where obscene amounts of money appear to have been spent on some training provision or seemingly bizarre events organized in the name of 'good training'. Kellaway (2000), for example, describes what she terms the 'ultimate nightmare in training programmes'. For a full week, a group of managers are transported to a training centre where they must relinquish every aspect of their ordinary lives and set up their own micro-society. Some are stripped of their belongings and labelled 'immigrants'. Others are chosen to form the 'elite' and enjoy a lavish lifestyle.

The rest are designated 'middles' and are threatened by the underclass and harassed by the elite. After several days of bitter warfare, the 'game' comes to an end and the remaining days are spent analysing what has transpired.

Reflective questions

Kellaway called this course 'The Course from Hell'.

1 Why do you think she has concerns about such a programme?

2 What might have been the rationale of the course designers?

Kellaway despairs at the expense of such provision, when the clues to improved managerial performance 'are not in simplified models of societies' but 'right under our noses'. Such an example suggests an almost unlimited HRD budget. In reality, most organizations are not like this. Resources for HRD are scarce and must be negotiated. It is not uncommon to hear of organizations cutting their budget when times are tough. This is why we refer to costs and resources as a complicating factor. Contrast the situation facing the trainer in two organizations with which the authors have close links – the Skipton Building Society, the sixth largest society in the UK, and Elite Packaging, a relatively small company that packages and distributes items to contract. The Skipton head office has a suite of comfortable, well-equipped training rooms, with state-of-the-art connections to web-based learning. In contrast, Elite Packaging, although it takes training seriously, has no dedicated training resources and must use the canteen for any group-based training sessions. So, while there may be sound reasons, in terms of learning principles, group size, learning environment and so on, to develop an intensive three-day team-building programme, with group sizes of no more than 12, some of these aspirations may have to be sacrificed in the face of budgetary constraints. At worst, for example, a company may decide that it cannot afford a tailor-made two-day interpersonal skills programme with active involvement on behalf of participants and must fall back on a generic e-learning package simply because of cost/resource constraints.

A key factor affecting the level of resources available to an HRD department will be the maturity and status of the function within the organization (see also Chapter 3) and the extent to which HRD is considered as input or a direct outcome of strategic considerations (Coleman and Keep, 2001).

Organizational context

Our final issue concerns the organizational context into which any training intervention is to be introduced, and the level of harmony and integration between learning and key aspects of organizational context, which will either help or hinder progress. This will include, crucially, the level of vertical integration between organizational strategy and HR strategy, and the extent to which HR strategies and approaches are themselves horizontally integrated and aligned to support and reinforce each other. As highlighted in Chapter 6, the role of performance management processes, and the relationship between these and learning interventions, is worthy of particular consideration. Harrison (2005) argues that one outcome of a performance management system should be to ensure continuous learning and development, as well as being a tool to assist in the identification of training needs. In other words, there is the potential for a performance management process to be a development tool in its own right. As discussed in Chapter 6, processes such as the provision of multisource feedback and appraisal can potentially add further value here. While the adoption of performance management by organizations is widespread, however, the nature of such systems varies significantly and may be a factor to consider in the selection of a particular development solution.

A further crucial aspect of context is organizational culture. Look back for a moment to the cartoon at the start of this chapter. Let's assume that the training need for some kind of teamwork is a legitimately identified need. The training implemented has clearly forced individuals to get 'upfront and personal' with members of their work team. But the boss has a problem. He is worried how others will view these kinds of techniques. One could almost hear him saying 'This isn't the sort of thing we do around here.' The practice may conflict with the values and beliefs that characterize the workplace or wider organization. This is not the place to discuss organizational culture in depth, suffice it to say that organizational culture can be the vital link between learners, the learning content and the transfer of learning into the workplace. Of course, there is a tension here. As noted by Swart et al. (2004), learning has a critical role to play in the development of organizational culture, yet organizational values, defence routines and taken-for-granted ways of working can provide real impediments and barriers to new learning. A paradox may result: 'Because of the way this organization learns, it cannot learn' (see also Chapter 9).

In sum, organizational context provides a crucial backdrop to the success of any training intervention. A critical analysis at an early stage, to identify barriers and enablers within the reality of the work situation, that is, where the training ultimately needs to be applied, will be important in influencing choice and ultimately success. By identifying and harnessing 'enablers', such as senior management support or a motivated body of line managers, the chances of successful learning can be maximized. In contrast, the identification of problems and barriers at an early stage allows these to be acknowledged and mediated against.

The discussion above presents a complex web of factors to be considered when deciding which particular learning intervention is best suited to addressing a particular learning need, and the subsequent planning and design. It is important to recognize that these factors will not all be of equal weight in any given situation, and that the specific context surrounding a learning need, and the priorities within this, will be of key importance. What is really driving investment in a particular training programme?

Reflective question

Think back to the case of Harvey Nichols in HRD in Practice 7.1.

Which of the factors explored above, and summarized in Figure 7.1, were particularly important in influencing the design of the learning programmes chosen?

Training and learning methods

We turn now to how these various design issues can be acknowledged, addressed and utilized in the delivery of training and learning. We seek to provide an overview of the broad range of learning solutions, many of which can be creatively blended together to provide bespoke solutions to meet individual, team and organizational needs.

In providing an overview of the options available, it is worth noting that these have been categorized by many different authors according to different criteria. Marchington and Wilkinson (1996) aim to provide a framework to assist in the analysis of learning methods, and differentiate according to two main criteria:

1 the extent to which methods are individually or group based

2 the extent to which they are self-directed and participative (andragogical) or have high levels of control by tutors, trainers and other experts (pedagogical).

These are represented visually as two axes, shown in Figure 7.3, and you are invited to position methods within the diagram.

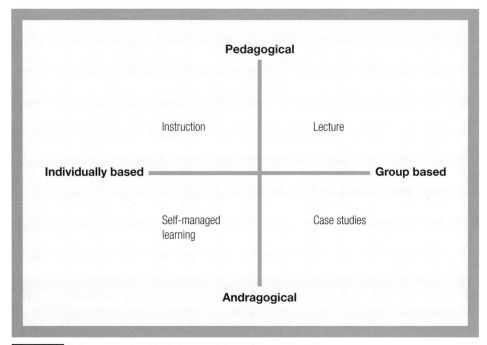

FIGURE 7.3 A framework of training and learning methods

SOURCE: Adapted from Marchington and Wilkinson (1996)

Focusing on the issue of control, Hackett (2003) provides an analysis of the extent to which training methods are trainer or learner centred and concludes that three main categories exist:

1 *Training-centred methods* such as the lecture, which has the obvious advantage of high levels of control by the trainer over content and pace of delivery.

2 *Learner-centred methods* such as self-development questionnaires and learning logs, which hand over this control, to a greater or lesser extent, to the learner.

3 *Coaching*, which Hackett claims is the only method to allow a 'learning partnership' to develop between trainer and learner.

No categorization of methods is perfect. Our approach draws on Mumford's (1997) review of methods in terms of their relationship to work. We suggest two broad categories of options, off the job and integrated, considering each method in terms of how it is distinct from, or integrated with, the actual performance of work-related tasks:

- *Off-the-job learning options:* lectures, discussions, case studies, role plays, business games, group dynamics, e-learning and off-the-job skill instruction. These methods tend to be constructed purely for the purpose of learning, rather than to achieve a task or workplace activity. They may be delivered either internally or externally. They include methods that may be delivered as part of a larger programme or course, or as a stand-alone option. The focus tends to be trainer centred rather than learner centred. Table 7.1 has more details, including the strengths and weaknesses of each option.

- *Integrated learning methods:* on-the-job training, coaching, shadowing, mentoring, exercise/project work, action learning, job rotation and secondment. These methods combine a concern for learning with the performance of tasks/workplace activities. They tend to enlist the support of 'helpers' to aid in the learning process, and are heavily dependent on the appropriate learning climate for success. They tend to be learner centred with the opportunity for recognition of individual needs, and based on experiential learning, harnessing the emotions and senses as well as cognitive capabilities. Table 7.2 has more details, including the strengths and weaknesses of each option.

As noted at the start of Chapter 6, the CIPD defines training as 'an instructor led, content based intervention, leading to desired changes in behaviour' and learning as 'a self directed, work-based process, leading to increased adaptive potential' (Sloman, 2005). According to this, the off-the-job learning options would mostly be considered as 'training', and the integrated options as 'learning'.

TABLE 7.1 Off-the-job methods

Method	Description	Benefits and strengths	Problems/points to watch
Lecture	A structured talk or presentation to convey required information, for example product knowledge, new policy/procedure	Suitable for large audiences. A cost-effective way of communicating key information. Sequence and structure can be carefully thought through. Trainer centred, with high degree of control over content	Limited opportunity for participation – communication tends to be one way, although questions may be usefully integrated. Ability of participants to assimilate and understand material may not extend much beyond 30 minutes. Heavily dependent on the quality of the delivery

Method	Description	Benefits and strengths	Problems/points to watch
Discussion	Free exchange of information and ideas, but working to a clear brief provided by the trainer, for example a discussion of barriers to effective internal communications	Seeks involvement of the trainee. Suitable where subject matter involves opinion, 'grey' areas. Also when attitudes need to be addressed. Good for getting engagement as regards application of learning and feedback to trainer	Discussions often stray off the point. Superficial discussion may be unhelpful, vague and woolly. Control issues need careful thought by trainer. Some degree of prior knowledge may be required to make discussion useful rather than purely opinion based
Case study	Presentation of scenario (real or fictitious) describing organizational practice and behaviour. Trainees are asked to analyse the documented problem and/or reflect on described practice, for example an unfair dismissal case, a financial problem, departmental reorganization	Seeks involvement of the trainee. Suitable where a careful look at the problem or set of circumstances, free from pressures of an actual event, is beneficial. Provides opportunities for exchange of ideas and encourages consideration of alternative solutions. Tests trainees' ability to apply theory to practice.Can provide examples of organizational good practice	Decisions taken in case study settings are removed from the reality of decision making. Unrealistic scenarios may predominate. Quality of debrief crucial for effectiveness. Overuse can result in trainees treating as a 'mechanistic' exercise
Role play	Trainees enact a role they may have to play at work, for example interviewing a customer or negotiating an agreement. Other trainees, or actors, may be employed to play the role of significant others to enhance credibility	Involves the trainee. Good for training where suitable behaviour needs practising. Trainee can practise, in a 'safe' environment, and receive personal feedback. Role plays that are videoed offer a particularly valuable resource for reflection and managing feedback	Some trainees may be fearful/embarrassed. Unreal situations may encourage atypical behaviours unlikely to be seen in reality. Requires clear purpose, sound briefs and good facilitation on behalf of trainer. Can be time-consuming and resource demanding
Business game	Trainees manage a range of organizational issues or problems on the basis of information given to them. Outcomes of decisions are fed back to trainees to influence subsequent decision making. Sophisticated games may be computer assisted	Involves trainees, practically, in dealing with management problems. Simulation of a real-life problem or scenario aids transfer of learning. Enables theory to be put into practice and consequences reflected upon	Limited or unreal outcomes from decisions made may undermine value of method. May result in trainee disengagement. Extent to which 'game' reflects reality is critical

Method	Description	Benefits and strengths	Problems/points to watch
Group dynamics	Trainees are put into groups to carry out a simulated exercise and behaviour is examined, for example group decision making, intergroup conflict, intragroup communication	Potentially powerful way to understand self and impact of self on others and vice versa. Increases insight and understanding of working with other people and getting work done through other people	Learning can be hurtful as well as helpful – the facilitator's role is critical in managing this. High levels of skills required on behalf of the facilitators. Danger of trainees treating exercises as just a bit of fun and/or opting out. Invariably time-consuming and resource demanding
E-learning	Learning is delivered through the internet or intranet	Can effectively overcome time, place, pace issues and barriers. Good for material that can be broken down into distinct blocks and is not subject to interpretation or change. Sophisticated technological applications enable high risk training to be undertaken safely and effectively, for example flight simulation. Usefully used as part of blended solutions	Much e-learning is little more than electronic page turning. May not be fit for purpose. Can isolate trainees. To cope effectively with skills requires sophisticated applications that are expensive. Learner support should not be ignored
Off-the-job skill instruction	A skill is taught by explanation, demonstration and practice, for example how to operate a computer	Most suitable for a wide range of psychomotor skills. Particularly good where task analysis reveals potential difficulties or blocks to achieving mastery	Part or whole approach may cause trainer difficulty re most appropriate strategy. Trainee likely to experience difficulty if asked to absorb large chunks of information or procedures before opportunity for practice. A good employee does not necessarily make a good instructor

TABLE 7.2 Integrated methods

Method	Description	Benefits and strengths	Problems/points to watch
On-the-job training	Sometimes referred to as 'sitting by Nellie'. Training is undertaken at the workplace, often involving demonstration followed by supervised practice. Often used for semi-skilled jobs but potential for developing individual skills in all types of work	Can effectively integrate work and learning. Realistic and immediate. Transfer problems minimized	Potential to learn good habits as well as bad. Choice of 'Nellie' is critical. To do well requires planning and an understanding of trainee/ learner

Method	Description	Benefits and strengths	Problems/points to watch
Coaching	An individual meets a coach on a one-to-one basis to work on a range of work-related issues, some of which may also include personal factors. Distinct from mentoring with its focus on specific behavioural change and/or performance improvement, for example customer service telephone training, leadership development	Targets individual needs. Enables trainee to practise skills in real situations under supervision and monitoring. Good for situations where trainee may be experiencing difficulties or problems. Potentially good role for line manager to adopt. Cost-effective and promotes devolvement of learning responsibility. Facilitates learning transfer	Not a substitute for basic skills and knowledge. Can be time-consuming and resource demanding. Frequently line mangers require coaching skills, so further resources are required. Trainees can become overdependent on coach. An appropriate (open) work culture/learning climate will enhance likelihood of success
Shadowing	Trainees observe a skilled, experienced practitioner at work, and discuss their perceptions with the practitioner. Process should require shadow to reflect on experience	Integrates work and learning. Enables trainee to witness first hand real day-to-day jobs and tasks being performed. Promotes wider participation in learning effort beyond HRD	Tends to be time-consuming and can slow down the person being shadowed. Real work can be mundane and boring, so the learning may be mundane and boring. Requires some structure, for example building in regular reflection and review
Mentoring	An appointed mentor supports and encourages trainee to manage their own personal development. The mentor, usually a senior professional or manager, helps the mentee find the right direction and developmental solutions to career and other issues	Develops the individual rather than training them. Particularly suitable for aspects of career development. Enables person to question assumptions, shift mental context. Good for addressing attitudes and feelings as regards work problems, issues and so on. Can assist individual to address organizational politics	Not appropriate for helping to enhance specific skills re performance. Time-consuming and resource demanding. Best over a longish period. Good mentors are hard to find. Mentoring relationships can be difficult and uneasy. Important that a mentor understands self before they mentor others
Exercise/ project	Trainees asked to undertake a particular work-related task leading to a required outcome, for example computerizing client records or setting up a staff absence control system	Suitable for any situation where trainee might benefit from practice following knowledge and theory input. Can be individual or group based. Much scope for the imaginative trainer to design appropriate and challenging exercises to test and further develop trainees' capabilities	Unrealistic exercises risk disengagement. Should be challenging but attainable. Design critical to ensure sufficient focus on learning rather than just on task

Method	Description	Benefits and strengths	Problems/points to watch
Action learning	Individuals work in groups, addressing real organizational problems. Emphasizes the importance of crucial questioning and reflection in learning. Can be project based	Integrates work and learning. Maximizes opportunities for experiential and social learning. Harnesses the power of critical reflection and learning as a force for individual and organizational change	If participants do not have a genuine organizational problem to focus on, initiatives may fail. Benefits from strong facilitation. Needs champions and sponsors within the organization for success
Job rotation	Moving around a number of jobs to build experience across job roles. Often a feature of graduate training programmes	Provides broad experience and awareness of aspects of a number of roles in a shorter period of time than via natural progression. Should broaden perspective and outlook. Chance to develop new skills, knowledge and networks	May prove frustrating, as potentially insufficient time to deliver in roles experienced. Resource hungry due to learning curves. Consistency of learning support via different line managers may vary
Secondment	Trainee spends a substantial period of time (typically 3–12 months) in a different job or with different responsibilities from normal. No special arrangements – just normal work	Provides experience of a new role and environment. Opportunities to develop new knowledge, skills, outlook and networks	Potential problems may arise in identifying appropriate job or role. Responsibility for learning and critical reflection lie solely with individual. Tensions may arise on resumption of old role

Activity

Form a group of four. It is likely that you will be familiar with at least some of the methods outlined in Tables 7.1 and 7.2. Think about the different methods you have experienced within university and outside. Do you rate some as more effective than others? Why? Discuss your findings.

Trends and issues

The continued popularity of traditional 'off-the-job' provision

Despite the promotion of creative, more learner-centred and work-based options by HR theorists and indeed the CIPD, respondents to the CIPD (2007a) *Learning and Development Survey* still rated formal training courses as one of the most effective methods of learning, with instructor-led, off-the-job training being one of the most frequently used methods. Bearing in mind that the targeted respondents were those who hold roles as learning, training and development managers, a significant gap between rhetoric and reality is suggested. Commenting on the adoption of particular methods in his critique of the survey, Wain (2007, p. 23) notes that 'irrespective of claims to the contrary, formal and traditional approaches remain highly significant in learning and development practice'.

So why do traditional methods remain so popular? It is important, first, to recognize that such approaches do have value, and the way they are designed, adopted and applied can be specifically tailored to meet organizational needs. The fact that a learning solution is conducted away from the job itself can be a real advantage. This is well illustrated in the case of role play, often used as a way of practising skills in a safe environment where it is important for the individual and the organization that mistakes are not made in reality, because of the scale or serious nature of potential negative consequences. Activities such as union negotiations and interviewing can fall into this category, as can work involving more vulnerable groups, with role play being used within criminal justice training programmes. Companies such as BT and HBOS have used professional actors in role-playing situations to provide additional realism and credibility to the training.

Nonetheless, it is somewhat puzzling that in the face of a plethora of alternative methods, many of which may well be more appropriate to meet the identified need, the traditional off-the-job course remains so popular. One explanation may lie in the approach organizations take to learning and development generally, and the nature of training needs identified and invested in. Drawing on Fonda and Hayes' (1986) typology where learning and development is not well developed within an organization and training needs are identified in an ad hoc way to meet immediate needs – for example the provision of health and safety training in response to a number of accidents, or customer care training in response to a number of complaints – traditional training packages may provide quick, cheap, easy and accessible ways of meeting those needs, and evidence that such needs have been addressed. This latter point reflects the pressure many organizations face to provide simple measures of their training effort. Annual reports regularly refer to an average number of 'training days' received by employees.

The more complex and advanced levels of skills needed on the part of trainers/facilitators to deliver alternative options may also play a part, as may the need to 'fit' learning solutions within the broader learning climate and culture within organizations. In other words, it may be indicative of a lack of capability and imagination on the part of the HR and training and development staff within them. Such a weakness is likely to be compounded if such staff perceive obstacles and barriers in trying to 'sell' new approaches to senior managers often steeped in traditional training practice.

Activity

In groups of three, visit the following website devoted to experiential learning – www.learningandteaching.info/learning/experience.htm.

Using material from this website, critically assess how the experiential learning cycle might be used as a basis for reducing the reliance on traditional off-the-job training.

The rise of e-learning

While the off-the-job course remains popular, there has been a shift in exactly how such provision is delivered. The ability to harness IT as a delivery tool in training and learning has witnessed considerable growth in recent years. E-learning and web-based training materials have been extensively adopted by a wide range of organizations including the education sector itself. Chapter 14 discusses this whole field in more depth. Here it is appropriate to note two key points.

First, some organizations have acted in significant ways on the basis of the enormous potential they see in such delivery. Consider the examples in HRD in Practice 7.2.

Three examples of e-learning

Yorkshire Bank

The National Australia Group, Europe, of which the Yorkshire Bank is a part, has introduced a 'Learning Campus' containing more than 30 modules of e-learning material covering the areas of legislative and compliance training. While it estimated an approximate cost of £10.7m per year had the material been delivered via workshops, delivery via the e-learning platform allowed the training to reach all staff in the UK at an estimated total spend of £230,000 (£2 per employee).

Hilton Hotels

Hilton Hotels has a 'Hilton University' website (www.hiltonuniversity.com). This states: 'E-learning is our innovative web-based training system that lets you choose what, where and when you learn.' According to the website, between 2002 and 2005, nearly 10,000 Hilton people completed over 100,000 e-learning programmes and 93% of these learners said they would recommend this form of learning to their friends and colleagues. The strongest 'likes' were the chance to learn at a time, place and speed that suited the learner.

Learn Direct

Learn Direct was developed by the University for Industry, with a remit from the UK government to provide high-quality, post-16 learning, which:

- Reaches those with few or no skills and qualifications who are unlikely to participate in traditional forms of learning
- Equips people with the skills they need for employability, thereby strengthening the skills of the workforce and increasing productivity
- Is delivered innovatively through the use of new technologies.

  According to its website (www.learndirect.co.uk), Learn Direct offers around 500 different courses covering a range of subjects, including management, IT, skills for life and languages, at all levels. More than three-quarters of the training courses are available online.

The second point to note is that despite the apparently glowing testimony of the participants on the Hilton Hotel's e-learning programmes, its overall effectiveness as a training method is far from proven. A key factor here may be the extent to which a lot of e-learning fails to address the basic principles of learning discussed earlier in this chapter. In other words, much e-learning can be little more than electronic page turning – not interactive and not geared to the needs of the individual trainee or learner (see, for example, Tynjala and Hakkinen, 2005; Gibb, 2008; also see Chapter 14).

Flavour of the month: coaching and mentoring?

Traditionally viewed as a relatively directive way of improving performance of a work-related task, the field of coaching has expanded considerably to address longer term work and career development, structured and organic approaches. Defined by the CIPD as 'an activity where an individual meets with a coach on a one-to-one basis to work on a range of work-related issues, some of which may also include personal factors' (Knights and Poppleton, 2007, p. 2), the approach taken to coaching in organizations may vary greatly. A more traditional approach would be seen in a call centre environment such as BT where coaching on a one-to-one basis to improve call handling skills on the part of customer service advisers. In contrast, the fund manager M&G offers coaching as part of its talent management strategy, while the coaching offer at Orange is focused on career development. Here individuals are encouraged to nominate themselves for the coaching programme, with participants receiving three 90-minute sessions with an internal career coach (CIPD, 2007b). Whatever the aims, focus and design of a coaching initiative, the skills of the coach and climate in which the coaching is taking place will be key to its success.

Coaching skills are also potentially valuable within a mentoring relationship, although the focus will be different, with the strength of mentoring being its long-term holistic approach. Clutterbuck and Klasen (2002, p. 16) believe that:

> mentoring derives its immense effectiveness in employee learning and development from being an integrated method that flexibly combines elements of the four other one to one development approaches, coaching, counselling, networking/facilitation and guardianship.

Often used to champion the needs of minority groups, its value to both mentors and mentees can be considerable. Cole (2005) discusses the case of a targeted mentoring programme introduced for black and minority ethnic health service employees. The scheme purports to offer mutual benefits, equipping the mentee to move up the NHS ladder and the mentor with a better understanding of the perspectives of ethnic minorities. Cole relates the experience of one mentee, Yvonne Coghill, who likened the mentoring to 'a laying on of hands' and reported that the impact on her self-confidence was 'transformational'. In another innovative initiative, Hampshire Constabulary has developed a gay mentoring scheme to help staff develop their careers. It reported that 90% of 2007 trainees opted for a mentor, with participants able to select a gay mentor if preferred (CIPD, 2008).

The best of both worlds: a blended approach?

Although loosely configured into a classification of 'off-the-job' and 'integrated' methods, this chapter has considered a wide range of potential training and learning methods. Of course, the most effective programmes tend to be those based on a sound analysis of learning needs and detailed consideration of the factors discussed earlier in the chapter. From this basis, effective solutions may well creatively combine a number of methods (see HRD in Practice 7.3). This is seen by the number of winners of the national training awards who have chosen to use some type of blended approach. (The website www.nationaltrainingawards.com/ gives details of previous winners and the rationale underpinning the programmes.)

HRD in Practice 7.3

The Bupa Personal Best programme

The Bupa care homes learning programme Personal Best is a good example of an organization using a blended approach to meet learning needs and enable its employees to 'go the extra mile' in terms of meeting the needs of residents. It was the overall winner of the CIPD People Management Award 2006. The programme delivered learning in the care homes themselves, using a modular approach, which included experiential learning, interviewing care home residents to develop a greater understanding and appreciation of their needs, and the development of individual action plans to specify actions to be taken in the future. One specific activity reported in *People Management* (Phillips, 2006) involved staff putting themselves in the place of residents, being lifted mechanically into bed and fed pureed food to learn for themselves what these experiences felt like. A series of customer service training modules has been developed to complement the Personal Best programme, and financial results were reported as being up 25% on the previous year.

Engaging 'hard to reach' groups

It is generally acknowledged that some methods of learning potentially act as barriers to some disenfranchised groups, who may be put off by the use of methods they associate with previous negative experiences. This is illustrated by the winner of the National Training Award 2005, the Lighthouse Project (www.thelighthouseproject.co.uk/), and which provides a good example of how the unique and individual nature of training needs will influence the methods chosen. This project was established in 1997 to meet the needs of severely disadvantaged groups, especially single parents, teenagers living alone and young families heavily dependent on benefits. Such groups lack basic skills and tend to be viewed as hard to reach and engage (see also Leitch, 2006). The Lighthouse Project identified a key reason as the inappropriate nature of the provision being offered, arguing for a more flexible and creative approach. It attempted, unsuccessfully, to source appropriate courses from local colleges, and then decided to design its own approach. This involved the delivery of the 'First Steps' programme in each of the project's four centres in the West Midlands. A number of sessions were delivered and adapted to meet individual needs, with the focus on 'achievement' providing the core of the programme. Participants were assessed continually by informal observation by tutors, and computer-generated evidence provided evidence of learning in literacy and numeracy, thus assisting in a level of accreditation towards a qualification.

Summary

- Effective and 'fit for purpose' training and learning require careful and thoughtful translation of identified needs into learning plans.

- This process is aided by the recognition of a range of factors, including the purpose and objectives of any training or learning intervention, an understanding of how learning principles can maximize effective learning, the characteristics of the learner or group of trainees, and the constraints of limited resources and organization context.

- Specific objectives, which can be clearly communicated and are measurable, avoid ambiguity and assist in designing fit for purpose training activity.

- Learning principles that can usefully be considered in the design of training or learning include:

  - learning is likely to be more effective when relevant feedback is provided

  - learning is likely to be more effective when the learner is actively involved.

- Fit for purpose training design can be considered as analogous to a combination lock – in the sense of good design 'unlocking' the door to individual learning.

- Groups of trainees, which reflect considerable individual differences, for example motivation, levels of experience, personality, can be problematic if available resources constrain the extent to which training can be 'tailored'.

- Training that is at odds with the culture of the organization will cause tensions and requires careful management.

- While resource constraints will influence what can be done in practice, a wide range of methods and practice is available to the trainer.

- A useful distinction is that between off-the-job learning options (including case studies, role play, business games) and integrated learning methods (including 'sitting by Nellie', action learning, coaching and mentoring).

- There is rarely one 'best' method. All methods have different strengths and weaknesses; the key is to match method(s) with needs.

- While a majority of organizations continue to make heavy use of off-the-job methods, recent years have seen methods such e-learning, coaching and mentoring rise in popularity.

- Blended learning, involving appropriate combinations of methods, is increasingly seen as the way forward, as this will enable more of the critical design factors to be addressed. Imaginative use of blended learning may well offer opportunities to meet the challenges of engaging 'hard to reach' or disenfranchised learners.

Discussion questions

1 What are three characteristics of SMART objectives? Why might setting objectives for interpersonal skills training be more difficult than for a range of PC training (Excel, Word and so on)?

2 What is a principle of learning? How can learning principles be integrated into the effective design of training or learning interventions? Which principles of learning are most relevant to you in your studies at university?

3 How might the notion of the 'integration of work and learning' be used to differentiate between different methods of training or learning?

4 What are two strengths and two weaknesses of e-learning?

5 Why are methods such as coaching and mentoring increasingly popular?

6 What is blended learning? Identify a training need where a blended learning solution might be most appropriate.

Further reading

Buckley, R. and Caple, J. (2007) *The Theory and Practice of Training*, 5th edn, London, Kogan Page.

Knowles, A. and Swanson, R.A. (2005) *The Adult Learner*, 6th edn, Burlington, MA, Elsevier.

Pettinger, R. (2002) *Mastering Employee Development*, Basingstoke, Palgrave – now Palgrave Macmillan.

Reid, M., Barrington, H. and Brown, M. (2004) *Human Resource Development: Beyond Training Interventions*, 7th edn, London, CIPD.

Sloman, M. (2005) *Training to Learning: Change Agenda*, London, CIPD.

References

Baldwin, T. and Ford, J.K. (1988) Transfer of training: a review and directions for future research, *Personnel Psychology*, **41**(1): 63–105.

Beard, C. and Wilson, J.P. (2006) *Experiential Learning: A Best Practice Handbook for Educators and Trainers*, London, Kogan Page.

Bloom, B.S. (ed.) (1956) *Taxonomy of Educational Objectives: The Classification of Educational Goals*, Handbook I, *Cognitive Domain*, New York, McKay.

Buckley, R. and Caple, J. (2007) *The Theory and Practice of Training*, 5th edn, London, Kogan Page.

CIPD (Chartered Institute of Personnel and Development) (2007a) *Learning and Development Survey*, London, CIPD.

CIPD (Chartered Institute of Personnel and Development) (2007b) 'What is on the job training?', fact sheet, London, CIPD.

CIPD (Chartered Institute of Personnel and Development) (2008) Police constabulary extends its gay mentoring scheme, *People Management*, **14**(7): 12.

Clutterbuck, D. and Klasen, N. (2002) *Implementing Mentoring Schemes*, Oxford, Butterworth Heinemann.

Cole, A. (2005) Minority support, *People Management*, **11**(19): 16–17.

Coleman, S. and Keep, E. (2001) *Background Literature Review for PIU Project on Workforce Development*, London, Cabinet Office.

Cromwell, S.E. and Kolb, J.A. (2004) An examination of work-environment support factors affecting transfer of supervisory skills training in the workplace, *Human Resource Development Quarterly*, **15**: 449–71.

Fonda, N. and Hayes, M. (1986) Is more training really necessary? *Personnel Management*.

Gibb, S. (2008) *Human Resource Development*, 2nd edn, Basingstoke, Palgrave Macmillan.

Hackett, P. (2003) *Training Practice*, London, CIPD.

Harrison, R. (2005) *Learning and Development*, London, CIPD.

Holton, E.F., Bates, R.A., Bookter, A.I. and Yamkovenko, V.B. (2007) Convergent and divergent validity of the learning transfer system inventory, *Human Resource Development Quarterly*, **18**(3): 385–419.

Honey, P. (2007) *The Trainer Styles Questionnaire*, Maidenhead, P. Honey.

Honey, P. and Mumford, A. (1992) *The Manual of Learning Styles*, Maidenhead, P. Honey.

Kellaway, L. (2000) *Sense and Nonsense in the Office*, London, FT/Prentice Hall.

Knights, A. and Poppleton, A. (2007) *Research Insight: Coaching in Organizations*, London, CIPD.

Knowles, A. and Swanson, R.A. (2005) *The Adult Learner*, 6th edn, Burlington, MA, Elsevier.

Kolb, D.A. (1984) *Experiential Learning: Experience as the Source of Learning and Development*, Englewood Cliffs, NJ, Prentice Hall.

Leitch, S. (2006) *Prosperity for all in the Global Economy: World Class Skills*, London, HM Treasury.

LSC (Learning and Skills Council) (2008) *National Employers Skills Survey 2007: Main Report*, London, LSC.

Marchington, M. and Wilkinson, A. (1996) *Core Personnel and Development*, London, IPD.

Mumford, A. (1997) *How to Choose the Right Development Method*, Maidenhead, P. Honey.

Phillips, L. (2006) BUPA stars, *People Management*, **12**(22): 30–3.

Skinner, B.F. (1950) Are theories of learning necessary?, *Psychological Review*, **57**: 193–216.

Sloman, M. (2005) *Training to Learning: Change Agenda*, London, CIPD.

Stammers, R. and Patrick, J. (1975) *The Psychology of Training*, London, Methuen.

Swart, J., Mann, C., Brown, S. and Price, A. (2004) *Human Resource Development: Strategy and Tactics*, Oxford, Butterworth Heinemann.

Tynjala, P. and Hakkinen, P. (2005) E-learning at work: theoretical underpinnings and pedagogical challenges, *Journal of Workplace Learning*, **17**(5/6): 318–36.

Wain, D. (2007) *Lies, Damned Lies and a few Home Truths: Reflections on the 2007 Learning and Development Survey*, London, CIPD.

Evaluation of HRD

8

David Devins and Joanna Smith

Chapter learning outcomes

After studying this chapter, you should be able to:

- Explain the importance of evaluation in HRD
- Understand the key ideas and perspectives relating to evaluation
- Explain how evaluation is connected to HRD policy
- Assess various methods of evaluating HRD
- Examine the future direction of HRD evaluation

Chapter outline

Introduction

Evaluation is a relatively young discipline, which has its roots in the work of Campbell and Stanley (1963), who were responsible for popularizing the distinction between experimental and quasi-experimental design. Over the years, the discipline has evolved and developed, and it is applied to many policies and practices, organizations, teams and individuals. It forms the core of many strategic planning processes, organizational development, HRD and individual development practices. In fact, some people suggest that there is very little that cannot be evaluated. One guru, when describing the scope of what can be evaluated, declared: '"Everything". One can begin at the beginning of a dictionary and go through to the end, and every noun, common or proper, calls to mind a context in which evaluation would be appropriate' (Scriven, 1980, p. 4). While cautioning against this all-embracing view, it is clear that evaluation of one form or another has a key role to play in the field of HRD at a range of levels – national, sectoral, organizational, divisional, team and individual – along with a wide range of strategic, tactical and operational activities.

A key question to ask is: Why do evaluation? Sometimes, it is because we have to – there is a contractual obligation to undertake an evaluation. It is often the case that someone, somewhere has provided some resources and they want to know what their money has been spent on, if it has made a difference, or if it could have been spent more wisely elsewhere. Demonstrating the impact of an HRD intervention is an important part of reinforcing its value and utility. Equally, evaluation may be done because there is a wish to learn from experience and improve the design of a programme, policies or practices. We may want to involve others in reflecting on the process or performance of an intervention to build capacity and share understanding. Clearly there are many reasons why we should evaluate; however, evaluation is often lacking or may be done as an afterthought and the gains to be had from a well-designed and implemented evaluation will not be realized.

Reflective questions

1 In your experience, what type of things do you evaluate?

2 Why do you do it?

3 How do you do it?

For further information about the evaluation community, see the UK's Evaluation Society – www.evaluation.org.uk/ – or the European Evaluation Society – www.europeanevaluation.org/.

Theoretical perspectives

There is no single universally accepted definition of the term 'evaluation', as the following selected quotes from the burgeoning evaluation literature illustrate:

The process of determining the merit, worth or value of something or the product of that process. (Scriven, 1991, p. 139)

Evaluation is the systematic application of social research procedures for assessing the conceptualization, design, implementation and utility of social intervention programmes. (Rossi and Freeman, 1993, p. 5)

Evaluation is the systematic assessment of the operation and/or outcomes of a programme or policy, compared to a set of explicit or implicit standards as a means of contributing to the improvement of social policy. (Weiss, 1998, p. 4)

The definitions highlight some common themes associated with evaluation, emphasizing:

1 systematic approaches

2 some 'thing' (processes, projects, programmes or policies)

3 outcomes and impact

4 utility.

In this chapter, 'evaluation' is used as a general term that encompasses these attributes, which, as we will see, can be applied to a variety of aspects of HRD.

It should be noted, however, that there is a wide range of types of evaluation – ex ante, summative, formative, comprehensive evaluation, theory-driven evaluation, utilization focused evaluation and meta-evaluation, to name but a few. The following key terms highlight the focus of the different approaches:

- *Ex ante evaluation:* at the start of the project/programme (also known as formative)

- *Interim evaluation:* during the project/programme (formative and summative)

- *Ex post evaluation:* at the end of the programme (summative).

Adopting a particular approach to evaluation often means adopting a particular approach to research and a particular view of the world, which has, at its extremes, the notions of positivism underpinned by an experimental approach and relativism underpinned by a constructivist approach.

From its roots in positivism ...

Underpinning much evaluation in the early days is the logic of experimentation. For more than 30 years, policy trials and rigorous social experiments have been a primary method of evaluating potential new policies, particularly in the USA, in advance of widespread policy implementation. These approaches generally involve the random assignment of individuals to treatment and control groups so that the impact of a policy intervention may be assessed. This approach is widely acknowledged as the 'gold standard' in terms of evaluation design. At its simplest, the logic of experimentation underpinning this approach involves a four-stage process:

1 Randomly assign research subjects to two or more matched groups

2 Apply a treatment (or in this case a policy instrument) to one group and not the other

3   Measure both groups before and after the treatment of one

4   Compare the changes in the treated and untreated groups.

The two groups are studied before and after the experimental treatment and at the same points in time, to allow comparisons and conclusions to be drawn about the effect of the intervention (see Figure 8.1). In this way, exogenous or confounding factors that might otherwise influence outcomes ought to be randomly distributed between the treatment and control group. As long as the samples in each group are large enough, differences in the outcomes of the two groups can be attributed to the 'treatment'.

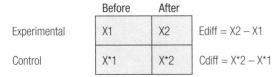

	Before	After	
Experimental	X1	X2	Ediff = X2 – X1
Control	X*1	X*2	Cdiff = X*2 – X*1

Effect of intervention = difference between Ediff and Cdiff

FIGURE 8.1 Classic experimental design

SOURCE: de Vaus (1993, p. 35)

The core element of this approach is the 'theory of causation'. It is argued that since the groups are randomly matched to begin with, the only difference between them is the application of the programme, and it is therefore only the treatment that can be responsible for the difference in outcomes. While one cannot observe causation, it has to be inferred from the repeated succession of one event by another. In a classic analysis, a causal relationship exists if:

•   the cause preceded the effect

•   the cause was related to the effect

•   we can find no plausible alternative explanation for the effect other than the cause.

Perhaps importantly in the field of policy evaluation, experimental design does not explain why an effect takes place nor does it seek to understand why an intervention works or does not work (Pawson and Tilley, 1997). The unique strength of experimentation is in describing the consequences attributable to deliberately varying a treatment (that is, 'causal description'). In contrast, experiments do less well in clarifying the mechanisms through which, and the conditions under which, causal relationships hold (that is, 'causal explanation'). Causal explanation is an important route to the generalization of causal descriptions, because it identifies which features of the causal relationship are essential to transfer to other situations, an outcome of considerable interest to policy planners. What experiments do best is improve causal descriptions; they do less well at explaining causal relationships. The experimental method does not set out to explain why an intervention works, and the experimental paradigm has often struggled to deliver clear answers to the questions posed by policy planners and decision makers in terms of 'what works' – the programmes, projects or actions taken to develop human capital. To understand why there is an inconsistency of outcomes, different questions need to be asked in terms of 'why' or 'how' the processes have affected behaviours.

1 Why would you use a scientific approach?

2 Can you find a good example? (Google it.)

3 What value does it have in the HRD context?

... to constructivism

In the 1970s, many social science disciplines were gripped by the debate on positivism, and witnessed the rise of oppositional perspectives known variously as 'interpretative', 'phenomenological' or 'hermeneutical', for example. This coincided with a move towards the usefulness of evaluation as a means of informing decisions or, most optimistically, enlightening decision makers and those involved in the development and implementation of policies and programmes (Weiss, 1980). Together, the 'oppositional' perspectives and the pragmatic approach to evaluation led to an approach referred to as 'constructivism' (or sometimes 'constructionism').[1] The constructivist paradigm has its roots in anthropological traditions. Instead of focusing on explaining, this paradigm focuses on understanding the phenomenon being studied through ongoing and in-depth contact and relationships with those involved. Relying on qualitative data and rich descriptions, the constructivists' purpose is 'the collection of holistic world views, intact belief systems and complex inner psychic and interpersonal states' (Maxwell and Lincoln, 1990, p. 508). In other words, who are the people involved in the programme and what do the experiences mean to them?

While there are a number of approaches to social constructivism (Gergen, 1985, 1994; Pearce, 1992; Shotter 1993; Burr 1995), the key features are as follows:

- The use of language, organized into conversations, discourses, narratives, and stories, provides the means by which we come to experience our world and construct 'reality'. Thus language, as a social resource, has a central role in the making of phenomena that may come to be accepted as real.

- Meanings are made through a relational process between people that become embedded into ongoing ways of talking, which in turn may become accepted versions of reality in a particular local context. The taken-for-granted view of the world provides a variety of truths and facts about a reality, which may be 'highly circumscribed by culture, history or social context' (Gergen, 1985, p. 267). The extent to which meanings continue to be accepted depends not on empirical validity but the day-to-day workings of social processes in a particular time and place. What comes to be accepted as real serves a function within a particular historical and cultural context with no claim to 'truth' beyond the context.

- By participating in different relationships in different contexts, we acquire various ways of talking, which can be used for the achievement of valued ends in different situations. Meanings are unlikely to remain constant since, as a consequence of our participation in different relationships, versions of reality are always open to further or revised specification, offering the possibility of new meanings to emerge via a social process leading to a new or revised version of reality.

The idea is that initiatives and programmes that go under the microscope cannot and should not be treated as 'independent variables'. Rather, all policies and interventions are constituted in complex processes of human understanding and interaction. Proponents of the constructivist approach, such as Guba and Lincoln (1989), see evaluators as facilitating an exchange of meaning between stakeholders, where, through dialogue, stakeholders jointly construct a consensus about an intervention. Through this lens, programmes work through a process of reasoning, change, influence, negotiation, persuasion and choice. While traditional evaluation emphasizes outputs and outcomes, this form of evaluation emphasizes processes and particularly the myriad of stakeholders who may be involved in developing and implementing an intervention, strategy, programme or project.

Reflective questions

1 Why would you use a constructivist approach?

2 Can you find a good example? (Google it.)

3 What value does it have in the HRD context?

Somewhere between positivism and relativism

Throughout recent decades there have been heated exchanges between the proponents of positivist and constructionist approaches to evaluation. Between the extremes of positivism and constructivism lies a pluralist view of evaluation, which calls for both breadth and depth in programme evaluation (Cronbach, 1982).

This approach is taken further by Rossi and Freeman (1993), who highlight a threefold distinction of evaluation activities based on analysis related to the conceptualization and design of interventions, monitoring or programme implementation, and assessment of programme utility.

This has developed into theory-based evaluation based on the premise that interventions are based on a theory – either implicit or explicit – which explains how and why it will work. The key to understanding what really matters about a programme is through identifying this theory (sometimes referred to as the 'programme logic model'). By combining outcome data with an understanding of the process, a great deal can be learned about the programme's impact and its most influential factors (Weiss, 1995).

A more recent development has been the advent of realist evaluation (Pawson and Tilley, 1997), which seeks to position itself as a model of scientific explanation avoiding the traditional epistemological poles of positivism and relativism. Realism's key feature is its stress on the mechanics of explanation and its contribution to a progressive body of scientific knowledge.

1. Are there any problems associated with combining outcome and process data?

2. What implications does it have for research methods?

3. Is this approach becoming more or less popular? Why/why not?

Evaluation of NHRD

Several models have been introduced to explore evaluation within the context of the organization and workplace training. However, much evaluation work today is conducted on national government programmes with government departments and quasi-government agencies. The concept of NHRD policies and practice was introduced in Chapter 3. While it may be difficult to define and varies from country to country, the general focus of NHRD has developed out of a government interest in workforce development as a strategic issue. In the UK in particular, NHRD is often focused on the development and utilization of skills in order to enhance competitiveness and alleviate social exclusion. The system remains fragmented, with a range of government departments and agencies responsible for various aspects of the system. The UK government is committed to the vision outlined in the influential Leitch (2006) review of skills, which sees the UK becoming a world leader in skills by 2020. At the heart of this raised ambition for NHRD lies a shared responsibility for employers, individuals and government to increase action and investment in education and training. One of the key debates surrounding public policy intervention is whether and how much public intervention is needed. The Leitch review is a prime example of the use of evidence drawing on a range of research and evaluation studies, often commissioned by government departments or quasi-government agencies, to develop thinking and set the agenda.

Activity

Working with a partner, find out about NHRD in England. Go to the Department for Innovation, Universities and Skills – www.dius.gov.uk/ – and the UK Commission for Employment and Skills – www.ukces.org.uk/.

For Scotland, go to www.scotland.gov.uk/Topics/Education, for Wales, go to http://new.wales.gov.uk/topics/educationandskills/?lang=en, and for Northern Ireland, go to www.delni.gov.uk/index/publications/pubs-sectoral/skills-strategy-ni.htm.

Thinking about a policy or programme related to NHRD:

1. What was it seeking to achieve?

2. What actions were/are required to take it forward?

3. What factors are/were critical to its success?

Evaluation frameworks – the ROAMEF cycle

A framework is critical to the successful development and implementation of evaluation. There is a wide range of frameworks to be applied to appraise and evaluate policy and NHRD. An example of one endorsed by the government is provided in the *Green Book* (HM Treasury, 2003), which is a systematic approach used to guide national government appraisals and evaluation in the UK. It provides a useful overview to illustrate the key characteristics of evaluation throughout the policy process – important when considering evaluation within the context of NHRD – however, it is only one of a wide range of frameworks that may be used to evaluate public policy.

Activity

Working in groups of three, each person checks one of the following frameworks for evaluation:

- http://ec.europa.eu/budget/sound_fin_mgt/eval_framework_en.htm – the European Commission

- www.berr.gov.uk/files/file40324.pdf – *Evaluating Science and Society Initiatives*

- www.wkkf.org/Pubs/Tools/Evaluation/Pub770.pdf – the *Kellogg Foundation Evaluation Handbook*.

Identify the key features of each framework and share your results.

The basic model of evaluation outlined in the *Green Book* is the ROAMEF (rationale, objectives, appraisal, monitoring, evaluation and feedback) cycle, shown in Figure 8.2.

The underlying rationale for policy intervention is usually founded in market failure, as discussed in Chapter 3, or where there are clear government distributional objectives (societal equity) that need to be met. The Leitch (2006, p. 3) review of skills embodies this approach to NHRD, where government investment must focus on market failures, ensuring a basic platform of skills for all and targeting help where it is most needed.

The *Green Book* outlines a circular process of evaluation, where the first step is based on a process or systems approach through an appraisal of the proposed intervention (ex ante evaluation). Towards the end of the process, an outcomes-oriented evaluation (ex post evaluation) is prescribed to determine whether the intervention has worked and, if so, to what extent.

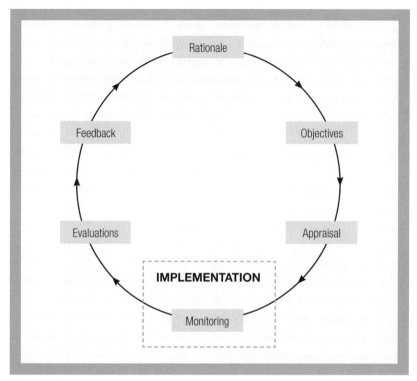

FIGURE 8.2 The ROAMEF cycle

SOURCE: HM Treasury (2003, p. 3)

Rationale

The Leitch review (2006) marshals both research and evaluation evidence to highlight that a skilled workforce has positive impacts on high-level economic aims such as productivity and GDP growth. At the same time, it provides evidence of a major skills deficiency, which is reflected in qualification levels at various levels when international comparisons are made. There is further evidence of different forms of market failure exerting an influence on policy, including:

- *Externalities:* leading to an underinvestment in training by employers where employers are concerned that, once trained, an employee will leave the firm before the firm has recouped its investment

- *Imperfect information:* leading to employees being unable to judge the quality of their training or appreciate the benefits

- *Credit market imperfections:* where low-paid employees in particular are likely to be credit constrained or unable to pay for training.

These market failures mean that the level of training provided by the market is likely to be inefficiently low from society's point of view. Well-designed interventions, engaging employers and providing high-quality flexible approaches to skills development, may help to bridge the gaps and improve NHRD.

Objectives

If an intervention is worthwhile, the objectives of the new policy, programme or project need to be clearly stated. Objectives may be expressed in general terms so that a range of options to meet them can be considered. There is usually a hierarchy of outcomes, outputs and targets that should be clearly set out. Objectives and their targets should be SMART:

- Specific

- Measurable

- Achievable

- Realistic

- Time bound.

An illustration of such an approach may propose an objective related to the development of skills, linked to an output in terms of number of training places and/or numbers completing training, which in turn may be linked to an outcome associated with the value of extra human capital or earnings capacity.

Appraisal

The purpose of appraisal is to help to develop an intervention that meets the objectives of government action. Appraisal emphasizes consideration of the costs and benefits of different intervention models (including a 'do nothing' model), with a view to identifying an approach that represents value for money. A key element of the appraisal is the treatment of uncertainty about the future, and techniques such as sensitivity and scenario analysis and methods may be used.

At the heart of appraisal lies the valuing of the costs and benefits of identified options. This can be a far from straightforward process, as the relevant costs and benefits to government and society of all options should be valued and the net benefits or costs calculated. As suggested earlier, HRD-related intervention at the micro- and macro-level needs to show a return like other expenditures and is often viewed as a cost rather than an investment. Costs can be expressed in terms of relevant opportunity costs, fixed, variable, semi-variable and step costs, and inputs may come from accountants, economists and other specialists depending on the type of appraisal. Benefits can be expressed in terms of taking into account the direct effects of interventions as well as wider societal effects using real or estimated market prices, or the results of commissioned research to ascertain the benefits associated with an intervention. Various other adjustments to the value of costs and benefits may be made to take account of equity, inflation and discounting.

Some form of appraisal of risk should also be part of this stage of the evaluation process and account for the overoptimism that characterizes many project appraisers, as well as assessing uncertainties associated with the development and implementation of the intervention.

Reflective questions

1 What is the purpose of appraisal?

2 Who should undertake appraisal?

3 What are the weaknesses of the *Green Book* approach to appraisal?

Monitoring

All organizations keep records and notes and discuss what they are doing. This simple administration becomes monitoring when it encompasses the systematic collection of data, particularly relating to the financial management and outcomes of a policy, programme or project during implementation. It is a key element of performance management, which seeks to ensure the successful implementation of an HRD intervention. An effective monitoring system will:

- ensure that management information is measuring what is important in terms of inputs (such as costs), outputs, outcomes and impact

- put in place controls to ensure that the data are accurate

- provide regular financial and progress reports.

Monitoring will help to answer questions at various points in the life of a project, such as: How well are we doing? What difference are we making?

Reflective questions

1 Why should we monitor?

2 Who should monitor?

3 What is the difference between monitoring and evaluation?

Evaluation

The section below on evaluation in the workplace provides a more detailed introduction to various models of evaluation of HRD and provides an opportunity to explore further the nature of evaluation within the organization context. However, within the ROAMEF cycle, evaluation is identified as a discrete activity to be completed towards the end, or at the end, of a programme. The main aim of this stage is to examine what has happened against what was expected to happen. A key element of this is to establish what would have happened in the absence of the intervention (the counterfactual). Other important concepts to consider when analysing data as part of an evaluation are additionality, displacement and deadweight. (Descriptions of these and many other concepts relevant to evaluation are available in the evaluation glossaries at www.oecd.org/dataoecd/29/21/2754804.pdf and www.un.org/Depts/oios/mecd/mecd_glossary/index.htm.)

Feedback

Feedback is a critical part of the process, as without it, recognition of the value of an intervention, potential improvements to the process identified though the evaluation, and the value of the evaluation itself will not be recognized. For some time, the challenge of connecting the outcomes of research and evaluation processes with the inputs that professionals and politicians use in making judgements and taking decisions has been recognized (Davies et al., 2000; Nutley et al., 2003) and forms an important dimension of the future of evaluation related to HRD intervention, which we will return to towards the end of this chapter.

Some observations on the ROAMEF approach

The ROAMEF framework, or variations of it, has become a central part of the approach to evaluation adopted by many organizations, especially those in the public sector, as a way of judging the success or otherwise of interventions. As well as being systematic and logical, the model is systemic as the feedback loop provides information about activities so that necessary improvements may be identified.

There are some obvious consequences for this model for the evaluation of NHRD. One of these is that evaluation appears as a distinct stage of the process and its placement towards the end of the process tends to mean that, in some instances, evaluation is something of an afterthought. In this case, evaluation tends to be completed towards the end of the programme, with a certain degree of pressure to undertake the activity quickly to come to a judgement on the 'success' or otherwise of the programme. However, as outlined above, it can encourage reflection and various types of evaluation and appraisal activities throughout the policy-making process (similar to the CIRO model outlined below). Furthermore, by adopting an approach that takes account of the interests of various stakeholders and cultural and contextual factors as part of the evaluation process, a more responsive approach can be adopted to evaluation (Stake, 2004). This shifts the emphasis of evaluation away from 'proving' towards feedback and learning.

Evaluation of HRD in the workplace

HRD is a collective process involving a range of people and activities. The purpose of evaluation will vary depending on the objectives of relevant stakeholders. Good workplace evaluation will engage stakeholders at the ex ante, interim and ex post stages outlined above. Harrison (2005, p. 144) argues for a participatory approach to evaluation 'that has been produced in collaboration with key partners'. However, the objectives of different stakeholders may vary and any evaluation may need to adopt a range of methods and measures to evaluate the success in meeting such objectives. Examples of varying stakeholder objectives for training for middle managers are outlined in Table 8.1. We will return to these later.

TABLE 8.1 Stakeholder objectives for training middle managers

Stakeholder	Possible objectives
Individual	Obtain formal qualification to improve promotion prospects within or outside the organization
Line manager	Develop independence and confidence in role and reduce reliance on them as middle manager becomes more autonomous
HR department	Ensure consistency between managers and ensure all such managers are working within a common competency framework
Finance department	Provide positive financial return on investment
Senior management team	Improve overall organizational performance and meet strategic organizational objectives

It is important that HRD practitioners are aware of the philosophical constructs of the positivist and constructivist approaches to evaluation. However, Kenny et al. (1979) caution those involved with the practical aspects of evaluation to take a pragmatic approach. They argue that a rigorous scientific approach, however desirable, is not practicable in most workplace settings. If evaluation does not take place and/or is not subject to some rigour, the success or otherwise of training and development interventions undertaken by organizations remains unmeasured and unproven. It can be safely asserted that Kenny et al.'s writings are no less relevant today. There is access to greater quantities and (it is hoped) greater quality of data from which to evaluate. The need to justify and measure success has arguably never been more at the forefront of business and society's thinking. Edwards (2005) recognizes the current societal phenomenon of measuring performance and satisfaction, from the success of schools and the individual child's progress within them, to how happy we are with our hotel bed, bus or burger. She notes that this process of measurement is prevalent within the workplace via competence frameworks and staff appraisals. Phillips (1994a, 1994b) identifies the dangers of such a climate as being self-fulfilling – evaluation for evaluation's sake.

Evaluation fits within the four-stage training model, referred to in Chapter 6, and shown in Figure 8.3.

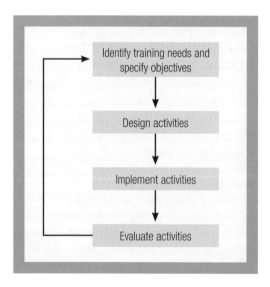

FIGURE 8.3 A four-stage training model

The potential danger here is to consider evaluation as the last activity of the cycle, that is, we evaluate at the end of a training and development intervention. The references made earlier to ex ante, interim and ex post should mean embedding evaluation as a continuing process throughout the cycle.

With the macro- and micro-contexts of evaluation of workplace training and development interventions in mind, it is appropriate to consider the purpose of evaluation and then critique some established models of evaluation in the workplace.

Purpose of evaluation

The evaluation of HRD activity at work involves the collection and interpretation of data. The results of this process can be used for a variety of purposes according to particular needs. For example, senior managers might need evidence that a programme of learning on customer service was having a measurable impact on performance.

Easterby-Smith (1994) identifies four distinct purposes of evaluation:

1 *Proving:* This shows that something happened. It may justify the costs of training, provide evidence for its ongoing delivery, and confirm it was the right thing to do (or, of course, the converse of these).

2 *Improving:* This identifies how the training intervention might be improved. The tendency is for this to be measured and acted on after the training has been completed. However, noting the need for ex ante and interim evaluation, this could be done at various stages of delivery.

3 *Learning:* Participants in HRD activities can review what they are learning, considering how to make changes in the context of the activity but also what might be used at work or in the future.

4 *Controlling:* This is often the focus of training departments. Evaluation results help to control the quality of training providers, the costs and the behaviour of the participants. Easterby-Smith (1994, p. 19) notes the proliferation of such a purpose, particularly in large public sector organizations such as the police. The need to ensure consistency between central and regional (or in the case of education, individual local schools) is growing, as the tension to allow autonomy and yet ensure national standards increases.

In addition to these purposes, it is also suggested that because evaluation is concerned with the collection and interpretation of data, the results can be used to persuade and influence others of the value of HRD activities (Mumford and Gold, 2004). It is a reminder that information can be used for a variety of purposes, as a representation of the facts or a version of events, told from a particular point of view (Clarke, 1999).

Evaluation models

Kirkpatrick's evaluation model

In 1959, Kirkpatrick published articles outlining techniques for evaluating training programmes. These articles described a four-level process for the evaluation of training.

This process has been commonly referred to as the Kirkpatrick model. The four levels are shown in Figure 8.4.

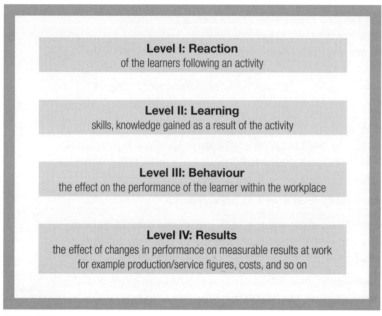

Level I: Reaction
of the learners following an activity

Level II: Learning
skills, knowledge gained as a result of the activity

Level III: Behaviour
the effect on the performance of the learner within the workplace

Level IV: Results
the effect of changes in performance on measurable results at work
for example production/service figures, costs, and so on

FIGURE 8.4 Levels of evaluation for training

SOURCE: Adapted from Kirkpatrick (1998)

This all seems quite logical and sensible but, as HRD in Practice 8.1 shows, it can be difficult to implement.

HRD in Practice 8.1

Evaluation is a tricky business

Rose spent three months evaluating evaluation activity and processes at National Westminster Bank. As a large organization with many operating divisions, the bank had around 12 different and separate HRD departments and functions. Rose found that most had the same simplistic approach – end of course questionnaires ruled, and most were read by the HRD staff involved in the delivery and then filed. No analysis or reporting occurred, except in a few isolated examples. Rose also established the reasons for this:

1 No higher level evaluation occurred because it was considered too time and resource intensive to do so.
2 No information beyond learner satisfaction was ever asked for by senior or operational managers.
3 HRD staff had what they believed they needed to validate and improve their work and performance.

Because Rose investigated evaluation as part of the requirement of her professional qualification, she became an expert on the research and writing on evaluation and so reckoned the situation she found was untenable. She designed a corporate approach to evaluation for implementation across the bank and then spent the next nine months getting it accepted corporately and in each of the bank's divisions. The approach didn't go into return on investment or anything overly sophisticated. But it did achieve the generation of data on changes in work behaviour and performance following learning and development events, and also the production of evaluation reports for every activity, which fed into quarterly and annual divisional and corporate reports on the value of investing in employee development. An improvement on what previously existed was achieved.

Basarab, cited in Kirkpatrick (1998), notes that the first two levels of the model refer to internal drivers for the training department to evaluate the effectiveness of its provision. The second two levels refer to external drivers, which evaluate the participants' contribution to business operations and overall organizational success.

Reaction

This first level measures the participants' reactions to the training and development intervention they have experienced. Typically, data are collected ex post, via 'happy sheets' or other forms of what Kirkpatrick (1998, p. 20) refers to as measures of 'customer satisfaction'. Figure 8.5 provides an example.

The reasons for measuring reactions are varied. It can help to measure what is learned by participants. It measures an emotional response, which, although not scientifically proven as accurate, does give relatively quick data from which to evaluate the effectiveness of the intervention. Both Kirkpatrick (1998) and Alliger et al. (1997) caution those interpreting data that positive reactions do not always equal a good training experience and negative reactions do not always equal a poor one. A baseline conclusion could be that positive reactions do not guarantee learning, but do make participants more amenable to further training and may encourage learning. Participants may also be more positive in their recounting of the experience to their manager and peers, thereby influencing future participants' expectations. Conversely, a

Performance and Development Review Training

Please give your views and comments regarding your day						
Excellent 4	Very good 3	Satisfied 2	Not satisfied 1 (please give details)			
How did you rate the content of the programme?			4	3	2	1
Comments						
How did you rate the facilitator?			4	3	2	1
Comments						
How did you rate the quality of handouts information?			4	3	2	1
Comments						
How did you rate the venue?			4	3	2	1
Comments						
How was the quality of catering?			4	3	2	1
Comments						
Were your overall objectives met?			4	3	2	1
Your objectives were:						
Any other comments:						

Thank you for your feedback

FIGURE 8.5 Reaction-level evaluation sheet

negative reaction may disengage a participant from learning and future training activities. The 'bad publicity' such reactions may produce in the wider workplace will not help the efforts of a training department when it promotes such interventions in the future.

Bramley (1999, p. 367) suggests that some basic questions should be asked before reaction data are gathered. What information is needed? How can it be collected? It is suggested that happy sheets do not predict learning or changes to behaviour. These sheets are therefore limited to collecting data on only the first level of Kirkpatrick's model. Bramley (1999) also suggests that for repeat interventions to different groups of participants, the gauging of reactions only needs to be done a few times. Unless the intervention changes, the range of reactions is likely to be the same.

This critique of Kirkpatrick's first level supports the suggestion above that the evaluation made at this level is an internal driver for the training department. Positive reactions can justify the intervention and garner support and funding for its repetition. Negative reactions can improve the quality of the intervention, from redesigning training aspects to changing the sandwiches served at lunchtime. The quality of the intervention can be improved prior to delivery. Reactions can also be gathered from participants during the training intervention. This may be done via interim 'happy sheets' or more qualitative focus groups. If there is a danger of negative reactions, such timely evaluation allows providers to amend and correct perceived shortcomings before the end of the event. This may result in more positive reactions later. Alliger et al. (1997) note that the 'usefulness' of learning is important for the application of training in the workplace. They urge designers to consider this at the planning stage. This relates to the need to engage relevant stakeholders from the outset in training intervention design. Workplace constraints and the perceptions of workers, when they return to their roles, are key to ensuring that these do not become blocks to effective learning and transfer of behaviour.

Activity

Working with a partner, consider the following questions:

1 How important are emotional reactions as measures of a successful training intervention?

2 Do you agree with Bramley that such data need only be collected a few times for the same event?

Learning

Tests of learning are undertaken to achieve educational and professional qualifications via assessments. The evaluation of learning from training interventions can follow the same process; however, this is often not designed into such interventions. It may be undesirable from the participants' viewpoint, too costly to administrate, or the learning taking place may be deemed too difficult to measure. Some interventions require assessment. Training to drive a forklift truck or to be a workplace first aider needs certification via formal testing. Other interventions, for example coaching or diversity training, may have more subjective outcomes, which do not require testing and can be difficult, if not impossible, to assess. There is also an argument that what is tested is not necessarily what is actually learned as a result of an intervention. Bramley (1999, p. 368) cautions that 'participation in an event does not equal learning'. A formula for measuring how much participants have learned can be expressed as the gain ratio:

$$\text{Gain ratio} \quad \frac{\text{Post-test} - \text{Pre-test}}{\text{Possible} - \text{Pre-test}} \times 100$$

Bramley (1999, p. 369) suggests that 'the average gain ratio across the group is a measure of the efficiency of the programme'. He argues that a group average of over 70% is needed to be efficient. If the percentage is lower, Bramley suggests splitting the group into those with pre-knowledge and those without. The ratios may vary and show the intervention is appropriate for one group but not another. There is another danger with high pre-knowledge. The success of individuals' test results may be high, but this shows the extent of their prior learning, not the success of this specific training intervention. The importance of effective training needs analysis and a link to job analysis is critical here to the efficiency of the intervention (see Chapter 6).

Behaviour

Although evaluation of learning can evidence the extent to which something is learned, it will not predict the extent to which such learning will be used effectively in the workplace. The third element of Kirkpatrick's model seeks to address this. Bramley (1999) suggests a worker's performance is a combination of their ability and motivation and the opportunity to display such learning. He argues for the 'hardwiring' of learning when applied in the workplace. Rock (2006) provides extensive physiological evidence for the importance of using the hardwired brain as opposed to using 'working memory'. The latter requires great physical and mental energy. For example, the first time someone drives a car, the levels of concentration and effort are significantly greater than for someone who has driven the same route for many years. So in the workplace, learning that can be regularly practised and re-enforced is likely to result in changed behaviour.

This assumes that the worker has learned well from the training intervention, and that their ability to apply the learning to the workplace is within their mental and physical capacity. For example, an update on employment law may inform line managers of their legal rights and responsibilities to help them manage their staff more effectively, but it alone is unlikely to equip them to represent the work organization in legal proceedings. Workers may be more motivated to apply learning if they see an immediate benefit to themselves and, if they are turned into business objectives, to the overall success of the organization. If changed behaviour is likely to result in a pay increase or promotion, it too is likely to be more motivating and therefore more readily applied.

However, workers need opportunities to apply their learning. Recruitment and selection training may only be applied once or twice a year by some participants, as job vacancies to which they may appoint come up infrequently. Opportunities may also be limited by an organization's culture. A training intervention that encourages creativity and enterprise may be stifled in the workplace by hierarchical organizational structures and an autocratic management style. Those having undertaken diversity training may be ridiculed in the workplace for perceived 'political correctness'. Unless such participants are confident of the messages learned, they may suppress any application in order to retain the respect of immediate work colleagues.

In order to maximize the application of learning, Bramley (1999, p. 370) recommends the use of practical 'performance tests', rather than written assessments, when evaluating at the learning level of Kirkpatrick's model. A study by Rouiller and Goldstein (1993, cited in Bramley 1999, p. 374) identified seven scales to measure the 'transfer climate'. The emphasis was on how line managers can influence the adoption of new behaviours after training. The scales focused on:

- goal setting

- the closeness of training behaviour to normal behaviour

- whether equipment was available in the workplace

- the autonomy of those trained to handle problems

- the degree of negative and positive feedback

- the impact of no feedback because line managers were too busy to provide it

- the degree of ridicule those trained received if they applied their learning.

From Rouiller and Goldstein's studies, the tests at the end of the training intervention only predicted 8% of participants' behaviour transfer scores (that is, participants could score highly in the test but perform badly in the workplace). The transfer climate measure, described above, predicted 46% (see Bramley 1999, p. 374).

Results

This level of the Kirkpatrick model is the most obviously business focused. It evaluates the extent to which a training intervention has had a positive impact on overall organizational success. Bloom (1964, cited in Wilson, 2005, p. 411) refers to the 'impact of learners' understanding, behaviour or attitudes'. The key here is to define what impact is sought from the training at its earliest development stage. Why has the intervention been commissioned? Who decided it should take place? What were the learning objectives? How do these objectives impact on organizational success? How will that success be measured?

Some outcomes of training interventions may be difficult if not impossible to measure (Edwards, 2005). Some interventions can give results that are relatively easy to measure numerically. Examples include the reduction in accidents following health and safety training, or an increase in sales after sales training. However, other interventions, such as coaching programmes for managers or diversity training, produce more subtle changes to behaviour and attitude, which may take years for statistical evidence of effectiveness to show.

Reflective question

How would you measure the results of diversity training?

It may be helpful, given the complex nature of evaluating results, to establish how this level will be measured at the design stage of training. To be truly effective, such measurements should be the decision of the relevant stakeholders. Referring back to Table 8.1, the differing objectives of each stakeholder need different measurements of effectiveness. Table 8.2 suggests what these might be.

TABLE 8.2 Evaluation of development training for middle managers

Stakeholder	Possible objectives	Measurement of results
Individual	Obtain formal qualification to improve promotion prospects within or outside the organization	Awarded formal qualification – x% of participants obtain formal qualification
Line manager	Develop independence and confidence in role and reduce reliance on them as middle manager becomes more autonomous	Less line management time spent in support of middle managers No costs (financial or reputation) to the organization as a result of middle managers' autonomous decisions Financial savings to organization as line managers able to focus on own tasks
HR department	Ensure consistency between managers and that all such managers are working within a common competency framework	Fewer examples of middle managers operating outside organizational policies and processes – x% compliance with company rules – measure increase from baseline pre-training
Finance department	Provide positive financial return on investment	Financial benefits (more sales, profit, less wastage) outweigh cost of programme
Senior management team	Improve overall organizational performance and meet strategic organizational objectives	Improved business reputation, higher market share, better labour turnover, reduced absenteeism, organizational objectives met on time (or early)

There is no end to the possible measures of effective results an organization could choose. However, to carry out all those suggested above would take significant time and expense. The key is to decide the measures at the planning stage and focus on these. The danger of this is that the measures chosen may not be the right ones. The cost of analysing data to provide evidence of results also needs to be factored in. One model for considering a range of measures of results is Kaplan and Norton's (1992) balanced scorecard. This combines financial and non-financial measures.

Activity

Working with a partner, go to www.balancedscorecard.org, the home page of Balanced Scorecard Institute. Explore how the process of the balanced scorecard might be used to measure results of HRD activity.

Another danger when trying to extract the direct cause and effect of HRD interventions is that extraneous factors may influence results. The improved market share may be due to better management training, but could be attributed to failings by an organization's competitors. Higher labour turnover after a training programme could evidence the unplanned result that managers have been trained for promotion, which they find sooner from other employers. The impact of government policies, the economic environment, and supplier and competitor behaviour are all examples of external factors that could influence results.

However, such limitations should not stop this level of evaluation from being attempted. It provides a direct link back to why the intervention was identified at the outset. It offers evidence for improvement or modification. It could provide justification to the training department and other stakeholders that the intervention is worthwhile and should be continued. Without such a business focus, any evaluation may 'miss the point' and, as Phillips (1994a) states, become evaluation for evaluation's sake.

Reflective questions

Think about some workplace training you have done or the course you are studying:

1 How would you evaluate its effectiveness?

2 How does your employer or course provider evaluate its effectiveness?

3 Does one aspect of Kirkpatrick's model apply more than the others?

The CIRO evaluation model

Harrison (2005, p. 144) offers an overall critique of the Kirkpatrick model, cautioning its use in the workplace: 'All generic models must be tailored to fit specific needs, and even Kirkpatrick does not always suit context.' This omission is arguably overcome by the use of another evaluation model, the CIRO, which refers to:

- Context

- Inputs

- Reactions

- Outcomes.

The model was developed by Warr et al. (1970) and Hamblin (1994), originally for the evaluation of management training (see Chapter 10). It supports the arguments made earlier in this chapter that evaluation activities should take place before, during and after the intervention.

Context

This is the ex ante aspect of evaluation. It aims to evaluate the context in which the training intervention took place. It will review the objectives and purpose of the training. Why was it commissioned? Who supported the intervention (and possibly, who did not)? It will evaluate how effective the preparation was for training. What briefings and support were put in place to ensure the training would meet its objectives? It should identify what worked and how the preparation and planning could be improved for future delivery. The context may also be wider in terms of the business climate in operation at the time of the intervention. If the training was delivered at a time of great success, would its outcomes be different at times of difficulty? Would managers be equally keen to release staff and engage in motivational activity to encourage behavioural change if the operating environment was less positive? Techniques for data collection would include interviews, questionnaires, briefings, written tests and feedback from others ahead of development.

Inputs

This evaluates the resources required to deliver the training intervention. There are tangible costs such as materials, external training consultant fees, room hire and subsistence. Harrison (2005, p. 145) recommends accurate records are kept as these costs are incurred for review after the event. There should be a measure between the resources used and the extent to which they met the learning objectives set at the 'context' stage above. It is important to account for hidden costs such as staff time away from their job. The opportunity cost of not undertaking the training should be higher than the cost of taking staff out of the workplace for hours or days, in order to justify its efficiency and effectiveness. It could be argued that this is attempting to 'measure the unmeasurable' (Edwards, 2005, p. 407). Measuring the cost of not doing something can be difficult to predict. Techniques for data collection would include session reviews, questionnaires, written or practical tests, feedback from others during events, and interviews.

Reactions

In many respects, this is similar in definition to the same term used in the Kirkpatrick model. It measures the emotional responses of participants to the training they have experienced. A broader range of reactions might be included here. For example, the reactions of the deliverers of the training and those of the managers, peers and subordinates to an individual's training will all inform the evaluation process. Harrison (2005, p. 145) notes that there should not be 'an indiscriminate use of happy sheets', but that such data collection must be used and relate back to the objectives of the training. Techniques for data collection would include questionnaires and interviews.

Outcomes

This stage of the CIRO model initially sounds similar to the results level of the Kirkpatrick model. However, Hamblin (1994) developed a four-level structure of analysis for outcomes. These levels integrate the internal and external drivers identified by Basarab above. Indeed, Warr et al. referred to a continuum of immediate, intermediate and ultimate outcomes (see Harrison 2005, p. 146). Hamblin's four levels are:

1 *The learner level:* measures what is learned by individuals, not unlike the learning level of Kirkpatrick's model.

2 *The workplace level:* measures changes in job behaviour (again not unlike the behaviour aspect of Kirkpatrick). Measurement may be in the form of appraisal, observation and from discussions with the individual, their peers and line manager.

3 *The team/departmental/unit level:* Hamblin includes within this level the operational measures (for example increases in production, reduced wastage) that can be attributed to a specific department.

4   *The organizational level:* these are the broader outcomes that may take time (years, possibly) to evaluate fully. It could include hard measures of increased share price or market share, or it could be softer outcomes of culture change, which, of course, could lead to the former.

Techniques for data collection would include questionnaires, interviews, debriefing meetings, feedback from others relating to behaviour and performance, measurements of performance and results achieved. HRD in Practice 8.2 shows the approach taken to data collection for a large programme of development for SME managers.

A development programme for SME managers

The development programme took place across England from September 2004 until April 2006 and allowed managers to obtain a grant of up to £1,000 towards any development identified following an in-depth assessment.

The aims of the evaluation were to:
- measure the impact of the programme on the participants' own performance
- measure the impact of the programme on their respective organizations
- assess how effective the brokerage models have been from the customer perspective
- inform policy on the way in which leadership and management provision can be embedded in Train to Gain.

The methodology consisted of:
- a postal/email survey of all local LSCs and Business Links
- six partnership case studies and telephone follow-up with ten Business Links
- stakeholder interviews with programme managers at the Centre for Enterprise
- a telephone survey of 500 participants on the programme and in-depth case studies with 20 participants
- a telephone survey of 216 intermediary organizations and a control group survey with 100 organizations.

Source: LSC (2006)

Activity

Working in groups of three, consider how you would evaluate a training event on communication for 10 participants in a management consultancy team. The task is to show that the three-hour event has had an impact on the participants and performance. Go to www.lancs.ac.uk/fss/projects/edres/ltsn-eval/ for a site devoted to resources for evaluators.

These evaluation models provide a systematic route for gathering data relating to HRD activities, allowing the purpose of evaluation to be met. There are limitations, in that the models are stronger when activities are clearly identified and completed in a limited time frame, such as training courses. HRD involves a wider view of learning at work and beyond, however, and there is often a time-lag between learning events and use. For example, completion of a professional qualification, such as the Chartered Institute of Marketing, may not lead to an immediate impact at work.

A further difficulty arises from the range of variables that affect learning at work, where it becomes more precarious to attempt to link impact at the different levels implied by the models above. For example, reactions to an HRD event may be strong but participants find they are prevented from applying learning to their work, because of the opinions of their fellow workers, the requirements of their managers, or the way the work is defined. These are features of an organization's learning climate (see Chapter 9).

Responsive models

The different purposes of evaluation and the difficulties of applying systematic models of evaluation have resulted in a number of approaches to evaluation, which take more account of the interests of different stakeholders and their requirements. Such approaches are referred to as 'responsive evaluation' (Stake, 2004) and give more attention to cultural and context factors and providing feedback for ongoing learning.

One approach, presented by Patton (1997), focuses on utilization by those who have an interest in what is happening, so that they can make decisions based on evaluation information as it emerges. The role of the evaluator is to facilitate such judgements 'rather than acting as a distant, independent judge'.

Another approach is concerned to make action possible, especially where learning is concerned with dealing with complex and difficult issues. This is referred to as 'action evaluation' (Rothman, 1997). Stakeholders can set goals, expressing values and motivations which can be shared with others in a project, and allowing for agreement on direction. Actions can be set and evaluated on a continuous basis.

Activity

Go to www.beyondintractability.org/essay/action_evaluation/ to find out more about action evaluation.

For more resources on helping learners to actively review HRD activities, go to www.reviewing.co.uk/.

Evaluation and organization change

Throughout this book, links have been made with the pressures on many organizations to change, leading to new definitions of what organizations do and how work is defined. For example, increasingly work is team based and requires interaction with others in different locations physically and virtually within and between organizations. Further, such work is frequently knowledge based and relies on the interactions of professionals and experts (see Chapter 9). Therefore organizations need to see change continuous with learning as a crucial capability to achieve this.

A number of approaches to supporting change through learning and evaluation have been presented. For example, Preskill and Torres (1999) present a model of evaluative enquiry based on key ideas relating to reflection, dialogue and the use of questions between change participants and stakeholders to surface assumptions and clarify values. The purpose of evaluation is to support learning and respond to the emerging patterns of information needs for decision making. The process is ongoing and becomes part of work practices on a continuous basis. In a similar vein, Rix and Gold (2000) develop the idea of a reflective infrastructure to support change agents leading complex projects, where evaluation is completed throughout the project and data are interpreted and fed back to help improve the operation of the project, especially where difficulties occur.

Future direction of evaluation

Evaluation continues to develop and evolve as a discipline and a practice in response to new threats and challenges. Globalization will continue to influence organizations and evaluation practice and the need to build evaluation capacity and to share experiences on an international scale will require new competencies and set new ethical challenges at both the macro- and the micro-level. A recent CIPD report (2008) identified future changes in terms of, for example, the prevalence of coaching and e-learning as key learning and development practices, and employers' preferences for the development of skills such as interpersonal skills and communications skills, and evaluation models and methods will need to take account of these developments as they evolve. For some time, the challenge of connecting the outcomes of research and evaluation processes with the inputs that professionals and politicians use in making judgements and taking decisions has been recognized in the literature, and if evaluation is to have an impact on policy and practice, there remains a need to develop approaches that facilitate this. A key challenge will be to incorporate these developments into the future education and training of evaluators and those who plan to undertake evaluations of HRD activity at the macro- and micro-levels. There have been some calls for professionalizing evaluators and providing standards and/or competencies to underpin their learning and development (Russ-Eft, 2008).

In April 2007, the CIPD published a report, *The Value of Learning: A New Model of Value and Evaluation* (Anderson, 2007). In many respects, the concerns of those evaluating learning in the workplace remain unchanged to those addressed by the models discussed earlier. However, the emphasis of this report by Anderson is keenly focused on the external aspects of the evaluation of learning. The concept of return on investment is not new. Phillips and Phillips (2001) stressed the need in some work organizations for a positive business return on the investment made in training the workforce. Kearns (2005) sought to find a calculation process to measure the economic return of individual learning. In simple terms, such measurements could be seen as a more sophisticated version of cost–benefit analysis. The focus for the early 21st century is the externality of training's success. Any benefits to the individual learner or training department are viewed as relatively insignificant if the training does not benefit the whole organization.

As identified by Anderson (2007), the benefit is the extent to which training interventions are aligned with, and help achieve, the strategic objectives of the organization. She dismisses a 'one size fits all set of metrics' (p. 2). Three key elements are identified for successful training and meaningful evaluation:

- the previously noted alignment
- the use of a number of evaluation methods
- working out which approaches are right for specific organizations.

What appears to frustrate many HRD professionals is the belief that training interventions in their organizations cannot be fully measured. In a CIPD survey (2006), 80% believed that their training interventions delivered far more than they could prove. However, only 36% of organizations surveyed specifically sought to evaluate training inputs against bottom line outputs. Detailed evaluation appears too time-consuming and of little interest to line managers. This appears contradictory to the earlier exhortations to involve line managers, as one of many stakeholders, in the evaluation process from the outset.

This is where the future of evaluation looks destined to change. Organizations are more concerned with investing in their 'human capital' (Anderson, 2007, p. 3). One perpetual feature of people is their potential to be both an asset and a liability. This can depend on their personal behaviour, response to management and general attitude to work. Using the 'capital' concept, the implication is of human resources as investments. In order to improve the return on this expensive investment, it needs to be nurtured – only then can this asset be truly appreciated. If it is starved of investment (that is, development), it may well turn out to be a costly liability for the organization. This is a significant change to the historical view of training in many organizations. When times were hard, the training investment was often the first to be cut. Organizations have woken up to the dangers of this short-termism.

Anderson identifies two new models of evaluation that emphasize the importance of strategic alignment and the definition of value in different organizations. The first, the value and evaluation process, is a linear model noting three elements, shown in Figure 8.6.

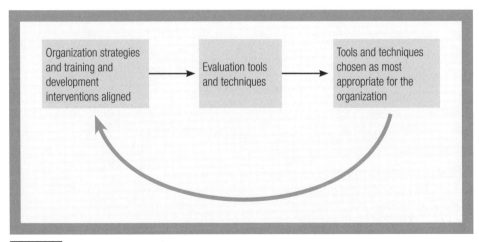

FIGURE 8.6 Value and evaluation process

SOURCE: Adapted from Anderson (2007, p. 5)

The second model consolidates the concept of return on investment. It also affirms the position of the graduate recruiters by introducing the concept of 'return on expectation'. The model identifies four values and evaluation practices that organizations may use, shown in Figure 8.7.

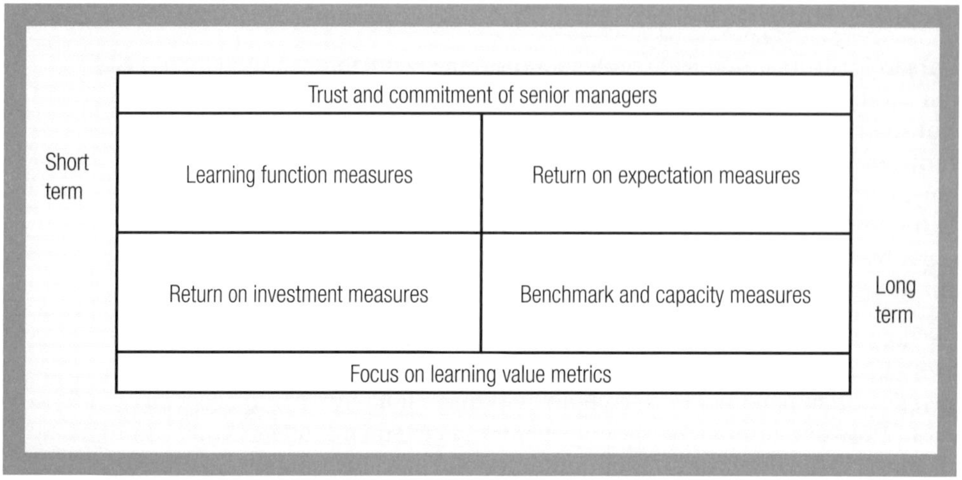

	Trust and commitment of senior managers		
Short term	Learning function measures	Return on expectation measures	
	Return on investment measures	Benchmark and capacity measures	Long term
	Focus on learning value metrics		

FIGURE 8.7 Measures of returns model

SOURCE: Adapted from Anderson (2007, p. 11)

Each approach to evaluation could be used exclusively or in conjunction with other approaches, subject to the needs of the organization, its strategic objectives, and the way training and development interventions are then aligned. Each approach identifies a different emphasis in the business; from short-term to long-term measures and from learning metrics to senior management commitment to evidence organizational strategic success.

Summary

- Evaluation has a key role to play in the field of HRD at a range of levels – national, sectoral, organizational, divisional, team and individual – along with a wide range of strategic, tactical and operational activities.

- Common themes associated with evaluation emphasize systematic approaches, something to evaluate such as processes, projects, programmes or policies, outcomes, impact and utility.

- The logic of experimentation underpins much evaluation theory but recent years have seen a shift towards a more pragmatic approach and a more pluralist view of evaluation.

- Evaluation of NHRD programmes is guided by a systematic approach referred to as the ROAMEF (rationale, objectives, appraisal, monitoring, evaluation and feedback) cycle.

- In the workplace, evaluation of HRD activity at work involves the collection and interpretation of data for a variety of purposes.

- The Kirkpatrick model describes a four-level process for the evaluation of training that underpins systematic approaches to evaluation. Other models give more attention to the importance of context in providing the rationale for training and the support that may or may not be provided.

- Different purposes of evaluation and the difficulties of applying systematic models of evaluation have resulted in a number of approaches to evaluation that take more account of the interests of different stakeholders and their requirements.

- Evaluation can be a vital part of change projects.

- Future approaches to evaluation need to ensure that HRD activities are aligned with and help to achieve strategic objectives.

Discussion questions

1 Can the value of HRD activity be proven?
2 Can evaluation ensure that public funds are spent efficiently and for the benefit of society?
3 How can different interests in HRD activity be satisfied in the workplace?
4 Should evaluation become a profession?
5 What is the value of evaluation in change projects at work?

Further reading

Hale, R. (2003) How training can add real value to the business, part 1, *Industrial and Commercial Training*, **35**(1): 29–32.

Holton, E. and Naquin, S. (2005) A critical analysis of HRD evaluation models from a decision-making perspective, *Human Resource Development Quarterly*, **16**(2): 257–80.

Russ-Eft, D. and Preskill, H. (2005) In search of the holy grail: return on investment evaluation in human resource development, *Advances in Developing Human Resources*, **7**(1): 71–85.

Tamkin, P., Yarnell, J. and Kerrin, M. (2002) *Kirkpatrick and Beyond: A Review of Models of Training Evaluation*, Brighton, Institute of Employment Studies.

Note

1   There are important differences between constructivism and constructionism. However, we do not intend to explore these differences here. See Patton (2002) for a fuller explanation.

References

Alliger, G.M., Tannenbaum, S.I., Bennett, W. et al. (1997) A meta-analysis of the relations among training criteria, *Personnel Psychology*, **50**: 341–58.

Anderson, V. (2007) *The Value of Learning: A New Model of Value and Evaluation,* London, CIPD.

Bramley, P. (1999) Evaluating training and development, in A. Landale (ed.) *Gower Handbook of Training and Development*, 3rd edn, Aldershot, Gower.

Burr, V. (1995) *Introduction to Social Construction-ism,* London, Routledge.

Campbell, D.T. and Stanley, J.C. (1963) *Experimental and Quasi-experimental Designs for Research,* Chicago, Rand McNally.

CIPD (Chartered Institute of Personnel and Development) (2006) *The Changing Role of the Trainer: Building a Learning Culture in your Organization*, London, CIPD.

CIPD (Chartered Institute of Personnel and Development) (2008) *Learning and Development: Annual Survey Report 2008*, London, CIPD.

Clarke, A. (1999) *Evaluation Research*, London, Sage.

Cronbach , L. (1982) *Designing Evaluations of Educational and Social Programs*, San Francisco, CA, Jossey-Bass.

Davies, H., Laycock, G., Nutley, S. et al. (2000) A strategic approach to research and development, in H. Davies (ed.) *What Works?*, Bristol, Policy Press.

De Vaus (1993) *Surveys in Social Research*, 3rd edn, London, University College London.

Easterby-Smith, M. (1994) *Evaluating Management Development, Training and Education*, 2nd edn, Aldershot, Gower.

Edwards, Z.C. (2005) Evaluation and assessment, in J. Wilson (ed.) *Human Resource Development*, 2nd edn, London, Kogan Page.

Gergen, K.J. (1985) Social constructionist inquiry: context and implications, in K.J. Gergen and K. Davis (eds) *The Social Construction of the Person,* New York, Springer Verlag.

Gergen, K.J. (1994) *Relationships and Realities,* Cambridge, MA, Harvard University Press.

Guba, E.G. and Lincoln Y.S. (1989) *Fourth Generation Evaluation*, Newbury Park, CA, Sage.

Hamblin, A.C. (1994) *Evaluation and Control of Training*, Maidenhead, McGraw-Hill.

Harrison, R. (2005) *Learning and Development*, 4th edn, London, CIPD.

HM Treasury (2003) *The Green Book: Appraisal and Evaluation in Central Government*, London, TSO.

Kaplan, R.S. and Norton, D.P. (1992) The balanced scorecard: measures that drive performance*, Harvard Business Review*, **70**(1): 71–9.

Kearns, P. (2005) *Evaluating the ROI from Learning: How to Develop Value-based Training,* London, CIPD.

Kenny, J. Donnelly, E. and Reid, M. (1979) *Manpower Training and Development*, 2nd edn, London, IPM.

Kirkpatrick, D.L. (1998) *Evaluating Training Programs*, 2nd edn, San Francisco, CA, Berrett-Koehler.

Leitch, S. (2006) *Prosperity for all in the Global Economy: World Class Skills*, HM Treasury, www.hm-treasury.gov.uk/media/6/4/leitch_finalreport051206.pdf.

LSC (Learning and Skills Council) (2006) *Impact Evaluation of the National Phase of the Leadership and Management Development Programme,* Coventry, LSC National Office.

Maxwell. J.A. and Lincoln, Y.S. (1990) Methodology and epistemology for social science, *Harvard Educational Review*, **60**(4): 497–512.

Mumford, A. and Gold, J. (2004) *Management Development: Strategies for Action,* London, CIPD.

Nutley, S., Percy-Smith, J. and Solesbury, W. (2003) *Models of Research Impact: A Cross Sector Review of Literature and Practice*, London, Learning and Skills Development Agency.

Patton, M. (1997) *Utilization-focused Evaluation*, 3rd edn, Thousand Oaks, CA, Sage.

Patton, M.Q. (2002) *Qualitative Evaluation and Research Methods*, 2nd edn, Thousand Oaks, CA, Sage.

Pawson, R. and Tilley, N. (1997) *Realistic Evaluation*, London, Sage.

Pearce, W.B. (1992) A 'camper's guide' to constructionisms, *Human Systems,* **3**: 136–61.

Phillips, J.J. (1994a) *Measuring Return on Investment*, vol. 1, Alexandria, VA, American Society for Training and Development.

Phillips, J.J. (1994b) *Measuring Return on Investment*, vol. 2, Alexandria, VA, American Society for Training and Development.

Phillips, J.J. (1997) *Handbook of Training Evaluation and Measurement Methods*, Houston, TX, Butterworth-Heinemann.

Phillips, P.P. and Phillips, J.J. (2001) *Measuring Return on Investment,* vol. 3*,* Alexandria, VA, American Society of Training and Development.

Preskill, H.S. and Torres, R.T. (1999) *Evaluative Inquiry for Learning in Organizations*, Thousand Oaks, CA, Sage.

Rix, M. and Gold, J. (2000) With a little help from my academic friend: mentoring change agents, *Mentoring and Tutoring*, **8**(1): 47–62.

Rock, D. (2006) *Quiet Leadership: Six Steps to Transforming Performance at Work,* London, HarperCollins.

Rossi, P.H. and Freeman H.E. (1993) *Evaluation: A Systematic Approach*, London, Sage.

Rothman, J. (1997) *Resolving Identity-based Conflict in Nations, Organizations, and Communities,* San Francisco, Jossey-Bass.

Russ-Eft, D. (2008) Expanding scope of evaluation in today's organizations, paper presented at the International HRD Conference, Lille.

Scriven, M. (1980) *The Logic of Evaluation*, Inverness, CA, Edgepress.

Scriven, M. (1991) *Evaluation Thesaurus*, 4th edn, Thousand Oaks, CA, Sage.

Shotter, J. (1993) *Conversational Realities*, London, Sage.

Stake, R.E. (2004) *Standards Based and Responsive Evaluation*, Thousand Oaks, CA, Sage.

Warr, P.B., Bird, M.W. and Rackham, N. (1970) *Evaluation of Management Training*, Aldershot, Gower.

Weiss, C.H. (1980) Knowledge creep and decision accretion, *Knowledge: Creation, Diffusion, Utilisation,* **1**: 381–404.

Weiss, C.H. (1995) Nothing as practical as good theory: exploring theory-based evaluation for comprehensive community initiatives for children and families, in J. Connell, A.C. Kubisch, L.B. Schorr and C.H. Weiss (eds) *New Approaches to Evaluating Community Initiatives: Concepts, Methods and Contexts*, Washington DC, Aspen Institute.

Weiss, C.H. (1998) Have we learned anything new about evaluation?, *American Journal of Evaluation*, **19**(1): 21–33.

Wilson, J. (ed.) *Human Resource Development*, 2nd edn, London, Kogan Page.

SECTION 2 CASE STUDY

Tackling a training and learning problem: the case of the Hull dinner ladies

Wide public interest in school dinners followed Jamie Oliver's campaign to raise awareness about the unhealthy provision and his attempts to change attitudes and behaviour in relation to healthy food in Britain's schools. Interestingly, it also raised the profile of another group of workers – dinner ladies – often unrecognized and undervalued in our society. Nora, one of the dinner ladies featured, became a star in her own right, and the issue of 'lunchtime supervisors' – to give them their 'proper' title – was brought into the public consciousness.

Following the campaign, Hull City Council began a free school dinner programme, offering free school meals to all primary school children. As part of the monitoring of the project, it was highlighted that there was a lack of training for lunchtime supervisors. Lunchtime supervisors provide supervision for children during the lunch break, both in the dining hall and outside in the playground, and should be distinguished from the catering staff who prepare and serve the food. Existing training was ad hoc and had no long-term impact on performance. In the absence of teaching staff during the hour and a half lunch break, the lunchtime supervisors are often in charge of the school and the pupils. In order to investigate the perceived lack of training, Hull City Council commissioned the

University of Hull to undertake a study of the training needs of lunchtime supervisors in 71 Hull primary schools.

All 71 schools were sent a survey to hand out to their lunchtime supervisors, asking questions about their role, their likes and dislikes, what they found challenging and the support they received. Six schools were selected to take part in a more in-depth study – chosen to vary in size, location and economic prosperity of the area. A representative from Hull University interviewed both the head teachers and the lunchtime supervisors over a period of several months. She spent a week working as a lunchtime supervisor and spoke to lunchtime supervisors, in groups and one to one, to understand what was required in the role and how the role was managed. A number of needs were identified:

- Head teachers wanted supervisors to be trained in playing with children to encourage playground activities
- The lunchtime supervisors themselves identified managing behaviour and resolving conflict as a key requirement
- The project manager highlighted developing confidence, understanding the role and understanding children's needs as critical requirements.

Additionally, as part of the investigation, a number of other contextual factors were highlighted; factors which it was considered important to acknowledge and address to help ensure the success of any training intervention:

- The government, in the form of Ofsted, measures the quality of lunchtime supervision as one factor in its assessment of school performance
- Hull City Council reports difficulties in recruiting lunchtime supervisors with the right skills. The work is low paid and confined to the lunchtime period
- Many of the existing dinner ladies left school without qualifications. Few had undertaken any sort of formal learning since leaving school
- The role of lunchtime supervisors tends to be undervalued by head teachers, teachers, children and even the dinner ladies themselves
- There was a lack of integration of the dinner ladies with the wider school team, highlighting the need to address the profile of the role and the need to change perceptions
- Some existing dinner ladies have been in the role for more than 20 years and believe their experience is sufficient and they therefore do not require training
- A number of existing staff have other part-time jobs, thus limiting their availability for training.

SOURCE: Stead, F., Griggs, V. and Holden, R.J. (2007) *The Case of the Hull Dinner Ladies: Interview with Faye Stead*, Leeds Metropolitan University

Questions

1 Consider the activities undertaken by Hull University to investigate the training needs of the dinner ladies. Would you consider these to be organizational-, job- or individual-level analysis?

2 Why might a training programme focusing on the needs as identified in the case be unsuccessful or insufficient?

Activities

1 Draw on the data collected and presented in the case study and develop two key competencies for the lunchtime supervisors, illustrating the mix of knowledge, skill and attitude in each competency statement.

2 Develop an outline proposal to meet the training needs identified. Include in the proposal:

- the method(s) to be used
- how the proposed training will reflect important ideas about learning and key principles of learning
- consideration of the characteristics of this particular group of trainees
- where the training might take place and when
- a consideration of resources and costs in relation to the proposed training.

3 Consider the evaluation of the proposed training. As in 2, develop an outline proposal, which addresses:

- an appropriate framework for the approach to be adopted for the evaluation
- how evaluation data might best be collected
- the value of the training activity to different stakeholders
- the extent to which the process of evaluation employed might further assist the learning of the dinner ladies.

SECTION 3 **LOOKING AT** HRD AT WORK

Workplace Learning and Knowledge Management

9

Jeff Gold, Rick Holden, Vivienne Griggs and Niki Kyriakidou

Chapter learning outcomes

After studying this chapter, you should be able to:

- Explain the meaning of workplace learning, Organizational Learning (OL) and Knowledge Management (KM)

- Understand key ideas relating to workplace learning such as the learning company

- Explain how knowledge is produced at work

- Understand how knowledge can be managed at work

- Assess how management development can be evaluated

Chapter outline

Introduction

The organization as a learning system

Organizational Learning

Knowledge creation and management

Summary

Introduction

The idea of high performance working as a route to competitive advantage – in an era of constant change from technology, global and local competition and high standards set by stakeholders and customers – is based on relationships of trust and commitment from enthusiastic employees who are empowered to use high skills and discretion in their work (Ashton and Sung, 2002). For HRD, it is now accepted that narrow conceptions concerned with training and work skills are insufficient – we are in the age of the learner and learning (Sloman, 2003). There is a shift in emphasis to how learning is occurring throughout an organization with a collective core competence of learning (Prahalad and Hamel, 1990). However, between the individual and the collective idea of a workplace or organization, there are the opportunities and situational factors that contribute to or prevent people from learning. That is, to a greater or lesser extent, a workplace provides space, an environment and a climate for learning, where most people gain and apply skills and knowledge every day of their working lives (Billett, 2006). Throughout the 1990s, many managers and leaders in organizations were attracted to the idea that their organization should become a 'learning organization' or 'learning company' (Pedler et al., 1991). By the start of the 2000s, this aspiration was extended to consider the importance of knowledge, its creation and management, stimulated by the increasing realization that many organizations were knowledge based, knowledge was the key ingredient of products and services (OECD, 1996) and that as knowledge workers, employees are a vital source of an organization's intellectual capital (Edvinsson and Malone, 1997). In this chapter, we will consider how this move to a more collective organizational view of learning at work provides new possibilities for HRD.

The organization as a learning system

A long-standing conundrum that has bedevilled many HRD practitioners is that despite their efforts to deliver training efficiently, this might not result in learning in terms of sustained changes in skills, behaviour and attitudes. Mayo (2005, p. 19), for example, suggests that a 'frightening amount of training' does not result in learning, for two reasons. First, training can be divorced from the workplace and so become irrelevant for those attending. Second, the training might not be supported by the context and environment of the workplace. Does this seem familiar?

Reflective questions

1   How effective are you in using training to change what you do?

2   What helps and what hinders you?

Taylor (1991) argued against the narrow focus on training through systematic models, which are simple and easily understood, and only suitable in stable environments. Thus in recent years, as environments have been less stable and more unpredictable, there has been growing interest in considering the contextual issues that affect learning at work, such as the motivation and interests of learners, but also factors like history and the response of others, such as managers, leaders and fellow workers. These elements together constitute a 'learning culture' at work. To consider the various factors requires a more systemic approach to HRD (Chiaburu and Tekleab, 2005) and an understanding of the organization as a learning system or what is usually referred to as 'workplace learning'.

This can be quite a challenge to managers and others because of the lack of awareness of taken-for-granted assumptions that dominate life in organizations. For example, Morgan's *Images of Organization* (2006) highlights the role of metaphor in explaining complex phenomena such as the workplace by crossing images and language. Thus an organization can be understood as a machine and this can feed into what decisions are made in the reality that follows. However, we must remember that metaphors are a way of talking and understanding and are not the reality – organizations are not machines but it can be useful to consider them as such. The danger arises, as Mintzberg (1990, p. 19) argued, when the idea of organization structure as 'machine bureaucracy' is accepted as the *only* way to structure an organization. In HRD, Marsick and Watkins (1999) have suggested that the machine metaphor lies behind the way learning is based on a deficit model of identifying gaps against a hard standard, with little room for considering attitudes, apart from how they can be manipulated to reinforce desired performance. One consequence is the way that accounting procedures reinforce the dominance of the machine metaphor by requiring measurement of the cause and effect links of HRD to the bottom line.

Workplace learning requires a challenge to the machine metaphor and attempts to employ alternative ways of understanding, with different metaphors such as organizations as systems. Thus, while the idea of workplace learning is hardly a new phenomenon, like many other aspects of what Gold and Smith (2003) have called the 'learning movement', there is often a link to how learning is a source of competitive advantage, especially in a knowledge-based economy (Harrison and Kessels, 2004); clearly, the implication is that learning is a good thing. One way of seeing the organization as a system for learning is by highlighting the interdependence between strategy, the role of managers and teams and knowledge transfer (Hirsh and Tamkin, 2005). Competency frameworks are often seen as a way of making such links manifest through performance management systems that declare development requirements that reflect business needs. However, research on the use of competencies suggests that the way they are used and the support that follows in learning is vital (Strebler et al., 1997), which highlights the working of what is referred to as the 'learning climate' or 'environment'. For example, based on research on apprentices, Fuller and Unwin (2003) suggest that a learning environment can be considered as more or less expansive or restrictive on a continuum. Expansive environments are characterized by access to learning and qualifications, career progression, the valuing of skills and knowledge and, crucially, managers as facilitators. It is not too difficult to work out the restrictive environment.

At the centre of an expansive learning environment lies the relationship between line managers and their staff. Recent research has again explored the importance of this relationship for learning and development (Hutchinson and Purcell, 2007). While it is often formal training programmes that are identified, it is managers who provide the structure and support that set the climate for learning, which also affects what happens after training has been completed, informally (Eraut et al., 1999). There is growing interest in selecting managers for the responsibility of supporting staff development and this includes allocating them the role of coach. Thus, the interdependent systemic view of workplace learning also seeks to engender a 'coaching culture', where, according to Clutterbuck and Megginson (2005, p. 44), coaching becomes the 'predominant style of managing and working together'. This view brings us closer to the performance of work and how this provides opportunities for learning (see below). Coaching is often associated with mentoring, although there are some differences, where mentoring usually focuses on longer term learning and development. It is usually carried out by someone more senior or experienced. HRD in Practice 9.1 shows how one organization used coaching to change the culture at work.

HRD in Practice 9.1

Coaching lifts morale at the Child Benefit Office

Managers at the beleaguered Child Benefit Office (CBO) no longer feel 'beaten into a place where they did what they were told' and this is thanks to coaching. Delegates at the CIPD's annual conference heard that staff morale has increased and firmly moved the CBO and its sister agency, the Tax Credit Office, away from a command and control culture.

Richard Summersgill, director of Child Benefit and Tax Credit Operations, part of HM Revenue & Customs said: 'When we inherited the culture in 2005, we were widely perceived as a failing organization, we had lots of flailing in the press and tens of thousands of unhappy customers. Much of it was down to

computers not doing what they were specified to do but it was a very difficult place for our people to work. Managers each day were getting different instructions; orders were being issued that had to be obeyed.'

Andy Farrar, Sommersgill's deputy, added: 'We needed a major transformation programme that recognized and unleashed dormant talent. We saw coaching as the cornerstone of that transformation.' The CBO and Tax Credit Office have spent 'tens of thousands of pounds' on coaching, but, according to Summersgill, it has 'more than paid off'.

Source: Adapted from Hall (2008)

Activity

Find out more about coaching at the International Coaching Federation – www.coachfederation.org.uk/. There is a free online journal on evidence-based coaching and mentoring at www.business.brookes.ac.uk/research/areas/ coaching&mentoring/. The European Mentoring and Coaching Council's site is at www.emccouncil.org/.

Moving towards a more systemic understanding of the workplace as a space for learning also requires a consideration of how there are different interpretations of the various activities and processes of work. It is within such activities and processes that people learn what they are allowed to do and what they should not do. For example, changes in processes advocated by management as part of a 'lean' production development usually require learning but employees may be reluctant, seeing this as a threat to their skills and their relationships with others (Bratton, 2001). There is a significant degree of uncertainty in how learning can be brought about in the workplace and Gold and Smith (2003) provide an image of the contested possibilities, shown in Figure 9.1.

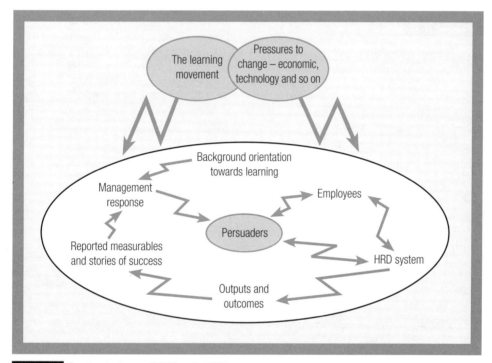

FIGURE 9.1 Contested possibilities in HRD

SOURCE: Adapted from Gold and Smith (2003)

This image begins to bring into play some of the less considered features of workplace learning. There is still a place for formality in the HRD system where training and other more recognized learning events are available and delivered. Outside the organization, in addition to the key considerations of pressures to change, there is also the learning movement, a part of the environment where recommendations, ideas and exhortations relating to learning and development are made but managers may or may not respond to these. It is suggested that some managers are more favourably disposed towards learning and development but this does not immediately become delivered learning. The jagged arrows indicate possible contests and the need for persuasion. Here there are key roles for managers as well as others who speak positively about learning, but there are also those who may not. Even if people complete activities, there is no certainty that learning follows (Antonacopoulou, 2001), nor that a precise cause and effect value can be shown – more likely is the spread of something good or otherwise by word-of-mouth storytelling.

Does this image come close to the way ideas about learning are spread in your organization or any organization you know?

The informal system

A systemic view of workplace learning extends understanding to consider any learning that takes place in the context of the workplace, and this has to include much of what occurs as a response to work issues, including mistakes, accidents, problems or just simple incidental conversations – indeed, anything that occurs at work which instigates and sustains a change in knowledge, skills and attitudes. However, when this occurs, learning may not be the word used by those involved. Some of it remains implicit and tacit (Reber, 2003), with little or no conscious awareness that it has happened or is being used. Alternatively, there might be some incidental but just-about recognized reaction to events, or a more deliberate use of events for the purpose of learning. These three possibilities are presented as a typology of informal or, as preferred by Eraut (2000a), 'non-formal learning'. Whatever changes have been made can remain local and protected by those involved so that the benefits or otherwise do not move to other parts of the organization. The important contrast to formal HRD is the way that skills development takes place naturally (Stuart, 1984), in a non-contrived manner, in response to the issues that occur almost every day at work, mainly from the work itself, especially through interactions with others such as customers and fellow workers. This calls for an embellishment of the systemic metaphor with the idea of what Felstead et al. (2005) call 'learning as participation'. There is now much interest in the everyday processes of learning, much of it informal, through participation in work practice. The influence of the work of Russian psychologist Vygotsky (1978) and the social-cultural theory of human development is noticeable. The theory highlights how learning occurs through participation in action and interactions with others, who can provide support to learn new skills. This process focuses on how mediation occurs through the use of 'tools' such as language, social signs and symbols to create new understanding in individuals. The linking of individual learners to their social and cultural context is part of what Beckett and Hager (2002) see as an 'emerging paradigm' of learning, which is:

- organic and holistic
- contextual
- activity and experience based
- found in situations where learning is not the main aim
- activated by individual learners rather than by trainers or teachers
- often collaborative or collegial.

Reflective questions

1 Do you often 'learn' when the main aim is not learning?

2 How influential are others in what you learn?

Fenwick (2008) has examined some of the key research in workplace learning over the past few years. The focus has been on the relationship between individual learning and the collective idea of the workplace. She found the idea of context to be particularly evident but with two contrasting possibilities of how the idea is understood. First, there is a view that context is a 'container' in which 'the individual moves' (p. 237). Within the container are the social and physical factors that make up an environment and this includes people and technology. It might also include the ways of talking and the various practices present. Second, there is the view of context as a 'web of relations', where individuals become inseparable from actions carried out jointly with others or a set of norms and values that are socially formed. This view is particularly pertinent to research on what are referred to as 'communities of practice' and a cultural view of organizing (see below). A key aspect of context relevant to both views is how power is analysed (Hager, 2004), although there is less research devoted to this.

However viewed, context is considered an essential component of models to take advantage of informal learning. For example, Marsick and Watkins (2001) provide a model for using informal and incidental learning, shown in Figure 9.2.

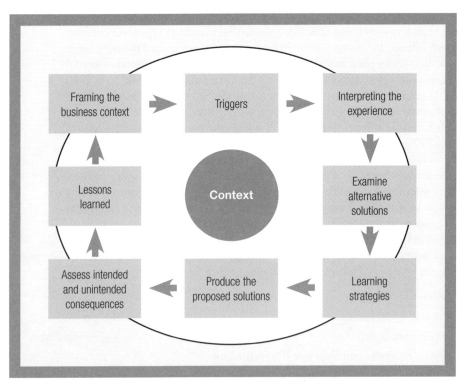

FIGURE 9.2 A model for informal and incidental learning

SOURCE: Marsick and Watkins (2001, p. 29)

The model shows how context provides everyday possibilities for learning, which begins with some kind of trigger. This may take the form of a challenge or a problem, perhaps a surprise. These all serve to create sufficient dissatisfaction to require some kind of further examination and assessment. Such interpretation is also affected by context, which can promote or even inhibit the examination. Marsick and Watkins (2001, p. 29) point out that while the model suggests progression, making sense is more likely to proceed as 'ebb and flow' rather than as a sequence. For example, lack of time and space can inhibit the move from interpretation to alternatives. Context includes history, which influences the choice of alternatives, and implementation may require new skills or special permissions, perhaps redefining roles and responsibilities. There may also be variations in providing resources for ambiguous projects. However, if action can be taken, outcomes can be assessed and lessons learned for future actions. If sustained, these can also feed into the context for further learning in the future. In this way, informal learning becomes more explicit and is available to be used by organizations, a theme we will explore below.

Billett (2006) also seeks to make the learning as participation metaphor in workplace learning more explicit, arguing for a workplace curriculum. A key point is that all organizations require employees to learn, and that it is 'erroneous' (p. 9) to refer to workplaces as informal learning environments, since by necessity an organization provides workers with 'affordances' to engage with learning at work, so that they can fulfil their role as defined by the division of labour. This also engenders various contests about the composition of the curriculum reflecting differing interests and goals. For example, more experienced workers might limit participation if they perceive a threat from new workers. There may also be cultural and historical norms that prevent access to participation, for example the so-called glass ceiling for women managers (see Veale and Gold, 1998). Peers and colleagues will also have an impact on learning experiences, depending on the impact on their interests. Managers, as we identified above, can play a key role in supporting staff to engage with opportunities (they can also hinder this process), although as Billett (2006, p. 33) argues, 'individuals themselves will ultimately determine how they participate in and learn through what is afforded them'.

Organizational Learning

The learning as participation metaphor as an elaboration of the systemic metaphor connects with ideas that organizations are learning on a continuous basis in a variety of ways. Indeed, learning is so embedded in what people do, how they work and the systems that connect the parts together, it becomes possible to consider OL as the source of life at work (Gibb, 2002). There is a great deal of attraction in considering OL as crucial to securing competitive advantage and change. A key idea is that if current ways of working – the organization's routines that accumulate through the experience of everyday working and responding to problems – are less likely to secure competitive advantage or the future life of the organization, then new ways must be found and learned (Antonacopoulou et al., 2005). However, this is not easy and one of the most useful contributions in OL has been made by Argyris (1999) and Argyris and Schön (1996).[1] Where current ways of working are accepted, change only occurs in response to errors or problems that need to be corrected to bring things back to normal. This is referred to as 'single-loop learning' and is the most common form of OL. There is no challenge to accepted routines and ways of working based on embedded assumptions accepted by everyone. A commonly used analogy to understand this is the use of a thermostat in maintaining the temperature of a room. By contrast, if ways of working are simply insufficient in the face of more difficult problems, such as changes in markets or technology, single-loop learning will not be enough because the embedded assumptions remain in place. What is required is a challenge to these assumptions and principles of working, a process referred to as 'double-loop learning'. An example would be an engineering company that focused on manufacturing, which increasingly found itself outcompeted on cost by overseas competition. The challenge to assumptions resulted in a new focus on design engineering, using the knowledge of its workers, allowing manufacturing to switch to lower cost producers if necessary. As we will see below, there is strong link between OL and using knowledge as the source of competitive advantage.

OL is broadly a field of study of 'the learning processes of and within organizations' (Easterby-Smith and Lyles, 2003, p. 9), and while it has certainly been important in recent years, as Mirvis (1996) has indicated, the foundation of OL lies in the development of systems ideas dating back to the 16th century. However, it wasn't until the 1950s that systems ideas began to be used in considering organizations, for example as social systems and processors of information. These alternatives to the dominant machine metaphor of organizations are now themselves taken for granted. The idea that organizations learn, like humans, is embedded, and yet organizations are not humans, but the idea of learning is transposed to organizations as if they were humans. For example, Dixon (1994) adapts Kolb's learning cycle (see Chapter 5) to form an organizational learning cycle based on the generation of information, its dissemination, integration and interpretation before its use in action. However, there are difficulties in moving from individual learning to other levels such as groups and teams and, of course, organizations. Fiol and Lyles (1985) argued that there was a lack of a clear definition of learning at levels beyond individuals and confusion with other terms such as adaptation and change.

One model of OL that attempts to link individual, group and organizational levels of analysis has been presented by Crossan et al. (1999). They argue that OL begins with learning at the individual level, then the group level before reaching the organizational level. There are four processes, working bidirectionally to create and apply knowledge. These processes, the '4Is model', are:

- *Intuiting:* individuals see patterns in their experience that provide new insights, which they translate into metaphors for possible communication to others.

- *Interpreting:* individuals explain their insights to themselves and then others, through talk, which then become possible ideas for application.

- *Integrating:* the group shares in the understanding and takes action as a consequence.

- *Institutionalizing:* the learning at individual and group levels becomes organizational through 'systems, structures, procedures and strategy' (p. 525) with which others can work.

Crossan et al. (1999) acknowledge that these processes, while forming a learning loop, are unlikely to flow without difficulty. For example, as outlined by Lawrence et al. (2005), power and politics are likely to play a role. Thus in the stages from intuition to interpretation, new ideas can be considered but take place against a background of what is rewarded and what is not. Any group will have a history of accepting or rejecting new ideas based on their interests. It is suggested that influence becomes crucial, requiring the control of resources, particular expertise that is seen as relevant and social skills that are in tune with cultures.

Another well-known OL model is Nonaka and Takeuchi's (1995) knowledge-creating model, as modified by Nonaka et al. (2000). The model is presented as a spiral of knowing that passes through conversion modes – these comprise the SECI model:

- *Socialization:* tacit knowledge of individuals shared with others

- *Externalization:* conversion of tacit knowledge into explicit metaphors, analogies, concepts and models

- *Combination:* new knowledge is combined with existing knowledge

- *Internalization:* whatever emerges from combination is enacted and becomes part of behaviour and accepted and so the process begins again.

Nonaka et al. (2000) also identify the importance of context, which can enable or inhibit the conversions. They conceptualize a context of shared space for knowledge creation, which they refer to as 'Ba'. This can be physical such as an office, or virtual, such as email or wiki, or mental, such as shared experiences. The nature of Ba varies with different phases. Thus Ba originates at the socialization phase, where face-to-face experiences are vital for the transfer of tacit knowledge.

Activity

Read more about Argyris at www.infed.org/thinkers/argyris.htm and Schön at www.infed.org/thinkers/et-schon.htm. Find out more about Nonaka's spiral and Ba at www.polia-consulting.com/A-Japanese-approach-of-KM-the-Ba.html.

These various OL models all imply or require some consideration of tacit knowledge, which, as we will consider below, is far from easy. There are other difficulties with OL models. For example, Weick and Westley (1996) suggest that the words 'organization learning' are an oxymoron, and are thus in contradiction. Preferring instead to consider the more active processes of learning and organizing since organization cannot be directly perceived, they also suggest using a cultural view of organizing to consider the dynamic of exploring and exploitation. This begins to tackle the assumption that organizations are single, unified entities. Yanow (2000) adopts a cultural view, for example, to consider the practice of groups and the values, beliefs and norms that are shared through talk, rituals, myths and stories. What we normally refer to as 'organizations' are composed of a variety of groups, practising or 'organizing' according to the local meanings and understanding created within the group. OL now becomes more concerned with this process of organizing, and learning at this local level can be as much about preserving what is valued and sustaining the life of the group as it is about change and innovation.

Communities of practice

The cultural view of OL connects with the importance of work practice as the source of knowing and the creation of knowledge, leading to the need for a practice-based understanding of how this occurs (Nicolini et al., 2003). For example, one of the most important contributions is the work on communities of practice (CoPs), where learning is mostly informal and improvisational, 'situated' in the practice of the work in a local context (Lave and Wenger, 1991). Learning occurs by becoming a participant in practice. Brown and Duguid (1991) use the idea of CoPs to show how the practice-based learning among technicians can be at variance to what others, such as managers outside the practice, consider to be the correct or 'espoused' way of doing things. It is practice in context that is learned, including the sharing of stories about practice and what is effective. This local knowledge can be very different to the abstract knowledge contained in work manuals or the talk of more senior managers. Yanow (2004, p. 12) highlights how local knowledge is frequently underprivileged in organizations at the expense of more theory-based and abstract knowledge, which is usually considered 'expert'. However, it is argued that local knowledge can also be expert. Thus salespersons and those working in the field are likely to learn about their practice of communicating with customers through their interactions, often in great detail. They learn about the lives and identities of those whom others might measure as numbers – both ways of understanding stem from different cultures that need to be considered in OL.

In recent years, CoPs have been recognized as a source of creativity and there has been an effort to formally recognize their value. In spite of the apparent informal and self-organizing quality around the demands of the situation, it is argued that they can be directed by managers and become more oriented towards 'their companies' success' (Wenger and Snyder, 2000, p. 145). There is widespread application of the idea of CoPs in the private and the public sector, often as part of KM techniques and toolkits.

However, there has also been criticism of the way CoPs have been commandeered by managers and consultants with too much focus on the formation of CoPs rather than the context of situated learning and the practice that occurs (Roberts, 2006). There is also a downplaying of the tensions, disagreements, contradictions and power issues in the way CoPs negotiate meanings (Marshall and Rollinson, 2004).

Nevertheless, research and debate continue about CoPs, and a crucial point remains concerning the importance of everyday practice that makes the life of any group at work, which is not always amenable to management control. Hager (2004) suggests that values of resistance to change and close boundaries are quite possible and presents a contrasting metaphor of construction, to bring together learners, context and articulation of learning.

The learning organization

Operationalizing CoPs has been one of the moves by managers in organizations to create learning organizations or learning companies. Thus while OL is a field of study, the learning organization (LO) is an attempt to make some of the ideas manifest in the workplace. In response, a range of models and formulas have been presented to provide guidance and even prescription. For example, in the UK, Pedler et al. (1991, p. 1) defined their version of the learning company as an 'organization which facilitates the learning of all its members and continuously transforms itself'. They included suggestions for the dimensions of a learning company, which provided differentiation from a non-learning company, including:

- A learning approach to strategy

- Participative policy making

- The use of ICT to inform and empower people

- Reward flexibility

- Self-development for all.

Of course, given the comments made earlier, it could be rather difficult to classify any organization as non-learning. Nevertheless, these dimensions give a flavour of the kinds of activities that could be pursued. Others, such as Peter Senge (1990a), suggested that learning organizations could be built on the basis of five disciplines:

- Personal mastery

- Shared vision

- Team learning

- Mental models

- Systems thinking.

Senge (1990b) was also keen to highlight the role of leaders as designers, teachers and stewards, whose job it was to challenge current mental models and support systemic thinking. In particular, leaders needed to work the idea of creative tension by developing a gap between current realities and feasible future possibilities. Thus the organization could engage with a generative learning process to create a new future, in contrast with adaptive learning, where the organization simply coped with the present.

Perhaps because of the idealistic nature of these models, there was little evidence of implementation and confusion on how to do this (Tsang, 1997). From the late 1990s, the idea of the LO remained popular and even appeared in government policy documents, along with other learning entities such as 'learning regions' or 'learning cities' (Longworth, 2006). The metaphor became one of a journey, possibly never completed but there is a retention of the persuasive appeal of the LO. Örtenblad (2004) suggests that the vagueness of the idea can be a source of creativity, although this is unlikely in bureaucratic structures. To help the journey of LOs, there are various diagnostic tools. For example, the Dimensions of the Learning Organization Questionnaire (DLOQ) is based on Watkins and Marsick's (1993) model, suggesting that the LO needs to consider dimensions at the people and the systems level (Yang et al., 2004). People-level dimensions include:

- Create continuous learning opportunities

- Promote enquiry and dialogue

- Encourage collaboration and team learning

- Empower people towards a collective vision

and the structural dimensions are:

- Connect the organization to its environment

- Establish systems to capture and share learning

- Provide strategic leadership for learning.

There are also outcome variables, such as the:

- Gain of organizational knowledge
- Increase of organization financial performance.

Another tool is provided by Garvin et al. (2008), who present three building blocks for measuring:

1 a supportive learning environment

2 concrete learning processes and practices

3 leadership behaviour that reinforces learning.

To some extent, the development of these tools is making the idea of the LO more meaningful, despite the scepticism among more critical observers (Sambrook and Stewart, 2002).

Activity

Go to www.partnersforlearning.com/instructions.html where you can find an online version of the DLOQ. Try another tool at www.conferenceboard.ca/humanresource/LPI/what.asp.

Action learning

The LO as a journey chimes with a process of learning that focuses on groups with difficult work issues. This is 'action learning', originally developed by Revans (1982) as a counter to theory-led management development activities. There continues to be ongoing debate as to the meaning of action learning (Pedler et al., 2005), but the basic idea is that work problems are identified that are not easy to solve.

Not exactly a principle but an indication of Revans' approach to action learning is his learning statement of $L = P + Q$, where L = learning, P = programme knowledge/instruction and Q = questioning insight. Revans (1998) gave more prominence to Q, which for him also stood for quandary, quiz and query. Less attention is given to P, which also stood for platitude, package and sometimes poppycock. Learners, through questions and support in a group, reflect on questions and decide what action to take to solve real problems (McGill and Beaty, 1995). The process becomes continuous through the need to report back to the group, and reflect on the action, results achieved and, most crucially, learning. The curriculum is determined by the learner against the context of work practice (McLaughlin and Thorpe, 1993). As trust and confidence in the process grows, participants can potentially ask more critical questions and take more challenging actions (Miller, 2003).

Knowledge creation and management

Since the late 1980s, when writers such as Drucker (1988) identified the need to change from the mechanistic command and control organization towards an information-based organization, knowledge and its creation and management have been considered as the source of lasting competitive advantage. The emphasis on knowledge has spawned a plethora of terms such as 'knowledge workers', 'knowledge-intensive organizations', the 'knowledge-based' view of the firm, 'knowledge societies' and so on. Knowledge has been seen as the key ingredient of products and services (OECD, 1996), and those who make, manipulate and apply it are part of an organization's intellectual capital (Edvinsson and Mallone, 1997) and a reason for investing in HRD as part of an organization's human capital accumulation (Garavan et al., 2001).

Information as knowledge

As indicated in other chapters (for example Chapter 16), advances made in the application of ICT, especially over the internet, allow the digitization, storage, retrieval, analysis and communication of information. In addition, there has been a convergence around microtechnologies, computing, telecommunications, broadcasting and optical electronics to make what Castells (2000) has seen as the new 'age of information', with revolutionary consequences. Part of this revolution is the way that information-processing devices incorporate feedback that allows the accumulation and transfer of information.

Reflective question

What assumptions are being made about the connection between information and knowledge?

It would seem that much of what is considered in KM is indistinguishable from information. For example, Mayo (1998, p. 36) defines KM as:

> the management of information, knowledge and experiences available to an organization – its creation, capture, storage, availability and utilization – in order that organizational activities build on what is already known and extend it further.

The information as knowledge equation is clearly prevalent in ICT-based commercial KM systems and more widely in a range of tools and devices. Even if the starting point is people, who learn something new, through codification and recording, this can be made available for searching by others anywhere in the world. This view of knowledge is clearly an option in deciding a strategy for managing knowledge (Hansen et al., 1999). Thus many organizations see KM as the installation of networked software and the allocation of roles to knowledge officers, company librarians, webmasters and information consultants. Capture and storage mean the resource can be counted as intellectual capital, even though there are many reasons why people in organizations may not use the KM tools available (Lubit, 2001). However, this is a partial view of knowledge and, as Machlup (1980, p. 27) reminds us, 'knowledge … has several meanings'. Scarbrough and Swan (2001, p. 8) suggest that the systems and technologies of KM tend to 'gloss over the complex and intangible aspects of human behaviour', including learning in the workplace, where, we argue, much of what really counts for knowledge is created and used in practice. It becomes difficult to separate knowledge from those who know, what Tsoukas (2000) refers to as a 'knowing subject', who always exists in some place of action, embedded in some collective way of life.

Knowing-that and knowing-how

While any discussion on knowing and knowledge is fraught with difficulty, it is common to use a distinction first made by Ryle ([1949]1984) between 'knowing-that' and 'knowing-how'. The former is concerned with concepts and abstractions that can be made explicit and communicable, based on facts and explanations. For individuals, it is their 'embrained' knowledge (that is, knowledge dependent on their conceptual skills and cognitive abilities), as suggested by Blackler (1995). This form of knowledge is highly valued in our society and can become public, available in a codified form, and easily stored and transferred, for example in books, journals and papers from internet databases. As suggested above, this is barely distinguishable from information.

By contrast, knowing-how is personal, based on knowing what to do according to the requirements of the situation. According to Blackler (1995), this is 'embodied knowledge', and is related to doing and practice that can also become collective knowing-how, as embedded knowledge in organization routines and norms. Eraut (2000b, p. 128) suggests that dealing with new or unexpected events 'cannot be accomplished by procedural knowledge alone or by following a manual'. This kind of knowing is 'tacit' and it is generally accepted that without consideration of the tacit dimension in knowledge creation and management, there is little benefit from the accumulation of codified knowledge generated by advances in ICT. As identified earlier, it is also the source and potentially the outcome of OL models, such as that of Nonaka et al. (2000). According to Polanyi (1967), tacit knowing, the key source of this idea, is not easy to put into words. For example, we can usually pick out a face we know from a large crowd but it would be difficult to say how we do this. As Polanyi states: 'this knowledge cannot be put into words' (p. 6). This makes some of the claims relating to tacit knowledge and its role in KM problematic, or, as Beckett and Hager (2002, p. 120) point out, there is a 'multiply ambiguous' nature of tacit knowledge with a variety of meanings (see Chapter 16). Thus Collins (2001), who is concerned with the transferability of tacit knowledge in science, provides the following classification:

1 *Concealed knowledge:* 'the tricks of the trade', deliberately concealed and not passed on to others, or not included in journals with insufficient space for such details.

2 *Mismatched salience:* there are an indefinite number of potentially important variables in a new and difficult experiment and the two parties focus on different ones.

3 *Ostensive knowledge:* words, diagrams, or photographs cannot convey information that can be understood by direct pointing, demonstrating or feeling.

4 *Unrecognized knowledge:* work performed in a certain way without realizing the importance of this – others pick up the same habit during a visit, and neither party realizes that anything important has been passed on.

5 *'Uncognized/uncognizable' knowledge:* humans do things such as speak acceptably formed phrases in their native language without knowing how they do it.

Gourlay (2006, p. 67) seeks to remove some of the ambiguity by suggesting that we use the term 'tacit knowledge' in those situations where there is evidence of action or behaviour 'of which the actors could not give an account', which is closer to Polanyi's view considered above. He argues that managers can create the conditions for experiences to influence tacit knowledge but this can also 'be in a negative direction' (p. 67), as defensive routines. This view also has the potential to bring KM closer to learning and, as argued by Spender (2008), helps to move theory towards the creation of knowledge. He presents an emerging typology of KM – 'knowledge-as-data, knowledge-as-meaning and knowledge-as-practice' – and suggests that the latter is best placed to deal with uncertainties, failures, 'not-knowing or knowledge-absence' (p. 166) as the source of creativity and the development of a methodology to explore, understand and manage the constraints that people in organizations have to face.

Activity

Work with a partner. How much tacit knowing is there in reading this question? Share your comments.

Try the following links to resources and publications on KM – www.kmre-source.com/ and www.kmnetwork.com/. Go to www.localdirect.gov.uk/assets/other/cd4-local-directgov-knowledge/ to examine a KM guide, including the use of CoPs.

Increasingly, it would seem that the opportunities for learning and knowledge creation in response to failures and knowledge gaps are becoming more evident, requiring new ways of organizing as a response. For example, project-based organizing enables a response to customer demand that expects differentiated goods and services in sectors such as fashion, the arts, software, digital and multimedia (Sydow et al., 2004). Such products and services need to be customized through negotiation rather than standardized for a mass market, and therein lies the space for 'not-knowing' and creativity. To take advantage of these possibilities so that learning can be shared requires devices such as project reviews, critical incident logs and informal sharing of ideas (Brady and Davies, 2004). HRD in Practice 9.2 provides an example of how one company seeks to learn from projects.

HRD in Practice 9.2

Learning in projects at Intraining NTP Consulting

First of all learning is a crucial part of what we do. Even when we have experience of a particular presenting issue, it is never exactly the same as our experience. Client briefs are always context specific and even if we are in familiar territory, there are always new facets to be considered.

Managing knowledge is something close to our hearts and we try to focus on two aspects. Learning before, during and after a project and double-loop learning, that is, having learned from what is happening, digging deeper and looking for insights that at first sight might be hidden from view.

While we are by no means perfect, we try to approach all our projects in this way. At the beginning of a project, we will pull the team together to decide on a methodology and try and draw the process. This draws out learning, before people can contribute to the diagrams based on their experience. We establish clear aims and objectives for the project for the client and any we might have. This approach also allows people who are not directly involved in the project to keep in touch and be brought in at a moment's notice to comment and review progress, ideas and problems so that a team approach is maintained.

Evaluation is built into all our projects as a 'learning history', which is an ongoing review and at the end when the final report is delivered. We try to make sure that people working on a specific project are supported by the whole team without interfering with progress and creating a committee. In this way, everybody can keep in touch and learn from what is going on.

Source: Mike Rix (2008, personal communication)

In addition, it is not just within projects that knowledge can be created. As suggested by Newell et al. (2004), a team may not have all the relevant knowledge for its work and needs to network with others. This process draws on what Nahapiet and Ghoshal (1998, p. 243) call 'social capital', defined as the 'sum of the actual and potential resources, available through, and derived from, the network of relationships possessed by an individual or social unit'. The use of social capital depends on trust and reciprocity. For sharing knowledge that feeds relationships to build social capital, there need to be opportunities to share knowledge, a degree of empathy, help and trust and a belief that the knowledge is accurate and reliable (von Krogh, 2003).

In addition to projects, customization can require an ongoing learning process between organizations and customers. Victor and Boynton (1998, p. 195) refer to this type of working as co-configuration:

> Mass customization … requires the company to sense and respond to the individual customer's needs. But co-configuration work takes this relationship up one level – it brings the value of an intelligent and 'adapting' product.

As a way of working, co-configuration is synonymous with knowledge creation and knowledge sharing. It is oriented to both individuals and groups and has the potential to link learning at the individual level to that of the organization. Daniels (2004) identifies two features of learning for successful co-configuration. First, learning for co-configuration where different departments representing different specialisms find a mechanism for dialogue to negotiate their practices. Second, through interaction with customers and others, learning is articulated so that knowledge can be shared. Both processes become interdependent in a dialogue around customer and practice.

Summary

- Difficulties in implementing systematic models of training have led to an interest in understanding the contextual issues that affect learning at work. Understanding the organization as a learning system is referred to as 'workplace learning'.

- Workplace learning requires the use of different ways of understanding organizations and contrasts to the dominant image of organizations as machines.

- Informal learning at work includes much of what occurs as a response to work issues, including mistakes, accidents, problems or just simple incidental conversations, although changes that occur often remain protected by those who made them.

- There is growing interest in how organizations can take advantage of informal learning by emphasizing participation to make learning more explicit.

- OL is concerned with the routines of working that accumulate through experience of working and dealing with problems and finding new ways of working where required. It requires a consideration of learning at different levels of the organization.

- A cultural view of OL can lead to a consideration of communities of practice, where learning is informal and situated in practice.

- The LO and action learning are ways managers and others have tried to stimulate and take advantage of OL.

- Knowledge, its creation and management have been considered as the source of lasting competitive advantage. There are different ideas relating to the meaning of knowledge, such as the distinction between knowing-that and knowing-how.

- Tacit knowledge is considered important to models of KM but difficult to capture or even 'put into words'.

- Projects and customization require new ways of working, sharing knowledge and learning in an ongoing process.

Discussion questions

1 Should line managers take responsibility for HRD?
2 How can informal learning be considered in organizations?
3 Do organizations learn? Can such learning be used for competitive advantage?
4 Is the learning organization achievable?
5 Can tacit knowledge be understood?

Further reading

Bratton, J. (2004) *Workplace Learning: A Critical Introduction*, Aurora, Ontario, Garamond Press.

Bresnen, M. and Goussevskaia, A. (2004) Embedding new management knowledge in project-based organizations, *Organization Studies*, **25**(9): 1535–55.

Davies, L. (2008) *Informal Learning*, Aldershot, Gower.

Duguid, P. (2005) 'The art of knowing': social and tacit dimensions of knowledge and the limits of the community of practice, *Information Society*, **21**(2): 109–18.

Elkjaer, B. (2004) Organizational learning: the 'third way', *Management Learning*, **35**(4): 419–34.

Pedler, M., Burgoyne, J.G. and Brook, C. (2005) What has action learning learned to become?, *Action Learning: Research and Practice*, **2**(1): 49–68.

Note

1   Argyris and Schön were themselves working with the ideas of Bateson (1972).

References

Antonacopoulou, E.P. (2001) The paradoxical nature of the relationship between training and learning, *Journal of Management Studies*, **38**(3): 327–50.

Antonacopoulou, E.P., Ferdinand, J., Graca, M. and Easterby-Smith, M. (2005) *Dynamic Capabilities and Organizational Learning: Socio-political Tensions in Organizational Renewal*, London, Advanced Institute of Management.

Argyris, C. (1999) *On Organizational Learning*, Oxford, Blackwell.

Argyris, C. and Schön, D.A. (1996) *Organizational Learning II*, Reading, MA, Addison-Wesley.

Ashton, D. and Sung, J. (2002) *High Performance Work Practices: A Comparative Analysis on Issues and Systems*, Geneva, International Labour Organization.

Bateson, G. (1972) *Steps to an Ecology of the Mind*, New York, Ballantine.

Beckett, D. and Hager, P. (2002) *Life, Work and Learning: Practice in Postmodernity,* London, Routledge.

Billett, S. (2006) Constituting the workplace curriculum, *Journal of Curriculum Studies*, **38**(1): 31–48.

Blackler, F. (1995) Knowledge, knowledge work and organizations: an overview and interpretation, *Organization Studies*, **16**(6): 1021–46.

Brady, T. and Davies, A. (2004) Building project capabilities: from exploratory to exploitative learning, *Organization Studies*, **25**(9): 1601–21.

Bratton, J. (2001) Why workers are reluctant learners: the case of the Canadian pulp and paper industry, *Journal of Workplace Learning*, **13**(7/8): 333–44.

Brown, J.S. and Duguid, P. (1991) Organizational learning and communities-of-practice: toward a unified view of working, learning, and innovation, *Organization Science*, **2**(1): 40–57.

Castells, M. (2000) *The Rise of Network Society*, Malden, MA, Blackwell.

Chiaburu, D. and Tekleab, A.G. (2005) Individual and contextual influences on multiple dimensions of training effectiveness, *Journal of European Industrial Training*, **29**: 604–23.

Clutterbuck, D. and Megginson, D. (2005) *Making Coaching Work*, London, CIPD.

Collins, H.M. (2001) Tacit knowledge, trust, and the Q of sapphire, *Social Studies of Science*, **31**(1): 71–85.

Crossan, M., Lane, H. and White, R. (1999). An organizational learning framework: from intuition to institution, *Academy of Management Review*, **24**: 522–37.

Daniels, H. (2004) Cultural historical activity theory and professional learning, *International Journal of Disability, Development and Education*, **51**(2): 185–200.

Dixon, N. (1994) *The Organizational Learning Cycle: How We Can Learn Collectively*, Maidenhead, McGraw-Hill.

Drucker, P. (1988) The coming of the new organization, *Harvard Business Review*, **66**(1): 45–53.

Easterby-Smith, M. and Lyles, M.A. (2003) Introduction: watersheds of organizational learning and knowledge management, in M. Easterby-Smith and M.A. Lyles (eds) *The Blackwell Handbook of Organizational Learning and Knowledge Management*, Oxford, Blackwell.

Edvinsson, L. and Malone, M.S. (1997) *Intellectual Capital*, New York, Harper Business.

Eraut, M. (2000a) Non-formal learning, implicit learning and tacit knowledge in professional work, in F. Coffield (ed.) *The Necessity of Informal Learning*, Bristol, Policy Press.

Eraut, M. (2000b) Non-formal learning and tacit knowledge in professional work, *British Journal of Educational Psychology*, **70**: 113–36.

Eraut, M., Alderton, J., Cole, G. and Senker, P. (1999) The impact of the manager on learning in the workplace, in F. Coffield (ed.) *Speaking Truth to Power,* Bristol, Policy Press.

Felstead, A., Fuller, A., Unwin, L. et al. (2005) Surveying the scene: learning metaphors, survey design and the workplace context, *Journal of Education and Work*, **18**(4): 359–83.

Fenwick, T. (2008) Understanding relations of individual collective learning in work: a review of research, *Management Learning*, **39**(3): 227–43.

Fiol, C.M. and Lyles, M.A (1985) Organizational learning, *Academy of Management Review*, **10**(4): 803–13.

Fuller, A. and Unwin, L. (2003) Learning as apprentices in the contemporary UK workplace: creating and managing expansive and restrictive participation, *Journal of Education and Work*, **16**(4): 407–26.

Garavan, T.N., Morley, M., Gunnigle, P. and Collins, E. (2001) Human capital accumulation: the role of human resource development, *Journal of European Industrial Training*, **25**(2/3/4): 48–68.

Garvin, D., Edmondson, A. and Gino, F. (2008) Is yours a learning organization?, *Harvard Business Review*, **86**(3): 109–16.

Gibb, S. (2002) *Learning and Development: Processes, Practices and Perspectives at Work*, Basingstoke, Palgrave Macmillan.

Gold, J. and Smith, V. (2003) Advances towards a learning movement: translations at work, *Human Resource Development International*, **6**(2): 139–52.

Gourlay, S. (2006) Towards conceptual clarity for 'tacit knowledge': a review of empirical studies, *Knowledge Management Research & Practice*, **4**(1): 60–9.

Hager, P. (2004) Lifelong learning in the workplace? Challenges and issues, *Journal of Workplace Learning*, **16**(1): 22–33.

Hall, L. (2008) Coaching lifts morale at Child Benefit Office, *People Management*, 2 October, p. 12.

Hansen, M.T., Nohria, N. and Tierney, T. (1999) What's your strategy for managing knowledge?, *Harvard Business Review*, **77**(2): 106–16.

Harrison, R. and Kessels, J. (2004) *Human Resource Development in a Knowledge Economy*, Basingstoke, Palgrave Macmillan.

Hirsh, W. and Tamkin, P. (2005) *Planning Training for your Business*, Brighton, Institute of Employment Studies.

Hutchinson, S. and Purcell, J. (2007) *Learning and the Line: The Role of Line Managers in Training, Learning and Development*, London, CIPD.

Lave, J. and Wenger, E. (1991) *Situated Learning: Legitimate Peripheral Participation*, Cambridge, Cambridge University Press.

Lawrence, T.B., Mauws, M.K., Dyck, B. and Kleysen, R.F. (2005) The politics of organizational learning: integrating power into the 4I framework, *Academy of Management Review*, **30**(1): 180–91.

Longworth, N. (2006) *Learning Cities, Learning Regions, Learning Communities*, London, Routledge.

Lubit, R. (2001) The keys to sustainable competitive advantage: tacit knowledge and knowledge management, *Organizational Dynamics*, **29**(3): 164–78.

Machlup, F. (1980) *Knowledge: Its Creation, Distribution, and Economic Significance*, vol. 1, *Knowledge and Knowledge Production*, Princeton, NJ, Princeton University Press.

McGill, I. and Beaty, L. (1995) *Action Learning*, London, Kogan Page.

McLaughlin, H. and Thorpe, R. (1993) Action learning – a paradigm in emergence: the problems facing a challenge to traditional management education and development, *British Journal of Management*, **4**(1): 19–27.

Marshall, N. and Rollinson, J. (2004) Maybe Bacon had a point: the politics of interpretation in collective sensemaking, *British Journal of Management*, **15**(Special 1): 71–86.

Marsick, V.J. and Watkins, K. (1999) Envisioning new organizations for learning, in D. Boud and J. Garrick (eds) *Understanding Learning at Work*, London, Routledge.

Marsick, V.J. and Watkins, K. (2001) Informal and incidental learning, *New Directions for Adult and Continuing Education*, **89**: 25–34.

Mayo, A. (1998) Memory bankers, *People Management,* 22 January: 34–8.

Mayo, A. (2005) What are the latest trends in training and development?, in CIPD, *Latest Trends in Learning, Training and Development*, London, CIPD.

Miller, P. (2003) Workplace learning by action learning: a practical example, *Journal of Workplace Learning*, **15**(1): 14–23.

Mintzberg, H. (1990) The design school: reconsidering the basic premises of strategic management, *Strategic Management Journal*, **11**(3): 171–95.

Mirvis, P.H. (1996) Historical foundations of organization learning, *Journal of Organizational Change Management,* **9**(1): 13–31.

Morgan, G. (2006) *Images of Organization*, London, Sage.

Nahapiet, J. and Ghoshal, S. (1998) Social capital, intellectual capital and the organizational advantage, *Academy of Management Review*, **23**(2): 242–66.

Newell, S., Tansley, C. and Huang, J. (2004) Social capital and knowledge integration in an ERP project team: the importance of bridging and bonding, *British Journal of Management*, **14**: S43–57.

Nicolini, D., Gherardi, S. and Yanow, D. (eds) (2003) *Knowing in Organizations: A Practice-based Approach*, New York, Armonk.

Nonaka, I. and Takeuchi, H. (1995) *The Knowledge-creating Company*, New York, Oxford University Press.

Nonaka, I., Toyama, R. and Konno, N. (2000) SECI, Ba and leadership: a unified model of dynamic knowledge creation, *Long Range Planning*, **33**: 5–34.

OECD (Organization for Economic Co-operation and Development) (1996) *The Knowledge-based Economy,* Paris, OECD.

Örtenblad, A. (2004) The learning organization: towards an integrated model, *Learning Organization*, **11**(2): 129–44.

Pedler, M., Burgoyne, J.G. and Boydell, T. (1991) *The Learning Company: A Strategy for Sustainable Development*, Cambridge, McGraw-Hill.

Pedler, M., Burgoyne, J. and Brook, C. (2005) What has action learning learned to become?, *Action Learning: Research and Practice,* **2**(1): 49–68.

Polanyi, M. (1967) *The Tacit Dimension*, Garden City, NY, Doubleday.

Prahalad, C.K. and Hamel, G. (1990) The core competence of the corporation, *Harvard Business Review*, **68**: 79–91.

Reber, A.S. (2003). Implicit learning and tacit knowledge, in B.J. Baars (ed.) *Essential Sources in the Scientific Study of Consciousness*, Boston, MIT Press.

Revans, R. (1982) *The Origins and Growth of Action Learning*, Lund, Studentlitteratur.

Revans, R. (1998) *ABC of Action Learning*, London, Lemons & Crane.

Roberts, J. (2006) Limits to communities of practice, *Journal of Management Studies*, **43**(3): 623–39.

Ryle, G. ([1949]1984) *The Concept of Mind*, Chicago, University of Chicago Press.

Sambrook, S. and Stewart, J. (2002) Reflections and discussion, in S. Tjepkema, J. Stewart, S. Sambrook et al. (eds) *HRD and Learning Organizations in Europe*, London, Routledge.

Scarbrough, H. and Swan, J. (2001) Explaining the diffusion of knowledge management: the role of fashion, *British Journal of Management*, **12**(1): 3–12.

Senge, P.M. (1990a) *The Fifth Discipline: The Art and Practice of the Learning Organization*, New York, Currency Doubleday.

Senge, P.M. (1990b) The leader's new work: building learning organizations, *Sloan Management Review*, **32**(1): 7–23.

Sloman, M. (2003) *Training in the Age of the Learner*, London, CIPD.

Spender, J.-C. (2008) Organizational learning and knowledge management: whence and whither?, *Management Learning*, **39**(2): 159–76.

Strebler, M., Robinson, D. and Heron, P. (1997) *Getting the Best out of your Competencies*, Brighton, Institute of Employment Studies.

Stuart, R. (1984) Towards re-establishing naturalism in management training and development, *Industrial and Commercial Training*, July/August: 19–21.

Sydow, J., Lindkvist, L. and DeFillippi, R. (2004) Project-based organizations, embeddedness and repositories of knowledge, *Organization Studies*, **25**(9): 1475–89.

Taylor, H. (1991) The systematic training model: corn circles in search of a spaceship?, *Management Education and Development*, **22**(4): 258–78.

Tsang, E.W. (1997) Organizational learning and the learning organization: a dichotomy between descriptive and prescriptive research, *Human Relations*, **50**: 73–89.

Tsoukas, H. (2000) Knowledge as action, organization as theory, *Emergence*, **2**(4): 104–12.

Veale, C. and Gold, J. (1998) Smashing into the glass ceiling for women managers, *Journal of Management Development*, **17**(1): 17–26.

Victor, B. and Boynton, A. (1998) *Invented Here: Maximizing your Organization's Internal Growth and Profitability*, Boston, Harvard Business School Press.

Von Krogh, G. (2003) Knowledge sharing and the communal resources, in M. Easterby-Smith and M.A. Lyles (eds) *The Blackwell Handbook of*

Organizational Learning and Knowledge Management, Oxford, Blackwell.

Vygotsky, L. (1978) *Mind and Society: The Development of Higher Mental Processes*, Cambridge, MA, Harvard University Press.

Watkins, K.E. and Marsick, V.J. (1993) *Sculpting the Learning Organization: Lessons in the Art and Science of Systemic Change*, San Francisco, Jossey-Bass.

Weick, K. and Westley, F. (1996) Organizational learning: affirming an oxymoron, in S. Clegg, C. Hardy and W. Nord (eds) *Handbook of Organization Studies*, Thousand Oaks, CA, Sage.

Wenger, E.C. and Snyder, W.M. (2000) Communities of practice: the organizational frontier, *Harvard Business Review*, 78(1): 139–45.

Yang, B., Watkins, K.E. and Marsick, V.J. (2004) The construct of the learning organization: dimensions, measurement, and validation, *Human Resource Development Quarterly*, 15(1): 31–55.

Yanow, D. (2000) Seeing organizational learning: a 'cultural' view, *Organization*, 7(2): 247–68.

Yanow, D. (2004) Translating local knowledge at organizational peripheries, *British Journal of Management*, 15(S1): 9–25.

Management Development

Jeff Gold, Joanna Smith and Catherine Burrell

10

Chapter learning outcomes

After studying this chapter, you should be able to:

- Explain the meaning of managers, management and Management Development (MD)
- Understand the importance of MD for individuals, organizations and the country
- Explain various approaches to assess the development needs of managers
- Understand how effective learning can be provided for managers
- Assess how MD can be evaluated

Chapter outline

Introduction

For many years, there have been concerns about the quality and quantity of managers in UK organizations and elsewhere, although it is still not clear as to whether this represents a problem (Burgoyne et al., 2004). For example, in an influential report by Porter (2003) on the UK economy, it was suggested that the capability of managers was a consequence of investment, the use of advanced technology and the employment of highly skilled labour, rather than its cause. Nevertheless, it has become conventional wisdom to support the view that Management Development (MD) is a good thing for individuals, organizations and the nation. The Leitch (2006) review of skills highlighted this view, by linking an improvement in management skills to the improvement in business performance. Recent research across Europe does indeed suggest that investment in MD impacts on organizational performance and productivity, although this link is seldom straightforward and is contingent on a number of factors, such as the priority given to, and support for, MD by those in senior positions (Mabey and Ramirez, 2005).

We certainly hope to explore such factors in this chapter, which reinforce a common understanding about managers and managing: management is a complex process contingent on the particular requirements of specific organizations. It involves more objective features such as technology and the nature of work but also highly subjective factors such as the attitudes of managers, staff, customers and their traditions, culture and history. These factors vary from one organization to another and affect the way managers work, learn and develop (Mumford and Gold, 2004). Further, in recent years, there has been a discernable growing interest in MD and how good practice can be extended across a variety of differing areas. For example, there has been much interest in MD in all areas of the public sector, including schools, hospitals and the health sector, local government and the civil service. There is also interest among community and voluntary groups – now referred to as the 'third sector'. Evidence of this interest was provided by the work of the Council for Excellence in Management and Leadership (CEML, 2002a), which also examined MD in the professions and SMEs.

You will have noticed that, increasingly, the term 'leadership' is used either alongside MD or as a replacement for it. We will briefly examine this process in this chapter (see Chapter 11 for more on Leadership Development). However, whatever term is employed, there are significant issues to consider relating to what might be considered good practice. In this chapter, we will focus on MD and take the view that even those who occupy senior positions as leaders in organizations will still need to be managers too. Further, many will have started their careers as trainees in an occupation before moving into positions where they have to manage others as well as themselves. They are therefore likely, to a greater or lesser extent, to be exposed to MD methods and processes. We will first consider the nature of such work and how MD might contribute towards its effective practice.

Managers, management and MD

In the UK, a large number of people are identified by the title 'manager' or 'leader'. There is also a wide variation of meanings attached to such titles. For example, in some organizations, senior staff are called managers or executives and other staff might be called leaders, such as 'team leaders'. Other terms might include coordinator and supervisor. This makes it difficult to calculate precisely the numbers of managers; however, the

Economic & Labour Market Review publishes quarterly figures of a range of indicators including employment by occupation. Thus in November 2007, there were over 29 million people in employment, of whom around 4.5 million or 15.2% were recorded as 'managers and senior officials' (www.statistics.gov.uk/elmr/11_07/). However, we suggest that many more people are likely to be involved in managing as an activity such as professionals and those in skilled trade occupations. As the economy becomes increasingly knowledge based and service driven (Moynagh and Worsley, 2005), more people are likely to be involved in managing, even if their title does not designate them as managers. Of course, there are many small business owners who can't avoid the activity of managing, although they may not be particularly skilled at doing so (CEML, 2002b).

Activity

You can find updated figures on the numbers of managers from the *Economic & Labour Market Review* at www.statistics.gov.uk/elmr/03_08/data_page.asp.

There are a variety of formal qualifications specifically concerned with management or business but many study areas would also include some aspect of management, for example hospitality, sports, events and so on. CEML (2002a) highlighted the growth in numbers to 11,000 of those achieving MBAs in 2000, but there are many other kinds of management qualifications at Masters and professional levels, offered in over 100 business schools in the UK. According to the Higher Education Statistics Agency (HESA, www.hesa.ac.uk/index.php), in 2006/07, there were over 300,000 students in the UK studying for business and administrative qualifications, an increase of around 30% since 1996. There are also a range of vocational qualifications in management leading to NVQs, although it is usual to indicate that the UK gives less emphasis to vocational qualifications compared to other countries (Tamkin et al., 2006). In addition, for many who study for management qualifications, there is usually an opportunity to focus on particular functional areas of management such as marketing, finance, HRM and HRD. Where the qualification leads to membership of a professional body – such as the CIPD or the Institutes of Chartered Accountants in England and Wales and Scotland – this can serve as an entry to general management later on. What is important is that all such qualifications, to a great or lesser extent, draw on a body of knowledge referred to as 'management'.

Reflective questions

1   Do you feel that your studies are preparing you sufficiently for management?

2   Do you believe that you have or will have the credentials to be a manager?

While management as an activity has been with us since the dawn of civilization, most accounts of management theory begin with the work of F.W. Taylor in the USA, who analysed work tasks and set the methods to find a 'one best way' to control work and eliminate waste. While Taylor worked in the latter part of the nineteenth century, the influence of his work gave birth to what has been called 'scientific management' and the assumption that through the systematic and rigorous study of work, basic principles will be found. In the twentieth century, the work of the French writer Henri Fayol (1949) set out the main management functions as planning, organizing, coordinating, command and control. These categories still form the main areas of coverage and theory presentation in management textbooks. Together, the work of Taylor and Fayol advocating managers as scientists and administrators has been called 'classical management', and debates continue on the value of this view of management in describing the work of managers (Caroll and Gillen, 1987). However, you will still find many courses and training events for managers based on classical management. In addition, since the 1930s, in what became known as the 'human relations school', there has been a growing influence of psychology and behaviour sciences. This opened up thinking on such issues as motivation, payment systems, conflict, groups and managing change – again, prime issues to this day for many management courses and another image for managers as behavioural scientists. Together, the theories and models from classical management and the human relations school still form much of the content of what is taught in management qualifications like the MBA. However, in recent times, there has been much criticism of this approach and the disconnection of such theories from actual practice (Bennis and O'Toole, 2005).

This is rather surprising, since we have known quite a lot about practice for some time. For example, in the UK, Stewart (1975) studied the work of hundreds of managers and found that they:

- worked at a brisk pace with little free time

- spent a lot time interacting with people

- based a lot of their work on personal choice

- do not work according to neat, well-organized models.

Kotter's (1982) work also found a lack of apparent organization or even strategic behaviour. Instead, managers spent a lot time dealing with a variety of issues through conversations. This might appear rather inefficient but was the way of getting things done. There was no formal plan as such but a more informal 'agenda' and then the building of a network of several others through whom objectives could be achieved. This informality is important for those who seek to help managers learn, as we shall see.

The turn towards the reality of what managers do has produced much research and new images. There are two, among several, that appeal to us. The first is derived from Watson's (1994) study of managers as they practised their work. He highlighted the value-laden and moral positions of managers. For Watson, 'management is essentially and inherently a social and moral activity', where success is achieved by 'building organizational patterns, cultures and understandings based on relationships of mutual trust and shared obligation among people involved with the organization' (p. 223).

The second image is one associated with the importance of conversations in management. Here, the manager creates meaning through talk with others, and through such talk provides clarity for others. Talk is crucial to practice and makes things happen if others respond positively. However, this is not always predictable and so managers need to argue persuasively in this process. This is an image of the manager as a practical author, presented by Shotter and Cunliffe (2003).

Consider each of the images presented. What are the implications for MD of such images?

The various images of managers provide different views on the meaning and practice of MD. For example, images that suggest management is a science or administrative activity are informed by a technicist perspective, which assumes that managers are rational, technical and morally neutral, and seek to find the best model to ensure organization goals are efficiently met (Holman, 2000). There is an implication here that managers need to formally learn ideas and models that fulfil this image, which would support this definition of MD:

> MD is a planned and deliberate process to help managers to become more effective.

However, when we consider some of the research on what managers actually do, we need a practice perspective that takes account of the moral and ethical work of managers and the necessity of working with others, usually informally, in a variety of situations and cultures. This might produce a different definition of MD:

> MD is a process of learning for managers through recognized opportunities.

The first definition suggests something to do with effectiveness, probably in an identified way or against some understanding of effectiveness, such as measurable results or particular but observable ways of behaving. It is likely to be clearly set out and specified in advance of events, for example a training programme on time management, consisting of preset objectives and attempts to measure outcomes. Further, such objectives and their measurement provide some link to organization effort to develop the right kinds of managers as required (Jansen et al., 2001). The key difference is how the second definition leaves the nature of the processes used as an open question – only those recognized as opportunities by managers will count. Indeed, the process might not be recognized until it has already happened, like reviewing the outcome of a meeting that did not produce the right result. However, the process could also be planned and deliberate, such as attending a seminar on age discrimination, but even then, what is learned may be surprising and has to be recognized. This makes MD less predictable and lacking in clarity at the outset because learning, as recognized, is more emergent (see Goldstein, 1999). The second definition focuses on helping managers to learn, without specifying what the learning is for or where it comes from; again, this might occur by considering events retrospectively or even while events are happening. It also implies a different interpretation on effectiveness, which we will consider below.

There is an inevitable tension between the definitions, one that can be seen in the way people talk about MD, represented in Figure 10.1. There is a definite preference usually for planning in MD and, as explained below, this provides for structure in presentation and delivery. It also helps to form the budget for MD. However, it is not easy to generalize about plans in terms of how managers should be developed (Burgoyne et al., 2004). There is also recognition of the importance of learning in MD, whether formally, informally or by accident. Ideally, MD in an organization might seek to benefit from both stances; indeed, it is likely that both deliberation and emergence are always present in MD.

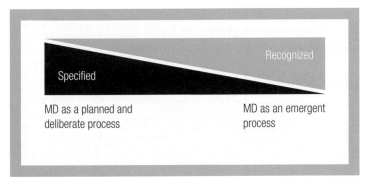

FIGURE 10.1 Planned vs. emergent MD

Both definitions can incorporate other terms, such as Management Training – usually events concerned with the acquisition of skills – and Management Education – a more formal process of acquiring knowledge and understanding, resulting in accreditation. A link between both, and certainly crucial to all definitions of MD, is the idea of Management Learning (ML), a bridging term between the various elements of training, education and development (Fox, 1997), covering a field of academic study of managers, learning and organizations. We will consider some of the key ideas on ML below.

Strategy and MD

The word 'strategy' has origins in the Greek term 'strategos', meaning the art of a general in overcoming an enemy. In the UK, just who the 'enemy' is when we consider MD depends on the level of the discussion. For many years, there have been concerns about the UK's productivity performance relative to competitor nations such as France, Germany and the USA, and the link this may have to the performance of managers (CEML, 2002a). There are also crucial issues relating to the reform and modernization of the public sector (PIU, 2000) and stimulating enterprise among SMEs (Leitch, 2006). For organizations facing competitive and global pressures, MD needs to link to strategy as an expression of business needs, while for individual managers, the 'enemy' may be the complexities of managing an increasingly diverse and knowledge-based workforce, and uncertainty over how their careers might develop (CIPD, 2003). We will consider some of the key issues at each of these levels.

The national scene

At the national level, there is an assumption that MD can make a contribution to national economic success. The reasoning is part of what Garavan et al. (1999, p. 193) refer to as a 'functional performance rationale' for MD, shown in Figure 10.2. Crucial to this argument is that the links can be proven and this puts great emphasis on the need to evaluate MD, which, as we shall see, is not always a simple process. However, even if the evidence is not entirely forthcoming, it has been assumed for many years that the UK needs to do more MD. The debates began in the 1960s but were given impetus in the 1980s by the publication of a range of reports highlighting the problem of management in the UK. The most prominent was Handy's (1987), which pointed out that all the UK's competitors – the USA,

Germany, Japan and France – were more serious about MD, although each had their own approach to it. This was supported by Constable and McCormick's report (1987), which revealed that many British companies made no provision for training managers.

Management development

Good managers

Successful performance of managers

Success in organisations

National economic success

FIGURE 10.2 MD and economic success

SOURCE: Mumford and Gold (2004)

It appears that things did improve during the 1990s and Thomson et al.'s surveys (1997, 2001) found a higher priority given to MD, although there were interesting variations between organizations. For example, an organization might declare MD to be a priority and show a policy for it but little evidence of training. The Council for Excellence in Management and Leadership was set up in 2000 to 'develop a strategy to ensure that the UK has the managers and leaders of the future to match the best in the world' (CEML, 2002a, p. 1), because 'good management and leadership is pivotal to investment, productivity, delivery of service and quality of performance'. It too found more attention given to MD, with many qualifications and opportunities available, but many organizations still unclear and unfocused about what they needed and difficulties about proving a positive return on investment in MD. It also proved difficult to ascertain whether the UK had a gap in managerial skills (Williams, 2002).

One of the CEML's crucial recommendations was the need to stimulate demand for MD from organizations and individuals and build links between demand and supply. This was recognized by the government's response (DTI/DFES, 2002). An action plan was drawn up for stimulating demand by benchmarking effective business practices so that organizations might be encouraged to stimulate demand for MD as part of a process to move up the value chain. A means to do this would be through Sector Skills Councils (SSCs), the voice of employers in 25 sectors in relation to skills issues, a role reinforced by the Leitch report. A government Leadership and Management Advisory Panel monitors progress of the action plan. In the English regions, management and leadership development are incorporated into regional economic strategies by RDAs. There are separate bodies for Scotland, Wales and Northern Ireland.

Working in a group of four, prepare short presentations on the various national and regional strategies on MD.

Check www.sfbn-mandl.org.uk/default.htm, a site on management and leadership development for all SSCs. You can find out more about the advisory panel at www.sfbn-mandl.org.uk/advisory_panel.htm. Check the regional economic strategy for northwest England at www.nwda.co.uk/areas-of-work/skills--education/leadership-and-management.aspx. For the Welsh Management Council, go to www.walesmanagementcouncil.org.uk/, and for Northern Ireland's strategy process, go to www.delni.gov.uk/management-and-leadership-development-strategy-for-ni-summary-of-consultation-responses. Scotland's approach is incorporated in the Scottish skills strategy at www.scotland.gov.uk/Publications/2007/09/06091114/0.

Organizations and strategy

MD could have a variety of purposes in an organization. Storey et al. (1994), for example, suggest that MD could be seen as:

- a device to engineer organizational change – in particular culture change

- a tool in pursuit of quality, cost reduction and profitability

- a way to structure attitudes

- a contribution to the development of a learning organization

- assistance with self-development.

Whatever the purpose, the conventional argument is that MD needs to link to an organization's strategy. However, for many organizations, this link is not made immediately, partly reflecting an organization's understanding of its strategy and the role of MD. Burgoyne (1988, p. 41) set out a 'ladder' of responses to MD, a reflection of an organization's 'maturity'. The six levels are shown in Table 10.1.

At each level, there is a degree of strategy, even at level 1 where managers are allowed to take advantage of MD possibilities, but in a totally unplanned way. For many managers, this informal and natural process of learning is the most common approach, especially in small organizations. At higher levels, there is some semblance of an articulation of the approach to MD and its purpose. At level 4, the link to strategy becomes clearer and this seems to be the priority in organizations that seek to integrate MD with organization goals, according to a CIPD (2003) survey. However, there can be a difference between the purpose of sustaining the current business model and developing managers to create future business models. The latter is implied in moves above level 4, but it also requires a more complex view of how strategies are formed. For example, Mintzberg et al. (1998) provide a learning approach to strategy, where learning by managers and others, often in unplanned ways from their work, can become recognized not just by managers themselves but by the organization as an input into strategy. Once again, we can see the importance of both a planned and emergent view of MD.

TABLE 10.1 Levels of maturity of organizational management development

Level 6: Strategic development of the management of corporate policy	MD processes enhance the nature and quality of corporate policy-making processes, which they also inform and help to implement
Level 5: MD strategy input to corporate policy formation	MD processes feed information into corporate policy decision-making processes on the organization's managerial assets, strengths, weaknesses and potential, and contribute to the forecasting and analysis of the manageability of proposed projects, ventures, changes
Level 4: MD strategy to implement corporate policy	MD strategy plays its part in implementing corporate policies through managerial human resource planning, and providing a strategic framework and direction for the tactics of career structure management, and learning, education and training
Level 3: Integrated and coordinated structural and development tactics	The specific MD tactics that impinge directly on the individual manager – career structure management, assisting learning – are integrated and coordinated
Level 2: Isolated tactical MD	There are isolated and ad hoc tactical MD activities, either structural or developmental, or both, in response to local problems, crises or sporadically identified general problems
Level 1: No systematic MD	No systematic or deliberate MD in structural or developmental sense, total reliance on natural, laissez-faire processes of MD

SOURCE: Burgoyne (1988, p. 41)

MD at level 6 is rarely reached by many organizations, but it implies a strong connection between what managers learn and do and the way strategy is formed and implemented. We might suggest two possibilities. First, there needs to be an understanding of the assumptions informing the strategy and how these need to be critically challenged. Second, managers can become futures thinkers, adopting techniques such as scenarios to engage in creative thinking about different possibilities for the future (Schwartz, 1991), and be more flexible in the development of business models (CMI, 2008).

To move in this direction would require some important changes of understanding in strategy formation. It is still probably the case that there is little involvement from MD and learning and development more generally in organization strategy (CIPD, 2007). Nevertheless, there is growing evidence of the importance of the impact of MD that is connected to strategy and organization performance. Mabey (2005), using data from 1,000 organizations – with responses from HR managers and line managers from three surveys in 1994, 2001 and 2004 – sought to show whether Management and Leadership Development (MLD) could be linked to organization measures such as commitment, performance and productivity. Figure 10.3 shows how the links work.

The most important finding was how employers took responsibility for MLD and sustained this over time. Thus, if this was perceived by managers, it improved the link between MLD, engagement and performance. Also important were the support of the board and the link to business objectives, which made MLD 'strategically driven', and the use of competencies. The evidence also supported earlier work by Mabey (2002) on the importance of the HR context, where taking a long-term view about managers was more likely to result in attention being given to MLD and the creation of a supportive context, which encouraged informal learning and related directly to work experience. Interestingly, HR managers were often unaware of the amount of development actually occurring, because of the difficulty of reporting informal learning, even though it was often seen as effective.

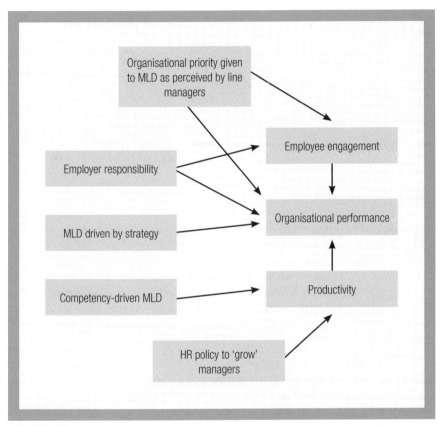

FIGURE 10.3 How MLD links to organization performance

SOURCE: Mabey (2005)

Providing effective MD

The different definitions of MD considered earlier in this chapter are made manifest when we focus on the issues surrounding the provision of MD and, in particular, how such provision can be done effectively. This becomes even more important when organizations in all sectors face a quickly changing environment, which requires a challenge to key assumptions about MD provision (Goodge, 1998). A crucial tension when considering effective MD provision relates to differences between the requirements of the organization and those of managers. For the organization, a strategy provides guidance on managerial requirements in terms of skills and performance.

Effectiveness concerns how well the requirements of the strategy are translated into the skills of managers through MD and then performance. However, given the contingent and unpredictable nature of managerial work, managers themselves may be less interested in the skill requirements being set by the organization, and more concerned with finding their own requirements for working more effectively and using MD to achieve this. We will need to consider both parts of this tension, and find some degree of reconciliation between them.

Effectiveness for the organization

For an organization to consider the connection between its strategy and MD, there needs to be some expression by management of what it means. To a greater or lesser extent, we all have our own views of what we mean by 'good management' but there is unlikely to be full agreement between us. Our responses will reflect our experiences, our knowledge and our prejudices. In organizations, management's views are likely to affect key decisions, such as who becomes a manager and what MD they will require, so it is important for an agreed view to be expressed and articulated in the interests of openness, fairness and legality. Organizations therefore seek a model of management and we can point to two types of model used:

1 *Generic models:* such models are said to apply to all managers in all contexts. This might include the various models of skills and abilities, developed through research or writers' wish lists. You can find such models in most textbooks on management and training packs. Perren and Burgoyne (2002) used many books and frameworks to develop 83 abilities for managers and leaders. For example, in the area of managing relationships, the following abilities were identified:

- bargain, sell and negotiated

- build empathy, relationships and trust

- create bearing and presence

- display assertiveness

- display humour

- listen to people

- present self and ideas.

2   *Organization models:* such models are defined by an organization and reflect the requirements as set out in the strategy and business plan and the meanings and values present.

Management competences

Both generic and organization models of management are often expressed in frameworks of management competences, which describe behaviours, attributes and skills needed for effective work performance, or the outputs of such work – an important distinction, as we will see. Competences (sometimes called capabilities) are seen as a way of aligning the objectives of an organization and activities such as selection, appraisal, reward and training and development (Holbeche, 1999), the linking mechanism for what we now call performance management. Alignment becomes possible because of the way competences provide the language for describing effectiveness, which allows for a more consistent way to assess people (Whiddett and Hollyforde, 2003). In larger organizations, competences are often specified at different levels to cover all employees, although we will consider their use mainly with managers.

There are two approaches to competences for managers, the behaviour approach and the standards approach. The behaviour approach for management competences, or more correctly 'competencies', concerns the abilities and underlying characteristics that allow a manager to achieve effective results; original work in this area is associated with Boyatzis (1982) in the USA. Abilities and underlying characteristics are difficult to assess directly and become evident in what a manager does, so most definitions of competency focus on behaviour. For example, the CIPD's (2008, p. 1) definition of competency is:

> the behaviours that employees must have, or must acquire, to input into a situation in order to achieve high levels of performance.

The work of Boyatzis and others, including the consultancy Hay Mcber, led to much interest in management competences and the idea that the frameworks could be applied in any context, that is, they provided a generic approach. However, there were doubts that generic approaches could accommodate differences in cultures and local meanings of terms such as planning and decision making. So organizations developed their own frameworks of competences based on collecting data from managers and others on their work and benchmarking against other frameworks already in existence. For example, a leading financial services organization has six clusters of competences:

- driving business vision and brand

- business judgement

- leading performance

- customer drive

- working with others

- drive, commitment and personal development.

You should be able to see how the alignment with strategy comes into view. Each cluster comprises difference competences. Thus 'leading performance' is composed of:

- inspiring trust

- driving execution and performance

- inspiring and developing others

- courageous leadership.

For each of these, there is a scale for scoring behaviour. These are often quite detailed but as an example, a high score for inspiring trust would be shown in behaviour where a manager 'demonstrates the highest level of personal integrity and ethical behaviour', while a low score would be shown in behaviour that 'compromises personal integrity and ethical behaviour'. This process is repeated for all clusters and all competences in the framework.

The standards approach focuses more clearly on the outputs of performance with specified performance criteria. In the UK, this approach finds expression in the National Occupational Standards (NOS) for management and leadership, which provide qualifications at four levels of management (supervisor to senior management) that conform to NVQ requirements. The standards were first developed in 1991 by the Management Charter Initiative. Through the use of a process of functional analysis, the key purpose of management and the key roles for performance were derived.. Each role is then broken into:

- units of competence

- elements of competence for each unit

- performance criteria.

Since 2000, the standards have been the responsibility of the Management Standards Centre (MSC), which completed the latest revision to the model in 2004, broadening coverage to include management and leadership. The roles are now identified as:

- managing self and personal skills

- providing direction

- facilitating change

- working with people

- using resources

- achieving results.

Each of these are then specified as units, for example, 'providing direction' has 12 units, including B1: 'Develop and implement operational plans for your area of responsibility'. For each of these, the outcomes of effective performance are stated along with skills, knowledge and understanding and underpinning behaviour. The MSC also adds new units as required.

Go to the home page of the Management Standards Centre – www.manage-ment-standards.org. You will find some examples and case studies of the use of the standards.

There are mixed opinions on competences for managers whether based on behaviour or standards. There are clearly some benefits if a planned and deliberate view of MD is taken. Strebler et al. (1997) point to the value of competences in identifying training needs and designing programmes for relevance. Winterton and Winterton (1997) suggested that competences generally add more coherence to an organization's training structure. Boyatzis (2008, p. 11) sees recent developments towards a more holistic view of competences to include emotional and social competency as the way to develop talent and distinguish 'outstanding performers in management'.

However, competences have been also subject to much critique, which continues to this day. Part of this critique is aimed at the NOS, which attempt to fit management work or functions into the NVQ/SNVQ framework. Research has suggested that the evidence collection required to complete a standards qualification involves too much bureaucracy and paper chasing (Swailes and Brown, 1999), which in turn leads to too much attention on meeting the standards rather than using them to change practice (Holman and Hall, 1999). In her research in private sector organizations, Grugulis (2000, p. 89) found that the standards became 'a distraction from developmental learning, rather than a contribution towards it'. More generally, management competences are seen as another 'one best way' approach to describing the work of managers, which can easily become a prescription for what managers do – they reduce the complexity and difficulty of management work into something technical and functional in the service of organization goals (Garavan and McGuire, 2001). Competences can become an expression of an organization's ideology – to be observed almost like a religion (Finch-Lees et al., 2005). This gives a certain degree of power to those who develop competences and those who use them to judge performance. As Holmes (1995, p. 36) argues, the very description of performance contained in competence statements also provides the knowledge of what should be done, and they become the 'legitimate way of talking about' performance.

Both generic and organization models of management, especially those expressed as management competences, formally provide the basis for an assessment of needs for MD. Many organizations try to help their managers to express MD needs as a personal development plan (PDP), completed after an appraisal interview. Completion of a PDP represents a commitment by an organization towards the MD of its managers and a crucial part of support to managers (Thomson et al., 2001). In a planned and deliberate approach to MD, appraisal interviews, as part of an organization's performance management system, are the most common method of assessing MD needs. A survey by the CIPD (2005) of over 500 companies found that 65% held annual appraisals, 27% had twice-yearly appraisals and 10% had rolling appraisals. In addition to appraisals, some organizations hold development centres (see Chapter 17), where trained observers, with the help of psychometric tests and group activities, can provide information about a manager's behaviour, which in turn can be used to express MD needs. Woodruffe (2000) highlights development centres as a means to help managers engage in continuous learning and adjust to fast-changing roles. Through appraisal and development centres, an organization can seek to effectively integrate activities such as MD with organization goals. However, we do need to consider more carefully the response of managers to such processes.

Effectiveness for managers

Given the findings relating to what managers actually do, it is not surprising that they may not always respond positively to what others plan for them as MD. There is even the possibility that the focus on what the organization deems appropriate may be greeted with cynicism and a sense of meaninglessness (Clarke, 1999). As a consequence, managers may find that MD lacks relevance to their concerns and what they receive as formal inputs become difficult to apply and therefore they see no value or reward in doing it. This is part of a 'vicious learning sequence' (Mumford and Gold, 2004, p. 90). By contrast, we can consider a more virtuous process, where MD concerns what is relevant to a manager's needs, who can then see the possibilities for use and value is obtained from application, which in turn creates an interest in more MD. This is part of the idea of a 'virtuous learning cycle', shown in Figure 10.4.

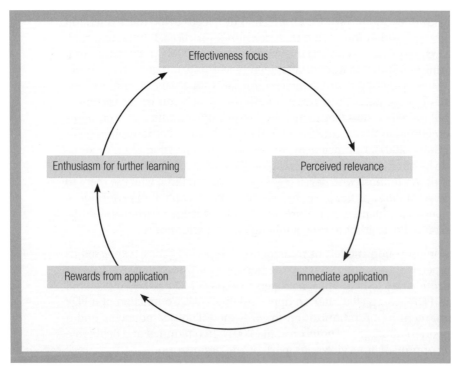

FIGURE 10.4 A virtuous learning cycle for MD

SOURCE: Mumford and Gold (2004, p. 91)

A crucial part of this more optimistic version of MD is the recognition of what is considered effective for managers, which requires greater concern for the issues faced by managers and how they learn from particular opportunities (Mumford, 1995). While such opportunities can be planned in response to organization requirements for managers, there is also more scope to consider how managers can learn from a wider variety of opportunities, whether planned for or not. Recalling our second definition, a process of learning for managers through recognized opportunities, we can start to see that 'effectiveness' revolves around questions such as:

* What is recognized as important for managers?

* How does learning occur?

* What opportunities are used?

Mumford and Gold (2004) summarize the position with a triangle of effectiveness, shown in Figure 10.5, which we will use to consider the key factors in providing MD.

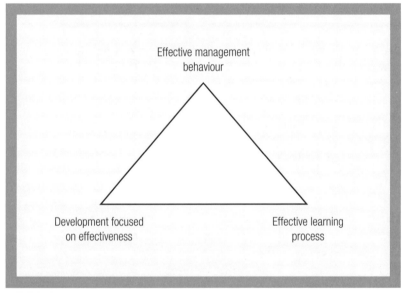

FIGURE 10.5 Triangle of effectiveness

SOURCE: Mumford and Gold (2004, p. 89)

Finding out the meaning of effective management behaviour for individual managers requires a move beyond the formal approaches to identifying needs through appraisals and development centres. Indeed, for many years research has pointed to the difficulties in using formal assessment processes in identifying the needs for MD. Part of this is the dual feature of assessment in providing data for judgements to be made on performance and reward, as well as to consider development needs. The most well-known study was completed in the 1960s by Meyer et al. (1965) of 92 managers who were being appraised. Since most regarded their performance as above average, any criticism was considered negative and resulted in defensive behaviour by managers. Appraisal research has continued to highlight the perception that it is a political process (Poon, 2004) and therefore difficult to manage and produce MD needs that are considered acceptable to managers. Similarly, development centres have been found to be fraught with tensions and difficulties, which affect the acceptance of results and performance motivation (Halman and Fletcher, 2000).

Feedback to managers

A key variable is the way managers respond to feedback, especially critical feedback (Cannon and Witherspoon, 2005). Feedback to managers can help managers improve their work and learn details, but there is a danger that feedback can impact on a manager's view of 'self', affecting self-belief and self-esteem (DeNisi and Kluger, 2000).

Activity

Working with a partner, explore these questions:

1 How do you respond to feedback?

2 How much criticism is acceptable to you?

For many managers, feedback can provide a rich source of learning, on a continuous basis, as shown in HRD in Practice 10.1.

HRD in Practice 10.1

Open forums at LBBC

LBBC is an engineering company that designs and manufactures advanced pressure vessel and autoclave systems. As part of the culture change we were going through, having split the business into two distinct business units, in early 2004 I felt it was necessary to set up a weekly open forum. It involved me sitting in the meeting room from 9:00 to 9:30 every Tuesday morning. Any employee could voluntarily come in and discuss any issue with me.

I felt it was necessary because of the uncertainty that is created during a period of change, particularly culture change, and, specifically, because:

- I was providing an opportunity for any employee to ask any question of me within the presence of other employees
- I was putting emphasis on the employees to ask questions if they were

unsure of a situation, hadn't heard or had misunderstood some of the more formal communications, that is, removing the excuse for people to say 'nobody tells me anything' or 'well I didn't understand that'.

The initial meetings were well attended and discussions mainly centred specifically around the cultural and structural changes we were going through. We then experienced a period of a core group of attendees, who were those most supportive of the changes and wished to explore the reasons for things happening and what might happen next. Latterly, attendance has dropped to mainly one individual regularly attending and occasionally others, particularly if I encourage attendance.

I continue to feel it has been a worthwhile activity, for the reasons given above, even with the recent poor attendance. If someone claims they don't know about an issue and have not been told, I can still remind them of the forum and that it is their responsibility to find out.

I was soon surprised at the benefits we were getting from the interactions between employees. What would start as a question to me soon became an open debate among the attendees, where the learning from those present was very good, as they recognized the fact that different people had different perspectives on a situation. This was a powerful exercise.

The next learning was how it became a great opportunity for me to gauge opinion on particular issues, either before I launched them or soon after launch. Through the open atmosphere we had created, I obtained some genuine thoughts and comments on many issues that I would not otherwise have sought. Sometimes these opinions would be more influential than those of my managers.

One example is an early meeting we had. As a consequence of the split, the design business would 'purchase' the fabrications from the manufacturing business, and there was initial doubt over their competitiveness. Design employees were arguing they would be better off buying from another organization. This was being debated in the forum, and I was told that I would never allow that to happen. Now I clearly disagreed with that, as it was critical to my reasons for the split, but the benefit was that the comment was made openly and I replied honestly in front of 8–10 people. They knew that I meant it. So it was their decision where they buy from, and they couldn't use the excuse of 'well, the boss wouldn't want us to go anywhere else.' This would have also applied to other situations.

Source: Howard Pickard, managing director, LBBC Ltd (personal communication)

One way an organization can try to balance out the feedback to managers, and possibly increase its acceptance to managers, is to develop schemes of multisource feedback where managers can be rated on their performance from different sources:

- their staff – upward appraisal

- fellow managers – peer appraisal

- others such as customers and clients

- a combination of all sources including immediate superiors – 360 degree feedback.

All these approaches widen the possibility for feedback to managers, although they are likely to make use of the dimensions of behaviour in the organization's management competence framework and they could deepen the difficulties of top-down judgement-oriented appraisals. In these approaches:

- Research suggests that *upward appraisal* needs to be anonymous because this removes a fear of reprisal and the tendency for too much kindness when staff ratings were known to managers (Antonioni, 1994). Upward appraisal depends on how confident managers feel that they can change behaviour – referred to as self-efficacy – and whether managers are oriented towards setting goals for learning (Heslin and Latham, 2004). If sustained, upward appraisal reinforces the behaviours being rated and communicates what and how staff want their managers to improve, so this may reveal crucial areas for improvement and learning (Reilly et al., 1996).

- *Peer appraisal* is generally accepted as the preferred approach for helping professionals to develop. For managers, however, there are some slight difficulties, since they have to work with each other and asking them formally to give feedback can be seen as a disturbance to relationships, especially where comparisons between managers are needed and teamwork is required (Peiperl, 2001).

- The potential of *360 degree feedback* is to provide a more accurate picture of a manager's behaviour, so long as the purpose of the feedback is clear and managers do not become confused (Handy et al., 1996).

Research suggests that managers are likely to give more significance to feedback from their own managers (Greguras et al., 2003) and that only small improvements in performance occur over time because of the complex range of factors present in feedback (Smither et al., 2005). However, it does seem that multisource feedback can have value for development purposes (McCarthy and Garavan, 2001) and the organization supports this through coaching (DeNisi and Kruger, 2000).

Whatever the source of feedback and whatever the content, whether this is translated into MD needs that are recognized by managers as being concerned with effective behaviour will depend on how far they match or inform a manager's self-appraisal and assessment. All managers have a subjective view – it cannot be otherwise – of their own performance informed by beliefs and ideas of what work requires and what needs to be done to meet particular goals (Campbell and Lee, 1988). Too many goals from different sources are confusing (Emsley, 2003). Managers also judge their behaviour and make changes if they see it as necessary; they will also be more critical and raise more issues if the process of self-appraisal is oriented towards MD needs. One obvious process is to ask managers to consider the problems and issues they are facing; it is even better if managers are able to reflect on their behaviour and identify what aspects of their work they need to improve and how MD can help this. We consider the importance of reflection in learning below.

Management learning

Effective MD requires a consideration of how managers learn. There are of course many explanations of learning and Chapter 5 presented some of the main theories and principles. However, in the field of MD, two particular theories have received attention. The first is Kolb's (1984) experiential learning cycle, as adapted by Honey and Mumford (2006) and the second is situated learning, drawn from the work of Lave and Wenger (1991).

Honey and Mumford (2006) employ a Learning Styles Questionnaire (LSQ) to indicate preferences for particular stages of the learning cycle, shown in Figure 10.6.

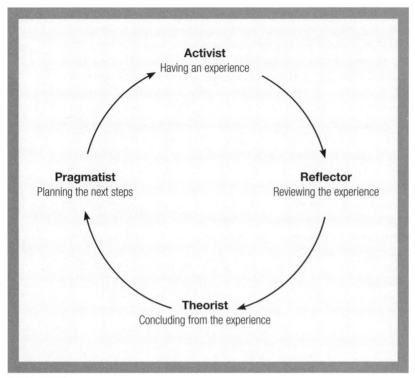

FIGURE 10.6 Honey and Mumford's learning cycle and styles

SOURCE: Honey and Mumford (2006)

Managers who complete the LSQ can begin to understand their preferences for learning and developers can consider such preferences in the design of MD activities, for example activists learn best from here-and-now tasks, and reflectors learn best when they can stand back, listen and observe. As well as preferences, managers can also consider what prevents them from completing the cycle or giving less attention to a particular stage. For example, an activist may also have a low preference for theorizing, drawing out conclusions from an experience, and this may affect how the manager derives learning from MD events. This can lead to a consideration of why this occurs, for example a manager's past experience or training may lead to habits of not learning how to develop conclusions that can then be considered for implementation. However, this might also be the consequence of what occurs in the manager's organization, for example when a manager returns from a training event with some possible ideas for action but there is no support to consider how this might done. Indeed, the structure of the job may prevent changes to work or there may be strong attitudes from others about new ideas from training events that prevent change. These factors are aspects of an organization's learning climate (Temporal, 1978). This provides a crucial link to situated learning, which takes a more social approach to learning and focuses more on a manager's participation in everyday activities.

Kolb's cycle and its adapted version by Honey and Mumford remain popular among managers and trainers; however, there has been criticism about the reliability of learning style assessments (Coffield et al., 2004) and the way they can decontextualize learning and overemphasize individual learners (Reynolds, 1997). Recently, there has been growing interest in the importance of social context and how aspects drawn from context, including interaction with others and the use of language, can affect whether learning is enabled or constrained (Holman et al., 1997). Situated learning gives more attention to such factors and highlights how most learning occurs through informal and incidental work situations as part of a manager's practice. This 'natural' learning would be recognized by most managers, although the particular features of situated learning might not normally be considered. The key ideas are drawn from the work of Russian psychologist Vygotsky (1982), where any action is mediated by the use of physical tools such as a pen in writing, and psychological tools such as language, acquired through interactions with others. These ideas were developed by Lave and Wenger (1991) and in a managerial context by Fox (1997), who explored how managers learn by participating in practice, whether at work or in MD events, by talking, watching others, and especially sharing stories about what works and what does not or what is acceptable. Any learning involves a change in practice, through new ways of talking and understanding, but such changes have to be considered sensible by those involved in the practice. Much of this becomes taken for granted, hence it is 'natural', but through reflection, the assumptions can be articulated and potentially challenged and new possibilities considered (see below).

Effective provision

The third angle of the effectiveness triangle in Figure 10.5 requires attention to development that is focused on effectiveness. As we have already seen, there are tensions when we consider effective behaviour and learning for managers and this continues when we examine provision. A quick 'google' of the term 'Management Development+UK' yielded 15,200,000 hits, and many of these are undoubtedly from those who can provide MD – it is clear there is no shortage of supply in MD. As found by CEML (2002a), the crucial issue is demand and, we would suggest, recognition by managers of appropriateness. Much of the provision is through formal programmes, events and training, although this could understate the importance and value of informal or less formal MD. To explore the possibilities, we will make use of a framework of types of MD, first presented by Mumford (1987) and more recently by Mumford and Gold (2004). This is shown in Figure 10.7.

The value of this typology becomes clear when we consider the two dimensions and then the different types of provision. First, one dimension is concerned with a manager's completion of tasks. At work, completion of tasks is usually high and contrasts with the occasions when a manager is away from work, at a conference for example. A second dimension relates to the concern for learning. A high concern occurs when learning is explicit and contrasts with occasions when it is not. When the dimensions are combined, we can explore the different possibilities.

Thus in type 1, there is low concern for learning but high concern for task – this is working normally without considering learning explicitly but we know learning is still occurring informally, as managers solve problems, interact with others and share stories. It is quite natural and situated in a context. However, it is haphazard, emergent, often accidental and usually unrecognized, but it is certainly relevant and real to managers. It is therefore important but managers may be as much constrained by their learning as enabled and they may also fail to recognize the opportunities when they arise.

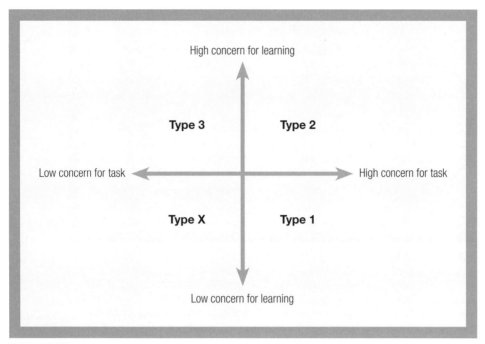

High concern for learning

Type 3   Type 2

Low concern for task ←——————————→ High concern for task

Type X   Type 1

Low concern for learning

FIGURE 10.7 Types of MD

SOURCE: Mumford and Gold (2004, p. 117)

By contrast, type 3 makes learning central and formal. MD can be planned in advance, possibly as a response to an identification of needs, with clear objectives and a structure for delivery. It is also likely to occur away from the difficulties of everyday practice. Here we can identify the many training and educational events that are available to managers, ranging from team-building programmes that make use of outdoor activities, to completion of an MBA or other accredited qualifications, or attendance on a one-day course on time management. Within such events, a large variety of methods can be employed, such as case studies, group exercises, reading and role plays (Huczynski, 2001). The value of such events is that managers have the opportunity to focus on learning, and if off-site, they can detach themselves from the hustle and bustle of work life. This is a crucial point, as one of the difficulties of this type of MD is that managers may not see the relevance of what is provided. This may be even more apparent if managers do not see a connection with what they 'need', even if the organization does (Antonacopoulou, 1999). There is also the difficulty of applying learning to work, an important feature of evaluation, which incorporates a concern for the transfer of learning (see below).

Type 2 provision offers some attempt to combine work with learning. This is a more proactive stance towards recognizing and using opportunities at work as the source of learning. If managers can do this, they make learning relevant and real, with immediate or probable application. Most obvious are new situations or problems that require a change to the usual ways of behaving (Davies and Easterby-Smith, 1984). It becomes crucial that managers combine the recognition of such situations with an understanding of how they learn. Kolb (1983) suggests a link between his version of the learning cycle and the stages of managing and solving problems; similarly, Mumford (1997) saw a connection between learning and dealing with management tasks, as shown in Figure 10.8.

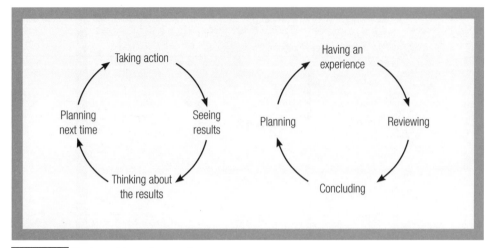

FIGURE 10.8 Task and learning cycles

SOURCE: Adapted from Mumford (1997)

Managers may be able to see how their learning preferences connect to how they work through problems. For example, a low preference for 'concluding' may also become manifest in a lack of time to consider the results of taking action in order to draw out clear conclusions. There will also be many opportunities for learning at work but it requires managers to recognize them, or even seek them out, to take advantage of them.

Of course, it is quite possible for managers to become disaffected with MD. We mentioned earlier the idea of a vicious learning sequence and one consequence of this may be to find that there is little further enthusiasm for MD or indeed work as a manager in general. Mumford and Gold (2004) refer to this as 'type X MD', a reminder that power and politics at work can affect how managers respond to MD and their work.

Reflection

Learning from work experiences such as problems, accidents or mistakes or even planned events held off-site can be made explicit through reflection on what happened, how and perhaps why. Reflection is recognized as a key feature of how professionals carry out their practice, referred to by Schön (1983) as 'reflection-in-practice', but it is important to make this process more deliberate through 'reflection-on-practice'. This can be done in a variety of ways such as writing logs of events, keeping a diary, writing short narratives of what happened or sitting with others to share views about events. Reflection completed in these ways can help managers become more aware of what they are doing and how, and can also reveal underlying patterns of behaviour that can help to identify new needs as well as ideas for change. Following the work of writers such as Mezirow (1990), managers have been encouraged to become 'critical reflectors'. This involves not just reflecting on what happened and how but also the assumptions that underpin a manager's understanding of what happened. Managers investigate not just what they think but the way they think, allowing them to explore their perspectives towards the difficult issues they face, with the potential to test the validity of their assumptions (Antonacopoulou, 2004). Gold et al. (2002) used a storytelling approach to reflection and then helped managers to examine their arguments within the story to reveal key assumptions and the history that lay behind the assumptions. This enabled managers to become critical of long-held beliefs that hindered action.

The skill of reflection can be used in a variety of approaches to MD that cross the typology in Figure 10.7. For example, self-development is an approach to MD where managers take responsibility for their own development, covering what they want to learn and how. The growing availability of e-learning resources and online communities provide good support for the self-developing manager. Organizations can support self-development with their own supply of resources, and help managers set a 'learning contract', although this gets close to a PDP and may inhibit managers. As Megginson and Pedler (1992) argue, self-development implies freedom for managers to choose what *not* to learn.

Reflection may also feature in action learning, where managers identify difficult problems, which they then share with other managers who provide challenge and support through probing questions, but not answers. A key assumption in action learning is that managers can overcome problems by working with other managers, their 'comrades in adversity' (Revans, 1982, p. 636). Managers always work on real projects or real issues that are important and this ensures that action is taken and learning is achieved. Revans expressed learning (L) as equal to programmed knowledge (P) plus questioning insight (Q), so that L = P + Q. Reflection is implied in the Q part of the equation. P concerns existing knowledge and was given a lower status by Revans, since managers faced with intractable problems were more likely to find questions and insight of greater benefit. This is a significantly different view of the world compared to the traditional MD diet (see McLaughlin and Thorpe, 1993). Action learning has proved to be an enduring approach to management development, with good examples of success, as shown in HRD in Practice 10.2.

Action learning with the All-sector Management & Leadership Programme Strategic Forum

In 2005, the Skills for Business project team at the Sector Skills Development Agency developed an action learning programme, which involved 23 owner-managers of small businesses in Guildford, Nottingham and Glasgow. The programmes were designed to run for six months and in the evaluation that followed, these were some of the success stories.

Business A predicts future profitability:
'I joined the programme because I wanted help in taking my company (financial services) to the next stage of creating a stable, profitable business.

This would then allow me to hand over the running of my business within the next five years. I have found the programme extremely useful, especially the sessions where the participants are discussing each other's problems. I have benefited greatly from this and have been able to bring the benefits directly back to my business. My challenge was the lack of profitability in my business, despite having more work than we could handle. During the programme, I have resolved to charge fees for the work I do and offer staged payments to clients, rather than relying on commissions as before. I was worried in case I would lose clients, but they have all accepted the new structure without any problems. This will significantly help my profitability and enable a future handover.'

Business B has developed a more open management style:

'I was appointed MD two months before the programme and wanted help to gain the confidence to change the company. This programme has really been invaluable. I have increased the level of promotional and PR activities – we produce newsletters and ask for referrals. I now give staff briefings to keep them all informed and we are starting to document our procedures. I am working on a culture change to create a more open style of management and increased staff empowerment. I found the group feedback sessions really useful in helping me to develop my ideas. Thank you!'

Business C has reduced wastage and improved production:

'I joined the programme after it had started but soon found it very helpful. I had not been in this role long and was having problems. I am now being appreciated as a leader. I have delegated almost 80% of my old roles and people are now coming to work earlier, probably as a result of me changing my style. I seem to be more approachable – people are asking me for help with their problems instead of hiding them. The point of the course seems to be about dealing with 'you', not the shop floor. I have been able to remove my self-made blocks. The business has benefited from reduced wastage and improved production. The programme has really helped me to gain the confidence and achieve these changes.'

Source: www.sfbn-mandl.org.uk/alfl_success_stories.htm

Evaluating MD

If MD provides good managers, and good managers are necessary for improving organization performance and even national economic and social success, then at each stage, evaluation become the means of proving the validity of such claims. However, it has long been recognized that it is difficult to show these cause and effect connections in MD (Smith, 1993). This makes evaluation models such as that developed by Kirkpatrick (1983) – which advocates a set of stages or levels for evaluation, from reactions of learners following an activity to a cost–benefit analysis (see Chapter 7) – difficult to implement.

Reflective question

Why do you think there are difficulties in implementing a staged approach to evaluation in MD? Write down your answers before you read more.

Staged or systematic models of evaluation are less appropriate for MD partly because, as identified above, managers can learn in different ways from different opportunities, and it is almost impossible to isolate the impact of one activity from another. Certainly, it is possible to evaluate reactions to a training event, often by completion of a questionnaire (often referred to as 'happy sheets'), but once managers return to work, unless they can clearly implement what they have learned from the training, which would mean attempting to isolate managers from other influences, it is nearly impossible to show a connection between undertaking training and improved performance. Management work is seldom ordered and predictable, so the mechanistic assumptions of staged or systematic models are less appropriate to all kinds of MD. However, this should not be an excuse to ignore evaluation in MD altogether and accept its value as an 'act of faith'. Given the amount of resources that can be invested in MD, there ought to be a process for assessing the value obtained. Alternative approaches to evaluation can be considered that take more account of the context of management work. For example, Warr et al. (1970) developed a model of evaluation for management training events (see Chapter 8 for more detail). This CIRO model covers:

- Context – the organization situation that requires change

- Inputs – methods used in the training

- Reactions – from managers about the training

- Outputs – immediate, intermediate (behaviour at work) and ultimate (impact on organization).

The model can employ a variety of different methods for collecting data and it can also be used for different purposes. Easterby-Smith (1994) has identified four purposes for evaluating MD:

- *proving:* showing that specified outcomes have been achieved as a consequence of MD

- *improving:* using data to provide a better MD activity

- *learning:* reviewing activities to assess value and identify possible actions beyond the MD activity

- *control:* to ensure there is information to show that MD activities operate efficiently.

Mumford and Gold (2004) add influence as a fifth purpose. Since evaluation is concerned with collecting data, such data can be used to persuade others about the value of MD. For example, results can be presented to show the success of a pilot programme or to argue for the continuation of a programme.

Activity

You have been asked by a senior manager to work out an evaluation approach for a team-building programme for junior managers. It is a two-day programme with an outdoor element followed by a work project for two months. What techniques can be used and for what purpose?

Try www.lancs.ac.uk/fss/projects/edres/ltsn-eval/links.htm for resources on collecting data for evaluation and http://reviewing.co.uk for a more experiential approach to reviewing training.

One of the reasons for the failure of systematic approaches to evaluating MD is the need to satisfy the different interests of those who need information about MD and the value it is providing, that is, the stakeholders, including employers, employees, trainers and providers, finance directors and so on. Of course, participating managers themselves have a strong interest in the value of MD. Therefore evaluation needs to take account of different interests and respond to their requirements – referred to as 'responsive evaluation' (Stake, 1975). One example of responsive evaluation is an approach presented by Patton (1997), which seeks to involve everyone who has an interest in evaluation in setting the direction of the evaluation process so that they can make use of the data in making decisions. In MD, this would allow evaluation to occur throughout a process and for different purposes. Where there are differences or ambiguities about the purpose and data to collect, stakeholder meetings should be held to allow dialogue and discussion. The recognition that there are different viewpoints in evaluation, indeed different versions of 'reality', and the need for understanding through talk and discussion are features of Guba and Lincoln's (1989) *Fourth Generation Evaluation*.

It might be argued that the main purpose of evaluation ought to be to help or empower managers as learners to take action. For example, Fetterman's (2002) model of empowerment evaluation is designed to enable programme participants to do their own evaluation so they can establish direction, work out what needs to be done and plan for the next steps. This would include looking beyond the immediate activity to the context and the communities that need to be involved. Similarly, action evaluation (Rothman, 1997) is concerned with enabling project participants to jointly set goals leading to actions and then evaluation. Goals set become the source of feedback and reflection. There can be a continuous process of defining/redefining goals and taking action as required for success. Where there is difficulty, goals need to be reconsidered and actions adjusted. This responsive and adaptive approach to helping managers to learn from events and difficulties is also a key feature of the problem of the transfer of learning in MD.

Transfer of learning

Planned type 3 MD activities always carry an inherent danger that because learning occurs off-site, participants may not be able implement new ideas and skills back at work. This is a problem for HRD in general (Cromwell and Kolb, 2004), but given the expense of MD and especially the deleterious effect on the motivation of managers, this is a particular concern. There has been keen interest to understand how and why the transfer of learning may or may not occur. Thus Baldwin and Ford (1988), in a review of research, identified that transfer of training occurs when skills and knowledge are learned, retained and generalized for application to various work activities and then maintained by repeated use (see Chapter 7). This process is influenced by the characteristics of the learner, such as motivation or personality. In addition, the work environment, including opportunities to use skills and support from peers and managers, can play a key role (Ford and Weissbein, 1997). Holton et al. (2007, p. 391) refer to all the influences as the 'transfer system' and have developed a Learning Transfer System Inventory (LTSI) to help organizations to discover the key barriers to transfer. The items in the inventory relate to:

1 Motivational factors relating to expectations that people have about applying new skills

2 Secondary influences concerning the degree of preparedness of learners and the belief or conviction by learners of their ability to use skills, referred to as 'self-efficacy' (Bandura, 1977)

3 Environmental elements such as supervisor support or sanctions and peer support

4 Ability elements relating to the opportunity to apply new skills, the energy and workload of learners and the way training is designed to link to work performance.

All these are assessed by the LTSI and plans can be made to ensure help can be provided to support managers and their learning. For example, Mabey (2002) identified how HRM practices such as planned career structures, succession plans and fast tracking contributed significantly to MD in organizations. Similarly, it has been found that the role of the 'boss' can be influential in helping managers to develop and learn (London, 1986). Specifically, where a manager's manager provides a coaching service, this is now seen as a crucial support for learning and performance improvement more generally (Hunt and Weintraub, 2002). Other help for MD can be found from more senior managers who act as mentors (Megginson et al., 2005), or by developing a manager's social capital, that is, developing a range of relationships with others who can be called upon when needed (Tymon and Stumpf, 2003).

Summary

- Recent research suggests that investment in MD impacts on organizational performance and productivity, although this link is seldom straightforward and is contingent on a number of factors, such as the priority given to MD and support for it by those in senior positions.

- The theories and models from classical management and the human relations school continue to form much of the content of what is taught in management qualifications like the MBA. However, there has been much criticism of this approach recently and the disconnection of such theories from the practice of managers.

- MD can be defined as 'a planned and deliberate process to help managers become more effective' or 'a process of learning for managers through recognized opportunities'.

- At the national level, there is an assumption that MD can make a contribution to national economic success. The reasoning is part of a 'functional performance rationale' for MD. In organizations there are various purposes for MD but there should be a link to strategy, although this will depend on the 'maturity' of an organization.

- Effectiveness in MD will reflect the model of management used in organizations, sometimes expressed as 'competences', although there are many criticisms of this approach. For managers, effectiveness requires a consideration of management behaviour, development focused on effectiveness and an effective learning process.

- Managers can take a more proactive stance towards recognizing and using opportunities at work as the source of learning. If managers do this, they make learning relevant and real, with immediate or probable application. Most obvious are new situations or problems that require a change to the usual ways of behaving.

- In action learning, managers identify difficult problems that they share with other managers who provide challenge and support through probing questions. A key assumption in action learning is that managers can overcome problems by working with other managers, their 'comrades in adversity'.

- Evaluation in MD is often an 'act of faith', but various approaches can be considered and take account of the context of management work, the interests of various stakeholders and utilization of ideas from learning in action at work.

Discussion questions

1 Is there a link between management learning and OD?
2 Are management competences a good way of measuring managers for development?
3 What is meant by effectiveness in MD and can it be achieved?
4 Can managers learn to learn? What can help or hinder management learning?
5 Can the value of MD be proven?

Further reading

Burgoyne, J. and Reynolds, M. (1997) *Management Learning: Integrating Perspectives in Theory and Practice*, London, Sage.

Cullen, J. and Turnbull, S. (2005) A meta-review of the management development literature, *Human Resource Development Review*, **4**(3): 335–55.

Mabey, C. and Lees, T.F (2007) *Management and Leadership Development*, London, Sage.

Mintzberg, H. (2004) *Managers not MBAs: A Hard Look at the Soft Practice of Managing and Management Development*, New York, Berrett-Koehler.

Mumford, A. and Gold, J. (2004) *Management Development: Strategies for Action*, London, CIPD.

Suutari, V. and Viitala, R. (2008) Management development of senior executives: Methods and their effectiveness, *Personnel Review*, **37**(4): 375–92.

Thomson, A., Mabey, C., Storey, J. et al. (2001) *Changing Patterns of Management Development*, Oxford, Blackwell.

References

Antonacopoulou, E.P. (1999) Training does not imply learning: the individual perspective, *International Journal of Training and Development*, **3**(1): 4–23.

Antonacopoulou, E.P. (2004) *Introducing Reflexive Critique in the Business Curriculum: Reflections on the Lessons Learned*, London, AIM Research Working Paper Series.

Antonioni, D. (1994) The effects of feedback accountability on upward appraisal ratings, *Personnel Psychology*, **47**(2): 349–56.

Baldwin, T.T. and Ford, J.K. (1988) Transfer of training: a review and directions for future research, *Personnel Psychology*, **41**: 63–105.

Bandura, A. (1977) *Social Learning Theory*, Englewood Cliffs, NJ, Prentice Hall.

Bennis, W. and O'Toole, J. (2005) How business schools lost their way, *Harvard Business Review*, **83**(5): 96–104.

Boyatzis, R. (1982) *The Competent Manager: A Model for Effective Performance*, New York, John Wiley and Sons.

Boyatzis, R. (2008) Competencies in the 21st century, *Journal of Management Development*, **27**(1): 5–12.

Burgoyne, J. (1988) Management development for the individual and the organization, *Personnel Management*, June: 40–4.

Burgoyne, J., Hirsh, W. and Williams, S. (2004) *The Development of Management and Leadership Capability and its Contribution to Performance: The Evidence, the Prospects and the Research Need*, Report 560, London, DfES.

Campbell, D. and Lee, C. (1988) Self-appraisal in performance evaluation: development versus evaluation, *Academy of Management Review*, **13**(2): 302–14.

Cannon, M.D. and Witherspoon, R. (2005) Actionable feedback: unlocking the power of learning and performance improvement, *Academy of Management Executive*, **19**(2): 120–34.

Carroll, S.J. and Gillen, D.J. (1987) Are the classical management functions useful in describing managerial work?, *Academy of Management Review*, **12**(1): 38–51.

CEML (Council for Excellence in Management and Leadership) (2002a) *Managers and Leaders: Raising our Game*, London, CEML.

CEML (Council for Excellence in Management and Leadership) (2002b) *Joining Entrepreneurs in their World*, London, CEML.

CIPD (Chartered Institute of Personnel and Development) (2002) *Developing Managers for Business Performance*, London, CIPD.

CIPD (Chartered Institute of Personnel and Development) (2003) *Managing Careers Survey*, London, CIPD.

CIPD (Chartered Institute of Personnel and Development) (2005) *Performance Management Survey*, London, CIPD.

CIPD (Chartered Institute of Personnel and Development) (2007) *Learning and Development*, London, CIPD.

CIPD (Chartered Institute of Personnel and Development) (2008) *Competency and Competency Frameworks Fact Sheet*, www.cipd.co.uk/subjects/perfmangmt/competnces/comptfrmwk.htm.

Clarke, M. (1999) Management development as a game of meaningless outcomes, *Human Resource Management Journal*, **9**(2): 38–49.

CMI (Chartered Management Institute) (2008) *Management Futures: The World in 2018*, London, CMI.

Coffield, F., Moseley, D., Hall, E. and Ecclestone, K. (2004) *Learning Styles and Pedagogy in Post-16 Learning: A Systematic and Critical Review*, London, Learning and Skills Research Centre.

Constable, J. and McCormick, R. (1987) *The Making of British Managers*, London, BIM/CBI.

Cromwell, S.E. and Kolb, J.A. (2004) An examination of work-environment support factors affecting transfer of supervisory skills training in the workplace, *Human Resource Development Quarterly*, **15**: 449–71.

Davies, J. and Easterby-Smith, M. (1984) Learning and developing from managerial work experiences, *Journal of Management Studies*, **21**(2):168–83.

DeNisi, A.N. and Kluger, A.S. (2000) Feedback effectiveness: can 360-degree appraisals be improved?, *Academy of Management Executive*, **14**(1): 129–39.

DTI/DfES (Department of Trade and Industry/ Department for Education and Skills) (2002) *Government Response to the Report of the Council for Excellence and Management in Leadership*, London, DTI/DfES.

Easterby-Smith, M. (1994) *Evaluating Management Development, Training and Education*, 2nd edn, Aldershot, Gower.

Emsley, D. (2003) Multiple goals and managers' ob-related tension and performance, *Journal of Managerial Psychology*, **18**(4): 345–56.

Fayol, H. (1949) *Administration Industrielle Generale*, English transl., London, Pitman Harper.

Fetterman, D. (2002) Empowerment evaluation: building communities of practice and a culture of learning, *American Journal of Community Psychology*, **30**(1): 89–102.

Finch-Lees, T., Mabey, C. and Liefooge, A. (2005) 'In the name of capability': a critical discursive evaluation of competency-based management development, *Human Relations*, **58**(9): 1185–222.

Ford, J.K. and Weissbein, D.A. (1997) Transfer of training: an update review and analysis, *Performance Improvement Quarterly*, **10**(2): 22–41.

Fox, S. (1997) From management education and development to the study of management learning', in J. Burgoyne and M. Reynolds (eds) *Management Learning*, London, Sage.

Garavan, T.N. and McGuire, D. (2001) Competencies and workplace learning: some reflections on the rhetoric and the reality, *Journal of Workplace Learning*, **13**(4): 144–63.

Garavan, T.N., Barnicle, B. and O'Suilleabhain, F. (1999) Management development: contemporary trends, issues and strategies, *Journal of European Industrial Training*, **23**(4/5): 191–207.

Gold, J., Holman, D. and Thorpe, R. (2002) The role of argument analysis and story-telling in facilitating critical thinking, *Management Learning*, **33**(3): 371–88.

Goldstein, J. (1999) Emergence as a construct: history and issues, *Emergence: A Journal of Complexity Issues in Organizations and Management*, **1**(1): 49–72.

Goodge, P. (1998) How do we make management development effective?, *Journal of Management Development*, **17**(1): 83–7.

Greguras, G., Ford, J. and Brutus, S. (2003) Manager attention multisource feedback, *Journal of Management Development*, **22**(4): 345–61.

Grugulis, I. (2000) The management NVQ: a critique of the myth of relevance, *Journal of Vocational Education and Training*, **52**(1): 79–99.

Guba, E. and Lincoln, Y. (1989) *Fourth Generation Evaluation*, Newbury Park, CA, Sage.

Halman F. and Fletcher C. (2000) The impact of development centre participation and the role of individual differences in changing self-assessments, *Journal of Occupational and Organizational Psychology*, **73**(4): 423–42.

Handy, C. (1987) *The Making of Managers*, London, NEDO.

Handy, L., Devine, M. and Heath, L. (1996) *360° Feedback: Unguided Missile or Powerful Weapon*, Ashridge, Ashridge Management Research Group.

Heslin, P. and Latham, G. (2004) The effect of upward feedback on managerial behavior, *Applied Psychology*, **53**(1): 23–37.

Holbeche, L. (1999) *Aligning Human Resources and Business Strategy*, Oxford, Butterworth-Heinemann.

Holman, D. (2000) Contemporary models of management education in the UK, *Management Learning*, **31**(2): 197–217.

Holman, D. and Hall, L. (1996) Competence in management development: rites and wrongs, *British Journal of Management*, **7**(2): 191–202.

Holman, D., Pavlica, K. and Thorpe, R. (1997) Rethinking Kolb's theory of experiential learning in management education, *Management Learning*, **28**(2): 135–48.

Holmes, L. (1995) HRM and the irresistible rise of the discourse of competence, *Personnel Review*, **24**(4): 34–49.

Holton, E., Bates, R., Bookter, A. and Yamkovenko, V. (2007) Convergent and divergent validity of the learning transfer system inventory, *Human Resource Development Quarterly,* **18**(3): 385–419.

Honey, P. and Mumford, A. (2006) *The Learning Styles Questionnaire: 80 Item Version*, Maidenhead, P. Honey.

Huczynski, A. (2001) *Encyclopaedia of Development Methods*, Aldershot, Gower.

Hunt, J. and Weintraub, J. (2002) *Coaching Managers: Developing Top Talent in Business*, San Francisco, Sage.

Jansen, P., van der Velde, M. and Mul, W. (2001) A typology of management development, *Journal of Management Development*, **20**(2): 106–20.

Kirkpatrick, D.L. (1983) Four steps to measuring training effectiveness, *Personnel Administrator,* November: 19–25.

Kolb, D. (1983) Problem management: learning from experience, in S. Srivastva (ed.) *The Executive Mind*, San Francisco, Jossey-Bass.

Kolb, D. (1984) *Experiential Learning*, Englewood Cliffs, NJ, Prentice Hall.

Kotter, J.P. (1982) *The General Managers*, New York, Free Press.

Lave, J. and Wenger, E. (1991) *Situated Learning: Legitimate Peripheral Participation*, Cambridge, Cambridge University Press.

Leitch, S. (2006) *Prosperity for all in the Global Economy: World Class Skills,* London, HM Treasury.

London, M. (1986) The boss's role in management development, *Journal of Management Development,* **5**(3): 25–34.

Mabey, C. (2002) Mapping management development practice, *Journal of Management Studies,* **39**(8): 1139–60.

Mabey, C. (2005) *Management Development That Works: The Evidence,* London, CMI.

Mabey, C. and Ramirez, M. (2005) Does management development improve organizational productivity? A six-country analysis of European firms, *International Journal of Human Resource Management,* **16**(7):1067–82.

McCarthy, A. and Garavan, T. (2001) 360° feedback process: performance, improvement and employee career development, *Journal of European Industrial Training,* **25**(1): 3–32.

McLaughlin, H. and Thorpe, R. (1993) Action learning – a paradigm in emergence: the problems facing a challenge to traditional management education and development, *British Journal of Management,* **4**(1): 19–27.

Megginson, D. and Pedler, M. (1992) *Self Development,* Maidenhead, McGraw-Hill.

Megginson, D., Clutterbuck, D., Garvey, B. et al. (2005) *Mentoring in Action: A Practical Guide for Managers,* London, Kogan Page.

Meyer, H., Kay, E. and French, J. (1965) Split roles in performance appraisal, *Harvard Business Review,* **43**(1): 123–9.

Mezirow, J. (1990*) Fostering Critical Reflection in Adulthood,* San Francisco, Jossey-Bass.

Mintzberg, H., Ahlstrand, B. and Lampel, J. (1998) *Strategy Safari,* London, Prentice Hall.

Moynagh, M. and Worsley, R. (2005) *Working in the Twenty-first Century,* Leeds, ESRC Future of Work Programme.

Mumford, A. (1987) Using reality in management development, *Management Learning,* **18**: 223–43.

Mumford, A. (1995) Putting learning styles to work: an integrated approach, *Industrial and Commercial Training,* **27**(8): 28–35.

Mumford, A. (1997) *How to Choose the Right Development Method,* Maidenhead, P. Honey.

Mumford, A. and Gold, J. (2004) *Management Development: Strategies for Action,* London, CIPD.

Patton, M. (1997) *Utilization-focused Evaluation,* 3rd edn, Newbury Park, CA, Sage.

Peiperl, M. (2001) Getting 360 degree feedback right, *Harvard Business Review,* **79**(1): 142–7.

Perren, L. and Burgoyne, J. (2002) *Management and Leadership Abilities: An Analysis of Texts, Testimony and Practice,* London, CEML.

Phillips, J. (1996) Measuring ROI: the fifth level of evaluation, *Technical and Skills Training*, April: 10–13.

PIU (Performance and Innovation Unit) (2000) *Strengthening Leadership in the Public Sector*, London, PIU, Cabinet Office.

Poon, J. (2004) Effects of performance appraisal politics on job satisfaction and turnover intention, *Personnel Review,* **33**(3): 322–34.

Porter, M.E. (2003) UK Competitiveness: Moving to the Next Stage, LSE lecture, 22 January.

Reilly, R., Smither, J. and Vasilopoulos, N. (1996) A longitudinal study of upward feedback, *Personnel Psychology,* **49**(3): 599–612.

Revans, R. (1982) *The Origins and Growth of Action Learning,* Bromley, Chartwell-Bratt.

Reynolds, M. (1997) Learning styles: a critique, *Management Learning,* **28**(2): 115–33.

Rothman, J. (1997) *Resolving Identity-based Conflict in Nations, Organizations and Communities,* San Francisco, Jossey-Bass.

Schön, D.A. (1983) *The Reflective Practitioner: How Professionals Think in Action,* London, Maurice Temple Smith.

Schwartz, P. (1991) *The Art of the Long View,* New York, Doubleday.

Shotter, J. and Cunliffe, A. (2003) Managers as practical authors: everyday conversations for action, in D. Holman and R. Thorpe (eds) *Management and Language*, London, Sage.

Smith, A. (1993) Management development evaluation and effectiveness, *Journal of Management Development,* **12**(1): 20–33.

Smither, J., London, M. and Reilly, R. (2005) Does performance improve following multisource feedback? A theoretical model, meta-analysis, and review of empirical findings, *Personnel Psychology,* **58**(1): 33–66.

Stake, R. (ed.) (1975) *Evaluating the Arts in Education: A Responsive Approach,* Columbus, OH, Merrill.

Stewart, R. (1975) *Contrasts in Management,* Maidenhead, McGraw-Hill.

Storey, J., Edwards, P. and Sisson, K. (1994) *Managers in the Making,* London, Sage.

Strebler, M., Robinson, D. and Heron, P. (1997) *Getting the Best out of your Competences,* Report 334, Brighton, Institute of Manpower Studies.

Swailes, S. and Brown, P. (1999) NVQs in management, *Journal of Management Development,* **18**(9): 794–804.

Tamkin, P., Mabey, C. and Beech, D. (2006) *The Comparative Capability of UK Managers,* Brighton, Institute for Employment Studies.

Temporal, P. (1978) The nature of non-contrived learning and its implications for management development, *Management Education and Development,* **9**: 93–9.

Thomson, A., Storey, J., Mabey, C. et al. (1997) *A Portrait of Management Development,* London, Institute of Management.

Thomson, A., Mabey, C., Storey, J. et al. (2001) *Changing Patterns of Management Development,* Oxford, Blackwell.

Tymon, W. and Stumpf, S. (2003) Social capital in the success of knowledge workers, *Career Development International,* **8**(1): 12–20.

Vygotsky, L.S. (1982) *Collected Works,* Moscow, Pedagogica.

Warr, P., Bird, M. and Rackham, N. (1970) *Evaluation of Management Training,* Epping, Gower Press.

Watson, T.J. (1994) *In Search of Management,* London, Routledge.

Whiddett, S. and Hollyforde, S. (2003) *A Practical Guide to Competencies,* London, CIPD.

Williams, S. (2002) *Characteristics of the Management Population in the UK: Overview Report,* London, CEML.

Winterton, J. and Winterton, R. (1997) Does management development add value? *British Journal of Management,* **8**(Special Issue): 65–76.

Woodruffe, C. (2000) *Development and Assessment Centres,* 3rd edn, London, CIPD.

Leadership Development

11

Paul Iles, Chitra Meetoo and Jeff Gold

Chapter learning outcomes

After studying this chapter, you should be able to:

- Explain the meaning of leaders, leadership and Leadership Development (LD)
- Understand the importance of LD for individuals, organizations and society
- Explain various approaches to identify effective leadership, including transformational, charismatic, servant and authentic leadership models
- Distinguish between leaders and leadership, and human and social capital development
- Understand how effective development can be provided for leaders
- Discuss how LD can be evaluated

Chapter outline

Introduction

Leaders and leadership

Models of leadership

Leader development and LD

Summary

Introduction

It would be something of an understatement to claim that leadership and the development of leaders are hot topics. In the UK, the Council for Excellence in Management and Leadership (CEML, 2002, p. 6), for example, highlighted a general need for more and better managers and leaders, and that 'new developments are putting emphasis on leaderships abilities'. It is leaders who transform organizations (Bennis, 1989) and develop the vision that empowers others to accept responsibility for achieving it, whereas managers transact administrative and operational matters, controlling and monitoring the efforts of others as a response to the vision and ideas generated by the leader. This image, and its implied links to improved performance, has been particularly striking and has attracted interest across all sectors of the economy (Cabinet Office, 2000; PIU, 2000; DTI/DfES, 2001). However, there remain key questions about the meaning of leadership, whether a definitive model of abilities can be identified and used, or even if there is any evidence of leadership affecting overall performance (PIU, 2000).

For example, a street-level impression of leadership soon produces an interesting list of names such as Churchill, Thatcher, Gandhi and, more often than not, Hitler. What meanings of leadership would cover this group? In addition, confusion about the abilities that make a good leader can divert attention from leadership; as suggested by Burns (1978, p. 1), 'If we know too much about leaders, we know far too little about leadership' and we probably still do.

In this chapter, we argue that 'Leadership' Development (LD) as theorized and practised has too often been equated with 'leader' development. This has resulted in a focus on the individual, as against attending to the social, political, collective and other contexts of action and meaning. The upshot of this has been that there may have been a misallocation of resources in the attempt to develop leadership capacity (Bolden, 2005). We will distinguish between leaders and leadership on the one hand, and leader development and LD on the other. There is a dearth of critical studies on approaches to LD, despite the increasing interest shown in this topic in recent years.

In this chapter, LD is about the development of leadership processes in context, which must consider the interactions between those appointed as leaders and those seen as 'followers', as well as the cultural, historical and contingent conditions always present in any leadership situation. Leader development can be seen as involving the enhancement of human capital, while LD is about the creation of social capital, extending the collective ability of people to effectively undertake leadership roles and processes. It is about helping them to understand how to join and build social networks, develop commitments and access resources. These 'leadership roles' come with and without formal authority. Thus it is necessary to understand and act on the interactions between the 'leader' and the socioeconomic and political environment, with leadership being an emergent property of this interaction. Social capital theory, following Day (2000) and Iles and Preece (2006), is drawn on in order to aid the conceptualization and application of LD in context.

Working with a partner, each person identifies three people they immediately associate with the term 'leader'. Once identified, consider what each person has done to make them a leader. Compare notes and then define leadership.

Why do you think there are so many meanings of leader and leadership?

Leaders and leadership

The term 'leadership', like many terms in HRD, is contested. Most definitions focus on 'vertical leadership' (Yukl, 1999) exercised by a individual leader who acts to influence followers through the principle of 'unitary command'; although in practice, most studies focus on dyads or leader–follower pair exchanges, such as the currently influential 'leader–member exchange' (LMX) theory (Graen and Uhl-Bien, 1995). A substantial body of research has shown that LMX quality is positively related to followers' attitudes, citizenship behaviour and organizational outcomes (Ilies et al., 2007).

Robbins (2005) sees leadership in terms of the ability to influence a group towards the achievement of goals, while Northouse (1997, p. 3) defines leadership as:

> a process whereby an individual influences a group of individuals to achieve a common goal.

In much of the literature, this simple dichotomy, like those between hand and brain, managers and workers explored in Chapter 3, is taken for granted (Crevani et al., 2007). For example, Hatch et al.'s (2006) interviews with leading CEOs found a series of 'epics', where the 'leader-as-hero' succeeds, like characters in ancient myths, against seemingly impossible odds to slay the dragon, win the heart of the fair lady and lead his people to victory or the promised land. As Mintzberg (1999, p. 4) puts it: 'we seem to be moving beyond leaders who merely lead; today heroes save'.

Note that this hero is almost always a 'he' – our conceptions of the 'romance of leadership' (Meindl, 1995) and 'heroic leadership' are strongly gendered (Fletcher, 2004). Interestingly, many of the critiques of this 'heroic' conception come from Scandinavia, a region in which the model of culture developed by Hofstede (1991) and discussed in Chapter 18 comes out as more 'feminine' than other regions, and often from women (for example Billing and Alvesson, 2000; Crevani et al., 2007).

Early approaches to leadership focused on leader 'traits', especially personality characteristics and the well-worn notion that leaders are born rather than made. It is an enduring view, despite failing to find much consistency across sectors and organizations, but one that Cattell and Stice (1954) could still argue persuasively for during the 1950s. This is a typical set of traits associated with good leaders:

- emotional stability

- enthusiasm

- conscientiousness

- tough-mindedness
- self-assurance
- compulsiveness
- dominance.

The influence and continued presence of the 'traits' argument still raises doubts about whether a leader can be trained, developed or otherwise. However, Conger (2004, p. 136) suggests the argument is irrelevant; leaders are 'born and made' and later life experiences, especially difficult and challenging tasks, and support through coaching or models of success are critical.

Activity

The trait and personality view of leadership remains a partial mystery, only clarified by the use of inventories that may cast some light. Go to www.personal.psu.edu/faculty/j/5/j5j/IPIP/, where you will be able to complete an online version of the International Personality Item Pool questionnaire. We will return to this in our discussion of 'transformational' leadership.

Doubts about trait models resulted in a focus on the behaviour of leaders, begun in the USA in the Second World War and continued ever since. The search was on for a model of leadership behaviour that resulted in a 'one best way' approach to leading, where training and development became possible. Many of these models continue to this day. Whether described by the 1950s' Ohio or Michigan studies in terms of structure and consideration of a concern for task and people, or by Blake and Mouton (1985) in terms of the team leader's concern for people and production, the most effective leader seemed to be attentive to the task and social-emotional relationship dimensions of leadership (captured in Bales' Interaction Process Analysis, discussed in Chapter 12).

However, it has become clear that such a model of leadership is decontextualized and individualistic; most research was conducted by psychologists on small groups and on the behaviour of team leaders or supervisors (self-reported by the leader or reported by team members) rather than leaders of large organizations, using attitudinal or perceptual measures. Other theorists developed more contingent theories of leadership, especially 'situational' theories stressing the need to adapt the leader's style to the demands of the situation. However, most also focused on leaders of small groups and the situation of followers, seen in terms of their maturity, on the leaders' position of power or their relationship with their followers (for example Fiedler, 1967, 1996; Hersey and Blanchard, 1982). Other similar theories include path-goal theory (House and Mitchell, 1974) and LMX theory (Graen and Uhl-Bien, 1995), as well as normative decision theory (Vroom and Yetton, 1973). Most allowed the measurement and identification of current behaviours or 'styles' of leadership, followed by adjustment as a result of new understanding and learning. Many leadership programmes continue to use such methods in some form or another.

Form a group of three. Go to www.nwlink.com/~donclark/leader/survstyl.html and print off the Leadership Style Survey. Complete it and work out your preferred styles. Discuss the implications of the results.

Managers and leaders

The focus on behaviour and styles during the 1950s and 60s suggested that leadership and management needed to be considered as variations within a role. For example, when faced with a member of staff considered to be immature or a novice, managers/leaders should adjust their style to become more directive, typically the behaviour of a manager. Further, writers such as Mintzberg (1973) studied chief executives but, in common with other studies of managers, found a pattern of pace, variety and fragmentation, with different roles required, such as monitor, negotiator, spokesperson but also figurehead and leader. At this point, we might need to reconsider whether a chapter on LD is required, sufficiently different from Chapter 10. Prior to the 1980s, 'leadership' and 'management' were rarely differentiated, usually being seen as interchangeable or overlapping activities (for example the meta-analyses of leadership training we discuss at the end involve both 'management' and 'leadership' development – often collectively referred to as 'managerial leadership training'). Where leadership was differentiated, it was seen as involving influence processes in small groups by supervisors or frontline managers, typically studied by psychologists using survey or experimental methods.

However, as Storey (2004) and Preece and Iles (2009) have noted, what is seen to constitute 'leadership' has also changed over time, and during the 1980s, we saw 'new paradigm' models such as the 'charismatic' and 'visionary' models of Bennis and Nanus (1985) and the 'transformational' model of Bass (1985). Here leadership was linked more closely with the facilitation of organizational change and transformation by senior leaders, not managers. In recent years, there has been a further shift: post-Enron, there is much more concern with integrity (Mangham, 2004), 'ethical leadership' (Iles and Macaulay, 2007; Hickey et al., 2007), context (Ray et al., 2004) and 'leadership competences' (Salaman, 2004). Further, the 1990s saw a concern with 'creating corporate culture', organizational symbolism and the need to bring about transformational leadership in large organizations facing new global challenges. This led to a renewed interest in earlier, more political and sociological accounts of leadership, such as the work of Burns (1978) and Weber (1978) on charisma.

One widely influential view compares management with leadership, often in the latter's favour: whereas managers are concerned with today, with delivery, targets, efficiency, utilization and authority, focusing on internal organizational issues, control and 'doing things right', leaders are held to be oriented to tomorrow, to development, direction, purpose and vision, and innovation. They focus on external issues, facilitation, empowerment and 'doing the right thing'. In contrast, Kotter (1990) has argued that organizations, needing to promote stability and change, require leaders and managers. Leading change is the focus of leaders, who need to increase urgency, build a guiding team, get the vision right, communicate for buy-in, empower action, create short-term wins, not let up, and make change stick. Manocha (2004) notes that many organizations still fail to acknowledge the difference between leadership and management.

In the UK, Adair and Adair (2006) developed a popular approach to LD based on action and change. Action-centred leadership is based on three areas of consideration, represented as three overlapping circles:

- achieving the task
- managing the team or group
- managing individuals.

For each area, a leader needs to consider a number of responsibilities:

- *achieving the task:* identify aims and vision for the group, purpose and direction
- *managing the group:* establish, agree and communicate standards of performance and behaviour
- *managing individuals:* identify and agree appropriate individual responsibilities.

This approach to LD has now gained worldwide popularity (find out more about action-centred leadership at www.johnadair.co.uk/).

Models of leadership

Today, leadership is the subject of a plethora of books, articles and conference papers, as well as government and corporate initiatives of various kinds. Whereas in the 1980s and early 1990s there was sustained interest in management, now there is the suggestion that management is not enough – we need leaders too – almost to the point where mere 'management' has become a negative word (for example Bennis and Nanus, 1985). The 21st century is a time of renewed academic and political interest in leadership (see, for example, Grint, 2005). Storey (2004) has pointed to the enormous growth of literature on leadership in recent years, while there has been a slower rate of growth in the LD literature. He also notes recent high-profile initiatives on leadership in the UK public sector (for example the National College for School Leadership, a new leadership centre for the NHS, new leadership initiatives in the police service and the Ministry of Defence), along with the publication of a variety of reports (for example Horne and Stedman-Jones, 2001). One example is the higher education sector, where the Leadership Foundation for Higher Education was founded in 2003 (Duckett, 2008). As Storey (2004, p. 5) observes, leadership is often underspecified, standing in 'for all the qualities that are desirable in a top team or responsible post-holder', and assumed to be the answer to a whole range of complex problems, all of which demand organizational change. Improved/enhanced organizational leadership is seen as the appropriate response in all sectors. The search has been for a model for developing leaders.

Transformational leadership

An influential model of leadership has come from Bass (1985, 1990), comparing 'transactional' leaders, exercising contingent reward and management by exception, with 'transformational' leaders, exercising idealized influence and inspirational motivation in a 'charismatic-inspirational' style. Such leaders stimulate organizational members intellectually and give them individualized consideration. In empirical studies, transformational leadership has usually been shown to be more highly correlated with extra effort, satisfaction with the leader, and perceptions of leader effectiveness. It is usually measured by the 360 degree Multifactor Leadership Questionnaire instrument (Bass and Avolio, 1993) against four dimensions:

- transformational leadership
- transactional leadership
- non-transactional leadership
- outcomes of leadership, such as effort, effectiveness and satisfaction.

Once completed, each leader receives a report, which includes:

- Descriptions of the leadership styles
- Scale- and item-level information at all rater levels
- A narrative of the leader's style
- Agreement levels along ratings
- Leadership outcomes
- How to build leadership competency
- Suggestions for interpreting the report.

One obvious follow-up to this process is to support development with a coach. Some have tried to relate transformational leadership to personality traits; for example, although results usually indicate small effects, such leaders often seem to be extravert, agreeable and open to experience (for example Bono and Judge, 2004).

Other theories also emphasize emotions and values in leadership and symbolic behaviour, making events meaningful for followers, in contrast to earlier 'rational' theories. Charismatic theories (for example Conger, 1989) are primarily interested in the leader's impact on the follower, and the behaviours used to achieve such effects. Followers apparently feel trust, admiration, loyalty and respect, and are motivated to do more than they are expected to do. Aware of task outcomes, followers transcend self-interest and make sacrifices for the sake of organizational goals. Charismatic theories stress articulating a vision, showing sensitivity to the environment, expressing confidence, modelling exemplary behaviour, and emphasizing collective identity, although Yukl (1999) notes that the core behaviours involved often vary from theory to theory, and sometimes from older to newer versions of the same theory.

In most studies, no practising leaders are actually observed, and the specificity and generalizability of the instruments have often been questioned (van der Weide and Wilderom, 2001), as well as the confusing combination of the emotional 'charisma' construct with the rational 'vision' construct (Khatri et al., 2001). Students of 'managerial behaviour' have often criticized leadership researchers for focusing on what leaders 'should' do, not what they actually do – as in Kotter's (1990) prescriptive model.

As noted earlier, transformational leadership subscribes to a 'heroic' model of leadership, with little interest in reciprocal influence processes or shared leadership, or how followers can challenge and change the visions of their leaders. Such frameworks carry the danger of once again proposing 'one best way' of leadership and decontextualizing it, in particular seeing it in terms of a set of individual leadership competencies. What is more, as Alimo-Metcalfe and Alban-Metcalfe (2001) have suggested, such a model is rooted in a strong US, male and private sector view of the heroic leader and, particularly post-Enron, is open to serious challenge. The Enron scandal is a reminder that while leaders can be celebrated as heroes, there are also 'dysfunctional' behaviours that involve corruption, bullying and 'toxic' behaviour by senior executives, sometimes referred to as the 'dark side' of leadership. Other terms used here include 'inauthentic' and 'pseudo-leadership'.

Activity

Enron was a large US company that employed 21,000 staff in 40 countries. However, its leaders, much praised until its collapse, had lied about profits and concealed its debts. To learn more about the Enron scandal, go to http://news.bbc.co.uk/1/hi/business/1780075.stm.

In Alimo-Metcalfe and Alban-Metcalfe's (2001) study of male and female British public sector health and local government managers during the development of a new transformational leadership questionnaire, factor analysis revealed nine key factors related to how UK public sector managers perceived the ideal 'near' transformational leader – in contrast to most US studies of 'far' leaders, for example chief executives. These factors are:

- a genuine concern for others
- political sensitivity and skills
- decisiveness, determination and self-confidence
- integrity, trustworthiness, honesty and openness
- empowering and developing potential
- inspirational networking and promotion
- accessibility and approachability
- clarifying boundaries and involving others
- encouraging strategic thinking.

A concern in the UK public sector with issues of ethics, integrity and external networks, as well as with organizational and interorganizational politics, has been found in studies of leadership in the public services in other countries (for example Iles and Macaulay, 2007; Hickey et al., 2007).

Emotional intelligence

Recent work has also stressed the importance of 'emotional intelligence' (EI) to leadership, especially transformational leadership. Salovey and Mayer (1990) have argued that people vary in their capacity to process emotional information and relate it to wider cognition. Goleman (1996) took this further by associating EI with leadership and business success. 'Successful people', higher in EI, were better able to perceive, understand, and regulate their emotions. Dadehbeigi et al. (2008a) suggest that EI is associated with leadership emergence, effective leader outcomes, leadership effectiveness and transformational leadership, showing the close links between EI and transformational leadership, although doubts remain about the validity of the EI concept:

- Is it saying anything new, as it seems to overlap with other variables?

- Its definition and operationalization – the reliance on self-report studies

- Is it a personality trait able to be translated into competencies, or a cognitive ability?

- Not all studies are supportive of a link between EI and leadership; is it able to be developed?

Dadehbeigi et al. (2008b) analysed an EI training programme for bank employees in Iran using real-life and work-related examples of the four EI competencies put forward by Goleman (1996) – self-awareness, self-management, social awareness and relationship management. EI increased after training, and service quality and financial performance improved. Cartwright and Pappas (2008) reviewed the literature on EI in the workplace and concluded that EI is likely to have implications for selection and development, especially in stressful jobs, and for service quality and customer/client interactions. Its association with leadership effectiveness is more limited, however.

Interest in EI is part of a wider interest in emotions in leadership, such as empathy and respect (Clarke, 2008), perhaps associated with the move from a manufacturing to a service and knowledge-based economy. Positive emotions play a crucial role in transformational leadership, for example through 'emotional contagion' (Johnson, 2008), while negative ones are central to 'toxic' leadership theories. Leadership can be related to 'emotional labour' (Iszatt-White et al., 2005). Respect is often treated implicitly, and often differently, in the leadership literature, and is particularly significant within 'servant leadership' (Greenleaf, 1977) and ethical leadership. Sendjaya et al. (2008) measured servant leadership, characterized by service orientation, holistic outlook and a moral-spiritual emphasis. Servant leadership has six dimensions:

- voluntary subordination
- authentic self
- covenantal relationship
- responsible morality
- transcendental spirituality
- transforming influence.

It also resembles transformational leadership, but is less oriented to organizational goals and more to followers' needs and interests. It also resembles another emerging model of leadership, 'authentic leadership' (Avolio and Gardiner, 2005), in emphasizing the deep awareness necessary of the leader's own and others' values and perspectives and the context in which they operate, but places a greater stress on spirituality.

Activity

You can find out more about servant leadership at www.greenleaf.org/whatissl/index.html. What do you see as the implications of servant leadership for LD? You may also wish to look at the emerging field of spirituality in organizations – see the *Journal of Management Spirituality and Religion*, www.jmsr.com.

Best practice models

Finding a model for LD is something that most large organizations seek. Fulmer and Wagner (1999), for example, undertook a survey of six selected 'best practice organizations' from an initial choice of thirty organizations. A key finding was the alignment of LD to support corporate strategy, with leaders seen to play a key role in implementing strategy. Very often, the connection is made by developing and using a competency framework for the organization, which can be varied locally, rather than using a generic model. There were key links to assessing leaders against the framework at development centres (see Chapter 10), coaching and mentoring and planning succession. As we saw in Chapter 10, competencies are seen by many large organizations as a way of linking MLD with organizational measures such as commitment, performance and productivity (Mabey and Gooderham 2005), hence the continued use and evolution of 'best practice' models (James, 2000). However, such specification of leadership behaviour is not always considered effective, because models can become prescriptive and normative, setting out what leaders should do and what they need to learn to become 'excellent', 'high performing' and so on.

Emergent and constructed views

In contrast to the search for best practice models, there is a view that what leaders do is contingent on the situation faced, including dependence on the responses and actions of others. We now consider leadership more as a social process (Barker, 2001), a dynamic and living activity where it is more difficult to predict the outcomes. The bigger the project – and leaders are expected to take responsibility for change projects – the more variables are present and the more difficulties might arise. Watson (2001) talks about the 'emergent manager', and this applies equally to leaders and leadership, which is better understood as a world of movement, emergent processes and relationships with others. Leadership only makes sense when followers and the context of action are brought into the equation. Those appointed as leaders need to accept what Antonacopoulou and Bento (2004, p. 82) call a 'learning leadership' approach to their development, focusing on 'discovering and experiencing leadership from within'. We suggest that this involves reflecting on events, seeking feedback, working with coaches, peers and mentors and experimenting with new ideas and behaviour.

Changes in the way we now think about leadership have opened up connections with the world of 'futures studies' (Micic and Gold, 2008), and Boydell et al. (2004) argue that instead of focusing on the personal qualities of leaders, we need to focus on the leadership challenges faced by communities, societies and organizations in a more collective way. They conceptualize leadership situations in terms of the challenges, contexts and characteristics of everyone involved, including those designated as 'leaders'. So the focus is on developing leadership rather than leaders (see also Grint, 2005), and on 'leaderful' organizations and 'distributed' leadership.

Leadership scenarios at Bupa

As part of the Bupa LD programme, I learned that scenario planning can be a useful tool in business. Stories about how scenario planning has been successfully utilized by other companies like Shell and the great value attributed to it and the resources poured into it by BT helped, as knowing that these companies and others valued scenario use sparked enthusiasm and made me want to find out more and take part. Thinking of a possible state of reality in the future and then imagining how that reality may have come about was useful; we all thought divergently at first, coming up with the maximum number of things that could happen. We used a structure of thinking about things we felt would happen in different periods in the future, for example likely and soon, or unlikely and far off. It was much easier to think about things that are likely to happen soon; harder to think what will happen in 5 or 10 years' time. We then thought about how these situations could have come to be in a more convergent style, and learned how to question our own use of language in order to make our statements more succinct and increase commitment.

To embed learning, we used a Bupa example, and created a story around it, working on a future scenario where Bupa was the leading healthcare company and more customer friendly, because all businesses interacted as one to provide customers with a seamless service. We considered what would lead to that being a reality in 2012. I can see the usefulness of scenario planning on a smaller scale within a smaller context like a department; a great tool to use to help visualize objectives and to achieve future goals.

Source: Susan George (personal communication)

Smircich and Morgan (1982) saw leadership as 'the management of meaning': leaders act by defining organizational reality through a process of interaction, developing a vision, articulating values and working on changing organizational culture. This shifts attention from the solo leader to collective construction processes. For example, Uhl-Bien (2006) sees leadership processes as those in which emergent coordination and change are constructed. Alvesson and Svenningsson (2003, p. 961) point out that normative leadership research sees 'the leader as consistent essence, a centred subject with a particular orientation'; however, leaders are not 'the autonomous, self-determining individual with a secure unitary identity … [at] the centre of the social universe' (Alvesson and Deetz, 2000, p. 98). A development of this approach is to take a social constructivist perspective on leadership (Sjöstrand and Tyrstrup, 2001). Another is to move away from the 'individualistic' focus of much leadership theory by focusing on 'shared' or 'distributed' leadership, to which we next turn.

Distributed leadership

Gibb (1954) distinguished 'focused' from 'distributed' leadership, contrasting the focus on sole leaders – usually heroic, transformational and charismatic CEOs – with shared, dispersed or distributed leadership. Here reciprocal influence processes operate and team structures and empowerment are seen to grow in importance. As we consider the move towards the social process of leadership, we can begin to see a dimension, ranging from the focus on the solo leader to a collective view of leadership, as shown in Figure 11.1.

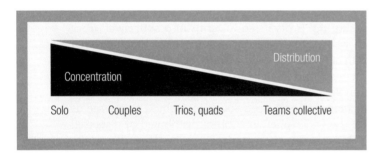

FIGURE 11.1 Leadership approaches
SOURCE: Ross et al. (2005, p. 131)

From the solo focus, we can point to approaches that embrace couples or trios and quads, as in leadership teams at executive levels. One person may nominally carry the title CEO or MD, but there is clearly a distribution of power and responsibility. Team leadership occurs at a variety of levels from the senior team to various teams that have a degree of autonomy for decision making (see Chapter 12). Beyond teams, the unit changes towards a collective view of shared leadership covering a whole area of work or a whole organization. The diversity of leadership approaches now evident presents those appointed as leaders, the solos, with something of a conundrum, because they carry responsibility but may not be able to control the way leadership is working. As Yukl (1999, p. 293) suggests:

> an alternative perspective would be to describe leadership as a shared process of enhancing the collective and individual capacity of people to accomplish their work roles effectively … the leadership actions of any individual leader are much less important than the collective leadership provided by members of the organization.

For House and Adtja (1997, p. 457), 'leadership involves collaborative relationships that lead to collective action': distributed leadership can be delegated, co-leadership, or peer leadership. As well as appealing to egalitarian values, distributed leadership may have practical benefits – reducing overload, allowing multiple development opportunities, motivating and engaging leaders and followers, and allowing all those with capabilities to address decision making.

Gronn (2000, p. 318) sees distributed leadership as an emergent property of a group or network of interacting individuals, arguing for:

> the centrality of conjoint agency. That is, the satisfactory completion of discretionary tasks is attributable to the concertive labour performed by pluralities of interdependent organization members.

For Gronn (2002), distributed leadership can be 'dispersed' and 'numerical', or 'conjoint' and 'concertive'. The first pair suggests that all organizational members can be leaders at some time; the second results from conjoint, synchronized agency and actions, either through spontaneous collaboration, intuitive working relationships, or as institutionalized practice, as in formal leadership teams. Leithwood et al. (2007) offer similar distinctions: planned alignment/spontaneous alignment (mostly positive) and spontaneous misalignment/anarchic misalignment (mostly negative). Similarly, Iles and Macaulay (2007) found that 'ethical leadership' in English local government was 'fragmented', and therefore incoherent, rather than positively distributed.

Here we will note that sometimes 'sharing' is discussed in terms of a shift away from bureaucratic command and control systems to decentralized structures and self-directed teams (see Chapter 12) and the growth of knowledge workers and the knowledge-intensive economy. Some argue that management and leadership now require complementary roles that 'share' leadership, for example the chair and CEO, CEO and COO, the football coach and a director of football, or manager and head coach in rugby. This we see as 'shared' leadership, one example of the wider phenomenon of distributed or dispersed leadership. Such distributed leadership is often characterized by interdependence, the complementary overlapping of responsibilities, and the coordination and management of interdependencies.

Distributed leadership represents something of a challenge to our understanding of leadership, and as Bennettt et al. (2003, p. 2) point out, there is 'little agreement as to the meaning of the term'. It is suggested that it is best to think of distributed leadership as 'a way of thinking about leadership' rather than as another technique or practice. Harris (2008) reviews the literature linking distributed leadership to organizational change, especially in educational settings, but points to the research challenges and methodological difficulties in conducting research on distributed leadership, with competing definitions and definitions of the term, often overlapping with shared and participative leadership. However, if we consider the growing number of situations where people work in professional or knowledge-based contexts, or in virtually dispersed global organizations, it is difficult to disagree with Gronn (2000, p. 333) when he states that 'all the indications are that distributed leadership is an idea whose time has come', although the word was first used in Australia in 1954 in contrast to 'focused' leadership (Gibb, 1954). What are needed are ways of helping leaders to understand the distribution of leadership (Ross et al., 2005).

Leader development and LD

Here we see LD as involving the development of knowledge, skills, attributes and experience as a means of enhancing the performance of leadership roles and processes. However, it seems that many leaders may have to go 'external' for their LD, as many of them may feel unable to show/admit internally that they need LD. HRD specialists may not believe they have the expertise to provide it. As Burgoyne et al. (2004, p. 49) argue, LD 'works in different ways in different situations', and any design for development needs to consider specific circumstances. Thus, there are a number of ways of categorizing LD, as with MD (Chapter 10). Mumford (1987) distinguished between 'unplanned accidental', 'planned on the job', and 'planned or programmed' learning experiences that occur outside work. LD can therefore involve formal education and training, conducted 'off the job' through short courses, qualification-based programmes, and in-company training (Woodall and Winstanley, 1998). External programmes can bring specialist competence, a wider perspective, and up-to-date knowledge; internal programmes can help to encourage team building and collaboration, and link development to strategic goals. Off-the-job methods include action learning, secondments, projects, coaching, mentoring and international assignments, as well as self-managed learning through reading and e-learning.

In many countries, there appears to be a move towards more experiential methods, such as outdoor development, action learning, coaching and mentoring (see, for example, Thomson et al., 2000; Williams et al., 2003; Suutari and Viitala, 2008). As Hirst et al. (2004, p. 324) argue:

> organizations should place greater emphasis on experiential learning so as to foster sustained behavioural and practice changes. Organizations can introduce formal mentoring and job rotation programs, 'stretch assignments,' and opportunities for more senior responsibilities to build the experience base. These activities have been found to be powerful stimulants of experiential learning.

Active, experiential LD can challenge participants' beliefs, skills and knowledge. In addition, the focus of LD has increasingly shifted away from functional knowledge and skills to more strategic and integrative issues and towards e-learning and self-managed learning to enhance flexibility and responsiveness. However, LD may require structured processes to help leaders to focus on learning, share lessons, and integrate them into the existing personal and organizational knowledge/competence bases. Uncertainties raised here include what knowledge and skills are necessary to carry out the executive role, and how best to learn these.

However, evidence for the effectiveness of LD has often been patchy. Many of the companies surveyed by Thomson et al. (2000) reported that development had often not met its objectives, and that measures of its positive impact were lacking. Most evaluation studies have been based on interviews or surveys with the professionals responsible for those activities (Thomson et al., 2000; Russon and Reinelt, 2004), hence an impartial view seems unlikely.

Leader development or LD?

Day (2000) notes that many currently popular LD practices (like 360 degree feedback, mentoring and action learning) were originally developed and implemented in organizations for other reasons, for example to improve performance management, enhance socialization, and increase productivity. Perhaps the most popular approaches, following the individualized, competence-based models of leadership discussed earlier, have been based on personal development programmes for developing leaders – 'leader development' as opposed to 'Leadership Development'. This reinforces the message that leadership is about the personal attributes or competencies of leaders (Boydell et al., 2004) and that such qualities or attributes can be developed through programmes of personal leader development. Such an approach has been described as 'an alienating social myth' (Gemmil and Oakley, 1997), encouraging learned helplessness among followers.

As we considered earlier, most models of leadership seek to set out best practice as the skills and attributes, or competences, required by those appointed as leaders. However, we also contrasted such models with a view suggesting that the work of leaders is contingent on the situation faced, and dependent on the responses and actions of others. In addition, as explained above, the focus of development can range from giving attention to solos, those appointed as leaders, towards seeing leadership as a social and potentially collective process that is distributed. Here we wish to develop these ideas by proposing a typology of modes of LD using two axes: how 'directed' or 'open' the approach adopted is, and whether it mainly addresses individual human capital development, termed 'leader development' by Iles and Preece (2006), or collective social capital development, LD. The distinction between 'directed' and 'open' was used by Iles and Yolles (2004) to refer to different action research (AR) approaches. 'Directed' or prescriptive approaches predefine the direction that an AR intervention will develop, as defined by the paradigms that underpin the methodologies:

- *Directed AR* operates through predefined or predetermined paradigms, for example most OD, team-building interventions, and competence frameworks.

- *Organic, open or emergent AR* operates through the mix of participants who determine the outcomes organically through group development in an emergent fashion, such as team 'syntegrity/syntegration' (Iles and Yolles, 2004) or, at an individual level, mentoring or coaching.

A similar approach has been proposed by Rodgers et al. (2003), using slightly different terminology. Figure 11.2 combines these two approaches to provide four quadrants to consider LD.

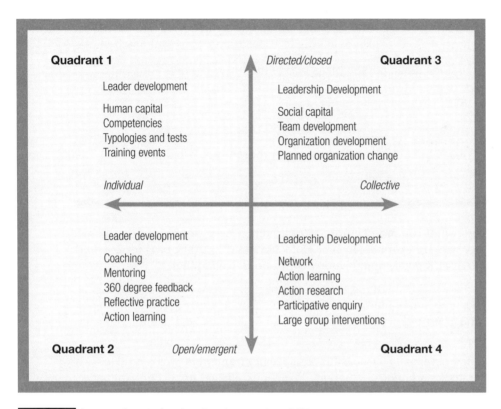

FIGURE 11.2 Approaches to leader development and LD

SOURCE: Adapted from Iles and Yolles (2004) and Rodgers et al. (2003)

Quadrant 1 approaches

What are commonly called LD programmes are often in fact leader development programmes, often involving a mixture of competency models, psychometric assessment of personality, emotional intelligence, team management profiles and training events around particular skills or issues. The focus of attention is on solo leaders or leaders as individuals, enhancing human capital. Storey (2004) identifies three LD interventions that fit into this quadrant, representing the most common offerings to leaders. These are:

1 *Learning about leadership and organizations:* mainly traditional ideas and theories, delivered in business schools and training workshops.

2 *Self-analysis, team analysis and leadership styles:* completed by individuals to create understanding of current styles but can also include psychometric tests, which can link to feedback and coaching in quadrant 2.

3 *Top-level strategy courses:* often aimed at the higher level leaders, delivered as executive courses or master classes. They can be expensive, depending on who delivers and where.

Activity

Form a group of three. Each person picks one of the following and finds out what is offered for executives, and how such programmes are delivered, with prices, if possible.

- Harvard Business School – www.exed.hbs.edu/programs/custom/

- London Business School – www.london.edu/programmes/mba.html

- INSEAD – http://executive.education.insead.edu/.

Research suggests that competency frameworks, both generic or organization based, often play a key role. For example, Income Data Services (IDS, 2003, p. 1) reviewed LD programmes in five UK public and private organizations. Noting that:

> it is now a fairly safe bet that most organizations … have come to regard the quality of their leadership as a significant business issue' … [and] as all our companies recognize, management and leadership roles are quite different and demand different competencies

the IDS shows how developing a leadership 'competency framework' was central to each of the five case studies. Change orientation, drive for excellence, impact and influence, strategic thinking and customer focus all featured strongly, with EI emerging alongside self-awareness and contrasting leadership styles, especially in the public sector. The programmes were often developed in partnership with a consultancy company, university or management college, and usually involved much emphasis on leading and developing people, strategic and innovative thinking, performance management and personal impact, making great use of e-learning, coaching and mentoring, secondments and attachments, which links to quadrant 2 approaches.

Quadrant 2 approaches

We suggest that experiential approaches and those focusing on reflection and feedback from others fall into this quadrant. Storey (2004) highlights the popularity of experiential programmes, perhaps using the outdoors and simulations (see also Chapter 10). An example would be a clinical leadership programme in a not-for-profit mental health organization in England that aimed to link effective leadership with personal skills and competencies in a transformational leadership framework (Storr and Trenchard, 2008). This involved 'adult learning' – involving presentations, groupwork, personal analysis and critical reflection following a Myers-Briggs test (and using diaries) and 360 degree feedback, case study presentations and home-based project work and action learning sets. Performance needs were identified through an appraisal process, with reference to the NHS Knowledge and Skills Framework and Leadership Qualities Framework. Similarly, the Third Sector Leadership Centre (Stewart and Birchall, 2008) provides a diagnostic tool to prompt leaders to identify the most appropriate development intervention, based on the skills and knowledge required and the time available to commit, from a range of options: action learning, assessment tools, coaching, competency frameworks, mentoring, qualifications, residential leadership programmes, secondments and volunteering, self-directed learning, and workshops and master classes.

HRD in Practice 11.2

The Academy of Chief Executives' experiential leadership development programme

An experiential programme run for chief executives in England by the Academy of Chief Executives (northeast) involved speaker sessions, issue sessions involving peer learning, coaching, an intranet, a retreat, national seminars and a 'leaders' quest' abroad. These LD initiatives address issues of networking, bonding and bridging, and especially issues of trust and social capital.

Participants reported:

'OK, there were two reasons to join: one was to keep learning and the second was to have a sort of sounding board … in most cases I found the quality of speakers has been good … most of it has been fresh and new and therefore stimulating, and I have been able to take ideas from it and put it into practice.'

'You actually get a different perspective – what you see as a problem, others see as a great opportunity, and they challenge what you are thinking, and sometimes when you are in it, you don't 'see the wood for the trees'. They don't provide a solution, but they set you on a path which gives you the possibility of finding a solution.'

'You can talk in confidence to a group of people … I assumed that there would be people there who would be much more experienced than me. I want to learn from that … to develop an understanding of the place of the chief executives, how they deal with issues, how they behave, what language they use, and the way they approach these things … This was my attitude – to really latch onto their coat tails and see what they do and how they work, what has made them successful.'

Source: Iles and Preece (2006); Preece and Iles (2009)

Experiential learning processes in LD may enhance self-confidence through feedback, the observation of others (whether peers or facilitators) and self-checking or 'self-monitoring' (Snyder, 1979, 1987). Here people regulate their own behaviour and monitor its social appropriateness, using social comparisons, in order to be favourably perceived by others. One such experiential learning process, discussed in Chapter 10, is action learning.

Mentoring and coaching have been referred to as examples of open LD (in particular, 'learning from role models'). Mentoring, where a more experienced manager/executive – the mentor is not usually the protégé's immediate boss – facilitates the learning and career development of a less experienced mentee, appears to be growing in popularity, providing both psychosocial (for example acceptance and encouragement) and career facilitation benefits (for example sponsorship, protection and exposure). Mentoring is oriented to support, rather than challenge or assessment, and can enhance the cognitive (for example more sophisticated strategic representations) as well as the mutual trust, respect and commitment dimensions of social capital. Coaching usually involves the integration of assessment, challenge and support. If linked to 360 degree assessment, it has the potential to enhance human and social capital by increasing weak and strong network ties (Granovetter, 1973) and acting as a link between leaders and LD. In recent years, there has been a strong growth in coaching for leaders, referred to as 'executive coaching'. Carter (2001) suggests this is due to the failure of traditional approaches to providing feedback to senior managers who often have to work in lonely or isolated contexts. Gray (2006) points to the importance of executive coaching in developing leaders and enhancing performance, although there are few qualifications so far for coaches. Difficulties can arise in the disturbance and anxiety that coaching may engender.

Quadrant 3 approaches

As Iles and Preece (2006) have pointed out, LD involves more than developing human capital or individual skills and intrapersonal competence – it also involves developing social capital, defined by Nahapiet and Ghoshal (1998, p. 243) as 'the sum of actual and potential resources within, available through and derived from the network of relationships possessed by an individual or social unit'. Day (2000) argues that there is a need to link leader development, based on enhancing human capital, and LD, based on creating social capital. LD is defined by Day as 'expanding the collective capacity of organizational members to engage effectively in leadership roles and processes' (p. 582). Unlike 'leadership competencies', social capital cannot be regarded as a commodity, and one sole actor or leader cannot have 'ownership rights'. LD therefore involves helping people to understand, in an integrative way, how to build relationships to access resources, coordinate activities, develop commitments and build social networks. Leadership roles refer here to those that come with and without formal authority, while 'leadership processes are those that generally enable groups of people to work together in meaningful ways' (Day, 2000, p. 582).

LD 'involves building the capacity of people to learn their way out of problems that could not have been predicted' (Dixon, 1993), or that arise from the disintegration of traditional organizational structures and the associated loss of sense making (Weick, 1993). This perspective on LD takes us closer to the distributed models of leadership discussed earlier and away from vertical leadership and its focus on the sole, heroic leader. As individuals, leaders need to invest time in building trust and respect from others and developing the shared and collective meanings that enable a virtuous form of distributed leadership to develop. Team development programmes (Chapter 12) are suited to the development of shared meanings, accepting that influence can be a reciprocal process of interdependence, the work of multiple leaders (Spillane, 2006).

The extension of teams into planned OD and change programmes (Chapter 12) promotes the sharing of leadership responsibilities, and involves using social/relational processes to help build commitments among members of a community of practice (Wenger, 1998), which may be internal and/or external to the organization. Organizations 'need to attend to both individual leader and collective leadership development' (Day, 2000, p. 582) in order to build leadership capacity. This focus in LD is therefore on the interaction between individuals and social and organizational environments (Fiedler, 1996), involving considerations such as 'how to relate to others, coordinate their efforts, build commitments and develop extended social networks' (Day, 2000, p. 582). LD is seen as potentially taking place anywhere, involving learning from work in the context of ongoing work initiatives tied to strategic imperatives.

Quadrant 4 approaches

Bennett et al. (2003, p. 3) suggest that distributed leadership is an 'emergent property of a group or network of individuals in which group members pool their expertise'. Networking is primarily about investing in and developing social capital, with a primary emphasis on developing support as well as on expanding definitions through exposure to others' thinking and forming commitments outside one's immediate work group. In this sense, it can build peer relationships across functional areas, leading to the creation of additional social capital, as well as linking LD with leader development if used in conjunction with feedback, coaching and mentoring.

Evaluation of LD

Despite the growth in LD, few evaluation studies have been conducted. Burke and Day (1986) conducted a meta-analysis of 70 studies of 'managerial leadership training' (from business and industry alone) covering seven methods, six content areas and four types of outcome criteria (subjective behaviour, subjective learning, objective results and objective learning) between 1951 and 1982. The results suggested that leadership training was moderately effective – different methods did not necessarily translate into enhanced knowledge or increased performance. Collins and Holton (2004) analysed 83 studies of 'managerial leadership development' between 1982 and 2001, including studies from education, the military, government and health fields, finding that significant improvements in knowledge and skills were attainable if practitioners focused on ensuring appropriate training and development.

Summary

- As theorized and practised, LD has too often been equated with leader development. This has resulted in a focus on the individual, as against attending to the social, political, collective and other contexts of action and meaning.

- Early approaches to the study of leadership focused on leader traits, especially personality characteristics and the well-worn notion that leaders are born rather than made. It is an enduring view, despite failing to find much consistency across sectors and organizations.

- From 1945, models of leadership to enable the development of leaders focused on behaviour and styles in particular situations, facing tasks and relationships with others.

- During the 1980s, there was a clear attempt to differentiate transformational leadership models from transactional models of management. Recent work has also stressed the importance of emotional intelligence to leadership.

- There is growing interest in approaches to leadership that contrast with sole leaders; this includes leadership processes shared across situations and distributed leadership.

- LD can vary according to the attention given to individual leaders or collective approaches and whether development is directed and prescribed or open and emergent.

- Most LD programmes focus on leaders and are directed and prescribed based on theories, skills and issues for the attention of those in senior positions.

- Experiential programmes are also popular and can involve attention to reflection and feedback from others including coaching. Action learning can also be used.

- Leaders need to invest time in building social capital and developing the shared and collective meanings that enable a virtuous form of distributed leadership to develop.

Discussion questions

1 Can we define leadership?
2 Is it possible to develop a best practice model of leadership for developing leaders?
3 Should LD be concerned with focusing on individual leaders only?
4 Does good leadership result in the enhanced performance of organizations?
5 How can reflection, feedback and coaching be used in LD?

Further reading

Gilpin-Jackson, Y. and Bushe, G. (2007) Leadership development training transfer: a case study of post-training determinants, *Journal of Management Development*, **26**(10): 980–1004.

Gold, J., Thorpe, R. and Mumford, A. (2009) *Handbook of Leadership and Management Development*, Aldershot, Gower.

Western, S. (2008) *Leadership: A Critical Text*, London, Sage.

References

Adair, J.E. and Adair, J. (2006) *How to Grow Leaders: The Seven Key Principles of Effective Leadership Development*, London, Kogan Page.

Alimo-Metcalfe, B. and Alban-Metcalfe, R. (2001) The development of a new Transformational Leadership Questionnaire, *Journal of Occupational and Organizational Psychology*, **74**(1): 1–28.

Alvesson, M. and Deetz, S. (2000) *Doing Critical Management Research,* London, Sage.

Alvesson, M. and Sveningsson, S. (2003) Good visions, bad micro-management and ugly ambiguity: contradictions of (non-) leadership in a knowledge-intensive organization, *Organization Studies*, **24**(6): 961–88.

Antonacopoulou, E. and Bento, R.F. (2004) Methods of 'learning leadership': taught and experiential, in J. Storey (ed.) *Leadership in Organizations*, London, Routledge.

Avolio, B.J. and Gardner, W.L. (2005) Authentic leadership development: getting to the root of positive forms of leadership, *Leadership Quarterly*, **16**(3): 315–38.

Barker, R.A. (2001) The nature of leadership, *Human Relations*, **54**(4): 469–94.

Bass, B. (1985) *Leadership and Performance Beyond Expectations*, Cambridge, MA, Harvard University Press.

Bass, B. (1990) *Bass and Stodgill's Handbook of Leadership*, New York, Free Press.

Bass, B. and Avolio, B. (1993) Transformational leadership: a response to critics, in M. Chemers and R. Ayman (eds) *Leadership Theory and Research: Perspectives and Directions*, San Diego, Academic Press.

Bennett, N., Wise, C. and Harvey, J. (2003) *Distributed Leadership,* Nottingham, National College for School Leadership.

Bennis, W. (1989) *On Becoming a Leader,* New York, Wiley.

Bennis, W. and Nanus, R. (1985) *Leaders: Their Strategies for Taking Charge*, New York, Harper and Row.

Billing, Y.D. and Alvesson, M. (2000) Questioning the notion of feminine leadership: a critical perspective on the gender labelling of leadership, *Gender, Work and Organization*, **7**(3): 144–57.

Blake, R. and Mouton, J. (1985) *The New Managerial Grid*, 3rd edn, Houston, TX, Gulf.

Bolden, R. (2005) *What is Leadership Development?*, Exeter, Leadership South West.

Bono, J.E. and Judge, T.A. (2004) Personality and transformational and transactional leadership: a meta-analysis, *Journal of Applied Psychology*, **89**: 901–10.

Boydell, T., Burgoyne, J. and Pedler, M. (2004) Suggested development, *People Management,* **10**(4): 32–4.

Burgoyne, J., Hirsh, W. and Williams, S. (2004) *The Development of Management and Leadership Capability and its Contribution to Performance: The Evidence, the Prospects and the Research Need*, Report 560, London, DES.

Burke, M.J. and Day, R.R. (1986) A cumulative study of the effectiveness of managerial training, *Journal of Applied Psychology,* **71**(2): 232–45.

Burns, J.M. (1978) *Leadership,* New York, Harper Row.

Cabinet Office (2000) *Strengthening Leadership in the Public Sector: A Research Study by the PIU,* London, PIU.

Carter, A. (2001) *Executive Coaching: Inspiring Performance at Work*, Brighton, Institute of Employment Studies.

Cartwright, S. and Pappas, C. (2008) Emotional intelligence, its measurement and implications for the workplace, *International Journal of Management Reviews,* **10**(2): 149–72.

Cattell, R.B. and Stice, G.F. (1954) Four formulae for selecting leaders on the basis of personality, *Human Relations,* **7**(4): 493–507.

CEML (Council for Excellence in Management and Leadership) (2002) *Managers and Leaders: Raising our Game,* London, CEML.

Clarke, N. (2008) Respect in leadership: the increasing need for empathy in managers, paper presented to the 9th International Conference on Human Resource Development Research and Practice across Europe, IESEG, Lille, May.

Collins, D.B. and Holton, E.F. (2004) The effectiveness of managerial leadership development programs: a meta-analysis of studies from 1982–2001, *Human Resources Development Quarterly,* **15**(2): 217–48.

Conger J.A. (1989) *The Charismatic Leader: Behind the Mystique of Exceptional Leadership*, San Francisco, Jossey-Bass.

Conger, J.A. (2004) Developing leadership capability: what's inside the black box?, *Academy of Management Executive,* **18**(3): 136–9.

Crevani, L., Lindgren, M. and Packendorff, J. (2007) Shared leadership: a postheroic perspective on leadership as a collective construction, *International al Journal of Leadership Studies,* **3**(1): 40–67.

Dadehbeigi, M., Shirmohammadi, M. and Ershadi, S. (2008a) Emotional intelligence and leadership: a literature review, paper presented to the 9th International Conference on Human Resource Development Research and Practice across Europe, IESEG, Lille, May.

Dadehbeigi, M., Shirmohammadi, M. and Ershadi, S. (2008b) Developing managers' and employees' emotional intelligence: an experimental study in a public bank, paper presented to the 9th International Conference on Human Resource Development Research and Practice across Europe, IESEG, Lille, May.

Day, D. (2000) Leadership development: a review in context, *Leadership Quarterly*, **11**(4): 581–611.

Dixon, N. (1993) Developing managers for the learning organization, *Human Resource Management Review,* **3**: 243–54.

DTI/DfES (Department of Trade and Industry/ Department for Education and Skills) (2001) *Opportunity for all in a World of Change*, White Paper, Cm 5052, London, HMSO.

Duckett, H. (2008) Academics on leadership, paper presented to the 9th International Conference on Human Resource Development Research and Practice across Europe, IESEG, Lille, May.

Fiedler, F. (1967) *A Theory of Leadership Effectiveness*, New York, McGraw-Hill.

Fiedler, F. (1996) Research on leadership selection and training: one view of the future, *Administrative Science Quarterly*, **41**: 241–50.

Fletcher, J.K. (2004) The paradox of post-heroic leadership: an essay on gender, power and transformational change, *Leadership Quarterly*, **15**(5): 647–61.

Fulmer, R.M. and Wagner, S. (1999) Leadership: lessons from the best, *Training and Development*, **53**(3): 28–32.

Gemmil, G. and Oakley, J. (1997) Leadership: an alienating social myth?, in K. Grint (ed.) *Leadership*, Oxford, Oxford University Press.

Gibb, C.A. (1954) *Handbook of Social Psychology*, Cambridge, MA, Addison-Wesley.

Goleman, D. (1996) *Emotional Intelligence*, London, Bloomsbury.

Graen, G.B. and Uhl-Bien, M. (1995) Relationship-based approach to leadership: development of leader-member exchange (LMX) theory of leadership over 25 years: applying a multi-level multi domain perspective, *Leadership Quarterly,* **6**: 219–47.

Granovetter, M. (1973) The strength of weak ties, *American Journal of Sociology*, **78**: 1360–80.

Gray, D.E. (2006) Executive coaching: towards a dynamic alliance of psychotherapy and transformative learning processes, *Management Learning,* **37**(4): 475–97.

Greenleaf, R.K. (1977) *Servant Leadership: A Journey into the Nature of Legitimate Power and Greatness*, New York, Paulist Press.

Grint, K. (2005) *Leadership: Limits and Possibilities*, Basingstoke, Palgrave Macmillan.

Gronn, P. (2000) Distributed properties: a new architecture for leadership, *Educational Management and Administration*, **28**(3): 317–38.

Hatch, M.J., Kostera, M., and Kozminski, A.K. (2006) The three faces of leadership: manager, artist, priest, *Organizational Dynamics*, **35**(1): 49–68.

Harris, A. (2008) Distributed leadership: according to the evidence, *Journal of Educational Administration,* **46**(2): 172–88.

Hersey, P. and Blanchard, K. (1982) *Management of Organisational Behavior: Utilizing Human Resources*, Upper Saddle River, NJ, Prentice Hall.

Hickey, G., Iles, P.A. and Macaulay, M. (2007) Mapping the ethics network in English local government, *Vieesoji Politika IR Administravimas,* **19**: 7–15.

Hirst, G., Mann, L., Bain, P. et al. (2004) Learning to lead: the development and testing of a model of leadership learning, *Leadership Quarterly,* **15**: 311–27.

Hofstede, G. (1991) *Cultures and Organizations*, New York, McGraw-Hill.

Horne, M. and Stedman-Jones, D. (2001) *Leadership: The Challenge for All?*, London, Institute of Management/DTI/DEMOS.

House, R. and Aditya, R. (1997) The social scientific study of leadership: quo vadis?, *Journal of Management*, **23**(3): 409–73.

House, R.J. and Mitchell, T.R. (1974) Path-goal theory of leadership, *Contemporary Business*, **3**: 81–98.

IDS (Income Data Services) (2003) *Leadership Development*, July, no. 753.

Iles, P.A. and Macaulay, M. (2007) Putting principles into practice: developing ethical leadership in local government, *International Journal of Leadership in Public Services,* **3**(3): 15–28.

Iles, P.A. and Preece, D. (2006) Developing leaders or developing leadership? The Academy of Chief Executives' programmes in the north-east of England, *Leadership* **2**(3): 317–40.

Iles, P.A. and Yolles, M. (2004) Knowledge migration and the transfer of knowledge in managing change in the national radio of Bulgaria, British Academy of Management Annual Conference, St Andrews, Scotland.

Ilies, R., Nahrgang, J.D. and Morgeson, J.P. (2007) Leader-member exchanges and citizenship behaviour: a meta-analysis, *Journal of Applied Psychology,* **92**: 269–77.

Iszatt-White, M., Kelly, S. and Rouncefield, M. (2005) *Leadership and Emotional Labour: Research Summary*, Lancaster, Centre for Excellence in Leadership.

James, K. (2000) *Leadership and Management Excellence: Corporate Development Strategies*, London, CEML.

Johnson, S.K. (2008) I second that emotion: effects of emotional contagion and affect on leader and follower outcomes, *Leadership Quarterly*, **19**: 1–19.

Khatri, N., Harvey, A. and Tirimizi, S. (2001) An alternative model of transformational leadership, paper presented to British Academy of Management Annual Conference.

Kotter, J. (1990) *How Leadership Differs from Management*, New York, Free Press.

Leithwood, K., Day, C., Sammons, P. et al. (2007) *Leadership and Student Learning Outcomes: Interim Report*, London, DCSF.

Mabey, C. and Gooderham, P. (2005) The impact of management development on the organizational performance of European firms, *European Management Review*, **2**(2): 131–42.

Mangham, I. (2004) Leadership and integrity, in J. Storey (ed.) *Leadership in Organizations: Current Issues and Key Trends*, London, Routledge.

Manocha, R. (2004) Spot the difference, *People Management*, February: 36–8.

Meindl, J.R. (1995) The romance of leadership as a follower-centric theory, *Leadership Quarterly*, **6**(3): 329–41.

Micic, P. and Gold, J. (2008) Future management: towards a model of futures learning for managers, paper presented to the 9th International Conference on Human Resource Development Research and Practice across Europe, IESEG, Lille, May.

Mintzberg, H. (1973) *The Nature of Managerial Work,* New York, Harper Row.

Mintzberg, H. (1999) Managing quietly, *Leader to Leader*, **12**: 24–30.

Mumford, A. (1987) Using reality in management development, *Management Education and Development*, **18**(3): 223–43.

Nahapiet, J. and Ghoshal, S. (1998) Social capital, intellectual capital and the organizational advantage, *Academy of Management Review*, **23**: 242–66.

Northouse, P.G. (1997) *Leadership: Theory and Practice*, London, Sage.

Nyhan, R.C. (2000) Changing the paradigm: trust and its role in public sector organizations, *American Review of Public Administration*, **30**(1): 87–109.

PIU (Performance and Innovation Unit) (2000) *Strengthening Leadership in the Public Sector,* London, PIU, Cabinet Office.

Preece, D. and Iles, P.A. (2009) Leadership development: assuaging uncertainties through joining a leadership academy, *Personnel Review*, **38**(3): 286–306.

Ray, T., Clegg, S. and Gordon, R. (2004) A new look at dispersed leadership: power, knowledge and context, in J. Storey (ed.) *Leadership in Organizations: Current Issues and Key Trends*, London, Routledge.

Robbins, S.P. (2005) *Organizational Behavior*, 11th edn, Upper Saddle River, NJ, Prentice Hall.

Rodgers, H., Frearson, M., Gold, J. and Holden, R. (2003) *International Comparator Contexts: The Leading Learning Project*, London, Learning and Skill Research Centre.

Ross, L., Rix, M. and Gold, J. (2005) Learning distributed leadership, part 1, *Industrial and Commercial Training*, **37**(3): 130–7.

Russon, C. and Reinelt, C. (2004) The results of an evaluation scan of 55 leadership development programs, *Journal of Leadership and Organizational Studies*, **10**(3): 104–7.

Salaman, G. (2004) Competences of managers, competences of leaders, in J. Storey (ed.) *Leadership in Organizations: Current Issues and Key Trends*, London, Routledge.

Salovey, P. and Mayer, J. (1990) Emotional intelligence, *Imagination, Cognition and Personality*, **9**: 185–211.

Sendjaya, S., Sarros, J. and Santora, J.C. (2008) Defining and measuring servant leadership behaviours in organizations, *Journal of Management Studies*, **45**(2): 402–24.

Sjöstrand, S. and Tyrstrup, M. (2001) Recognised and unrecognised managerial leadership, in S. Sjöstrand, J. Sandberg and M. Tyrstrup (eds) *Invisible Management: The Social Construction of Leadership,* London, Thomson.

Smircich, L. and Morgan, G. (1982) Leadership: the management of meaning, *Journal of Applied Behavioral Science*, **18**(3): 257–73.

Snyder, M. (1979) Self-monitoring processes, in L. Berkowitz (ed.) *Advances in Experimental Social Psychology,* vol. 12, New York, Academic Press.

Snyder, M. (1987) *Public Appearances/Private Realities: The Psychology of Self-monitoring*, San Francisco, Freeman.

Spillane, J. (2006) *Distributed Leadership*, San Francisco, Jossey-Bass.

Stewart, J.A. and Birchall, D. (2008) Leadership development for third sector leaders in the health and social care sector, paper presented to British Academy of Management Conference, Harrogate, September.

Storey, J. (ed.) (2004) *Leadership in Organizations: Current Issues and Key Trends*, London, Routledge.

Storr, L. and Trenchard, S. (2008) Clinical leadership: from swampy lowlands to giddy heights – leadership in action, paper presented to the 9th International Conference on Human Resource Development Research and Practice across Europe, IESEG, Lille, May.

Suutari, V. and Viitala, R. (2008) Management development of senior executives: methods and their effectiveness, *Personnel Review*, **37**(4): 375–92.

Thomson, A., Mabey, C., Storey, J. et al. (2000) *Changing Patterns of Management Development*, Oxford, Blackwell.

Uhl-Bien, M. (2006) Relational leadership theory: exploring the social processes of leadership and organizing, *The Leadership Quarterly*, **17**(6): 654–76.

Van der Weide, J. and Wilderom, C. (2001) Leadership behavior of highly effective middle managers, paper presented to British Academy of Management Annual Conference.

Vroom, V.H. and Yetton, P.W. (1973) *Leadership and Decision-making*, Pittsburgh, PA, University of Pittsburgh Press.

Watson, T.J. (2001) The emergent manager and processes of management pre-learning, *Management Learning,* **33**(2): 221–38.

Weber, M. (1978) *Economy and Society*, 2 vols, Los Angeles, University of California Press.

Weick, K.E. (1993) The collapse of sensemaking in organizations: The Mann Gulch disaster, *Administrative Sciences Quarterly*, **38**: 628–52.

Weick, K.E. (1996) *Sensemaking in Organizations*, Newbury Park, CA, Sage.

Wenger, E. (1998) *Communities of Practice*, Cambridge, Cambridge University Press.

Williams, S.D., Graham, T.S. and Baker, B. (2003) Evaluating outdoor experimental training for leadership and team building, *Journal of Management Development*, **22**(1): 45–59.

Woodall, J. and Winstanley, D. (1998) *Management Development: Strategy and Practice*, Oxford, Blackwell.

Yukl, G. (1999) An evaluation of conceptual weaknesses in transformational and charismatic leadership theories, *Leadership Quarterly*, **10**: 285–305.

Teams and Team Development

12

Paul Iles and Chitra Meetoo

Chapter learning outcomes

After studying this chapter, you should be able to:

- Appreciate the importance of teams and team working in HRD

- Understand the key differences between groups, teams, self-managing work teams and self-directed teams

- Assess the benefits to individuals, society, teams and the organization of introducing teamwork in organizations

- Assess the impact of diversity on team processes and team performance

- Analyse the nature of team building and team development and the methods used to facilitate it in HRD

- Assess the importance of intergroup team building in HRD

Chapter outline

Introduction

Teams have been in existence in organizations for many years. Here, we will first distinguish between groups and teams before exploring team working, seen here in terms of a team's arrangements, process, behaviour and organization. We will then look at team development: creating new teams (team building) or reviewing and improving the performance of existing ones (team development). We will discuss and evaluate methodologies such as the Team Climate Inventory, task-oriented team development/GRPI, Belbin's team roles, the Team Role Inventory, Bales' Interaction Process Analysis, team coaching and outdoor development, before assessing the importance of intergroup team building in HRD.

Teams and groups

Reflective questions

1 How would you define a 'group'?

2 How would you define a team, as distinct from a group?

Interestingly, while 'group' is a neutral term, 'team' is value laden, and is usually used positively – groups of workers are often called 'teams' and their bosses 'team leaders' for this reason (in contrast, words like gang, mob and ringleader are often used pejoratively).

For some, a key characteristic of a team is a 'common fate', for others, it is an explicit or implicit social structure (for example roles, status, norms). An important dimension is team leadership, an issue considered in more detail in Chapter 11. For some, face-to-face interaction is key (but what of virtual teams who never meet?). For most, a group, rather than a 'category', comes into being when two or more individuals perceive themselves to be members of the same social category, and when they define themselves as members. Group membership has social and psychological consequences, especially for social identity, affecting members' behaviour even when others are not present. Formal groups are established with relatively clear, official roles, rules and goals; informal groups emerge without prescribed goals and relationships.

Stewart (1999 p. 325) defines a team as: 'a group of people working in an interdependent manner to achieve a commonly understood goal', whereas Katzenbach and Smith (2004, p. 5), discussing 'real teams' rather than groups or so-called teams, introduce mutual accountability and shared commitment, defining a team as:

> a small number of people with complementary skills who are committed to a common purpose, performance goals, and approach for which they hold themselves mutually accountable.

Thus, teams are both different from, and more than, groups; they are now often seen as the key building blocks of organizational life. A group of people therefore becomes a team when team members know they have a common goal, commitment towards those objectives, and how these objectives/goals are to be met, with mutual accountability (Stewart, 1999). According to Levy (2004, p. 142), a team 'needs to have the power to control how it operates'.

However, cohesive, smoothly operating teams may have adverse consequences for other units, so attention should be paid to linking teams to their wider external and internal environments. For cohesive teams, Kanter (1982) points out the dangers of:

- *Suboptimization:* too high team spirit can generate insularity and parochialism

- *Turnover:* such teams may have issues in accepting new members

- *Rigidity:* it may be hard to change roles, norms, procedures and prior decisions

- *Territorialism:* such teams may feel others don't understand them, and, overrating their unique contribution and expertise, resent apparent intrusion into their work

- *Not invented here:* there may be reluctance to share and accept influence from others

- *Life cycle:* such teams may wish to continue beyond their period of maximum effectiveness.

An example of 'good teams going wrong' is provided by the largely autonomous 'dream team' at the Nut Island sewage works in the 1990s. It was performing difficult, dangerous work without complaint, putting in unpaid overtime, handling its own staffing and training decisions, and acting with great esprit de corps and commitment to the mission; yet it contributed to the catastrophic failure of the mission (Levy, 2001). A cohesive, committed team and distracted, disengaged senior mangers passed through a negative feedback spiral: an isolated 'self-managing' team with a strong identity, ignored by distracted senior managers when asking for help or giving warnings of trouble ahead, feels betrayed and resentful, and an 'us against the world' mentality, suspicious of 'outsiders', heightens its sense of heroism. It disguises its problems, management fails to expose the team, so it makes up its own rules, masking deficiencies. Finally, management and the team ignore each other until external events break the stalemate. Appropriate performance measures linked to internal operations and corporate goals, which are in turn linked to senior management visibility and recognition and rotation of personnel are steps that might avoid such a fate.

Some projects might continue long after they should have been closed down, in part because of enthusiastic 'champions' and highly cohesive project teams ignoring or marginalizing dissidents, practising self-censorship and 'keeping the faith' by 'believing in the project'. Without putting 'sceptics' on the team, a well-defined review process and an 'exit champion' ready to decommission a project, such ill-run projects might cause heavy losses before being finally abandoned (Janis, 1982; Royer, 2004).

Team working

Team working can be a means of shifting power and authority from higher levels to employees. Ingram et al. (1997, p. 118) point out that 'the most effective linkages between business activities are forged by people and the way in which they work together in groups'. In order to enable successful implementation of teams, organizations need to heavily invest in team building and team development, which makes HRD central to effective team performance.

The growth of team-based work

Frederic Taylor initiated the early analysis of how people worked together in a group in the early 1900s (Linstead et al., 2004). 'Scientific management' was focused on production/manufacturing: 'the way to create the most efficient division of labour could best be determined using scientific management techniques rather than intuitive or informal rule-of-thumb knowledge' (George and Jones, 2005, p. 33).

Taylorism tended to focus more on the power of managers, rather than the needs and wants of employees. For Cooper (2005, p. 7):

> the limitations of scientific management in knowledge-based and service-based economies is recognised, but the legacy of 'management by tasks' remains deeply embedded in organizations.

Later, 'socially-based manufacturing methods including lean production, cellular manufacturing, just-in-time component supply and team working' (Winfield and Kerrin, 1996, p. 49) were developed, as well as further investigation into how best to build and develop teams.

Teamwork in organizations

The increasing need for flatter organizational structures in knowledge-based economies has given rise to more responsibility, authority, autonomy and flexibility being expected from individuals. The idea of delegating responsibility to groups has often been promoted within HRM (for example innovative work practices or high performance work systems), as well as in lean manufacturing and business process re-engineering. Task design and supervisory behaviours have been invoked to explain the enhanced performance held to result from teamwork, resulting in higher effort, engagement, commitment and motivation through participation and discretion.

Teamwork usually involves delegation of responsibilities and decentralization of decision making. This may impact on attitudinal outcomes like job satisfaction, involvement, commitment and trust, which may then affect behavioural outcomes such as turnover and absenteeism, and extra-role behaviours such as organizational citizenship. These may then impact on operational outcomes such as productivity, quality, innovation and flexibility (see Figure 12.1). These impacts may also be enhanced by structural changes brought about by teamwork, such as less complexity, reduction of throughput time and reduction of losses. Operational outcomes may then lead to enhanced financial outcomes such as added value, profitability and costs in a 'performance chain' (Delarue et al., 2008).

Survey-based research on the links between teamwork and organizational performance (often measured operationally, such as productivity, quality, customer satisfaction; or financially, such as value-added or return on capital employed; or attitudinally/behaviourally, such as job satisfaction or absenteeism) is largely supportive. Teamwork can further enhance performance if combined with structural changes such as decentralization and delayering (Delarue et al., 2008). Team working is often introduced alongside other HRM changes, such as training or reward changes, for example profit sharing, or team-based reward systems.

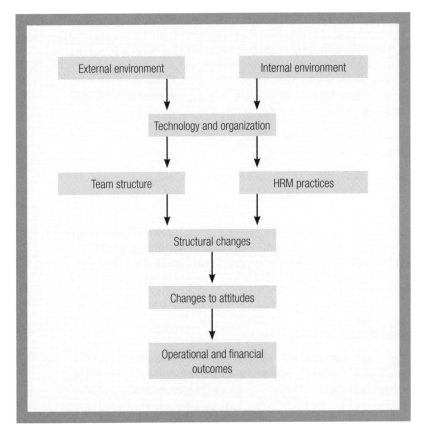

FIGURE 12.1 Teamwork and organizational performance

SOURCE: Adapted from Delarue et al. (2008, p. 144)

Different types of team working

Many different types of teams are used within organizations, such as top teams, cross-functional teams, problem-solving teams, project teams, virtual teams, self-managed work teams, task force teams, quality circle teams, sales teams and self-directed teams.

Cross-functional teams have become more popular alongside matrix organizations; individuals from different functions come together for a particular project or task. Organizational performance can be improved through adoption of a successful cross-functional team (for example Proehl, 1996; Dufrene et al., 1999). Dyer (1995, p. 5) argues that high performance arises when teams work on a specific problem and gain 'maximum creativity in as short a time as possible' before adjourning; they can also be problem-solving teams, individuals coming together to solve identified problems, dissolving when the problem is solved (Torrington et al., 2005; Robbins, 2005). Van Mierlo et al. (2006, p. 295) argue that having the appropriate level of social support in a team environment 'appears to be most effective in encouraging team members to assume individual responsibility'.

Another rising team is the virtual team: geographically dispersed members may have little or no face-to-face contact, instead keeping in touch through modern communications technologies, for example emails and videoconferencing (Kreitner et al., 2002), working across space, time and organizational boundaries. Virtual teams can also show elements of cross-functional teams/problem-solving teams, bringing together people from different specialist or geographical areas to resolve a problem.

Others make different distinctions. Katzenbach and Smith (2004) distinguish between task forces/project teams, that is, teams that recommend things, working groups that make or do things, and supervising teams that oversee things. Hackman (1987) identifies four different kinds of teams:

- Manager led

- Self-managing

- Self-designing

- Self-governing.

Self-managed work teams (SMWTs) and self-directed teams (SDTs) have been around for the last half-century, since the sociotechnical systems (STS) movement (Trist and Bamforth, 1951; Emery and Trist, 1960), which argued that social and technical systems needed to be optimized together, as inattention to one component could produce problematic results. The semi-autonomous team evolved from STS, addressing employees' social needs (Maslow, 1954) alongside technical knowledge to bring the best out of employees, while giving them freedom to choose the best way to get high performance. The late 1980s saw the notion of SMWTs gaining popularity as a means of designing high performance/high commitment teams.

These semi-autonomous groups enjoyed higher levels of trust, autonomy and flexibility; management shifted responsibility for team success onto team members (Levy, 2001). For van Mierlo et al. (2006, p. 282):

> autonomy refers to control over (aspects of) task performance and is typically considered something positive, bringing health and satisfaction to the employee who disposes of it, and efficient work processes, profit, and satisfied clients to the employer who grants it.

Different authors give different definitions. Glassop (2002, p. 227) defines a self-managing work group as 'a group of interdependent individuals that have accepted responsibility for a group task and share this responsibility by monitoring and controlling the contributions of its members'. Similarly, Spreitzer et al. (1999, p. 340) define SMWTs as 'groups of interdependent individuals that can self-regulate their behaviour on relatively whole tasks', while Cappelli and Neumark (2001, p. 748) argue that such teams 'give their members authority over decisions that in other contexts are made by supervisors, such as how to perform their tasks or, in more advanced situations, which tasks to perform'.

Delarue et al. (2008) suggest some dimensions on which team design may differ:

- degree of self-management

- nature of team membership

- team structure and size, breadth of job definition, degree of autonomy

- team composition

- type of tasks performed

- technology and equipment in use.

Consequently, different types of teamwork may be associated with different organizational outcomes. We can see teams as lying on an autonomy–interdependence dimension, from a self-directed team to a group of workers, as shown in Figure 12.2. The four quadrants are:

- *quadrant A:* some types, for example professional service teams, could be situated here, with high levels of autonomy but low interdependence between team members

- *quadrant B:* here a group would show both low interdependence and low autonomy.

- *quadrant C:* SMWTs usually experience high interdependence, but may still have low autonomy, due to decision-making powers resting with managers or leaders

- *quadrant D:* SDTs may lie here, showing both high autonomy and high interdependence.

Thus, many organizations may use team development methodologies to prepare teams to move to quadrant D.

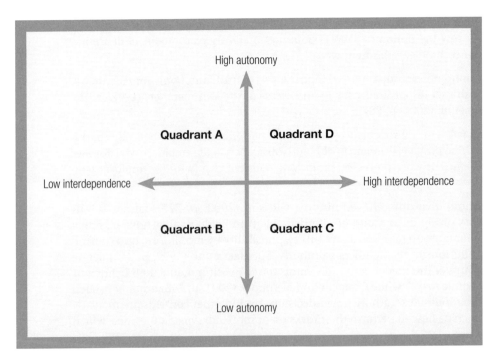

FIGURE 12.2 Autonomy–interdependence matrix for teams

SOURCE: Adapted from Delarue et al. (2008)

Although autonomy and flexibility often seem essential in team working, a study of team working in the UK Inland Revenue identified target-based team working, where these played little part (Procter and Currie, 2004), and interdependence, especially outcome interdependence, was driven by work targets.

Team building and team development

The terms 'team building' and 'team development' are often used synonymously in HRD, but sometimes distinctions are made between putting a new team together (team building) and working with an existing team (team development). Interest rose out of the early OD work of Lewin, in particular on training groups (T groups) at the National Training Laboratories in the USA after 1945. Changing attitudes and behaviour, such as racial prejudice, was more effective through a team's direct experience of the issues in a group setting or T group rather than lectures or other input (Burke, 2003).

T groups and team building

T groups typically consist of groups of people undergoing training and development as 'strangers' who had never worked together before; an unstructured agenda, with emphasis on direct experience of the 'here and now', and a focus on personal change, growth and development were key features. Classical T groups had no formal leader or instructor, instead a facilitator intervened at appropriate moments to ask questions and give feedback. Flip charts were used to record the group experience for later feedback and analysis.

However, two main issues emerged around the use of T groups:

- *Psychological damage:* Some participants seemed psychologically damaged by the feedback received on behaviour and attitudes, but as the session ended after one or two days, little in the way of counselling was provided.

- *Transfer of training:* Participants may have learned something powerful about themselves or others in the T group, but this learning was difficult to transfer to the workplace (not just an issue with T groups).

T groups also helped to lead to other initiatives, such as action learning (see Chapter 11) and team development interventions, which differs somewhat from classic T groups, in that:

- The participants are usually members of intact, pre-existing work teams, not strangers.

- The focus is as much on the past and future plans as the present.

- The activities are more structured, usually short activities such as group consensus/ranking exercises, tower building and other practical activities, and outdoor development exercises like treasure hunts, raft building and abseiling. Feedback and debriefing on issues such as learning, team working, listening, communicating, decision making, trusting, facilitating, leadership, supporting and managing conflict may then follow.

- The facilitator is typically more directive and interventionist, providing input, feedback, discussion and assessment as well as facilitation.

- The focus is on teamwork, group issues, team learning and development, rather than solely on personal growth.

- Flip charts continue to be used, but also more modern technology: camcorders, computers and projectors capture what happens, which is used later for analysis of performance and to encourage reflection on learning and what the team could do differently next time.

Team building has continued to be popular, in part because issues raised can be worked on 'back in the office' (and any 'damage' is more likely to be addressed, given the continuous nature of many team-building initiatives).

Assessing team development needs

Just as individual training needs assessment is often recommended before training and development interventions are implemented, the HRD needs of teams are often assessed through training needs analysis: questionnaires, focus groups, observation and interviews identify issues such as skill levels, skill mix, team interaction and task achievement. The Team Climate Inventory (TCI) (Anderson and West, 1994) seeks to assess the shared perceptions of policies, practices and procedures in teams, including:

- *Communication:* how members interact, and the structure and style of team meetings

- *Participation:* in decision making and other activities

- *Safety:* how safe people feel, and how much interpersonal trust there is

- *Cohesiveness:* how cohesive the team perceives itself to be, and is perceived by others

- *Task style:* how the team approaches tasks and pursues objectives

- *Vision:* the team's vision or mission, and objectives and targets

- *Innovativeness:* how creative the team is.

The TCI can be used to assess team dynamics and climate.

Team development interventions

Reacting to the frequent emphasis in much team building on improving interpersonal relationships, Beckhard (1972, p. 24) listed four purposes for team building, pointing out that

> unless one purpose is defined as the primary purpose ... people then operate from their own hierarchy of purposes and, predictably, these are not always the same for all members.

The purposes of team building are to:

- *set goals or priorities* – we might now also add mission, vision or purpose

- *analyse or allocate the way work is performed* – according to team members' roles and responsibilities

- *examine the way the team is working* – its processes, such as norms, decision making, or communications

- *examine interpersonal relationships* among members.

In their work on healthcare systems, Rubin et al. (1978) introduced the concept of 'task-oriented team development' (the GRPI model) – any team-building intervention needs to address issues of goals, roles, procedures and interpersonal relationships, in that order. Many team problems, seen as relationship problems or a 'lack of chemistry', are often addressed through interpersonal training involving attention to communication issues, for example 'the issue is a lack of communication'. In practice, these are often caused by goal or role problems – either members disagree over goals, think they are pursuing the same goals when they have not been discussed, or they have changed without everyone being aware of the changes; or there is lack of role or procedural clarity. Interpersonal relationship issues may then be a symptom of the failure to agree goals, or clarify roles and procedures, not the cause of the team problems. Team builders need to address goal (or mission, vision or purpose) issues first, role issues second, procedural issues third, and only then interpersonal issues.

Goal issues

As Katzenbach and Smith (2004, p. 7) point out:

> The best teams invest a tremendous amount of time and effort exploring, shaping and agreeing on a purpose that belongs to them both collectively and individually. This 'purposing' activity continues throughout the life of the team.

Poor teams fail to coalesce around a common mission, purpose or aspiration, translated into specific (for example SMART) performance goals (here, we see the A as 'agreed', as well as the more common 'achievable'). Indeed, 'when purposes and goals build on one another and are combined with team commitment, they become a powerful engine of performance' (p. 7). Specific goals help to define distinctive work products, facilitate clear communication, maintain focus, build team identity, achieve small wins, and motivate and energize the team to pursue attainable but challenging goals.

Teams may come together for various purposes:

- to develop a new product
- to develop an improved service
- to organize an event such as a conference, launch or farewell party
- to raise money for charity.

The goal or purpose provides a reference point and helps in decisions about what information is necessary, as well as providing a basis on which to measure performance and progress.

Reflective questions

Think of a 'team' you have worked in, whether in full or part-time work, at college or university, or in a community/voluntary context.

1 How clear were you about what was required of you, or the team as a whole?

2 What did the team sponsor or leader want you to do, for what reason, and by when?

3 What was the 'big picture'? Where did the team's work fit in to what was happening elsewhere, inside or outside the organization?

4 Were objectives SMART – specific, measurable, agreed/achievable, realistic, timed?

5 Was success judged in concrete, recognizable terms? What did success look like?

6 What resources were available to the team? Were they realistic?

7 Were there any things the team was not able to do, or was not told?

Source: Adapted from Fleming (2004, p. 26)

Role issues

Teams are often brought together because members are thought to possess distinctive, necessary and complementary skills, not possessed by any one individual. Requirements include technical or functional expertise, problem-solving and decision-making skills, and interpersonal skills. Teams are also often powerful vehicles for developing skills.

Team members can approach team tasks and roles with different levels of energy and attitude, or commitment, towards the role and/or task. One way of looking at this is to develop an 'energy investment model', with attitude/commitment on one axis and 'energy' on the other, as in Figure 12.3. It is then possible to map, across time, the contributions of team members. Teams do not want contributors who are 'walking dead' – low energy levels combined with negative attitudes. But do all teams want everyone to be 'players' – members with high energy and high, positive attitudes? 'Spectators' – positive in attitude but low in energy – may be shy, undervalued, or feel any contributions will be marginalized, put down or ignored. They may be thinkers rather than doers (reflectors or theorists rather than activists, in the language of Chapter 5). Teams may want to give them the option to play more, as long as the team values their efforts.

'Cynics' – high in energy but with apparently negative attitudes – may also have valid perspectives: they may be unsure about the direction in which the team is heading, feel it is 'throwing the baby out with the bath water' or themselves to be defenders of the 'true identity' of the team, or think things have not been fully thought through. Cynics may turn into the 'walking dead', spreading apathy or suspicion, but may also be converted, if listened to or included, into 'players', using their energy for positive ends – not putting a brake on anything ('seen it all before', 'it can't work here') but ensuring that actions taken are well considered, with objections raised in constructive rather than overly critical ways.

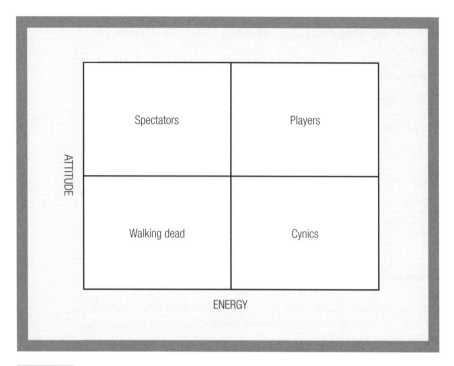

FIGURE 12.3 Roles team members play in change processes

SOURCE: Adapted from Miller (2008, p. 10)

The roles played by team members should be clear, overlapping, but not conflicting, and teams should employ a mix of roles and skills sufficient for the tasks before them. Stewart (1999, p. 28) supports this by acknowledging that:

> whatever the form of team-working being introduced, the team members need to be clear about what the team is set up to achieve and understand their role within the team.

Role conflict or role ambiguity might be explored through role analysis – role requirements are defined and analysed through 'focal' role occupiers initiating an analysis of the role, its rationale, and its associated duties. Tasks and behaviours can be added or subtracted until the incumbent and the team as a whole are satisfied with the role description, allowing role profiles to be developed, and other roles to be analysed and clarified in turn (Dayal and Thomas, 1968).

Role negotiation may then be used to enable each role holder to change some of their duties, responsibilities or behaviours in return for changes in the others' behaviours, duties or responsibilities. Such changes can be written up in the form of a contract, with further meetings to determine if such contracts have been honoured and to evaluate their effectiveness (Harrison, 1972; Iles and Auluck, 1993).

Activity

Form groups of three. Each person answers the following questions. Share your findings with the other two.

- What skills do you think you have developed, at work, college/university, or in the wider community?

- What are your achievements?

- What have you learned from working in teams?

- How do you prefer to operate in a team?

- What do you value in the way other team members operate?

- What do you think you can contribute to a team?

- What are your interests? What do you see as a worthwhile challenge?

- What concerns do you have about working in a team?

Source: Adapted from Fleming (2004, p. 30)

Questions like these stimulated more formal work into what made for a high-performing team, leading Belbin (1981, 1993) to the identification of team roles contributing to high performance, to which we now turn.

Belbin's model of team roles

In the early 1980s, Belbin developed a profile, the Team Role Inventory, to assess the individual strengths and weaknesses of team members; high team performance seemed to be associated with teams balanced in terms of the roles undertaken by each team member (Senior, 1997). Belbin's (1981, 1993) work has been widely used in the past two decades in elucidating the strengths and weaknesses of individual team members and their contribution to team dynamics and performance.

Theoretically, Belbin's work can be traced to bureaucratic (the need for specialization to match job competencies) and human relations theories (good interpersonal relationships are important to organizational functioning). The distinction between task-oriented and relationship-oriented or social-emotional/maintenance-oriented roles in groups has also been influential (Bales, 1950). Belbin (1981, 1993) argues that if team members all have similar weaknesses, the team as a whole may tend to have a similar weakness. In contrast, if team members have similar strengths, they may compete for tasks and responsibilities. A team role (not to be confused with a functional role) is defined by personality, ability, current values and motivation, field constraints, work experience and role learning.

More specifically, Belbin tries to:

- Define an individual's current preferences (a moment in time or a snapshot of the person here and now)

- Identify their typical team behaviour against the Team Role Inventory

- Assess their suitability to a team role, chosen from one of nine (originally eight) types: plant, resource investigator, coordinator, shaper, monitor evaluator, team worker, implementer, completer finisher and a specialist.

Assessments are not strictly psychometric personality tests, because they measure preferred behaviour, not personality factors or dispositions. Up until 2001, analysis was based on findings from the Team Role Inventory, a simple questionnaire completed by the individual, a Self Perception Inventory (SPI), and then by the peer group for the purpose of assessing preferred behaviours and characteristics that are either beneficial or detrimental to a team. Seven sections, comprising ten descriptive statements, each section having ten points allocated by the respondent between the ten sentences, assess:

1   Potential contribution to the team

2   Shortcomings relating to teamwork

3   Personal influence towards group tasks

4   Relationships with other team members

5   Personal job satisfaction in teamwork

6   Leadership style within stressful constraints

7   Personal problems experienced when working in groups.

This SPI typically consists of about 80 questions, determining the profile that an individual may show when taking a role.

Nine clusters of behaviour are assessed, called team roles (see Table 12.1).

TABLE 12.1 Belbin's team roles

Role abbreviation	Team role type	Description	Team contribution	Allowable weaknesses
PL	Plant	Creative, imaginative, unorthodox	Solves difficult problems	Ignores incidentals. Too preoccupied to communicate effectively
RI	Resource investigator	Extrovert, enthusiastic, communicative	Explores opportunities	Overoptimistic. Loses interest once initial enthusiasm has passed
CO	Coordinator	Mature, confidant, a good chairperson	Clarifies goals, promotes decision making, delegates well	Can be seen as manipulative. Offloads personal work
SH	Shaper	Challenging, dynamic, thrives on pressure	Possesses the drive and courage to overcome obstacles	Prone to prevarication. Offends people's feelings
ME	Monitor evaluator	Sober, strategic and discerning. Sees all options	Judges accurately	Lacks drive and ability to inspire others

Role abbreviation	Team role type	Description	Team contribution	Allowable weaknesses
TW	Team worker	Cooperative, mild, perceptive and diplomatic	Listens, builds, averts friction	Indecisive in crunch situations
IMP	Implementer	Disciplined, reliable, conservative and efficient	Turns ideas into practical actions	Somewhat inflexible. Slow to respond to new possibilities
CF	Completer finisher	Painstaking, conscientious, anxious. Searches out errors and omissions	Delivers on time	Inclined to worry unduly. Reluctant to delegate
SP	Specialist	Single-minded, self-starting, dedicated	Provides knowledge and skills in rare supply	Contributes on a narrow front. Dwells on technicalities

SOURCE: www.belbin.com

Certain types of combination could potentially result in tensions and conflicts – pairing a shaper (SH) with a monitor evaluator (ME), a resource investigator (RI) with a specialist (SP), or a plant (PL) with an implementer (IM) without facilitator intervention may well result in conflict.

The profiling questionnaire has now been replaced by the Belbin e-interplace software package to more reliably:

- improve self-awareness and personal effectiveness
- foster mutual trust and understanding between work colleagues
- match people to jobs for the purpose of selection and career planning
- enhance team building and team development.

Observer assessment has been added to the e-interplace system to provide feedback on how others see the person undertaking the self-assessment and provide a more robust profile than assessment based purely on self-report.

Belbin uses the nine team roles to create four work roles, defined as a mix of tasks and responsibilities undertaken by individuals or within a team. A colour classification system to clearly differentiate between the four categories of work is used to avoid ambiguities and misunderstandings and enable managers to assign a type of work to a subordinate most suited to that particular category of work role. It is a simple way of allocating resources to tasks that can be delegated to a team member.

It is now usually recognized as dysfunctional that membership of any given team should remain static. Further perspectives within the team need to be widened, and facilitating career moves within the organization offers one means of achieving this aim, while also offering the advantage of growing a 'bigger person'. Another way is to arrange periodic swaps of members within existing teams in order to deepen understanding of the broader field.

One issue is that of the stages of a team's development, discussed later, linked to the need for different team roles at different stages:

- identifying needs
- finding ideas (needs plants, shapers and coordinators)
- formulating plans
- making ideas
- establishing organization
- following through (needs completer finishers and implementers).

Emotional intelligence seems to be linked to the coordinator and resource investigator roles, but not to the shaper or completer roles (Davies and Kanaki, 2006; Aritzeta et al., 2007).

Just as there are 'horses for courses', there are 'teams for pitches'; Belbin distinguishes negotiators (resource investigators and team workers) from manager/workers (implementers and completer finishers), and intellectuals (monitor evaluators and plants) from team leaders (coordinators and shapers). High-performing teams need to have a balanced representation of all team roles.

However, doubts remain as to the psychometric properties of the Belbin inventory. Davies and Kanaki (2006) showed that personality dimensions associated with the SYMLOG Interpersonal Effectiveness Profile based on the Interaction Process Analysis (IPA) of groupwork developed by Bales (1950) were clearly and strongly related to team roles. The dominance (upward) dimension was associated with the roles of implementer, coordinator and resource investigator, while the accepting authority (forward) dimension was associated with the roles of monitor evaluator and completer finisher, and negatively associated with plant and shaper. The friendly (positive) dimension was positively associated with team worker and plant.

Aritzeta et al. (2007) have shown that the evidence for the construct validity of Belbin is mixed, but that the model and the inventory show adequate convergent validity. However, there were strong associations between some team roles, indicating weak discriminant validity among some scales. Much research to measure the relationship between Belbin's team roles and organizational performance has shown generally positive results (Senior, 1997; Blenkinsop and Maddison, 2007; van de Water, 2008).

HRD in Practice 12.1

Using Belbin's Team Role Inventory in a PR/advertising top team

One example of how Belbin's Team Role Inventory might be used in team building is given by a PR/advertising company (cited in Swart et al., 2005). The company used it to improve the performance of its senior management team, and to identify individual team styles and interactions. The data were combined with observations of problem-solving activities to analyse team role behaviours, team contributions and miscommunications and misunder-

standings between team members.   ance and identify not just individual
Members could identify how to change   training needs but also organizational
behaviour to improve team perform-   issues.

Procedural issues

Within teams, there will be many members with experiences of things going wrong and teams adopting faulty procedures, such as meetings that overrun their allotted time, or teams that postpone decisions.

Teams need to ensure that they are open to new ideas and constantly look at what they are doing, and how, in order to make improvements (Fleming, 2004), including asking:

- Why are we meeting?

- How often do we need to meet?

- Who will chair meetings?

- How do we solve problems and make decisions – by consensus, voting, the leader?

- How will decisions be communicated?

- How will success be judged?

- How will we monitor progress against goals and objectives?

- How are we functioning in terms of openness, cooperation, communication, conflict, use of talents, dealing with issues and problems, lessons learned?

One example of the importance of considering team procedures is given by the study of US cardiac surgery teams by Edmondson et al. (2004). Implementing new processes and adopting new technologies required a focus on the active management of learning by team leaders. The best team leaders were 'partners' – accessible, asking for input and admitting their errors. Effective teams were designed for real-time learning, leaders framed motivating learning challenges, and an environment of 'psychological safety' that fostered communication and innovation was developed (similar to the TCI of Anderson and West, 1994). The authors recommended that leaders should be chosen not just for technical expertise, but also for their ability to create learning environments. Knowledge sharing and learning are particularly evident in 'communities of practice' (Wenger and Snyder, 2004), informal self-organizing groups bound together by shared expertise and a passion to drive strategy, generate new business lines, promote best practice, develop skills and recruit and retain talent. Managers need to bring the appropriate people together, provide a facilitating infrastructure, such as time, sponsors, links with HRD and support teams, and measure value in innovative ways.

Meyer (2004) argues that traditional, results-oriented performance measurement systems fail to support multifunctional teams, and may indeed undermine them; the system should help the team, not top managers, monitor progress, and the team itself must play a lead role in designing its own measurement system, creating new, relatively few, process measures to track delivery, within the context of strategic goals and understandings.

Interpersonal issues

An influential way of looking at interpersonal processes in groups and teams is Bales' Interaction Process Analysis (IPA), a method for analysing the 'systems of human interaction' (Bales, 1950, p. 257) in, originally, small face-to-face groups. Bales' contribution to the analysis of small groups was in distinguishing team process, how the group went about its business, from team task or content, what the group's goals were, with a primary focus on process. The IPA consists of 12 complementary-paired group processes, further subdivided into four major functions, describing interaction/communications issues or problems (Table 12.2).

TABLE 12.2 System of process categories in the IPA, related psychosocial group functions, and common communications problems

General category A: positive (and mixed) actions	
1	Seems friendly
2	Dramatizes
3	Agrees
General category B: attempted answers	
4	Gives suggestions
5	Gives opinions
6	Gives information
General category C: questions	
7	Asks for information
8	Asks for opinions
9	Asks for suggestions
General category D: negative (and mixed) actions	
10	Disagrees
11	Shows tension
12	Seems unfriendly

Bales' (1950) IPA coding scheme identifies four general categories of communication/interaction behaviour, two associated with task behaviour and two with social-emotional behaviour:

- *positive social-emotional area:* positive actions (expressive – shows solidarity, shows tension release, agrees)

- *active task area:* attempted answers (instrumental – gives suggestions, give opinions, gives orientation)

- *passive task area:* questions (instrumental – asks for orientation, asks for opinions, asks for suggestions)

- *negative social-emotional area:* negative actions (expressive – disagrees, shows tension, shows antagonism).

How the team addresses issues of task and social-emotional process reveals important data about its interpersonal workings, structures, and priorities as a 'microscopic' social system. The model uses a 'unit of speech or process' (p. 259) as the unit for coding and analysis: sentences or utterances, noted either with the observer/coder present, or from audio recordings. IPA analysis generates three descriptions of team interaction processes:

1 positive or negative social-emotional reactions, and task focus on questions or answers

2 relative amounts of orientation, evaluation, control, decision, tension management, and integration behaviours

3 relative frequencies of the 12 category types, reflecting the communications strategies commonly employed by the team.

The mutually exclusive categories of the IPA have been criticized because single codes require that one judgement be made about what may be a subtle and complex statement. On the other hand, the method has also been recognized as innovative, because it identifies the presence and importance in group interaction of both task and relational functions as demonstrated by actual verbal behaviour.

One way IPA can be used in team building is in a 'fishbowl' activity. Here a group is split into two teams, one seated in an 'inner circle' and one acting as observers in an outer circle. While the inner team performs a task (for example a consensus activity of the 'lost on the moon/at sea/in the desert' kind, or a strategy discussion activity), the outer observers each take one team member and analyse their performance in the team task according to the IPA profile (for example does the team member ask questions, give opinions, manage tensions and so on). At the end of the activity, each observer gives feedback on the performance of one team member; roles are then reversed and the observer group now takes the inner circle, to be observed by the new, outer circle group. The whole exercise could also be recorded and analysed later with reference to, for example, how well the team performed its task (content, for example decision making) as well as how well it performed in terms of its process (for example managing tension or conflicts, communicating).

Although the concept of 'emotional intelligence' is usually applied to individuals such as leaders and managers, it can be applied to teams (Druskat and Wolff, 2004), as effective teams seek to build relationships inside and outside the team, with mutual trust, team identity and a sense of team efficacy providing a strong basis for cooperation and collaboration. Teams that allow emotions to surface, perhaps through posters and storyboards, and understand how they can affect the team's work are more likely to be effective. Teams must pay attention to the emotional issues involved on three levels – team to individual, team to itself and team to external actors. From the perspective of the individual, there is a need for interpersonal understanding, perspective taking, confronting and caring. From the perspective of the team, there is a need for self-evaluation, seeking feedback, creating resources such as time and procedures to manage emotions, creating a positive, optimistic environment, and a proactive problem-solving style. From an external perspective, there is a need for organizational understanding and the building of external relationships and networking.

HRD in Practice 12.2

Team building in a community drug team

A community drug team in East Dorset, consisting of members drawn from five professions and three different employing agencies, used task-oriented team development and the GRPI model to resolve issues of mistrust and poor teamwork (for example not passing information on training courses on to other members). A particular focus was dealing with goals. Should the team focus on research, training, direct services to clients, service development, support and advice or liaison, service coordination and evaluation? Line manager pressure, member interest and desire for credibility with colleagues may push the team to more direct user contact, but at the expense of other goals and priorities. Initially, ill-defined goals and mission were clarified and specific objectives set and agreed with senior managers, such as setting up specific user groups and a family support service.

In order to clarify roles, the team defined generic and profession-specific skills; some members had specific professional requirements (for example appearing at court for probation workers). It also attempted to resolve role conflicts (given that each member was also a member of other teams) through role analysis and role negotiation, adopting a 'coordinated team' structure, where the team leader, a clinical psychologist, obtained agreed authority and accountability.

In order to clarify procedures, the team agreed to record new referrals in a common book, and allocate cases by workload and case characteristics through a key worker system. All cases, and case closures, were reviewed at clinical meetings, with minuted weekly meetings. All team correspondence, and one set of notes, were accessible to all members.

In order to improve relationships, the team attempted to meet frequently, share projects, include everyone at monthly lunches, train together, and identify joint training needs, including using outside facilitators. In addition, the team spent a first week at an event to generate a common identity and knowledge base, developed further through corporate PR and articles in professional journals. Given staff changes and the formation of specific subgroups such as a women's group, periodic team maintenance was felt to be necessary.

Team building through outdoor development

Team development interventions in the UK commonly use outdoor development, or 'ropes and slopes' involving physical challenges of some sort, for example in mountain or marine environments. Some common questions for team building generally and outdoor development in particular include:

- What does it offer in terms of a learning experience?

- For what purposes can it be used?

- What issues need to be taken into account in running an event and ensuring transfer to the workplace?

Outdoor development involves:

- Use of outdoor activities to provide a problem or a challenge

- Individual/group attempts to solve a problem or face up to a challenge

- Competitive or non-competitive tasks (individual or group)

- Review of task through feedback, analysis and reflection

- Use for personal development, team building and leadership skills.

Its characteristics may have some or all of the following:

- A powerful experiential learning

- An unfamiliar environment

- A real environment

- An open-ended design

- Emotional intensity

- Psychological safety

- Physical safety.

However, there is little evidence that comprehensive evaluation happens; a survey in 1997 found that only 3% of organizations using outdoor development used pre/post-test comparisons. However, 95% claimed that learning transferred to the workplace, 47% claimed a contribution to corporate objectives, and 79% claimed increased effectiveness in the workplace (Badger et al., 1997). A rigorous evidence base on this issue is still lacking, however.

HRD in Practice 12.3

Team-building events at the Littlewoods Organization

In the 1990s, the Liverpool-based Littlewoods Organization was experiencing problems, in particular the departments associated with gaming and football pools, due to the rise of the National Lottery, which was undermining its cus-tomer base. It responded in various ways, by downsizing, seeking alternative channels such as electronic gaming, and buying companies, often London-based, that had experience in these areas. In order to develop a common culture, members from London and Liverpool participated in team-building events in the Lake District with outside facilitators. The activities included getting team members across a barrier, cooperating with others in building a 'house' with stones while blindfold, using planks and barrels to cross a lake, and engaging in a 'treasure hunt' against other teams – searching the fells for clues as to the whereabouts of a prize (in this case, a bottle of champagne buried on an island in the middle of a lake). Analysis and feedback were used to identify patterns also shown in the workplace (for example not listening, not cooperating, not taking the initiative, failing to take responsibility).

Team development stages

A popular topic in team building has been the notion that teams go through a series of 'stages' as they develop. Tuckman (1965) identified five stages of team development (see Figure 12.4):

- *forming:* characterized by dependence on the 'leader'

- *storming*: independence/counterdependence

- *norming*: interdependence

- *performing:* interdependence

- *adjourning/mourning:* exit, break-up, moving on, for example rituals are often used to address emotional issues of loss and grief in project teams, for example reunions, parties, gifts.

Effective leaders will aspire to bring fully fledged teams to the performing stage as quickly as possible to attain high performance.

Tuckman's stages have been widely used and accepted in academic and practitioner worlds, although some have questioned their linear nature (do all teams have to go through all stages in the same order? Can teams slip back/regress to an earlier stage?), as well as the applicability of a model derived from the study of experimental/training groups to real-world teams.

The stages are as follows:

- *Forming*: At the first stage of team development, people are only just coming together to form a team. This stage is characterized by anxiety about the composition of the team, and people are concerned with what the team is for and 'who fits where'. Thus, team members focus their attention on the leader/chair/sponsor, and tend to assess whether to trust them or not, while having to depend on them for their roles and responsibilities. Members are often polite and guarded. This may cause the leader to focus more on individual tasks, while providing links among the team members to encourage interaction. In this scenario, decision making is fragmented, with individuals often focusing only on their own performance. Team leaders need to think about preparation, including what they want out of it, who will be coming, what they will expect, and what experience/ skills/knowledge they bring, as well as how to 'break the ice', perhaps by getting members to share experiences and ideas.

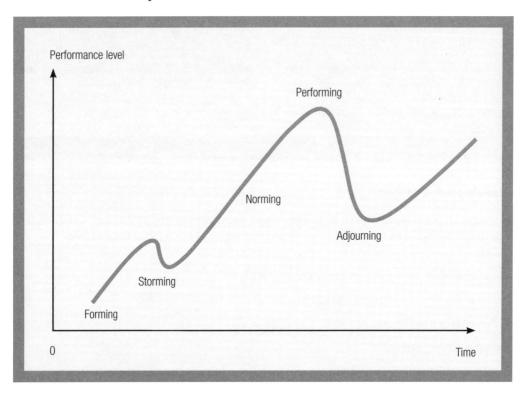

FIGURE 12.4 Tuckman's team development stages

- *Storming:* Tuckman (1965) suggests that teams go to storming when members reach a level of familiarity and are comfortable interacting with each other (Levi, 2001). As members become more familiar with each other, they test each other and role boundaries through challenges and may 'jockey for position', which can lead to confusion, demotivation, emotional resistance or rebellion. Team members are still experimenting at this stage and are concerned with 'how we work together'. Levy (2001, p. 41) asserts that in this instance the team members start to realize that the project might be more difficult than they had anticipated, and 'may become anxious, defensive, and blameful'. These issues will need to be worked through; the team leader may try to resolve conflicts by interacting with team members either individually or as a team, inviting questions and opinions while noting verbal and nonverbal reactions. The decision-making process can be adversarial, with challenges and threats to the leader, raising concerns for the sponsor, and frequent rumours, scapegoating and splits within the team into 'us and them'. The storming stage is important, bringing to the fore different perspectives on issues.

- *Norming*: Once a certain level of understanding is reached, the group starts trusting the processes and begins to organize itself around tasks, rules, systems and procedures. As there is group cohesion, views may be exchanged openly and new ideas actively sought. Team members may interact and facilitate team processes, enhancing mutual support and cooperation and establishing a shared group identity and purpose (Levy, 2001). Decision making becomes part of the process, while team rules/norms, such as punctuality, positively impact on performance. However, there might still be some difficulties, and a danger of slipping back to storming, especially if newcomers are introduced. This may be handled through constructive discussion and negotiation, since levels of communication between team members are much higher.

- *Performing:* This is where the team has matured and is able to operate effectively as a team, with higher degrees of trust among team members, mutual support and dynamic interaction. The team focuses fully on problem solving, information sharing, tolerance, energy and collective decision making and cooperation (Tuckman, 1965; Senior, 1997; Levy, 2001). There are constructive attempts to complete tasks when roles allow for flexible and effective work. Not all teams manage to successfully reach this stage, as they may get stuck in earlier, more conflicting stages, or slip back. Many team leaders will try to get through all the previous stages as quickly as possible to achieve goals, but this may be a mistake, masking unresolved issues and conflicts. The team leader may even take on more of a coaching role to help team members identify their team development needs.

- *Adjourning:* Tuckman later identified a fifth stage (perhaps accompanied by *mourning*), whereby the team is psychologically prepared beforehand for break-up or dissolution. Some teams may have planned endings, such as problem-solving or project teams. When team goals or objectives are achieved, members disperse. Guzzo and Dickson (1996) argue that after a few years of working together, a team's prolonged existence can be harmful for performance, increasing the need for the adjourning stage to bring freshness to the team. Too much cohesion can harm team creativity by reducing conflict and challenge, encouraging complacency, and enhancing the likelihood of 'groupthink'. Here, as we saw earlier on some of the dangers of team working (in particular, the Nut Island case), teams may ignore crucial information and distort reality, partly in the interests of maintaining group cohesion, so that discussion of threats is avoided, silence is interpreted as consent, and self-censorship prevails. Members voicing dissent may be seen as disloyal, traitors or 'not one of us'.

One way of avoiding groupthink is through greater team diversity, as the more diverse range of capabilities team members bring to a team, the more flexible that team will be in meeting changing demands. Teams that allow for varied and differing perspectives while enabling members to work towards common problems can enhance their performance through organizational learning. Archival studies in the US financial sector have shown positive relationships between top team heterogeneity and strategic change, especially the adoption of innovative strategies. Although Northcraft et al. (1995) argue that diversity in the team impacts on the amount of time it takes for a team to move through the first three stages, diverse teams may be more creative in the long run (see Chapter 13 for a fuller discussion of diversity).

Other teams may be unsuccessful in reaching the performing stage because they have failed to work through issues arising in earlier stages. Levy (2001) points out that a team's life is often a roller coaster of successes and failures; teams may go through different levels of performance during low or high periods when members are trying to resolve issues.

After Tuckman, there have been many different models of team development put forward (McGrath, 1990; Ancona and Caldwell, 1990; McIntyre and Salas, 1995), but Tuckman (1965) is still widely used and consulted when developing a team because of the clarity and simplicity of stage definition.

Activity

If you are introducing teamwork in your current workplace or doing a team-based project in your college/university, would you use Tuckman's team development stages, outdoor development, Belbin's roles, or all three? Explain your decision.

Team coaching

Coaching is usually seen as a one-to-one intervention, but Clutterbuck (2007, p. 77) argues it can also be applied to:

> Helping the team improve performance, and the processes by which performance is achieved, through reflection and dialogue.

This is similar to individual coaching, but is more complex, and has some extra dimensions:

- confidentiality
- scope of the relationship
- speed of decision making.

Team coaching has been less studied, but similar models to individual coaching apply, ranging from directive (for example GROW model) to non-directive (for example process consultation). Unlike a facilitator, the team coach is more engaged and 'inside' the team. Unlike team building, dialogue is more frequent and more intensive (Clutterbuck, 2007).

Reflective question

Thinking of an organization you are familiar with or you currently work for, what learning would you need to make an effective team coach?

Intergroup team building

Most team building focuses on developing internal relationships in the team. However, some methodologies have been developed to focus on intergroup or inter-team relationships, especially in terms of managing intergroup/inter-team conflict. One such technique, 'organizational mirroring', involves a host group (for example a unit, team, or department, or a function, like 'educational psychologists') receiving feedback from other groups (for example other teams, units, departments, or functions like 'head teachers') about how it is perceived. A study of social workers and nurses in Bradford, for example, showed how negative perceptions of each other affected referral rates of, in particular, Asian women (Iles and Auluck, 1988). Another development, 'three-dimensional mirroring', involves two separate groups building and sharing two or three lists. One concerns perceptions of how the group sees itself, another how it perceives the other group. A third might involve predictions of how the other group will perceive it. The two groups then meet separately to discuss the implications of the two lists, and then meet together to resolve priority issues between the two groups, and action plans are then devised (Blake et al., 1965).

An alternative, devised by Fordyce and Weil (1971), gets each group to devise three lists:

- *a positive feedback list:* attributes or behaviours that the group likes and values about the other group and wishes it to keep or continue doing

- *a bug list:* things the group dislikes about the other group and wishes it to stop doing

- *an empathy list:* what it thinks the other group is saying about it, or what it wants the other group to start doing.

The two groups share their lists and the total group builds a key list of unresolved issues and priorities. Subgroups are then formed to work on each item and report back to the whole group for action planning and evaluation. Such techniques can be used to address diversity issues, such as facilitating successful joint work by male and female or black and white colleagues (Iles and Auluck, 1988).

Summary

- There are several types of team now being commonly used in organizations, for example cross-functional teams, project teams, virtual teams and self-managed work teams. However, this list is not exhaustive.

- T groups have been in use to build teams since the 1950s. The classical T groups used mainly strangers and focused on issues in the 'here and now' and the personal growth of the trainee. The use of T groups has grown in the UK but the problems of training transferability became a common issue. This has been overcome by the use of team development and outdoor training activities.

- Team development needs may be assessed through such instruments as the Team Climate Inventory.

- Another example is task-oriented team development or GRPI, focusing on team goals, roles, procedures and interpersonal relationships. Bales' Interaction Process Analysis may be used to develop interpersonal skills in a team.

- Belbin's team role profiling is widely used to analyse preferred team roles, despite continuing doubts about its psychometric properties.

- Tuckman's team development stages are still widely used in organizations to train teams at different levels of development. Tuckman (1965) came up with five stages – forming, storming, norming, performing and adjourning.

- Relations between teams may be explored and improved through a variety of techniques of intergroup team building.

Discussion questions

1 Why would you wish to introduce team working?
2 When do you think team building would be useful?
3 Do you see any problems arising from a cohesive, conflict-free team?
4 How autonomous should self-directed teams be?
5 If a team seems to be experiencing conflict, would you send it on an outdoor development course?

Further reading

Ancona, D. and Caldwell, D. (1990) *Information Technology and Work Groups: The Case of New Product Teams*, Hillsdale, NJ, Lawrence Erlbaum.

Benders, J. and van Hootegem, G. (1999) Teams and their context: moving the team discussion forward beyond dichotomies, *Journal of Management Studies*, **36**(5): 609–28.

Jong, A., de Ruyter, J. and Lemmink, J. (2005) Service climate in self-managing teams: mapping the team member perceptions and service performance outcomes in a business-to-business setting, *Journal of Management Studies*, **42**(8): 1593–620.

Mankin, D., Cohen, S.G. and Bikson, T.K. (1995) *Teams and Technology*, Boston, MA, Harvard Business School Press.

Spencer, J. and Pruss, A. (1992) *Managing your Team*, London, Piatkus.

Staniforth, D. and West, M. (1995) Leading and managing teams, *Team Performance Management: An International Journal*, **1**(2): 28–33.

Wellins, R.S (1992) Building a self-directed work team, *Training and Development*, December: 24–8.

West, M.A., Tjosvold, D. and Smith, K.G. (ed.) (2003) *International Handbook of Organizational Teamwork and Cooperative Working*, Chichester, John Wiley & Sons.

Woodcock, M. (1989) *Team Development Manual*, 2nd edn, Brookfield, VT, Gower.

References

Anderson, N. and West, M. (1994) *Team Climate Inventory*, Windsor, NFER Nelson.

Aritzeta, A., Swailes, S. and Senior, B. (2007) Belbin's team role model: development, validity and applications for team-building, *Journal of Management Studies*, **44**(1): 96–118.

Badger, B., Sadler-Smith, E. and Michie, E. (1997) Outdoor management development: use and evaluation, *Journal of European Industrial Training*, **21**(9): 318–25.

Bales, R.F. (1950) *Interaction Process Analysis: A Method for the Study of Small Groups*, Reading, MA, Addison-Wesley.

Beckhard, R. (1972) Optimizing teambuilding efforts, *Journal of Contemporary Business*, **1**(3): 23–32.

Belbin, M. (1981) *Management Teams: Why they Succeed or Fail*, London, Heinemann.

Belbin, M. (1993) *Team Roles at Work*, Oxford, Butterworth Heinemann.

Blake, R.R., Shepherd, H.A. and Mouton, J.S. (1965) *Managing Intergroup Conflict in Industry*, Ann Arbor, MI, Foundation for Research on Human Behavior.

Blenkinsop, N. and Maddison, A. (2007) Team roles and performance in defence acquisition, *Journal of Management Development*, **26**(7): 667–82.

Burke, W. Warner (2003) *Organization Change: Theory and Practice*, Thousand Oaks, CA, Sage.

Cappelli, P. and Neumark, D. (2001) Do 'high performance' work practices improve establishment-level outcomes?, *Industrial and Labour Relations Review*, **54**(1): 737–75.

Clutterbuck, D. (2007) *Coaching the Team at Work*, London, Nicholas Brealey.

Cooper, C.L. (ed.) (2005) *Leadership and Management in the 21st Century: Business Challenges of the Future*, New York, Oxford University Press.

Davies, M.F. and Kanaki, E. (2006) Interpersonal characteristics associated with different team roles in work groups, *Journal of Managerial Psychology*, **21**(7): 638–50.

Dayal, I. and Thomas, J. (1968) Operation KPE: developing a new organization, *Journal of Applied Behavioral Science*, **4**(4): 473–506.

Delarue, A., van Hootegem, G., Procter, S. and Burridge, M. (2008) Teamworking and organizational performance: a review of survey-based research, *International Journal of Management Reviews*, **10**(2): 127–48.

Druskat, V.U. and Wolff, S.B. (2004) Building the emotional intelligence of groups, in *Harvard Business Review on Teams that Succeed*, Harvard Business School Press.

Dufrene, D., Sharbrough, W., Clipson, T. and McCall, M. (1999) Bringing outdoor challenge education inside the business communication classroom, *Business Communication Quarterly*, **62**(3): 24–36.

Dyer, W.G. (1995) *Teambuilding: Current Issues and Alternatives*, 3rd edn, Reading, MA, Addison-Wesley.

Edmondson, A., Bohmer, R. and Pisano, G. (2004) Speeding up team learning, in *Harvard Business Review on Teams that Succeed*, Harvard Business School Press.

Emery, F.E. and Trist, E. (1960) Socio-technical systems, in C.W. Churchman and M. Verhulst (eds) *Management Sciences: Models and Techniques*, vol 2, Oxford, Pergamon.

Fleming, I. (2004) *Teamworking Pocketbook*, 2nd edn, Arlesford, Management Pocketbooks.

Fordyce, J.K. and Weil, R. (1971) *Managing with People: A Manager's Handbook of Organization Development Methods*, Reading, MA, Addison-Wesley.

George, J.M. and Jones, G.R. (2005) *Understanding and Managing Organizational Behavior*, 4th edn, Upper Saddle River, NJ, Pearson/Prentice Hall.

Glassop, L.I. (2002) The organizational benefits of teams, *Human Relations*, **55**: 225–40.

Guzzo, R.A. and Dickson, M.W. (1996) Teams in organizations: recent research on performance and effectiveness, *Annual Review of Psychology*, **48**: 307–38.

Hackman, J.R. (1987) The design of work teams, in J. Lorsch (ed.) *Handbook of Organizational Behavior*, Upper Saddle River, NJ, Prentice Hall.

Harrison, R.C. (1972) When power conflicts trigger team spirit, *European Business*, Spring: 27–65.

Iles, P.A. and Auluck, R.K. (1988) Managing equal opportunity through strategic organization development, *Leadership and Organization Development Journal*, **4**(3): 3–10.

Iles, P.A. and Auluck, R.K. (1993) Inter-agency team development, in C. Mabey and B. Mayon-White (eds) *Managing Change*, 2nd edn, Milton Keynes, Open University Press.

Ingram, H., Teare, R., Scheving, E. and Armistead, C. (1997) A systems model of effective teamwork, *The TQM Magazine*, **9**(2): 118–27.

Janis, I. (1982) *Groupthink*, 2nd edn, Boston, Houghton Mifflin.

Kanter, R,M. (1982) Dilemmas in managing participation, *Organizational Dynamics*, **11**(1): 5–27.

Katzenbach, J.R. and Smith, D.K. (2004) The discipline of teams, in *Harvard Business Review on Teams that Succeed*, Harvard Business School Press.

Kreitner, R., Kinicki, A. and Buelens, M. (2002) *Organizational Behavior*, 2nd edn, Maidenhead, McGraw-Hill.

Levi, D. (2001) *Group Dynamics for Teams*, Thousand Oaks, CA, Sage.

Levy, P.F. (2004) The Nut Island effect: when good teams go wrong, in *Harvard Business Review on Teams that Succeed*, Harvard Business School Press.

Linstead, S., Fulop, L. and Lilley, S. (2004) *Management and Organization: A Critical Text*, Basingstoke, Palgrave Macmillan.

McGrath, J. (1990) Time matters in groups, in J. Gallegher, R. Kraut and C. Egido (eds) *Intellectual Teamwork: Social and Technological Foundations of Cooperative Work*, Hillsdale, NJ, Lawrence Erlbaum.

McIntyre, R.M. and Salas, E. (1995). Measuring and managing for team performance: emerging principles from complex environments, in R.A. Guzzo and E. Salas (eds) *Team Effectiveness and Decision Making in Organizations*, San Francisco, Jossey-Bass.

Maslow, A. (1954) *Motivation and Personality*, New York, Harper.

Mayo, E. (1945) *The Social Problems of an Industrial Civilization*, Boston, MA, Harvard University Press.

Meyer, C. (2004) How the right measures help teams excel, in *Harvard Business Review on Teams that Succeed*, Harvard Business School Press.

Miller, D. (2008) *Brilliant Teams: What to Know, Do and Say to Make a Brilliant Team*, Harlow, Prentice Hall.

Northcraft, G.B., Polzer, J.T., Neale, M.A. and Kramer, R. (1995) Productivity in cross-functional teams: diversity, social identity, and performance, in S.E. Jackson (ed.) *Diversity in Work Teams: Research Paradigms for a Changing World*, Washington DC, APA Publications.

Procter, S. and Currie, G. (2004) Target-based teamworking: groups, work and interdependence, *Human Relations Journal*, **57**(12): 1547–72.

Proehl, R.A. (1996) Enhancing the effectiveness of cross-functional teams, *Leadership and Organization Development Journal*, **17**: 3–10.

Robbins, S.P. (2005) *Organizational Behaviour*, 11th edn, Upper Saddle River, NJ, Pearson Education.

Royer, I. (2004) Why bad projects are so hard to kill, in *Harvard Business Review on Teams that Succeed*, Harvard Business School Press.

Rubin, I.M., Plovnick, M.S. and Fry, R.F. (1978) *Task-oriented Team Development*, New York, McGraw-Hill.

Senior, B. (1997) Team roles and team performance: is there really a link?, *Journal of Occupational and Organizational Psychology*, **70**(3): 241–58.

Spreitzer, G., Cohen, S. and Ledford, G. (1999) Developing effective self-managing work teams in service organizations, *Group & Organization Management*, **24**(3): 340–66.

Stewart, R. (ed.) (1999) *Gower Handbook of Teamworking*, Aldershot, Gower.

Swart, J., Mann, C., Brown, S. and Price, A. (2005) *Human Resource Development: Strategy and Tactics*, Oxford, Elsevier Butterworth Heinemann.

Torrington, D., Hall, L. and Taylor, S. (2005) *Human Resource Management*, 6th edn, London, Pearson Education.

Trist, E. and Bamforth, K. (1951) Some social and psychological consequences of the longwall method of coal getting, *Human Relations*, **4**: 3–38.

Tuckman, B. (1965) Developmental sequence in small groups, *Psychological Bulletin*, **63**(6): 384–99.

Tuckman, B. and Jensen, M. (1997) Stages of small group development, *Group and Organizational Studies*, **2**(4): 419–27.

Van de Water, H., Ahaus, K. and Rozier, R. (2008) Team roles, team balance and performance, *Journal of Management Development*, **27**(5): 499–512.

Van Mierlo, H., Rutte, C.G., Vermunt, J.K. and Kompier, M.A. (2006) Individual autonomy in work teams: the role of team autonomy, self-efficacy, and social support, *European Journal of Work and Organizational Psychology*, **15**(3): 281–99.

Wenger, E. and Snyder, W. (2004) Communities of practice: the organizational frontier, in *Harvard Business Review on Teams that Succeed*, Harvard Business School Press.

Winfield, I. and Kerrin, M. (1996).Toyota motor manufacturing in Europe: lessons for management development, *Journal of Management Development*, **15**(5): 49–56.

HRD and Diversity

13

Helen Rodgers, Victoria Harte and Jim Stewart

Chapter learning outcomes

After studying this chapter, you should be able to:

- Identify and examine the complex debates emerging in the literature about diversity in organizations
- Critically evaluate the varying views of the meaning of diversity in relation to managing and valuing diversity
- Describe and assess the role of HRD in facilitating diversity in organizations
- Explore cases of diversity in relation to key themes arising from the literature
- Reflect on individual diversity awareness and sensitivity

Chapter outline

Introduction

Diversity and HRD

Conceptual and theoretical meanings of diversity

Issues and concerns in diversity

Delivering diversity through HRD

Summary

Introduction

This chapter is concerned with the notion of 'diversity' and its connections with HRD. Diversity is a relatively new term and concept, which has come into common usage only in the past 15 years or so. Its origins lie in attempts to create more interest and commitment in work organizations to the principles and aspirations associated with the earlier term and concept of 'equal opportunities' in relation to the treatment of people at work (Kandola and Fullerton, 1998). A simple distinction can be drawn between the terms on the basis that equal opportunities is based on a moral argument, translated in some countries, including the UK, the USA and all members of the EU, into legal requirements governing the way employers treat actual and potential employees. In contrast, diversity refers to an argument in favour of similar principles and aspirations based not specifically on moral grounds but on the business and other benefits that can be achieved by treating actual and potential employees fairly and with dignity (Kandola and Fullerton, 1998). This is not to say that applying the notion of equal opportunities cannot and does not bring organizational benefits or that the case for diversity does not have a moral dimension. It is simply a matter of emphasis. However, there are also differences in understanding of the idea of 'fairness' in relation to the two concepts, which we will explore later.

Reflective questions

1 What do the words 'fair' and 'fairness' mean to you?

2 Where and how do you think you came to have your understanding of these words?

Diversity and HRD

Organizations face a number of challenges with regard to diversity because a central principle is that all employees will be treated with fairness, dignity and respect. This requires that all employees also operate and behave in accordance with that principle. In practice, this requires a workplace culture that acknowledges and responds positively to the different needs of individuals and a work environment where difference and potential are nurtured and valued. These requirements for particular organizational cultures, workplace environments and individual behaviour show an immediate and significant connection with and role for HRD. According to Stewart (2007), the purpose of HRD is to change behaviour at both individual and organizational levels. As Figure 13.1 shows, organizational-level behaviour is a function of what is referred to as 'core competence' and 'culture'.

Stewart argues that, at individual levels, behaviour is a function in part of knowledge, skills and values. The distinction between the two levels is primarily analytical, since it is only individuals who actually behave, separately and collectively. But the collective behaviour we call 'organization culture' influences the separate behaviour of individuals, and the same is true in reverse. This means that if organizations wish to create workplace cultures and environments that are supportive of treating all employees with fairness, dignity and respect, HRD will have a critical role in bringing about the necessary changes in individual and collective behaviour. We will explore how that might be done in practice later in the chapter. We will move now to examine the meaning of the notion of diversity in more detail.

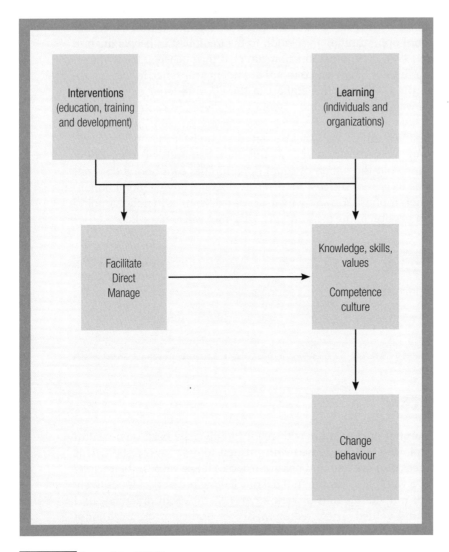

FIGURE 13.1 A model of HRD

Conceptual and theoretical meanings of diversity

The debates outlined in this section suggest that the conceptual shift from equality to diversity is wrought with complexity. Many of the theoretical debates acknowledge the historical evolution of the terms 'equality' and 'diversity' and register the incongruity of terms (Bentley and Clayton, 1998; Winstanley and Woodall, 2000). In the late 1990s, there was a shift from an equal opportunities (EO) focus to a diversity focus, argued on the basis that the EO approach was insufficiently holistic in its attempts to eradicate discrimination. In addition, the case for diversity emerges out of the critique of the EO approach and its inability to deliver demonstrable organizational results, despite 30 years of legislation (Rodgers et al., 2004; EOC, 2007). The changing social, demographic and geographic drivers impacting on 21st-century organizations have also shifted the need towards increased representation of diverse social groups in the workforce. This presents a number of conceptual challenges for those with an interest in managing and developing people.

The issue of equality management has existed since the 1970s and 80s when employers and trade unions had their own policy approaches (Greene and Kirton, 2004), albeit somewhat simplistic compared to today's approach to equality and human rights (EHR). However, in the late 1980s, Jewson and Mason (1986) brought about a shift to, in what was considered at the time, a more refined approach to dealing with equality. This shift was known as the 'sameness' approach, which became embedded as part of the traditional liberal EO agenda. The theoretical underpinnings of the sameness approach were that employees were 'treated the same'. This approach is still widely used today in both EHR and managing diversity approaches, although the latter is dependent on how an organization interprets and implements a diversity policy. However, despite the sameness approach still being widely used, there has been another shift in the equality management movement, which happened in tandem with the trend of the late 1980s and 90s towards deregulation, flexibility, new managerialism and HRM (Greene and Kirton, 2004). This shift involved a move away from the traditional liberal EO approach, that is, the sameness agenda, towards an approach concerned with recognizing employees as different and valuing that difference and the diversity among individual employees and potential employees (Kirton and Greene, 2004). This shift could be considered a further refinement or a more sophisticated approach to dealing with equality (Liff, 1997). There are obvious conflicts between the sameness and difference approaches as well as conceptual problems. Paradoxically, employees should not and cannot be treated as the 'same', but equally social justice and equality cannot be fully achieved with the diversity approach where employees are seen as different and their differences valued. This has provoked further discourse from Greene and Kirton (2004) who, from a trade union perspective, suggest that sameness and difference need to coexist, reflecting that the common ties between individuals should be recognized.

Furthermore, the coexistence of sameness and difference strengthens a more collectivist and moral framework of diversity management as opposed to an individualist, utilitarian framework for managing diversity. The principles of western management are dominated by a focus on the individual from recruitment and selection through to development and progression, while also recognizing the benefits of performance and employee engagement through teams.

These conceptual differences create challenges for organizations mainly in the drive to acknowledge the different needs of individuals and to create environments where the differences and potential of individuals can be nurtured and valued. Adopting a diversity approach in organizations is an attempt to eradicate discrimination on a number of levels. For example, individuals' personal characteristics are often used for job segregation. Individual perceptions and prejudice can often affect the effectiveness of recruitment and development practices in organizations, which may result in a number of detrimental consequences, including various forms of bullying, harassment and discrimination.

In organizations, diversity may take many forms and mean different things, from the need to attend to changes in an organization's environment, through changes in labour market profiles to the changing expectations of people engaged in the work process. Thus, while the foundation for diversity is rigorously embedded within the multicultural nature of 21st-century organizations, understanding what it is to practise or 'do' diversity is often unclear and this is the key challenge for those involved in developing organizations and individuals. This challenge can be clearly seen in what is referred to as 'talent management', where a fundamental question facing those who engage in the process is whether to adopt an exclusive approach, which defines and treats only some employees as talented – an employees as different approach, or an inclusive approach, which defines and treats all employees as talented – an employees as the same approach (see Tansley et al., 2007 for a discussion of this issue).

On 1 October 2007, reflecting these conceptual developments in the UK, three commissions concerned with the rights of different social groups were combined under one umbrella. What were previously known as the Commission for Racial Equality (CRE), the Disability Rights Commission (DRC) and the Equal Opportunities Commission (EOC) merged to became the Commission for Equality and Human Rights (CEHR), formed to protect the rights of individuals across a diverse mix of interests.

Issues and concerns in diversity

So far we have discussed the theoretical underpinnings of diversity and how it might be applied in practice in society, economy and organizations. We have also discussed the drivers of diversity in those same contexts. But to what extent does actual practice match the theory, in other words, as with HRM/HRD more widely (McGoldrick and Stewart, 1996; Legge, 2004), is there a gap between the rhetoric and reality? Clearly, the potential existence of such a gap is a major issue and concern for those involved in managing diversity.

What is diversity?

The CEHR's vision is to create, promote and protect 'a society built on fairness and respect. People confident in all aspects of their diversity.' It is an independent advocate for equality and human rights in Britain and aims to reduce inequality, eliminate discrimination, strengthen good relations between people and promote and protect human rights. The commission enforces equality legislation on age, disability, gender, gender reassignment, race, religion or belief and sexual orientation and encourages compliance with the Human Rights Act 1998. One of its key objectives is to use influence and authority to ensure that equality and human rights remain at the top of agendas for government, employers, media and society, in their campaign for social change and justice (CEHR, 2008).

Despite this recent change and refocusing of the three aforementioned commissions, it is interesting to note that the remit of the CEHR remains unchanged on what it considers central to equality and human rights. However, there are other schools of thought that extend and go beyond these areas to include numerous other elements that are believed or considered to be important to the issue of diversity (Mavin and Girling, 2000;

CIPD, 2005). These include economic status, family/marital status, nationality, spent convictions, part-time working, carer responsibilities, political/opinion affiliation, educational qualifications, languages and work experience. These are clearly outside the remit of the CEHR – what might be termed as the 'standard' or 'established' scope of EO – or even what might be 'justifiably' subject to legislation.

Rhetoric versus reality

In relation to EHR and the CEHR, is there a gap between the rhetoric of the commission and what happens in reality? Can legislation really protect everyone in the workplace from discriminatory practices from similar level or senior colleagues? Policies pursued by the former EOC that purport to reduce gaps in gender salaries and other forms of discrimination offer some indication through assessing whether their targets were met. Rodgers et al. (2004) suggest that while many organizations claim to operate EO policies, detailed assessment of the effectiveness of such policies (aside from statistical monitoring) is often neglected and in many instances this perpetuates inequality and lack of diverse representation at senior levels in organizations.

The most recent publication from the EOC (2007) on gender outlines how a revolution that began in the 1970s remains unfinished with regard to the roles that men and women undertake in society in relation to the workplace and family and home life. This accords with the judgement of the CIPD on progress with diversity policies more generally (Line, 2008). A lot of work is still to be done, as the most recent statistics on gender from 2005 (EOC, 2006) might illustrate (see Table 13.1).

TABLE 13.1 Progress in achieving gender equality

Employment	
Part-time employment	42% of working women aged 16–64 in 2005 worked part time, as opposed to 9% of working men. Part-time work is the most common alternative working arrangement for women
Employment by age	60% and 40% of working women aged 25–44 in 2005 worked full time and part time, as opposed to 96% and 4% of working men respectively
Employment by disability	54% and 46% of working women aged 16–59 in 2005 were disabled working full time and part time, as opposed to 87% and 13% of working men respectively
Employment by ethnic group	57% and 43% of white working women aged 16–64 in 2005 worked full time and part time, as opposed to 91% and 9% of white working men respectively
	68% and 32% of Indian working women aged 16–64 in 2005 worked full time and part time, as opposed to 91% and 9% of Indian working men respectively
	73% and 27% of black Caribbean working women aged 16–64 in 2005 worked full time and part time, as opposed to 87% and 13% of black Caribbean working men respectively

Pay and income	
Full-time and part-time earnings	There is a 17.1% gender pay gap between women and men who work full time and a 38.4% gender pay gap between women and men who work part time
Annual full-time earnings	There is a 27.1% gender pay gap between women and men
Individual pension income	There is a 47% lower weekly income gap between women and men in retirement
Individual salary income	There is a 27% lower weekly income gap between women and men in full-time employment and a 25% lower weekly income gap between women and men in part-time employment

SOURCE: Adapted from EOC (2006)

It is clear from the above snapshot data that there are still inequalities in gender in relation to salaries and income. However, what isn't clear is how the CEHR intends to address these issues of inequality. It suggests that if a number of goals are achieved over the next 10 years, it can complete the revolution. One of the suggested goals is to 'close the income gap between men and women' but it doesn't elaborate on exactly how it might or will do this. This is an example of rhetoric not reflecting reality. Furthermore, the commission reveals that it is unable to 'give direct legal assistance to everyone' but can offer advice through its helpline and online resources. Unfortunately, this applies to individual cases, where there are no opportunities to push the boundaries of the law, create legal precedents or clarify and improve the law. This in itself could appear unfair and discriminatory.

In relation to diversity rather than EO, and more so managing diversity, what is rhetoric and what is reality? This is a question that still remains largely unanswered, mostly due to a lack of critical evaluative research, the misinterpretation of managing diversity, the misuse of the term 'managing diversity', the use of the term by senior management within organizations for the wrong reasons and the sheer number of definitions of diversity that are almost as diverse as the subject itself (CIPD, 2005). Were things simpler when the term EO was the only term referred to? Is the sophistication in the use of the terms 'diversity', 'difference' and 'managing diversity' muddying the waters? Some say 'yes' (Greene and Kirton, 2004) and some say 'no' (CIPD, 2005). The views of Greene and Kirton and the CIPD are at opposite ends of the continuum. A gap between the rhetoric and reality still seems to exist, but it appears to be more than that for some – there is the view that managing diversity is still a rhetorical concept (Mavin and Girling, 2000).

It is argued that there are distinct differences between the concepts of EHR and managing diversity (Mavin and Girling, 2000; Greene and Kirton, 2004; CIPD, 2005). That said, it is suggested that this also may be a rhetorical claim (Mavin and Girling, 2000). EHR is about human rights for individuals in respect of their age, disability, gender, gender reassignment, race, religion or belief and sexual orientation and ensures equality, ethics and social justice, protected by legislation, holistically. But the approach to EHR within the workplace in organizations is about individuals within homogeneous categories or social groups – groups of women, black and ethnic minorities, people with disabilities and so on – that is, people with an assumed sameness who are ensured of a voice, a fair hearing. In addition to this is the strengthening of these collective groups in organizations where there is trade union representation. Managing diversity is somewhat more complex. As discussed earlier, it has many guises. Much of the existing literature suggests that it can be broadly categorized as 'doing little more than reiterating the traditional arena of EO' (Cooper and White, 1995; Ellis and Sonnerfield, 1995; Copeland, 1998). This would suggest 'EO in managing diversity's coat'. A research report from Greene and Kirton (2004) suggests that managing diversity is something that could only happen once basic levels of EO had been achieved. The following comment from a trade union officer from the GPMU particularly resonates with Greene and Kirton's (2004, p. 17) view of managing diversity:

> It's about valuing the people you've already got in the company and giving them opportunities ... We're still at the level of talking about equality ... overcoming barriers as opposed to that kind of diversity view of managing people to fulfil their potential.

Furthermore, Rodgers et al. (2004) remark, leading and managing with a diversity agenda presupposes that equality or the treatment of 'like as like' on the basis of characteristics such as gender, age, race, disability, sexual orientation, religion and employment status already exist, or are implicit within an organization's norms, therefore allowing diversity through difference to be nurtured, valued and celebrated.

Another view of managing diversity goes far beyond the conventional approach to EO, such as compliance to legislation and targeted homogeneous group initiatives, and views it as an explicit strategic approach to managing the 'difference' of individuals, as opposed to 'sameness' (Mavin and Girling, 2000). One notion would be to enable sameness and difference to coexist and recognize both these in individuals throughout an organization. However, this would be an extremely challenging pursuit. This is also recognized by Greene and Kirton (2004). They suggest that the sameness and difference approaches are seen as appropriate strategies, albeit within different contexts. While recognition of the heterogeneity of social groups is important, as well as the diversity of interests within social groups, the collective aspects of group membership are also seen as significant. Finding a harmony between individuals and groups in one single approach seems almost impossible. Viewing women as homogeneous single interest groups does not recognize their differences, but can they be viewed as heterogeneous on a collective basis, particularly when an issue of inequality relates to equal pay, for example? Furthermore, this particular debate is not new and fears of 'throwing good after bad' have led to calls for approaches that build on existing EHR interventions (Liff, 1997; Dickens, 1999; Cornelius, 2002).

HRD in Practice 13.1

The BBC, the UK national public service broadcast organization, uses both terms, equal opportunities and diversity, in its policy statements, as detailed below.

The BBC's commitment

Diversity for the BBC is a creative opportunity to engage the totality of the UK audience. That includes diverse communities of interest, as well as gender, age, ethnicity, religion and faith, social background, sexual orientation, political affiliation and so on.

Delivering on our commitment to equal opportunities and diversity is important to the BBC for a number of reasons. For example, the audiences that we serve are increasingly diverse. The BBC is also a public service broadcaster funded by a licence fee paid by all sections of UK society.

- The BBC is committed to reflecting the diversity of the UK audience in its workforce, as well as in its output on TV, on radio and online.
- The BBC also has a number of legal obligations to comply with current legislation, for example around the Disability Discrimination Act (DDA).
- The BBC has set itself diversity workforce targets.

The BBC is a member of the major industry networks on disability and ethnicity, as well as of the main UK employer forums which bring together organizations committed to driving progress on diversity.

Our equal opportunities statement

The BBC is committed to promoting equal opportunities for all, irrespective of colour, race, religion or belief, ethnic or national origins, gender, marital/civil partnership status, sexuality, disability or age.

The BBC is committed to reflecting the diversity of the UK and to making its services accessible to all. This applies both to our output and to the people who work here.

The BBC aims to create and sustain an inclusive work environment which provides equality of opportunity for everyone.

Find out more about the BBC's approach to diversity by visiting www.bbc.co.uk/info/policies/diversity.shtml#commitments.

Reflective questions

1 What do you think of the practice of framing a commitment using the language of diversity and a policy statement in the language of equal opportunities?

2 Does the content of the BBC document suggest a difference between diversity and EO or are they essentially the same? Why?

Costs and benefits of diversity policies

While a plethora of legislation underpins employment contracts, many theorists suggest that commitment to a diversity agenda has other benefits, but why should an employer want to push the boundaries set by law? Equal opportunity is often seen as treating everyone in exactly the same way. But to provide real equality of opportunity, people often need to be treated differently in ways that are fair and tailored to their needs. Currently, employer attention to pushing the boundaries of diversity and the management of diversity is based on the economic argument; it makes sound business sense to use the talents of many diverse social groupings and individuals in order to achieve the economic outcomes required to sustain an organization's effectiveness. In their ground-breaking book *Diversity in Action: Managing the Mosiac*, Kandola and Fullerton (1998) make a distinction between proven benefits, debatable benefits and indirect benefits.

Proven benefits include:

- the recruitment of scarce labour and skills
- reduction in employee turnover
- reduction in absenteeism
- enhanced organizational flexibility.

Proven benefits can be explicitly quantified and tracked by the organization.

Debatable benefits include:

- enhanced team creativity and problem solving
- improved decision making
- improved customer service and responsiveness
- improved quality.

Debatable benefits are less quantifiable but are generally thought to add to the organization's capacity and effectiveness.

Indirect benefits include:

- improved morale
- increased job satisfaction
- better public image
- increased competitive edge.

Indirect benefits enhance the work experience and add to the organizational ethos and general sense of employee engagement. Other authors take up the idea of a wider set of advantages offered by a diversity approach as representing social justice, attending to the fulfilment and satisfaction of employee needs and expectations and extending the organization's corporate reputation.

This social justice argument is based on the belief that everyone should have a right to equal access to employment and, when employed, they should have a right to equal pay and equal access to training and development, as well as being free of any direct or indirect discrimination, harassment or bullying. This is often described as the right to be treated fairly. In addition to this, the employee needs and expectations argument asserts that people aspire to work for employers with good and fair employment practices and to feel valued at work. To be competitive, organizations need to derive the best contributions from everyone. Skill shortages and difficulties in filling vacancies are forcing more organizations to recruit from more diverse talent pools and to offer different employment packages and working arrangements. Creating an open and inclusive workplace culture is integral to achieving this type of employment model. The links between diversity and corporate reputation present a compelling argument for employers. Healthy businesses flourish in healthy societies and the needs of people, communities and businesses are interrelated. Social exclusion and low economic activity rates limit business markets and their growth. Thus businesses need to consider corporate social responsibility (CSR) in the context of diversity. CSR is usually thought of as being linked to environmental issues, but an increasing number of employers take a wider view, seeing the overall image of an organization as important in attracting and retaining both customers and employees. Indeed, it can be argued that CSR is part of the 'new' psychological contract emerging between a firm and the community or communities in which it operates.

Building on these arguments, many organizations and employers in the UK and Europe have implemented what we might term 'diversity policies'. Most diversity policies are voluntary initiatives by employers to recruit, retain and develop employees from diverse social groups. Such employers range across business organizations, national governments, equality agencies, trade unions and nongovernmental organizations. There are a number of basic fundamentals that any organization needs to consider before embarking on the implementation of a diversity policy. First, the identification of what the policy is intended to achieve. Not all organizations set out to achieve the same goals when addressing diversity. This is a key consideration because benefits for individuals, groups and the organization will be dependent on goals being achievable and realistic and not the rhetorical form that may be used to express them. Second, costs are another significant consideration associated with, for example, the implementation of large-scale HRD programmes to change internal cultures as part of diversity policy goals. Other costs linked with complying with the laws on discrimination and opportunity costs associated with the diverting of management time in executing the policy and change programmes also need careful consideration. These costs are a mixture of explicit and implicit and care needs to be taken to ensure that costs are, as far as possible, identified and managed.

HRD in Practice 13.2

Diversity at Pearson

'At Pearson, everything we create – ideas, stories, newspapers, images, books, websites – is only as good as our people's minds and imaginations. We're proud of them and their talent, enthusiasm and ambition. Our goal is to be the best company to work for in the world: a place where people want to work and where they treat people as they want to be treated themselves. Our first step is to provide recruitment and development programmes, benefits and a culture that rivals anywhere else' (Sir David Bell, director for people, Pearson).

You can find out more about Pearson's diversity policy by visiting its website at www.pearson.com/.

Reflective questions

1 What do you think are the goals being pursued at Pearson?

2 How realistic and achievable are these goals?

Assessing benefits

In 2003, the European Commission (EC, 2003) commissioned a report to examine the measurement of costs and benefits of workforce diversity policies against a background of the implementation of new anti-discrimination directives throughout the EU and increased investment in workforce diversity policies by businesses. Its findings provide extremely informative evidence on diversity policies, their measurement, the type of measurement and outcomes from the implementation of such policies. Two principal benefits that organizations seek from their investments in diversity policies were identi-fied and these are linked to economic gains. This has a direct connection with the business case for diversity.

The two economics benefits are (EC, 2003):

- *Strengthening long-term 'value-drivers':* tangible and intangible assets that allow companies to be competitive, generate stable cash flows, and satisfy their share-holders. These include building a differentiated reputation with key stakeholders and customers, and improving the quality of human capital within a company.

- *Generating short- and medium-term opportunities to improve cash flows:* for example by reducing costs, resolving labour shortages, opening up new markets, and improving performance in existing markets. These are also known as 'return on investment' benefits.

One point to note is that the research was qualitative in design and so these benefits are reported rather than actually measured for the research project. So far, there is little evidence of quantitative assessment or systematic measurement of benefits and outcomes. Additional benefits of having strategic, achievable and operational diversity policies that foster inclusivity and respect for the dignity of the individual are that organizations free themselves of costly lawsuits, hostile environments and divisive conflict-ridden cultures (Iles and Hayers, 1997).

Assessing costs

Organizations face four types of additional cost when they invest in workforce diversity policies. These are (EC, 2003):

- *costs of legal compliance:* potential costs include record-keeping systems, training of staff and communication of new policies.

- *cash costs of diversity:* the main cash costs are specialist staff, education and train-ing, facilities and support, working conditions and benefits, communication, employment policies and monitoring and reporting processes. Some of these are one-off and short term but most are long-term, recurring expenses.

- *opportunity costs of diversity:* opportunity costs represent the loss of benefits because a scarce resource cannot be used in other productive activities. These include diversion of top management time, diversion of functional management time and productivity shortfalls.

- *business risks of diversity:* many programmes designed to change corporate cultures take longer than planned to implement or fail completely. This 'execution risk' is widely understood among companies. Sustainable diversity policies are an outcome of a successful change in corporate culture.

It will be clear from the EU research and the points made here that measuring the costs and benefits of diversity policies is highly complex and probably impossible to achieve in any exact form in practice.

Do we value diversity?

The relationship between costs and benefits raises the question of whether we, as a society, value diversity in its own right, in the UK. It is fair to say that there are differences within our society, illustrated by contentious political parties in regional areas of the UK and conflict-ridden cultures displaying a disregard and lack of respect for individuals and groups in society. The current government demonstrated its commitment to diversity when it published a new equality Bill entitled *Framework for a Fairer Future* on 26 June 2008, which sets out its approach to addressing inequalities in society, social mobility being one of these. The Commons address by Harriet Harman outlined the government's view of those inequalities and described what it believed these are:

> addressing those inequalities and creating a fairer society is important for three reasons. First, fairness is important for the individual. Secondly, fairness is important for our society – a society that is equal and fair is one that is more at ease with itself. Thirdly, fairness is important for our economy – diversity makes us outward facing and helps us to compete in the global economy.

It appears that the government's rationale represents basic approaches to tackling the issues of a diverse and inclusive society. Considering that migration to the UK is not a new phenomenon – it started at the end of the Mesolithic times (4000 BC) – it seems that fostering an inclusive society is not and has not been easy. Even though society is more civilized today than it was in 4000 BC, there are still many hurdles to overcome, perhaps best illustrated currently in relation to race and religion. These points relate to the government's focus on individuals and society as a whole. The government considers its focus on the economy to be equally important. The UK organizations that support the UK economy are charged with competing in the global economy from a diverse perspective. An approach that many organizations take to adopting this perspective involves strategic input from their HRM/HRD departments. Stewart and Beaver (2003) suggest that an increasing number of organizations are recognizing that effectively managing their HR necessitates recognition and incorporation of the global context.

As a consequence of globalization and the changing nature of the labour market, partly due to an increase in migration to the UK, organizations can no longer settle for culturally and ethnically homogeneous workforces, thus transferring the onus to employers to adopt a different approach to managing increasingly diverse workforces, which is argued to be good for organizations and their ongoing survival (Stewart and Beaver, 2003). This approach encompasses the 'business case for diversity' – linking the effective and efficient management of a diverse workforce to the direct success of an organization and the economic benefits associated with this. This focus on managing a diverse workforce has clear implications for HRM and HRD. HRM policies and activities are mainly associated with recruitment and selection, rewards and the development of specific diversity policies, while HRD is mainly focused on learning interventions to support the implementation of these policies and the achievement of associated objectives. We now move onto delivering diversity through the use of HRD interventions.

Delivering diversity through HRD

From the late 1990s onwards, it became clear that 'diversity management' was a necessity for all 'successful' organizations. Littlefield (1995) identified training as a key intervention to solve diversity problems across 50 countries. Given the opposing debates discussed earlier, two key questions for managers and leaders are:

- What are the problems we face in relation to EHR and diversity?

- What initiatives can be put in place to help us move in the right direction?

While the development of an HRD agenda for diversity has grown substantially over the past few years, identifying the right development areas for organizations and understanding the needs of individuals in embracing diversity presents a number of challenges.

Training: what type/s and who gets it?

Previous research (Harris, 1991) suggests that the number of organizations providing diversity training has increased significantly over the years, and that two-thirds of companies conducted diversity training for managers and almost 40% provided training for all employees. Yet the current statistical evidence, presented in Table 13.1 above, suggests that segregation, an unequal distribution of roles and discrimination still prevail in organizations.

The definition of diversity training varies from organization to organization and depends on how the concept of diversity is understood by those championing the diversity agenda. Most organizations that provide training offer awareness and/or skill-based training in an attempt to sensitize employees to the issues presented by diversity in the workplace, yet the nature and outcome of diversity training is rarely scrutinized.

HRD interventions can take many forms. A number of HRD activities will be necessary as part of major change programmes associated with achieving the successful implementation of diversity policies and achieving genuine respect, fair treatment and opportunities for all in practice. Such programmes are called for by the CIPD (Line, 2008) and feature in many organizations' approach to managing diversity (Michielsens et al., 2008). The approach of the civil service featured in HRD in Practice 13.4 is a good example. However, not all organizations can or choose to adopt major cultural change but instead rely on and select from a range of different HRD interventions. Before detailing some of these, it is worth making the point that some or all may be included in cultural change programmes. The key difference is that in those programmes HRD activities form part of an integrated strategy.

Probably the most common HRD intervention is some form of awareness training aimed at all or most employees. Diversity awareness training has grown out of attempts to implement EO policies related to particular categories and groups, for example race awareness and sexism awareness training. The intellectual rationale for this intervention is that individual behaviour needs to change and this in turn requires individual attitudes to be changed through raising awareness of the existence of (illogical) rationale for and negative effects of, for example, sexist beliefs and attitudes (Stewart, 1996). However, the success of this type of intervention is hard to measure. The attempts that have been made suggest mixed results and there is some evidence that they can reinforce and deepen the very attitudes they are supposed to change (Stewart, 1996; Home Office, 2002). A further argument against awareness training is that it shifts responsibility from the organization to individual employees. In any case, the assumed causal relationship between individual attitudes and individual behaviour has yet to be established (Stewart, 1996).

HRD in Practice 13.3

Bladerunner wins right to compete in the Olympics

He's known as the fastest man on no legs. Oscar Pistorius, South African paralympic champion, has broken all the flat sprint records in his class and now wants to compete in the able-bodied Olympics. He regularly blurs the line between able-bodied and disabled as he races along on his carbon-fibre legs. Not that the young South African cares for that word – disabled. And for that reason, he believes – despite having no limbs below the knees – that he should be allowed to compete in the Olympics. Pistorius says: 'It would mean that I could compete at a better level. I would be the first paralympic to compete so I would be basically be setting a benchmark.'

But the world of athletics is divided over this, with critics claiming that his carbon-fibre blades, called Cheetahs after the animal, give him an unfair advantage – lengthening his stride and giving him extra spring. In January 2008, the International Association of Athletics Federations (IAAF, the athletics governing body) banned Pistorius from competing in the Olympics as an able-bodied athlete.

Pistorius, now aged 21, was born with crucial bones missing – at the age of one he had both legs amputated below the knee. But from the moment he could walk, he has approached life at a run. Pistorius is a world-record holder for the 100, 200 and 400 metres. Crucially, he won gold at the 2004 Paralympics, and that's when the criticism began as he set his sights further.

In May 2008, in an appeal against the IAAF ban, the Court of Arbitration for Sport said in a statement that the IAAF had not proved competition rules had been contravened: 'On the basis of the evidence brought by the experts called by both parties, the panel was not persuaded that there was sufficient evidence of any metabolic advantage in favour of the double amputee using the Cheetah Flex-Foot.'

The panel emphasized that their verdict only applied to the individual case of the South African. It was also stressed that any advancements in the prosthetic limb technology used by Pistorius could be contested by the IAAF again: 'The panel does not exclude the possibility that, with future advances in scientific knowledge, and a testing regime designed and carried out to the satisfaction of both parties, the IAAF might in future be in a position to prove that the existing Cheetah Flex-Foot model provides Oscar Pistorius with an advantage over other athletes.'

Source: Excerpts from *Daily Mail*, June 2007; BBC News 16 May 2008

Discuss your responses to the following with fellow students or colleagues:

1 What are your reactions to the Pistorius case?

2 Consider the case in relation to the sameness and difference perspectives advocated in the diversity literature.

3 Consider the implications of the ruling in the light of awareness raising and behaviour changes for individuals and organizations.

Other researchers (Alban-Metcalfe and Alban-Metcalfe, 2005) make the distinction between awareness raising and the building of skills in operating within a diverse workforce. Distinctions are made in the mode of delivery and the outcome from the different HRD interventions. Awareness training is usually a classroom-based activity and may be useful to impart knowledge, provide wider perspectives and offer new ways of thinking and seeing. More specifically, it can be used to correct the myths and stereotypes that permeate an organization and increase employee sensitivity to diversity issues (Nagamootoo et al., 2005).

Advantages of the awareness training approach are that it can be focused on particular workplace contexts, planned and delivered across organizations relatively easily and cover large numbers of people at a reasonable cost. However, the classroom-based approach has been criticized for its generalized nature in not being able to meet the needs of individuals, particularly its inability to impart skills and influence the types of behavioural change to enable the cultural shifts towards truly embracing diversity in the workplace.

Skills-based training builds on awareness training by attending to the behavioural aspects of the individual and providing new tools and techniques to promote more effective interactions between different individuals, the aim being to promote behavioural change. The underlying rationale for skills-based training comes from Bandura's (1986) social learning theory, which proposes that participants will learn more through behaviour role modelling. In terms of developing skills based on diversity sensitivity, participating in role play encourages rehearsal and practice of managing diversity-related issues. Here individuals are offered a safe and supportive environment in which to develop their skill sets and receive one-to-one feedback or reinforcement about their behaviour development from an experienced coach.

The claims made of the skills-based approach are that it assists learning and development on an individual basis and promotes deep, long-term learning and behavioural change. It can be tailored to consider specific workplace contexts and is more interactive than the class-based exchanges often used in awareness training. However, it is time-consuming and costly and for these reasons tends to be targeted at senior members of the organization.

While the two approaches offer a different set of advantages and outcomes, most studies (Nagamootoo et al., 2005) suggest that a mix of both awareness training and skills-based training is suitable for organizations, where the balance should be guided by organizational context. Using both awareness training and skills development assists organizations to answer the why, what and how of embracing a diversity culture.

However, as Stewart (1996) suggests in the light of plausible evidence for a causal relationship between individual attitude and individual behaviour, the shift of responsibility to the individual needs to be matched with an organizational commitment to a sustainable momentum for change. Awareness training should not be seen as a one-off 'quick fix' intervention and should change to reflect the ever changing demands of the organization and strategy. In addition, skills-based training should be supported by effective coaching and development long after the initial intervention.

A common group-based HRD intervention is a programme to inform, communicate and educate employees of the organization's diversity policy and the rights and responsibilities of all employees arising from the policy. This is likely to be the minimum HRD intervention used by any organization adopting a diversity policy. Delivery of these programmes does not have to be face to face and methods utilizing e-learning, for example, may be used by large employers. Additional programmes are also usually developed and delivered for those with particular responsibilities within a diversity policy, for example those involved with recruitment and selection. Many of these will be managers.

While it is important for organizations to consider meaningful diversity training throughout the organization, so that individuals can keep ahead of the game, there is a large body of evidence (Schein, 1985; Bass and Avolio, 1993; Alban-Metcalfe and Alban-Metcalfe, 2005) to suggest that senior managers, leaders and those promoting the public face of the organization are key to creating the right environment and developing appropriate strategies to enable the delivery of a diversity agenda. It is also important to recognize the important role played by line managers in offering support and promoting opportunity for their staff with fairness, dignity and respect and in deciding what merit is in the process of appraising staff. However, diversity tends to feature separately from MLD and so programmes on recruitment and selection are often designed and delivered by HR staff and departments rather than HRD or MD staff and departments. Both these interventions were well established before the term diversity came into common usage and were standard interventions associated with EO policies.

More recent HRD interventions have focused on both individuals and groups associated with diversity policies. Individual interventions include coaching and mentoring, for example for women to support their development as managers. While coaching and mentoring programmes may be aimed at groups such as women or members of black and minority ethnic groups, the methods themselves are one to one and so the HRD activities support individuals. Group-based HRD interventions include use of action learning sets as well as support networks. These methods were also utilized as part of implementing EO policies but have become more common as part of approaches to managing diversity. So too have what are known as positive action programmes as used by the civil service for example (see HRD in Practice 13.4). These are HRD interventions aimed at underrepresented groups to help overcome barriers to particular careers. Again although such programmes were originally developed under the banner of EO, they have been taken up to a greater extent under the banner of managing diversity.

We would argue that there has been little if any progress in designing and developing new HRD interventions to support diversity since those developed to support the achievement of EO. Perhaps one significant development is that of diversity leadership programmes for senior managers. There has arguably been little progress here though, as pointed out by Line (2008). So, our conclusion is that HRD theory and practice has yet to initiate any meaningful response to managing diversity.

HRD in Practice 13.4

Diversity policy in the UK civil service

The UK civil service launched a diversity policy and change programme in 2005 based on a 10-point plan, as follows:

- targets
- measurement and evaluation
- diversity champions network
- leadership and accountability
- recruitment
- development
- behaviour and culture change
- efficiency and location reviews
- mainstreaming diversity
- communication.

While HRD is identified as a separate if key point (development), it does in fact encompass all other points, for example LD (see http://leadersunlimited.nationalschool.gov.uk/ for more detail) and training and development in recruitment practices and as a central part of the strategy to achieve behaviour and culture change. More details of the plan can be found at www.civilservice.gov.uk/documents/pdf/diversity/10_point_plan_nocover.pdf.

Activity

Access the website www.civilservice.gov.uk/documents/pdf/diversity/10_point_plan_nocover.pdf to consider the following questions:

1 What is the main contribution of HRD to the effective implementation of diversity policies in the UK civil service?

2 Is the use of and contribution set for HRD appropriate and realistic?

3 What other contributions might have been sought from HRD interventions in securing the aims and objectives of the 10-point plan?

Use your responses to these questions to produce a short statement describing the role of HRD in achieving effective diversity policy in organizations. Compare and contrast your statement with those produced by fellow students or colleagues.

LD and the links with diversity

Alban-Metcalfe and Alban-Metcalfe (2005) draw a distinction between the way in which managers and others act competently in response to diversity and the way in which they act in a 'transformational' or a transactional way as leaders in influencing the climate and culture of an organization. They draw on the works of Schein (1985) and Bass and Avolio (1993) in demonstrating the strong links between leadership and organizational culture, whereby the process by which leaders influence culture is by the creation and reinforcement of organizational norms and behaviour. Furthermore, in HR terms, recruitment, selection and placement decisions are all influenced by prevalent values and norms (Bass, 1998). Alban-Metcalfe and Alban-Metcalfe's (2005) research indicates that acting competently and performing these competences transformationally (showing concern, inspiring, supporting, enabling, showing respect for the dignity of others) are more conducive to building and valuing cultures of diversity than performing these competences transactionally (being directive, disempowering, lacking respect).

Leaders and others concerned with valuing diversity then need to examine the norms and behaviours associated with the recruitment and development, appraisal and performance of their workforce and consider their own behaviours and actions in the context of their daily work. HRD through LD programmes has a clear contribution to make to achieving most of these outcomes but especially the last. As we have seen in this brief section, it also has a contribution in all aspects of diversity management from basic communication of policy through awareness training and skills development to achieving cultural change. Many of the functions and processes described in other chapters of this book will be applicable to supporting managing diversity, for example the design and delivery of HRD to management and team development. So we can conclude with the confident assertion that HRD is currently and will remain an essential component of managing diversity in any and all its forms and approaches.

Summary

- The notion of 'diversity' had clear links with and grew out of earlier notions associated with equal opportunities. There are no clear distinctions or agreed differences between the two concepts and some argue there is in fact no difference.

- Partly because of the above, diversity and managing diversity are complex concepts and activities.

- Central to this complexity is the range of different and sometimes competing arguments in favour of achieving effective diversity management in work organizations. These include moral imperatives, achieving business benefits, compliance with legislation, contributing to achieving social justice and applying the principles of corporate social responsibility.

- An added feature of the complexity is specifying the groups covered by diversity, whether it is in fact useful to apply the term to particular and specified groups and the challenge of achieving respect, fairness and dignity in the treatment of all individual current and potential employees.

- Arising from the former point on groups versus individuals is the problem of deciding whether to treat individuals the same or each individual differently or, perhaps more accurately, the problem of doing both at the same time.

- Two additional and related significant issues with managing diversity are first separating rhetoric from reality or principles from practice and second assessing the impact of attempts to apply principles in practice. A particular and important example of the second difficulty is establishing, specifying and measuring the costs and benefits of investing in managing diversity.

- HRD is clearly a significant and important component of any attempt to achieve effective diversity management policy and practice in work organizations. This is most clearly the case because of the link between individual and collective behaviour and effective diversity management.

- HRD practice has a number of contributions to make with perhaps the central one being achieving cultural change to facilitate effective diversity management.

- Additional HRD interventions include the communication of organizational policies, awareness training, skills development and positive action programmes.

- A range of standard activities within HRD professional practice will be relevant to these contributions, including the design and delivery of HRD interventions and the provision of management and team development programmes. Leadership Development may, however, be the most significant and important HRD contribution to achieving effective diversity management in work organizations.

Discussion questions

1 In 2004, *Business Week* revealed that US research showed:

    on average, companies with the highest percentage of women among their top officers had a return on equity 35% higher than those with the fewest high-level women. Total return to shareholders was 34% higher for the companies with the most executive women vs those with the fewest. (Alimo-Metcalfe and Brutsche, 2005)

    So why are so few women at the top? Is it because women simply don't have the qualities required of modern business leaders, or current organizational assessment processes are biased in ways that reduce the entry of women to the most senior organizational positions? What evidence and arguments do or would support each of these explanations?

2 There is considerable evidence to suggest that black and minority ethnic employees are rated lower in performance evaluations than white employees (Friedman et al., 1998), especially when the raters themselves are white (Alban-Metcalfe, 2005). Furthermore, black and minority ethnic, female and disabled managers face a number of factors that appear to be stunting their career progression, including a lack of supervisory support, a lack of constructive and critical feedback and 'out group' status in organizations (Alban-Metcalfe, 2005). What assumptions and norms do you suggest are influencing the management

and evaluation processes underway here? What policies and practices might an HRD professional consider implementing in order to change this situation?

3 What role and contribution can team development play in achieving effective diversity management?

4 Which target groups in organizations will be most likely to benefit from diversity skills development programmes and why?

5 Which target groups in organizations are most likely to benefit from awareness training and why?

6 What features and components would you include in a leadership development programme designed to increase the effectiveness of diversity management?

Further reading

CEHR (Commission for Equality and Human Rights) (2008) *Talent not Tokenism: The Business Benefits of Workforce Diversity*, London, CBI Human Resources Policy Directorate.

Ghilardi, L. (2006) *Intercultural City, Making the Most of Diversity: The Contribution of Outsiders to Entrepreneurship and Innovation in Cities: The UK Case*, London, Noema Consultancy.

Home Office (2002) *Training in Racism Awareness and Cultural Diversity*, London, Research, Development and Statistics Directorate.

References

Alban-Metcalfe, J. (2005) Perceptions and prospects: diversity issues among managers in local government, paper presented at HRD Conference, Leeds.

Alban-Metcalfe, J. and Alban-Metcalfe, J. (2005) A 360⁰ approach to diversity and the development of skills-based training, paper presented at HRD Conference, Leeds.

Alimo-Metcalfe, B. and Alban-Metcalfe, J. (2005) Leadership: time for a new direction?, *Leadership*, 1(1): 51–72.

Alimo-Metcalfe, B. and Brutsche, M. (2005) Gender and leadership: does it really matter?, paper presented at HRD conference, Leeds.

Bandura, A. (1986) *Social Foundations of Thought and Action: A Social Cognitive Theory*, Englewood Cliffs, NJ, Prentice Hall.

Bass, B.M. (1998) *Transformational Leadership*, Mahwah, NJ, Lawrence Erlbaum.

Bass, B.M. and Avolio, B.J. (1993) Transformational leadership and organizational culture, *Public Administration Quarterly*, 17(1): 112–21.

Bentley, T. and Clayton, S. (1998) *Profiting from Diversity*, Aldershot, Gower.

CEHR (Commission for Equality and Human Rights) (2008) *Talent not Tokenism: The Business Benefits of Workforce Diversity*, London, CBI Human Resources Policy Directorate.

CIPD (Chartered Institute of Professional Development) (2005) *Change Agenda: Managing Diversity; Linking Theory and Practice to Business Performance*, London, CIPD.

Cooper, M. and White, B. (1995) Organisational behaviour, in S. Tyson (ed.) *Strategic Prospects for HRM*, London, Institute of Personnel and Development.

Copeland, L. (1988) Valuing diversity, part 2, pioneers and champions of change, *Personnel*, July: 44–9.

Cornelius, N. (ed.) (2002) *Building Workplace Equality: Ethics, Diversity and Inclusion*, London, Thomson.

Dickens L. (1999) Beyond the business case: a three-pronged approach to equality action, *Human Resource Management Journal*, 9(1): 9–19.

EC (European Commission) (2003) *The Costs and Benefits of Diversity: A Study on Methods and Indicators to Measure the Cost-effectiveness of Diversity Policy in Enterprises*, Directorate-General for Employment, Social Affairs and Equal Opportunities, europa.eu.int/comm/employment_social/fundamental_rights/prog/studies_en.htm.

Ellis C. and. Sonnerfield, J.A. (1995) Diverse approaches to managing diversity, *Human Resource Management*, **33**(1).

EOC (Equal Opportunities Commission) (2006) *Facts about Men and Women in Great Britain*, Manchester, EOC.

EOC (Equal Opportunities Commission) (2007) *The Gender Agenda*, Manchester, EOC.

Friedman, R.A., Kane, M. and Cornfield, D.B. (1998) Social support and career optimism: examining the effectiveness of network groups among black managers, *Human Relations*, **51**(9): 1155–77.

Greene, A.M. and Kirton, G. (2004) Views from another stakeholder: trade union perspectives on the rhetoric of 'managing diversity', Warwick Papers in Industrial Relations, Number 74, Warwick University, Industrial Relations Unit.

Harris, P. (1991) *Managing Cultural Differences*, Houston, TX, Gulf.

Home Office (2002) *Training in Racism Awareness and Cultural Diversity*, London, Research, Development and Statistics Directorate.

Iles, P. and Hayers, P.K. (1997) Managing diversity in transnational project teams: a tentative model and case study, *Journal of Managerial Psychology*, **12**(2): 95–117.

Jewson, N. and Mason, D. (1986) The theory and practice of equal opportunities policies: liberal and radical approaches, *Sociological Review*, **34**(2): 307–34.

Kandola, R.S. and Fullerton, J. (1998) *Diversity in Action: Managing the Mosaic*, London, CIPD.

Legge, K. (2004) *Human Resource Management: Rhetorics and Realities*, Basingstoke, Palgrave Macmillan.

Liff, S. (1997) Two routes to managing diversity: individual differences or social group characteristics, *Employee Relations*, **19**(1): 11–26.

Line, F. (2008) Diversity: done and dusted?, paper presented at CIPD conference Developing the Profession, University of Nottingham, 26–27 June.

Littlefield, D (1995) Managing diversity seen as core economic value, *People Management*, **1**(12): 15.

McGoldrick, J. and Stewart, J. (1996) The HRM-HRD nexus, in J. Stewart and J. McGoldrick (eds) *HRD: Perspectives, Strategies and Practice*, London, Pitman.

Mavin, S. and Girling, G. (2000) What is managing diversity and why does it matter?, *Human Resource Development International*, **3**(4): 419–33.

Michielsens, E., Urwin, P. and Tyson, S. (2008) Implementing diversity employment policies: examples from large London companies, paper presented at CIPD conference Developing the Profession, University of Nottingham, 26–27 June.

Nagamootoo, N., Birdi, K. and Adams, M. (2005) Diversity training: how can we make it more effective?, paper presented at HRD conference, Leeds.

Rodgers, H., Frearson, M., Holden, R. and Gold, J. (2004) Equality, diversity and leadership: different journeys, variegated landscapes, paper presented at the HRD conference, Limerick University.

Schein, E.H. (1985) *Organizational Culture and Leadership*, San Francisco, CA, Jossey-Bass.

Stewart, J. (1996) *Managing Change through Training and Development*, 2nd edn, London, Kogan Page.

Stewart, J. (2007) The ethics of HRD, in C. Rigg, J. Stewart and K. Trehan (eds) *Critical Human Resource Development: Beyond Orthodoxy*, Harlow, FT/Prentice Hall.

Stewart, J. and Beaver, G. (2003) *Human Resource Development in Small Organisations*, London, Routledge.

Tansley, C., Turner, P.A., Foster, C. et al. (2007) *Talent: Strategy, Management, Measurement*, London, CIPD.

Winstanley, D. and Woodall, J. (2000) *Ethical Issues in Contemporary Human Resource Management*, Basingstoke, Palgrave Macmillan.

14

E-learning

Jim Stewart

Chapter learning outcomes

After studying this chapter, you should be able to:

- Explain the meaning of e-learning
- Describe the history and origins of e-learning
- Describe some common characteristics of e-learning within HRD
- Evaluate arguments and engage in debates about the meaning of e-learning and what constitutes e-learning approaches to HRD
- Critically assess claims about the benefits and advantages of e-learning approaches within HRD practice

Chapter outline

Introduction

Background and origins

Definitions and meanings

Contexts and applications

Debates and controversies

Current and future developments

Summary

Introduction

This chapter examines what is now referred to as 'e-learning'. We include the word 'now' here because e-learning has emerged as an accepted and dominant term from a range of other possible terms and acronyms associated with a set of approaches to learning and development that share similar and common characteristics. As with other terms and concepts associated with HRD, the concept of e-learning is not as straightforward as it might at first seem. It is obviously associated with learning, but what, how and why are critical questions, with argument and debate about the correct answers. The 'e' of e-learning would appear to be easy to define – it is generally taken to be an abbreviation of 'electronic' – and so e-learning would appear to mean electronic forms of delivering learning. But there is dispute about what constitutes 'electronic' when referring to e-learning. So this chapter will include an examination of various views and perspectives of e-learning, with no definitive answers being provided.

Reflective questions

1 What do you think is included in the term 'electronic'?

2 What do think are the advantages and disadvantages of learning using electronic media?

You might find it useful to visit www.elearningage.co.uk, the home page of the *e.learning age* magazine.

Background and origins

The origins of e-learning can be clearly linked to approaches designed to accommodate learning at a distance (see Stewart and Winter, 1994 for a full discussion of this). Historically, these approaches were referred to as 'correspondence courses', since they were based on paper-based learning materials sent and received through the post, as are letters, or 'correspondence'. Correspondence courses traditionally did and still do generally lead to a qualification and are aimed at individuals wishing to change or advance their career. The term is not much used today, but when it is, the meaning continues to be associated with qualification courses taken and paid for by individuals. Another feature already implied is that of learning at a distance and this feature is the key one of the related term 'distance learning'. This term can have a variety of meanings but is generally accepted to describe learning that has the following features:

- The learner is not immediately or continuously in the presence of, or supervised by, a trainer or tutor

- The learner does, however, benefit from the services of a training or tutoring organization

- These services may include support from a distance provided by a trainer or tutor

- These services always include learning materials provided by the training or tutoring organization

- The materials can take a variety of forms and media, and courses usually utilize a mix of these forms and media.

It is clear from these features that the concept of distance learning refers to a separation of learners in time and space from those who support them The points above deliberately use the terms 'training/trainer' and 'tutoring/tutor'. This is to denote the possibility of distance learning being used by employers for their employees and by educational institutions for their students. Distance learning has a history of being used for both purposes and in both contexts of HRD practice. Correspondence courses have the longest history of distance learning for purposes of education and qualification provision, but the term has traditionally been applied to courses supplied by commercial organizations rather than educational institutions. Perhaps the most famous and certainly one of the first examples of the latter is the UK Open University, which was established in 1968 and accepted its first students in 1970. While not directly attributable to the creation of this institution, the name introduces yet another term, that of 'open learning'. This approach is argued to offer and provide flexibility and autonomy to learners, so that they can determine:

- What is learned

- How it is learned

- When it is learned

- Where it is learned

- At what pace learning occurs.

HRD in Practice 14.1

E-learning for widely dispersed staff

The communications company Siemens utilizes e-learning to deliver training to staff widely dispersed across the globe. For example, a team of six or seven engineers working on a project in Africa need training but it is not cost-effective to bring them back to Europe for a short training session. Their project has a limited life and so it is also not cost-effective to set up a training infrastructure in their work site.

E-learning is the answer that impressed a training manager from Royal and Caribbean Cruise Lines, who has similar problems of widely dispersed and mobile staff. He was also impressed with the apparent facility of web-based training to deliver a common standard of training wherever staff happen to be.

Source: Based on Brockett (2008)

The ways in which the Open University and other similar institutions operate, and indeed how many if not all commercial and employer-based open learning programmes also operate, make it clear that flexibility and learner autonomy have limits. The Open

University, for example, has a limited number of courses and so limits the 'what', their academics and course designers decide how to produce and present learning materials and so impose strict limits on the 'how', and as a university working to an academic year, limits are also imposed on the 'when' and the 'pace' of learning. These characteristics are therefore statements of ideal rather than actual conditions of learning. Even so, they suggest a conceptual difference between distance learning and open learning. This difference rests on the aim and ideal of learner autonomy as a central feature of open learning, and the existence of distance as a central feature of distance learning. It is possible to imagine an open learning programme with no separation in time or place between learners and those who support them. It is also possible to imagine a distance learning programme with no learner autonomy to determine the what, how, when, where or pace of learning. So the two concepts are separate and different. Despite this conceptual difference, common usage often links open and distance learning together as a single approach to learning, or, alternatively, views distance learning as a form of open learning (see Stewart and Winter, 1994).

Activity

Form groups of four. Consider the following questions and then discuss your answers and attempt to reach a consensus response:

1 To what extent do you think the ideal conditions of open learning are possible in a formal, qualification-based programme?

2 To what extent and in what ways do you think that distance learning and open learning are similar and different?

3 What problems do you think learners will experience from being distant in time and place from their trainers/tutors?

4 How do you think these problems can best be overcome?

5 What are your views on the suitability of open and distance learning programmes for educational programmes and employer-based programmes for employees?

To explore the ideas that underpin open learning in higher education in the UK, visit www.olf.ac.uk/. You might also visit www.elearning.ac.uk/, the site of the Joint Information Systems Committee e-learning programme, which aims to identify how e-learning can benefit learners, practitioners and educational institutions.

As we have seen, both open and distance learning programmes can come in a variety of different forms and media. The first and traditional form was paper-based texts. These texts are different from presentations from books. For example, it is considered effective practice in paper-based distance learning materials to make maximum use of white space and, related to this, to use larger font sizes than normally found in books. Over the years, research into such materials has produced a number of other guidelines to make the materials less daunting and more attractive and easy to use:

- *Presentation:* as well as white space and font size, other aspects include high-quality paper, the use of colour, print quality reproduction and attractive and high-quality packaging/binding and cover materials.

- *Layout:* this refers to the presentation of the content. Guidelines recommend breaking up the text with boxed content such as summaries, activities and illustrative examples. The use of headings and subheadings is also encouraged, as is breaking up the text with diagrams, graphics and photographs.

- *Ease of use:* it is suggested that the content is organized into a logical structure and then broken up into manageable chunks, which are presented as a series of discrete units. Opinion varies on what is a manageable chunk but a useful guideline is no more than 15 minutes of reading followed by an activity of some sort, with the whole unit being capable of completion in no more than one hour. There are three more items under this heading:

  - the use of clear objectives so that learners know what they are working towards

  - the use of a clear and consistent 'signposting' system, that is, different symbols to guide learners as to what they should be doing at any given point, for example different symbols for reading, responding to questions, an activity and taking a break

  - the provision of a study guide, which includes an explanation of the signposting system.

- *Interactivity:* this is probably the most significant and distinguishing feature of open and distance learning materials. It covers many items including learner activities and exercises, provision and use of self-assessment questions and model answers to enable self-monitoring of learning and progress, and provision of trainer/tutor support for assessment of assignments and/or provision of guidance and advice on the content. Use of language and writing style is also included under this heading. The advice is to aim for language use consistent with a daily newspaper rather an academic tome and to adopt a conversational style to engage the learner.

You might recognize some of these features from this book and others you read as a student. This is simply because features that have been found to support learning in the paper-based texts used in open and distance learning programmes are now routinely used in student textbooks for the same reason – to support and facilitate learning. What is of more interest here is that the same features have been and are applied in different forms and media utilized in open and distance learning. The Open University leads the way in use of alternatives to paper-based text through the use of television, radio, video and audio tapes among others. The use of different forms and media also leads to new names, such as technology-based training or learning and, in higher education, resource-based learning, which encompasses paper as well as technology-based materials. The 1980s and 90s saw more modern technologies such as PCs being utilized, although the Open University used computers for assessment and other activities from the start. This led to further names, such as computer-based training and computer-assisted learning. In fact, such media had a longer history than was recognized at the time, since what was referred to as 'programmed learning' was used with specially developed machines from the 1950s. Other technological advances led to interactive video and later digital video interactive, compact disc video and compact disc read only memory (CD-ROM). All these later developments relied on digital technology and, in some cases and to a certain extent, computer hardware. One point of commonality to do with all these media, from paper to computer programmes, is that their development was not, initially at least, for educational or learning purposes. To an extent, the main purpose was either information storage and processing or entertainment. Opportunities for utilization in support of learning were recognized after the media became established in other arenas and for other purposes. This is an important point, which we return to later. We will now move on to looking more closely at e-learning and the relevance of the discussion so far for understanding the potentialities and limitations of this approach to HRD.

Definitions and meanings

A useful starting point in examining the meaning and definitions of e-learning is to restate that it is connected to and is part of a long history of approaches developed as alternatives to face-to-face instruction, whether that face-to-face instruction occurs in a college classroom or an employer's training centre. Given that this is the case, e-learning shares with all other media and technology the same features, characteristics and practice of open and distance learning. It is often an attempt to deliver learning at a distance and provide more autonomy to learners themselves over the what, how, when, where and the pace of learning. In common with other developments in open and distance learning media and technology, it is also justified on learning and cost saving benefits. These claimed benefits are often questionable, as they have been with earlier media and technology (Stewart and Winter, 1994). What is less questionable is that e-learning as a form and medium of open and distance learning is subject to the same principles of effectiveness as earlier media and technology. In other words, the guidance given above on what supports effective learning through open and distance learning approaches also applies to e-learning. So presentation, layout, interactivity and ease of use, while having a different context for application, will be just as important in e-learning as they are in paper-based texts (Sambrook, 2003). In fact, the principles are always applied differently in different media and technology since each different form has its own requirements, possibilities and limitations, but what helps and what hinders learning remains largely constant.

An initial point of debate in defining e-learning rests on which technologies to include and which to exclude. For example, Sambrook (2003) defines e-learning as any learning activity supported by ICT. This is similar to a CIPD (2003) definition that asserts e-learning to be any learning that is delivered, enabled or mediated by electronic technology. Both definitions have a focus on particular technology and seem to be in agreement, although 'electronic' may be narrower in scope than ICT. However, in a later publication, the CIPD (2004a) elaborated its definition to emphasize what it describes as 'connectivity', on the basis of which it excludes any stand-alone technology such as CD-ROMs. Sambrook (2003) discusses the same point and the arguments of various authors and decides that CD-ROMs are included in her definition. So, there is clearly disagreement here on what exactly constitutes e-learning.

In the same publication, the CIPD (2004a) provoked a different debate by introducing a further elaboration of its definition by adding the words 'that is, for the explicit purpose of training in organizations' (p. 2). This narrows the definition even more and would, if accepted and applied, exclude any and all learning that meets the technological part of the definition but which occurs in non-work contexts such as students learning in universities. This element of the definition is clearly too restrictive and so will be rejected here. But that still leaves the problem of deciding what is included and what is excluded in terms of technology. Practice has moved on since both definitions were offered and it is a fast moving and developing field. In addition, the CIPD 2003 report claims that the term e-learning was first used in 1999 and so the term is still very young in its life cycle. For these reasons, it is reasonable not to expect or need a precise definition. A debate about the inclusion of CD-ROMs will not take us very far. One point of relevance to note, however, is that Web 2.0 technology (see later section) utilizes and emphasizes the potential of connectivity even more than previous technology and so there may be case for giving greater weight to that factor in deciding on a definition. Nevertheless, the use of ICT for education and training purposes seems to be a useful defining feature of e-learning.

A further area of debate in understanding the meaning of e-learning is the role of what is referred to as 'stuff and stir'. The use of these words was introduced by Rossett (cited in CIPD, 2003) to distinguish between the content of learning and the process of learning. This is a well-established distinction in HRD and refers to what is to be or is learned (the stuff) and the how or way it is learned (the stir). Stuff and stir are applied specifically in e-learning for this distinction. The argument is that stir is more important and significant in defining e-learning and making it effective. Examples of stir are the collaborative learning tools such as virtual classrooms and online discussion boards. There is a clear link here with the notion of 'connectivity' and so perhaps an explanation for the CIPD excluding CD-ROMs from its definition. In this view, learning content (stuff) delivered by ICT but without supporting collaborative processes (stir) is not considered to be e-learning. This argument may in part be based on not utilizing the full functionality and associated benefits of ICT. As we saw earlier, support for open and distance learning can be in a variety of forms and does not rely necessarily on collaborative processes. Since ICT can and does provide these other forms of support, it seems a little esoteric to exclude those programmes that do not provide online collaboration from the meaning of e-learning. A possible reason for doing so might be to support a case that e-learning is a genuine fundamental departure from what has gone before. But any familiarity with ICT programmes without collaborative stir will lead to the conclusion that they are simply open and distance learning programmes that utilize new and different technology. In addition, open and distance learning programmes, including those that are primarily paper based, have for many years sought to include collaborative processes using whatever technology was available at the time. The Open University is perhaps a good but by no means only example of this, with its personal tutor telephone system, study groups and summer schools. So it seems reasonable to conclude that e-learning is primarily a continuation of established approaches to HRD, which utilizes the latest technology to deliver learning content, while supporting learners and facilitating learning. This is what all HRD practice, including all forms of open and distance learning, seeks to achieve. E-learning simply utilizes particular forms of technology to achieve those aims.

Contexts and applications

There are a number of significant factors that explain the rise in the popularity and use of e-learning. According to a CIPD (2004b) survey, one of these is undoubtedly the role of vendors. Both technology companies and those already selling technology-based education and training products identified the potential for utilizing ICT in developing new products. The former companies developed products to support the stir of e-learning. These are generally referred to as 'learning platforms' – computer programs that enable and support a variety of applications to aid learning through ICT. A major market for these products has been and remains educational institutions such as colleges and universities, although large employers have also adopted commercially available systems. The latter companies developed the stuff of e-learning and so brought products to market that required ICT hardware and software. Early examples of these were mainly in the form of CD-ROMs but they quickly became more sophisticated and relied on the availability of learning platforms. Technology companies developing the learning platforms also developed stuff to accompany their system products. The education market is less significant for learning content than large employers. Respondents to the CIPD survey were clear that those companies selling products related to e-learning were a major factor in driving adoption and increases in use.

An additional factor has been public policy. Sambrook (2003) identifies a focus by national governments and their agencies on, for example, lifelong learning as part of the explanation (see Chapter 15), and a similar focus on work-based learning by governments as part of their policy initiatives is also relevant. So, the use of and growth in e-learning has been in part the outcome of public policy support and funding and other government-led initiatives for its promotion. The notions of lifelong learning and work-based learning are not directly relevant here, but Sambrook provides a useful model of the latter that helps to explain government interest. The model distinguishes between:

- *learning in work*, which denotes learning through and on the job

- *learning at work*, which denotes learning that occurs at the place of work but away from the job, for example in a training or learning centre

- *learning outside work*, which denotes learning relevant to work but occurring perhaps at home or at a college.

The UK government has been keen to promote the latter two of these in order to improve skills and economic performance, and e-learning is seen as relevant to both these contexts. Similar arguments apply to lifelong learning and enabling and promoting that through e-learning has been part of the UK government's strategy on vocational education and training (see Chapter 3).

Activity

Working with a partner, visit the following sites:

Learn Direct – www.learndirect.co.uk

National Extension College – www.nec.ac.uk/info/?usca_p=t

National Open College Network – www.nocn.org.uk/Homepage

Find out how these institutions have sought to advance e-learning to support skills development in the UK.

This brief examination of some of the reasons for the growth in the use of e-learning suggests a number of different contexts of practice. One is society and communities. E-learning is seen by governments as a way of increasing the amount of learning as well as spreading the range of people involved. A second context is formal education. The rise in use of e-learning in this context is also associated with government policy in the UK, since they provide the majority of funds for education. Such funds have been directed in part at promoting e-learning at all levels of education from compulsory schooling to degree-level education at universities. The emphasis has been more on the flexibility and autonomy of open learning rather than creating distance learning in these contexts. But most programmes associated with government policy and funding have elements of both. The final major context of practice is that of work organizations. This has occurred mostly in large employers and has had a greater emphasis on distance rather than open learning, although again most programmes have elements of both.

In relation to the work and employment context, e-learning has not seen the continued growth anticipated in earlier years. The most recent survey in the UK (CIPD, 2008) showed 47% of respondents using more e-learning than previously and 26% saying they don't use or no longer use e-learning. An additional interesting finding of the survey is that while over half of those surveyed use e-learning, the figures for the public sector are 82% but only 42% for the private sector – clearly a much higher rate of usage in the former compared with the latter. The survey has no data on the question, but it might be that this greater use in the public sector is related to the policies of national government, in that they are likely to have more influence on HRD practice in the public sector. Indeed, some of the respondents in that sector will be government organizations at national, regional and local levels.

Research has shown a variety of benefits of e-learning (Pollard and Hillage, 2001), which include the ability to learn 'just in time' at the pace and convenience of the learner, providing updateable materials and cost-effectiveness in delivery. In addition, there has always been the possibility of collaborative working and learning, with participants spread over large distances. Worries about access to ICT have now diminished and with the growth of telephonic broadband systems (such as www.skype.com) and Web 2.0 technologies, there is significant potential for further development of e-learning. Several large organizations use e-learning as a key feature of their corporate universities as part of their KM strategies (Stewart and Tansley, 2002).

The application and use of e-learning raised a number of issues of significance for HRD practice. The first is the role of the HRD professional. There is an established debate on this issue (see Chapter 2) and so e-learning is only one element. However, there is an argument that there has been a shift in emphasis in recent years from training to learning and that the role of the HRD professional has and is changing accordingly (Sambrook and Stewart, 2000; Brown et al., 2006). It may be that the recent introduction and rise in use of e-learning has some connection with the changing role of the HRD professional. Less emphasis on direct and face-to-face instruction, or training delivery, is certainly a feature of the claims on the changing role. Use of e-learning, as with other forms of open and distance learning, certainly demands less direct training delivery. Another claimed feature of the changing role reflects increasing responsibility for initiating and managing learning being passed to individual employees in work organizations. This too – as with open learning more generally, with its focus on learner autonomy – is enabled and supported to an extent (but see next section) by e-learning. A requirement for changed attitudes towards training and learning on the part of HRD professionals and employee learners is highlighted as critical to the success of e-learning by over 90% of respondents in the CIPD (2008) survey. This finding supports the general arguments on the role of the HRD professional and individual employees in managing their own learning. Similar findings on the changed roles and relationships between learners and those who support them have been revealed in research into the use of e-learning in higher education (Arbaugh and Duray, 2002; McPherson and Nunes, 2006). It seems to be the case therefore that the application and use of e-learning have significant implications for HRD practice and the role of HRD professionals.

HRD in Practice 14.3

Online academies at 02

The mobile phone provider 02 uses what it refers to as 'online academies' to help staff make sense of and access learning and development products and content. According to its HR director, the main problem before launching the academies was that employees found it difficult to find and make sense of the training and development opportunities available to them. To help overcome this, each of the company's nine directorates now has its own online learning portal, referred to as an 'academy'. Each is designed and presented to reflect the nature of the business and work of each directorate and, at the time of writing, the academies have over 5,000 learning items such as articles, self-assessment instruments and case studies. The academies will also be integrated in the company performance management system and 360 degree feedback tool. According to the HR director, another expected and intended benefit is to have a ready-made vehicle for launching any development across the business.

Source: Based on Phillips (2008)

A second issue questions to some degree the nature and extent of this argued shift in role for HRD professionals. A clear lesson of experience of e-learning to date is that it is not a panacea and so cannot be applied to all learning needs, and that even where it is relevant and useful, it needs to be utilized as part of an overall design and set of methods. The 'mixing' of e-learning with other methods is now generally referred to as 'blended learning'. The effectiveness of blended learning as opposed to using e-learning as a single approach is supported by 95% of respondents to the CIPD (2008) survey. It is also supported by research in employment contexts (Bonk and Graham, 2006) and education contexts (Mortera-Guttierrez, 2006) as being more effective than using e-learning alone. The particular mix of methods can and does vary according to the particular learning being sought, but as a rule of thumb, it is argued that e-learning is effective in relation to learning knowledge-related content but needs to be combined with other methods when developing skills. This is also argued to be particularly the case in relation to social and interpersonal skills. There is nothing new in these arguments, as similar points have been made in relation to all forms of and media used in open and distance learning (Stewart and Winter, 1994). They do suggest, however, that there is still a place and role for direct, face-to-face training delivery in the role of HRD professionals.

Reflective questions

1 What are the key differences for trainers between face-to-face delivery and the use of e-learning?

2 What difference in skills do the two roles demand?

A third and final issue raised by the application of e-learning is another element of the argued new role for HRD professionals. We do not have to accept the arguments on connectivity in defining e-learning to recognize that online collaboration is a feature of many e-learning programmes. This suggests a new context and set of tools for HRD professionals in supporting and facilitating learning. Encouraging discussion and interaction among learners, designing and applying activities and exercises, facilitating participation and answering questions are all part of the normal and established role of the HRD professional in direct and face-to-face delivery. The same kinds of contributions are also required in supporting online interaction but this shift in context is argued to be so significant that it constitutes a different role and new and different skills. This role and the associated skills go beyond those that arise simply from using new and different technology, or so it is argued (see for example Salmon, 2004). A new term has come into common usage instead of trainer, tutor or facilitator to accompany the new role and that is e-learning 'moderator'. The role of e-moderator is said to be different to face-to-face roles and there is extensive research and comment on how the role needs to be performed and the knowledge and skills required to perform it effectively.

We can conclude this section by saying that e-learning can be and is being applied across all the major areas of HRD practice. Although well established, e-learning has not been applied in any of these areas to the extent once predicted. It also seems to be clear that the effective use of e-learning requires, in most if not all cases, well-designed combinations of blended learning and that its use has some implications for the role of HRD professionals. These last two points are the subject of some debate and so e-learning still retains some controversies. We will identify what those are and examine some of them next, before speculating on the future of e-learning in the final section.

Activity

Work in pairs. Visit the E-learning Network at www.elearningnetwork.org/ for some ideas and links to best practice guides and the Centre for Learning and Performance Technologies at www.c4lpt.co.uk/index.html for a useful introductory guide to e-learning and links to e-learning tools.

Think about the following questions and then discuss your answers with your colleague.

1 Which contexts of HRD practice do you think are most relevant for the use and application of e-learning?

2 What reasons might there be to explain a slowdown in the use of e-learning?

3 The CIPD survey reports some employers ceasing to use e-learning. What do you think might explain their decision?

4 How might the skills of an effective e-moderator differ from those of an effective face-to-face trainer or tutor?

Debates and controversies

We have already seen that defining e-learning is a matter of some debate and controversy. This is related in part to the differing views on the extent to which e-learning represents a radical new departure in HRD practice or is simply a continuation of established approaches under the wider approach of open and distance learning. Our view here is clearly in support of the latter. This view receives some support from the work of Sambrook (2003) and her colleagues (Sambrook et al., 2001). Work by these researchers on the use of e-learning by employees shows first that attitudes towards and confidence in learning per se and then specific learning materials in particular and finally e-learning as an approach influence responses to and effectiveness of e-learning. In other words, e-learning is not seen by learners as a radical or significant departure from previous learning experiences by learners themselves. A second finding of this research is that a range of factors common to most approaches to and methods of learning influence learners' responses to and the effectiveness of e-learning. The most significant of these factors was found to be 'user friendly'. That factor might be applied to any form of learning experience but it is certainly one that has been applied for many years in open and distance learning. A final outcome of this work was use of the notion of 'getting in, getting on, getting out'. As applied to e-learning, this refers to ease of entry to the materials, engaging with the materials and exiting the materials. Again, this notion could be applied to most if not all forms and approaches to HRD practice. But it clearly applies to all open and distance learning materials.

Another focus of debate and controversy is the extent to which practice is led by the 'e' or by the 'learning' of e-learning. We saw earlier that many professionals believe that growth in the use of e-learning was in part driven by vendors, suggesting that technology rather than learning principles led the development of e-learning. A recent focus of this debate has been on what are referred to as 'learning objects'. These are the 'stuff' of e-learning and have been subject to international attempts to set technical standards by intergovernmental agencies. Friesen (2004), an educationalist, makes a strong argument based on three objections against the process adopted to set these standards. The objections are:

1   the difficulty in specifying a learning object from a purely technical perspective

2   a challenge to the assumption that learning objects and related technical standards can be pedagogically neutral

3   the undue (according to Friesen) influence of the US military/industrial complex in intergovernmental agencies and the standard setting process.

Friesen's basic argument is that the case of standards for learning objects is illustrative of the development of e-learning being led by technology and technical specialists rather than by educational, HRD and learning specialists. No doubt technology specialists will take a different view, but Friesen does show that there is debate and controversy over the emphasis on and significance of e-learning.

The work by Sambrook (2003) cited earlier highlights two further areas of debate and controversy. The first of these is the costs and benefits of e-learning. Sambrook argues that the full costs are almost impossible to establish and so therefore is any worthwhile cost–benefit analysis. Evaluation of HRD activity is always difficult (see Chapter 7) but, according to Sambrook, this is particularly true of e-learning. However, there is a well-established view that e-learning brings cost savings and learning benefits. Similar arguments on cost savings and learning benefits have been made in the past for new technologies in open and distance learning but with very little evidence to support them (Stewart and Winter, 1994). It seems that this is another continuing thread connecting e-learning to previous approaches to HRD practice. A second debate centres on the issue of trust. Many e-learning platforms have a monitoring function that enables the activity, engagement and progress of individual users (learners) to be checked by those with administrative access to the system. The extent to which such functionality is utilized signals the level of trust, or otherwise, placed by the provider of e-learning in individuals using the programmes. We can say from personal experience that, in the leisure retail industry, e-learning programmes to deliver food hygiene training are sold with the monitoring function as a major selling point. The issue of trust is also related to the notion of learner autonomy in open learning since any degree of monitoring suggests a low level of learner autonomy.

The discussion of trust raises two final and related controversial issues. The first is the potential for control and standardization presented by e-learning. A claimed benefit is to guarantee that all learners receive and so experience the same learning. This claim is questionable on the grounds that individuals are unique and so experience the same phenomena differently and uniquely. The more important point is the desirability of attempting to achieve standardization. Related to this is the role of the HRD professional and the extent to which it is desirable that this includes monitoring, control and standardization. Answers to this question may vary from context to context, for example a lecturer in a university may take a different view to an employee development officer in a commercial work organization. However, it is a question that arises when considering the use of e-learning and one likely to generate much debate.

Reflective questions

1 What for you are the main areas of controversy in e-learning?

2 Given such controversy, why do you think e-learning has proved so popular?

These topics of debate and controversy highlighted here are by no means exhaustive and there are others within research and practice of e-learning. Most will continue into the future. New topics may emerge as e-learning and in particular the use of new technologies continue to develop. We will now turn our attention to speculating on those developments.

Current and future developments

We have seen that a wide range of HRD contexts have adopted e-learning. The spread of contexts is likely to continue in the future, in part influenced by new technological possibilities. E-learning is already used in all levels of education and in all types of work organizations as well as at societal levels. Three contexts that could encompass its use to greater degrees in the future are first within communities, second among voluntary and social groups and third by individuals for their own personal development. No doubt some use in these contexts already happens. What we are suggesting here is that these contexts will be areas of future growth in use.

This growth will be facilitated by technology. Two current developments are likely to be significant. The first is the emergence of social networking enabled by Web 2.0 technology within the internet. A key feature of this is the ability of individuals and groups to build and control their own networks. Some sites that utilize Web 2.0 such as Second Life are already being used by universities for educational purposes. But the same technology enables communities and voluntary and social groups to utilize the same systems for their own purposes, which are likely to include learning and development at some point. What is likely to facilitate more individual and personal use is technology that enables what is referred to as 'm-learning' (mobile-learning). As Sambrook (2003) identifies, m-learning is likely to grow in the future and the argument here is that this will lead to a greater use of e-learning by individuals for their own personal learning and development.

These speculations are based on current knowledge of current technologies. What is not conjecture is that by the time these speculations are read, technologies and applications of existing technologies not currently known will have emerged and they may lead to different developments. However, as with existing e-learning, the developments are unlikely to represent radical or new departures in the essence of HRD practice or the ways in which people learn.

This chapter has explored the origins and development of e-learning as well as the meaning of the term. A clear conclusion to be reached is that e-learning is not a universal panacea for all HRD needs and that it cannot provide a solution to all HRD problems. That said, e-learning does have relevance to a wide range of contexts of HRD practice. Gaining benefit from its application in those contexts is more likely to be achieved by adopting well-researched principles of effective learning, in particular those which have been established in open and distance learning. There is a danger, however, that technology and the work of technical specialists will have greater influence than HRD professionals and other learning specialists. The role, contribution and influence of these two groups are only one of many debates and controversies within the research and practice of e-learning. Debates and controversies are likely to continue and to be added to as new possibilities emerge through new technologies and applications. These are also likely to open up different contexts of practice to e-learning systems and programmes. In summary, we might say that e-learning has brought some benefits to HRD practice and has potential to bring more. But realizing and achieving that potential is by no means automatic or guaranteed.

Summary

- E-learning is a relatively new approach to and method of HRD practice.

- It can be seen as a continuation of well-established approaches within the wider approach known as open and distance learning.

- Effective use of e-learning requires the application of sound learning principles that are relevant to all forms of HRD practice.

- The principles developed in open and distance learning are of particular relevance.

- There is a strong case based on research and practice that e-learning should always be combined with other methods through blended learning.

- E-learning has implications for the role of HRD professionals and in particular that associated with the claimed new role of e-moderator.

- The use and application of e-learning generates a lot of debate and controversy, which are likely to continue as new approaches such as m-learning become established.

Discussion questions

1 What are the arguments for and against viewing e-learning as a radical new departure in HRD practice?

2 What are the key possibilities and limitations of e-learning?

3 What are the key implications of e-learning for the role of HRD professionals?

4 What are the key issues involved in the control and monitoring capabilities of e-learning for learners?

5 What are the key issues for HRD professionals arising from the same capabilities?

6 What further debates and controversies do you anticipate from the application of e-learning in different contexts and from new technologies?

Further reading

Bates, A. (2005) *Technology, E-learning and Distance Education*, London, Routledge.

Carr-Chellman, A.A. (2005) *Global Perspectives on E-learning: Rhetoric and Reality*, London, Sage.

Garrison, D.R. and Anderson, T. (2002) *E-Learning in the 21st Century: A Framework for Research and Practice*, London, Routledge.

Salmon, G. (2004) *E-moderating: The Key to Teaching and Learning Online*, 2nd edn, London, Routledge Falmer.

Sloman, M. (2002) *The E-Learning Revolution: How Technology is Driving a New Training Paradigm*, New York, Amacom.

References

Arbaugh, J.B. and Duray, R. (2002) Technological and structural characteristics, student learning and satisfaction with web-based courses: an exploratory study of two on-line MBA programmes, *Management Learning*, 33(3): 331–47.

Bonk, C.J. and Graham, C.R. (2006) *The Handbook of Blended Learning: Global Perspectives, Local Designs*, San-Francisco, CA, Jossey-Bass.

Brockett, J. (2008) Cruise firm 'raids' Siemens for ideas, *People Management*, September: 11.

Brown, L., Murphy, E. and Wade, V. (2006) Corporate e-learning: human resource development implications for large and small organizations, *Human Resource Development International*, 9(3): 415–27.

CIPD (Chartered Institute of Personnel and Development) (2003) *E-learning: The Learning Curve,* London, CIPD.

CIPD (Chartered Institute of Personnel and Development) (2004a) *Inclusive Learning for All*, London, CIPD.

CIPD (Chartered Institute of Personnel and Development) (2004b) *E-Learning Survey Results*, London, CIPD.

CIPD (Chartered Institute of Personnel and Development) (2008) *Annual Learning and Development Survey*, London, CIPD.

Friesen, N. (2004) Three objections to learning objects and e-learning standards, in R. McGreal (ed.) *Online Education Using Learning Objects*, London, Routledge.

McPherson, M.A. and Nunes, J.M. (2006) Organizational issues for e-learning: critical success factors as identified by HE practitioners, *International Journal for Educational Management*, 20(7): 542–58.

Mortera-Gutierrez, F. (2006) Faculty best practices using blended learning in e-learning and face to face instruction, *International Journal on E-Learning*, 5(3): 313–37.

People Management (2007) TK Maxx tries on e-learning, *People Management*, June.

Phillips, L. (2008) Online academies prove to be good call for 02, *People Management*, October.

Pollard, E. and Hillage, J. (2001) *Exploring e-Learning*, Report 376, Brighton, Institute for Employment Studies.

Salmon, G. (2004) *E-moderating: The Key to Teaching and Learning Online*, 2nd edn, London, Routledge Falmer.

Sambrook, S. (2003) E-learning in small organizations, *Education and Training*, 45(8/9): 506–16.

Sambrook, S. and Stewart, J. (2000) Factors influencing learning in European learning orientated organizations: implications for management, *Journal of European Industrial Training*, **24**(4): 209–19.

Sambrook, S., Geertshuis, S. and Cheseldine, D. (2001) Developing a quality assurance system for computer based learning materials: problems and issues, *Assessment and Evaluation in Higher Education*, **26**(5): 417–26.

Stewart, J. and Tansley, C. (2002) *Training in the Knowledge Economy*, London, CIPD.

Stewart, J. and Winter, R. (1994) Open and distance learning, in S. Truelove (ed.) *Handbook of Training and Development*, 2nd edn, Oxford, Blackwell.

SECTION 3 CASE STUDY

Talent management

The following two case studies provide examples of two different approaches to talent management.

Gordon Ramsay Holdings employs over 900 staff and the organization has restaurants in London, the USA and Europe as well as consultancies in Dubai and Tokyo. Gordon Ramsay is co-CEO (the other is his father-in-law). He works closely with restaurant personnel and identifies creative talent in the workforce. The emphasis within the organization is on developing talent rather than recruiting it in. As an example of this approach, the organization frequently places a home-grown senior chef in charge of a new restaurant. As part of the training for heading up a new restaurant, chefs are sent on a sabbatical to improve their cooking skills. These sabbaticals last between six and twelve months and usually involve working in prestigious restaurants outside the UK. Chefs are not required to return to the organization at the end of the sabbatical but most do.

SOURCE: CIPD (2007) *Research Insight, Talent Management*, London, CIPD, June: 5–6

M&G is the investment arm of Prudential plc with offices in the UK, Europe and South Africa. The nature of fund management means that the flows of funds often follow individuals, who can attain high-profile status but can also lose it, which can then damage the business. The company has developed coaching as a key part of its talent management strategy. The training and development team works directly with individuals, line managers and the HR team to determine development needs on an ongoing basis. They provide a small internal coaching team who focuses on initial development diagnosis and then recommends a range of options including training, shadowing, secondment, mentoring and coaching. External coaches are also used to support individuals who are seen to have potential and are placed in new roles to develop their capabilities. These external coaches are a diverse group of experienced coaches with a variety of skills, background and expertise. The training and development team helps to identify relevant coaches for individuals but the coachee chooses their coach in order to ensure ownership of the coaching relationship. The relationship lasts until the coach and coachee agree that the objectives have been met.

SOURCE: CIPD (2007) *Research Insight, Coaching in Organizations*, London, CIPD, Oct: 11–13

1   Evaluate the key similarities and differences between these two approaches to talent management?

2   How effective is each approach at retaining talented individuals?

3   What other development initiatives might be considered to support these approaches?

SECTION 4 **LOOKING AROUND**
HRD IN DIFFERENT CONTEXTS

Contrasting Contexts of HRD Practice

Vivienne Griggs and Rick Holden

15

Chapter learning outcomes

After reading this chapter, you should be able to:

- Understand the nature and characteristics of the voluntary/community sector and the small and medium-sized enterprise (SME) sector within the UK economy

- Explore the critical features of these two sectors in relation to HRD

- Assess the positive and negative forces influencing HRD practice in these organizational contexts

- Reflect on key issues affecting a more strategic, planned and focused approach to HRD within these organizational contexts

Chapter outline

Introduction

The voluntary and community sector: the 'third' sector

Challenges and opportunities for HRD in the third sector

HRD in SMEs

Small business learning

Summary

Introduction

> The most valued knowledge for HR management is likely to come from learning to apply HRM theories and techniques in particular organizational contexts. (Tyson, 1999, p. 51)

Much research on HRD has focused on large private sector organizations. To what extent can this be applied to organizations operating in different organizational contexts? What impact do the size, sector and ownership of a business have on its learning and development strategy? The range of contexts is considerable. Some commentators argue that the differences between sectors such as service and manufacturing are of great interest. The significance of cross-cultural management and the public sector are further examples and indeed these are acknowledged elsewhere in this book. It is beyond the scope of one chapter to address all potential contextual factors. Our focus is more modest. We address two organizational settings: the voluntary and community sector, and SMEs. These are underrepresented in the literature and present a challenging and distinctive context for HRD. Through attention to these two contexts, we aim to highlight that important differences do exist and to provide detailed, critical illustration in order that the implications for a 'contingency' approach to HRD practice are identified and captured.

Reflective questions

1 If you were to observe the management of people in a large retail store, an environmental charity and a small plumbing firm, what similarities and differences would you expect to see?

2 How might these impact on HRD in each of these organizations?

The voluntary and community sector: the 'third' sector

The voluntary sector within the UK describes businesses that are not owned by the government or private individuals in order to make a profit. Terms such as the 'charity sector', the 'not-for-profit sector' and the 'third sector' are often used interchangeably. Peter Drucker, the influential management writer, refers to it as the 'social sector'. The sector includes organizations registered with the Charity Commission, as well as a wide variety of others, including housing associations, places of worship, trade unions, sports and recreation clubs, and small voluntary groups. Definitions have been widely discussed (Salamon and Ahneier, 1992; Billis and Glennerster, 1998; Myers and Sacks, 2001; Parry et al., 2005) and yet there is still a lack of consensus (Blackmore, 2004). Kendall and Knapp (1995) described it as a 'loose and baggy monster' – reflecting the diversity and difficulty of categorization. While acknowledging this complexity and the imprecise boundaries, for the purposes of this chapter, we will use the UK government's definition of the sector. The Cabinet Office created the Office of the Third Sector in May 2006, and proffers the following description (www.cabinetoffice.gov.uk/third_sector/about_us.aspx):

The third sector is a diverse, active and passionate sector. Organizations in the sector share common characteristics:

- non-governmental

- value-driven

- principally reinvest any financial surpluses to further social, environmental or cultural objectives.

The term encompasses voluntary and community organizations, charities, social enterprises, cooperatives and mutuals both large and small.

In the UK, the Department for Business, Enterprise & Regulatory Reform (BERR) has principal responsibility for the sector (see www.berr.gov.uk/bre/benefits/third-sector/page44021.html for further information on the third sector).

The importance of the third sector

According to Clark (2007), there are 600,000 paid employees in the third sector, accounting for 2.2% of the UK workforce. The sector has grown by nearly 80,000 employees (14.9%) since 2000, and commentators suggest that there are no signs of this growth in size and significance slowing down (Reichardt et al., 2007). The rate of increase (26%) has been much higher than that of the private sector (11%) and the public sector (14%) (NCVO, 2006). In what Salamon (1994) refers to as 'associational revolution', he positions this growth of the sector in a wider global picture, not just in the UK.

The following are some statistics relating to the third sector (Cabinet Office, 2008):

- Total public funding (from local and central government) reported by the voluntary and community sector has doubled from less than £5bn in 1996–97 to more than £10bn in 2004–05

- Since 2004, the government has invested more than £350m in the capacity of the third sector to respond to people's needs through specific programmes

- In 2004–05, the UK's charity sector had a total income of about £27.6bn, an increase of over £800m from the previous year, representing about 2% of the UK's GDP

- The number of registered charities rose from around 120,000 in 1995 to more than 164,000 in 2005, and there are also hundreds of thousands of small community groups

- There are around 55,000 social enterprises, and indications that the numbers are rising

- Research in 2003–04 found that 56% of third sector organizations reported an increase in activity in the previous year, and 67% of them expected activity to grow in the next three years.

The growth of the third sector has been partly due to changes in government strategy. The increase in the number of organizations in the voluntary sector started in the 1980s with the introduction of care in the community (Community Care Act 1990), which moved from public provision in hospitals to providers from public, private and voluntary organizations. This has further developed with the Labour government's focus on partnership working. Kendall (2003) suggests that it is linked to almost 20 years of public sector delivery being contracted out by local and central government. This mixed economy of care has therefore resulted in a change in funding arrangements for voluntary organizations, which now receive their financial support in large part from the public sector. This in turn has implications for the management of the organizations as they are required to tender for services and are subject to performance measures on these contracts. Consequently, voluntary organizations are competing with public and private sector companies for the funding.

One implication of the change in practice from an annual block grant to the purchasing or contracting out of specific services is that voluntary organizations are increasingly tendering for contracts to carry out pieces of clearly defined work with specific performance standards (Courtney, 1994). Government funding is targeted in particular areas to support the political agenda. Public service agreements set out the government's priorities, funding for projects will be targeted at these and therefore changes in the government's priorities will influence the funding available for different voluntary sector organizations or projects. Hence, in the same way public sector organizations are shaped by the political agenda, the altered approach to the provision of funding to voluntary organizations means that they are also subject to greater political influence.

Distinctive characteristics

Clearly, some of the management issues will be common across all types of organization, whether they are in the public, private or voluntary sector. Parry et al. (2005) suggest that HRM in the voluntary sector may have similarities to the public sector because of the lack of profit motive and the employees' commitment to the organization's aims. Some studies have started to look at HRM in the sector but few have specifically examined HRD. From the literature, we have identified some characteristics that are relevant to the learning climate of the organization:

- *A mixed workforce:* One of the defining characteristics of the sector is the large numbers of volunteers working alongside the paid workforce. The majority of voluntary sector organizations continue to rely heavily on volunteers. The *2005 Citizenship Survey* estimates that 11.6 million people formally volunteer at least once a month in England (Kitchen et al., 2006), which has a fundamental impact on the nature of management. In terms of learning and development, surveys show a mixed approach to the voluntary workforce, with some organizations concentrating their efforts solely on paid employees. Trustees of voluntary organizations are also volunteers and this further complicates workforce dynamics. Walton (1996) highlights a gap in HRD literature to the learning needs of non-employees.

- *Culture:* It is claimed that the sector has a distinctive culture due to the participative forms of decision making and the values linked to the particular cause or mission of the organization (Cunningham, 2001). If staff choose to work in these organizations because they believe in their aims, intrinsic motivation may be more of a driver than extrinsic rewards. This has an impact on the psychological contract of employees, and the normal exchange process of employment is fundamentally altered. A unitarist style of operation is a potential corollary of this.

- *Complexity of stakeholders:* Billis and Glennerster (1998) discuss multiple stakeholders as a dominant characteristic and stakeholder ambiguity as a key distinguishing feature of voluntary agencies. In an organization with a profit motive, a clear exchange process is often evident. Good performance may be linked to increases in pay, and organizational objectives may be achieved through a range of financial incentives. Employees therefore have a clear understanding of the traditional management relationship and are accountable to the shareholders/owners of the business. In voluntary organizations, accountability is often to a number of different groups, further exacerbated by the public sector relationship outlined above. This is supported by the experience of Tony Lee, the ex-operations director for Nat West and subsequently chief officer for the Muscular Dystrophy Campaign, who claims that the contrast between the sectors is that the commercial world is much simpler as there are far fewer stakeholders (Hill, cited in Myers and Sacks, 2001).

- *Management processes:* Kellock Hay et al. (2001) talk about the 'unique sectoral characteristics that can complicate the management process'. Issues they highlight, such as resource scarcity and diverse stakeholder objectives, will impact on learning and development processes in these organizations. The complexity of decision making and the management by committees often typical of these organizations can make decision making a long and complex process. The highly individualistic characteristics and the value-led nature may influence the way people are managed (Armstrong, 1992). This is likely to provide a wide diversity of approaches. The management role held by trustees also presents something of a dichotomy. Managers of organizations are employed by the trustees but have an interest in ensuring the development of appropriate knowledge and skills. As a group of volunteers, often difficult for organizations to recruit, there may be real learning and development issues for these roles. Diplomatic handling of the relationship will be required.

- *Resources:* By their nature, these operations are lean in terms of overheads, budgets are tight and spending needs to be clearly justified. Although employee costs can total up to 70% of a voluntary organization's budget, people management in the sector has traditionally taken a back seat to the more pressing concerns of fundraising and delivery (Zacharias, 2003). The range of financial sources also tends to be greater than in other sectors and funding streams may be irregular and unpredictable, making long-term planning difficult (Armstrong, quoted in Parry et al., 2005).

Reflective question

What impact do you think the distinctive characteristics discussed above are likely to have on learning and development in such organizations?

Challenges and opportunities for HRD in the third sector

Evidently, some of these distinctive features create a challenge for HRD. From an internal perspective, we will consider resources/funding for training, the role of learning and development, and workforce and stakeholder diversity. External influences present additional challenges and following consideration of these, HRD in Practice 15.1 outlines one particular charity facing a number of obstacles to the development of a more strategic approach to training and development, while HRD in Practice 15.2 discusses a voluntary organization where the level of learning has been maximized as a pathway towards achieving its organizational goals.

Internal challenges

In their investigation of change management in the voluntary sector, Kellock Hay et al. (2001) identified the lack of time and resources for training as a barrier to change. Parry et al. (2005) found that finding money for training can be problematic in the voluntary sector as it cannot be budgeted for in service contracts. The timescale for the payback of learning and development may be an issue linked to the nature of funding. If contracts are short term, investment in longer term learning and development initiatives may be difficult to justify. One consequence of budgetary constraints is that training is often supply driven rather than demand led. Organizations will undertake training when grants or subsidies are offered, but this opportunistic approach to training makes a strategic approach difficult to achieve.

Research shows that over two-thirds of voluntary sector SMEs do not have a dedicated HR specialist (Newsome and Cunningham, 2003). A strong commitment from trustees and managers to learning and development may overcome this lack of specialist skills, but in some organizations, there is a lack of recognition of the value of training and development. This may be an indication that the training and HR needs of these employees are not being met.

The complexity of stakeholders and workforce diversity are clearly significant for HRD. Training needs will be at three levels: the trustees, the paid workforce and the volunteers. In the charity area, Bruce (cited in Harrison, 2005) identified leadership training at board level as a major priority, because of the importance of boards in ensuring:

- effective strategic planning and marketing
- skills development plans incorporating a wide range of learning approaches, including coaching, mentoring and peer group learning, are in place
- the promotion of a learning culture
- operational managers are skilled in their people management and development roles.

The issue of voluntary workers is highlighted by Walton (1996), who argues that this group is often overlooked in the HRD literature.

External challenges

These are some of the external challenges:

- *Employment legislation:* Externally driven change, such as increases in employment legislation, necessitates training to ensure compliance in these areas.

- *Recruitment and retention problems:* 'The Social Care Employers' Consortium is lobbying central government for increased resources so that the sector can recruit, retain and train the professional staff it needs' (Zacharias, 2003).

- *Competing for talent with the private and public sectors:* The changes in the sector highlight a need to become more competitive. Courtney (1994) refers to a survey of voluntary organizations, which found that 60% of senior appointments were made from outside the sector, which he claims is an indictment of current management training within the sector.

- *Performance measurement:* The Treasury requires that organizations in receipt of public funds demonstrate value for money (Amos-Wilson, 1996), which has implications for the increasing number of organizations in this sector delivering publicly funded programmes.

- *Changing skill requirements:* The external changes to the sector are also changing the traditional skill requirements. Securing sustainable funding through a tender process and the management of performance measures linked to these contracts necessitate a more commercial orientation than has been required in the past. The interrelationships of different services provide new opportunities for networking and relationship management.

HRD in Practice 15.1

Learning and development at a mental health charity

A mental health charity provides support for vulnerable adults in a large UK city. There are approximately 60 paid employees and a similar number of volunteers. Volunteers are mainly counsellors and are required to have a recognized counselling qualification. Training and development for paid employees is inconsistent across the organization, as some managers have been proactive in this area, whereas others have had little involvement. In the past, staff have applied for 'whatever took their fancy'. Consequently, a small number who showed an interest have done lots of training – whether it was relevant or not

– and other people have chosen not to do any at all. Evaluation of training has been based on comment sheets completed at the end of the event.

The barriers to learning and development noted by the personnel officer include:

- The range of stakeholders: the clients, the staff, the executive committee, the local healthcare professionals, the funders (government and private bodies) and other partnership organizations (other charities and heathcare providers).

- The role of the personnel officer is process and procedurally driven, and there is no specific learning and development function.

- There is no senior support for HR, the personnel officer feeling that she is often ignored. The strategy is dominated by the chief executive who has a strong focus on service delivery but does not recognize the importance of learning and development.
- There is a strong counselling culture, in line with the services provided. This manifests itself in a strong people orientation, treating everyone as individuals. One symptom of this is a reluctance to adopt any generic HR policy, which has hampered a strategic approach to HRD.

Three drivers for change have begun to impact on the receptiveness of the organization to an HRD strategy:

- A staff satisfaction survey highlighted that people felt they weren't getting enough of the right sort of training.
- The appointment of a new senior director, who had previously worked in a larger social care charity with a strong training ethos.
- The government introduced a competitive tendering process for allocating funds to charity organizations. It is believed that staff skills, qualifications and experience will be considered as part of the selection criteria.

Source: Griggs and Holden (2008)

Activity

What steps would you take to improve the effectiveness of learning and development in the case of this mental health charity?

Opportunities for learning and development

Despite a number of potential barriers and constraints for learning and development in the voluntary sector, there is considerable evidence of good practice. For example, Clutterbuck and Dearlove (1996) cite the Royal National Institute for the Blind, which offers a comprehensive training programme for managers, including the option of taking a Certificate of Management Studies. Zacharias (2003) highlights a charity for the homeless in London called Broadway, which overcame recruitment difficulties by developing an 'intensive programme of core skills and on the job training'. Hill and Stewart (2000) identify a range of good practice in a youth and community work charity, where the very nature of the charity and its strong people focus appear to have a positive effect on HRD.

In fact, the distinctive qualities of the sector may themselves facilitate a learning culture. Beattie (2006) claims that there is greater evidence of caring behaviour in the voluntary sector, where these person-centred values may generate a more receptive learning climate. Studies of Knowledge Management projects show how vital culture and social relations are. Consequently, high levels of staff engagement could mark a commitment to continuous learning.

The diverse working relationships may present clear opportunities for the development of staff. In private organizations, individual performance is often rewarded despite attempts to encourage teamwork. Where the workers share a common goal linked to strong personal values, the approach to good performance is likely to be less individualistic. Collaboration in working practices could therefore lead to greater knowledge sharing and creation of ideas. The level of empowerment and commitment could indicate that self-directed learning is appropriate for trustees and other voluntary roles.

Partnership working with public and private sector organizations provides opportunities for learning networks and communities of practice. Public sector organizations working within the same domain, for example housing or child services, are likely to have common goals that should encourage collaborative working. Similarly, local charities are sometimes affiliated to a national charity and would therefore share best practice and learning: 'Networking and partnerships can play a major role in ensuring that advice, guidance and support are shared across the voluntary sector. Umbrella organizations have a key role to play in this process' (NCVO, 2006).

Development in the accreditation of courses offers an effective enhancement to organizations that do not have the budget to compete on salaries or fringe benefits. Volunteers are sometimes people who have been out of the workforce for a variety of reasons and the provision of work experience through volunteering may be a path into paid employment. This can be enhanced through training and qualifications. Opportunities for employees may also be attractive as part of an employment package that cannot compete with salaries of the private sector. Courtney (1994) states that voluntary organizations are a major employer of paid and unpaid people with low academic attainment and suggests that the development of NVQs could provide accreditation and hence recognition of their extensive skills and experience. It could be argued therefore that learning and development have a particular focus in this sector. Similarly, the importance of workplace learning (see also Chapter 9), rather than a reliance on formal training provision, may be a key feature for organizations without the budget for expensive training courses. HRD in Practice 15.2 describes a voluntary organization attempting to maximize learning as a pathway towards achieving its organizational objectives.

HRD in Practice 15.2

Home-Start Leeds

Home-Start Leeds is a family support charity providing support to parents with young children. The service involves recruiting and training volunteers to visit families at home who have at least one child under five to offer informal, friendly and confidential support. It is a locally managed scheme but affiliated to Home-Start, which provides the operating principles, guidance and support.

Home-Start Leeds is run by a group of 12 trustees, who are themselves volunteers and are responsible for the governance function in the scheme, which can involve providing leadership and direction and ensuring that legal requirements are met. They employ a team of approximately 20 paid staff and delegate to them the responsibility for the operational management of the scheme. One key job role is that of coordinator, whose responsibilities include the recruitment and training of volunteers, matching suitable volunteers to families requiring support, liaising with the appropriate statutory bodies in the area and obtaining sustainable funding for the scheme. The direct support for families is provided by a team of 200–300 volunteers. Trustees receive induction training from the chair of trustees and Home-Start, and ongoing guidance and support from other trustees and the scheme manager.

Paid staff have a four-week induction programme planned by their line manager and job shadow an existing member of staff for the first six weeks. Coordinators also undertake an introduction to counselling course as part of their initial training. All paid staff have a six-weekly support and supervision meeting with their line manager, when individual development plans are discussed. The emphasis is on a broad range of learning experience rather than formal training provision, so staff would be encouraged to read appropriate literature, identify sources of information and support, or discuss issues with members of internal and external networks.

Sharing of learning is encouraged and supported; all coordinators share an open-plan office and do not have computers on their desks, so there is a genuine emphasis on talking to each other as a means of problem solving. There are team meetings every two weeks to look at core elements of their work – as such, continuous professional development is embedded into their day-to-day operations.

Volunteers are required to undertake a mandatory 50-hour preparation course before they are matched to a family. This training is developed and delivered by the coordinators. One-to-one support is provided by the coordinators if participants require additional help. The course is accredited by Open College Networks and participants therefore have the option to go for assessment and receive a qualification. Further training is optional, although through monthly support and supervision meetings with coordinators, they would be referred to appropriate training if training needs are apparent. Those looking for a career path are often keen to attend but not everyone participates in ongoing training.

In addition, volunteers are encouraged to attend a range of events, for example guest speakers from other related organizations, such as Children's Centres, and are sent literature on relevant information and learning opportunities. There is also a mentoring scheme for volunteers so a new person would be matched with someone with greater experience to support their development. A further opportunity is a work experience programme, which is offered to volunteers who are working towards careers in social care and family support. They can apply for a six-month placement with the Home-Start team to broaden their experience. The work experience programme is funded by the LSC. A steering group has been established to focus on the ongoing learning and development of volunteers.

Home-Start Leeds has received IiP accreditation. One of the trustees with previous experience of IiP in a local authority suggested it might be beneficial for the scheme to consider. Due to the strong emphasis on development in the organization, they recognized the value of the opportunity for reflection and review offered by IiP but were initially discouraged by the cost. Because of the underrepresentation of voluntary organizations working towards IiP, funding was offered. There was a high level of participation in the review process and it triggered the work experience project.

Collaborative working is strongly encouraged; steering groups operate as a form of action learning sets to address key issues or new projects, and the workforce is well represented at external networks.

Source: Pemberton et al. (2008)

HRD is positioned strongly within Home-Start Leeds, although there is no formal training and development or HRD function. The case demonstrates a variety of learning initiatives and how these have been tailored to the particular context in which Home-Start operates.

Activity

From the HRD practice evident within Home-Start Leeds, draw out some illustrative examples of the issues discussed so far in this chapter.

We have identified some unique features of the voluntary sector, which impact on learning and development, providing both opportunities and potential barriers. However, the start of our discussion was the initial difficulty over definition of the sector and this is due in part to the wide diversity of companies and we must be careful therefore not to overgeneralize the characteristics. Paton et al. (2007) suggest that organizational domains such as housing or social welfare may have greater significance for management than whether the organization is private, public or voluntary. Clutterbuck and Dearlove (1996) suggest that size may be a more important determinant than sector, so a small computer training company will have more in common with a small charity than with a computer giant such as IBM. The influence of the size of business and the implications for HRD in SMEs is the focus of the rest of this chapter.

HRD in SMEs

To really succeed in an increasingly competitive climate, every small business manager needs to get the best from their employees. Despite the time pressures they face, no small business manager can afford to cut corners on training – either for their employees, or themselves. (John Denham, secretary of state for innovation, universities and skills, 2008, www.dius.gov.uk/news_and_speeches/press_releases/management)

Much of the literature on which our prevailing understanding about HRM and HRD is based reflects policy and practice in large organizations. However, over 60% of the UK's workforce are employed in organizations with fewer than 100 employees. It has become customary to talk about SMEs, as the alternative grouping to large organizations. The EU and the UK government regard a business with 250 or fewer employees as an SME.

SMEs are a significant component of the economy. Figure 15.1 indicates that at the start of 2006, SMEs accounted for more than half of the employment (58.9%) and turnover (51.9%) in the UK. Many commentators argue that it is useful to further disaggregate the SME grouping and talk of the importance of small businesses (0–49 employees). Figure 15.1 shows that small enterprises alone accounted for 47.1% of employment and 37.2 % of turnover.

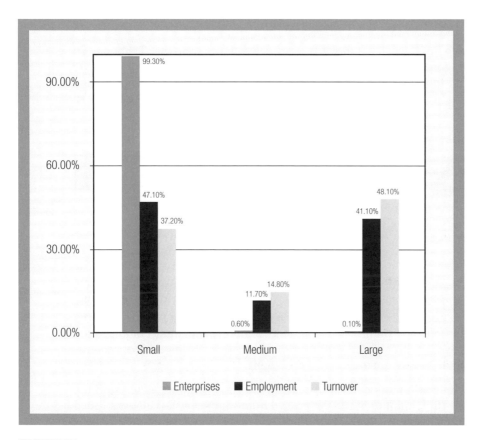

FIGURE 15.1 Share of enterprises, employment and turnover by size of business, 2006
SOURCE: BERR statistical press release, 2007

Given that there are so many of them, it is perhaps unsurprising that the SME sector features prominently in government thinking about economic growth and competitiveness. Suggestions of recurrent weakness in the UK's VET performance have implicated the small business sector for some time (Johnson, 1999; PIU, 2001; SBS, 2004; Johnson and Devins, 2008). While the indications are that the sector will continue to grow, a key feature of current government policy on workplace learning is the belief that the UK needs to 'raise its game' (Leitch, 2006) in terms of productivity and skills within SMEs. Recognizing the significance of the sector in terms of employment and its potential as a driver of future economic growth, the government has declared its goal to make the UK the best place in the world to start and grow a business (SBS, 2004).

We now explore the suggestion of apparent weaknesses in HRD within the SME sector, and the barriers and difficulties facing SMEs in relation to undertaking training and development are discussed. While official data on the level of training in SMEs present a cause for concern, there is a danger in how this is interpreted. We then explore an alternative view of HRD in SMEs: one that recognizes the potential for a significant level of ongoing learning closely related to the unique situation and needs of businesses within this sector.

A training paradox?

A range of research has indicated that size is a key determinant as to the likelihood of a firm undertaking formal training. For example, Matlay's (1999) research with over 6,000 SMEs found that over 85% of respondents from SMEs admitted to not having provided their workforce with any training over the previous 12 months (see Table 15.1).

TABLE 15.1 Provision of training by small businesses

Economic sector	No training (%)	Up to one day	2–3 days	4–5 days	6–10 days	Over 11 days
Manufacturing	86.37	6.72	1.75	1.56	0.29	3.31
Services	85.16	6.44	2.16	1.87	0.56	3.57

SOURCE: Matlay (1999)

While showing some improvement, more recent official statistics largely support Matlay's conclusions. According to data from the *National Employers Survey 2007* (LSC, 2008), establishments with 25 or more staff are much more likely to provide training, both on and off the job, than smaller establishments. Similarly, the smaller organization is less likely to have a training plan and training budget. Over one-third of organizations with less than 25 staff make any such provisions.

It is particularly interesting to look at how many SMEs have been accredited with the Investors in People (IiP) standard. It will be recalled from Chapter 4 that IiP, established in 1991, is the UK government's 'flagship' training and development standard (Hoque et al., 2005). Its objective is to assist organizations to improve business performance through enhanced HRD practice. However, as noted by Smith and Collins (2007), there would appear to be considerable doubts as to its value to the vast majority of SMEs. While 44% of organizations with 250 employees or more are IiP accredited, less than 2% of SMEs have this standard (www.iipuk.co.uk). A key conclusion drawn by Smith and Collins is that small firms 'are not standard' and there are real difficulties in matching IiP requirements with the individual requirements of SMEs.

Interestingly, while there are compelling data to suggest a lack of formal training provision, SMEs appear highly positive about the value and potential benefits of training. Over 90% of Matlay's respondents indicated a positive or very positive attitude towards training. An apparent paradox emerges – positive views about training yet no provision. Exploration of this paradox is revealing and offers insight into a more realistic assessment of HRD practice within SMEs. Two interrelated themes are critical: an understanding of the smaller business and an understanding of small business learning.

Understanding the small business sector

A degree of consensus has emerged over recent years, based on research within SMEs, that such organizations are complex. A complex scenario is compounded when we consider the nature of managing in a small business. Storey (1994), Johnson (1999) and Ashton and Sung (2001) all point out that far too often policy makers have not understood that a small business is not a small large business and that it is a mistake to apply large firm solutions to small enterprises. Hill and Stewart (1999) argue that managing in a small business is highly individualized and difficult to relate to any 'textbook' formula of the management of training and development.

TABLE 15.2 Characteristics of large vs. small firms

Large	Small
Long-term orientation	Short-term orientation
Predictive and planned business activity	Reactive and unplanned business activity
Annual budgetary planning	Weekly cash flow
Control and governance via board of directors	Dominance of owner/manager
Bureaucratic, hierarchical	Flatter, employees closer to 'boss'
Professional managers	Businesspeople
Likely to have HR specialists	Unlikely to have HR specialist
More likely to have a trade union	Less likely to have a trade union

Activity

Form a group of three or four. Consider Table 15.2 and think about your work experience. Have you worked in what we are calling an SME? What features of the organization can you recall that might be attributed to its size? Compare your experiences.

While acknowledging the danger of an overly simplistic generalization, Harrison (1997, p. 50) sums up the differences as follows:

> Management and development in the smaller as compared with the larger organization operates in context of more flexible labour, more individualized employment relationships, a clearer and shared perception of the primary goal and a greater awareness of the need for change.

These 'structural' factors create difficulties for SMEs in entering and making full use of the training market. A number of perceptions about available training make matters worse. These include concerns about:

- the cost of training

- the availability of directly relevant training

- uncertainty and ignorance about products such as NVQs and IiP (Matlay, 2004).

In response to such difficulties, there has been no shortage of publicly funded initiatives that have sought to help SMEs to access and engage in a greater level of training and development activity. However, the track record of such initiatives is not good. The case below provides some illustration of the problems encountered.

HRD in Practice 15.3

'Business as usual': the case of the learning broker

The Human Resource Development Unit within Leeds Metropolitan University was commissioned to do an independent evaluation of an initiative to enhance the demand for workplace learning among SMEs within the metal engineering sector in south Yorkshire. This sector is still significant in terms of employment and output in this region. The evaluation revealed constraints and weaknesses in the small business training market.

A number of interrelated problems combined to undermine the impact of the initiative:

- Many organizations simply brought forward training they were planning to do anyway. The existence of a training grant culture undermined the initiative. Companies appeared happy to chase a grant to assist with training needs already identified rather than engage in a more fundamental review of how training could play a role in medium-to-long-term business development.

- An evident tension existed between pressures on the broker to meet measurable, short-term targets and longer term organizational training and development needs. There were missed opportunities, for example for a broker-initiated consideration of systems of production and whether to move away from old trades in favour of more modern technology.

- The broker himself was an employee of the employers' body representing the businesses in this sector and thus his freedom of action to provide objective advice was compromised by his own position in the network of vested interests.

The researchers concluded that the relationship between small firms and some form of expert training intermediary was one that could be developed further in the future, but not without significant shifts in thinking in terms of levels, use and conditions attached to public monies allocated to enhance demand for skills within the small business sector.

For a fuller discussion of such issues, see, for example, Thursfield and Holden, 2004; Holden et al., 2006. Also visit the

Our discussion has sought to explain the relatively weak demand for formal training on behalf of the SME sector. It also provides some insight into the constraints facing publicly funded initiatives to enhance demand. However, our understanding of SME perceptions about, and practice of, HRD requires one further consideration.

Small business learning

In response to the apparent paucity of training activity within small businesses, a number of commentators (see, for example, Byrne et al., 2002) raise the issue of whether this is correctly identified as a lack of training or more a problem of definition. In other words, learning activity may well be taking place but be of a character and nature that does not sit comfortably with any commonly understood definition of formal training, that is, it is mainly off the job and provided by external sources. Hill and Stewart (2000) argue the need for alternative ways of understanding HRD in small businesses. A closer look at some of their research findings is valuable. They examined HRD policies and practice in three SMEs using a model of HRD that typically underpins IiP policy and practice as a benchmark. In the main, this confirms the sort of analysis highlighted earlier – a lack of formal training together with few formal systems to identify, access and evaluate training activity. However, Hill and Stewart suggest that closer scrutiny of what was happening in these SMEs reveals some interesting practice. One technical manager interviewed noted that workforce training and development activities were ad hoc, 'with a reliance on the *informal sharing of expertise* on the shop floor' (emphases added). The same manager suggested that mistakes were treated as 'learning opportunities' and employees were encouraged to make suggestions for improved working practice on the basis that 'they are the experts'. In another case, while no formal appraisal system operated, it transpired that all employees did participate in informal individual development interviews, which was felt to have a real impact in terms of morale and communication. Hill and Stewart (2000) wondered whether such practice was any less effective than the kinds of formal processes prescribed in the training and development texts, which supposedly characterize practice within the large firm paradigm. They argue that the nature of training and development in small firms mirrors the characteristics of the businesses themselves – 'both are essentially informal, reactive and short-term in outlook'.

As a result of the growing body of research, Gold and Thorpe (2008) suggest there is a growing recognition that 'informal learning should be given prominence'. They note that the government's 2004 action plan for small business (SBS, 2004), which seeks to provide a more 'joined up service', is attempting to stimulate demand and work with informal learning. They cite the Council for Excellence in Management and Leadership (CEML, 2002) as providing a valuable guiding theme. CEML argues the need for any intermediary, broker or support agency to 'join the SMEs in their world'. A useful instrument developed by the CEML is the Business Improvement Tool for Entrepreneurs (BITE) (CEML, 2002). Essentially, the tool is an instrument for a business conversation. Used in this way, the tool can be seen as a facilitator of dialogue, free of jargon. The tool is composed of short questions, under the headings of:

- decisions, strategies and setting goals

- creating personal drive

- communicating with others

- motivating others

- delegating to others

- winning business

- developing systems and procedures.

Any trainer seeking to make use of BITE needs to familiarize themselves with the seven sections and use them flexibly and sensitively as the conversation develops.

Research on the use of BITE (see, for example, Davis, 2003; Devins and Gold, 2003; Holden et al., 2006) has indicated that the tool can play a role in developing a depth of understanding about small businesses and the role of learning, broadly defined, as a contributor to business success. HRD in Practice 15.4 provides an illustration.

HRD in Practice 15.4

Learning at Doctor Wu's

According to the *Lonely Planet (England) Travel Guide*, Doctor Wu's in Leeds is a 'funky little bar ... somewhere to escape the craziness of the city and revel in the laid back atmosphere'. The bar hosts live music most nights. Steve, Ben and Rick (Ben's father) established the business in 2003. For 18 months or so, Steve and Ben ran the bar on a day-to-day basis with the help of a full-time bar manager and 12–15 part-time employees – mostly students or recent graduates 'deferring their career plans'.

Although the bar seemed to be doing well – packed out on Fridays and Saturday nights – the accounts were more sobering; a small loss in 2003–04 turned into a bigger loss in 2004–05. This was unsustainable. Conscious of the need to do something, the directors rather haphazardly looked around for simple solutions. Open longer? Open shorter? Do food? Get some business coaching? The latter looked potentially helpful – focused and one on one – but was simply too expensive. The business was introduced to BITE by a colleague of Ben's father at the university. BITE got them beyond the day to day. Discussion developed on how the business could ensure survival and generate some growth.

Three issues emerged as crucial: the ability of the business to provide a return to three directors, sales growth and wastage. Steve favoured selling, while Rick and Ben wanted to keep going. Rick began to address certain strategic issues, and Ben thought carefully about the week-by-week work. Rick had an 'informal' discussion with their accountant and the bank. He also had long chat with his brother – himself an accountant. Ben sought to tap his network – reps, suppliers, ex-tutors from college. An experienced restaurateur for whom Ben had worked on and off during school and university was particularly helpful in highlighting a number of 'tricks of the trade'.

Over the course of six months, the following actions were put into practice:

- Ben and his father 'bought out' Steve.
- A dual pricing mechanism (via a membership scheme) was introduced to maximize revenue on busy nights.
- The bar was refurbished, in part to maximize the available space.
- Reps were invited in to talk to staff about the products, the best ways to serve (minimize waste) and so on and to help organize special nights (a rum night, a whisky night).
- A 'no wage' placement student was recruited to manage sound and acoustics.

The weekly staff meeting introduced by Ben was revelatory. Staff took on different responsibilities, for example for particular nights of the week in terms of type of music, overseeing a limited snack menu, and graphic art and design for promotions. It became increasingly noticeable that the staff were a close bunch – reliable, hard working and sharing a strong identification with the bar and its ethos. Most of them helped out with the refurbishment in September 2005 for nothing.

Financially, turnover increased, and in 2005–06 the business broke even and subsequently generated a small profit in 2006–07.

Source: Holden and Walmsley (2007)

There is minimal evidence of 'training' in this case, but it is instructive to speculate on the role of learning in assisting the business to recover from its precarious position in 2005.

Reflective questions

1 Is there evidence of learning taking place at Doctor Wu's?

2 How would you seek to describe the characteristics of any learning that you can identify.

BITE was no panacea for the difficulties faced by Doctor Wu's, but it did provide the directors with a valuable insight into the business, which, combined with effective integration of work and learning on a day-to-day, week-by-week basis, rather than any formal injection of training, enabled the business to survive and grow.

Clearly there is a need to recognize and emphasize the importance of 'informal' learning and the case study reinforces this point. Research has also begun to shed light on the characteristics of this 'informal' learning. Drawing on the influential work of Lave and

Wenger (1992) in terms of 'situated learning', Raffo et al. (2000) explore how entrepreneurs operate in the cultural industries – media, fashion design, publishing and so on. They conclude that most small business learning occurs through the 'interactions of individuals' in day-to-day practice and is firmly located within the working context: 'Practical business knowledge is not easily developed in formalized external training contexts away from the reality of a trainee's business experience and activity' (Raffo et al., 2000, p. 219).

The authors note the importance of networks for small businesses. The significance of networks has been recognized in the literature for some time (see, for example, Blundel and Smith, 2001; SBS, 2002). However, it is only relatively recently that researchers have begun to focus on this point in the context of learning (Taylor and Thorpe, 2000; Saquet, 2000; Anderson et al., 2001). There is evidence in Taylor and Thorpe's research of a social dimension to small firm owner/manager decision making that appears to be significant, challenging the view that the owner/manager's learning might be more akin to operating as an 'intellectual Robinson Crusoe'. Taylor and Thorpe (2000) also draw particular attention to the importance of social networks outside work or business-related contexts.

Conceptually, Theodorakopoulos and Wyer (2001) have developed a model that usefully captures this emerging understanding. The basis for their model is that small business learning is messy, untidy and fraught with difficulties. Networking is an integral part of small business learning – learning is 'built' through relationships. This includes interface with key 'others' as diverse as customers, suppliers, the bank and the accountant. Closer to home, key relationships are those with staff, and an owner/manager's friends and family. While some effective learning may result from 'fleeting interfaces', significant areas of understanding and insight often require the build up of a longer term, trusting relationship. The authors argue that 'strategic' learning is likely to be evident when there is:

- a recognition of the need to nurture teamwork

- a willingness and ability, on behalf of the owner/manager, to constantly reflect on their view of reality, comparing this with those of key informants, and, on the basis of this, experimenting and trying out new things

- an ability to filter out the irrelevance of much formal, externally provided training and to integrate pertinent externally generated learning with existing, subjective experience-based understanding.

In terms of an understanding of small business learning, the model, shown in Figure 15.2, powerfully illustrates the need for an in-depth understanding of the role of networks and networking activities within a highly specific context.

SMEs as learning organizations

Chapter 9 contains fuller discussion of ideas about organizational learning and learning cultures. Even if we could agree what such an entity looked like, it might be stretching the point somewhat to argue that Doctor Wu's is a 'learning company'. But perhaps we can begin to see why some commentators feel that a problem in the research and writing on organizational learning is a relative neglect of size. Hendry et al. (1995) suggest that

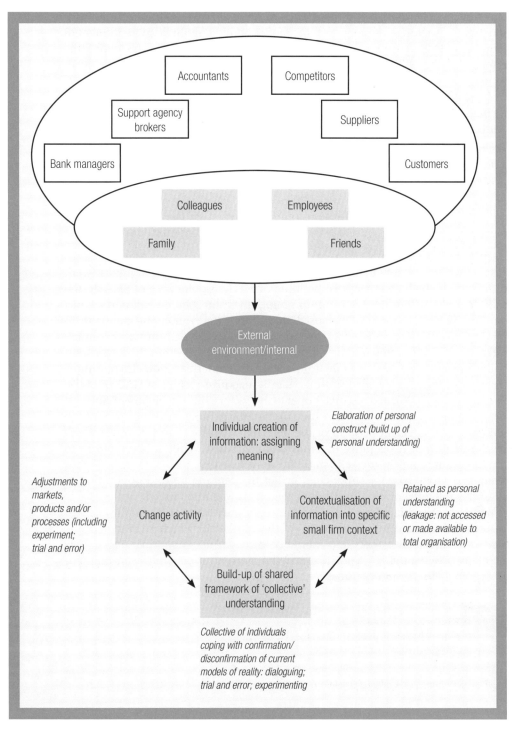

Text inside the figure:

Accountants

Competitors

Support agency
brokers

Suppliers

Bank managers

Customers

Colleagues

Employees

Family

Friends

External
environment/internal

Individual creation of
information: assigning
meaning

*Elaboration of personal
construct (build up of
personal understanding)*

*Adjustments to
markets,
products and/or
processes (including
experiment;
trial and error)*

Change activity

Contextualisation of
information into specific
small firm context

*Retained as personal
understanding
(leakage: not accessed
or made available to
total organisation)*

Build-up of shared
framework of 'collective'
understanding

*Collective of individuals
coping with confirmation/
disconfirmation of current
models of reality: dialoguing;
trial and error; experimenting*

FIGURE 15.2 A model of small business learning

SOURCE: Theodorakopoulous and Wyer (2001)

SMEs may have real learning advantages, such as more effective internal communications and that work teams – as bigger fish in smaller ponds – might be more influential in the learning of SMEs. Their research into adaptation and learning in SMEs lends some support for a view that SMEs, by virtue of their size, may find it easier to harness individual and team learning and translate this into organizational learning. This focus is consistent with the notions of integrating work and learning and tacit knowledge and learning (see also Chapter 9). Harrison (2002, p. 225) concludes that many SMEs have the potential to come close to a notion of the 'learning organization', albeit often 'subconsciously':

> They are fast, reactive, well informed about their external and internal environments, and foster a climate of continuous learning leading to the development of knowledge that is used to innovate and advance. They operate like this not necessarily because there has been any conscious decision to do so, or even an awareness that this is happening, but simply because it is in this way that those organizations thrive and manage to attract and retain high-calibre people.

In this section we have sought to discuss HRD practice in SMEs, clearly a highly different context from that which characterizes the large firm. The significance of SMEs to the skills policy agenda within the UK is not in doubt, given their relative importance as employers and potential sources of increased productivity, innovation and competitiveness. While conventional wisdom portrays a picture of weak demand and a much greater likelihood that training and development will be evident within the larger than the smaller business, we have sought to question this interpretation. Increasingly, research suggests that this paints an unnecessarily negative picture of HRD in SMEs. Johnson and Devins (2008), in a research paper to the Sector Skills Development Agency,[1] summarize the basis for this well when they argue that existing measures of training activity do not take sufficient account of the 'informal, flexible nature of much workforce development that takes place in small organizations'. While it is important to recognize the nature and character of small business learning, this is not to cede that there remains a strong case for enhancing further the demand for and application of skill within the SME workplace. Government rhetoric is well intentioned. However, it is practice that engages with, responds to and is directly relevant to SMEs that is likely to increase organizational demand for skills. If the market in which such practice is deployed is less driven by targets and more accommodating, supportive and understanding of the SME world, HRD practice and the learning it generates can add real strategic capability to the small business.

Summary

- We have addressed how our understanding of HRD might need to be sufficiently flexible and nuanced in order for us to appreciate its positioning and its contribution in alternative contexts to that of the large private firm. Our focus has been the voluntary and community sector and SMEs.

- While drawn from research in small businesses, Storey's (1994) words, 'a small business is not just a small large business', have a powerful ring to them for all alternative scenarios to the large private sector firm.

- Across the sectors, we have explored key differences, such as the absence of any specialist HRD position/function, short-term orientation, complexity of stakeholders, and nature of the workforce.

- Different and distinctive interpretations of HRD practice have been identified and illustrated, such as the power of informal learning, integration of work and learning, and collaborative learning.

- Critically, in terms of HRD practice, there is no neat formula that can be easily transferred from the large private firm into a charity such as Home-Start Leeds or a small business like Doctor Wu's. To say that no aspects of good practice are transferable would, of course, be nonsense. Rather, we have argued for sensitivity to context and how managers and employees face subtly different demands, are accustomed to different cultures and face different business pressures because of the context.

- Ultimately, HRD practice needs to be contingent on the situation if it is be most effective in supporting the development of individuals who work within such contexts and the organization as a whole. A number of the examples and case studies in the chapter clearly indicate that this is not just rhetoric, demonstrating how their brand and style of HRD and their approach to HRD practice can achieve the contribution to which all protagonists of HRD aspire.

Discussion questions

1 Identify four differences between a large private sector firm and either an organization in the voluntary/community sector and/or a small business. What implications do such differences have for the practice of HRD?

2 Why is the complexity of stakeholders in voluntary organizations relevant to learning and development?

3 Why did we question the prevailing evidence about the level of training and development undertaken by small organizations?

4 Why might there be a danger in encouraging a small business/charity to achieve the IiP standard? What benefits might IiP offer in this context?

5 Recall two examples where informal learning appeared to have real impact. Why do you think this was the case?

6 In what ways are Home-Start Leeds and Doctor Wu's similar and in what ways are they different? What do you feel is the critical characteristic of HRD in each of these organizations?

Further reading

Armstrong, M. (1992) A charitable approach to personnel, *Personnel Management*, December.

Bridge, S., O'Neill, K. and Cromie, S. (2003) *Understanding Enterprise, Entrepreneurship and Small Business*, Basingstoke, Palgrave Macmillan.

Harrison, R. (2005) *Learning and Development*, 4th edn, London, CIPD.

Hill, R. and Stewart, J. (1999) Human resource development in small organizations, *Journal of European Industrial Training*, **24**(2/3/4): 105–17.

Kellock Hay, G., Beattie, R., Livingstone, R. and Munro, P. (2001) Change, HRM and the voluntary sector, *Employee Relations*, **23**(3): 240–55.

Note

1   The Sector Skills Development Agency was established to support, develop and fund the UK's network of employer-led Sector Skills Councils (SSCs). However, following recommendations in the Leitch review, it was closed in 2007 and replaced by the UK Commission for Employment and Skills, with a brief to play a central role in raising the UK's skills base, improving productivity and competitiveness, increasing employment and making a contribution to a fairer society.

References

Amos-Wilson, P. (1996) Management training in UK NGOs: a small survey, *Journal of European Industrial Training*, **20**(1): 15–19.

Anderson, V., Boocock, G. and Graham, S. (2001) An investigation into the learning needs of managers in internationalising small and medium sized enterprises, *Journal of Small Business and Enterprise Development*, **8**(3): 215–32.

Armstrong, M. (1992) A charitable approach to personnel, *Personnel Management*, December.

Ashton, D. and Sung, J. (2001), *Lessons Learned from Overseas*, Centre for Labour Market Studies, University of Leicester.

Beattie, R.S. (2006) Line managers and workplace learning: learning from the voluntary sector, *Human Resource Development International*, **9**(1): 100–19.

Betts, J. and Holden, R. (2003) Organizational learning in a public sector organization: a case study in muddled thinking, *Journal of Workplace Learning*, **15**(6): 280–7.

Billis, D. and Glennerster, H. (1998) Human services and the voluntary sector: towards a theory of comparative advantage, *Journal of Social Policy*, **27**(1): 79–98.

Blackmore, A. (2004) *Standing Apart, Working Together: A Study of the Myths and Realities of Voluntary and Community Sector Independence*, London, NCVO.

Blundel, R.K. and Smith, D. (2001) Business networking: SMEs and inter-firm collaboration: a review of the literature, Sheffield, DTI/Small Business Service.

Byrne, J., Galt, V., Ibrahim, G. et al. (2002) *Barriers to Training in Small and Medium Sized Enterprises*, Centre for Growing Business, Nottingham Trent University.

Cabinet Office (2008) Key third sector statistics, www.cabinetoffice.gov.uk/third_sector/Research_and_statistics/Key_statistics.aspx.

CEML (Council for Excellence in Management and Leadership) (2002) *Joining Entrepreneurs in their World: Improving Entrepreneurship, Management and Leadership in UK SMEs*, London, CEML.

Clark, J. (2007) *The UK Voluntary Sector Workforce Almanac*, London, NCVO.

Clutterbuck, D. and Dearlove, D. (1996) *The Charity as a Business: Managing in the Public Sector, Learning from the Private Sector*, London, Directory of Social Change.

Courtney, R. (1994) Directions in voluntary sector management, *Management Development Review*, **7**(3): 33–6.

Cunningham, I. (2001) Sweet charity! Managing employee commitment in the UK voluntary sector, *Employee Relations*, **23**(3): 192–206.

Davis, M. (2003) Working with intermediaries to reach entrepreneurs, report prepared for CEML on piloting BITE, Centre for Enterprise, Leicester.

Devins, D. and Gold, J. (2003) Encouraging small business development and learning through intermediaries: initial findings from a pilot intervention, paper presented at British Association of Management Conference.

Gold, J. and Thorpe, R. (2008) Training, it's a load of crap: the story of the hairdresser and his suit, *Human Resource Development International*, **11**(4): 385–99.

Griggs, V. and Holden, R.J. (2008) Interview with mental health charity personnel officer, Leeds Metropolitan University.

Harrison, R. (1997) *Employee Development*, London, CIPD.

Harrison, R. (2002) *Employee Development*, 3rd edn, London, CIPD.

Harrison, R. (2005) *Learning and Development*, 4th edn, London, CIPD.

Hendry, C., Arthur, M. and Jones, A. (1995) *Strategy through People: Adaptation and Learning in the Small-medium enterprise*, London, Routledge.

Hill, R. and Stewart, J. (1999) Human resource development in small organizations, *Human Resource Development International*, **2**(2): 103–23.

Hill, R. and Stewart, J. (2000) Human resource development in small organizations, *Journal of European Industrial Training*, **24**(2/3/4): 105–17.

Holden, B.T. and Walmsley, A. (2007) *The Dr Wu's Story: Interview with Ben Holden*, Leeds Metropolitan University.

Holden, R.J., Nabi, G., Gold, J. and Robertson, M. (2006) Building capability in small businesses: tales from the training front, *Journal of European Industrial Training*, **30**(6): 424–40.

Hoque, K., Taylor, S. and Bell, E. (2005) Investors in people: market led voluntarism in vocational education and training, *British Journal of Industrial Relations*, **43**(1): 133–51.

Johnson, S. (1999) *Skills Issues in Small and Medium Sized Enterprises*, National Skills Task Force, Research Paper 13, Nottingham, DfEE.

Johnson, S. and Devins, D. (2008) *Training and Workforce Development in SMEs: Myth and Reality*, SSDA Catalyst, Issue 7, Sector Skills Development Agency.

Kellock Hay, G., Beattie, R., Livingstone, R. and Munro, P. (2001) Change, HRM and the voluntary sector, *Employee Relations*, **23**(3): 240–55.

Kendall, J. (2003) *The Voluntary Sector: Comparative Perspectives in the UK*, London, Routledge.

Kendall, J. and Knapp, M. (1995) A loose and baggy monster: boundaries, definitions and typologies, in J. Davis-Smith, C. Rochester and R. Hedley (eds) *An Introduction to the Voluntary Sector*, London, Routledge.

Kitchen, S., Michaelson, J., Wood, N. and John, P. (2006) *2005 Citizenship Survey: Active Communities Topic Report*, London, Department for Communities and Local Government.

Lave, J. and Wenger, E. (1992) *Situated Learning: Legitimate Peripheral Participation*, Cambridge, Cambridge University Press.

Leitch, S. (2006) *Prosperity for all in the Global Economy: World Class Skills*, London, HM Treasury.

LSC (Learning and Skills Council) (2008) *National Employers Survey 2007: Key Findings*, Coventry, LSC.

Matlay, H. (1999) Vocational education and training in Britain: a small business perspective, *Education and Training*, **41**(1): 6–13.

Matlay, H. (2004) Contemporary training initiatives in Britain: a small business perspective, *Journal of Small Business and Enterprise Development*, **11**(4): 504–13.

Myers, J. and Sacks, R. (2001) Harnessing the talents of a loose and baggy monster, *Journal of European Industrial Training*, **25**(9): 454–64.

NCVO (National Council for Voluntary Organizations) (2006) *The UK Voluntary Sector Almanac 2006: The State of the Sector*, London, NCVO.

Newsome, K. and Cunningham, I. (2003) More than just a wing and a prayer: Identifying human resource capacity among small and medium sized organisations in the voluntary sector, Department of Human Resource Management, University of Strathclyde.

Parry, E., Kelliher, C., Mills, T. and Tyson, S. (2005) Comparing HRM in the voluntary and public sectors, *Personnel Review*, **34**(5): 588–602.

Paton, R., Mordaunt, J. and Cornforth, C. (2007) Beyond nonprofit management education: leadership development in a time of blurred boundaries and distributed learning, *Nonprofit and Voluntary Sector Quarterly*, December: 148S–162.

Pemberton, A., Griggs, V. and Holden, R. (2008) *HRD within Home-Start Leeds: Interview with Ann Pemberton*, Leeds Metropolitan University.

PIU (Performance and Innovation Unit) (2001) *In Demand: Adult Skills in the 21st Century*, PIU, Cabinet Office.

Raffo, C., O'Connor, J., Lovatt, A. and Banks, M. (2000) Attitudes to formal business training and learning amongst entrepreneurs in the cultural industries: situated business learning through 'doing with others', *Journal of Education and Work*, **13**(2): 215–30.

Reichardt, O., Kane, D. and Wilding, K. (2007) *The UK Voluntary Sector Almanac: The State of the Sector 2007*, London, NCVO.

Salamon, L.M. (1994) The rise of the nonprofit sector, *Foreign Affairs*, **73**(3): 111–24.

Salamon, L. and Ahneier, H. (1992) *In Search of the Non Profit Sector 1: The Question of Definition*, working paper no 2, Baltimore, MD, Johns Hopkins University Institute for Policy Studies.

Sauquet, A. (2000) *Small Business Training and Competitiveness: Building Case Studies in Different European Cultural Contexts*, Brussels, European Commission.

SBS (Small Business Service) (2002) *Small Business and Government: The Way Forward*, www.sbs.gov.uk.

SBS (Small Business Service) (2004) *A Government Action Plan for Small Business: Making the UK the Best Place in the World to Start and Grow a Business*, www.sbs.gov.uk.

Smith, A.J. and Collins, L.A. (2007) How does IiP deliver the lifelong learning agenda to SMEs?, *Education and Training*, **49**(8/9): 720–31.

Storey, D.J. (1994) *Understanding the Small Business Sector*, London, Routledge.

Taylor, D. and Thorpe, R. (2000) The owner manager – no isolated monad: learning as a process of co-participation, paper presented at 23rd ISBA Conference.

Theodorakopoulos, N. and Wyer, P. (2001) Small business growth and the use of networks, paper presented at 24th ISBA Conference.

Thursfield, D. and Holden, R.J. (2004) Increasing the demand for workplace training: workforce development in practice, *Journal of Vocational Education and Training*, **56**(2): 289–305.

Tyson, S. (1999) How HR knowledge contributes to organisational performance, *Human Resource Management Journal*, **9**(3): 42–52.

Walton, J. (1996) The provision of learning support for non-employees, in J. Stewart and J. McGoldrick (eds) *Human Resource Development: Perspectives, Strategies and Practice*, London, Pitman.

Zacharias, L. (2003) Small change, *People Management*, **1**: 24–7.

Continuing Professional Development and Lifelong Learning

Jeff Gold and Joanna Smith

Chapter learning outcomes

After studying this chapter, you should be able to:

- Explain the meaning of continuing professional development (CPD) and lifelong learning (LL)

- Understand the key drivers for the necessity of CPD and LL

- Assess the benefits to individuals, society and groups and the economy, and the tensions between these

- Explain the nature of professional work and the various methods of CPD

- Assess the importance of LL and its practice

Chapter outline

Introduction

For a number of years now, it has become axiomatic that learning should not cease once individuals have completed their period of formal education and training; instead, it is important for everyone to become a lifelong learner. Although the idea of learning throughout life has a long pedigree, especially among liberal-minded educationists, during the last quarter of the 20th century and into the 21st, Green (2002, p. 611) suggests that lifelong learning (LL) has become a 'dominant and organizing discourse in education and training policy'. Bagnall (2000, p. 20) states that LL 'is now featured in practically every imaginable agenda for social change, educational policy preamble and mission statement'. Impetus in the 1990s was provided by the OECD (1996a) and the European Commission (EC, 1995) and along with other terms such as 'learning companies', 'learning regions' and 'learning societies' (Coffield, 2000a), LL became seen as a response to significant changes in the way work is practised and the rapidity with which such changes impact on practice, with the concomitant effects on the requirements for skills and learning – this is the 'speed of change' argument for LL (Tamkin, 1997). Allied to this is the recognition that economic success can no longer rely on large numbers of the workforce with basic skills; instead, there is a need for people to reskill in line with the requirements of work or to aspire to move into more highly skilled work. The importance of skills for productivity was recognized by the Leitch review (2006) and the UK government's response to the review (DIUS, 2007) and, crucially, it was recognized that the gaps in learning and skills were a principal reason for a failure by organizations to compete in global markets but also for individuals to participate in economic activity. Thus, we can see how the LL movement embraces an economic imperative to compete globally as well as to enhance and widen participation and inclusion of greater numbers in the workforce. The latter is part of the social cohesion argument for LL, where through the acquisition of skills, individuals become more employable and are able to find work to match their talents, thereby contributing to and benefiting from social and economic prosperity. Further, they have the ability to manage their lives throughout their lives, 'from the cradle to the grave' – referred to as the 'life cycle' argument for LL. In addition, learning can spread to all contexts of life such as home, community as well as work – part of the 'life-wide' argument (EC, 2001).

In many of these arguments for LL, much is made of the developments in knowledge-intensive work as part of the knowledge economy and knowledge society (Rohrbach, 2007). For growing numbers of workers, knowledge is vital to the process of work and also the main constituent of the output of work, whether as a tangible product or intangible service. Increasingly, work occurs in knowledge-based organizations employing knowledge workers (Newell et al., 2002). Professional workers especially are able to make claims for their expertise in particular fields of knowledge work and such workers are usually members of a professional body that protects and enhances their professional status, for example solicitors belong to the Law Society. As we will explain below, a key characteristic of professional work is the command of an underpinning body of knowledge. Therefore, in response to the rapid changes in such knowledge that is vital for the claim of expert status, it has become increasingly recognized that all professionals need to undertake continuing professional development (CPD). Professional bodies such as the Law Society and the Chartered Institute of Personnel and Development (CIPD) seek to engender LL for their members as CPD as a representation of good professional practice (Roscoe, 2002). As a consequence, there are now various policies, approaches and methods that enable, support and sometimes pressurize professionals to build on their qualifications by undertaking CPD. In this chapter, we will consider how this occurs. We will first revisit some of the key drivers for CPD and LL. We will then explore the importance of CPD for professional work and the methods used before extending our analysis towards LL.

Key drivers

As with all arguments presented, those made in favour of LL and CPD, as well providing facts, are also attempts to persuade people to do something about their learning. If we have entered the 'risk society' (Beck, 1992), we apparently must do something about our learning. Such arguments therefore have a rhetorical quality (Edwards, 2001). Nevertheless, few can doubt that there are significant and interconnected technological, economic and social changes that underpin the arguments. Change was the principal reason presented in the Fryer report (NAGCELL, 1997), although it is also interesting to note that the report was cautious about learning being seen as the only response to change. It was, however, crucial to the development of government policy on LL in the UK. Of course, throughout history, people have learned to cope with change and, even today, many people are able to deal with change without reference to policies for LL or CPD. Such informal learning still represents the most common form of learning in all forms of work practice, although it is quite possible to use informal learning more deliberately and consciously (see Gold et al., 2007).

Reflective questions

1 What is your response to the idea of the 'risk society'?

2 How do you feel about the prospect that you must consider learning for the rest of your life?

The key dimensions of change that impact all areas of work are:

- globalization
- competition and deregulation
- technology
- knowledge
- social
- political.

We will provide brief coverage of each with consideration to LL and CPD.

Globalization

Changes in the global economy such as the growth of world trade and market liberalization accompanied by highly mobile capital, labour and information (Scase, 1999) are consistently invoked as a rationale for LL. The emerging economies of India, China and others are seen as a reason for western nations such as the UK to invest more in higher level or 'world class skills' (Leitch, 2006) in order to compete and innovate. It is argued that low-skill work will decline, which risks feeding a growing division and polarization between those with skills who are able to participate in the provision of high value-added services as part of the knowledge-driven economy and those who cannot. What is referred to as an 'hourglass' structure appears to be emerging in the labour market, where large numbers of workers are employed in low-skill occupations at low pay, while others such as professionals and knowledge workers enjoy high pay in high-skill occupations (Campbell et al., 2001; Moynagh and Worsley, 2005). On the grounds of participation and avoidance of division, it becomes crucial to enable a movement into higher skilled work and this puts a significant onus on how products and services are specified in terms of skill requirements. Wilson and Hogarth (2003) assert that higher specification denotes a more advanced level of production systems, which in turn demands a higher skill intensity in production and a higher demand for skills.

Competition and deregulation

This is strongly connected to globalization, where many jobs have been exposed to low-cost competition. However, even among professionals, who traditionally enjoyed a degree of protection from competitive forces, there is now recognition that a response must be made. For example, professionals and professional firms like lawyers and accountants are able to compete with each other and market their services. For example, auditing was a traditional service offered by accountants but competition and technological developments forced down profits, making it a low-cost service that could be provided by less expert staff (Powell et al., 1999). As a consequence, many accountancy firms have sought to provide high value-added services through an offer of consultancy (Hanlon, 1997), a process that has also fed the development of a 'new' profession – management consultancy – although some might question the professional status of such a process (see below). There have also been significant developments in the legal profession, where a recent review in England and Wales encouraged competition and the removal of restrictive barriers so that consumers can benefit (Clementi, 2004). It allowed non-lawyers to become partners in law firms and envisaged that law firms could consist of a range of legal professionals such as solicitors, barristers, licensed conveyancers and others (referred to as 'legal disciplinary practices'), and, in future, different professions will be able to establish a firm (referred to as 'multidisciplinary practices').

Many professionals such as lawyers, accountants and architects work for a firm. Traditionally, where competition between professionals was not accepted, such firms were organized as professional partnerships (Greenwood et al., 1990), with professionals left to develop roles according to preferences but with little strategic direction from partners. It has been suggested that competition and deregulation require a more commercial and market-oriented approach, giving more emphasis to managing, planning and strategy. Thus, according to Cooper et al. (1996), a new archetype of professional organization emerged, referred to as the 'managed professional business'.

Technology

There has always been a link between learning and changes in technology. However, the application of the microchip to so many domains of employment has been a fundamental cause of the necessity for LL and CPD. What are loosely referred to as the 'new technologies' have had an ongoing impact on workplace organization, size, design and production of products and services, location of production, the employment relationship and contract and so on. Castells (1996) highlights probably the most important feature of the IT revolution, through ICT, as knowledge generation combined with processing and communication devices, with a feedback loop that enables accumulation and production of further innovations. Developments in emerging technologies such as biotechnology and nanotechnology not only provide the opportunity for new products and services but also are considered to be drivers of change requiring new and different forms of expertise. For example, there is the emerging profession of the nanoscientist with the Institute of the Nanotechnology (www.nano.org.uk/).

Knowledge

The generative capacity of ICT is a fundamental feature of the knowledge-based economy allowing innovation in ideas, products and services, facilitated by the creation of knowledge networks (OECD, 1996b) where geography and distance provide no barriers to the sharing of knowledge. The focus on knowledge gives more emphasis to the skills of workers who can be recognized as knowledge workers, a key source of any organization's intellectual capital (Stewart, 1997). As we will show below, most claims for expertise made by professionals and others are based on a command of knowledge, although there are different kinds of knowledge that must be considered. However, for now, we will focus on the knowledge made available through ICT. Thus professionals who need to update their understanding increasingly turn to online and electronic sources, in contrast to a reliance on printed journals and books. For example, lawyers working in the employment field are able to join a mailing list to obtain the latest decisions from tribunals, which will affect their service to clients. They can also download seminars as part of their CPD (www.cpdwebinars.com/).

While knowledge provides the basis for expertise, it also becomes more possible to reconfigure work around different combinations of expert knowledge. For example, an implication of nanotechnology is the need to form multidisciplinary teams of scientists, engineers and medical researchers to share knowledge and create new solutions. Increasingly, experts will need to work across disciplinary boundaries though dialogue and negotiation (Daniels, 2004). In addition, since the solutions to many basic problems are now available online, experts and professionals will need to learn from customers and clients on how to provide value-added services that cannot be found elsewhere.

Social

There are trends and patterns emerging that affect the recognition of expertise and the granting of status. For example, a changing demographic profile has implications for the kinds of services that are needed and the skills to support their provision. One trend noted is the decline of deference to those in authority, including many professionals such as the health professions (Kuhlmann, 2006). This means that status, and often high fees, cannot be taken for granted. There is said to be a decline in the trust placed in professionals and a move towards making them more accountable, including a clearer demonstration that they are competent (Watkins and Drury, 1995).

With the availability of knowledge, status can be challenged and new claims for expert recognition can be made. It is increasingly being recognized that different generations have different expectations of services and how time between work and leisure is spent. The so-called 'generation Y' (Loughlin and Baring, 2001), for example, seem to want to spend their lives meaningfully and usefully, based on equity and fairness for which they are prepared to use collective strength – perhaps via an online facility (Zemke et al., 2000).

Political

The various factors above have forced governments and bodies such as professional associations to take a more strategic view of LL and CPD. There have been responses and reforms throughout the western world to education systems and qualifications as well as HRD (Eurydice, 2001). In the UK, and especially following the Fryer reports (NAGCELL, 1997, 1998), there has been a range of initiatives to engender a culture of LL so that everyone is oriented towards skill development in order to respond to and take advantage of change. In an age of skills shortages, there has been emphasis on removing the barriers of those excluded from opportunities, through discrimination or lack of self-belief, to become involved.

services and work-based learning. For the Scottish strategy on lifelong learning, go to www.scotland.gov.uk/Publications/2003/02/16308/17750, and for Wales, go to www.elwa.ac.uk/ElwaWeb/elwa.aspx?pageid=2061.

Despite the political pressure, the rhetorical quality of the arguments presented by governments is not necessarily translated into practice. For example, in the UK, policies that emphasize opportunities and learning can be hampered by the polarization of the high and low skills requirements of production and service provision (Green, 2006).

Many professionals work in the public sector. For example, local government employs a variety of professional staff such as accountants, architects, social workers, teachers and so. Similarly, many professional staff can be found in the health service and the civil service. A discernable feature of work in such contexts is the various attempts to reform public services by giving more power to managers to complete change initiatives. Usually termed 'new public management' (Pollitt, 2000), it is recognized that there is significant potential for tension to arise between the values of professionals and the managerialist techniques employed. This is also bound to affect the learning and development of professionals in terms of which issues should be given prominence – professional or organizational. However, there is also recognition that professionals can become managers and leaders within the public sector, with more attention given to including such skills in their training (Gold, 2002). This may not prevent resentment among professionals who dislike attempts by others to direct their work (Exworthy and Halford, 1999).

Professionals may also resent attempts by their professional association to complete CPD. Although relatively unknown until the 1960s, most professional associations now have a CPD policy on the basis that the knowledge professionals use, the tasks performed and the roles completed become dated (Gear et al., 1994). Some professional associations, such as the Law Society, have a mandatory policy on CPD where lawyers are required to complete a minimum of 16 hours a year on activities recognized as CPD. This approach is referred to as a 'sanctions' model of CPD (Rapkins, 1995). Other associations, such as the Institute of Logistics and Transport, have a voluntary policy where the association suggests that members complete CPD but does not invoke sanctions against those who do not – referred to as a 'benefits' model. As we show below, the model adopted is a reflection of the status of a profession and the degree of guardianship provided by the professional association. While there does appear to be some confusion around policies, implementation and how CPD is undertaken (Woodall and Gourlay, 2004), there is considerable pressure on professionals to undertake CPD.

Professional work and CPD

In western societies, professional life and status are key attractors and in the UK it is estimated that around 20% of the workforce either hold or seek a professional qualification. The Skills Task Force (STF, 2000) identified a 50% rise in the professions from 1981 to 1998, with continued growth into the 2000s. Professionals are considered vital to support the growth in services but also manufacturing, where professionals are considered necessary for achieving technological and productivity gains. While professionals can be found in all advanced societies performing similar work (Brecher, 1999), in the UK, many professions have been a feature of life for over two centuries and some can trace their roots to pre-Enlightenment days. For example, law, medicine and the ministry have been termed the 'status professions', with their origins in medieval times as university disciplines to be studied by the sons of the aristocracy (Elliott, 1972). Since then, many areas of life have been professionalized and it is argued that this process has been a key contributor to the view of Britain as a meritocratic society (Perkin, 1989). There are currently over 350 professional associations in the UK (www.dfes.gov.uk/europeopen/eutouk/authorities_list.shtml lists all the regulated professional associations and provides links to all their websites). All professionals are recognized for their expertise because of the complexity of decisions faced by non-professionals in relation to particular aspects of life. According to Dietrich and Roberts (1997), this complexity of decisions provides the 'economic basis' for professionalism, where clients who are faced with ignorance seek the services of those they recognize as experts. Of course, more needs to done to arrive at fully fledged professionalism but through a recognition of expertise, organization and institutionalization into professional associations can follow (Witz, 1992). Over time, recognition of the need for particular kinds of expertise becomes more solid and grants power to those who have the credentials and command of the required knowledge to act and practise as professionals (Boreham, 1983).

Reflective questions

1 Is this explanation of professionalism one that matches the common understanding of those called 'professionals' in modern life?

2 What would be meant by someone acting 'unprofessionally'?

Freidson (2001) has presented an ideal type of professionalism composed of five interdependent elements:

1 specialized work that is grounded in a body of theoretically based discretionary knowledge and skill, which is given special status

2 an exclusive jurisdiction created and controlled by occupational negotiation

3 a sheltered position within labour markets based on the qualifying credentials of the occupation

4 a formal training programme to provide qualifying credentials

5 an ideology that asserts a commitment to quality and doing good.

You can use these elements to assess various claims for professionalism. For example, Gold et al. (2003) examined the status of HRD professionals. It was shown that HRD had partial claims for professionalism – an emerging body of theoretical knowledge that underpinned practice, with a growing number of dedicated journals and a growing importance attached to learning at work, which assisted HRD professionals in establishing an occupational division from others. However, it still remained possible for anyone to claim the ability to practise HRD, that is, membership of the relevant professional association, the CIPD, did not grant a licence to practise.

Professional knowledge

It should be clear from the above that knowledge plays a central role in professional work. Here it is customary to distinguish between what Eraut (2000a) refers to as 'public knowledge' and 'personal knowledge'. The former is knowledge that is explicit, communicable and provides the content of formal learning programmes, which lead to certification and professional accreditation. It can also be formally stated as 'codified knowledge' in abstract terms and abstraction distinguishes the professions from other groups (Abbott, 1988). Novices are accepted into the realm of a profession by proving their understanding of theories and models and their application within a range of practical situations. However, to progress from novice to expert requires learning within situations through practice and this is mostly achieved informally (Cheetham and Chivers, 2001). Such 'personal knowledge', although drawn from theories and models, is more extensive and accumulates as 'tacit knowledge'. This knowledge is highly situated, difficult to copy and, like all tacit knowledge, might even be difficult to talk about (Gourlay, 2006). As Eraut (2000a, p. 128) suggests, it 'cannot be accomplished by procedural knowledge alone or by following a manual'. Schön (1983) highlighted tacit knowledge as an aspect of 'reflection-in-action', which is the ability of professionals to respond spontaneously to surprise through improvisation, without thought. He contrasted such knowing with 'technical rationality', composed of formulable propositions within a distinct product of a body of knowledge aimed at problem solving, predictability and control.

These distinctions between codified and tacit knowledge do provide something of a complication for professionals and professional associations that seek to develop policies and requirements for CPD. Clearly, because abstract knowledge can be presented in codified form, through books, journal articles, websites and so on, it forms the basis of educational programmes for professional qualification and CPD. However, tacit knowledge is gained through practice, informally within various contexts, usually through interaction with others – clients, fellow professionals and so on. The difficulty here is recognizing or articulating that learning has occurred. However, for most professionals, it is the most common form of learning. As we shall see below, CPD presents professional associations and their members with a number of dilemmas and paradoxes (Megginson and Whitaker, 2003).

CPD policies and practices

In order to protect and advance the claims for expert status, most professional bodies have developed CPD policies for their members, undertaken following the completion of the initial qualification that allows entry to the profession. Madden and Mitchell (1993, p. 12) have defined CPD as:

> The maintenance and enhancement of the knowledge, expertise and competence of professionals throughout their careers, according to a plan formulated with regard to the needs of the professional, the employer and society.

As we can see from this definition, there are two key features of CPD. First, it is a planned and formulated process, and second, the focus is almost entirely on individual professionals. As we will see, on both counts, these features have been subjected to some criticisms in recent years.

Most professional associations seek to help their members 'manage' CPD by providing guidance on planning, implementing and monitoring. In this way, CPD models are similar to the systematic approaches to training based on a series of steps to follow (Grant et al., 1999). Figure 16.1 provides a CPD model showing a typical series of steps.

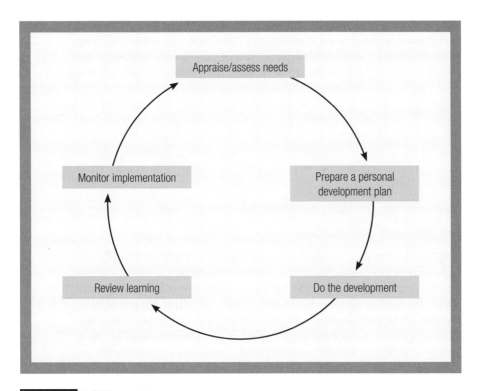

FIGURE 16.1 A CPD model

Although shown as a cycle, the usual starting point is an appraisal and assessment of needs. Because much professional work occurs in relationships with clients, it is difficult for those outside the relationship to make judgements about needs. Where performance is difficult to observe and is knowledge based, it is difficult to impose performance management processes such as appraisal and assessment from the outside (Reilly, 2005). It is therefore suggested that professionals should take responsibility to appraise and assess themselves. Of course, this also provides the potential for distortion in judgements. Also, many professionals work in organizations where, as part of a performance management system, they may be appraised and assessed by line managers for a variety of purposes including development. For example, Redman et al. (2000) examined appraisal in an NHS hospital and found strengths in personal development planning along with setting objectives, although there was some inconsistency in implementing the appraisal process. Nevertheless, professional associations are likely to focus on their members as individuals and make them responsible for their CPD. For example, the Institute of Chartered Accountants in England and Wales (ICAEW) requires its members to use their professional judgement to:

- reflect on the knowledge and skills required for their role

- consider the responsibilities and expectations placed upon them

- identify learning and development needs.

It is left to members to work out what needs should be met, but the ICAEW suggests that technical knowledge, business awareness, IT skills and 'soft' skills such as negotiation, time management and team leadership skills may be included. It is also left to members to identify how the needs are met by identifying particular inputs; we refer to this as the 'input approach' to CPD. The ICAEW offers the following suggestions, which are not untypical for CPD:

- focused discussion with colleagues

- online research

- reading

- study of regulations and standards

- researching a particular type of issue related to a role

- researching legislation applicable to a role.

Attending courses and seminars would also be typical for CPD, although the ICAEW does not specify the achievement of a certain number of hours or points nor a requirement to attend a certain number of courses or seminars. However, other professional associations are more prescriptive. For example, since 1985, CPD has been has been compulsory for members of the Law Society, with solicitors encouraged to take responsibility for their own development to meet the requirement of a minimum of 16 hours of CPD per year, of which at least 25% must consist of participation in accredited training courses for providers authorized by the Law Society (www.lawsociety.org.uk/professional/continuing/solicitors/cpdscheme.law). In addition, members are also required to attend a management course stage before the end of their third CPD year. Again, the policy sets out a wide range of activities that may be included, such as:

- work shadowing

- mentoring and coaching

- preparation and delivery of training courses

- distance learning and the use of audiovisual materials.

Depending on the power of the professional association, members may be required to complete a record of what inputs they identify and complete as part of their CPD. For example, the Law Society operates on an annual cycle and each solicitor returns a completed training record, an example of which is shown in Table 16.1.

We can notice the way such a record would require the specifying of particular inputs and conforms to a standard view of professional learning, where CPD is seen as a way of 'topping up' the initial period of compulsory education in qualifying as a professional. The record becomes a demonstration that CPD is being taken seriously (du Boulay, 2000).

TABLE 16.1 Sample training record for solicitors

Date	Training activity (for course attendance, indicate course title, provider name and reference, otherwise state how activity was undertaken)	Comments	Number of hours credit
10.11.03	Attendance at update on Revenue Law (inhouse) 123/ABCD video and discussion	Provided a review of the provisions in the budget which need to be taken into account when advising on personal investments and will planning	2 hours and 10 minutes
12.12.03	Time spent on building portfolio of evidence for NVQ in management	Prepared and gathered evidence in respect of units on budgeting and recruitment interviews	3 hours

SOURCE: The Law Society

This approach to managing CPD through the recording of inputs undertaken can be seen as a feature of control by professional associations. Taylor (1996), for example, suggests that monitoring is a feature of most CPD schemes and can become a pointless exercise, where the end becomes recording rather than the use of inputs by professionals in their work. This also raises the crucial issue for any training activity – the extent to which it is transferred to work practice. There have been some studies of CPD that point to the difficulties of transfer. For example, Bolton (2002, p. 322) studied chiropractors' views of CPD and found little impact on practice. CPD was not seen as 'instrumental in improving the care of patients', even though they had positive views on what they did in CPD. Allery et al. (1997) studied 100 GPs and consultants and found that organized education only accounted for one-third of changes to practice and that most of these occurred through a combination of organizational and social factors. HRD in Practice 16.1 shows an example of how one professional, a leading solicitor in Leeds, took control of his own CPD.

HRD in Practice 16.1

CPD in the legal profession

'I am a Leeds-based lawyer with a long interest in and involvement with management. Like most lawyers, I am probably intelligent enough to know when I need external input or knowledge and arrogant enough to either ignore it or persuade myself that I can manage without it. Against that background, the hardest part of engaging in the CPD process leading to a Masters was acknowledging my need for such education and the considerable value it would add.

I have been delighted with the value that has been added both to my firm and to me personally by every stage of the programme; not only has the process been stimulating and thought-provoking, it has generated clear and tangible results in my firm in the form of real differences of approach and insights, which have informed and improved management processes.

An example of the direct application of the learning gained would be the impact

A criticism of input-driven approaches to CPD is that they pay insufficient attention to the context of practice and the ability and motivation of professionals to make attempts to change their practice. Eraut (2001, p. 8) considers many models of CPD as 'one-dimenional' because of the difficulty in considering application and continued learning. A further difficulty occurs for professionals who work in organizations that prioritize organizational needs against those of individual professionals and learners more generally (Jones and Fear, 1994).

Because there are restrictions with an input-driven approach to CPD, some models have also incorporated the outcomes of learning. This allows professionals to justify that learning has taken place through an impact on practice. This also allows CPD to be widened to include different forms of learning and how such learning might be shared with others as well as enhancing performance (Grant, 1999). One interesting development by a number of professional associations is to support CPD by the creation of online communities. For example, the CIPD (www.cipd.co.uk/community) has created a number of professional communities as well as providing downloads of tools and podcasts. The Institution of Engineering and Technology (www.kn.theiet.org/) has set up a knowledge network composed of different specialisms, which allows members to participate in online and physical events.

The shift towards outcomes does seem to have widened the scope of CPD and also recognizes that professional learning can occur within and from practice, including informal events and in collaboration with others (Cordingley et al., 2003). Thus, working with a mentor or coach and developing learning contracts can all be included. The onus is now on proving that learning has occurred. There is more attention to reflection, perhaps in learning logs or diaries as part of a process of continuous review as well as recording (Gibbons, 1995). We can see here the important influence of Kolb's (1984) learning cycle and Schön's (1983) notion of reflection-on-action and even critical reflection (Gold et al., 2002).

Nevertheless, despite the extension towards outcomes, there still remain problems, given the complexity of professional work. For example, many professionals achieve outcomes by working with others, so it becomes impossible to attribute outcomes achieved to a single professional, although CPD schemes focus on individual professionals as the learners. A further difficulty arises in who judges what counts as CPD. Professional associations are the main arbiters on the meaning of CPD for their members and this can create restrictions. For example, in a study of professional learning in context, Thorpe et al. (2004, p. 12) found that surprise, contradiction and ambiguity were not uncommon in informal learning at work. One recently qualified professional learned that, in contrast to her training, the work was more 'hands-on' with work 'piling up' and little 'time to reflect'. The importance of such features is that they are all part of the personal learning that we identified earlier as being crucial to working as a professional, which goes beyond the theories and procedures (Eraut, 2000a), although it might not be recognized by professional associations as CPD. Recently, Gold et al. (2007) explored what they called the 'missing perspective' in CPD – how professional learning occurs in the course of practice. Their study of solicitors in a law firm highlighted the significant and powerful ways in which professionals learned in their practice, which added to their knowledge and understanding, both explicitly and tacitly, but also generated new ideas and new understandings that provided an immediate and relevant form of CPD.

Lifelong learning

If CPD is concerned with professional learning, for everyone else there is LL. This is a simple idea, even a tautology, that everyone learns throughout their lives. In some respects, the idea of LL is broad and all-encompassing, stretching to any aspect of life where we learn to do something different – understand ideas and learn facts, skills and so on. As Field (2006, p. 2) states, LL 'covers pretty much everything – and rightly so'. Nevertheless, for the reasons we outlined earlier, LL has increasingly been seen as a requirement of participation in the knowledge society (Rohrbach, 2007) and as a contribution to social and economic wellbeing at home, in the community and at work. For example, in the UK, the Inquiry into the Future for Lifelong Learning (www.niace.org.uk/lifelonglearninginquiry/Default.htm) has identified the following themes as relevant to the future of policy and practice in LL:

- prosperity, employment and work

- demography and social structure

- wellbeing and happiness

- migration and communities

- technological change

- poverty reduction

- citizenship and belonging

- crime and social exclusion

- the roles of public, private and voluntary sectors

- environmental sustainability.

Models of lifelong learning

The broad view of LL finds much favour with writers and practitioners who have for many years taken a more humanist approach to learning and development. It is a model of LL that seeks to help people to participate in a free democracy, especially those who lack privileges in general education opportunities and other spheres of life. It is a model of emancipation and social justice (Schuetze and Casey, 2006), which can appear ideal-istic and utopian, although there are some clear influences of this model in policies that seek to support learning for disadvantaged communities. Schuetze and Casey identify two other models of LL that seek to enhance access and participation. These are a cultural model that aims to support individuals to seek fulfilment in life and self-realization and an 'open society' model in which LL is concerned with the development of a learning system for those who want to and are able to participate. As a contrast to each of these models, most policies relating to LL, while recognizing the wider meanings, tend to emphasize the importance of human capital development as part of an economic imper-ative for learning in the face of rapid technological advances and globalization of markets (Preston and Dyer, 2003). In reality, this narrows the focus and connects LL to NHRD agendas and models (see Chapter 3). This tends to see LL as an aspect of the VET system that is necessary to provide sufficient skills for a country to gain competitive advantage. The narrowness of the vocational slant but the prominence given to it often underlies some of the key debates around LL.

Reflective question

To which of these models would you give prominence?

Skills and LL

The human capital model of LL underpins recent attempts in the UK to raise skill levels. For example, the Leitch review (2006) set 2020 as a target to achieve 'world leader' status, benchmarked by the upper quartile of OECD figures. This would be indicated by:

- 95% of working age adults achieving functional literacy and numeracy

- more than 90% of workforce adults qualified to at least level 2 where feasible

- shifting the balance of intermediate skills from level 2 to level 3 and improving the esteem, quantity and quality of intermediate skills

- more than 40% of the adult population qualified to level 4 and above.

In Chapter 4, we set out the key principles of the NQF based on NVQs or SVQs. Vital to the acceptance of this framework is the use of qualifications as a measurement by proxy of skills in an economy, a process referred to as 'credentialism'. An obvious criticism of using qualifications as a measurement tool is that it drives the system – in the sense that only qualifications count as learning. As Coffield (2000b, p. 5) argued, learners become 'intent on increasing their credentials rather than their understanding'. In most cases, informal learning is more likely, especially for adults in the work context, and this is not always amenable to certification (see below).

In Chapter 4, we also considered the academic/vocational divide in the UK, manifest in the different types of qualification available. This divide is a product of the UK's cultural and historical tradition, which has valued thinking over doing. However, there is a growing move to remove this divide and create a more unified pathway for learners to progress in paths of their choice. For example, in 2004, the NQF was extended to include academic qualifications up to doctorate level. This is shown in Table 16.2.

TABLE 16.2 The revised 2004 National Qualifications Framework in the UK

National Qualifications Framework		Framework for higher education qualification levels
Original levels	Revised levels	
5 Level 5 NVQ Level 5 Diploma	8 Specialist awards	D (doctoral): doctorates
	7 Level 7 Diploma	M (masters): masters degrees, postgraduate certificates and diplomas
4 Level 4 NVQ Level 4 Diploma Level 4 BTEC Higher National Diploma Level 4 Certificate	6 Level 6 Diploma	H (honours): bachelors degrees, graduate certificates and diplomas
	5 Level 5 BTEC Higher National Diploma	I (intermediate): diplomas of higher education and further education, foundation degrees, higher national diplomas
	4 Level 4 Certificate	C (certificate): certificates of higher education
3 Level 3 Certificate Level 3 NVQ A levels		
2 Level 2 Diploma Level 2 NVQ GCSEs Grades A*–C		
1 Level 1 Certificate Level 1 NVQ GCSEs Grades D–G		
Entry Entry Level Certificate in Adult Literacy		

SOURCE: www.qca.org.uk/libraryAssets/media/qca-06-2298-nqf-web.pdf

In September 2008, further revisions to the framework were introduced to help understanding and measurement (for further details, go to www.qca.org.uk/qca_19674.aspx). This will provide a credit value for how much time a qualification takes to complete – the size of a qualification, and how difficult it is – the difficulty as indicated by the level.

One of the key benefits of the revised framework is the clarity it provides for those seeking to move from vocational education into higher education. This is seen as part of an agenda to widen participation in higher education and a contributor to social justice as well as economic competitiveness. However, there is still a need for universities and colleges to consider how they can develop the curriculum to make their programmes more relevant to those seeking a vocational education. In the UK, Lifelong Learning Networks were established in 2005 to enhance progression opportunities for vocational learners, providing a 'bridge' from vocational education to higher education, covering nearly all universities and colleges. HRD in Practice 16.2 shows some examples of LL from the West Yorkshire Lifelong Learning Network.

LL in West Yorkshire

Lifelong learning, often used synonymously with adult education, continuing education and work-based learning, is a term that has been introduced quite recently in education-speak, but has a history going back centuries. Born out of the apprenticeship and Mechanics Institute movements, LL was associated with the development of the individual in terms of their work and personal prosperity. In the 20th century, it became more associated with political and social development, becoming embedded in community-based adult education. Into the 21st century, LL has once again become more associated with work. For many it provides a second chance. This is a typical case study.

As a mother and housewife, Sharon wondered what she was doing with her life. She enrolled on a foundation degree in e-technology at a local further education college, before progressing to an honours degree at university. With this achievement, she gained employment in a web-based e-learning company.

For others, lifelong learning has simply been an opportunity to develop their own career, as this case study shows.

Taking the opportunity of the new skills-based training introduced in the 1980s, Rachel took up a place on a youth training scheme in engineering. By studying part time at her local college and university, over the years she gained an ONC and HNC in Mechanical Engineering and is now studying for a BEng in Computer-aided Engineering. This commitment to learning has resulted in a successful career – from an engineering apprentice, she has progressed to become a general engineer and now a design engineer.

In these cases, the individual and employer benefited from the learning that took place, but both case studies were from a time of economic growth. As we move into a recession and associated redundancies, LL will be needed to effect career changes needed for the individual to fit into the new economy.

Source: Stephen Challenger, director, West Yorkshire Lifelong Learning Network (personal communication)

Read more about Lifelong Learning Networks at www.hefce.ac.uk/widen/lln/ and www.lifelonglearningnetworks.org.uk/.

A key activity of the network is to set up progression agreements between institutions to allow recognition of credit for learning and transfer. It has also helped in the development of foundation degrees, which have been developed with employers and allow the combination of academic study and workplace learning, making them relevant to performance at work. These are mainly delivered in further education colleges but are validated by universities.

Foundation degrees are one of the ways, along with apprenticeships, in which the UK is seeking to stimulate interest in intermediate skills qualifications (Wilson et al., 2005) and to attract students from different backgrounds and non-traditional learners into higher education (www.fdf.ac.uk/ has more on foundation degrees). The supply of intermediate skills has for several years been identified as a source of weakness in the UK. For example, the National Skills Task Force (2000) found a mismatch in technical and craft jobs and had concerns about qualified adults when compared to France and Germany. Such skills are usually classified at level 3 in the NQF, and the National Skills Task Force suggested that intermediate skills needed to include communications, innovation and problem solving, in addition to the technical skills and personal attributes such as motivation, judgement, leadership and initiative. However, the precise meaning of intermediate skills will vary between occupations and sectors. This means that a term such as 'craft' in one sector might be more or less complex compared to other sectors and be categorized at different levels in the NQF (Smeaton and Hughes, 2003).

A crucial element in learning intermediate skills seems to be their development at work in a programme of structured learning. This immediately creates difficulties for those who do not have access to work contexts due to low educational attainment and a lack of basic skills. The Moser reports (1993, 1999) have sought to highlight these problems. In schools, there have been national literacy and numeracy strategies, but the Leitch report (2006) found that 6.8 million adults had numeracy problems and 5 million were not functionally literate. In response, the government has set a target of 95% of adults to have these basic skills by 2020 as part of its Skills for Life strategy (DfES, 2004) (see the Skills for Life Strategy Unit at www.dfes.gov.uk/readwriteplus/Who_We_Are). In addition, in order to encourage adults to undertake training, whether they are in employment or between jobs, there are plans for lifetime Skills Accounts, containing the power to purchase learning from a quality assured source. These appear similar to attempts to improve adult participation in learning through Individual Learning Accounts in 2000. These allowed individuals to choose programmes of subsidized learning and by 2001, there were 2.5 million members but the programme was suspended in October 2001 and then abolished due to evidence of abuse and fraud by some providers. Thursfield et al. (2002) were critical of their design and implementation, so it remains to be seen whether Skills Accounts will fare better.

Of course, most learning and development is undertaken in a work context, although much of it is not accredited. In 2005, according to the National Employers' Skills Survey (NESS, 2006), 61% of the workforce in England had received training in the previous 12 months but this varied according to organization size. Most of it will be concerned with improving skills or knowledge and there will be some connection to organization performance. This is most people's experience of LL and gives rise to Boshier's (1998) comment that LL is 'human resource development in drag'. However, this is not always the case and during the 1990s, some organizations began to provide employee-led development (ELD) schemes, which allowed employees to choose learning programmes that were not necessarily work related. Such attempts to stimulate adults to undertake learning have a long history in the UK (Corner, 1990), for example Cadbury's provided support for non-work-related learning in the early 20th century. Perhaps the most well-known recent scheme is the Ford Motor Company's Employee Development and Assistance Programme, developed in collaboration with trade unions in 1988, first in the US and then in the UK. Under the scheme, all employees are entitled to £200 a year for non-work-related learning and health/fitness sessions. The apparent success of this scheme, and growing enthusiasm for ideas like the learning company in the 1990s, saw a growth of such schemes and support from the government (DfEE, 1997). Holden and Hamblett (1998) point to the assumption that ELD is a 'good thing' based on a mutuality of interests between employers and employees, allowing the establishment of a learning culture at work. However, the idea that ELD can eventually link to organization success and competitive advantage is seen as problematic and avoids difficult considerations of how skills are formed and products and services are specified and designed (Hamblett and Holden, 2000).

Reflective question

If your employer offered you £200 for any non-work-related learning, would it increase your desire to learn at work?

While not all ELD schemes are collaboratively developed with trade unions, there is evidence that recognition of unions can lead to more effective HRD strategies (Green et al., 1999). Under the provisions of the Employment Act 2002, organizations can grant recognition to union learning representatives (ULRs), who can promote training and learning to union members and consult with employers on issues concerning training and learning. They can also establish learning agreements with employers to provide joint mechanisms for coordinating and monitoring learning activities. ULRs can also draw funding from a union learning fund (www.unionlearningfund.org.uk/) provided by the government for projects to promote workplace learning. Wood and Moore (2005) completed a survey of union learning and found positive outcomes for unions and employers, although this mainly occurred where there were already cooperative relations between unions and management.

Informal or non-formal learning

Most LL is recognized in formal terms – employees undertake training, students attend courses, apprentices complete qualifications and so on. However, a moment's reflection will soon reveal how much informal learning occurs, mainly through interactions with others on an everyday basis. Even on formal programmes, there is likely to be a great deal of interaction that is not strictly in line with the formal requirements but probably vital to it (Field, 2006). As we outlined earlier with professionals, personal learning acquired informally through practice, surprises and ambiguity in work are all part of the accumulation of experience. Such processes are also vital to LL more generally and this is becoming increasingly recognized. For example, in SMEs, informal learning – by exploring, experimenting, problem solving and mistakes – is now understood as a key feature of the 'world' of entrepreneurs (CEML, 2002). Marsick and Watkins (1990, p. 12) point to the need for informal learning to 'deliberately encourage' in order to make it more effective through processes such as mentoring, team working, providing feedback and trial and error working. They also highlight how much incidental learning occurs every day but this is usually unconscious.

Eraut (2000b, p. 12) sees the term 'informal learning' as too much of a 'catch-all' label that covers all learning that is not formal, but the term is also confused with aspects of dress and ways of talking. He prefers the term 'non-formal learning' to contrast with formal learning. He sets out three types of non-formal learning:

1 *Implicit learning:* learning that occurs without intention and awareness at the time it has taken place but becomes part of experience, used unconsciously in future events.

2 *Reactive learning:* learning occurs spontaneously in response to events – there might be awareness that learning has occurred but there is little time to consider this except through reflection.

3 *Deliberative learning:* learning from events is recognized through reviewing and reflecting on actions, and time is provided to allow this to happen.

These views of learning are seen as a source of tacit knowledge, which has a particular value for organizations in the process of creating knowledge (see Chapter 9). For example, Nonaka and Takeuchi's (1995) knowledge-creating model begins with tacit knowledge by individuals that is then expressed to others, although there are doubts about the degree to which tacit knowledge can be expressed (Beckett and Hager, 2002). Nevertheless, in many organizations where knowledge is essential to the production and provision of services, proactive efforts are being made to surface knowledge from non-formal learning to provide new ways of doing things (Garvey and Williamson, 2002). Essential to this is knowledge sharing through reviewing and reflecting on experiences.

Review and reflection on experiences are often seen as key features of self-directed learning by adults who take responsibility for their own learning. Mezirow (1990), for example, sees critical reflection as a route to new ideas and 'transformative learning'. This requires a challenge to assumptions so that new possibilities can be identified. Self-directed learning is mainly characterized by projects where the learning is owned and controlled by the learner. The individual chooses what to learn, when to learn and how, and for many people such choices are available both formally and non-formally, according to preferences. Increasingly, individuals gain access to learning programmes through online sources and e-learning packages (see Chapter 14).

Summary

- LL has become a key idea in education and training policy, stimulated by the speed of change in knowledge-intensive work and technology. Professionals need to undertake CPD to preserve and advance their status as professionals.

- There are significant and interconnected technological, economic and social changes that underpin the arguments for LL and CPD.

- Professionals are considered vital in advanced societies and are recognized for their expertise because of the complexity of decisions faced by clients and consumers.

- Professional knowledge is composed of codified and abstracted knowledge and its application, which results in tacit knowledge.

- Most professional bodies have developed policies for CPD for their members in order to protect and advance claims for professional status.

- CPD is generally understood as a planned and formulated process of learning with an individual focus but there is growing interest in practice-based learning.

- LL has increasingly been seen as a requirement of participation in the knowledge society as well as a contribution to social and economic wellbeing where learning stretches to any aspect of life.

- LL underpins attempts to raise skill levels through credentialism, measured by qualifications gained at different levels.

- In the UK, there are difficulties of a vocational/academic divide in skills and qualifications, which policies are seeking to address.

- In the workplace, most LL is connected to improving skills or knowledge for organization performance but there are schemes that allow employees to undertake non-work-related learning.

- Informal and tacit learning are now recognized as vital features of LL.

Discussion questions

1 Why should we all become lifelong learners?
2 Can we compel professionals to complete CPD?
3 How can professionals demonstrate that they are up to date in their knowledge and skills?
4 Should LL be work related?
5 Who should be responsible for LL?
6 Can informal learning be recognized more fully?

Further reading

Candy, P.C. (1991) *Self-Direction for Lifelong Learning*, San Francisco, Jossey-Bass.

Coffield, F. (1999) Breaking the consensus: lifelong learning as social control, *British Educational Research Journal*, **25**(4): 479–99.

Kennedy, A. (2005) Models of continuing professional development: a framework for analysis, *Journal of In-service Education*, **31**(2): 235–50.

Longworth, N. and Davies, W.K. (1996) *Lifelong Learning*, London, Kogan Page.

Sadler-Smith, E. and Smith, P. (2006) Technical rationality and professional artistry in HRD practice, *Human Resource Development International*, 9(2): 271–81.

Yeo, R.K. (2008) How does learning (not) take place in problem-based learning activities in workplace contexts?, *Human Resource Development International*, 11(3): 317–30.

References

Abbott, A. (1988) *The System of Professions*, Chicago, University of Chicago Press.

Allery, L.A., Owen, P.A and Robling, M.R. (1997) Why general practitioners and consultants change their clinical practice: a critical incident study, *British Medical Journal*, **314**: 870–4.

Bagnall, R. (2000) Lifelong learning and the limits of economic determinism, *International Journal of Lifelong Education*, **19**: 20–35.

Beck, U. (1992) *Risk Society: Towards A New Modernity*, London, Sage.

Beckett, D. and Hager, P. (2002) *Life, Work and Learning*, London, Routledge.

Bolton, J. (2002) Chiropractors' attitudes to, and perceptions of, the impact of continuing professional education on clinical practice, *Medical Education*, **36**: 317–24.

Boreham, P. (1983) Indetermination: professional knowledge, organization and control, *Sociological Review*, **31**: 693–718.

Boshier, R. (1998) Edgar Faure after 25 years, in J. Holford, P. Jarvis and C. Griffin (eds) *International Perspectives on Lifelong Learning*, London, Routledge.

Brecher, T. (1999) *Professional Practices: Commitment and Capability in a Changing Environment*, London, Transaction.

Campbell, M., Baldwin, S., Johnson, S. et al. (2001) *Skills in England 2001: The Research Report*, Nottingham, DfES.

Castells, M. (1996) *The Rise of the Network Society*, Oxford, Blackwell.

CEML (Council for Excellence in Management and Leadership) (2002) *Joining Entrepreneurs in their World*, London, CEML.

Cheetham, G. and Chivers, G. (2001) How professionals learn in practice, *Journal of European Industrial Training*, **24**(7): 247–92.

Clementi, D. (2004) *Report of the Review of the Regulatory Framework for Legal Services in England and Wales*, London, Department for Constitutional Affairs.

Coffield, F. (2000a) Introduction: a critical analysis of the concept of a learning society, in F. Coffield (ed.) *Different Visions of a Learning Society*, Bristol, Policy Press.

Coffield, F. (2000b) The structure below the surface: reassessing the significance of informal learning, in F. Coffield (ed.) *The Necessity of Informal Learning*, Bristol, Policy Press.

Cooper, D., Greenwood, R., Hinings, C.R. and Brown, J. (1996) Sedimentation and transformation in organizational change: the case of Canadian law firms, *Organization Studies*, **17**(4): 623–47.

Cordingley, P., Bell, M., Rundell, B. et al. (2003) *The Impact of Collaborative CPD on Classroom Teaching and Learning: How Does Collaborative Continuing Professional Development (CPD) For Teachers of the 5–16 Age Range Affect Teaching and Learning?*, London, EPPI-Centre.

Corner, T.E. (1990) *Learning Opportunities for Adults*, London, Routledge & Kegan Paul.

Daniels, H. (2004) Cultural historical activity theory and professional learning, *International Journal of Disability, Development and Education*, **51**(2): 185–200.

DfEE (Department for Education and Employment) (1997) *Successful Strategies for Employee Development Schemes*, London, DfEE.

DfES (Department for Education and Skills) (2004) *Skills for Life: Improving Adult Literacy and Numeracy*, London, DfES.

Dietrich, M. and Roberts, J. (1997) Beyond the economics of professionalism, in J. Broadbent, M. Dietrich and J. Roberts (eds) *The End of the Professions?*, London, Routledge.

DIUS (Department of Innovation, Universities and Skills) (2007) *World Class Skills: Implementing the Leitch Review of Skills in England*, London, DIUS.

Du Boulay, C. (2000) From CME to CPD: getting better at getting better?, *British Medical Journal*, **320**: 393–4.

EC (European Commission) (1995) *Teaching and Learning: Towards the Learning Society*, White Paper, Brussels, EC.

EC (European Commission) (2001) *A Memorandum on Lifelong Learning*, Brussels, EC.

Edwards, R. (2001) Researching the rhetoric of lifelong learning, *Journal of Education Policy*, **16**(2): 103–12.

Elliott, P. (1972) *The Sociology of the Professions*, Basingstoke, Macmillan.

Eraut, M. (2000a) Non-formal learning and tacit knowledge in professional work, *British Journal of Educational Psychology*, **70**: 113–36.

Eraut, M. (2000b) Non-formal learning, implicit learning and tacit knowledge in professional work, in F. Coffield (ed.) *The Necessity of Informal Learning*, Bristol, Policy Press.

Eraut, M. (2001) Do continuing professional development models promote one-dimensional learning?, *Medical Education*, **35**: 8–11.

Eurydice (2001) *National Actions to Implement Lifelong Learning in Europe*, Brussels, Eurydice.

Exworthy, M. and Halford, S. (1999) Professionals and managers in a changing public sector: conflict, compromise and collaboration, in M. Exworthy and S. Halford (eds) *Professionals and the New Managerialism in the Public Sector*, Buckingham, Open University Press.

Field, J. (2006) *Lifelong Learning and the New Educational Order*, Stoke on Trent, Trentham Books.

Freidson, E. (2001) *Professionalism*, Cambridge, Polity Press.

Garvey, R. and Williamson, B. (2002) *Beyond Knowledge Management*, Harlow, Pearson.

Gear, J., McIntosh, A. and Squires, G. (1994) *Informal Learning in the Professions*, Department of Adult Education, University of Hull.

Gibbons, A. (1995) A personal approach to CPD, in S. Clyne (ed.) *Continuing Professional Development*, London, Kogan Page.

Gold, J. (2002) *Towards Management and Leadership in the Professions*, London, CEML.

Gold, J., Holman, D. and Thorpe, R. (2002) The role of argument analysis and story-telling in facilitating critical thinking, *Management Learning*, **33**: 371–88.

Gold, J., Rodgers, H. and Smith, V. (2003) What is the future for the human resource development professional? A UK perspective, *Human Resource Development International*, **6**(4): 437–56.

Gold, J., Thorpe, R., Woodall, J. and Sadler-Smith, E. (2007) Continuing professional development in the legal profession: a practice-based learning perspective, *Management Learning*, **38**(2): 235–50.

Gourlay, S. (2006) Towards conceptual clarity for 'tacit knowledge': a review of empirical studies, *Knowledge Management Research and Practice*, **4**: 60–9.

Grant, J. (1999) Measurement of learning outcome in continuing professional development, *Journal of Continuing Education in the Health Professions*, **19**: 214–21.

Grant, J., Chambers, E. and Jackson, G. (eds) (1999) *The Good CPD Guide: A Practical Guide to Managed CPD*, Sutton, Reed Business Information.

Green, A. (2002) The many faces of lifelong learning: recent education policy trends in Europe, *Journal of Education Policy*, **17**(6): 611–26.

Green, A. (2006) Models of lifelong learning and the 'knowledge society', *Journal of Comparative Education*, **36**(3): 307–25.

Green, F., Machin, S. and Wilkinson, D. (1999) Trade unions and training practices in British workplaces, *Industrial and Labor Relations Review*, **52**(2): 179–95.

Greenwood, R., Hinings, C.R. and Brown, J. (1990) 'P2 Form' strategic management: corporate practices in professional partnerships, *Academy of Management Journal*, **33**(4): 725–55.

Hamblett, J. and Holden, R. (2000) Employee-led development: another piece of left luggage?, *Personnel Review*, **29**(4): 509–20.

Hanlon, G. (1997) A shifting professionalism: accountancy, in J. Broadbent, M. Dietrich and J. Roberts (eds) *The End of the Professions?*, London, Routledge.

Holden, R. and Hamblett, J. (1998) Learning lessons from non-work related learning, *Journal of Workplace Learning*, **10**(5): 241–50.

Jones, N. and Fear, N. (1994) Continuing professional development: perspectives from human resource professionals, *Personnel Review*, **23**(8): 49–60.

Kolb, D. (1984) *Experiential Learning*, Englewood Cliffs, NJ, Prentice Hall.

Kuhlmann, E. (2006) Traces of doubt and sources of trust: health professions in an uncertain society, *Current Sociology*, **54**(4): 607–20.

Leitch, S. (2006) *Prosperity for all in the Global Economy: World Class Skills*, London, HM Treasury.

Loughlin, C. and Barling, J. (2001) Young workers' work values, attitudes, and behaviours, *Journal of Occupational and Organizational Psychology*, **74**(4): 543–58.

Madden, C.A. and Mitchell, V.A. (1993) *Professions, Standards and Competence: A Survey of Continuing*

Education for the Profession, Department of Continuing Education, University of Bristol.

Marsick, V. and Watkins, K.E. (1990) Towards a theory of informal and incidental learning, in V. Marsick and K.E. Watkins (eds) *Informal and Incidental Learning in the Workplace*, London, Routledge.

Megginson, D. and Whitaker, V. (2003) *Continuing Professional Development*, London, CIPD.

Mezirow, J. (1990) *Fostering Critical Reflection*, San Francisco, Jossey-Bass.

Moser, C. (1993) *Learning to Succeed: A Radical Look at Education Today and a Strategy for the Future*, London, Heinemann.

Moser, C. (1999) *A Fresh Start: Improving Literacy and Numeracy*, London, DfEE.

Moynagh, M. and Worsley, R. (2005) *Working in the Twenty-first Century*, Leeds, ESRC Future of Work Programme.

NAGCELL (1997) *Learning for the 21st Century*, www.lifelonglearning.co.uk/nagcell/.

NAGCELL (1998) *Creating Learning Cultures: Next Steps in Achieving the Learning Age*, www.lifelonglearning.co.uk/nagcell2/index.htm.

National Skills Task Force (2000) *Skills for All: Research Report from the National Skills Task Force*, London, DfEE.

NESS (National Employers' Skills Survey) (2006) *National Employers' Skills Survey*, Coventry, Learning and Skills Council.

Newell, S., Robertson, M., Scarbrough, H. and Swann, J. (2002) *Managing Knowledge Work*, Basingstoke, Palgrave – now Palgrave Macmillan.

Nonaka, I. and Takeuchi, H. (1995) *The Knowledge-creating Company*, New York, Oxford University Press.

OECD (Organization for Economic Co-operation and Development) (1996a) *Lifelong Learning for All*, Paris, OECD.

OECD (Organization for Economic Co-operation and Development) (1996b) *The Knowledge-based Economy*, Paris, OECD.

Perkin, H. (1989) *The Rise of the Professional Society: England Since 1880*, London, Routledge.

Pollitt, C. (2000) Is the emperor in his new underwear?: An analysis of the impacts of public management reform, *Public Management*, **2**(2): 181–99.

Powell, M.J., Brock, D.M. and Hinings, C.R. (1999) The changing professional organization, in D.M Brock, M.J. Powell and C.R. Hinings (eds) *Restruc-turing the Professional Organization*, London, Routledge.

Preston, R. and Dyer, C. (2003) Human capital, social capital and lifelong learning: an editorial introduction, *Compare*, **33**(4): 429–36.

Rapkins, C. (1995) Professional bodies and continuing professional development, in S. Clyne (ed.) *Continuing Professional Development*, London, Kogan Page.

Redman, T., Snape, E., Thompson, D. and Ka-Ching Yan, F. (2000) Performance appraisal in an NHS hospital, *Human Resource Management Journal*, **10**(1): 48–62.

Reilly, P. (2005) Get the best from knowledge workers, *People Management*, 29 September: 52–3.

Rohrbach, D. (2007) The development of knowledge societies in 19 OECD countries between 1970 and 2002, *Social Science Information*, **46**(4): 655–89.

Roscoe, J. (2002) Continuing professional development in higher education, *Human Resource Development International*, **5**: 3–10.

Scase, R. (1999) *Britain Towards 2010: The Changing Business Environment*, London, ESRC.

Schön, D.A. (1983) *The Reflective Practitioner: How Professionals Think in Action*, London, Maurice Temple Smith.

Schuetze, H. and Casey, C. (2006) Models and meanings of lifelong learning: progress and barriers on the road to a learning society, *Compare*, **36**(3): 279–87.

Smeaton, B. and Hughes, M. (2003) *A Basis for Skills: Investigating Intermediate Skills*, London, Learning and Skills Development Agency.

Stewart, T.A. (1997) *Intellectual Capital: The New Wealth of Organizations*, New York, Doubleday.

STF (Skills Task Force) (2000) *Skills for All: Research Report from the National Skills Task Force*, London, DfEE.

Tamkin, P. (1997) Lifelong learning: a question of privilege?, *Industrial and Commercial Training*, **29**(6): 184–6.

Taylor, N. (1996) Professionalism and monitoring CPD: Kafka revisited, *Planning Practice and Research*, **11**(4): 379–89.

Thorpe, R., Woodall, J., Sadler-Smith, E. and Gold, J. (2004) Studying CPD in professional life, *British Journal of Occupational Learning*, **2**(2): 3–20.

Thursfield, D., Smith, V., Holden, R. and Hamblett, J. (2002) Individual learning accounts: honourable intentions, ignoble utility?, *Research in Post-compulsory Education*, **7**(2): 133–46.

Watkins, J. and Drury, L. (1995) The professions in the 1990s, in S. Clyne (ed.) *Continuing Professional Development*, London, Kogan Page.

Wilson, J.P., Blewitt, J. and Moody, D. (2005) Reconfiguring higher education: the case of foundation degrees, *Education and Training*, **47**(2): 112–23.

Wilson, R. and Hogarth, T. (eds) (2003) *Tackling the Low Skills Equilibrium: A Review of Issues and some new Evidence*, Coventry, University of Warwick, Institute of Employment Research.

Witz, A. (1992) *Professions and Patriarchy*, London, Routledge.

Wood, H. and Moore, S. (2005) *An Evaluation of the UK Union Learning Fund: Its Impact on Unions and Employers*, London Metropolitan University, Working Lives Research Institute.

Woodall, J. and Gourlay, S.N. (2004) The relationship between professional learning and continuing professional development in the UK: a critical review of the literature, in J. Woodall, M. Lee and J. Steward (eds) *New Frontiers in HRD*, London, Routledge.

Zemke, R., Raines, C. and Filipczak, B. (2000) *Generations at Work: Managing the Clash of Veterans, Boomers, Xers, and Nexters in your Workplace*, Washington, DC, American Management Association.

Graduates and Graduate Employment

17

Rick Holden, Niki Kyriakidou, Crystal Ling Zhang and Jim Stewart

Chapter learning outcomes

After reading this chapter, you should be able to:

- Identify significant trends in the UK graduate labour market
- Locate interest in graduates and 'graduate jobs' within ideas about the knowledge economy, human and social capital
- Understand certain tensions in terms of the supply of and demand for graduates
- Assess claims that graduates may increasingly be underutilized
- View the transition from university to work as problematic

Chapter outline

Introduction

When discussing the contents of this chapter, we asked ourselves if we knew of any country in the world where the number of graduates as a proportion of the working population was declining. We could think of none. Indeed, all the evidence, empirical and anecdotal, suggests considerable growth, leading to a key question: are graduates the new vanguard of HRD? In recent years, all European countries have increased the numbers of students in higher education (HE). Official data from China (www.chinato-day.com/edu/a.htm) indicates that in 2004 there were 2.8 million graduates from colleges and universities, an increase of over 33% since the previous year. In Finland, 70% of young people enter HE. In the UK, there is a specific policy to increase the number of young people entering HE to 50% by 2010. All this is powerful testimony to the prevailing assumption that HE and people with the benefit of a higher education (that is, graduates) are a desirable societal asset. Indeed we would go a step further and suggest that the dominant view held by governments across the globe is that more graduates equal greater economic prosperity. Since the Lisbon summit in 2000 (see www.ec.europa. eu/internal_market/smn/smn21/s21mn14.htm), for example, European social and economic policy has been predicated on the assumption that increased skill levels as a result of education and training hold the key to success of Europe in terms of global competition (Purcell et al., 2003). Successive national governments since the late 1980s have developed policies to increase participation and widen access to HE in the belief that the resulting increased output of graduates will bring economic and social prosperity.

Reflective question

Consider these two quotes:

'Graduates are the generators of the business in five or ten years time' (head of global HR consulting PricewaterhouseCoopers, *Financial Times*, 8.8.08)

'Despite economic boom Chinese graduates face a struggle for jobs ... with three out of five university leavers expected to join the ranks of the unemployed' (Jonathon Watts, *Guardian*, 9.8.06)

Is the seemingly inexorable rise of a graduate labour force a driver of economic growth or simply a response to such growth?

The knowledge economy

The question posed above takes us to the heart of a debate about the supply of and demand for graduate labour. A key context for this are powerful ideas about the rise of the knowledge economy. Briefly, the orthodox argument unfolds as follows. A knowledge economy is developed around a more 'professional' (and thus educated) workforce. It has witnessed a fundamental shift away from a set of traditional industries dominated by unskilled and semi-skilled work to one where most work is now knowledge work. The growth in jobs within the knowledge economy is for jobs requiring high levels of education and skill. Knowledge has replaced capital as a key element in production and thus graduates, with their high levels of knowledge and skill, are in considerable demand. This follows from the argument that economies in the developed regions and countries of the world have progressed from situations where land was the major factor of production (feudal economies) through periods when capital was the major factor of production (industrial economies) to the situation now where labour is the major factor of production (knowledge economies) (see Stewart and Tansley, 2002).

Of course, labour has always been significant but the argument is that the form of labour has changed from physical in feudal and industrial economies to emotional and social labour and especially intellectual labour in knowledge economies. This analysis is significant in relation to claims of the necessity of education at higher levels, since it is assumed that the development of the knowledge and skills necessary for social and intellectual labour requires longer, different and higher level education and training than the development of the knowledge and skills necessary for physical labour. Governments bolster the 'economy needs more graduates' perspective with powerful 'human capital' arguments (investment in skills through education and training; see, for example, Becker, 1964), noting the evidence of a graduate earnings premium. Thus, in terms of HRD and the knowledge economy, graduates are indeed at the vanguard – they are a critical resource to enable the knowledge economy to grow and flourish.

National and regional policies are clearly influenced by such assumptions. For example, the UK government's White Paper, *The Future of Higher Education*, argued:

> Demand for graduates is very strong and research shows that 80% of the 1.7 million new jobs which are expected to be created by the end of the decade will be in occupations which normally recruit those with higher education qualifications. (DfES, 2003)

Within the Yorkshire & Humberside Regional Economic Strategy (Y&HRDA, 2006), graduates are identified as critical if the region is to achieve its ambitious targets of regeneration and growth. It talks of 'reversing the brain drain', which has seen the region suffer a net loss of graduates, and equates graduate capability with 'high skill levels', 'enterprise' and 'innovativeness', the key 'drivers', it maintains, of growth within its 'priority' sectors of digital technology, bioscience, advanced engineering, healthcare and environmental technologies.

However, a closer look at this whole thesis suggests that reality falls some way short of the hype. And, in terms of the focus of this chapter, as soon as one begins to question the pervasiveness of the knowledge economy, a whole bundle of questions appears in relation to the graduate labour market and graduate employment. Where better to see the knowledge economy emerging in its full glory than the USA, the most advanced industrial economy in the world? Yet this claim sits uneasily with the data. Drawing on US Bureau of Labor Statistics, Brown and Hesketh (2004, p. 47) note that no more than 30% of all Americans are in occupations requiring a bachelor's degree: 'For every job requiring a degree there are two that do not.' They also note an extract from one of George Bush's government initiatives to develop the workforce:

> Most new jobs will arise in occupations requiring only work-related training (on-the-job training or work experience) even though these occupations are projected to grow more slowly. This reflects the fact that these occupations accounted for about 7 out of 10 jobs in 2000. (Brown and Hesketh, 2004, p. 47)

Others raise similar concerns and questions. Grugulis (2007), exploring the myths and realities of the knowledge economy, points out that while one can see a rise in knowledge-intensive workplaces (R&D, consultancies, advertising and marketing agencies), she distinguishes between such knowledge-intensive forms and 'knowledgability in work', where customer service staff, clerks and call centre workers know a great deal about the work they do but tasks are constrained and discretion limited.

Activity

In groups of three or four, compare your work experience. Think about the jobs that exist in the places where you have worked. Extend this to work you are familiar with – perhaps jobs held by your immediate family. Discuss the levels of skill in these jobs. Compare your findings with the evidence discussed thus far.

In the context of the UK, and in some contrast to the official government predictions noted above, the Leitch report (2006) on UK skills argues that most of the 'skills gaps' are at an intermediate level[1] and not at degree level. Keep (2005) is more critical, arguing that Taylorism is alive and well. Substantial numbers of organizations in certain sectors of the UK economy compete on costs and not skill levels. The pressure, if anything, is to deskill. This is an entirely rational response, he argues, to the economic environment in which such organizations find themselves. HRD managers face a dilemma; they are under pressure from the rhetoric of good practice to upskill – perhaps recruit a graduate – yet under an equal but countervailing pressure from the reality of survival in a 'low skills equilibrium' marketplace (see Chapter 4).

In the face of such questions, the pervasiveness and dominance of the knowledge economy thesis begins to crumble somewhat. If large sections of the economy do not sit comfortably with knowledge economy characteristics and if sections of the knowledge economy in fact require relatively minimal levels of skill, this is of critical importance in the context of a rapidly increasing graduate population – one set to further increase over the forthcoming years. It raises questions such as:

- Is the continued expansion of HE justifiable on principally economic grounds?

- What evidence is there of segmentation within the graduate labour market; a distinction perhaps between an elite graduate labour force (principally from the traditional pre-1992 universities) and a larger 'rump' in terms of the jobs they do and the salaries they receive?

- What of the graduates emerging this year and the next and the next – what prospects do they face in terms of the utilization and development of their 'high level' skills?

- What of the transition into employment after HE? Might this be increasingly troublesome and difficult for a larger number of graduates year on year?

- What implications are there for the very notion of 'graduateness' and graduate identity if the expectations and aspirations inculcated in the process of HE (and rehearsed annually at graduation ceremonies up and down the land) turn out to be at odds with reality?

Subsequent sections of this chapter pick up these issues. A clearer picture of the graduate labour market and developing trends is a useful starting point.

The graduate labour market

Rising numbers of graduates

In the mid-1950s, the proportion of graduates was less than 5% in most European countries and the UK was then little different. However, expansion in the university sector saw the respective proportion doubling in many countries within 10 years (Brennan et al., 1996), and this has continued to rise. In the UK throughout the 1990s and 2000s, the overall numbers of students in HE have risen sharply, driven by a mixture of aggressive recruitment by some institutions and more recently by public policy seeking to widen and expand university entry (Table 17.1).

TABLE 17.1 Trends in student numbers at UK HE institutions, 1994/95–2006/07

	1994/95	2005/06	% increase	2006/07	% increase
Undergraduate	1,231,988	1,790,740	45%	1,803,425	46%
full-time	946,919	1,198,820	27%	1,208,645	28%
part-time	285,069	591,925	108%	594,780	109%
Postgraduate	335,325	545,370	63%	559,390	67%
full-time	129,711	234,220	81%	243,070	87%
part-time	205,614	311,150	51%	316,320	54%
All students	**1,567,313**	**2,336,110**	**49%**	**2,362,815**	**51%**

SOURCE: UK Universities (2008)

Interestingly, while Table 17.1 indicates a substantial increase in the numbers of students within HE in the UK, OECD (2007) data show Britain slipping down the league table in terms of its production of graduates. From third position in 2002, the UK has slipped to tenth place, having been overtaken by Australia, Denmark, Finland, Iceland, Italy, the Netherlands, New Zealand, Norway and Poland.

Although not all graduates return to the labour market, the vast majority do. The research of Purcell et al. (2005), based on samples of graduate leavers in 1995 and again in 1999, suggests a high percentage of graduates in full-time employment. With the government committed to ensuring that 50% of young people under 30 participate in HE (DfES, 2003), it seems likely that the supply of graduate labour will continue to expand. What may be more questionable, however, is the continued ability of the labour market to accommodate, fully, this increase in higher level skills. We will return to this issue later in the chapter.

Alongside the substantial increase in the number of 'new' graduates available to recruiters, year on year, their composition has also changed radically. This relates to the government policy of widening participation in HE. As well as raising absolute numbers, the current government in the UK is also committed to enabling groups not normally associated with entering HE to gain access and benefit from the assumed and claimed benefits of a university education and holding a degree.

Activity

Conduct a 'straw poll' among colleagues on your course. How many are 'new' entrants into HE – in the sense that none of their immediate family have a degree? Note the social characteristics, that is, family background, ethnicity, age and so on, of any new entrants. Then consider the 2006 government report *Widening Participation in Higher Education* (www.dfes.gov.uk/hegateway/ hereform/wideningparticipationnov06/index.cfm) and assess the government's objectives to widen participation in HE.

One result of the policy noted in the above report is to alter the previously established and conventional view of a 'typical graduate'. For example:

- Although considerable inequities persist (see also Galindo-Rueda et al., 2004), young people from all socioeconomic backgrounds are much more likely to go to university today as compared to 15 or 20 years ago. 'In fact the growth in HE participation amongst poorer students has been remarkably high, mainly because they were starting from such a low base' (Galindo-Rueda et al., 2004).

- HE is a major success story for ethnic minorities. In relation to the government's target of getting 50% of young people into HE, Modood (2006), drawing on DfES data, indicates a participation rate of 56% for black and minority ethnic groups in England compared with 38% for whites.

- Graduation in the UK is no longer the almost exclusive preserve of the under-25s – one in four of 'new' graduates are now over 25 years of age (HESA, 2006). In some universities, there is an almost equal balance between young and 'mature' graduates – many of the latter gaining their qualifications through part-time study. While the number of full-time students has increased substantially, the number of part-time students (at undergraduate level) has more than doubled (see Table 17.1).

- Increasingly, graduates emerge from new degree programmes. In 2005/06, the Higher Education Statistics Agency (HESA, 2006) reported that nearly 50,000 students were studying mass communications (media studies, publicity studies and so on). In 1996, no such category existed.

It might be expected that the introduction of student fees, and the potential increase in the level of current fees once the legal cap is withdrawn, will have a dampening effect on demand for HE. A report from the Higher Education Policy Institute (HEPI, 2007) argues differently and its most recent projections are based on an assumption that student fees will have minimal or even no effect on demand. Demand for graduates is likely to be a factor, in that it has an effect on supply, which in turn affects demand for

HE, that is, high demand for graduates from the labour market will lead to an increase in supply of graduates, which will increase demand for places in HE institutions. The potential impact of the economic climate on demand for graduates raises further questions. In HRD in Practice 17.1, Tesco, the UK's largest supermarket, indicates that its demand for graduates will be unaffected by any economic downturn. However, HRD in Practice 17.1 also suggests that other sectors, for example banking, may see significant declines. Thus, while the underlying trend seems to be one of increased participation in HE, the short-term sensitivity of demand remains more questionable.

HRD in Practice 17.1

Graduate recruitment in a recession

According to the Association of Graduate Recruiters' Graduate Recruitment Survey 2009 (www.agr.org.uk/news/agr_in_the_news/id.100.html), 'the party's over ... for now at least'. The report says that the number of graduate vacancies in the UK is to drop in 2009, the first time since 2003. Vacancies overall are expected to decrease by 5.4%, with most employers blaming the economic downturn for the cuts. The financial sector appears to be hardest hit, with banks expecting a massive 28% cut in the number of vacancies.

While economic uncertainty has led some graduate recruiters to reduce the number of jobs they are offering, others appear to be bucking the trend. The AGR reports that the engineering sector expects an 8.3% rise in graduate jobs. An Institute of Career Guidance (www.icg-uk.org) news item reports that Tesco is to maintain its commitment to quality graduate training schemes and it will not be reducing its graduate recruitment in 2009. Lorna Bryson, head of resourcing UK operations for Tesco, is reported as saying:

> While other employers are cutting back on hiring, we remain committed to hiring quality people who could end up going all the way to the top of the business. For example, back in 1979, Sir Terry Leahy, our current chief executive, joined as a management trainee. It's not all about working in stores. Tesco offers 15 different schemes for UK graduates from legal services and Tesco.com to property and engineering and buying and merchandising. We are looking for the Terry Leahy's of tomorrow – graduates who want to join one of the few British employers that still offers jobs with enough training and development opportunities to provide a career for life.

Changing graduate jobs

There have also been radical changes in the distribution of jobs in the graduate labour market in the past two decades. The growth in graduate jobs within the IT industry has been significant, and also within fields such as the media and a range of new healthcare professions. A key piece of research from Elias and Purcell (2003) has looked at how the increased numbers of graduates over recent years have been absorbed into the labour market. Table 17.2 describes a classification of graduate occupations based on the data (occupations are based on the 1990 Standard Classification of Occupations).

TABLE 17.2 Classification of graduate jobs

Type of occupation	Description	Examples
Traditional graduate occupations	The established professions, for which, historically, the normal route has been via an undergraduate degree programme	Solicitors Medical practitioners HE, FE and secondary education teachers Biological scientists/biochemists
Modern graduate occupations	The newer professions, particularly in management, IT and creative vocational areas, which graduates have been entering increasingly since educational expansion in the 1960s	Chartered and certified accountants Software engineers, computer programmers Primary school and nursery teachers Authors/writers/journalists
New graduate occupations	Areas of employment to which graduates have increasingly been recruited in large numbers; mainly new administrative, technical and 'caring' occupations	Marketing and sales, advertising managers Physiotherapists, occupational hygienists Social workers, probation and welfare officers
Niche graduate occupations	Occupations where the majority of incumbents are not graduates, but within which there are stable or growing specialist niches which require HE skills and knowledge	Entertainment and sports managers Hotel and accommodation managers Midwives, nurses Buyers (non-retail)
Non-graduate occupations	Graduates are also found in jobs that are likely to constitute underutilization of their HE skills and knowledge	Sales assistants Filing and record clerks Routine laboratory testers Debt, rent and cash collectors

SOURCE: Elias and Purcell (2003)

Elias and Purcell (2003) argue that using the new classification, although the majority of graduates are absorbed into graduate positions, the growth has happened among new graduate occupations rather than traditional and well-established modern ones. This is clearly indicated in Figures 17.1 and 17.2, which show the growth in employment across the range of Elias and Purcell's categories by gender. The rise in new graduate jobs for both male and female graduates is notable.

Graduate start-up: the new flavour of the month?

An interesting question to be asked of the Elias and Purcell (2003) research is the influence of the size of the organization in terms of new and niche graduate jobs. The UK government has been trying for some years to stimulate demand for graduates among SME establishments (see, for example, McNair, 1998; SBS, 2000). In a report to the Small Business Service, however, Holden et al. (2005) argue that policy has largely been 'running blind' as a result of a failure of research to provide meaningful insight into the uniqueness and complexity of the graduate labour market in the context of the small business sector. While there have been reports suggesting perceptions of 'mutual unattractiveness' (see, for example, Johnson and Pere-Verge, 1993; Westhead and Matlay, 2005), there has been a failure to examine rigorously the reality of graduate employment in such organizations. It is clear from statistics from the Higher Education Statistics Agency (at last reporting on size in terms of first destination employment) that graduates do find employment in small businesses (HESA, 2007). Evidence from 2003–04 suggests that approximately 30% of HE leavers obtain first destination graduate[2] employment within SMEs (Holden et al., 2007).

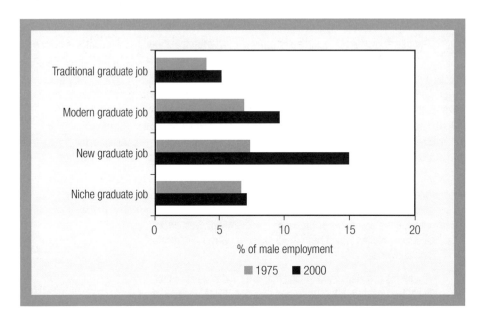

FIGURE 17.1 Male graduate employment

SOURCE: Elias and Purcell (2003)

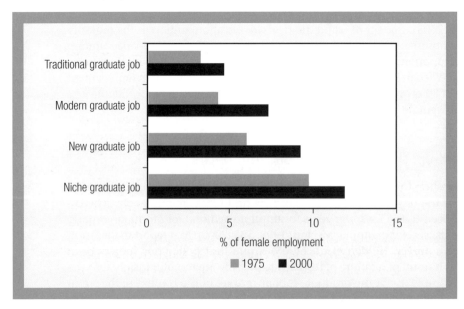

FIGURE 17.2 Female graduate employment

SOURCE: Elias and Purcell (2003)

While the size of organization in terms of first destination graduate employment remains an issue for further research, government interest appears to have shifted to a new imperative. The drive is now to encourage new graduates to start their own business. In 2004, the government established the National Council for Graduate Entrepreneurship, with a key policy objective to reduce the time-lag between completion of HE and start-up. This also translates into a regional agenda. The Yorkshire and Humberside Regional Development Agency (Y&HRDA, 2006), for example, reports that 'whilst trends in start-up are going in the right direction ... we are short of meeting the target of doubling graduate start-up rates by 2010'.

At the level of the university, start-up support appears in various forms, for example modules on start-up, specific units managing support and dedicated training provision and incubator services. Business Start-Up at Leeds Metropolitan University, for example, runs an annual 'summer school' for aspirant graduate entrepreneurs. However, available data suggest that the numbers remain small – about 4% of the graduate labour market (Green and Saridakis, 2007).

Reflective question

What exposure to entrepreneurship or enterprise have you experienced in your course thus far?

Activity

Visit your university's website and search for the sort of things it does in the name of enterprise/entrepreneurship education and training and its rationale for such provision.

An important conceptual ambiguity should be also be highlighted. There exists a tension between a view of enterprise and entrepreneurship as being intimately linked with business start-up and much broader notions; ones that see the values inherent within attitudes of enterprise and entrepreneurship as applicable in all sorts of walks of life (see Gibb, 2005). This said, it remains to be seen if the efforts of government and universities will, over time, have some real impact on the numbers of graduates who choose to start their own business on completion of HE. The ambiguity noted above is further addressed later.

In sum, therefore, the graduate labour market holds many contrasts and some apparent contradictions for understanding supply and demand. What is clear is that for those involved in it – graduates and recruiters – it has been something of a roller coaster ride during the 1990s and 2000s. The radical expansion in supply has triggered a heightened level of debate about its impact on the labour market. While the work of Elias and Purcell (2003) may offer some solace to today's students approaching graduation, it masks a number of critical tensions that greatly affect the lives of graduates approaching and entering the labour market and indeed their employers, and it is to these that the chapter now turns its attention.

The utilization of graduate labour

> One in three graduates is in a job that does not require a degree (*Financial Times*, 24.11.2006)

This quote captures well the tension we noted above; the question of whether increasingly there may be a mismatch between the high-level skills inherent within a degree programme and the nature of work subsequently undertaken by many graduates. This raises fundamental questions about the nature of what constitutes a 'graduate job' and a 'graduate career'.

The blue-chip corporate 'milk round' still flourishes, albeit with notable changes in the use of web-based technology to attract and engage graduate recruits. The promise is much as it has been – exciting, challenging, stretching jobs that build fully on HE. A report for the Centre for Research in Employment and Technology in Europe in 1998 argued that employers wanted graduates to 'hit the ground running' (Rajan et al., 1998), implying a virtuous circle of existing capability, utilization and opportunity for further development. Little has changed. HRD in Practice 17.2 illustrates the recruitment of graduates at Herbert Smith, a multinational law firm.

HRD in Practice 17.2

Herbert Smith

According to its website (www.herbert-smith.com), Herbert Smith is a leading and full-service international legal practice with a 1,300-lawyer network across Europe, the Middle East and Asia. For graduates, the website indicates that 'training and practising at Herbert Smith LLL prepares you for much more than life as a lawyer; it sets you up for a life rich in opportunities and variety'. The careers part of the website (www.herbertsmith.com/Careers/) provides pro-files and stories from recently recruited graduates. For example:

> Within days of walking into Herbert Smith, Katherine Fortey, a new graduate recruit, found herself playing a key role in a complex international finance deal that was important not only to the client but also to the firm. According to Katherine, 'I've never learnt so much and learnt it so quickly ... before working on the Ripplewood deal I'd had a two-week introduction to the firm and a four-day introduction to finance.'

Research-based case studies lend some testimony to such scenarios. Holden and Hamblett (2007), for example, report that graduates are clearly drawing considerably on their degree and being stretched well beyond it in their first year of working. One graduate, an engineer, notes in interview:

> By the second week there were new jobs coming in and I was soon onto new jobs and starting from scratch and with quite a bit of responsibility ... thinking about it now [six months after joining the firm] I certainly didn't expect to be doing anything like this within the first year of starting ... I am being asked to try and achieve a very stiff challenge.

On the basis that impact on organizational performance is a reasonable 'proxy' measure for 'utilization', then studies indicating that graduates 'add value' provide support for the argument that organizations can fully exploit the capabilities embodied within a graduate. The economic strategy for the Yorkshire and Humberside region (2006–15), for example, argues strongly that high-level skills appear to make a telling difference to business performance. The strategy document cites a study of South Yorkshire's advanced manufacturing and metals industries showing that firms that recruited graduates were performing significantly better than those who did not in terms of innovation and employment growth (Y&HRDA, 2006, p. 15). Nationally, the Knowledge Transfer Partnerships[3] programme annually reports a significant bottom line impact as a result of the recruitment of graduates (www.ktponline.org.uk/). In terms of graduate perceptions, a research report suggests that graduate satisfaction with work and employment is generally high, and although the report lacks detail, it does suggest that both employment contexts and financial benefits meet graduate expectations (Truss et al., 2006). Such evidence suggests something of a virtuous cycle.

However, there is evidence that sits less comfortably with the sort of scenarios noted above. Consider HRD in Practice 17.3 in the context of the discussion in this part of the chapter.

HRD in Practice 17.3

Waiting on tables

In a study of the utilization of hospitality graduates, Holden and Jameson (1999) note the experience of one organization that has recruited one or two graduates into its growing vegetarian restaurant business. One of the partner's discusses Lucy, the most recent graduate recruit: 'She's one of the few people who actually works across all the restaurants ... she's also the best person I've ever employed. She's quite stunning really, she has a real understanding of what we're about as a company.'

This is a glowing testimony for Lucy, in many ways the 'star' of recent graduate recruits. But the same partner is acutely aware that, for all that, Lucy actually spends 70% of her time waiting on tables. He comments:

My problem is this ... this is a fairly small company, growing but still small. How much can you afford to have people doing, you know, project-type stuff ... They've got a certain level of intelligence, they've reached a certain maturity and they've got a bit of background knowledge ... what worries me with graduates is how much of that knowledge they ever get to apply in something like this.

Of course, the context here is clearly that of a small business and there is some evidence to suggest that such problems may be more acute within the SME sector than within large organizations (see also Chapter 12 and, for example, Holden et al., 2005; Pittaway and Thedham, 2005).

Large-scale research is thin on the ground. However, the *Financial Times* (24.11.07) headline 'Rise in graduates overqualified for their jobs' refers to research undertaken by the

LSE's Centre for Economic Performance (www.ft.com/cms/s/0/42c631d2-9a2f-11dc- ad70-0000779fd2ac.html?nclick_check=1; see also Green and Zhu, 2008). The findings indicate that the proportion of non-graduate jobs has 'risen sharply since 1992', and also reveal a growing educational divide. Graduates from 'new' universities appear to be much more likely to end up in non-graduate jobs than their 'Oxbridge' counterparts. The research only covers graduates over the age of 25 to allow those surveyed time to settle into their careers, but nevertheless shows that for male and female graduates, the proportion in non-graduate jobs was approximately one-third. The authors conclude that the evidence provides a sharp 'counter' to the government's arguments to increase the supply of grad- uates. It should also be noted that this research follows earlier work in the same vein, which purports to show that less than 15% of graduates employed were using their degree (Green et al., 2003). However, research such as this provides only a broad picture of what is happening, without necessarily providing any insight into reasons. A recent study into the experience of graduates working as call centre operators found that they themselves make active choices to engage in non-graduate work and jobs following graduation for various reasons related to lifestyle and other choices (Blenkinsopp and Scurry, 2007). The same study also found that such choices can lead to changes in career aspirations and also a situation where graduates become stuck in non-graduate jobs because of their own initial decisions on graduation.

Clearly, we have a somewhat ambiguous picture. The evidence from the work of Green et al. seems to be at odds with that from Elias and Purcell, where even in the new cate- gories of new graduate jobs and niche graduate jobs, over 80% are reported to be 'using' their skills. Part of the ambiguity might be explained by what is meant by 'using' one's degree as compared to 'using one's skills' (see below). Further conceptual ambiguity is reflected in an ongoing failure to pin down just what is a 'graduate job'.

We conclude that there are sufficient empirical data to question the prevailing ortho- doxy of justifying an expansion of HE on the basis that the knowledge economy is a reality – a reality requiring an ever increasing supply of graduates. We turn now to a closely related theme, that of the employability of graduates in the context of their capa- bilities on completion of their HE.

Graduate employability

Well prepared for employment?

The REFLEX (Flexible Professional in the Knowledge Society) project, initiated by the European Commission in 2001, surveyed graduates, five years after graduation, in 13 European countries. The survey addressed graduates' HE and employment experiences, the competences they believed were required in their workplaces, their roles and respon- sibilities within the workplace, and their attitudes to their HE in the light of those experiences. In a summary of the findings, Brennan (2008) notes that UK graduates were much less likely to believe that they were well prepared by their HE to perform their first destination graduate jobs. A substantial proportion of UK graduates did not believe that their initial graduate employment required education to degree level. The survey also asked graduates to comment on the level of education required by their current jobs, that is, the jobs held after five years. Findings here provide further evidence that although salary levels and levels of unemployment are broadly comparable, UK HE has a somewhat different relationship to the labour market than other European countries (Figure 17.3).

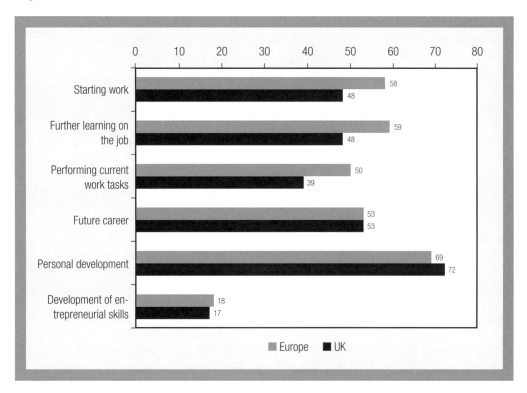

FIGURE 17.3 Perceptions of the degree programme five years on: 'A good basis for …'

SOURCE: Brennan (2008)

Brennan also reports some evidence from the research that UK employers put greater emphasis on 'where' rather than 'what' the graduate has studied, 'giving some support for the view that it is the "selection" function rather than the "training" function that is most important in UK higher education' (Brennan, 2008, p. 4).

A bachelor's or a master's degree?

Against a background of a process of harmonization of European HE systems since the 1999 Bologna Declaration (for more on this, visit the UK Higher Education in Europe Unit at www.europeunit.ac.uk), a number of commentators have begun to question if there is a shift afoot in how employers perceive the value of a first degree as an entry qualification into the labour market. According to research undertaken by Arthur et al. (2007) as part of the REFLEX project, employers and university leaders are increasingly expressing reservations about the value of a bachelor's degree as an initial entry qualification.

1 What are your intentions on completion of your degree, a job or a further qualification?

2 Are you at all concerned that your degree may not lead to employment of your choice?

Little (2008) cites studies that report, for example, German employers' concerns that those with only a bachelor's degree will need more in-house training. This would shift responsibility for such work-related training from university to the employers themselves. Little (2008, p. 389) questions if 'continuing international pressures towards the master's degree' could in fact lead to a 'devaluing of the bachelor's degree' within the UK. She concludes, however, that such shifts are less likely or at least will be slower in the UK. This is because of a stronger influence within the UK of the professions. In other words, a first degree in the UK is more likely to be followed by relevant employment and continuing development aligned to professional bodies. This said, Little (2008) acknowledges the likelihood of a heightening tension in the perceived responsibilities between HE and employers in terms of initial work readiness. This theme is further addressed below.

The skills agenda

There is an influential body of opinion that believes the concerns about underutilization are overplayed. Influenced heavily by the voice of the employer, a set of issues has emerged that refer to matters held, conventionally, under a banner of 'the skills agenda'. What skills do new graduates need as they leave behind their three or four years within HE and begin to take a significant step down a career pathway? Firmly wedded to the notion that the knowledge economy is a reality and will produce graduate jobs and absorb the ever increasing supply of graduates, this has been the focus of the UK government – as it seeks to justify the expansion – and vice chancellors up and down the land – as they seek to indicate how their institution will best add value. In other words, successful absorption into the labour market is simply about matching skills acquired through HE and the degree programme with those required and demanded by employers.

HRD in Practice 17.4

Microsoft

Stephen Uden, head of skills and economic affairs at Microsoft, sees forging greater links between universities and business as 'the key to the higher-end skills issues. There are not enough people coming out of schools and universities with the right skills.'

'We can't take employers out of the system so I have always been a big advocate of employers being involved in the system', he says.

Concerned by IT skills' shortages in its own industry, Microsoft, which has 2,500 employees in the UK, became involved in an initiative, called Revitalise IT, led by e-skills UK, the Sector Skills Council for business and IT. Employers work with universities and schools to change attitudes and stimulate demand among young people for technology-related degrees and careers. The network also supports universities in developing courses that reflect the needs of the IT industry.

As Uden explains, 'It is creating a vehicle for discussion between stakeholders. Universities want to teach stuff that's relevant and, because students are paying to go to university now, they are asking about earnings. We are finding universities are very interested in doing this.'

But Uden admits that this kind of practice is new. 'There has previously been a bit of a barrier between the sectors. Universities and industry did not talk.'

Now, he explains, 'universities are making a genuine effort to engage business, and by and large the business community has stepped up to the challenge too. It bodes well for the future.'

Source: News item (2008) *People Management*, 15 May

The characteristics of graduates are the determinant of their employability (Holmes, 2001, 2006). The skills agenda is not wholly without a research base. In 1995, based on research among its membership, the Association of Graduate Recruiters published an important piece of work looking ahead to the next century (AGR, 1995). Among its conclusions were that graduates need a range of skills beyond the 'technical', as well as attributes such as team working, problem solving and self-reliance. Similarly, on the basis of research with graduates, Harvey et al. (1997) argued that they needed 'transformative skills' – graduates who can do more than respond to change but anticipate and lead change – and to be 'critical lifelong learners' as they leave HE. The influence of such research and the political rhetoric underpinning it can be seen in several characteristics of today's HE provision:

- Enterprise in HE: initiatives stretch back to 1987 with the first Enterprise in Higher Education programme (Elton, 1991). More recently, notable initiatives have been the DTI-funded Science Enterprise Challenge, which focused on disciplines in science, engineering and technology and a wide range of Higher Education Academy-funded resources and tools for teaching staff (www.heacademy.ac.uk/ourwork/learning/employability/links).

- Higher Education Funding Council Centres of Excellence in Teaching and Learning: one such centre is based at Sheffield Hallam University, Embedding, Enhancing and Integrating Employability (E3I). According to the website (www.hefce.ac.uk/learning/tinits/cetl/final/show.asp?id=69), E3I's 'holistic approach advocates embedding and integrating a coherent range of employability features in programmes, benefiting all students, developing attributes needed for success in their chosen paths and lifelong development, and supporting widening access to employment'.

- Personal effectiveness skills: few undergraduate degree programme are now without some sort of recognition and acknowledgment of the need to complement studies with personal, professional, work-related skills and development. All business studies' students at Leeds Metropolitan University take a personal, academic, career and effectiveness programme. It runs through all three years of their course. Students in year two, for example, are asked to complete a reflective portfolio that addresses their developing personal skills in the context of their future employment and career aspirations. Elsewhere, Higson and Bullivant (2006) provide an interesting account of an Aston University initiative to encourage students to reflect on their employment experience, while Major (2006) describes the provision of career information to enhance the employability of undergraduate travel and tourism management students at Northumbria University.

Activity

In groups of three or four, visit the Graduates Yorkshire website – www.graduatesyorkshire.co.uk. View the case studies, and then draw up a list of what you feel employers are saying they want from graduates by way of skills and capabilities. Do you feel these are the skills and capabilities you are developing through your degree course?

Before we leave this theme of employability, it is important to note the concerns of those who see fundamental flaws in this skills agenda. Holmes (2001, 2006), for example, presents a critique of, and an alternative to, this dominant approach to employability. He contends that neither skills nor attributes are empirical phenomena so they cannot be identified through empirical investigation. Thus, lists and frameworks of skills are largely meaningless. Of greater importance is the notion of 'identity' and how and in what ways a graduate might acquire a sense of graduate identity. Critical is the understanding of graduates 'getting in and getting on' (Holmes, 2006, p. 2) within an organization after university. Holmes's arguments resonate with the view of Angot et al. (2008), who, on the basis of research with a number of graduates within French companies, question orthodox notions of the construction of 'professional identity'. Some of these identities, the authors suggest, are 'born of cynicism and disillusion' engendered by their experience. Similarly, Holden and Hamblett (2007), on the basis of their research with graduates at various points over their first year in employment, maintain that the situational context of learning about self for new graduates in employment renders much of the well-meaning personal and career development-type programmes within degree programmes of questionable relevance.

Transition

Much of the existing literature relating to graduates and graduate employment has tended to focus on entry into the labour market (recruitment) or, alternatively, issues of mobility and retention. Jenner (2008) argues that there has been little focus on the 'evolving nature of the relationship or the systems that support it'. Shaw and Fairhurst (2008) argue that graduate development managers need to re-examine their development schemes to ensure 'they not only meet the needs and expectations of the organization but also the individuals for whom they are designed'. The context for this suggestion is the notion that graduates in the latter half of the 2000s might be regarded as a new generation of graduates: 'generation Y' or 'millennials'. They discuss and illustrate how McDonald's has adjusted and tuned its graduate development programme to meet the perceived needs and attributes of these generation Y graduates.

Clearly tensions exist in terms of the employability, development and utilization of graduates. These are poorly understood for one very obvious reason. There has been insufficient research looking closely at the real experience of graduates in supposedly graduate jobs across different sectors and over a sufficiently long period of time to enable meaningful insight. The transition from HE to work is a difficult and complicated business. Of course, we are not the first to make such an observation. Nicholson and Arnold (1991), Arnold and McKenzie Davey (1992) and Connor and Pollard (1996) have all suggested a transition characterized by expectation mismatch with respect to the nature of work, line manager support, training and development and career management. Jenner (2008) suggests that transition models highlight the pivotal role of good support on joining an organization and the need for new graduates to be 'socialized' to their new surroundings.

HRD in Practice 17.5 provides an indication of how one major graduate recruiter endeavours to manage what it acknowledges is 'difficult'.

HRD in Practice 17.5

Kentz Engineers and Constructors

Kentz Engineers and Constructors is an international company with approximately 7,000 staff in Europe, Africa, the Middle East and Asia. The company provides a range of engineering and construction services. The oil and gas markets are prominent in the work of the company. According to its website (www.kentz.com/careers/graduates), the company 'places a huge emphasis on graduate development and everyone from the CEO downwards is committed to developing graduates in order to allow them to reach their full potential and achieve their career aspirations'.

In an article describing Kentz's approach to graduate deployment, O'Donnell et al. (2008) note the following model used to plan and guide graduate development.

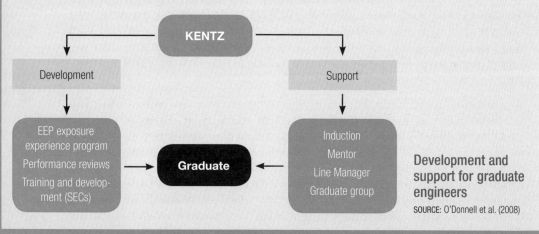

Development and support for graduate engineers

SOURCE: O'Donnell et al. (2008)

The authors argue that the Kentz model enables the company to help engineering graduates rapidly 'perform as junior engineers' and be ready to 'step up into design engineer, field engineer or project engineer'. Critical is the provision of mentoring, for example, in part as regards socialization but also in respect of 'agreeing objectives and standards with the mentee' and more broadly 'monitoring progress through work rotations'.

The case of Kentz reflects what might be considered to be the prevailing orthodoxy in terms of how the transition from HE to work might best be managed.

However, research by Fineman and Gabriel (1996), Holden and Hamblett (2007) and Jenner (2008) suggests that, even within the likes of Kentz, the reality may be somewhat different to the rhetoric. Jenner (2008, p. 436) highlights the contested nature of organizational life. In a case of graduate development within British Aerospace, she shows how graduate training, development and career management are best understood as discursive practice; 'shared understandings about the nature of work are constructed through a communication nexus of key stakeholders'. Holden and Hamblett (2007) rely on the testimony of five graduates in different employment settings to tell their stories of the ups and downs of the transition process over their first year of employment. Two extracts are presented below; one from a graduate working in the hospitality industry and one from a graduate engineer:

I'm starting to develop my manager voice as well, which is quite good, it gets the meaning across ... Another one that actually happened just three days ago, I was checking some rooms. As I walked past a room, I couldn't believe it, one of my guys was just sitting there watching TV. Everybody knows that that's unacceptable and I made it quite clear that I wasn't happy, and that little incident went all the way round the department, so now everyone is on a bit of eggshells around me ... But the porters ... they are all Polish ... had started to build their own little Polish mafia downstairs, so trying to control that is interesting ... the difference between me five or six months ago where I was sort of 'hi guys, how you doing?', you know, shaking hands and all that, now 'what are you doing?' if they are not on the floors and all that I want to know why, why I have seen them in the smoking room fifteen times and all that in the last ten minutes, do you know what I mean? (Holden and Hamblett, 2007, p. 536)

And certainly I suppose I did come across that in the first couple of months and it was just people are trying to sound you out as much as you're trying to sound them out ... I had one engineer and he tried to put some simple filing in my tray even though we've got a filing clerk. I'd handed something to him to sign as checker and he knows for a fact that it just needed to be put in the tray for the filing clerk to file it away and he purposely came and sat it on my in-tray, so I picked it up, walked back to his desk and put it in his in-tray and said, 'I'm not the ******* file clerk.' And walked off and you could see he was like, 'well actually yeah this lad does stand his ground as well, we won't bother him' ... But he was just doing it to test the waters and see ... after that happened, another engineer said 'My, that took some guts doing that.' I said, 'Why,

I'm not his filing clerk.' He said, 'I know but if you hadn't done it he'd have kept doing it. You're obviously learning quick!' (Holden and Hamblett, 2007, p. 552)

Reflective question

Contrast the lived experience of these two graduates with your exposure to personal and career development. Do they sit together comfortably?

Holden and Hamblett use the terms 'fragmentation' and 'cohesion' to help explain the lived reality of the transition into work over a period of a year. They note that from time to time and for all their respondents, such activities generate 'problems' – moments of fragmentation are experienced as mistakes occur. New experiences are encountered and as a result the role and the ways to perform effectively in role are assimilated and they move towards cohesion. The words of Joanna, another one of the graduate respondents, provide the authors with an insightful way of thinking about transition:

> She talks about learning 'from the inside'. We find this a particularly pregnant phrase. It suggests that 'things' look different 'from the inside'; that an 'outsider' might never really be made privy to the heart of the matter. We would sum the point thus: 'Conventions' are much bigger inside than they appear from the outside. (Holden and Hamblett, 2007, p. 574)

Thus, the authors remain sceptical that HE can simply equip students with employability skills or that neatly packaged induction programmes within the workplace can really address issues of power, identity and a sense of 'feeling at home'. The reality of 'learning about the job' and 'learning about self' are such that the HE curriculum and managers with responsibility for new graduates need a more nuanced, less mechanistic approach to assisting the HRD process for their graduate recruits.

Graduates: human and social capital

In 2007, Bill Gates, of Microsoft fame, addressed a group of new Harvard graduates. He said:

> Be activists. Take on big inequities ... You have an awareness of global inequity, which we did not have. And with that awareness you likely have an informed conscience that will torment you if you abandon those people whose lives you could change with very little effort. (www.networkworld.com/news/2007/060807-gates-commencement.html)

Gates is referring to the potential for graduates to contribute to social capital. The notion of social capital refers to the value that social networks and social relationships have within a society. It has its roots in debate and discussion about democracy (see, for example, de Tocqueville, 1998), and the value of education (Dewey, 1899). The publication of Robert Putnam's *Bowling Alone* in 2000, which warned that our stock of social capital – 'the very fabric of our connections with each other' – has renewed interest in how best to build and sustain social structures and networks.

A degree of consensus exists that education, and within this particularly HE, has an important role to play in engendering and fostering social capital. In Scotland, for example, the 2007 HE spending review argued that 'the societal impact of higher education in improving people's lives is clear and it is not purely economic' (Scottish Government, 2007, p. 10). The report cites the *Wellbeing Scotland* report, which indicates that graduates are healthier, less obese, have longer life expectancy, commit less crime and participate more fully in civic society (Universities Scotland, 2007). Graduates, it argues, play a major part in creating effective, confident, good citizens. On average, graduates contribute more to the creation of social capital – a further rationale for the increase in graduate numbers noted earlier. Even after adjustments are made for income and wealth (graduates typically earn above average salaries), societies with higher proportions of graduates demonstrate higher proportions of volunteerism, take more action on environmental issues and hold more positive attitudes towards race and gender equality. We might conclude by suggesting, therefore, that the contribution of graduates to social capital may be larger than the direct labour market and macroeconomic effects. Thus, graduates who find themselves unemployed or, more likely, underemployed can sleep easily, confident in the knowledge that they are making a valuable contribution to society simply by virtue of 'being a graduate'.

It was argued in Chapter 1 that higher education is a site and context of HRD practice. The focus on graduate employment provides a clear example of and support for this argument. The notion of 'employability' in particular indicates that HE has a role in developing knowledge and skills of relevance to the labour market, which are transferable to, and applicable in, employment. In some cases and in particular those linked to the 'old' professions of, for example, medicine and law, HE provides training as well as education and develops specialist knowledge and skills that have little or no value outside particular occupations (see, for example, Urwin and Hedges, 2006). In other cases, the argument is that HE can and should develop generic knowledge and skills that are relevant to all or at least a range of occupations and job roles, and this is the basis of the case for focusing on employability. A fundamental question, arising from the notion of employability, is the extent to which these generic knowledge and skills require a university education to develop. And, relatedly, there is the question of the extent to which these knowledge and skills are exclusively associated with what is termed a 'graduate job' and a 'graduate career'.

Summary

- Globally, the number of graduates as a proportion of the working population is rising.

- The UK's target is for 50% of young people to participate in HE.

- The high level of skills and capabilities associated with graduate labour raises the prospect that graduates might be regarded as the new vanguard of HRD.

- A key rationale for the expansion of HE is based on the demands of the knowledge economy. In reality, such arguments have serious flaws.

- The relationship between HE and the graduate labour market is significant. Current trends are for HE to emphasize the importance of 'employability' as a component of any degree course. New initiatives also promote enterprise and entrepreneurship.

- A picture of a complex graduate labour market emerges, raising issues about:

  - the changing profile of graduate jobs

  - whether a substantial minority of graduates may be overqualified and under-utilized in the work they do after qualifying

  - graduate identity and the very notion of what is 'graduateness'.

- The prospects of further tensions appear in the context of the process of the harmonization of European HE systems since the Bologna Declaration. Reports from some European countries suggest that employers are questioning the value of a bachelor's degree.

- The transition from HE into work remains problematic. While research raises interesting questions about a possible new generation of graduates (generation Y), the transition process is often fragmented, uneven and difficult to manage, raising doubts as to the real value of the whole employability agenda within HE.

- While graduates may conventionally be considered as human capital, recent research suggests that their contribution to social capital may actually outweigh any direct labour market effect.

Discussion questions

1 Why might graduates be regarded as the 'vanguard' of HRD?

2 What are the main factors driving the increase in the supply of graduates?

3 In the context of a UK target of 50% of young people participating in HE, what is the current situation? Explore how this may vary by gender, ethnicity and social class.

4 What are the different types of jobs in Elias and Purcell's (2003) 'new' classification of graduate jobs?

5 What is meant by the 'skills agenda'? How does your degree course purport to enhance employability?

6 Is the successful deployment of graduate labour simply a matter of matching the skills acquired through HE with those required and demanded by employers? How does research on the transition from HE into work shed light on this 'matching' process?

7 What is social capital and what might be an important relationship between graduate labour and social capital?

Further reading

Brooks, R. and Everett, G. (2008) The impact of higher education on learning, *International Journal of Lifelong Education*, 27(3): 239–54.

Brown, P. and Hesketh, A. (2004) *The Mismanagement of Talent: Employability and Jobs in the Knowledge Economy*, Oxford, Oxford University Press.

HEA (Higher Education Academy) *Learning and Employability*, Series 1 and Series 2, www.heacademy.ac.uk.

HESA (Higher Education Statistics Agency) (2007) *Destinations of Leavers from Higher Education Longitudinal Survey*, Cheltenham, HESA.

Purcell, K., Elias, P., Davies, R. and Wilton, N. (2005) *The Class of '99: A Study of the Early Labour Market Experience of Recent Graduates*, Warwick Institute for Employment Research.

Preston, D.S. (ed.) (2002) *The University of Crisis*, Amsterdam, Rodopi Press.

Prospects UK, An overview of the graduate job market, www.prospects.ac.uk.

Notes

1 Clarity about the exact meaning of intermediate skills is difficult. The OECD considers both level 2 and level 3 qualifications (for example NVQ level 2 and 3 qualifications) in the UK to be 'intermediate' level. Intermediate-level skills may also be defined in relation to intermediate-level jobs. The UK's National Skills Task Force proposed that these include associate professional occupations, clerical and secretarial occupations, and craft and skilled manual jobs. It gave examples of intermediate-level job titles, including traditional skilled trades, such as fitter, welder and bricklayer, and an immense range of non-craft occupations such as nurse, hairdresser, estate agent, office manager, laboratory technician, insurance broker and sales representative (see also Smeaton and Hughes, 2003).

2 HESA make an important distinction between 'graduate' and 'non-graduate' jobs.

3 Knowledge Transfer Partnerships (KTP) is Europe's leading programme helping businesses to improve their competitiveness and productivity through the better use of knowledge, technology and skills that reside within the UK knowledge base. Each partnership employs one or more recent graduates to work on a project, which is core to the strategic development of the business. The forerunner of the KTP programme was the Teaching Company Scheme (see also Senker and Senker, 1994).

References

AGR (Association of Graduate Recruiters) (1995) *Skills for Graduates in the 21st Century*, Cambridge, AGR.

Angot, J., Malloch, H. and Kleymann, B. (2008) The formation of professional identity in French apprentice managers, *Education and Training*, **50**(5): 406–22.

Arnold, J. and McKenzie Davey, K. (1992) Beyond unmet expectations: a detailed analysis of graduate experiences during the first three years of their careers, *Personnel Review*, **21**(2): 45–68.

Arthur, L., Brennan, J. and de Weert, E. (2007) *Employer and Higher Education Perspectives on Graduates in the Knowledge Society*, Open University, Centre of Higher Education Research and Information.

Aston, L. and Bekhradinia, B. (2003) *Demand for Graduates: A Review of the Economic Evidence*, Oxford, Higher Education Policy Institute.

Becker, G.S. (1964) *Human Capital: A Theoretical Analysis with Special Reference to Education*, New York, Columbia University Press.

Blenkinsopp, J. and Scurry, T. (2007) Hey gringo!: the HR challenge of graduates in non-graduate occupations, *Personnel Review*, **36**(4): 623–37.

Brennan, J. (2008) *The Flexible Professional in the Knowledge Society (REFLEX): Overview Report*, Open University, Centre for Higher Education Research and Information.

Brennan, J., Kogan, M. and Teichler, U. (1996) Higher education and work: a conceptual framework, *Higher Education Policy Series*, 23.

Brown, P. and Hesketh, A. (2004) *The Mismanagement of Talent: Employability and Jobs in the Knowledge Economy*, Oxford, Oxford University Press.

Connor, H. and Pollard, E. (1996) *What Do Graduates Really Do?*, Report No. 308, Brighton, Institute of Employment Studies.

DfES (Department for Education and Skills) (2003) *The Future of Higher Education*, White Paper, Cm 5735, London, TSO.

De Tocqueville (1998) *Democracy in America*, Ware, Wordsworth.

Dewey, J. (1899) *The School and Society*, Chicago, University of Chicago Press.

Elias, P. and Purcell, K. (2003) *Measuring Change in the Graduate Labour Market*, Research Paper No. 1, Warwick Institute for Employment Research.

Elton, L. (1991) Enterprise in higher education: work in progress looking back over the first three years, *Education and Training*, **33**(2): 5–9.

Fineman, S. and Gabriel, Y. (1996) *Experiencing Organizations*, London, Sage.

Galindo-Rueda, F., Marcenaro-Gutierrez, O. and Vignoles, A. (2004) *The Widening Socio-economic Gap in UK Higher Education*, London, Centre for the Economics of Education.

Gibb, A. (2005) *Towards the Entrepreneurial University*, Policy Paper 003, Birmingham, National Council for Graduate Entrepreneurship.

Green, F. and Y. Zhu (2008) Overqualification, job dissatisfaction, and increasing dispersion in the returns to graduate education, Discussion Papers in Economics, 0803, University of Kent.

Green, F., Mayhew, K. and Molloy, E. (2003) *Employer Perspectives Survey*, London DfES.

Greene, F. and Saridakis, G. (2007) *Understanding the Factors Influencing Graduate Entrepreneurship*, Birmingham, National Council for Graduate Entrepreneurship.

Grugulis, I. (2007) *Skills, Training and Human Resource Development*, Basingstoke, Palgrave Macmillan.

Harvey, L., Moon, S. and Geall, V. (1997) *Graduates' Work: Organizational Change and Students' Attributes*, UCE Birmingham, Centre for Research into Quality.

HEPI (Higher Education Policy Institute) (2007) *Demand for Higher Education to 2020 and Beyond*, www.hepi.ac.uk/pubs.

HESA (Higher Education Statistics Agency) (2006) *Students and Qualifiers Data Tables*, www.hesa.ac.uk/index.php/component/option,com_datatables/Itemid,121/.

HESA (Higher Education Statistics Agency) (2007) *Destinations of Leavers from Higher Education Longitudinal Survey*, Cheltenham, HESA.

Higson, H. and Bullivant, N. (2006) Preparing Aston Business School students to reflect on their employment experience, in N. Becket and P. Kemp (eds) *Enhancing Graduate Employability in Business and Management, Hospitality, Leisure, Sport and Tourism*, York, Higher Education Academy.

Holden, R.J. and Hamblett, J. (2007) The transition from higher education into work: tales of cohesion and fragmentation, *Education and Training*, **49**(7): 516–88.

Holden, R.J. and Jameson, S.M. (1999) A preliminary investigation into the transition and utilisation of hospitality graduates in SMEs, *Tourism and Hospitality Research*, **1**(3): 231–42.

Holden, R.J., Jameson, S.M. and Lashley, C. (2005) Graduate transition into employment in hospitality SMEs: on a road to nowhere?, *Industry and Higher Education*, **19**(1): 65–73.

Holden, R.J., Jameson, S., and Walmsley, A. (2007) New graduate employment within SMEs: still in the dark?, *Journal of Small Business and Enterprise Development*, **14**(2): 211–27.

Holmes, L. (2001) Reconsidering graduate employability: the graduate identity approach, *Quality in Higher Education*, **7**(2): 111–19.

Holmes, L. (2006) Reconsidering graduate employability: beyond possessive instrumentalism, seventh International Conference on HRD Research and Practice Across Europe, University of Tilburg, 22–24 May.

Jenner, S. (2008) Graduate development, discursive resources and the employment relationship at BAE Systems, *Education and Training*, **50**(5).

Johnson, D. and Pere-Verge, L. (1993) Attitudes towards graduate employment in the SME sector, *International Small Business Journal*, **11**(4): 65–70.

Keep, E. (2005) Keynote Speech, Sixth International Conference on HRD Research and Practice Across Europe, Leeds.

Leitch, S. (2006) *Prosperity for all in the Global Economy: World Class Skills*, London, HM Treasury.

Little, B. (2008) Graduate developments in European employment: issues and contradictions, *Education and Training*, **50**(5): 379–90.

McNair, S. (1998) *Graduates and Small Businesses*, DfEE Briefing Paper, Sheffield, DfEE.

Major, B. (2006) Enhancing travel, tourism and hospitality management graduates employability, in N. Becket and P. Kemp (eds) *Enhancing Gradate Employability in Business and Management, Hospitality, Leisure, Sport and Tourism*, York, Higher Education Academy.

Modood, T. (2006) Ethnicity, Muslims and higher education entry in Britain, *Teaching in Higher Education*, **11**(2): 247–50.

Nicholson, N. and Arnold, J. (1991) From expectation to experience: graduates entering a large corporation, *Journal of Organizational Behaviour*, **12**(5): 413–29.

O'Donnell, H., Karallis, T., Sandelands, E. et al. (2008) Corporate case study: developing graduate engineers at Kentz Engineers and Constructors, *Education and Training*, **50**(6).

OECD (Organization for Economic Co-operation and Development) (2007) *Education at a Glance: OECD Indicators*, Paris, OECD.

Pearson, R., Perryman, S., Connor, H. et al. (1999) *The IES Annual Graduate Review 1998–1999*, Report No 354, Brighton, Institute of Employment Studies.

Pittaway, L. and Thedham, J. (2005) Mind the gap: graduate recruitment in small businesses, *International Small Business Journal*, **23**(4): 403–26.

Purcell, K., Elias, P., Davies, R. and Wilton, N. (2005) *The Class of '99: A Study of the Early Labour Market Experience of Recent Graduates*, Warwick Institute for Employment Research.

Putnam, R. (2000) *Bowling Alone: The Collapse and Revival of American Community*, New York, Simon & Schuster.

Rajan, A., Chapple, K. and Battersby, L. (1998) *Graduates in Growing Companies: The Rhetoric of Core Skills and Reality of Globalisation*, Tunbridge Wells, Centre for Research in Employment and Technology in Europe.

Scottish Government (2007) *Scottish Budget Spending Review 2007*, Edinburgh, Scottish Government.

Senker, P. and Senker J. (1994) Transferring technology and expertise from universities to industry: Britain's teaching company scheme, *New Technology, Work and Employment*, **9**(2):81–92.

Shaw, S. and Fairhurst, D. (2008) Engaging a new generation of graduates, *Education and Training*, **50**(5): 366–78.

SBS (Small Business Service) (2000) *TCS Delivers Results for Business, Universities and Graduates*, London, SBS.

Smeaton, B. and Hughes, M. (2003) *Investigating Intermediate Skills*, London, Learning and Skills Development Agency.

Stewart, J. and Tansley, C. (2002) *Training in the Knowledge Economy*, London, CIPD.

Truss, C., Soane, E., Edwards, C. et al. (2006) *Working Life: Employee Attitudes and Engagement*, research report, London, CIPD.

UK Universities (2008) *Higher Education in Facts and Figures, Summer 2008*, UK Universities, London.

Universities Scotland (2007) *Wellbeing Scotland: The Contribution of Higher Education to Scotland's Wellbeing*, Edinburgh, Universities Scotland.

Urwin, P. and Hedges, P. (2006) Undergraduate student perceptions of quantitative skills abilities, and subsequent performance in quantitative skills testing, in N. Kyriakidou (ed.) *International Reflections on Education and Business*, Athens, Institute of Education and Research.

Westhead, P. and Matlay, H. (2005) Graduate employment in SMEs: a longitudinal perspective, *Journal of Small Business and Enterprise Development*, **12**(3): 353–65.

Y&HRDA (Yorkshire and Humberside RDA) (2006) *The Regional Economic Strategy for Yorkshire and Humber 2006–2015*, Yorkshire and Humberside RDA.

Cross-cultural HRD

Niki Kyriakidou, Crystal Ling Zhang and Paul Iles

Chapter learning outcomes

After studying this chapter, you should be able to:

- Compare the 'institutionalist' and 'culturalist' positions in comparative HRD

- Define the concept of culture

- Analyse some key theoretical perspectives on culture

- Evaluate the implications of the above perspectives on international and cross-cultural HRD

- Analyse the role and importance of training and development in international enterprises, especially in the preparation and effectiveness of international employees

- Critically analyse intercultural and cross-cultural training (CCT), including e-CCT

- Analyse HRD in international organizations, joint ventures and in knowledge transfer, with particular reference to China and the Middle East ·

Chapter outline

Introduction

Comparative HRD: the nationality thesis

Institutionalist approaches and national business systems

What is culture?

The concept of culture and HRD

HRD in international enterprises

Cross-cultural/intercultural training

International knowledge transfer and HRD

Summary

Introduction

With increasing globalization, issues of culture and cultural awareness have become more important. However, national differences in values and practices persist, and various models have been developed to analyse cultural differences, linked to differences in behaviour. This chapter explores the importance of 'institutionalist' and 'culturalist' explanations of national differences in institutions, values and behaviours. The development of international managers and other staff has become imperative, and cross-cultural training (CCT) in particular has grown in importance. The chapter discusses different types of global or international staff, especially the kinds of competences and skills needed to perform effectively in the light of cross-cultural adjustment problems. It analyses the kinds of training and development strategies necessary for effective performance, using various case studies to illustrate effective practice. Finally, the chapter explores the role of HRD in joint ventures and knowledge transfer, especially the role expatriates can play in coaching and mentoring locals, with particular reference to China and the Middle East.

Comparative HRD: the nationality thesis

The nationality thesis argues that globalization does not necessarily force countries, sectors and firms towards a convergence in their structure, culture, patterns of behaviour and HRD policies and practices. Institutional and cultural legacies continue to exert an influence, for example US firms differ from German firms in the strategic role played by HRD, the role of the unions and their commitment to training and development. Different frameworks have been developed to analyse and examine this issue; the most significant contributions to the debates so far have come from culturalist and institutionalist approaches (Vo, 2009).

Institutionalists argue for the importance of different national institutions or 'business systems' in explaining comparative differences in HRD. Culturalists argue for the continuing importance of national culture in explaining such differences, explaining organizational structure and practice as a collective enactment of beliefs and values or shared cognitive structures, ideas and understandings (for example Hofstede, 2001). We shall explore culture in more detail below. The claim here is that organizational patterns and processes, and managerial beliefs and behaviours, are driven by shared understandings and ideas. In contrast, institutionalists argue that this approach fails to consider cultural patterns as dynamic and emerging characteristics linked to historical development, with close relationships to specific institutions and social groups.

HRD in particular is performed differently in different countries, as we saw in Chapter 4, and HRD policy and practice remains diverse. Globalization is often overstated; most trade is not global, but uneven, mostly regional and conducted between relatively distinct national economies. Most international enterprises are not genuinely 'transnationals', but national companies with international business operations – most of their income, employment, strategic decisions, board composition and share ownership are still mainly rooted in their home country, and nation-states remain significant global players, with distinctive laws and regulations.

Institutional theorists claim that organizations are socially constituted, rooted in institutional settings. They analyse national institutions and their interactions with business and management as 'national business systems'. Usually the state, the financial and educational/HRD systems, the industrial relations system, and the network of business associations such as chambers of commerce are seen as key institutions affecting business and management. These institutions all impact on enterprises' HRD processes, such as how firms go about training and development. For example, Germany and Japan may be seen as 'collaborative' business environments, in contrast to the more 'competitive' Anglo-Saxon US/UK models.

Institutionalist approaches and national business systems

Institutional perspectives therefore see national institutional arrangements as relatively robust, demonstrating significant inertia in the face of pressures for changes. They focus on macro-level societal institutions, in particular those that govern 'access to critical resources, especially labour and capital' (Whitley, 1999, p. 47), and look to differences in the organization and the activities of the state, the capital, labour and financial systems, and the route taken by different countries to industrialization and modernization. Systematic analysis of the major national institutions and the interactions between these institutional arrangements is termed the 'national industrial order' by Lane (1992) in her analysis of British financial versus German production-oriented capitalism, and 'national business systems' by Whitley (1999) in his analysis of divergent capitalisms and the different paths taken by nations. This is the term we will use here.

Whitley (1999) distinguishes three 'ideal types' of national business systems:

1 *Particularistic:* lacking trust in formal institutions, with a weak or predatory state, weak collective intermediaries and norms governing transactions, and paternalistic authority relationships, for example China. This leads to flexibility and 'opportunistic hierarchies'. Opportunistic hierarchies rarely develop complex and stable organizational capabilities, owner control is typically direct and personal, coordination is highly personal and non-routinized, and flexibility is the response to the unpredictable environment.

2 *Collaborative*: interlocking institutions encouraging cooperative behaviour such as Japan, Germany, Austria and Sweden. This leads to 'cooperative hierarchies' and corporatist/interventionist approaches, as we saw in Chapter 3. Owners and managers share authority with employees and partners, and skilled manual workers are typically integrated into the organization as core members and 'social partners'.

3 *Arm's-length*: flexible entry and exit within an institutionalized formal system, with competitive capital markets. The state acts as a regulator, and training is seen more as a matter for individual firm investment than a matter for coordinated collaboration between the state, employers and unions, for example the USA, and California in particular, as we saw in Chapter 3. This leads to 'isolated hierarchies', where independence between collective actors is low, formal procedures govern interrelationships, and owners tend to be remote from managers. Firms are reluctant to share authority, and organizational competences and competitive capabilities are highly firm specific.

However, there is a danger of overgeneralization. Whitley (1999), for example, claims that Japan and Germany are examples of collaborative business environments generating cooperative hierarchies, but there are significant differences between the Japanese and German education and training system, such as the development of the internal labour market in large Japanese firms, as opposed to the great support German firms receive from the system of education and technical/vocational training, which focuses on skill development that is responsive to economic needs (Lane, 1995). German firms are strong in professional specialization and career advancement within functional hierarchies, in contrast to the rotation of generalist managers often practised in Japan.

The institutional perspective is criticized as being overdetermined by national stereotypes, and neglecting the potential for human agency. It is also difficult to apply in transitional periods. In his study of retail practices in China, Gamble (2003) argues that it is difficult to assess what exactly constitutes the contemporary Chinese 'national business system', and thus what the distinctive Chinese approach to HRD actually is. So we also need to explore culturalist perspectives.

What is culture?

Although there is no standard definition of culture, the concept of culture is deeply rooted in human history. 'Culture' usually refers to the shared attitudes, beliefs and behaviours that individuals learn from the family and society in which they live – a dynamic process, impacting on everything that people do and think. We learn culture through interaction, observation and imitation in order to participate as members of a social group.

Activity

Various definitions of culture in different contexts can be found at www. answers.com/culture&r=67.

In groups of four or five, discuss the differences in national cultures. List some components of your own national culture. Write down your definition of culture in no more than 20 words.

Culture is typically defined as:

> the system of shared beliefs, values, customs, behaviours, and artefacts that the members of society use to cope with their world and with one another, and that are transmitted from generation to generation through learning. (Bates and Plog, 1990, p. 7)

Culture is therefore often seen as the set of commonly held and relatively stable beliefs, attitudes and values that exist within an organization (organizational or corporate culture) or society (national or societal culture). It influences the way organizations and managers undertake and implement decision making and resolve problems (Hall, 1984). Culture is embodied in symbols, rituals and heroes, and reflected in organizational communication, such as manners, dress codes, social rules and norms and role models.

Cultural dimensions

According to Kluckhohn and Strodbeck (1961), there are six fundamental dimensions for cultural analysis:

- Who are we, and how does society conceive of people's qualities, for example good, bad, lazy, capable of being changed?

- How do we relate to the world – existence?

- What do we do? In some countries, this question refers to what someone does, in others to what someone is.

- How do we relate to each other? For example, do we think of ourselves as individuals or members of a social/professional group?

- How do we think about time? According to Harris et al. (2004), western societies see time as a commodity to be managed effectively. Other societies, for example Mediterranean countries and many Asian countries, have looser relationships with time.

- How do we think about space, for example room size, physical space between two people when they are talking to each other? Northern European and Japanese people often desire more distant relationships than many African or southern European peoples.

Perhaps the most influential cultural theorist has been Hofstede (2001), whose typology of cultural dimension is widely used in cross-cultural research. Initially in a survey of IBM employees, Hosftede found:

- National differences in behaviour and attitudes

- Such differences did not change much over time

- National cultural values were more significant than work-related values, such as those related to profession/age/gender/position in the organization

- People bring their ethnicity and culture to the workplace.

Hosftede's cultural dimensions are as follows (adapted from www.geert-hofstede.com/geert_hofstede_resources.shtml):

- *Power distance* (PD) focuses on the degree of equality, or inequality, between people in the society. A high power distance ranking indicates that inequalities of power and wealth have been allowed to grow and are generally accepted. In organizational terms, PD relates to the centralization of power and degree of autocratic leadership (Harris et al., 2004).

- *Individualism* (IDV) focuses on the degree to which the society reinforces individual or collective achievement and interpersonal relationships. High IDV indicates a larger number of looser relationships, and low IDV typifies societies of a more collectivist nature.

- *Masculinity* (MAS) focuses on the degree the society reinforces the traditional masculine work role model of male achievement, control and power. High MAS indicates that the country experiences a high degree of gender differentiation, while low MAS indicates low levels of differentiation and discrimination between genders, with females treated relatively equally to males.

- *Uncertainty avoidance* (UA) focuses on levels of tolerance for uncertainty and ambiguity within the society. High UA indicates rule-oriented societies that develop laws, rules, regulations and controls in order to reduce uncertainty. Low UA indicates a society that is less rule oriented, more readily accepting of change and more risk oriented.

- *Long-term orientation* (LTO) focuses on the extent to which a society exhibits a pragmatic, future-oriented perspective rather than a conventional historic or short-term point of view. Countries scoring high on this dimension have a long-term perspective, easily accept change and emphasize thrift and investment, for example China. Cultures scoring low on this dimension, for example many West African societies, believe in absolute truth, are traditional and have a short-term perspective.

In organizational settings, taking the two dimensions of UA and PD together, you can see differences in the way employees think about organizational structure and operations, as shown in Table 18.1.

TABLE 18.1 Thinking about organizational structure and operations

Dimensions	Structure and operations	Countries
Low UA, high PD	Personal bureaucracy	Hong Kong, India
High UA, high PD	Full bureaucracy	Japan, France
Low UA, low PD	Marketplace bureaucracy	UK, Scandinavia
High UA, low PD	Workflow bureaucracy	Israel, Germany

SOURCE: Adapted from Brooks (2003)

For example, in societies with high UA and high PD, such as Japan and France, the key element is the standardization of work processes by specifying work contents (Harris et al., 2004). Employees in high UA and low PD societies, such as Israel and Germany, tend to work in organizations where roles and procedures are clearly specified and coordination and control are achieved through qualifications and skills acquisition.

Schwarz (1990) developed his classifications because of difficulties with Hofstede's classifications; collectivism/individualism have some values in common, and the dichotomy implies a polar distinction in which individual and collective goals cannot be coincident (Gouveia and Ros, 2002). Schwarz (1990) included seven dimensions of analysis:

1 conservatism

2 hierarchy

3 mastery

4 affective autonomy

5 intellectual autonomy

6 egalitarian commitment

7 harmony.

Steenkamp (2001) argues that Schwartz's classification is superior in its theoretical grounding, but has not been empirically tested.

Another well-known approach is based on the work of Trompenaars (1997), who defines culture as an instrument to solve problems. There are three universally shared problem areas: human relationships, time and nature. Trompenaars and Hampden-Turner (1997) consequently identify seven bipolar dimensions:

- Universalism versus particularism

- Communitarianism versus individualism

- Neutral versus emotional

- Diffuse versus specific cultures

- Achievement versus ascription

- Human–time relationship

- Human–nature relationship.

Each dimension represents a dilemma for acting and deciding (www.7D-culture.com/Content/dim1_htm provides further explanation of these dimensions). People are often forced to choose. For example, in the UK, we would tend to favour universal in terms of preferences for rules for everyone to be followed, whereas in Spain, there might be a preference to work out rules based on the particulars of a situation. If people are unaware of these preferences, this is likely to result in misunderstandings and difficulties.

Reflective question

How aware are you of your cultural preferences?

Hofstede's work in particular has received sustained criticism, especially since the publication of the second edition of the original book (Hofstede, 2001), particularly in terms of methodology. McSweeney (2001, 2002) finds national culture implausible as a systematically causal factor of behaviour, arguing that both functionalist and other paradigms are needed for future research into national culture and for understanding social behaviour in different national cultures.

The concept of culture and HRD

The increasing drive of most international corporations to standardize managerial practices across nations has been influenced by national cultural values as companies search for effective international practices. Little research has been conducted on the impact of culture in the area of HRD (McGuire et al., 2002). As Ardichvili and Kuchinke (2002, p. 145) report:

International and comparative research is one of the fastest growing areas of scholarly inquiry in HRD. All international HRD studies, regardless of specific topics of investigation, sooner or later refer to culture. Therefore, the treatment of culture in international HRD research is a matter of central importance.

Culture and perceived 'cultural distance' have been shown to affect entry modes of international enterprises, such as acquisition, greenfield site or joint venture (JV) (Holliman et al., 2008). Interventionist models of HRD tend to be more commonly found in societies showing lower IDV and LTO, but lower UA than countries showing 'voluntarist' models, as Chapter 4 has shown.

National culture may particularly impact HRD; some Asian or Latin employees may expect training styles to be formal, deferential and directive (high PD), resisting group work that mixes hierarchical levels or involves direct, open criticism or feedback. Scandinavians may expect HRD to be informal and participative, and see direct feedback as welcome. People from high UA cultures, for example Japan, may be unhappy with experiential training, for example action learning and outdoor development, which involve some risk and uncertainty, preferring more structure. Learning styles may vary also with culture (see Zhang et al., 2006; Zhang and Iles, 2008; and HRD in Practice 18.1).

HRD in Practice 18.1

Kellogg, Brown and Root

Kellogg, Brown and Root (KBR) was formed in 2001 when Halliburton, the US firm, brought together three business units dealing with defence and civil infrastructure, oil and gas projects, and petrochemical projects into one subsidiary. KBR has global revenues of nearly $6bn and operates in over 100 countries. It has a workforce of 45,000, of which 12,000 are located in the UK.

The attraction and retention of managerial talent was seen as vital to the formation of effective teams appropriate for the different projects. However, a previous attempt to 'export' a competency framework developed at the Houston headquarters of Halliburton had been unsuccessful. During 2002 and 2003, KBR drove through a massive project to create a global competency framework. This was achieved by the creation of global steering groups clustered around over 100 'job families'. The outcome was a series of definitions of the core skills of individual jobs. These job-specific competencies were supplemented by 39 'transferable managerial behaviours' applicable to most KBR managers, whatever their country of location. The system is supported by an online database, and forms the basis of performance management and career planning, by enabling senior management across the whole company to search for talent in other countries. The link to the corporate intranet assists younger managers to plan their careers by accessing information on the skills needed for their current job or any post anywhere in the company.

Source: Carrington (2003, in Edwards and Rees, 2006, p. 182)

Taking Hosftede and Trompenaars' cultural dimensions into consideration, try to identify and critically analyse the difficulties a management development scheme like that developed in KBR might encounter in practice, in terms of definitions of the core skills of individual jobs.

Discuss your answers with your group members, supporting your arguments from your experience and what you have read so far in this chapter.

For Redding (1994), most research has been positivist and descriptive; more interpretative and ethnographic methods using semi-structured interviews or observation studies could be employed (Mallory et al., 2008). Many researchers, however, continue to rely on Hofstede (2001), even in studies of China, which was not included in the original study (Hong Kong, Singapore and Taiwan, which were, show different profiles). We can illustrate these problems with regard to Chinese culture.

Chinese culture and HRD

Hofstede (2001) appears to assume that national territory corresponds to cultural homogeneity, but China is not homogeneous, instead displaying strong regional differences and many minority ethnic/religious subcultures. The words 'individualism' and 'collectivism' appear to differ in meaning in different countries (Mead, 1994). Japanese employees may be more loyal to their organizations, while Chinese employees may well be more loyal to their families. However, both adopt the principle of collectivism, not western individualism.

The fifth Hofstede variable, LTO or Confucian dynamism – the capacity to adapt traditions to new situations, a willingness to save, a thrifty approach to scarce resources, a willingness to persevere over the long term and subordinate one's own interests to achieve a purpose, and a concern with virtue (Hofstede and Bond, 1988; Hofstede, 1991) – did not appear in his original work, but was identified as important by Chinese scholars among Chinese employees.

Other studies have taken different approaches. Using Confucian ideas more directly, they show significant generational diversity in cultural values. Liu (2003) has used interview and survey studies in two factories in northeast China, where recent organizational reforms (performance-based reward, less job security and so on) have led to differences in assumptions, beliefs and values between first generation, pre-reform employees and second generation, younger employees, hired post reform. Confucianism influences the way employees perceive the organization as a symbolic family, amplified by an earlier Maoist-era ideology emphasizing group rewards. Younger workers expressed unhappiness with regard to harmony at the expense of poor performance, and differed in their interpretation of bureaucracy, security, stability and loyalty. They saw these factors in less relational, more conditional, contractual and calculative ways, more like many young westerners.

Li and Nimon (2008) have also shown generational differences among Chinese workers, distinguishing between the social reform, Cultural Revolution, consolidation, and pre-liberation generational cohorts. The Cultural Revolution cohort, born in the 1940s and 50s, was least satisfied with recent economic reforms and their current position. It was more likely to work in state-owned enterprises, especially when compared to the younger 'social reform' cohort. These two studies illustrate that culture can change and is not static; we need to take generational diversity into account when considering culture. Gamble (2003) also warns us that cultures should be considered not as a static monolith but a shifting and changeable repertoire with diverse strands.

Cultural arguments linking Chinese economic performance to Confucian values therefore neglect the ways in which culture changes – cultures interact with, and influence, each other. Confucian culture stresses practical realism and pragmatism. China has always flourished when open to other cultures (for example the Tang Dynasty, 618–907) than when culturally closed. Ideas have been introduced from outside, indigenous elements reinterpreted, links built with foreign ideas, and cultural elements refocused, for example education redirected to science and technology rather than the humanities. An about-turn on Confucian values may also occur, with li (profit) put ahead of yi (justice), and 'outdated' values, for example gender inequality, may be rejected.

There are, however, attributes of Chinese culture not found in the west, such as guanxi (interpersonal relations), which remains of key importance for conducting business. Authority may be based on interpersonal relations rather than legal rationality. Guanxi is essential if approval is to be granted in order to access resources, generating personal obligations in response to requests for assistance by someone in the network.

Another distinctive cultural attribute is the concern for loss of 'face'. The Chinese do not usually attempt to convince others that they know best; dialogue and encouragement are more important than linear communications or persuasion.

Reflective question

What do you think the consequences of these Chinese cultural values might be on HRD policies and practice?

Culture and HRD in the Middle East

The Middle East is often neglected in many western HRD textbooks, although some books and journal issues specifically addressing HR issues in the Middle East have recently appeared (for example Budhwar and Mellahi, 2006).

One issue is what actually constitutes the Middle East. Some definitions include, for example, Cyprus and Turkey, while others restrict the term to the 'Levant'; but, however defined, it is very diverse in terms of language, religion, governance and economic development – some countries are major importers of labour, and others rely heavily on the remittances of migrant labour. Literacy and education levels also vary widely. However, across the region, some common issues for HRD include:

- the influence of national and international politics
- the impact of religion, ethnicity and culture
- the influence of western multinationals
- the significance of gender.

In much of the region, gendered inequality in career paths is widespread, especially for rural and poor women, although in some countries, upper-class women are afforded better career opportunities than in many western countries; reported discrimination in Turkey, for example, is lower than the EU average, and women play an increasingly active economic role, including at senior levels. In Iran, gender segregation in employment has also opened up other career opportunities for women, who have made great advances in university education.

Management styles in the Arab world, especially the Gulf states, may be seen as distinctive, constituting a 'fourth paradigm' (Weir, 2000, 2003), although Budhwar and Mellahi (2006, p. 296) claim that there is no 'Middle Eastern model'.

This style is held to consist of:

- family businesses
- autocratic but consultative ownership
- a rhetoric of consultative decision making within an essentially hierarchical structure; joint decision making may be seen as a weakness, and one-to-one consultation is preferred (Muna, 1980).

From the perspective of Hofstede (2001), Arab cultures are seen as high in masculinity, relatively high in long-term orientation, and middling on individualism, uncertainty avoidance and power distance. Some researchers have noted that HRD often reflects Islamic values (Tayeb, 1997) and that an 'Islamic work ethic' can be identified, influencing a range of attitudes towards organizational change and commitment. In particular, the family is the cornerstone of social life, with social identity and loyalty oriented to the 'wider' extended family, despite the diminution in size of the typical household and the tendency of younger generations to have a more independent life (Suliman, 2006). In much of North Africa, as we saw in China, more individualized work values have also emerged, especially among younger generations educated abroad and with access to western media (Budhwar and Mellahi, 2006; Yahiaoui and Zoubir, 2006).

A distinctive feature of Arab HRM is the role of networks; like Chinese guanxi, interpersonal connections are rooted in family and kinship ties but extend into business and organizational life. This phenomenon is often termed 'wasta' in the Gulf states or 'piston' ('pull', 'clout' or 'connections') in French-influenced North Africa. Although the importance of networks is evident elsewhere – such as the role of military and university connections in Israel – wasta in the Arab world is often professionalized, with mediators interceding on behalf of clients to obtain advantages in jobs, documents, tax breaks, training and university admissions. Such practices may help to humanize the workplace, but Arab critics often condemn such 'intercessionary' wasta as illegal or unethical – unlike guanxi in China, the phenomenon is less publicly acknowledged. However, they often continue to seek and provide wasta benefits for themselves, their relatives and their friends. Nepotism is also common in Iran, especially for senior managerial positions, and favouritism also remains an issue in Turkey (Hutchings and Weir, 2006).

In many Middle East countries, the public sector remains dominant, although some countries, such as Jordan and Turkey, have embarked on structural adjustment and privatization programmes to reduce government expenditures and turn around unprofitable state-owned businesses (Budhwar and Mellahi, 2006). These are often accompanied by changes in HRD policies away from centralized civil service models towards the expansion of training and performance management/talent management initiatives. Generally, international enterprises apply more 'strategic' HRD and better pay and training than local organizations, although with greater pressures on performance (Budhwar and Mellahi, 2006). However, in the Gulf states, training and development programmes are far more extensive in the public sector (Suliman, 2006).

HRD in international enterprises

Internationalization and the effective use of international HR located outside the home/ parent country are major issues affecting firms in an increasingly global economy. Key questions include: why and how do enterprises adopt different HRD policies and practices in areas such as training, talent management and career development? One framework developed by Budhwar and Mellahi (2006) draws attention to the influence of:

- national-level factors – culture and the national business system

- contingent factors – organizational size, structure, ownership, stage of internationalization, life cycle stage

- organizational-level corporate and HRD strategies.

Here we will view an international enterprise's HRD policies and practices as the product of an interaction between three factors (Shen, 2005):

1 *Home (parent) country factors:* such as domestic, cultural, legal, political and economic factors. Multinationals often remain deeply rooted in the national business systems of their country of origin, rather than being global, rootless, footloose entities (see Ohmae, 1990).

2 *Host country (local) factors:* such as cultural context, as reflected in local regulations and practices, for example the Chinese and Arab contexts explored earlier.

3 *Firm-specific factors:* for example senior management's attitudes towards internationalization and the international strategy, structure, and corporate culture of the firm.

Perlmutter (1969, p.11) argued that the international enterprise can choose four generic orientations to HRD, depending on its orientation to 'foreign people, ideas and resources':

1 *Ethnocentric:* here the international enterprise takes an 'international' approach, exporting the home system and making strategic decisions at headquarters, with mother–daughter relationships with subsidiaries. Key positions like CEO and finance director are filled with parent country nationals (PCNs), that is, expatriates; for example, a Japanese bank in Thailand may be run mostly by Japanese. This approach is more common in some sectors, for example banking and

finance, and in some countries, especially those high in uncertainly avoidance, for example Germany and Japan. It has the advantage of maximizing global efficiency and standardization, but minimizes local responsiveness – local managers who may know their local labour and product markets well are marginalized – and worldwide learning – all strategic ideas and initiatives tend to come from the home country headquarters. For example, a French manager in a Chinese–French JV producing handicrafts for the French market may employ the HRD practices of the French parent company (Mallory et al., 2008).

2 *Polycentric:* here the enterprise adopts a 'multinational' or 'multidomestic' approach, adapting its HRD policies to the local system, for example the role of guanxi in China, and wasta in the Middle East. Local subsidiaries enjoy much autonomy as 'sisters', and host country nationals (HCNs) occupy important positions. This strategy is more common in some sectors, for example advertising and food, where local responsiveness is important and in enterprises from some countries, for example European countries.

In addition, some positions, for example HRD director, are also most likely to be filled by locals, as cultural differences in motivation and reward may be seen as important. However, the strategy minimizes standardization, as each subsidiary can go its own way. Worldwide learning is inhibited, as ideas and innovations in one subsidiary tend to stay there. One reason for this is that HCNs are unlikely to be promoted to positions in other countries, or to headquarters.

3 *Geocentric:* here the enterprise takes a 'global' approach to operations. Through global sourcing of talent and global training programmes, it promotes employees to positions and subsidiaries regardless of nationality. It is likely to employ many transcountry/third country nationals (TCNs) to maximize global standardization as well as worldwide learning – using similar HRD vehicles to spread learning – and local responsiveness – by using HCNs or 'cosmopolitan' TCNs rather than 'ethnocentric' PCNs. This strategy is characteristic of transnational companies seeking to maximize global efficiency, national responsiveness and worldwide learning. Firms may thus create new HRD systems, different from home and local systems.

4 *Regiocentric:* here the enterprise uses a 'regional' approach, with managers from a particular region, for example Europe, East Asia, North America, enjoying regional (but not global) autonomy. Common HRD policies are developed across the region (but not globally), for example within Europe, there may be regional sourcing of talent and pan-European mobility, but this may not extend to Asia or North America.

Cultural distance between countries is also seen as an issue. Where subsidiaries are located in 'distant' countries, enterprises seem to prefer to deploy PCNs, although they may be less willing to go in these situations. In addition, the age of the subsidiary affects choice: the longer a subsidiary has been in operation, the fewer PCNs may be used, as the need for 'control' may be diminished in long-standing, presumably successful, affiliates.

Enterprises may have several motives for using international transfers:

- to fill positions with technically qualified staff
- to facilitate management development

- to facilitate organization development through knowledge transfer and the development of common corporate structures, culture and policies.

However, expatriates may experience problems, resulting in various degrees of 'failure', such as early return and underperformance – often judged more likely for US rather than European expatriates. They may struggle to adapt to the local culture, language, laws and customs, and their families (spouses and children) may also struggle to adapt. Both parties may be operating outside their 'comfort zone'. This is often described in terms of 'culture shock' and problems of 'cultural adaptation', or the degree of psychological comfort with the host country. This involves work, interaction and general adjustment (Waxin and Panaccio, 2005). HRD has a key role to play here, as job satisfaction and organizational socialization have been found to play important roles in the adjustment of Taiwanese expatriates in the USA by Liu and Lee (2008).

Reflective question

Why do expatriates/PCNs often find it hard to adapt to different cultures?

Expatriation often demands a high degree of interaction between members of different cultures. Western expatriates from individualist cultures are likely to value independence and self-sufficiency, whereas collectivists may value social relationships, gift giving and reciprocity (Tan et al., 2005). Expatriates behaving in a 'masculine' manner, asserting themselves and engaging in competitive behaviour, may not be well received in more collectivist/feminine cultures. Self-presentation and saving face may be more evident here, and the expatriate may need to 'give face, save face and above all avoid causing loss of face' (Hutchings and Murray, 2003, p. 37).

These adjustment/adaptation problems may be reduced if careful attention is paid to systematic HRD. Often the PCN may be recruited in an informal way – approached over a vacancy at a coffee break or by the water cooler – using general or purely technical selection criteria – loyalty, commitment, professional competence – to meet immediate organizational needs. Rarely is the nature of the 'assignment' taken into account. Is it to:

- fill a position?
- open a new branch or process?
- operate in a JV?
- transfer knowledge to locals?

or is it a mixture of all these?

Rarely is the subsidiary taken into account; however, doing so may build trust. The person's motives for going are also not often considered. Is it to:

- travel?
- enjoy an adventure?
- escape a job, a career, a personal difficulty?
- pursue an interest in international issues?

- pursue an interest in the specific country or culture?

- advance a career?

Whether these expectations are aligned with company expectations or in conflict with them is also not often considered.

If the assignment is to be a long-term one, with significant degrees of interaction with locals, for example a CEO or HR director position for three years, rather than a technical 'troubleshooting' assignment expected to last three days, then it is worth investing in more systematic HRD processes. The candidate's interest and experience, qualifications, linguistic abilities, and cross-cultural competences may all be taken into account. For example, does the candidate:

- Have experience of residence or education abroad?

- Speak more than one language?

- Demonstrate openness to new experiences, empathy, respect and a lack of ethno-centrism?

- Show good communication skills, including nonverbal communication?

- Show an interest in an international career, or the specific job, company, and/or culture?

- Show a tendency to avoid narrow stereotyping?

- Show adaptability, flexibility and a tolerance of ambiguity?

In addition, the company will need to take diversity issues into account:

- childcare issues and dual career issues may mean a reluctance to travel

- partners may find visas, work permits and jobs commensurate with their skills and experience hard to get

- companies may falsely assume that customers or partners overseas will not accept women in senior positions, and so be reluctant to hire them.

National laws on equal opportunity need to be taken into account, for example many Japanese companies in the UK and USA have often run into problems by discriminating against women or non-Japanese employees.

Alternative forms of international working are being used by international enterprises in response to a dual career couple and work–life balance issues, as well as the desire to reduce expatriation costs and respond to localization pressures from governments. Such international assignments include short-term assignments, international commuting and frequent flying. Sparrow (1999) includes among 'international' staff home-based managers focusing on different global markets, internationally mobile managers, technical professionals and transitional managers. These roles all have implications for the type of HRD required and the skills that need to be developed.

In addition, using HCNs (locals) more widely carries distinct advantages – they are often cheaper to employ, not just in terms of salaries but in terms of travel, accommodation and family costs, and they are familiar with the local laws, culture, government officials and local languages. They may also allow the company to present a 'local' face, and demonstrate that it is a good corporate citizen by offering opportunities to locals, enhancing its reputation with key stakeholders such as government and customers.

However, the company may doubt the loyalty or commitment of locals to act in the interests of corporate control, locals may find communication with corporate headquarters difficult, not knowing the language fluently or the people well, and they may be blocking 'developmental' international opportunities for talented, promising, high-potential PCNs.

Another alternative is to use TCNs; they may be cheaper than PCNs, and are often cosmopolitan 'career internationals', with substantial international experience outside their own countries and probably good linguistic skills also. However, there may be local resentment – TCNs may be seen as blocking HCNs' opportunities, or they may come from politically sensitive countries.

Other alternatives may be to practise 'inpatriation', bringing subsidiary staff, whether TCNs and HCNs, to the headquarters to transfer knowledge, test suitability, socialize into company culture, and build multicultural teams. 'Virtual' assignments through international collaboration on projects by videoconferencing, email and telephone rather than physical travel are becoming more common. The use of a greater variety of shorter assignments – troubleshooting, contractual assignments, rotational assignments, knowledge transfer activities, training, personal development, short-term commuters, frequent flyers – is also increasing.

All such initiatives can be assisted by cross-cultural training (CCT), to which we now turn.

Reflective questions

1   Why do expatriates often report adjustment/adaptation problems on repatriation to their home country?

2   Why do you think alternatives to expatriation have grown in popularity?

Cross-cultural/intercultural training

It is common to assess cross-cultural/intercultural competences through interviews, assessment centres and personality tests, sometimes created specifically for international working. CCT may also be offered before departure and in-country, as well as before and after repatriation, which may be even more of a culture shock than expatriation. Failures to cope may be expensive for the employee, for example loss of self-confidence and reputation, stress, and for the company, for example loss of business opportunities and damage to the brand. These costs may be reduced by better preparation. Personality dimensions, in particular openness, may be related to CCT performance, as are adaptability, teamwork and communication, as measured by a group discussion exercise (Lievens et al., 2003). This suggests that attention must be paid to recruitment and selection, including selection for CCT. However, selection is still often haphazard and unsystematic, based on job knowledge and technical competence.

CCT is defined by Brislin and Yoshida (1994, p. 2) as:

> formal efforts to prepare people for more effective interpersonal relationships and for job success when they interact extensively with individuals from cultures other than their own.

Tarique and Caliguri (2004, p. 284) see it as any:

> planned intervention designed to increase the knowledge of expatriates to live and work effectively and achieve general life satisfaction in an unfamiliar host culture.

CCT is often proposed as an anticipatory mechanism to enhance cultural adjustment, and Black and Mendenhall's (1990) review showed that it had a strong positive impact on self-confidence, interpersonal relationships with locals, perceptions of host culture, and expatriate adjustment and performance. A meta-analysis by Deshpande and Viswesvaran (1992) also showed positive results, especially on expatriate job performance.

Several CCT models have been put forward. Black and Mendenhall (1990) distinguish three kinds of training:

1 *factual training:* for example presentation of 'cultural knowledge' through lectures, handouts, DVDs and so on

2 *analytical training:* for example courses presenting analytical models such as those of Hofstede or Trompenaars

3 *experiential training:* for example action learning, outdoor training, multicultural team-building activities involving direct experience of working with people from other cultures.

They argue that such types vary according to the rigour of the training process and the degree to which modelling processes are used. As one moves from factual to analytical to experiential training, more rigour is introduced, and a greater variety of modelling processes employed. Which models are most appropriate depends on:

- *Degree of culture novelty:* the more 'culturally distant' the country is, for example China vs. France for a British person, the more experiential methods may be necessary

- *Degree of interaction with HCNs:* the more interaction is anticipated for the PCN, for example long vs. short stay, job as HR director or CEO rather than technician, the more experiential the method required.

Gudykunst and Hammer (1983) differentiate training methods based on two criteria:

1 *process or method of delivery,* for example didactic (cognitive) vs. experiential (emotional/behavioural)

2 *content,* for example culturally general vs. culturally specific. One example is the culture assimilator, which presents collections of critical incidents to which people have to respond with their best explanation – these can be either culturally specific or general.

Such training can be work or private life oriented, or both. In addition, it can occur in a classroom or training room, at work, or in virtual environments. Four categories of CCT can therefore be distinguished, as shown in Figure 18.1.

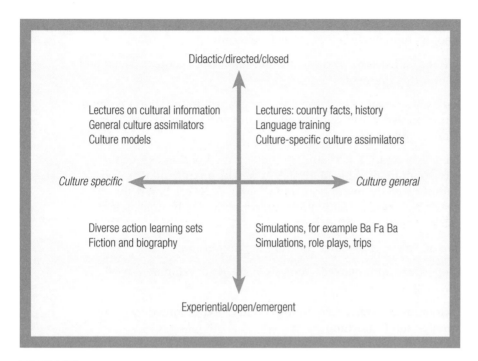

Didactic/directed/closed

Lectures on cultural information
General culture assimilators
Culture models

Lectures: country facts, history
Language training
Culture-specific culture assimilators

Culture specific ← → *Culture general*

Diverse action learning sets
Fiction and biography

Simulations, for example Ba Fa Ba
Simulations, role plays, trips

Experiential/open/emergent

FIGURE 18.1 Models of cross-cultural training

In a meta-analysis on the effectiveness of CCT, Mendenhall et al. (2004) found that lectures, presentations, culture assimilators and discussions were the most frequently used methods. These didactic methods were useful for knowledge transfer, but less effective in changing behaviour and attitudes and enhancing adjustment and performance. However, many findings were non-significant, suggesting that other factors, like the type of assignment being prepared for, affected the impact of didactic training. Pre-departure training, especially imparting basic information, seems to positively affect the accuracy of prior expectations and subsequent adjustment (Caliguri et al., 2001). Waxin and Panaccio (2005) found that CCT accelerated the adjustment of expatriates, but that this was moderated by prior international experience, that is, it had its largest impact on those managers with little prior international experience, and cultural distance, where it tended to have most effect. The type of CCT employed also had an effect; experiential methods were generally more effective, especially if culturally specific.

One example of the use of experiential methods in CCT is given by Lewis (2005), who highlights the use of dramas and other simulations as a more rigorous method in, for example, exploring decisions to invest. Another is 'blended action learning' (combining face-to-face action learning sets in five European partner countries and an e-learning platform called the 'Cultural Fluency Club') to develop cross-cultural skills and cultural awareness of SME leaders (Stewart, 2008). The executive training programme for European companies in Japan also mixes language training, seminars, company visits and in-house training in a hybrid blend of experiential and analytical methods in small groups (Lievens et al., 2003).

According to Tarique and Caliguri (2004, p. 285), designing effective CCT involves:

- Identifying the type of global assignment for which CCT is needed. Is the position technical, functional, high potential, or strategic/executive?

- Determining specific CCT needs. What are the organizational context, individual needs and level of the assignment?

- Establishing goals and measures to determine effectiveness in the short and long term, such as the cognitive, affective and behavioural changes necessary to enhance adjustment and success.

- Developing and delivering CCT, for example content, methods and sequencing. Here models of culture may be addressed, as well as mixing didactic and experiential methods seen as appropriate and whether these are best delivered pre-departure, post-departure, or both. Basic information may be appropriate pre-departure, deeper learning post-departure.

Tarique and Caliguri describe a three-stage programme, comprising:

1 an online pre-departure training needs analysis assessing development needs, followed by a briefing session

2 an initial CCT programme after arrival in the country, accompanied by continued e-support and personal coaching

3 at a later date, the provision of more sophisticated training, again with e-support.

Other factors to be considered are:

- Intranet-based training, multimedia and distance/blended learning may all be useful here.

- Evaluating the programme's success, against stated goals. Adjustment may be measured by interviews, surveys and appraisal records that balance CCT with other HR practices, especially recruitment, selection, reward, appraisal and career/talent management.

- Considering the training needs of HCNs and TCNs, not just PCNs, as in JVs (discussed later).

HRD in Practice 18.2

Breaking down the boundaries at Pfizer

A lack of communication between Pfizer's global R&D unit in Nagoya and the rest of the company had been hampering its contribution, said Tim Kendall, communications group manager, Pfizer global R&D. Despite the unit being crucial – it is responsible for early-stage drug development – Kendall admitted that 'global decisions were being made without consultation from Nagoya. The company gave up trying to communicate.'

A 2004 survey of the 400 staff at the site revealed large gaps in communications skills: 96% didn't feel satisfied they were able to present in English, and almost all respondents were not satisfied with their ability to participate in teleconferences or negotiations with US and UK colleagues. And although 65% said cross-cultural skills were important in their job, 89% said CCT was needed.

A training programme was implemented, covering language skills and cross-cultural awareness. Manager programmes, comprising flexible classroom study and e-learning, were mandatory. But the process was two-way, said Kendall. UK and US colleagues were also given CCT so they could understand Japanese communication styles better. A booklet with tips and information was distributed.

Kendall said: 'For example, Japanese people don't tend to interrupt so they would often say little during discussions, waiting for an opportunity to speak. The booklet made US and UK colleagues aware of this, reminding them to invite them to participate.'

A repeat survey carried out in Nagoya this year showed that, following the training, more than 30% said they were satisfied with their ability to present in English. Feedback from US and UK colleagues also showed that Nagoya's contribution had 'vastly improved'.

Source: Evans (2007) *People Management*, 3 May

According to Briscoe and Schuler (2004), other issues in CCT include:

- Who delivers CCT?

- What are the effects of language differences?

- Who takes responsibility?

- Should CCT be exported, or employees brought to regional or centralized training centres?

- Should each subsidiary/JV develop its own CCT?

- Should CCT be localized, or integrated?

In the HRD processes of multinational enterprises, both transfer (of home HRD practices to affiliates) and adaptation (of HRD to local practices) processes occur. These transfer processes often involve knowledge transfer, whether of technology or HRD processes such as better training or career/talent management policies and practices (Collings and Scullion, 2007).

International knowledge transfer and HRD

One question is what term best describes 'knowledge transfer processes'? Jankowicz (1999) uses metaphors of 'export sales' and 'new product development' to discuss knowledge transfer across cultural and linguistic boundaries. In the first case, the assumption is made that both parties share the same conceptual background and assumptions, whereas in the second case, the two parties are seen as equal collaborators. Every language encodes phenomena differently, so the meaning encoded by one party may be subtly different from that encoded by the other. Jankowicz (1999, p. 319) argues that instead of knowledge transfer, the term 'mutual knowledge creation' is preferable, as it refs to the negotiation of new understanding; Iles and Yolles (2003, p. 3) prefer the term 'knowledge migration'.

A number of factors have been found to affect such knowledge migration: a knowledge-sharing environment, ICTs, and organizational structure.

Knowledge migration may flow from a knowledge source, that is, the knowledge base, often in the 'west', such as the corporate HQ of an international enterprise, to a knowledge destination or sink, often in the 'south' or 'east', such as an affiliate or JV in China or the Middle East (Figure 18.2). The process may be facilitated by a 'knowledge intermediary' such as a consultant or academic, a project team, or expatriates.

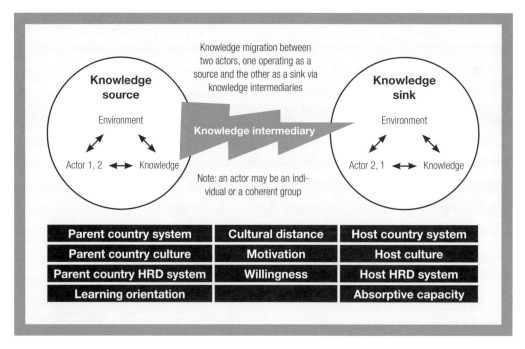

FIGURE 18.2 Knowledge migration in international enterprises and JVs

SOURCE: Adapted from Iles and Yolles (2002, 2003)

The process of transfer is often seen as covering several stages, from 'identifying the knowledge to the actual process of transferring the knowledge to its final utilization by the receiving unit' (Minbaeva et al., 2003, p. 587). The process is usually seen as a transfer from headquarters, for example in the USA, UK or Japan, to the overseas subsidiary, although it could be a 'reverse transfer', from subsidiary to headquarters. A firm's HRD processes may constitute a significant source of competitive advantage over local, indigenous firms, and may be critical to the firm's successful operations. Therefore transferring such processes, and using HRD processes to help transfer other processes, is crucial to effectiveness. Grant et al. (2000, pp. 115–16) argue that 'the movement of knowledge between different geographical locations is central' to the process of adding value in international enterprises.

In addition to concerns over whether knowledge of western HRD practices can be unprob-lematically transferred in the way suggested, a further question arises as to whether it is appropriate to attempt to transfer western HRD practices to other contexts, as the public services of developing countries face different problems and in different contexts. Within JVs, one-way 'transplant' programmes are often less successful than more collaborative, process-oriented approaches that make use of local expertise as to what is needed and how it may be delivered in ways that suit local conditions and circumstances.

Expatriate managers may be given the job of transferring knowledge through training, coaching or mentoring, as in the Anglo-Chinese retail store studied by Gamble (2003). The effectiveness of this depends on their willingness and ability to do this, which in turn depends, as Figure 18.2 shows, on the 'learning orientation' of the source and its strate-gic objectives. Effectiveness of transfer is also affected by parent country and host country characteristics, such as the national culture and institutional/business systems, as well as the cultural distance between source and sink. In addition, the learning or 'absorptive capacity' of the sink affects how well transfer occurs.

The ability and willingness of local personnel to learn will also determine how well they acquire HRD knowledge. Effective communication is vital for the transfer of knowledge. The importance of motivation and willingness in the transfer of knowledge has also been widely recognized. Valuing different cultures, building relationships, listening and observing, coping with ambiguity, managing others, translating complex ideas, and taking action are all necessary, and can be enhanced by HRD.

International JVs and HRD

Many international enterprises have entered into a variety of strategic partnerships, mergers and acquisitions, JVs and other more limited projects. 'Alliances' refer to generic forms of cooperation, and equity JVs are a special case, cemented by ownership sharing through equity holdings. However, JVs, especially international JVs, often fail, associated with differences in culture, HRD practices and management style (Iles and Yolles, 2002, p. 3).

JVs constitute entities with particularly complex sets of HRD practices due to the high levels of interaction between employees of different corporate and national backgrounds with collaborating partners (see, for example, Schuler et al., 1993; Dowling et al., 1994). JVs also need to use HRD and career management practices to reduce psychic distance and encourage identification, therefore HRD plays a significant role in affecting JV success. Particularly important issues are:

- the appropriate selection of JV personnel

- the use of experienced PCNs

- CCT

- the joint training of HCNs and PCNs

- building a unique JV culture through HRD, taking elements of host and home culture as well as new elements not found in either.

Clearly alliances involve sharing people and HRD practices, and HRD issues, especially orientation to the JV and issues of corporate and national culture, will be key. JVs provide significant opportunities for organizational learning, especially the transfer of culturally embedded knowledge if trust is developed and substantial non-contractual inputs invested (Fitzgerald, 2000). Benefits are likely to be appropriated asymmetrically, according to the organizational learning capacity of the partners (Pucik, 1988). A vital part of a learning infrastructure includes HRD policies supporting the protection of competitive advantage, especially the transfer and accumulation of knowledge, enabling parents to learn more about each other, more from each other, and more from the alliance itself – learning that can also be useful for other units and alliances. Some partners may emphasize learning, others may not, and 'the behaviours and styles of managers in organizations have a significant impact on the ability and willingness of a firm to learn' (Schuler, 2001, p. 317). HRD policies and practices may support or inhibit knowledge flows, sharing and development, and establishing mechanisms to enhance trust may benefit the relationship between alliance partners (Schuler, 2001).

Summary

- Despite the claims of some that globalization will lead to a convergence of management practices, including HRD, national differences persist.

- To understand comparative and cross-cultural HRD, it is necessary to take both an institutionalist and culturalist perspective, but also to see that countries and organizations can, within parameters, make different strategic choices.

- It is difficult to describe, for example, the contemporary Chinese business system – it consists of a mixture of models. In addition, Arab culture and Chinese culture seem to be undergoing rapid change, with the emergence of more individualistic values.

- The influence of family and networks (in Arab culture, wasta, in China, guanxi) remains powerful, and exerts a great influence on HRD, such as who is selected to provide training, or who is selected for training and development initiatives.

- HRD is important for international enterprises, especially in preparing international staff of various kinds – not just long-term expatriates.

- CCT, especially 'experiential' training, is particularly important in enhancing adjustment and effectiveness.

- HRD also plays a key role in transferring or migrating knowledge across borders, between the enterprise and its subsidiaries, expatriates and locals, and between parties in JVs in particular.

Discussion questions

1   Are organizational or individual differences in culture likely to be more or less strong than national cultural differences? Give examples for your answer.

2 Think about the strengths/weaknesses of cultural dimensions. How will these impact in business, especially in HRD? Why might they be of interest to managers?

3 Why should CCT programmes vary, depending on the type of global assignment under consideration?

4 What factors would you need to take into account in designing and evaluating an e-CCT programme? When would this be preferable as a CCT method?

5 You are a British consultant working in a multinational company, developing an induction programme for expatriate assignees in South Africa. Identify and analyse the cultural and HRD factors that might affect this. How you will overcome such barriers?

Further reading

Adekola, A. and Sergi, B. (2007) *Global Business Management: A Cross-cultural Perspective*, Aldershot, Ashgate.

Brewster, C. (2007) HRM: the comparative dimension, in J. Storey (ed.) *Human Resource Management: A Critical Text*, 3rd edn, London, Thomson Learning.

Fang, T. (2003) A critique of Hofstede's fifth national culture dimension, *International Journal of Cross Cultural Management*, **3**(3): 347–68.

French, R. (2007) *Cross-cultural Management in Work Organizations*, London, CIPD.

Ibarz, T. (2005) Multilingual and multicultural HRD, in J.P. Wilson (ed.) *Human Resource Development: Learning and Training for Individuals and Groups*, 2nd edn, London, Kogan Page.

Lee, L.-Y. and Croker, R. (2006) A contingency model to promote the effectiveness of expatriate training, *Industrial Management & Data Systems*, **106**(8): 1187–205.

Schuler, R.S., Jackson, S.E. and Luo, Y. (2004) *Managing Human Resources in Cross-border Alliances*, London, Routledge.

Woodall, J. (2006) International management development, in T. Edwards and C. Rees (eds) *International Human Resource Management: Globalisation, National Systems and Multinational Companies*, Harlow, FT/Prentice Hall.

References

Ardichvili, A. and Kuchinke, P. (2002) The concept of culture in international and comparative HRD research: methodological problems and possible solutions, *Human Resource Development Review*, **1**(2): 145–66.

Bates, D. G. and Plog, F. (1990) *Cultural Anthropology*, New York, McGraw-Hill.

Black, J.S. and Mendenhall, M. (1990) Cross-cultural training effectiveness: a review and a theoretical framework for future research, *Academy of Management Review*, **15**: 113–36.

Briscoe, D.R. and Schuler, R.S. (eds) (2004) *International Human Resource Management*, 2nd edn, London, Routledge.

Brislin, R. and Yoshida, T. (1994) *Intercultural Communication Training: An Introduction*, New York, Sage.

Brooks, I. (2003) *Organisational Behaviour: Individuals, Groups and Organisation*, 2nd edn, London, Prentice Hall.

Budhwar, P.S. and Mellahi, K. (eds) (2006) *Managing Human Resources in the Middle East*, London, Routledge.

Caliguri, P.M., Philips, J., Lazarova, M. et al. (2001) Expectations produced in cross-cultural training programs as a predictor of expatriate adjustment, *International Journal of Human Resource Management*, **12**(3): 357–72.

Carrington, L. (2003) Nine day wonder, *People Management*, 12 June: 42–3.

Collings, D.G. and Scullion, H. (2007) Global staffing and the multinational enterprise, in J. Storey (ed.) *Human Resource Management: A Critical Text*, London, Thomson.

Deshpande, S.P. and Viswesvaran, C. (1992) Is cross-cultural training of expatriate managers effective? A meta-analysis, *International Journal of Intercultural Relations*, **16**: 295–310.

Dowling, P.J., Schuler, R.S. and Welch, D.E. (1994) *International Dimensions of Human Resource Management*, 2nd edn, Belmont, CA, Wadsworth.

Edwards, T. and Rees, C. (2006) *International Human Resource Management: Globalisation, National Systems and Multinational Companies*, Harlow, FT/Prentice Hall.

Fitzgerald, S.P. (2000) Building personal and procedural trust through Sino-American joint ventures: the transfer of culturally embedded knowledge, paper presented to the 7th International Conference on Advances in Management, Colorado Springs, July.

Gamble, J. (2000) Localizing management in foreign-invested enterprises in China: practical, cultural and strategic perspectives, *International Journal of Human Resource Management*, **11**(5): 883–903.

Gamble, J. (2003) Transferring human resource practices from the United Kingdom to China: the limits and potential for convergence, *International Journal of Human Resource Management*, **14**(3): 369–87.

Gouveia, V.V. and Ros, M. (2002) The Hofstede and Schwarz models for classifying individualism at the cultural level: their relation to macro-social and macro-economic variables, *Psicothema*, **12**(Suppl.): 25–33.

Grant, R.M., Almeida, P. and Song, J. (2000) Knowledge and the multi-national enterprise, in C. Millar, R. Grant and C. Choi (eds) *International Business: Emerging Issues and Emerging Markets*, Basingstoke, Macmillan – now Palgrave Macmillan.

Gudykunst, W.B. and Hammer, M.R. (1983) Basic training design: approaches to intercultural training, in D. Landis and R.W. Brislin (eds) *Handbook of Intercultural Training: Issues in Theory and Design*, vol. 1, Elmsford, NY, Pergamon.

Hall, E.T. (1984) *The Dance of Life: The Other Dimension of Time*, Garden City, NY, Anchor.

Harris, H., Brewster, C. and Sparrow, P. (2004) *International Human Resource Management*, London, CIPD.

Hofstede, G. (1991) *Cultures and Organizations: Software of the Mind*, London, McGraw-Hill.

Hofstede, G. (2001) *Culture's Consequences: Comparing Values, Behaviors, Institutions, and Organizations across Nations*, 2nd edn, Thousand Oaks, CA, Sage.

Hofstede, G. and Bond, M.H. (1988) The Confucius connection: from cultural roots to economic growth, *Organizational Dynamics*, **16**(4): 5–21.

Holliman, D.M., Mallory, G.R. and Viney, H.P. (2008) What role does managerial perceptions of cultural difference play in the selection of foreign markets and appropriate entry strategy?, paper presented to British Academy of Management, Harrogate, September.

Hutchings, K. and Murray, G. (2002) Australian expatriates' experiences in working behind the bamboo curtain: an examination of guanxi in post-communist China, *Asian Business and Management*, **1**: 373–93.

Hutchings, K. and Weir, D. (2006) Understanding networking in China and the Arab world: lessons for international managers, *Journal of European Industrial Training*, **30**: 272–90.

Iles, P.A. and Yolles, M. (2002) International joint ventures, HRM and viable knowledge migration, *International Journal of Human Resource Management*, **13**: 624–41.

Iles, P.A. and Yolles, M. (2003) International HRD alliances in viable knowledge migration and development: the Czech academic link project, *Human Resource Development International*, **6**(3): 301–24.

Jankowicz, D. (1999) Towards a meaningful HRD function in the post-communist economies of Central and Eastern Europe, proceedings from the

Academy of Human Resource Development Annual Conference.

Kluckhohn, F. and Strodbeck, F. (1961) *Variations in Value Orientations*, Evanston, IL, Row Peterson.

Lane, C. (1992) European business systems: Britain and Germany compared, in R. Whitley (ed.) *European Business Systems, Firms and Markets in their National Contexts*, London, Sage.

Lewis, M.M. (2005) The drama of international business: why cross-cultural training simulations work, *Journal of European Industrial Training*, **29**(7): 593–8.

Li, J. and Nimon, K. (2008) The importance of recognising generational differences in HRD policy and practices: a study of workers in Qinhuangdao, China, *Human Resource Development International*, **11**(2): 167–82.

Lievens, F., van Keer, E., Harris, M. and Bisqueret, C. (2003) Predicting cross-cultural training performance: the validity of personality, cognitive ability and dimensions measured by an assessment centre and a behavior description interview, *Journal of Applied Psychology*, **88**(3): 476–89.

Liu, C. and Lee, H. (2008) A proposed model of expatriates in multinational corporations, *Cross Cultural Management*, **15**(2): 176–93.

Liu, S. (2003) Cultures within culture: unity and diversity of two generations of employees in state-owned enterprises, *Human Relations*, **56**(4): 387–41.

McGuire, D., O'Donnell, D., Garavan, T. et al. (2002) The cultural boundedness of theory and practice in HRD?, *Cross Cultural Management: An International Journal*, **9**(2): 25–44.

McSweeney, B. (2001) The essentials of scholarship: a reply to Geert Hofstede, *Human Relations*, **55**(11): 1363–72.

McSweeney, B. (2002) Hofstede's model of national cultural differences and their consequences: a triumph of faith – a failure of analysis, *Human Relations*, **55**(1): 89–118, www.it.murdoch.edu.au/~sudweeks/b329/readings/mcsweeney.doc.

Mallory, G., Yu Yang, G. and Ray, T. (2008) I did it my way: the impact of national culture on operational decision making by managers working overseas, paper presented to British Academy of Management, Harrogate, September.

Mead, R. (1994) *International Management: Cross-cultural Dimensions*, Oxford, Blackwell.

Mendenhall, M., Stahl, G., Ehnert, I. et al. (2004) Evaluation studies of cross-cultural training programs: a review of the literature from 1988–2000, in D. Landis and J. Bennett (eds) *The Handbook of Intercultural Training*, Thousand Oaks, CA, Sage.

Minbaeva, D.B., Pedersen, T. Bjorkman, I. et al. (2003) MNC knowledge transfer, subsidiary absorptive capacity, and HRM, *Journal of International Business Studies*, **34**(6): 586–99.

Muna, F. (1980) *The Arab Executive*, London, Macmillan.

Ohmae, K. (1990) *The Borderless World*, London, Collins.

Perlmutter, H.V. (1969) The tortuous evolution of the multi-national company, *Columbia Journal of World Business*, **4**: 9–18.

Pucik, V. (1998) Strategic alliances, organizational learning, and competitive advantage: the HRM agenda, *Human Resource Management*, **27**(1): 77–93.

Redding, S.G. (1994) Comparative management: jungle, zoo or fossil bed?, *Organization Studies*, **15**(3): 323–59.

Schuler, R. (2001) HR issues in international joint ventures and alliances, in J. Storey (ed.) *Human Resource Management: A Critical Text*, 2nd edn, London, Thomson Learning.

Schuler, R., Dowling, P.J. and de Cieri, H. (1993) An integrative framework of strategic international human resource management, *Journal of Management*, **19**(2): 419–59.

Schwartz, S. (1990) Individualism-collectivism: critique and proposed refinements, *Journal of Cross Cultural Psychology*, **21**(2): 139–57.

Shen, J. (2005) Towards a generic international human resource management model, *Journal of Organizational Transformation and Social Change*, **2**(2): 83–102.

Sparrow, P. (1999) International recruitment, selection and assessment, in P. Joynt and R. Marlin (eds) *The Global HR Manager: Creating the Seamless Organization*, London, CIPD.

Steenkamp, J.B. (2001) The role of national culture in international marketing research, *International Marketing Review*, **18**: 30–44.

Stewart, J.A. (2008) A blended action learning programme to develop cross-cultural skills for SME leaders, paper presented to British Academy of Management, Harrogate, September.

Suliman, A. (2006) Human resource management in the Arab Emirates, in P.S. Budhwar and K. Mellahi (eds) *Managing Human Resources in the Middle East*, London, Routledge.

Tan, J., Hartel, C., Panipucci, D. and Strybosch, V. (2005) The effect of emotions in cross-cultural expatriate experiences, *Cross Cultural Management*, **12**(2): 4–15

Tarique, I. and Caliguri, P. (2004) Training and development of international staff, in A. Harzing and J. van Ruysseveldt (eds) *International Human Resource Management*, London, Sage.

Tayeb, M. (1997) Islamic revival in Asia and human resource management, *Employee Relations*, **19**: 352–64.

Trompenaars, F. (1997) *Riding the Waves of Culture: Understanding Diversity in Global Business*, New York, McGraw-Hill.

Trompenaars, F. and Hampden-Turner, C. (1997) *Riding the Waves of Culture: Understanding Cultural Diversity in Business*, 2nd edn, London, Nicholas Brealey.

Vo, A.D. (2009) *Transformation in the Management of Human Resources and Labour Relations in Vietnam,* Abington, Woodhead.

Waxin, M.F. and Panaccio, A. (2005) Cross-cultural training to facilitate expatriate adjustment: it works!, *Personnel Review*, **3**(1): 51–67.

Weir, D. (2000) Management in the Arab world: a fourth paradigm?, in A. Al-Shamali and J. Denton (eds) *Arab Business: The Globalisation Imperative*, Kuwait, Arab Research Centre.

Weir, D. (2003) Human resource development in the Middle East: a fourth paradigm, in M. Lee (ed.) *HRD in a Complex World*, London, Routledge.

Whitley, R. (1999) *Divergent Capitalisms: The Social Structuring and Change of Business Systems*, Oxford, Oxford University Press.

Yahiaoui, D. and Zoubir, Y.H. (2006) Human resource management in Tunisia, in P.S. Budhwar and K. Mellahi (eds) *Managing Human Resources in the Middle East*, London, Routledge.

Zhang, L.C. and Iles, P. (2008) Do we turn into pumpkins? The experience of British-educated returnees to China, British Council conference, Going Global 3, London, 3–5 December.

Zhang, L.C., Allinson, C.W. and Hayes, J. (2006). Acculturation through British higher education: a qualitative exploration in the malleability of cognitive style and acculturation process in Chinese students following cross-cultural experience, 18th Congress of the International Association for Cross-Cultural Psychology, Athens.

The Future of Human Resource Development

19

Julie Beardwell, Jeff Gold, Paul Iles, Jim Stewart and Rick Holden

Chapter learning outcomes

After studying this chapter, you should be able to:

- Appraise the status of HRD

- Consider some of the trends for the future of HRD

- Understand the use of various tools to consider the future

- Evaluate the arguments provided in support of current debates

Chapter outline

Introduction

HRD and the future

Future trends and HRD

Futures tools and HRD

Summary

Introduction

In Chapter 1, we introduced you to HRD by considering the case of Terminal 5 at Heathrow Airport in London. We highlighted how, despite the best endeavours of the various groups involved to prepare for, lead and manage the important stages of the opening days of T5, there seemed to be other forces at work, which caused the mayhem and damage to reputations that followed. Whether this could have been predicted, we will never know, and even if it was possible, it would still have been highly likely that a lot of what happened was beyond the scope of human intelligence to predict. What we can say is that we all face a future, which, to some degree, can be predicted by considering various trends and indicators. Nevertheless, the consideration of these will always be in the present and based on the past; more challenging is the prospect that much of the future cannot be known – it is to a great degree unknowable (Stacey, 1992). Perhaps the best we can do is to work intelligently with trends and indicators to reduce uncertainty, and work creatively and speculatively where prediction is too difficult or impossible. As Stacey (2002) pointed out, there is a difference between an uncertain future and a complex future, where the latter is characterized by a large number of factors interacting dynamically, making it impossible to determine logical patterns for understanding. Perhaps too much reliance on the certainty of trends and indicators resulted in the 'credit crunch' difficulties which began in 2008. How many organizations were ready for this by using creative thinking around different future possibilities?

It has been suggested that analytical and creative thinking are required to work on the future (PIU, 2001), where the former is concerned with prediction and the latter with complexity and multiple future possibilities. Figure 19.1 shows a dimension of possibilities. In this chapter, we will apply both kinds of thinking to HRD.

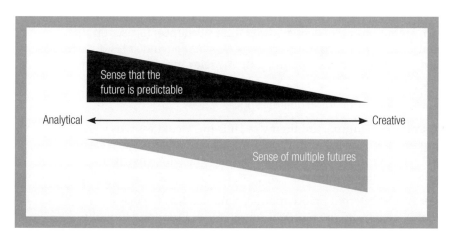

FIGURE 19.1 Analytical and creative approaches to the future

SOURCE: PIU (2001, p. 15)

HRD and the future

For a number of years now, the status of HRD, as a domain of practice and a field of study, has been seen as contentious and ambiguous (Mankin, 2001). As we have indicated, HRD has its origin in a limited view of training and has close links with HRM and OD. These historical roots tend to help and hinder the progress of HRD. There is help in the form of the infusion of ideas and theories from different directions, as we have seen throughout this book. In addition, for those who practise HRD, there is a means of claiming enhanced professional status through membership, in the UK, of the CIPD. For one of the fastest growing professions in recent years, the CIPD offers a qualification process and a certain degree of control on who can enter the profession, although such control is not yet exclusive. Thus it is still possible to practise HRD (and HRM) without membership of the CIPD. HRD could also be hindered by the CIPD through a loss of its independence and claims for a unique identity centred around knowledge, skills and learning (Gold et al., 2003). Further, HRD does not seem to have its own body of theory, which is often seen as the basis for any area of practice that can be called professional (Freidson, 2001). While there have been growing efforts to develop a theoretical base in HRD, with the development of journals, conferences, books and so on, there is still no clear agreement on the boundaries of HRD as a body of theory or how theory should be constructed. In the 1990s, McGoldrick and Stewart (1996) examined the relationship between HRD and HRM. Part of their purpose was to argue the 'space' for HRD within academic practices of teaching and research. Later research and writing by the editors of this book have focused on the connections between HRD and other related areas, including the learning organization (LO) (Tjepkema et al., 2002) and Knowledge Management (KM) (Stewart and Tansley, 2002). The latter two concepts have an obvious relationship with the notion of OL. In an article in *The Learning Organization,* Stewart (2005) argued a connection between LO and OL and OD and mentioned the long accepted connection between OD and HRD.

In the preceding paragraph, we used six different abbreviations denoting a focus of academic teaching and research that claims a distinctive if not a truly unique academic space. Yet every one of these spaces draws on the same core disciplines and, to a varying extent, which is a matter of degree rather than substance, focuses on the same social and organizational practices in its research. Stewart concluded his article with a section subtitled 'A battle of the acronyms', a theme relevant here. This theme has three arguments:

1 HRD is indeed engaged in a battle for academic space.

2 The internal debate on the meaning and theory of HRD has weaknesses as well as strengths, an argument advanced in the pages of *Human Resource Development International* (Poell, 2007). One of those weaknesses is to reduce the effectiveness of HRD in the battle of the abbreviations.

3 The battle itself, because of internal preoccupations with academic space, threatens the potential benefits to the material conditions of humanity brought about by the work of each of the abbreviations. As Stewart (2005, p. 93) put it:

> A third and final conclusion is that the concept of HRD and that of the LO have much in common. Both are human constructs which provoke debate and dispute and, at their best, dissent in work organizations. And, out of that debate, changes in the material conditions of work are made possible. Both concepts have the potential for real (beneficial) effects on the real experience of real people (no postmodernist I). I believe that researchers and writers working with both concepts should never forget that potential.

What follows from these arguments is that there may be little point or benefit in attempts to settle the debates on meaning and theory in relation to HRD. Indeed, some would argue against a specification of HRD if that would mean closing off new and emerging areas of study (Lee, 2001). Does it matter to, and does it help, professional practice to draw hard and fast lines between HRD, HRM, OD, LO and the rest? Is it even possible to draw such lines? And will the world in general and the world of professional practice in particular be the poorer or worse than it is or might be without those lines? These are big questions to which this book might be seen as an attempt to answer 'yes'. We editors are not so sure. The book may give some reasons for saying 'yes' and may make some contribution to settling arguments and debates. But we do not believe this is the point. The real point is that the book informs knowledge and understanding and so helps and advances practice.

So, as we consider the future of HRD, it would seem that theory and practice are at a crossroads. Perhaps this book is part of a trend that pushes HRD towards growth and increasing influence. This would match one of the options presented by Torraco (2008), which points to an increasing acceptance of HRD research and practice throughout work organizations, communities, schools and colleges. Further, HRD will play a leading role in trends such as diversity, cross-cultural understanding and ethical competence as well as economic growth. Of course, this option was seen as the trend before the downturn in economic activity towards the end of 2008. Nevertheless, if HRD is accepted as a path for learning and development, its influence will grow.

Of course, there is Torraco's contrasting option, which sees a decline in influence and a reduced role or even elimination of HRD. This does become a possibility if economic recession results in cost cutting, a problem that traditionally beset training in the past. In this option, HRD researchers become disconnected from the problems facing organizations and are seen as irrelevant.

The flux that emerged at the end of 2008 has and will clearly create the need for learning and change. The question is, will HRD be able to keep up, cope and respond? This was one of the findings from a survey by Ruona et al. (2003), where HRD professionals were criticized for not changing fast enough in responding to global and organization requirements. Although it was recognized that HRD had grown quickly, there were doubts that this would continue into the future. However, we would argue that HRD practitioners and researchers can play a leading role in responding to change and difficulties. Along with Ulrich (2007), we argue that the HRD community can create and add value with and to the people, organizations, institutions, nations and indeed the whole world. This can be done by working analytically with trends and creatively with future unknowns, as indicated in Figure 19.1. Such work draws on ideas and theories from futurism, a field concerned with the study of the future and the use of knowledge to enable the identification of choices and options (Slaughter, 1999). Futurists need imagination, the ability to test out thoughts and ideas in practice and learn from failure. We begin with some trends that we believe will provide opportunities for HRD research and practice in the future.

Future trends and HRD

'Trend' is a frequently used term in futurism and can have a variety of meanings. Here we might employ the meaning used by Lindgren and Bandhold (2003, p. 168), where a trend is seen as long-term change that is usually irreversible but which may 'creep up imperceptibly'. One way of identifying trends is through a survey of opinions. For example, Ruona et al.'s (2003) survey in the USA identified, unsurprisingly, the trends of:

- *globalization:* crossing the boundaries of time, space, geography and culture

- *technology:* affecting how work is done and how learning occurs

- *changing organizations and workforce:* demographics, diversity, location, skills levels.

Throughout this book, we have highlighted all these trends in some way. Our intention here is to focus on some of the trends that might be considered further.

Trend 1: hard times ahead

We are currently in the midst of what is described as the biggest global financial crisis since the Wall Street Crash of 1929 and the Great Depression that followed. Whatever the outcome of this contemporary crisis, it is clear that many businesses, especially but not exclusively in the banking and financial services industry, are experiencing hard times and will probably continue to do so throughout 2009 and possibly even beyond that. It is almost a cliché to say that expenditure and other resources allocated to the HRD function in work organizations are hit first and hardest in times of economic and financial difficulty. This reaction may not be restricted to work organizations and may also be true of NHRD, especially since national governments have to commit to unexpected and unplanned expenditure to attempt to counteract the current crisis. But, a cliché is not only a stereotype, it can also be based in truth. And so it is with HRD being hit first and hardest. We can say with some confidence that the short- and medium-term outlook for HRD practice and HRD practitioners is going to be one of hard times in accessing, securing, defending and holding on to resources to fund HRD processes and activities.

It is also true, however, that HRD professionals are used to having to argue and negotiate for resources in non-receptive climates. Of course, there always have been and always will be exceptions to this, where top and senior decision makers recognize the value and benefits of expenditure on HRD, seeing it as an investment rather than a cost. In most cases, however, HRD expenditure is seen as a cost and therefore a saving in expenditure that can easily be made. The experience of this has produced some general principles and lessons that can be applied. The first is that the value and benefits of HRD have to be highlighted and emphasized as a response to attempts to cut expenditure. HRD professionals believe in the value and benefits, often as an act of faith, but a second principle is that others do not and so have to be persuaded in their own terms. What this means is that 'value' and 'benefit' are not objective givens and depend on personal and individual perceptions, influenced by specific personal, professional and individual circumstances. For example, what is of value and a benefit will, in general, be different for a sales director, finance director, production director or a chief executive. So acts of persuasion have to be presented in terms that appeal to these different perceptions and interests. This example also indicates a third principle, which is that HRD professionals have to be skilled in organization politics. Carrying on with the example, the chief executive's view is likely to carry more weight in decisions in all circumstances, and that of the finance director more than other directors in most circumstances but certainly in those of economic and financial difficulty. So while the status and meaning of value and benefit presented in financial terms may be open to challenge on conceptual and theoretical grounds, that language is usually significant in persuading key decision makers. A final principle related to that of organizational politics comes from the advice of Revans (1982) on achieving change in organizations, which is to find the answers to three simple questions: Who knows? Who cares? Who can? These people are the allies whom HRD professionals need to build into a strategic coalition if they are to access, secure and defend resources in hard times.

Trend 2: the young

Don Tapscott, writing in the *Guardian* (2008), argues that the group he calls the net-geners ('the first to grow up digital') influenced Barack Obama's victory by tapping into the organizing power of social networks such as Facebook. More generally, Tapscott argues that the different attitudes the net-geners bring to work, together with their familiarity with the latest communication technologies, provide a powerful force for change in terms of how we work:

> The net-geners arrive at work, eager to use their social networking tools to collaborate and create and contribute to the organization. However, they are shocked to find technological tools more primitive than the ones used in school.

Tapscott is not alone in advocating youth as force for change within the world of work. Howe and Strauss (2007) refer to the 'millennials', offering an analysis of young people born after 1982, explaining how they differ from their 'baby boomer' and 'generation X' parents, and their characteristic behaviour, attitudes and expectations in terms of work and employment. The head of young person recruitment for Ernst & Young in the USA indicates that, by 2010, over 50% of the company's workforce will be 'generation Y'. He indicates that the company is changing and will continue to change to accommodate a shifting skill set characterized by, for example, 'a love of technology and demand for feedback' (Black, 2007). Of course, it is a cliché to say that young people in education today are tomorrow's organizational human resources, but it is pertinent to ask how young people might influence and shape HRD in years to come. Three observations on the relationship between young people and the future of HRD are noted below.

Youth unemployment

Of the world's unemployed, 50% are young people. Global recession may worsen such statistics and ensure that youth unemployment is not the preserve of the relatively unskilled and unqualified. Globally, two popular solutions to tackle this problem are apprenticeships (or similarly focused VET initiatives) and entrepreneurship. The rationale for the first is that apprenticeships can reduce the number of unqualified young people entering the labour market through enhancing employability and so on. However, it is premised on the assumption that the number of jobs suitable for those with apprentice-level qualifications can match a significant increase in supply – a questionable assumption, certainly in developed countries. The second neatly links the supposed characteristics of young people (energy, innovation, risk taking and so on) with assumptions that there can be significant employment growth through business start-ups. It is difficult to be critical of such policies other than to question whether their impact can be anything other than marginal. The political unpalatability of youth unemployment may force governments to initiate solutions with significant implications for HRD, such as guaranteed internships and training schemes, preferential recruitment schemes for young people, alongside the greater use of job sharing, sabbaticals and community work.

Skills and qualifications

Bob Reese, the president and chief executive of the International Youth Federation, is reported as bemoaning the fact that 'there is no sense of what the market is going to need and what skills young people are going to need' (Murray, 2008). But should we really be surprised by such uncertainty? In reality, research suggests an uncomfortable mix of clarity and uncertainty. In Chapter 17, we noted the ambiguity surrounding the notion of the knowledge economy and that this is reflected in tensions in the demands made of higher education and graduates. Undoubtedly for some, the knowledge economy will offer rich rewards and superb developmental opportunities. But for how many? At the other end of the jobs hierarchy, no amount of wishful thinking can remove the fact that, for the foreseeable future, a proportion of any youth cohort will take up employment in jobs where qualifications are not needed and only the most rudimentary skills are required. How can the champions of the dominant paradigm within education, one that espouses qualifications for worthwhile employment, square this circle?

A powerful player influencing the skills and qualifications agenda for young people is clearly that of the employer. Of course the employer has a legitimate stake in the discourse on how a society utilizes its young people within the labour market. But the power of this voice seems increasingly questionable and unhelpful. It has contributed to a 'creeping vocationalism' (Holden, 2006) within school and university curricula. Even 'personal' development initiatives within education seem principally geared to addressing the employer's agenda. It is doubtful if this power will recede in years to come. Indeed, all the evidence suggests the contrary. Consider, for example, the activities of Bosch, Siemens and ThyssenKrupp – three of Germany's largest industrial groups – that all work with kindergartens to try to get children interested in science. Such steps are being taken as long-term measures to ensure the supply of highly skilled engineers in years to come. Broadly similar thinking underlies the initiatives being taken by three UK companies in respect of qualifications (see the case study at the end of this chapter). Here, McDonald's, Flybe and Network Rail are to award their own qualifications. Such moves follow concerns raised by employers that schools and colleges are failing to equip youngsters for the world of work and, according to Prime Minister Gordon Brown, such awards will be one of 'the qualifications of the future' (Goff, 2007). Both these examples might appropriately be considered under a heading of education-business partnership. Such 'partnerships', we suggest, will become more prominent in the future. While cynics may suggest that the initiatives of the likes of Bosch and Siemens are best managed by the marketing function in terms of 'capturing' future customers, it is likely that responsibility for managing them will be the HRD professionals of tomorrow. How HRD addresses and manages the tension between the broad interests of individual (personal) HRD and narrower, commercial interests, which such partnerships highlight, provides an important future research agenda.

Learning and development

There is also the question of the impact of young people on the design and delivery of learning within organizations in the future. According to Prensky (2001), a generation of new learners, 'digital natives', are now part of the global workforce. These are the younger members of a workforce who began playing Pac-Man and Nintendo in the mid-1980s. The significance may be compounded by a further cohort of young people now entering the labour market raised on newer computer games (including virtual worlds such as Second Life) and the beginnings of the exodus of baby boomers from the workforce. The juxtaposition of these two forces may mean that organizations will have to incorporate substantially new approaches to the design and delivery of training in order to engage employees appropriately. Kapp (2007, p. 14) argues similarly:

> The level of complexity, realism and cognitive engagement of video games has changed dramatically over the past few decades. Kids playing video games in the early 1980s played considerably different games from kids in the year 2007. The influence of games on learning style, expectations and business acumen is just now becoming visible. As today's gamers start to enter the workforce, the differences will be even more profound and accelerated.

Shaw and Fairhurst (2008) suggest that, in the UK, the learning styles and expectations of generation Y graduates are very different from earlier generations. Drawing on the experience of McDonald's, which has recruited substantial numbers of generation Y graduates, Shaw and Fairhurst (2008, p. 374) suggest that future graduate development schemes will need to utilize the latest technology

> to deliver audio-visually rich, multi-tasking challenges which require a collaborative approach, offer instant feedback whilst at the same recognizing that its participants may not see the need for nor indeed take responsibility for their own development.

T-Mobile, for example, already deploys social networking in its induction of graduates to encourage a corporate spirit among new recruits. Specifically, Facebook is used to

> engage graduates after we've offered them a job, to get them to know each other and to network before they actually start with us … we also encourage their managers to join as well. (Davis, 2008)

Apple provides a glimpse of the possible use of the virtual world for learning and development, and again there is a link to the younger generation. Apple has long recognized the need for more innovative and engaging online learning and training environments, 'especially to meet the needs and preferences of younger, "net generation" sales staff' (Cross et al., 2007, p. 3). Apple uses Second Life and other virtual worlds that allow experimentation and exploration of new and innovative learning experiences.

Of course, we must not get carried away. Robust evidence on learning style shifts on behalf of young vis-à-vis older employees remains thin on the ground. There are, however, two interesting areas for HRD. First, the extent to which organizational learning policy and practice should be influenced by the 'apparent' aspirations and expectations of young people, and second, the extent to which it can manage 'fit for purpose' web-based learning technology, which may well be more amenable to young people, in the broader interests of a diverse workforce.

Trend 3: talent

A rapidly growing trend in HRD is the interest in 'talent' and 'talent management' (TM). There has been a great expansion in articles using these terms, many consultancies have developed TM products and services, and professional bodies such as the CIPD in the UK have recently commissioned and published research in the area (for example Tansley et al., 2007). Most of the interest has been stimulated by work by McKinsey consultants and concerns with the so-called 'war for talent' (for example Michaels et al., 2001). There are several reasons for the growth of TM:

- the growth of the knowledge economy has put a premium on talent, especially professional and managerial talent

- globalization has made competition for talent now a global, not just a national, issue, with the rise of the BRIICS (Brazil, Russia, India, Indonesia, China and South Africa) as major regional, and even global, economic actors and employers

- changing demographics, especially ageing populations in Japan, China and many western countries in particular, have meant that the retirement of the baby boomers has resulted in a loss of talent, with fewer younger replacements coming through

- changing values among younger generations (for example CSR, ethics, work–life balance) have resulted in less organizational loyalty and commitment, and more idiosyncratic, 'boundaryless' careers, making retention of talent a growing problem

- technological changes have meant that employee tracking and talent inventories and banks have become more available to organizations.

In addition, TM shows the increasing importance of economic theories to HRD, especially those concerning the importance of human capital, human capital management, and labour market segmentation (such as further developments of the 'flexible firm' model), as well as the growth in influence of marketing theories in HRD. The argument here is linked to 'employer branding'. Just as customer branding is important to give customers reasons to believe in a product/service enough to buy and advocate it to others, an employer brand has become more important to give applicants reasons to choose an employer (for example 'employer of choice' strategies) and advocate it to others, and to give existing employees reasons to stay, and advocate the company to others. Different 'offers' or 'propositions' will need to be targeted at different groups of employees and potential employees, just as different offers are made to different customer groupings. According to Huselid (2003), it makes no sense if business and marketing strategies are differentiated and HR strategies are not. His position is that companies need to identify 'A' positions – business-critical roles where performance is variable and high value can be added – and match 'A' employees to those roles, that is, those showing consistently high performance and/or potential. Similarly, B positions and people need to be identified, and also C positions (candidates for elimination or outsourcing?) and C people (candidates for redundancy and outplacement?).

This is an 'exclusive' view of TM – talent is confined to a small group of key employees critical to the business through performance or potential, and scarce development resources should be focused on this group, with a disproportionate impact on overall organizational performance. In practice, many organizations do take this view, targeting TM initiatives at either senior managers or 'high-potentials', whether in the US (for example Cappelli, 2008), the UK (for example Tansley et al., 2007) or China (for example Chuai et al., 2008), although not all will take an exclusive perspective on 'positions' as well as 'people'. This perspective is linked to more traditional concerns with 'succession planning', often associated with the early identification of potential, fast-tracking and intensive development, although not all believe that such 'planning' is possible in contemporary fast-changing business environments, or that 'potential' is the appropriate, or easily measurable, dimension (Cappelli, 2008). Demand and supply are seen as less predictable or measurable than implied by advocates of succession planning.

Other organizations take a more inclusive view, seeing talent as potentially occurring at all levels in all roles, or as occurring in several key functions, for example a health authority cited by Tansley et al. (2007) that saw talent in the managerial, clinical and service leadership fields. In China, some companies studied by Chuai et al. (2008) also took a more inclusive view. Some saw TM as targeted at a differentiated, exclusive group, others as concerned with the overall development of organizational competence. Others again saw TM as about ensuring a smooth continuity of talent supply. Those who take a more inclusive view often argue that a focus on individual talent or human capital development distracts attention from the development of social capital (for example trust, relationships) and the importance of teams, leadership, networks, organizational culture, routines and processes in affecting organizational performance (for example Iles and Preece, 2006; Preece and Iles, 2009).

Trend 4: corporate social responsibility

One of the key trends impacting on HRD is corporate social responsibility (CSR), sometimes referred to as corporate responsibility. CSR 'is about how companies conduct their business in an ethical way, taking account of their impact economically, socially, environmentally and in terms of human rights' (CIPD, 2008a, p. 1). CSR is not synonymous with ethics but has a strong ethical base (CIPD, 2003). The debate about CSR has grown in recent years, partly in response to a number of high-profile cases involving financial mismanagement, for example Enron, or the alleged use of sweatshop labour, for example Adidas and Nike, but also as a result of a greater awareness of environmental issues. The current financial and economic crisis is likely to make CSR more important than ever as companies seek to retain or rebuild trust. A report from Business in the Community (2008, p. 1), a UK membership organization that aims to mobilize business for public good, suggests that:

> Responsible businesses will have confidence in the products they are buying and selling; internal controls in place to reduce risk and maximize opportunity; and will be focused on long-term success (economic, social and environmental) rather than just short term returns.

If it is to make a sustainable difference, CSR has to be more than just PR or window dressing, it needs to be embedded in the organization's culture, which is where HRD can make a significant contribution. Much of CSR is about changing attitudes and actions and this can be achieved through training and development. However, it seems that there is still a lot of scope for improvement in this area, as few companies include ethics in induction training (Marchington and Wilkinson, 2008). The provision of learning opportunities more generally can also contribute to CSR as it can demonstrate a commitment to the ethical treatment of employees. Volunteering can be used to link training and development with CSR initiatives, for example the BBC offers staff development opportunities through volunteering with selected partners in the community (Simms, 2007).

Trend 5: diversity

The management of diversity can also reflect CSR in a number of ways such as employing people who are representatives of the local community and the introduction of 'dignity at work' policies (CIPD, 2008b). Managing diversity is of increasing importance to organizations as demographic trends continue to alter the composition of the workforce. Labour force projections estimate that, by 2020, 23.5% of the workforce will be over 50 and there will be a small increase in female participation and a slight decline in male participation in the workforce (Madouros, 2006). The past few years have also seen an increase in the number of migrant workers from central and Eastern Europe seeking employment in the UK, although numbers have declined recently due to the current financial crisis. The CIPD (2008b) suggests a number of ways in which HRD can support the effective management of an increasingly diverse workforce, including:

- building diversity concepts into team-building programmes to increase awareness of the need to handle different views

- developing and implementing awareness-raising programmes about diversity

- including diversity in induction training

- training line managers about diversity.

All these trends may be served by what is referred to as 'Critical HRD' (CHRD) (see Elliott and Turnbull, 2005; Rigg et al., 2007). A major focus and purpose of CHRD is to identify and highlight the social and cultural dimensions, purposes and impact of HRD as well as the narrow economic dimensions that traditionally characterize theory and practice. The ideas around CHRD have featured only marginally in this book but they have potential for greater relevance and utility in relation to the trends identified here. So, if these trends prove to have validity, CHRD may become a more influential source of theory and approaches to practice.

Futures tools and HRD

While trends imply a degree of predictability, much of the future is more difficult, if not impossible, to predict. We can talk about the future, but this is, by necessity, speculative. However, futures research and futures ideas are less concerned with the accuracy of predictions and more oriented towards assisting decisions. Learning about the future provides possible options on how the future will proceed. Futures writers such as Bell (1997) suggest that the purpose of futures work is concerned with heightening awareness about the future to help other disciplines, such as HRD, make better decisions. There are a variety of possible outcomes in the future, but action can only occur in the present and such actions can be part of an argument for how the future will be enacted. This would seem particularly important for those involved in HRD, given the options for HRD presented above by Torraco (2008).

Futurists believe that there is great value in considering the variety of possible futures, both positive and negative, orthodox and unconventional. To support learning about the future, a range of tools and methods has been developed. For example, a future search conference (FSC) seeks to bring together a large range of stakeholders who have a joint interest in an issue so that they can share intentions and create plans. According to Weisbord and Janoff (2000), the basic principles of an FSC are:

- getting a cross-section of the whole 'system' in one room

- exploring the whole before seeking to act on any part

- focusing on common ground and desired futures

- treating problems and conflicts as information, not action

- letting participants self-manage and take responsibility for action.

Dewey and Carter (2003) report the results of an FSC held in Florida in 2001 entitled Shaping the Future: Leading Workplace Learning and Performance. The event lasted three days and was attended by 64 participants. Working in groups, the participants considered past and present trends, analysis of present reality leading to common ground themes that could be developed into agreed ideas for plans. Through discussion and dialogue, the final area of common ground included:

- creating synergy between research and practice

- leveraging available technology without losing the human touch and social component of learning

- striking a healthy balance between work life and personal life

- striving to create humane workplaces

- acknowledging intellectual capital as the life blood of the organization – the true bottom line

- developing a sense of social responsibility

- embracing globalization

- embracing multiculturalism

- partnering in the fundamentally changing role for education

- managing knowledge and learning effectively

- developing partnerships and collaboration internal and external to the organization

- fostering lifelong learning.

Based on the beliefs and values of the participants, this list is broadly expressed in positive terms and is inevitably constrained by their understanding in 2001. We do not know if there was any follow-up activity or review. Certainly, most of the ideas were and are part of what people in HRD often talk about and have done so over the past decade; they do seem to lack a critical or alternative stance. However, another futures method, scenarios, can produce more varied results.

In developing scenarios, participants with a variety of views create different stories of future possibilities. De Geus (1988, p. 70) argued that scenarios 'are the scenery into which actors walk' through the creation of a number of 'internally consistent stories of possible futures'. An example of this approach is provided by Gold et al. (2003), where scenarios were developed concerning the future of the HRD profession in the UK to the year 2020. Following a process developed by Ringland (1998), a group drawn from different sectors of the HRD field developed over 120 key factors considered to be important to the future of the HRD profession. These were clustered into themes, which then provided the framework for developing scenarios. The result was four scenarios, shown in Figure 19.2.

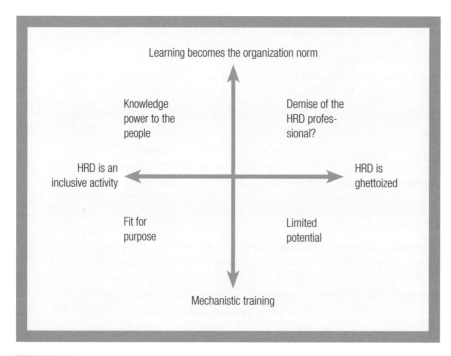

FIGURE 19.2 Future of the HRD profession

SOURCE: Gold et al. (2003, p. 448)

The two dimensions of the grid in Figure 19.2 are based on the analysis by the group and set the limits for the development of scenarios. Thus the vertical dimension, referred to as 'shaping', varies between two possible situations. In the first, learning becomes the organization norm, implying that, by 2020, the arguments to support learning as the source of prosperity and wellbeing for individuals, organizations, nations and the world will have been won. By contrast, the second situation of mechanistic training indicates that, by 2020, HRD research and practice will continue to struggle to make learning important and its influence felt. The horizontal dimension, referred to as 'inclusivity', ranges from high inclusivity, where HRD becomes an activity of significance to everyone, to a view where HRD is limited to a select few. By combining these dimensions, as shown in Figure 19.2, four scenarios were developed, brief descriptions of which now follow:

1 *Knowledge power to the people:* a highly positive scenario where the learning society has been achieved and learning is highly valued throughout society. This scenario is perhaps most closely linked with the theorizing and aspirations central to CHRD.

2 *Demise of the HRD professional?:* a scenario of mixed fortunes for HRD, where learning is accepted as the norm but not for everyone; instead a selective approach is adopted. For many, learning is reduced to techniques and HRD expertise is minimized. For the select few, providing opportunities to develop talent becomes standard and a privilege.

3 *Fit for purpose:* another scenario of mixed fortunes, where learning opportunities are available for a wide group of people but these opportunities are constrained and narrowed by the particular requirements of organizations, which are specified in an HRD plan and delivered top down against targets.

4 *Limited potential:* the most pessimistic scenario, where a low status is given to learning and HRD activities are limited to a select few with little room for creativity and new ideas.

Futurist writers Rogers and Tough (1996, p. 495) once stated that 'facing the future is definitely not for wimps', and if we reflect on these scenarios six years after they were written, we can see that HRD still remains at a point where elements of all scenarios seem to apply. Certainly as a profession, HRD has sought to advance towards an inclusive future and the learning and knowledge-based society. There are fears that this movement is not enjoyed by everyone, and in the UK especially, there has emerged a polarization between organizations that pursue a high-skill and knowledge route to performance improvement and those where low skill remains the requirement of work (Lloyd and Payne, 2004). HRD continues to be a low-level consideration in strategic discussions in many organizations and especially in the large numbers of SMEs where survival is frequently the primary interest. During a recession, with the need to control costs, this is unlikely to change. Paradoxically, recession could provide a good opportunity to invest in skill development and talent, especially among young people through apprenticeships. It is argued that organizations that have apprentices show a higher quality of work and profit (Kenyon, 2005). However, we do know that successful completion of apprenticeships does depend on a positive approach to HRD in the form of learning opportunities to participate in skilled work (Fuller and Unwin, 2003) and this would require a higher profile for HRD in an organization's strategy.

Summary

As we have identified in this chapter, and throughout this book, HRD as a field of research and practice has come a long way in a relatively short period of time. There are some clear trends emerging that provide good opportunities for creating and adding value to a broad range of stakeholders at all levels of activity. We firmly believe that this can be achieved and we very much hope that we have enrolled you in this process. In the midst of a great deal of uncertainty, difficulty and change in the world, what better response can there be but an exploration of learning and a critical examination of our assumptions for our future lives together. Good luck to you all.

References

Bell, W. (1997) The purposes of futures studies, *The Futurist*, Nov–Dec: 42–5.

Black, D. (2007) Interview in *InBiz*, BBC Radio 4, 17 January.

Business in the Community (2008) *Corporate Responsibility and the Financial Crisis: Business in the Community's Response*, briefing note, www.bitc.org.uk.

Cappelli, P. (2008) *Talent on Demand: Managing Talent in an Age of Uncertainty*, Boston, Harvard Business School Press.

CIPD (Chartered Institute of Personnel and Development) (2003) *Corporate Social Responsibility and HR's Role*, London, CIPD.

CIPD (Chartered Institute of Personnel and Development) (2008a) *Corporate Social Responsibility*, fact sheet, September, www.cipd.co.uk/subjects/corpstrtgy/corpsocres/csrfact.htm.

CIPD (Chartered Institute of Personnel and Development) (2008b) *Diversity: An Overview*, fact sheet, November, www.cipd.co.uk/subjects/dvsequl/general/divover.htm.

Chuai, X., Preece, D. and Iles, P. (2008) Is talent management just 'old wine in new bottles'?, *Management Research News*, 31(12): 901–11.

Cross, J., O'Driscoll, T. and Tronsden, E. (2007) Another life: virtual worlds as tools for learning, *eLearn Magazine*, www.elearnmag.org/subpage.cfm?article=44-1&section=articles.

Davis, P. (2008) Interview in *InBiz*, BBC Radio 4, 17 January.

De Geus, A. (1988) Planning as learning, *Harvard Business Review*, 66(2): 70–4.

Dewey, J. and Carter, T. (2003) Exploring the future of HRD: the first future search conference for a profession, *Advances in Developing Human Resources*, 5(3): 245–56.

Elliott, C. and Turnbull, S. (eds) (2005) *Critical Thinking in HRD*, Routledge, London.

Freidson, E. (2001) *Professionalism*, Cambridge, Polity Press.

Fuller, A. and Unwin, L. (2003) Fostering workplace learning: looking through the lens of apprenticeships, *European Educational Research Journal*, 2(1): 41–55.

Goff, H. (2007) McDonald's serves up. diplomas, www.news.bbc.co.uk/l/hi/education/7209276.stm.

Gold, J. Rodgers, H. and Smith, V. (2003) What is the future for human resource development professionals? A UK perspective, *Human Resource Development International*, 6(4): 437–56.

Holden, R.J. (2006) Editorial, *Education and Training*, 48(1).

Howe, N. and Strauss, B. (2000) *Millennials Rising: The Next Greatest Generation*, New York, Vintage Books.

Huselid, M.A. (2003) Presentation to DTI Accounting for People seminar, London, 18 July.

Iles, P.A. and Preece, D. (2006) Developing leaders or developing leadership?, *Journal of Leadership and Organizational Studies*, 10(3): 104–7.

Kapp, K.M. (2007) *Gadgets, Games and Gizmos for Learning: Tools and Techniques for Transferring Know-how from Boomers to Gamers*, San Francisco, John Wiley & Sons.

Kenyon, R. (2005) The business benefits of apprenticeships: the English employers' perspective, *Education and Training*, 47(4/5): 366–73.

Lee, M. (2001) HRD: a refusal to define HRD, *Human Resource Development International*, 4(3): 327–41.

Lindgren, M. and Bandhold, H. (2003) *Scenario Planning: The Link between Future and Strategy*, Basingstoke, Palgrave Macmillan.

Lloyd, C. and Payne, J. (2004) *Just Another Bandwagon? A Critical Look at the Role of the High Performance Workplace as a Vehicle for the UK High Skills Project*, SKOPE Research Paper No. 49, ESRC Research Centre on Skills, Knowledge and Organizational Performance.

McGoldrick, J. and Stewart, J. (1996) The HRM–HRD nexus, in J. Stewart and J. McGoldrick (eds) *HRD: Perspectives, Strategies and Practice*, London, Pitman.

Madouros, V. (2006) *Labour Force Projections, 2006–2020*, London, ONS.

Mankin, D.P. (2001) A model for human resource development, *Human Resource Development International*, 4(1): 65–85.

Marchington, M. and Wilkinson, A. (2008) *Human Resource Management at Work*, London, CIPD.

Martin, G., Reddington, M. and Kneafsey, M.B. (2008) *Web 2.0 and HR: A Discussion Paper*, London, CIPD.

Michaels, E., Handfield-Jones, H. and Axelrod, B. (2001) *The War for Talent*, Boston, Harvard Business School Press.

Milne, R. (2008) Sector that catches them young, *Financial Times*, 17 June.

Murray, S. (2008) Youthful force for change in society in 'Investing in Young People', *Financial Times*, 25 January, p. 1.

PIU (Performance and Innovation Unit) (2001) *Benchmarking UK Strategic Futures Work*, London, PIU.

Poell, R.F. (2007) W(h)ither HRD? Towards a self-conscious, self-critical, and open-minded discipline, *Human Resource Development International*, 10(4): 361–3.

Preece, D. and Iles, P.A. (2009) Leadership development: assuaging uncertainties through joining a leadership academy, *Personnel Review*, 38(3): 286–306.

Prensky, M. (2001) *Digital Game-based Learning*, Maidenhead, McGraw-Hill.

Revans, R. (1982) *The Origins and Growth of Action Learning*, Bromley, Chartwell-Bratt.

Rigg, C., Stewart, J. and Trehan, K. (eds) (2007) *Critical Human Resource Development*, Harlow, FT/Prentice Hall.

Ringland, G. (1998) *Scenario Planning*, Chichester, Wiley.

Rogers, M. and Tough, A. (1996) Facing the future is not for wimps, *Futures*, 28(5): 491–6.

Ruona, W., Lynham, S. and Chermack, T. (2003) Insights on emerging trends and the future of human resource development, *Advances in Developing Human Resources*, 5(3): 272–82.

Shaw, S. and Fairhurst, D. (2008) Engaging a new generation of graduates, *Education and Training*, 50(5): 366–78.

Simms, J. (2007) Hands up, *People Management*, 31 May.

Slaughter, R. (1999) Professional standards in futures work, *Futures*, 31: 835–51.

Stacey, R.D. (1992) *Managing the Unknowable: Strategic Boundaries between Order and Chaos in Organizations*, San Francisco, CA, Jossey-Bass.

Stacey, R.D. (2002) *Strategic Management and Organizational Dynamics: The Challenge of Complexity*, London, FT/Prentice Hall.

Stewart, J. (2005) The current state and status of HRD research, *The Learning Organization*, 12(1): 90–5.

Stewart, J. and Tansley, C. (2002) *Training in the Knowledge-based Economy*, London, CIPD.

Tansley, C., Turner, P. and Foster, C. (2007) *Talent: Strategy, Management, Measurement: Research into Practice*, London, Chartered Institute of Personnel.

Tapscott, D. (2008) Generation expects, *Guardian Work*, 8 November, p. 1.

Tjepkema, S., Stewart, J., Sambrook, S. et al. (2002) *HRD and Learning Organisations in Europe*, London, Routledge.

Torraco, R.J. (2008) The future of human resource development, *Human Resource Development Review*, 7(4): 371–3.

Ulrich, D. (2007) Dreams: where human resource development is headed to deliver value, *Human Resource Development Quarterly*, 18(1): 1–8.

Weisbord, M. and Janoff, S. (2000) *Future Search*, 2nd edn, San Francisco, Berrett-Koehler.

SECTION 4 CASE STUDY

Workplace qualifications

In January 2008, it was announced that a number of large organizations will be able to award their own qualifications equal to GCSEs, A levels and degrees. The QCA has given awarding powers to McDonald's, Network Rail and Flybe, thus allowing them to confer nationally accredited certificates from autumn 2008.

Employers will follow the Qualifications and Credit Framework, which uses a modular system. Learning will be work based and assessment will be via a mixture of coursework, examinations and observation by supervisors. Employees will complete modules to earn credits that can build up to a complete course:

- McDonald's will train employees for a level 3 certificate (equivalent to an A level) in basic shift management. The certificate will take a year, during which trainees will learn about the day-to-day running of a restaurant, including finance, hygiene and HR.

- Flybe, the budget airline, will award certificates from level 2 (equivalent to GCSE) to level 4 (equivalent to degree level) to cabin and engineering staff taking part in its airline trainer programme.

- Network Rail will introduce engineering qualifications covering technical issues and health and safety. Most trainees are expected to receive certificates at levels 2 and 3 but the organization will be able to award up to level 8 (equivalent to PhD).

In each case, the process will be scrutinized by the QCA to ensure that the awards meet the designated level.

Questions

1 To what extent can these work-based qualifications raise skills levels among the workforce and the unemployed?

2 To what extent can these training courses help with employee retention?

3 How might the effectiveness of these training courses be measured?

A letter *n* after a page number denotes a note number on that page.

F

G

M

N

O

P/Q

INDEX

U

V

W

Y/Z